Rand Morimoto
Andrew Abbate, MCSE
Eric Kovach, MCSE
Ed Roberts, MVP (Windows Server)

# Microsoft®
# Windows®
# Server 2003

# INSIDER
# SOLUTIONS

**SAMS**    800 East 96th Street, Indianapolis, Indiana 46240

# Microsoft Windows® Server 2003 Insider Solutions

International Standard Book Number: 0-672-32609-4

Library of Congress Catalog Card Number: 2003111830

Printed in the United States of America

First Printing: November 2003

06   05   04          4   3   2

## Trademarks

All terms mentioned in this book that are known to be trademarks or service marks have been appropriately capitalized. Sams Publishing cannot attest to the accuracy of this information. Use of a term in this book should not be regarded as affecting the validity of any trademark or service mark.

## Warning and Disclaimer

Every effort has been made to make this book as complete and as accurate as possible, but no warranty or fitness is implied. The information provided is on an "as is" basis. The authors and the publisher shall have neither liability nor responsibility to any person or entity with respect to any loss or damages arising from the information contained in this book.

## Bulk Sales

Sams Publishing offers excellent discounts on this book when ordered in quantity for bulk purchases or special sales. For more information, please contact

**U.S. Corporate and Government Sales**

**1-800-382-3419**

**corpsales@pearsontechgroup.com**

For sales outside of the U.S., please contact

**International Sales**

**1-317-428-3341**

**international@pearsontechgroup.com**

**Associate Publisher**
Michael Stephens

**Acquisitions Editor**
Neil Rowe

**Development Editor**
Mark Renfrow

**Managing Editor**
Charlotte Clapp

**Project Editor**
George Nedeff

**Copy Editor**
Kate Givens

**Indexer**
Erika Millen

**Proofreader**
Linda Seifert

**Technical Editor**
James V. Walker, MCSE

**Contributing Writers**
Amanda Acheson, MCSE
Chris Amaris, MCSE, CISSP, CCNA
Heath Abbate, MCP
Jon D. Skoog, MCSE
Joe R. Coca Jr., MCSE
Kenton Gardinier, MCSE, CISSP, MCSA

**Team Coordinator**
Cindy Teeters

**Designer**
Gary Adair

**Page Layout**
Michelle Mitchell
Ron Wise

**Graphics**
Tammy Graham

# Contents at a Glance

# Table of Contents

## 7    Managing Desktops           139

**Part VIII    Business Productivity Solutions**

# About the Authors

**Rand H. Morimoto, MCSE**   Rand Morimoto has been in the computer industry for more than 25 years and has authored, co-authored, or been a contributing writer for more than a dozen books on Windows 2003, Security, Exchange 2000, BizTalk Server, and remote and mobile computing. Rand is the president of Convergent Computing, an IT consulting firm in the San Francisco Bay Area that has been one of the key early adopter program partners with Microsoft implementing beta versions of Microsoft Exchange Server 2003, Sharepoint 2003, and Windows Server 2003 in production environments more than two years before the product releases. Besides speaking at more than 50 conferences and conventions around the world in the past year on tips, tricks, and best practices on planning, migrating, and implementing Exchange 2003, Rand is also a special advisor to the White House on cyber-security and cyber-terrorism.

**Andrew Abbate, MCSE**   Andrew Abbate has been in the computer industry for more than 10 years and is a specialist in AD and Exchange migration planning and implementations, firewall and security planning and implementation, Layer 2 and 3 switching, and wide area connectivity. Andrew possesses an MCSE/MCSA as well as holding certifications from numerous firewall, hardware, and software vendors. Andrew's experiences with companies ranging from 20 to 20,000 employees have afforded him a unique perspective on IT best practices.

**Eric Kovach, MCSE**   Eric Kovach has been in the IT services industry for nine years and is a Microsoft Certified Systems Engineer (MCSE) for both Windows NT 4.0 and Windows 2000. Eric received his bachelor of arts degree in philosophy from San Jose State University. Eric is a contributing writer for the Sams Publishing book *Windows Server 2003 Unleashed* along with a co-author of the Microsoft published 64-bit Windows Evaluation Guide. Eric has helped many medium and large corporations with the design, migration, and maintenance of their networks.

**Ed Roberts, Microsoft MVP (Windows Server)**   Ed Roberts has been involved in the computer industry for more than 19 years. Ed is the president of Roberts Technologies, an IT consulting firm based in central California. Mr. Roberts is also the president and founder of the Orange County NT User Group, which is a nonprofit corporation for community benefit based in Orange County, California. Having been involved with Windows NT since its 3.1 beta program, Ed has worked with Fortune 1000 corporations as a regional systems manager, senior systems engineer, and as a Microsoft consulting practice manager. Ed has been a presenter and advisory board member for several conferences including SoftBank Expo's "Windows Solutions" and "Windows NT Intranet Solutions" and the IDG World Expo's "Windows 2000 Conference and Expo," which coincided with the Windows 2000 Server launch. He has also been designated as a Microsoft "Most Valuable Professional" on the Windows Server platform.

# Dedications

*I dedicate this book to my sister Lisa and my brother Bruce.
Thank you for all your support over the years! I never realized the
support I got from you two until I started watching my own kids
and how between hits, fights, and screaming, there's really a love
and support shared between brother and sister.*

**—Rand H. Morimoto, MCSE**

*I dedicate this book to my parents. Without their support of my
interest in computers, I wouldn't be where I am today.*

**—Andrew Abbate, MCSE**

*I dedicate this book to my parents, Carmen and Richard Kovach,
who devoted their lives to the success of their three sons through
ceaseless support and inspiration.*

**—Eric Kovach, MCSE**

*I dedicate this book to my patient and understanding wife Patrizia
and my loving children Natalie, Nathan, Ashley, and Julia.*

**—Ed Roberts, Microsoft MVP (Windows Server)**

# Acknowledgments

**Rand H. Morimoto, MCSE**  We want to thank our acquisitions editor, Neil Rowe, who gave us the opportunity to write this book. To all those on the Sams Publishing team, including Mark Renfrow, Kate Givens, and George Nedeff, thank you for your edits and changes to put all the words in the right order and the management of this book to completion. Thank you to our technical editor, James Walker, for validating every page of content of the book for technical accuracy. We also want to thank all the consultants, consulting engineers, technical specialists, project managers, technical editors, and systems engineers at Convergent Computing who were valuable resources we called upon for the thoughts, suggestions, best practices, tips, and tricks that made up the content of this book.

And thank you to our dozens of early adopter clients who, in many cases, were our guinea pigs as we worked together years before the product release, helping us build case experience and knowledge of the technology.

Last but not least, to my wife Kim, thank you for taking care of the kids nonstop as I wrote evenings, nights, mornings, and on weekends for this book and the *Exchange Server 2003 Unleashed* book simultaneously. To Kelly and Andrew, thank you for being good while daddy wrote.

**Andrew Abbate, MCSE**  This book wouldn't have been possible without the support and assistance of a lot of people. I'd like to thank Rand for the opportunity to write this book and for always being there to answer the many questions of a new author. Thank you to my co-workers for all the tricks I've learned from them over the years. A big thanks goes to all of my friends for not giving me too hard a time about over using the "sorry, I have to work on the book" excuse. I'd also like to thank them for occasionally forcing me to go play golf to keep myself sane during this project.

**Eric Kovach, MCSE**  First and foremost I'd like to thank Rand Morimoto for giving me the opportunity to work on this project. I could not have done it without his continuous reassurance, generous advice, and invaluable mentoring. I'm also indebted to Jon Skoog and Amanda Acheson, the contributing writers who helped me. Their efforts and expertise truly make this book an in-depth and comprehensive work. Thank you to James Walker, not only for checking my facts, but also for making content recommendations that make this book more readable and technically valuable. I'd like to acknowledge all of my co-workers at Convergent Computing, a group of technical professionals who never hesitate to share their boundless knowledge or help me through a problem. Most notably, thanks go out to Andrew Abbate, who in addition to co-authoring this book has provided me with mentoring support and guidance over the past several months. Last, but not least, I'd like to thank my girlfriend Leanne Mackenzie for her patience, support, and encouragement throughout this process and especially during those many weekends and evenings that found me working on this book.

# We Want to Hear from You!

As the reader of this book, *you* are our most important critic and commentator. We value your opinion and want to know what we're doing right, what we could do better, what areas you'd like to see us publish in, and any other words of wisdom you're willing to pass our way.

As an associate publisher for Sams Publishing, I welcome your comments. You can e-mail or write me directly to let me know what you did or didn't like about this book—as well as what we can do to make our books better.

*Please note that I cannot help you with technical problems related to the topic of this book. We do have a User Services group, however, where I will forward specific technical questions related to the book.*

When you write, please be sure to include this book's title and author as well as your name, e-mail address, and phone number. I will carefully review your comments and share them with the author and editors who worked on the book.

Email:      feedback@samspublishing.com

Mail:       Michael Stephens
            Associate Publisher
            Sams Publishing
            800 East 96th Street
            Indianapolis, IN 46240 USA

For more information about this book or another Sams Publishing title, visit our Web site at www.samspublishing.com. Type the ISBN (excluding hyphens) or the title of a book in the Search field to find the page you're looking for.

# Introduction

When we set out to write this book, we didn't want it to be just another installation and migration book, but rather a serious resource guide for Windows experts to find tips, tricks, and best practices for implementing and supporting key Windows Server 2003 technologies. The authors started working with Windows Server 2003 (then codename Whistler) just days after the code for Windows 2000 was locked, when most organizations were getting a first chance to see the Windows 2000 server product. With more than three years of experience working with Whistler in early beta and production implementations, the authors of this book have provided a resource to help you make Windows 2003 technologies work properly. When given a choice of different ways of implementing the technologies, you can turn to this book for the best practices of successful field implementations.

This book is organized into eight parts, each part focusing around a core technological solution area, with several chapters making up each part. The parts of the book are as follows:

- **Part I: Security Solutions**—This part focuses on the key security areas that are the biggest challenge for administrators to get right. The three chapters in this part of the book cover best practices for securing a Windows Server 2003 environment, security relative to a wireless environment, and the use of smartcards in a secured access environment.

- **Part II: Management and Administration Solutions**—This part of the book comprises six chapters specific to core tips, tricks, and best practices around managing and administering a Windows 2003 environment. Topics include best practices for distributing administration, managing user rights and permissions, managing desktops, and administering Windows 2003 servers remotely. Additionally, this section covers Group Policies and the best ways of leveraging Group Policy Objects, the Group Policy Management Console, and performing centralization administration tasks within Windows 2003. This part of the book also includes an entire chapter focused on daily, weekly, and monthly maintenance practices to keep the Windows 2003 networking environment in optimal operating condition.

- **Part III: Design and Implementation Solutions**—With Windows 2003 and the second generation of Active Directory, along with new tools for planning, implementing, and administering the Windows Active Directory, this part focuses on the insider solutions and lessons learned in the most successful Windows and Active Directory designs and implementation solutions. This part includes a chapter on advanced Active Directory design concepts, specific tips and tricks for implementing Windows 2003 and Active Directory, as well as best practices at implementing DNS, DHCP, WINS, and domain controllers.

- **Part IV: Migration and Integration Solutions**—Migrations to Windows 2003 and Active Directory can either be hard or easy depending on the migration method you use. This part of the book focuses on Windows NT 4.0 and Windows 2000 migrations to

Windows 2003 as well as integrating Unix, LDAP, and Novell Networks into a Windows 2003 Active Directory environment.

- **Part V: Remote and Mobile User Solutions**—This part of the book focuses on mobility access to a Windows 2003 environment. This includes VPN access, dial-up communications to Windows 2003, Web access to Windows 2003–based resources, and new components built in to Windows 2003 Terminal Services that help organizations provide better remote and mobile access to the Windows 2003 networking environment.

- **Part VI: Business Continuity Solutions**—As organizations become dependent on their networks and network communication systems, the need for a fault-tolerant environment with recoverability becomes extremely important. This part of the book has one chapter on proactive monitoring and alerting to be notified of looming system problems before a major system failure. Another chapter in this part of the book focuses on various methods of creating fault tolerance in the Windows 2003 environment.

- **Part VII: Performance Optimization Solutions**—Whereas some organizations view performance optimization as a method of consolidating servers and systems, other organizations view performance optimization as a method of enhancing the operational efficiency of system operations. This part of the book covers both system optimization based on tuning practices and consolidation processes to minimize the number of server systems in a networking environment. The chapter on storage area networking devices describes how you can provide better scalability, redundancy, and manageability of stored information.

- **Part VIII: Business Productivity Solutions**—This last part of the book addresses file management, indexing, and information query options in Windows 2003 that leverage the built-in Windows 2003 technologies that meet business operational productivity initiatives.

We hope that our real-world experience in working with Windows Server 2003 and the real world best practices and insider solutions provided in this book will be valuable in your successful implementation of Windows 2003 technologies in your networking environment.

# PART I

## Security
## Solutions

# 1

# Securing Windows Server 2003

**M**any challenges face IT administrators. One of today's biggest tasks is securing the environment. Companies are more permissive about allowing partners to access data on their networks. At the same time, companies are stricter when it comes to securing that data and those communications. The challenge for the IT professional is to strike a balance between usability and security. Previously, Microsoft wasn't much help in this arena. Early versions of Windows suffered from numerous security flaws that the industry was happy to advertise. With the huge number of Windows machines in use all over the world, Windows became the favorite target of hackers and griefers who knew their work would have the biggest impact if they attacked Windows.

Microsoft has made great strides to improve the security of its operating systems and applications. All software must pass rigorous tests to check for known flaws, buffer overrun susceptibility, and other potential security issues before it is released to consumers. Windows 2003 was built during the beginning of this security focus and reaped the benefits of Microsoft's increased awareness of the need to produce secure software.

# Improved Default Security in Windows 2003

To improve security in Windows Server 2003, Microsoft reduced the attack surface area of the operating System. This was done by

- Creating stronger default policies for the file system Access Control Lists (ACL)
- Redesigning IIS
- Providing a systemic way to configure a server based on predefined roles
- Reducing the total number of services
- Reducing the number of services running by default
- Reducing the number of services running as system

More specifically, in Windows Server 2003, Microsoft disabled 19 services and modified several services to run under lower privileges. For example, installing Windows Server 2003 does not install IIS 6 by default. You must explicitly select and install it or choose Web Server as the system role via the Configure Your Server Wizard. When a server is upgraded to Windows Server 2003, IIS 6 will be disabled by default. If IIS 6 is installed, it will default to a locked down state. After installation, IIS 6 will accept requests only for static files. It must be intentionally configured to serve dynamic content. All time-outs and settings are set to aggressive security defaults. IIS 6 can also be disabled using Windows Server 2003 group policies to prevent rogue administrators from opening unauthorized Web servers.

Windows 2003 has stronger default ACLs on the file system. This, in turn, results in stronger default ACLs on file shares. For example, the everyone group has been removed from default ACLs.

Two new user accounts have been created to run services with lower privilege levels. This helps to prevent vulnerabilities in services from being exploited to take over systems. DNS Client and all IIS Worker Processes now run under the new Network Service account. Telnet now runs under the new Local Service account.

Right out of the box, Windows 2003 is built as a secure system. The system installs only the components it needs to operate rather than installing additional services by default. Windows 2003 defaults to settings that eliminate a large number of potential security holes by not supporting legacy operating systems that are known to be less than secure. During the installation of Windows 2003 the system will warn you that it will be unable to authenticate Windows 9x clients and Windows NT 4.0 clients prior to Service Pack 3. This is because Windows 2003 sets two specific settings in the Domain Controller Security Policy:

- Microsoft network server: Digitally sign communications (always)—Enabled
- Network security: LAN Manager Authentication level—Send NTLM response only

Although these settings can be altered to allow the legacy operating systems to authenticate, it is not recommended to do so. This would reopen the security holes this policy is designed to close. Many administrators will remember the days when Web sites could issue LanMan (LM) requests of a host and the host would offer up the username and the LM hash of the password. The LM hash is a very weak encryption that can be broken quite rapidly via a brute force attack. Although the LM hash is stored in a non-reversible encryption, the encryption algorithm is commonly known. By having a program generate a password and apply the algorithm to it, the result can be compared to the stolen hash to see if they match. If they do, the source password is known and the system is compromised. This is exceptionally fast if the password exists in a dictionary. Going beyond the scope of Windows 2003, it is a very good idea to disable the local storage of LM hashes on all systems in the network via Group Policy Object (GPO). To define the group policy setting that limits the storage of the LM Hash Value, follow these steps:

1. For the Group Policy object, choose Computer Configuration, Windows Settings, Security Settings, Local Policies, and then click Security Options.

2. In the list of available policies, double-click Network Security: Do Not Store LAN Manager Hash Value on Next Password Change.

3. Click Define This Policy Setting, choose Enabled, and then click OK.

## Improvements over Windows 2000

Perhaps the single greatest improvement in security over Windows 2000 is not a technology but a procedure. Windows 2000 installed Internet Information Server by default, it installed OS2 and Posix subsystems, and it offered little insight into the implications of installing various services and applications. Windows 2003, on the other hand, introduces the Configure Your Server Wizard. This wizard launches by default when a Windows 2003 server is first built. It asks the installer what the intended role of the server is and makes the appropriate changes on the system. Files are installed, service securities are set, and the administrator can feel comfortable that the system hasn't installed unnecessary services. This alone eliminates the largest cause of system insecurity—misconfiguration.

## New Security Technologies Introduced in Windows 2003

One of the new technologies introduced in Windows 2003 is Internet Information Services 6. IIS was redesigned in Windows Server 2003 to further improve security for Web-based transactions. IIS 6 enables you to isolate an individual Web application into a self-contained Web service process. This prevents one application from disrupting other applications running on the same Web server. IIS also provides built-in monitoring capabilities to find, fix and avoid Web application failures. In IIS 6, third-party application code runs in isolated worker processes, which now use the lower-privileged Network Service logon account. Worker process isolation offers the capability to confine a Web site or application to its root directory through Access Control Lists (ACL). This further shields the system from exploits that walk the file system to try to execute scripts or other built-in code.

Windows 2003 has also improved network communication security through the support of strong authentication protocols such as 802.1x (WiFi) and Protected Extensible Authentication

Protocol (PEAP). Internet Protocol Security (IPSec) support has been enhanced and further integrated into the operating system to improve LAN and WAN data encryption.

Microsoft introduced the Common Language Runtime (CLR) software engine in Windows Server 2003 to improve reliability and create a safer computing environment. CLR verifies that applications can run without error and checks security permissions to ensure that code does not perform illegal operations. CLR reduces the number of bugs and security holes caused by common programming mistakes. This results in less vulnerability for hackers to exploit.

Another technology introduction in Windows 2003 is the concept of Forest Trusts. Windows Server 2003 supports cross-forest trusts, allowing companies to better integrate with other companies that use the Active Directory. Setting up a cross-forest trust with a partner's Active Directory enables users to securely access resources without losing the convenience of single sign-on. This feature enables you to use ACL resources with users or groups from the partner's Active Directory. This technology is a great boon in situations where one company has acquired another. Establishing a cross-forest trust allows the two companies to immediately start sharing resources in a secured manner.

The idea of single sign-on is further improved by the introduction of Credential Manager. This technology provides a secure store for usernames and passwords as well as links to certificates and keys. This enables a consistent single sign-on experience for users. Single sign-on enables users to access resources over the network without having to repeatedly supply their security credentials.

Windows Server 2003 supports Constrained Delegation. Delegation in this context means allowing a service to impersonate a user or computer account to access resources on the network. This new feature in Windows Server 2003 enables you to limit this type of delegation to specific services or resources. For example, a service that uses delegation to access a system on behalf of a user could now be constrained such that it could only impersonate the user to connect to a single specific system and not to other machines or services on the network. This is similar in concept to the ability to limit a user to attaching to a restricted list of systems.

Protocol Transition is a technology that allows a service to convert to a Kerberos-based identity for a user without knowing the user's password or requiring the user to authenticate via Kerberos. This enables an Internet user to authenticate using a custom authentication method and receive a Windows identity. This technology is now available in Windows 2003. This can be very useful for companies that are planning to heavily leverage Kerberos as a centralized point of authentication for both Windows and Linux systems.

Windows Server 2003 now offers .NET Passport Integration with Active Directory. This enables the use of Passport–based authentication to provide partners and customers with a single sign-on experience to Windows–based resources and applications. By leveraging .NET Passport services, companies can often reduce their cost of managing user IDs and passwords for applications with large numbers of external users. Microsoft has gone to great lengths to ensure that .NET Passport information is stored as securely as possible to foster confidence in the industry and help grow the technology.

Although Windows 2000 supported encrypted folders, Windows Server 2003 now allows offline files and folders to be encrypted using EFS as well. Offline Files, or client-side caching, was introduced in Windows 2000 and allows mobile users to work with a local copy of a file while disconnected from the network. When the user reconnects to the server, the system reconciles the changes with the older versions of the documents on the server. This allows files to continue to be protected when cached locally on a mobile computer.

Stronger encryption technologies for EFS are available in Windows 2003. Windows Server 2003 now supports encryption for EFS that is stronger than the default Data Encryption Standard (DESX) algorithm. By default EFS will use the Advanced Encryption Standard (AES-256) for all encrypted files. Clients can also use Federal Information Processing Standards (FIPS) 140-1 compliant algorithms, such as the 3DES algorithm, which is also included with Windows XP Professional.

# Securing the Hatches

Today, the whole world is looking at security. As the world becomes more information connected, issues of information privacy are on everyone's mind. Several government mandates have been issued in the area of securing identity information for medical histories and for information regarding children.

Commerce across networks in the arena of business to business and business to consumer have all raised questions about whether credit card information is being stored securely or whether online transactions are safe. These issues have spawned many technologies and the corporate world has adopted many of these for internal security. As access to information becomes easier and easier, it is more and more critical to ensure that data and data transmissions are protected.

**Security and Company Reputation**

In today's market, if a company is to keep its customers, the customers must have faith in the company. Large online retailers are dependant on the confidence of their customers in their security in order to continue doing business. So long as customers feel secure that their financial information is being transmitted and stored securely, they will continue to do business with a company online.

If one of these online retailers was to become compromised and information such as credit card numbers was stolen, it could potentially destroy the company. The reputation of the company is tied directly to its security. Failure to be diligent in securing the hatches of a company can quickly lead to its downfall.

## Implementing Transport Layer Security

The concept of Transport Layer Security (TLS) is that conversations between networked devices should be held in a manner such that any other device that might have intercepted the communications will be unable to use the information. TLS, which is similar to SSL, is based on an x.509 certificate which must be published from a trusted Certificate Authority (CA). TLS can do the following:

- Detect message tampering
- Detect message interception
- Detect message forgery

To use TLS for client/server communication, the following steps are used:

1. Handshake and cipher suite negotiation.

2. Authentication of parties.

3. Key-related information exchange.

4. Application data exchange.

By default TLS will accept any cipher; this can be locked down further by GPO to limit the cipher choices through modification of the following Registry key:

HKEY_LOCAL_MACHINE\SYSTEM\CurrentControlSet\Control\SecurityProviders\SCHANNEL\ Ciphers

You will find multiple cipher choices listed and can enable or disable them as appropriate.

The TLS Handshake Protocol involves the following steps:

1. A "client hello" is sent from the client machine to the server, along with a random value and a list of supported cipher suites.

2. A "server hello" is sent in reply to the client along with the server's random value.

3. The server sends its certificate to the client to be authenticated and it might request a certificate from the client as well. This results in a "Server hello done" message. The client sends the certificate if it was requested by the server.

4. The client then creates a random Pre-Master Secret and encrypts it via the public key from the server's certificate. This encrypted Pre-Master Secret is then sent to the server.

5. Upon receipt of the Pre-Master Secret, the server and client each generate the session keys and Master Secret based on the Pre-Master Secret.

6. The client sends a "Change cipher spec" message to the server to indicate that the client will begin using the new session keys for encrypting and hashing messages. The client also sends a "Client finished" message.

7. The server receives the "Change cipher spec" message and switches its record layer security state to use symmetric encryption based on the session keys. The server sends a "Server finished" message to the client.

8. The client and server can now exchange data over the secured channel that they have established. All data and communications sent from client to server and from server to client are encrypted using the session key.

## Requiring Digital Signing

Older implementations of Small Message Block (SMB) communications were susceptible to what is known as a *man-in-the-middle* attack. A man-in-the-middle attack occurs when an attacker masquerading as one of the legitimate parties inserts messages into the communications channel. This allows the attacker to send its own credentials and causes the other host to accept its connection. By placing a digital signature into each SMB, which is verified by both the server and the client, there is a mutual authentication that verifies the validity of both the server and the client. If this security setting is enabled on a server, the clients must support digital signing of communications or they will be unable to communicate with the server.

This can be configured in the Default Domain Controller Security Settings under Security Settings/Local Policies/Security Options/Microsoft Network Server: Digitally Sign Communications (always)—Enabled.

## Leveraging PKI

Not surprisingly, certificate-based technologies require access to certificates. Specifically, certificates that have been issued by a trusted Certificate Authority. Companies have the option of using an external trusted Certificate Authority such as Verisign, SecureNet, or Globalsign. One advantage of using one of these external Certificate Authorities is that Internet Explorer comes preloaded with these as trusted root authorities. This means that clients won't have to contact those root CAs and prompt the user to accept the certificate. The other option is for a company to establish its own Certificate Authority. This could be a root CA or an Enterprise CA that was built based on a certificate provided by another Root CA.

If a company is going to issue its own certificates, client machines can be preloaded with the certificate via GPO settings. For example, if a company will be using digital certificates in their intranet, they might push a server certificate to the clients to define the server as an Intermediate Certification Authority. To push a certificate to clients, do the following:

1. Launch the GPO editor.

2. Choose User Configuration, Windows Settings, Internet Explorer Maintenance, Security, Authenticode Settings.

3. Choose Import Existing Authenticode Settings.

4. Click Modify Settings.

5. Click Import. This launches the Import Certificates Wizard.

6. Click Next.

7. Click Browse, and then browse to the certificate file. Choose Open and then click Next.

8. Choose Browse and select the appropriate certificate store.

9. Choose Next and then click Finish.

The Wizard will inform you that you are about to install a certificate claiming to be from a particular source. If this information is valid, select "yes". The Wizard will inform you that the certificate was successfully installed.

## Installing Certificate Services

Installing certificate services in Windows Server 2003 requires taking a Windows 2003 server and adding the Certificate Services component on the server. The process of adding Certificate Services to a Windows 2003 is as follows:

1. Choose Start, Control Panel, Add or Remove Programs.

2. Click Add/Remove Windows Components.

3. Check the Certificate Services box.

4. A warning dialog box will be displayed, as illustrated in Figure 1.1, indicating that the computer name or domain name cannot be changed after you install Certificate Services. Click Yes to proceed with the installation.

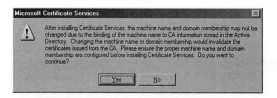

**FIGURE 1.1**  Certificate Services warning.

5. Click Next to continue.

6. The following screen, shown in Figure 1.2, enables you to create the type of CA required. In this example, choose Enterprise Root CA and click Next to continue.

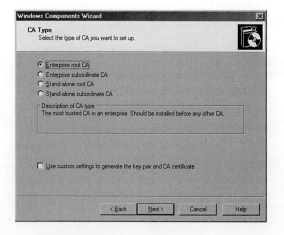

**FIGURE 1.2**  Selecting the type of CA server to install.

7. Enter a common name for the CA—for example, CompanyABC Enterprise Root CA.

> **If IIS Is Installed on the Server, a Dialog Box Will Appear**
>
> If IIS is installed on the server, a dialog box will appear noting that the IIS services will be temporarily stopped. When prompted whether it is okay to stop and restart the IIS service, choose Yes unless the service is actively in use at the time of certificate services installation.

8. Enter the validity period for the Certificate Authority and click Next to continue. The cryptographic key will then be created.

9. Enter a location for the certificate database and then the database logs. The location you choose should be secure, to prevent unauthorized tampering with the CA. Click Next to continue. Setup will then install the CA components.

10. If IIS is not installed, a prompt will be displayed, shown in Figure 1.3, indicating that Web Enrollment will be disabled until you install IIS. If this box is displayed, click OK to continue.

**FIGURE 1.3**   IIS warning in the CA installation procedure.

11. Click Finish after installation to complete the process.

## Importance of Physical Security

Network security is essentially useless if the servers involved aren't physically secured. Computers don't know the difference between a local break-in and a legitimate password recovery. Although security information is stored in the Active Directory, the Active Directory still consists of a database stored on servers. This information is laid out in a specific structure and a person with physical access to a hard drive that contains an NTDS.DIT file, a sector editor, and sufficient knowledge can compromise the security database.

Servers should always be located in locked data centers. Access to these data centers should be limited and audited. Security logs [%systemroot%\System32\config\SecEvent.Evt] should be duplicated in a separate location to prevent tampering. Applications like Microsoft Operations Manager, which centralize management of event logs, are useful for this task. Implementation of a syslog server will also work well for this.

Access to secured data centers should require multiple forms of authentication. For example, rather than just rely on a badge reader, the lock might consist of a combination of a badge reader and a PIN code that must be entered. This way, theft of a badge would not be enough to compromise the data center.

## BEST PRACTICE

### Certificate Server Integrity

Building an internal certificate server is not a trivial event and although it can be done in the 11 relatively simple steps noted in this chapter, certificate server security needs to be taken very seriously by organizations. Certificate authority only provides security and a sense of security when the integrity of the certificate creation process is ensured. If anyone can walk up to an organization's certificate server and create a certificate, no one would know whether the certificate they have is one issued by the real certificate administrator or by an unauthorized individual. If no one knows the validity of the certificate, the security of the data transmission, logon authentication, or data encryption has been greatly compromised.

Because an enterprise or root certificate server is authoritative for an organization's domain name (such as companyabc.com), that organization would not want its root certificate server compromised. If no one trusted whether any certificate-based authentication for the organization is valid, the organization has no credibility to its certificate-based security because someone who has unauthorized access to the certificate server could potentially issue certificates on behalf of the organization.

When building their enterprise or root certificate server, many large organizations distribute the task of certificate creation, hardware management, and system operations. The hardware is secured in a place that has extremely limited access. Creating certificates must be done on the server console, not set up for remote access. Access to the server requires two to three individuals to log on and access the appropriate utilities to create a certificate. All steps are videotaped and securely stored.

This whole process, although it seems to be extremely time- and process-intensive, is common for an organization because it protects the integrity of the organization's certificates.

Great care must be taken in ensuring that the creation of a Root CA is done in a secure and auditable fashion. A compromise of the Root CA essentially compromises every Enterprise and Subordinate CA that was built with a certificate from the Root CA. This, in turn, compromises every certificate issued by the CA hierarchy.

# Know Who Is Connected Using Two-factor Authentication

Usernames and passwords have long been the standard for user authentication. Windows NT improved on this concept by adding a *machine account* that was needed to log into a domain. Although this was good for domain logins it could be bypassed to attach to network resources via pass-through authentication. Many companies need stronger methods of authentication. This is especially critical when dealing with remote users. Modem pools and VPN devices are relatively easy to find. Malicious hackers can spend time trying to get through these devices with relative impunity. This concern is addressed by the concept of two-factor authentication such as smartcards and biometric authentication.

## Utilizing Smartcards

A *smartcard* is a portable programmable device containing an integrated circuit that stores and processes information. Smartcards traditionally take the form of a device the size of a credit card that is placed into a reader but they can also be USB-based devices or integrated into employee badges. Windows 2003 and Windows XP have native support for smartcards as an authentication method. Smartcards are combined with a PIN, which can be thought of as a password, to provide two-factor authentication. Physical possession of the smartcard and knowledge of the PIN must be combined to successfully authenticate.

To use a smartcard, a domain user must have a smart card certificate. The administrator must prepare a Certificate Authority (CA) to issue smart card certificates before the CA can issue them. The CA needs both the Smart Card Logon and Enrollment Agent certificate templates installed. If smart card certificates for secure e-mail messages are to be used, the administrator must also install the Smart Card User certificate template.

To configure a Windows-based Enterprise CA to Issue Smart Card Certificates, follow these steps:

1. Log on to an Enterprise CA. Be sure to use a domain administrator account.

2. From the Start menu choose Programs, Administrative Tools, Certification Authority.

3. In the Certification Authority console, expand your domain, right-click the Certificate Template container, and select New, Certificate Template to Issue.

4. In the Enable Certificate Template dialog box, select Smartcard User, and then click OK.

5. Right-click on the Certificate Template container, and click Manage. This will open up the Certificate Templates MMC.

6. In Select Certificate Template MMC, right-click on the Smartcard User and select Properties.

7. Click on the Security tab. Click on the Add button and choose the group for which you want to add smartcard access (in this example, a Smartcard Users group whose members are employees with smartcards was added to Active Directory).

8. Select Read and Enroll for Permissions as shown in Figure 1.4, and then click OK.

## Leveraging Biometrics to Enhance Security

*Biometrics* refers to unique biological information that can be used to determine the identity of a user. This, combined with a name/password authentication, provides a two-factor authentication that cannot be duplicated. Thumbprints, bone density, and retinal patterns are all commonly used with biometric security.

Third-party biometric solutions leverage proprietary authentication mechanisms to work in tandem with existing authentication protocols in network operating systems. Technologies like retinal scanners are usually standalone devices whereas items like fingerprint readers can integrate into the user's keyboard.

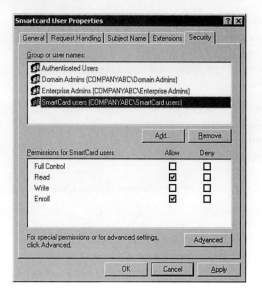

**FIGURE 1.4**  Adding a group for smartcard logon authentication.

# Using Templates to Improve Usage and Management

One of the biggest keys to effective security is the standardization of the application of security policies across the environment. Windows 2003 continues to support this concept with the use of the Security Configuration and Analysis MMC plug-in. This plug-in enables you to convert your own security policies into a template file that can be applied to other servers. This ensures that servers are configured identically. This can be exceptionally useful for systems configured to sit outside a firewall that are not members of an Active Directory domain and thus aren't managed by Group Policy Objects.

## Using the Security Configuration and Analysis Tool

The Security Configuration and Analysis tool, which is available in Windows 2003 from the MMC Snap-in, is designed to read specific security information from a server and compare it to a template file. This enables you to create standard templates and see whether servers in their environment conform to those settings.

To perform an analysis of a system, do the following:

1. Select Start, Run, mmc.exe and then click OK to launch the MMC snap-in.

2. Add the Security Configuration and Analysis snap-in.

3. Right-click the Security Configuration and Analysis scope item, and choose Open Database.

4. Choose a database name and then click Open.

5. Pick a security template, and then open it.

6. Right-click the Security Configuration and Analysis scope item and choose Analyze Computer Now, then click OK.

The system will display all local security settings and show the template recommendation from the database. By comparing local settings to a standard template created by the administrator, settings can be made consistent without steamrollering any required local security settings.

## Leveraging Secure Templates

Groups such as the National Security Agency or the National Institute of Standards and Technology have built what they consider to be secure templates for such roles as Domain Controller, Web Server, Application Server, and others. By using these templates as a starting point, you can build customized templates that take NIST or NSA guidelines into account. This makes it much easier to build a secure template as these groups specialized in knowing and understanding computer security.

# Patrolling the Configuration

After you have gone through a server and locked it down to your satisfaction, it is important to audit those settings against third-party tools to ensure that nothing was missed. It's also valuable to know that your network meets the standards of a well-recognized security entity such as the NSA or NIST.

With requirements like the Health Insurance Portability and Accountability Act (HIPAA) or Graham Leach Bliley Act (GLBA), many companies are now required to provide documentation to prove that they have taken the necessary steps to secure the sensitive information on their networks. Third-party analysis tools provide an objective and impartial assessment of network security. Although some assessment technologies are very thorough, they are no replacement for an audit by a reputable company that specializes in security audits.

## Auditing the System Security

The event log is an excellent way to track activity on a server. The local security policy allows you to enable or disable various auditing events, which are explained in the following list:

■ *Audit account logon events.* This setting audits each instance of a user logging on to or off of another computer in which this computer was used to validate the account. Account logon events are generated when a domain controller authenticates a domain user. The event is logged in the domain controller's security log. Similarly, logon events are generated when a local computer authenticates on a local user. In this case, the event is logged in the local security log.

- *Audit account management.* This setting audits each instance that a user account or group is created, changed, or deleted. It also generates events when a user account is renamed, disabled, or enabled. Password setting or changing is audited as well.

- *Audit directory service access.* This security setting audits each event of a user accessing an Active Directory object that has its own system access control list (SACL) specified.

- *Audit object access.* This security setting audits the event of a user accessing an object, such as a file, folder, Registry key, or printer that has its own system access control list (SACL) specified.

- *Audit policy change.* This setting audits incidences of a change to user rights assignment policies, audit policies, or trust policies.

- *Audit privilege use.* This setting audits each instance of a user exercising a user right.

- *Audit process tracking.* This setting audits detailed tracking information for events such as program activation, process exit, handle duplication, and indirect object access.

- *Audit system events.* This setting audits when a user restarts or shuts down the computer or when an event occurs that affects either the system security or the security log.

## Using the Microsoft Baseline Security Analyzer

### MBSA and the Latest Copy of the mssecure.xml File

MBSA attaches to the Microsoft Web site to pull the latest copy of the mssecure.xml file. If a machine that will run MBSA does not have Internet access, you can download the XML file and place it on the machine running MBSA. Remember to update this file regularly to be aware of critical updates on the target systems.

The Microsoft Baseline Security Analyzer is a tool designed to determine which critical security updates are currently applied to a system. MBSA performs this task by referring to an XML (Extensible Markup Language) file called mssecure.xml. This file is continuously updated by Microsoft to account for all current critical fixes. By leveraging the HFNetChk tool technology MBSA is able to audit the target system against the current list of fixes. This XML file holds information about which security updates are available for particular Microsoft products beyond just the operating system. This file holds the names and titles of security bulletins as well as detailed information about product-specific security updates, including the following:

- Files in each update package

- Versions and checksums

- Registry keys that were applied by applications

- Information about which updates supersede others

- Related Microsoft Knowledge Base article numbers

## Using Vulnerability Scanners

One of the most valuable methods for checking the security of a server is through the use of a vulnerability scanner. Vulnerability scanners are based on a constantly updated database of known security flaws in operating systems and applications. The scanner attaches to the target system on various ports and sends requests to the system. Based on the responses, the scanner checks its database to determine whether the conditions for an exploit exist on the system. These potential exploits are then compiled into a report and are presented to the administrator. Most vulnerability scanners have the option to do intrusive testing as well. Great care should be taken when performing intrusive testing. Intrusive testing is the only way to truly validate the results of the vulnerability testing. For example, a report item might list that a particular script is marked as executable via the Web services and that it could be exploited to cause the Web server to crash if it is passed a parameter containing a nonstandard character. You might believe that this is a false positive because you have assigned NTFS permissions to the script to only allow a single account to access the script; that account is one that you control and it can never send a nonstandard character. The only way to be sure would be to have the scanner attempt to exploit that apparent flaw. This would need to be done during a maintenance window in case the exploit succeeded. Only after performing this validation could you be certain that the vulnerability was not actually present.

Some popular vulnerability scanners are as follows:

- Microsoft Security Baseline Analyzer

- Internet Security Systems: RealSecure

- Nessus

- GFI LANguard Network Security Scanner

- Cerberus Internet Scanner (CIS)

## Auditing the File System

Windows 2003 possesses built-in mechanisms to audit file system access. This enables you to see who is accessing or attempting to access specific files and when the access occurs. This type of auditing is only supported on NTFS drives. To audit this type of access, you must first enable the Object Access Auditing. This feature can be enabled via the Default Domain Security Settings, under Local Policies/Audit Policy/ Audit Object Access. As shown in Figure 1.5, set this to audit both Success and Failure in order to track both types of events. Follow these steps to audit access of a particular file or folder:

**Managing the Auditing on a Server**

The role of managing the auditing on a server can be delegated to a non–administrator account by granting the Manage Auditing and Security Log rights via Group Policy. This enables you to delegate this role without giving full administrator rights. This can be especially useful for remote site administrators who only manage a subset of servers and users.

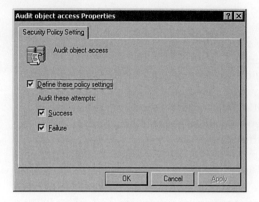

**FIGURE 1.5** Setting the security auditing function.

1. Navigate via Explorer to the file or folder in question.

2. Right-click the item to be audited, click Properties, and then Security.

3. Click Advanced, and then click the Auditing button. Click Add. Enter the name of the group or user of which you would like to track the actions and click OK.

4. In the Apply Onto drop-down box, choose the location where you want the auditing to take place.

5. In the Access box, indicate what successes and failures you want to audit by selecting the appropriate check boxes.

6. Click OK, OK, and OK to exit when done.

# Securing the File System

Windows 2003 stores all its data in the file system. User data, application data, and operating system files all live in the file system. To secure Windows 2003, these files need to be secured. Threats from outside the network, accidental deletion of system files, or access from an unauthorized internal group can all result in the loss of data or the compromising of confidential data. Windows 2003 supports many mechanisms to secure the file system.

## Locking Down the File System via NTFS

Way back in Windows NT 3.1 Microsoft introduced the NT File System (NTFS). NTFS was a great breakthrough over the FAT file system in many areas. Support for larger drives, support for nonstandard block allocation sizes, and the ability to define security on a file or folder level all gave NTFS a big advantage over FAT. The ability to secure files and folders individually via NTFS permissions is the basis of Windows 2003 as a securable file server.

Windows 2003 has made great strides in the area of default system NTFS permission on the file system. Windows no longer defaults to having the everyone group listed for all resources. Instead, it defaults to allowing authenticated users the ability to read and list files and folders. By default,

Windows 2003 will allow authenticated users to bypass traverse checking. This works hand in hand with the upgrades to client operating systems like Windows 2000 Professional and Windows XP Professional that now allow drives to be mapped at a point below the share point. So although a share might exist that looks like \\Server\users$ with departmental directories with hundreds of user directories below them, a user can now be mapped directly to his own directory without having to share the user directory explicitly and without having to grant the user rights to anything other then his own directory. Although the user might not be able to read or list the departmental directories it is unnecessary if the goal is only to give him access to his own home directory. This greatly simplifies the application of NTFS permissions.

## Locking Down Group Membership

One of the most important ways to keep a network secured is to ensure that users are not granted membership to groups that provide more rights than they really need. Similarly it is critical not to fall into the trap of simply making all administrators domain administrators just to ensure that they have sufficient rights to perform their daily duties. Windows 2003 has continued to make great strides in the area of granularity when it comes to assigning rights to administrators.

The area of group membership that is often overlooked by administrators is the local administrative groups on member servers and on workstations. Because these groups aren't centrally managed, it is easy to forget that they are out there. Administrators often add user's domain accounts into their local administrator group so that they can work on installing a new software package but often forget to remove that membership after the project is finished. This results in a number of users having elevated rights on their own workstations. This puts them at risk of unwittingly installing spyware or other applications that could put the network at risk.

One way to control membership of these local groups is through the application of Group Policy Objects. By defining the Administrators group as a Restricted Group you can define what accounts are allowed to be present in that group. If a local administrator adds an additional account the change will not be persistent. This enables you to easily control group memberships across the network. This parameter is found in Computer Configuration/Windows Settings/Security Settings/ Restricted Groups. Simply add the group you want to restrict and add the members that are allowed to be present.

## Keeping Users Out of Critical File Areas

Operating system files are the lifeblood of the operating system. Corruptions or deletions of these files can quickly cripple a server. Aside from application of security patches, there is no reason for an administrator to need write access to system files. Having the ability to do so only makes the administrator a threat to the stability of the system. Accidental file deletion or renaming through either operator error or malicious scripts can be prevented by locking down access to the system files. Allow the Administrator account to retain Full Control of the files in the %systemroot% directory but don't allow general administrative groups to have rights to these files. Discourage administrators from logging on to systems as Administrator. Instead have them use their normal account and use the "run as" feature if they need to run a program with elevated rights.

# Securing Web Services

Web Servers are one of the most common implementations of Windows 2003 and due to their role of serving users outside the domain they are especially vulnerable and need to be well-secured. New Web-related exploits are found practically daily and if Web servers are to remain secure, they must be up-to-date on available patches for the operating system as well as for the Web services.

## Using SSL

> **Bandwidth Usage and SSL**
> The use of SSL does not affect bandwidth usage. It does, however, place an additional CPU load on both the client and the server. If an existing Web application is going to be switched to SSL communications, the overall capacity of the system will be reduced. This overhead can be mitigated on the server via the use of hardware-based SSL accelerators.

One of the biggest concerns with Web servers is making sure that secure conversations are not intercepted via packet sniffing. Because the Internet is a pretty nebulous cloud with questionable security it is up to you to ensure that end-to-end communications with end users are secure. One of the most common ways to do this is with Secure Socket Layer communications. SSL runs above TCP/IP and below HTTP. SSL performs three primary functions:

- *SSL server authentication.* This allows a client to validate a server's identity. SSL-enabled client software can use public-key cryptography to check to see if a server's certificate and public ID are valid. It can also check to see if the certificate has been issued by a certificate authority (CA) listed in the client's list of trusted CAs. If, for example, a user were sending a credit card number over the Internet to make a purchase, he would want to verify the receiving server's identity.

- *SSL client authentication.* This allows a server to validate a user's identity. Using a similar technique as that used for server authentication, SSL-enabled server software can validate that a client's certificate and public ID are valid. It can also check to see that a trusted certificate authority issued them. If, for example, an online retailer wanted to send confidential information to a customer, it would want to verify the recipient's identity.

- *Encrypting SSL connections.* SSL requires that all information sent between a server and a client be encrypted by the sending software and decrypted by the receiving software. This provides a high degree of confidentiality and security. SSL includes a mechanism for detecting data that was tampered with. This further protects transactions performed over SSL connections.

## Scanning the Web Servers for Vulnerabilities

Web servers are especially vulnerable to attack by hackers and griefers. By their very nature Web servers are often open to anonymous access and are located in lightly secured networks. Web servers are very popular targets and as such, vulnerabilities are regularly found in Web services. In order for you to secure systems against these vulnerabilities, you must be aware of them. The easiest way to do this is to scan the Web servers for vulnerabilities regularly.

Many companies offer services specifically designed to regularly scan Web servers for other companies and provide them with reports on discovered vulnerabilities. This is an excellent option for companies that lack the resources or expertise to perform these scans in-house.

## Keeping Up With Patches

Keeping up with patches is absolutely critical for the security of Web servers. The vast majority of the critical fixes produced for Windows are based on flaws discovered on Web servers. This isn't so much because Web services are inherently insecure but because there are so many Windows-based Web servers on the Internet; they can't help but provide a tempting target for hackers. Microsoft has entire teams of engineers and software developers that are dedicated to solving these vulnerabilities as soon as they are discovered. Their job is to get these hotfixes out to administrators. The easiest way to manage these patches is with the Software Update Service.

The SUS server allows you to point all of your Web servers to a single server for downloading patches. You need only to check the logs on the SUS server to see if new patches are available. You can test these patches in a lab environment and then approve a patch for distribution. At that point, the Web servers that are configured to point to the SUS server will automatically install the patches and optionally reboot themselves.

> **Patches and Automatic Rebooting**
> If servers are configured to reboot automatically after patches that request a reboot, you could face a situation where all of the load-balanced Web servers reboot themselves at the same time. This could result in several minutes of downtime for the site depending on how long the servers take to reboot.

## Locking Down IIS

Windows 2003 IIS (version 6.0) surpasses its predecessor by integrating many of the features of the old IIS Lockdown Tool. The IIS Lockdown Tool worked by disabling unnecessary features within IIS based on the planned role of the server. This served to reduce the potential points of attack available to hackers. This was layered with URLScan, a utility that intercepted input from client machines and ran it through an internal check to determine if it was trying to send malicious data such as out-of-band characters or scripts. By default, IIS 6 installs with just the features needed to fill its defined role. It is able to specify exactly what ISAPI and CGI code is allowed to run on the server and has default behaviors for handling HTTP verbs and headers that are designed to execute WebDAV. IIS 6 maintains a UrlScan.ini file with a specific section for DenyUrlSequences. This replaces some of the features of URLScan. Similarly IIS 6 has a mechanism for limiting the length of fields and requests. This plugs many of the older IIS vulnerabilities. If these settings are too restrictive for a specific Web application, the parameters can be modified via Registry settings:

- HKEY_LOCAL_MACHINE\System\CurrentControlSet\Services\HTTP\Parameters\ AllowRestrictedChars

- HKEY_LOCAL_MACHINE\System\CurrentControlSet\Services\HTTP\Parameters\ MaxFieldLength

- HKEY_LOCAL_MACHINE\System\CurrentControlSet\Services\HTTP\Parameters\ UrlSegmentMaxLength

- HKEY_LOCAL_MACHINE\System\CurrentControlSet\Services\HTTP\Parameters\ UrlSegmentMaxCount

Although URLScan 2.5 will run on IIS 6, most administrators will find it unnecessary because most of the security features in IIS 6 are better than those in URLScan 2.5. URLScan 2.5 is highly recommended for use with older IIS 5.0 servers.

# Keeping Files Confidential with EFS

Windows 2003 supports the Encrypting File System on NTFS volumes. EFS enables a user to encrypt a file such that only he can access it. When a user initially uses EFS to encrypt a file, the user is assigned a key pair (public key and private key). This is either generated by the certificate services or self-signed by EFS depending on whether there is a CA present. The public key is used for encryption and the private key is used for decryption.

When the user encrypts a file, a random number called the File Encryption Key (FEK) is assigned to the file. The DES or DESX algorithm is used to encrypt the file with the FEK as the secret key. The FEK is also encrypted with the public key using the RSA algorithm. In this way, a large file can be encrypted using relatively fast secret key cryptography while the FEK is encrypted with slower but more secure public key cryptography. This provides a high level of security with less impact on overall performance.

## Leveraging Standalone EFS

Windows 2000, 2003, and XP all support EFS. They are capable of generating their own key pair for EFS if a domain level certificate is unavailable to them. EFS on a machine that does not belong to a domain has a number of differences than a machine that is a domain member. For example, Windows 2000 has a default setting that allows any local Administrator account to decrypt any user's encrypted files on that machine. This makes machines vulnerable to sector editor attacks as the local password store can be compromised. Windows XP and Windows Server 2003 do not have this behavior.

If a user encrypts a file and loses the certificate store of both the user and the local DRA, it will be impossible to decrypt the files. Similarly, due to the lack of a central key database for non-domain EFS users, a user could intentionally delete the DRA certificate and the certificate store and render the files unrecoverable.

When using EFS in a non–Active Directory environment, some key best practices should be followed to simplify management and improve local security:

- Windows 2000 computers should have the default DRA private key removed stored separately from the system.

- Use a SYSKEY mode with a boot floppy or master password that must be entered prior to system boot. The floppy or master password should be stored separately from the system. This helps protect the local account store from attack.

- Build machines using sysprep and custom scripts to configure a central recovery agent. This can be achieved via a run-once Registry key that removes the existing local DRA and inserts a

> **Existing Encrypted Files and Utilizing the Default Domain Recovery Agent**
>
> If a machine or user with standalone EFS is migrated to an Active Directory environment with an enterprise CA, clients will continue to use the self-signed certificates. They will not automatically enroll for a new certificate once they are joined. However, the default domain recovery agent will take effect for all new files. Existing encrypted files will utilize the default domain recovery agent once they are modified.

centralized DRA. This change must be performed after the sysprep mini-setup that generates the default DRA. The preferred practice is to use a Microsoft CA to issue a DRA certificate for the central recovery agent.

## Common Pitfalls with Encrypted File System Implementations

One of the easiest traps to fall into with Encrypted File System (EFS) is to allow users to enable EFS on their own machine without access to a domain wide recovery agent. Clients will create their own key pair and administrators might not have the capability to recovery encrypted files if the user loses the local key pair. Active Directory allows you to prevent users from enabling EFS until such time that a proper CA has been put in place to enable managed EFS on the clients. The easiest way to do this is via GPMC:

1. Open the Group Policy Management Console MMC snap-in.

2. Navigate to the appropriate container where the GPO should be applied.

3. Right-click on the GPO and select Edit as shown in Figure 1.6.

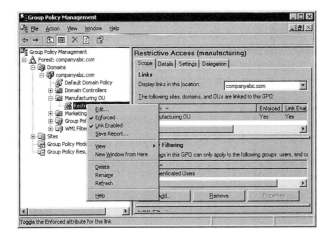

**FIGURE 1.6**
Editing the GPO in Group Policy Management Console.

4. Navigate to \Computer Configuration\Windows Settings\Security Settings\Public Key Policies.

5. Right-click the folder named Encrypting File System.

6. Click Properties.

7. Uncheck the box marked Allow Users to Encrypt Files Use Encrypting File System

8. Click OK.

# Bulletproof Scenario

CompanyABC is a small software company with offices all over the world. CompanyABC supports roaming salespeople who travel from office to office. CompanyABC prides itself on its ability to make resources available to the end users. CompanyABC has security policies in place that require encrypting all data on databases and file servers as well as all communications between computers. CompanyABC requires strong authentication for access to any and all systems.

Bob is an employee at CompanyABC. Bob works in sales travels often. He needs near constant access to contact databases and e-mail and has a fancy new notebook with a wireless network interface and Windows XP.

This section will take a look at a typical day for Bob and highlight the security features that enable Bob to perform his daily tasks in a secure manner.

Bob has just arrived in a remote office and needs to access a document that he has stored on a file server back at the corporate headquarters. Bob has been given access to a conference room to use as a temporary office. Bob boots up his notebook and is prompted to enter his smartcard. Bob places his smartcard-enabled employee badge into the smartcard reader in his notebook and is asked for a PIN. Bob enters his PIN and is authenticated to the notebook. As Bob's notebook launches Windows XP, it sends a DHCP request via the wireless network interface. Along with this DHCP request, Bob's system sends a ClassID that was configured on his system when it was first imaged. Luckily for Bob, the MAC address of his wireless card was entered into a RADIUS server that all of the wireless access points use to authenticate users at a hardware level. This allows the access point to process Bob's DHCP request. The request reaches a DHCP server located on an isolated network in the office. This Network site behind a firewall only allows VPN traffic to reach a specific pair of load-balanced VPN servers. Because the ClassID on Bob's machine matches the ClassID on a scope on the DHCP server, Bob's machine is given a valid IP address.

Bob launches his VPN connection and attaches to the local VPN server. Bob now has an L2TP connection secured with IPSec to the office network. At this point, a domain login prompt appears and Bob authenticates himself to the network via his Active Directory login. Pleased with his progress, Bob decides to reward himself with a nice cup of coffee. Knowing that the kitchen requires badge access to enter, Bob removes his employee badge from the notebook and walks to the kitchen. By removing his badge, the smartcard driver tells the system to lock itself.

This is a behavior that is configured on the notebook. While Bob is away, other users cannot gain access to his notebook. Bob returns shortly and unlocks his notebook via the smartcard and PIN combination. Because Bob has access to the corporate network, he decides to access his document on the server back at HQ.

When Bob's notebook requests the file from the server, the server informs Bob's notebook that it requires Transport Layer Security to access the resources. Bob's notebook and the server exchange certificates and random values and create a pre-master secret. This secret is used to generate their session keys. These session keys are used to encrypt the communications. When Bob's notebook told the server which ciphers it supported it informed the server that it only supports Microsoft Enhanced DSS and Diffie-Hellman SChannel Cryptographic Provider, which is the way the notebook was configured when it was first imaged. The server accepts this cipher and the channel is established.

The document Bob wants is sitting in his personal folder. This folder is encrypted via EFS based on a certificate that was issued to Bob by the corporate Certificate Authority. Because Bob's notebook possesses the correct key, he is able to decrypt the file to view it. Bob has also enabled several coworkers to decrypt the file so that it can be shared.

Bob, being just computer savvy enough to be dangerous, decides that this is just too much effort to get to a single file. Knowing that he is going to need to access this file again the next day at another office, Bob decides that he is going to create a local cached copy of the file through offline folders. Luckily, a Windows XP client with a Windows 2003 backend allows Bob's offline copy to remain encrypted. Now when Bob loses his notebook at the airport again, the company doesn't have to worry about a loss of intellectual property.

# Summary

In this chapter, you learned that Microsoft has taken great steps toward making communications and storage more secure. Windows 2003 represents the latest efforts of Microsoft in this area. You saw the importance of taking a layered approach to security. No single technology in Windows 2003 is the end-all, be-all of security. These technologies work together to help secure the intellectual property of the company both locally and abroad.

We've seen that although securing a system is very important, it's equally important to audit and test that security constantly. Monitoring activities in a network and recognizing signs of attack are critical in protecting a network.

Technologies like smartcards and biometrics help to strengthen the authentication process of Windows. Technologies like TLS and SSL help ensure that once authenticated, transmissions are still performed in a secure manner.

Files can be encrypted and still be shared among controlled lists of users. By storing files in an encrypted manner, systems become less vulnerable to data theft as a result of hardware theft. This enables companies to allow more access to their data without reducing the overall security of the environment.

It is always important to realize that today's "unbreakable" security will become tomorrow's plaything. 128-bit encryptions that used to take years to crack can be cracked in mere seconds by today's more powerful computers. Security is a commitment, an ongoing process that must be constantly monitored and maintained. It must grow as a company grows in order to remain useful.

# 2

## Implementing Secured Wireless Technologies

The security issues that face companies that implement wireless networks are many. It's like trying to secure a public network jack placed on the outside of your building. It just invites people to try and break into the network.

Trying to enforce the physical security that you've provided for your servers and backbone networking equipment isn't possible. This chapter discusses the alternatives in a wireless environment so you can at least tell who's accessing your network and from where.

You're going to look at how Windows Server 2003, along with the features included with your wireless networking equipment, can make it more difficult for attackers to take advantage of your public network jack.

**Moving Target**

The industry standard for wireless security is a moving target at this time. The target standard is IEEE (Institute of Electrical and Electronics Engineers) 802.11i. As of the writing of this book this standard is still in draft. It outlines wireless security guidelines for hardware manufacturers and software developers.

# Working Through Walls

Radio Frequency (RF) waves travel well through most solid objects. This creates a complicated scenario when dealing with physical security on your network. The placement of access points and their antennas requires some careful planning and site surveys.

## Common Mistakes When Planning Access Point Placement

When considering coverage and number of access points, physical placement is very important in a wireless network. Taking into account the surrounding building architecture, distances and possible sources of interference become critical. RF propagation patterns can be affected in many ways. You're going to look at some of the points to take into consideration while creating your WLAN layout.

### Considering Signal Attenuation

*RF attenuation* refers to the reduction of signal strength between the wireless AP and the client station. Attenuation is represented in decibels (dB). Decibels are 10 times the logarithm of the signal power at a particular input divided by the signal power at an output of a specified medium. An application of this formula is listed in Table 2.1.

**TABLE 2.1**

**Sample Attenuation Results**

| RF Signal | Medium | Loss | Attenuation |
|---|---|---|---|
| 200mw | Office wall | 100mw | 3dB |
| 200mW | Office window | 100mW | 3dB |
| 200mW | Metal Door | 150mW | 6dB |

Inside a building structure attenuation is caused by common construction materials such as wood, metal, and concrete. Additional items that come into play when considering loss are metal storage shelves, partitions, and people.

Examples of some common objects that cause signal attenuation are listed in Table 2.2.

**TABLE 2.2**

**Common Attenuation Causes and the Resulting Loss**

| Medium | Attenuation |
|---|---|
| Plasterboard office wall | 3dB |
| Office window | 3dB |
| Cinder block wall | 4dB |

## TABLE 2.2

**Continued**

| Medium | Attenuation |
| --- | --- |
| Glass wall (metal frame) | 6dB |
| Metal door | 6dB |
| Metal door (brick wall) | 12.4dB |

Outside the building structure attenuation is based on *free space* loss formulas. These formulas take into account the power of the transmitting station, distance, and the receiving station sensitivity. Other factors might be objects that might obstruct a portion of the RF propagation pattern.

Administrators need to take into account that RF signals between the client and the AP can be attenuated by various metal objects. These objects act like antennas and drown out the usable signal. When designing a WLAN layout make sure to be aware of building materials such as the following:

- Metal studded walls

- Steel I-beams

- Rebar reinforced concrete

- Heating and air-conditioning ducts

- Wire mesh reinforcements in walls

- Elevator shafts

- Window coatings that contain metal

WLAN administrators can reduce the ease of the "man in the middle" attacks by placing access points near the middle of the building structure. Window coverings that contain metal coatings can reduce the signal emitted into the parking lot or surrounding areas. Grounding metal studded walls can also help create a barrier to signal propagation into unwanted areas.

### Planning Signal Coverage

Omni-directional antennas transmit the RF signals in all directions at basically the same level. Think of the shape of a doughnut surrounding the center of the antenna.

802.11b access points generally have greater transmission range than 802.11a. This is because of the wavelength of the RF signal. The 2.4GHz of 802.11b has a longer wavelength and loses less power over distance.

Access points available from enterprise class vendors enable users to set the radio transmission power level. The maximum transmit power level allowed by the Federal Communications Commission in the Unite States for an 802.11b transmitter is 1 watt (1,000 milliwatts).

Directional antennas transmit the RF signals in a single direction. This type of antenna is best used for narrow coverage requirements such as hallways. Another application of this type of device is for long distance point-to-point transmission.

Coverage of the desired areas can be increased by deploying multiple overlapping access points. By knowing the requirements of the network you can either give the end users constant signal levels, such as 11MB/sec or allow throughput down to 1MB/sec.

The SSIDs, power output, and overlapping channels are important. By mapping out your network application requirements you can place the appropriate antennas and number of access points in the correct areas.

### Reducing Interference

Your wireless network signals are susceptible to multiple sources of interference. By keeping your access points higher in your room layout, such as above false ceilings and mounted to beams in warehouse structures, you should avoid most common sources of interference.

Rogue access points can create havoc on your wireless LAN design. You can avoid the rogue access point from hijacking your clients by removing the rogue from the desired connections within your client's wireless network interface card (NIC).

> **Avoiding WLAN Conflicts**
>
> Knowing the frequencies of the WLAN can help avoid conflicts. IEEE 802.11 is the standard for WLANs. The frequency, or band, that 802.11b uses from 2.4 to 2.5GHz. 802.11a operates in the range of 5.725 through 5.875 GHz.

Appliances such as microwaves and portable phones operate at the same frequencies as 802.11b and 802.11g networks. By avoiding placing your access points too near these appliances you can reduce your likelihood of interference with such devices.

### Considering Distance

Indoor distances can be affected by physical obstructions and RF-producing appliances. The average maximum distances are about 300 feet, but can differ greatly depending on access point power and antenna placement. As mentioned previously, signal strength, and therefore distance, can be decreased due to interference and attenuation.

Outside applications can be much greater due to the lack of interference. The use of directional antennas and amplifiers can extend the distance to kilometers in range.

### Turning Down the Volume

Although using the highest possible signal level gives the longest range, this might not always be desirable. By testing signal level tests and checking for overlapping channels, it might be necessary to lower the transmit power to reduce overlapping coverage.

Using the wireless AP configuration utilities, it might be prudent to lower the radio output. This approach would be best applied where access points are near the exterior of buildings or on the edge of desired WLAN RF coverage.

### Connecting to Power

One of the last things people often think about when deciding where to place their access points is power. An important item to consider is how to get the proper power to any access points up above false ceilings or mounted to beams high above the warehouse floors.

The saving grace in scenarios where power isn't readily accessible via an AC receptacle is called *power over Ethernet (POE)*. POE is supported by most enterprise level access point vendors. Some are as simple as an in-line power injector. Other vendors have special network switches that support POE.

### Bridging Versus Broadcasting

Wireless bridging devices can be used for temporary network links or where wiring is impractical. Bridging between two wireless devices lowers the ability of attackers from being able to associate with your wireless network. Using wireless bridges also allows for point-to-point or point-to-multipoint connections.

A popular use of wireless bridges is from building to building using directional antennas. This can either be a temporary or permanent installation. Using RF signal amplifiers and high gain antennas can transmit the signal for several miles.

# Managing Spectrums to Avoid Denial of Service

Should you choose 802.11a, 802.11b, or 802.11g? Depending on your current investment and infrastructure you might be able to avoid brute force denial of service attacks just by "changing the channel." This can be accomplished by using a lesser used frequency or compression scheme.

Keeping in mind that approved IEEE standards will have an affect on which implementation wireless technology manufacturers will roll out. These decisions also are going to be affected by market conditions and adoption rates. You should choose the most compatible wireless equipment that meets your company's application needs.

## Choosing Your Channel

802.11a uses 12 non-overlapping channels from 5.725 through 5.875 GHz. This might be a good alternative for reducing interference by devices such as cordless phones, Bluetooth devices, and microwaves. This would be recommended for smaller businesses that don't require strong security.

**IEEE 802.11a Not Yet Finalized**

The IEEE 802.11a standard has not been finalized as of the writing of this book. Therefore, manufacturers have been slow to implement security or other add-ons to 802.11a-based equipment.

802.11b and 802.11g non-overlapping channels:

- Channel 1 (2.412 GHz)
- Channel 6 (2.437 GHz)
- Channel 11 (2.462 GHz)

## Protecting Yourself from Internal Interference

In larger wireless network deployments many of the interference and RF signal problems that arise come from internal sources. By knowing the physical layout of your buildings as well as the existing RF interference you can work around or reduce these problems down the road.

Conducting an RF site survey of your environment is critical to protecting your WLAN from interference and obstructions. After you map out the signal levels take note of both internal and external access points.

Keep an accurate inventory of authorized access points. Using the reports from your site survey software, you should document the location and MAC address of each of your access points. Performing ongoing site surveys will make you aware of new rogue access points.

Creating a company or organization operations policy concerning authorized wireless access points will greatly reduce your administrative nightmares. By creating a method in which to incorporate wireless access points where rogues are popping up you can keep your end users happy.

## Protecting the Wireless Network

Keeping people from snooping around your network probably isn't going to happen. What you can do is reduce the ability for them to successfully gain access to your network resources. This will need to take place on several fronts. You'll need to lock down your systems as well as your wireless access points.

There are many vendors of wireless access points, bridges, and network cards. The amount of security features that they implement varies. Depending on your company's budget and the age of the equipment in place you might want to start with the basics:

- Ensure AP and NIC firmware is up to date
- Mount AP out of reach to avoid "hard reset"
- Change your AP's default administrator password
- Don't allow remote management
- Change your SSID name
- Don't broadcast your SSID
- Use MAC layer filtering
- Activate WEP (some older/entry level APs don't support 802.11x)
- Use 802.11x for dynamic key exchange (best security)

By taking these measures you will be able to keep the honest people honest. Those who have the time and tools might still be able to access the wireless network. That's where the next layer of defense comes into play. To protect the company's data, the internal networking equipment and operating systems need to have the same if not more security in place.

# Implementing Support for Secure 802.1x Technologies

Windows Server 2003 has the capability to implement 802.1x port-level security. This security capability is comprised of several components and each of them needs to be configured to pass the appropriate information to the others. All of the components in this process need to be 802.1x-compliant.

802.1x is the IEEE standard that defines port-based network access control. It also defines the method for passing the Extensible Authentication Protocol (EAP) messages. There are three parts of a Windows Server 2003–based 802.1x-compliant system:

> **RFC 2716**
>
> Microsoft introduced a Request for Comment (RFC) in 1999 called RFC 2716. This document describes EAP-TLS. Transport Level Security (TLS) provides for mutual authentication, encrypted negotiation, and key exchange between two end points. Combined, the two technologies are referred to as EAP-TLS.

- *Supplicant.* User or client that wants to be authenticated (Windows XP SP1 or later)

- *Authenticator.* Access point that is 802.1x-compliant (be sure to check with the manufacturer's documentation prior to choosing your equipment)

- *Authentication Server.* Microsoft IAS Server (RADIUS) registered with Active Directory

# Taking Advantage of Windows Server 2003 Security Features

Windows Server 2003 enables you a great deal of security and flexibility when it comes to the management of wireless networks and clients accessing them. By using Active Directory, DHCP, DNS, and Internet Authentication Services you can secure and audit remote computers as well as wireless users.

Group Policies are probably the primary tools for wireless network administrators. The ability to control most, if not all, of the wireless client's settings is a great way to ensure security compliance.

## Configuring the Wireless Network (IEEE 802.11) Policy

Windows Server 2003 Active Directory domains support a new Wireless Network (IEEE 802.11) Policies Group Policy extension. This extension enables you to configure the wireless network settings that are part of the Computer Configuration Group Policy.

Wireless network settings in the Wireless Network (IEEE 802.11) Policies Group Policy extension include the global wireless settings, list of preferred networks, WEP settings, and IEEE 802.1x settings. All the settings that are available in the Association and Authentication tabs in the Properties dialog box for a wireless network on a Windows XP (SP1 and later) or Windows Server 2003 wireless client are included in this configuration tool.

## Wireless Network (IEEE 802.11) Policies

The Wireless Network (IEEE 802.11) Policies do not apply to Windows XP clients prior to Service Pack 1. They also will not apply to the Microsoft 802.11x Authentication Client wireless clients.

You can configure wireless policies from the Computer Configuration/Windows Settings/Security Settings/Wireless Network (IEEE 802.11) Policies node in the Group Policy MMC snap-in. Figure 2.1 shows the location of the Wireless Network (IEEE 802.11) Policies node.

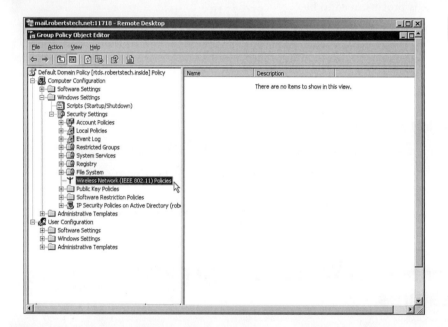

**FIGURE 2.1**
Wireless network (802.11) policies node.

## Wireless Network (802.11) Policies Node

The Wireless Network (802.11) Policies node is not available from the Windows Server 2003 Administrators Pack. You must configure this directly on the server or via Terminal Services.

## Single Wireless Network Policy

Only a single wireless network policy can be created for each Group Policy object.

There are no Wireless Network (802.11) policies by default. To create a new policy you must right-click on Wireless Network (IEEE 802.11) Policies in the console tree of the Group Policy Object Editor and then click Create Wireless Network Policy. The Create Wireless Network Policy Wizard will start. The wizard enables you to configure the name and description for the new wireless network policy.

After creating the new wireless policy you need to double-click on the name of the new policy in the Details pane to make the necessary modifications to implement their desired settings.

## Choosing the Proper Wireless Network Policy Properties

Now that the new wireless network policy has been created you need to go through each of the options on the General and Preferred Networks tabs and choose the appropriate settings for the wireless network. Figure 2.2 shows the options available on the General tab.

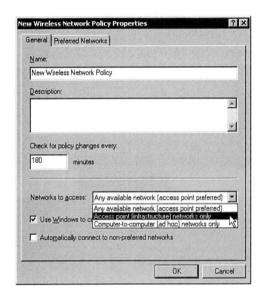

**FIGURE 2.2**    Wireless network policy General Properties tab.

Within the General tab you can configure the following properties:

■ *Name.* Enables you to specify a friendly name for the wireless network policy.

■ *Description.* Gives a description for the wireless network policy.

■ *Check for Policy Changes Every.* This setting specifies the interval, in minutes, after which clients check for changes to the wireless network policy.

■ *Networks to Access.* Enables you to choose which of the following networks the wireless client is allowed to create connections:

Any Available Network (Access Point Preferred)

Access Point (Infrastructure) Networks Only

Computer-to-Computer (Ad Hoc) Networks Only

Use Windows to Configure Wireless Network Settings for Clients—This check box enables the WZC service.

Automatically Connect to Non-preferred Networks—This check box enables the client to connect to wireless networks that are not configured in the Preferred Networks tab.

Within the Preferred Networks tab, shown in Figure 2.3, you can configure the following properties:

- *Networks*. This box displays the list of preferred wireless networks

- *Add/Edit/Remove*. These buttons enable you to create, delete, or modify the settings of a new or selected preferred wireless network.

- *Move Up/Move Down*. These buttons enable you to move the selected preferred wireless network up or down in the Networks list.

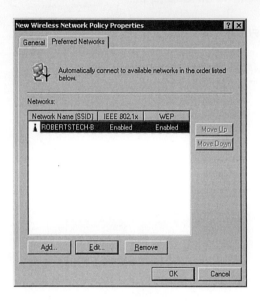

**FIGURE 2.3**    Wireless network policy Preferred Networks properties tab.

---

**WPA**

As of the writing of this book configuration for Wi-Fi Protected Access (WPA) was not available. Inclusion of WPA authentication and encryption settings is being considered by Microsoft in future Service Packs for Windows Server 2003 and Windows XP clients.

---

By double-clicking on any of the preferred wireless networks listed in the Networks list you can edit the properties of that network. Figure 2.4 shows the options that are available for modification.

The first tab at the top of the dialog box is Network Properties. This tab has the following options:

- *Network name (SSID)*. This field specifies the wireless LAN network name, also known as the Service Set Identifier (SSID).

- *Description*. This box enables you to give a short description of this wireless network.

- *Data Encryption (WEP Enabled)*. This check box specifies whether WEP is enabled for this wireless network.

- *Network Authentication (Shared Mode)*. This check box specifies whether 802.11 shared key authentication is used to authenticate the wireless client. If disabled, open system authentication is used.

- *The Key Is Provided Automatically*. This check box specifies whether a WEP key is provided via some means other than manual configuration. Checked keys are provided either on the wireless network card or through 802.1x authentication provided by an IAS server.

- *This Is a Computer-to-Computer (Ad Hoc) Network*. This check box specifies whether the client's wireless LAN network is operating in ad hoc mode.

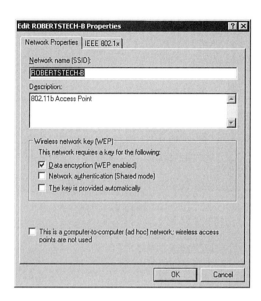

**FIGURE 2.4**    Wireless Network Policy preferred networks options.

The other tab that is available for settings of the preferred wireless networks is the IEEE 802.1x tab. Figure 2.5 shows the available configuration options.

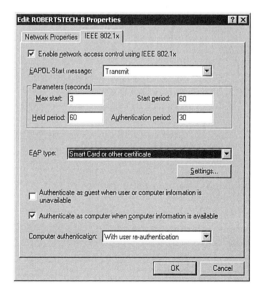

**FIGURE 2.5**    IEEE 802.1X properties options.

On the IEEE 802.1x tab you can configure the following settings:

- *Enable Network Access Control Using IEEE 802.1x*. This check box specifies whether you want to use IEEE 802.1x to perform authentication for this wireless network. This box also enables all the other settings on this tab.

- *EAPOL-Start Message*. This pulldown box enables you to select the transmission behavior of the EAPOL-Start message when authenticating. The following options are available:

  *Do Not Transmit*. This option specifies that EAPOL-Start messages are not sent.

  *Transmit*. This option sends, if needed, an EAPOL-Start message.

  *Transmit per 802.1x*. This option sends an EAPOL-Start message, upon association, to initiate the 802.1x authentication process.

- *Max Start*. This box specifies the number of successive EAPOL-Start messages that are transmitted when no response is received from the initial EAPOL-Start message.

- *Start Period*. This box specifies, in seconds, the interval between the retransmission of EAPOL-Start messages when no response to the previously sent message is received.

- *Held Period*. This box specifies, in seconds, the period that the authenticating client will not perform any 802.1x authentication activity after it has received an authentication failure indication from the authenticator.

- *Authentication Period*. This box specifies, in seconds, the interval for which the authenticating client will wait before retransmitting any 802.1x after authentication has been initiated.

- *EAP Type*. This pull-down box lists the EAP types that correspond to EAP DLLs installed on the client computer that are suitable for wireless access. The two main choices are Smart Card or Other Certificate or Protected EAP (PEAP).

- *Settings*. This button enables you to configure the properties of the selected EAP type.

- *Authenticate as Guest When User or Computer Information Is Unavailable*. This check box specifies whether the computer will attempt to authenticate as a guest when either user or computer credentials are unavailable.

- *Computer Authentication*. This pull-down box enables you to specify the way in which computer authentication works with user authentication.

Under Computer authentication, the three possible settings are as follows:

- *With User Authentication*. When users are not logged on to the computer, authentication is performed using the computer credentials. After a user logs on to the client computer authentication is maintained with the computer credentials. When the wireless client travels to a new wireless access point authentication is performed using the user's credentials.

- *With User Re-authentication*. When users are not logged on to the computer, authentication is performed using the computer credentials. After a user logs on to the client computer, authentication is performed using the user credentials. When a user logs off the computer, authentication is performed with the computer credentials. This is the recommended setting because it ensures that the connection to the wireless AP is always using the security credentials of the computer's current security context (computer credentials when no user is logged on and user credentials when a user is logged on).

- *Computer Only*. Authentication is always performed by using the computer credentials. User authentication is never performed.

## Incorporating Certificates into Wireless Security

One of the best ways to protect not only the WLAN, but also the whole network is called Private Key Infrastructure (PKI). On Windows Server 2003 this solution is also known as Certificate Services. Certificate Services can either be managed internally or outsourced to a trusted third party.

> **Automatic Computer and User Certificate Allocation**
>
> Windows Server 2003 Enterprise or Data Center Edition acting as the enterprise CA server is required for the automatic computer and user certificate allocation.

The computer and user certificates can be issued through Group Policies. This is best performed at an Organizational Unit (OU) level. It is recommended that an OU be created for the WLAN users.

Automatic computer certificate allocation can be performed. This might be desirable when a large number of users are going to be using your PKI infrastructure.

## Configuring Certificate Services

Administrators of medium to larger Windows 2000 or Windows Server 2003 environments will probably have already deployed a PKI infrastructure. There are several roles involved in a well-managed PKI architecture; they include the Enterprise root Certificate Authority (CA), Issuing CA, and Subordinate CA.

If this is the first instance of PKI in the Windows Server 2003 environment perform the following steps:

1. In the Control Panel, open Add or Remove Programs, and then click Add/Remove Windows Components.

2. In the Windows Components Wizard page, select Certificate Services, and then click Next.

3. On the next Windows Components Wizard page, select Enterprise root CA.

4. Click Next and then type the desired name in the Common Name for This CA field, and then click Next.

5. Accept the default Certificate Database Settings, and then click Next and finally Finish.

This will create the very base for the PKI architecture. In a truly secure environment the Enterprise root CA server is removed from the network and physically protected. This is to protect the integrity of the private key.

## Configuring Internet Authentication Services (IAS)

The network's remote and wireless clients need to be authenticated to access the domain. This service is provided by the Remote Access Dial-In User Service (RADIUS) or IAS role in your network. The IAS server is registered with the Active Directory. By having the two services aware of each other, a single sign-on environment can be maintained.

The Microsoft IAS-based RADIUS Server provides centralized authentication, authorization, and accounting (AAA). IAS is also a RADIUS Proxy because it can forward RADIUS requests to other RADIUS Servers for AAA. IAS can also be used to authenticate VPN clients, wireless access points, and Ethernet switches that support 802.1x.

**BEST PRACTICE**

### Plan Ahead

Plan ahead when choosing the version of Windows Server 2003 to build your IAS server. You need to know how many clients and outside RADIUS server groups you are going to be supporting.

Windows Server 2003 only supports up to 50 clients and two remote RADIUS server groups. Each RADIUS client must resolve to a single IP address. If the RADIUS client's fully qualified domain name resolves to multiple IP addresses only the first address will be used.

Windows Server 2003 Enterprise and Datacenter Editions can support unlimited RADIUS clients and remote RADIUS server groups. You can also configure RADIUS clients by specifying an IP address range.

## Configuring EAP-TLS Authentication

EAP-TLS is the method by which the wireless client and the IAS server exchange authentication and certification.

On your IAS server perform the following steps:

1. Open the Internet Authentication Service snap-in.

2. In the console tree, click Remote Access Policies.

3. In the details pane, double-click Wireless Access to Intranet. The Wireless Access to Intranet Properties dialog box is displayed.

4. Click Edit Profile, and then click the Authentication tab.

5. On the Authentication tab, click EAP Methods. The Select EAP Providers dialog box will be displayed.

6. Click Add. The Add EAP dialog box will be displayed.

7. Click Smart Card or Other Certificate, and then click OK. The smartcard or other certificate type will be added to the list of EAP providers.

8. Click Edit. The Smart Card or Other Certificate Properties dialog box will be displayed.

9. The properties of the computer certificate issued to the IAS computer will be displayed. Click OK.

10. Click OK to save changes to EAP providers. Click OK to save changes to the profile settings.

11. Click OK to save changes to the remote access policy.

> **Acceptable Computer Certificate**
> This dialog box verifies that IAS has an acceptable computer certificate installed to perform EAP-TLS authentication.

# Configuring the Wireless Client

Windows XP (with SP1, or later) is the preferred client in a WLAN environment. 802.1x and automatic wireless configuration, also known as Wireless Zero Configuration (WZC), are included in Windows XP. WZC is enabled when you choose Use Windows to Configure My Wireless Network Settings check box in your Wireless Network Connection Properties dialog box. WZC really comes into play when you have group policies configured on your Windows Server 2003 domain controllers.

> **Customers Who Participate in Microsoft's Premier Support**
> Microsoft provides the 802.1x Authentication Client for Windows 98 and Windows NT 4.0 Workstation to customers who participate in Microsoft's Premier Support.

You've seen WZC in action when you see the "One or more wireless networks are available" message in the notification area of the desktop. If you don't have group policies configured, the following defaults will apply:

- The SSID is acquired from the wireless AP beacon

- Network authentication is open

- Data encryption is disabled

- Shared key authentication is disabled

- IEEE 802.1x authentication for this network is disabled

If the default settings don't conform to your wireless network the user must manually configure each option to match the wireless AP and your Windows Server 2003 security settings.

## Configuring Wi-Fi Protected Access (WPA)

Windows XP (Post SP1) clients can take advantage of a stronger encryption standard known as WPA. WPA is an interoperable interim standard that has been developed by the Wi-Fi Alliance. WPA is a replacement for WEP, which has many known and published vulnerabilities. To take advantage of this new standard you will need to make sure that all your WLAN components are compatible.

## Required Updates

To implement WPA to protect your data you'll need to verify or update the software/firmware at the following:

- Wireless Access Point parameters includes WPA information element, WPA two-phase authentication, TKIP, Michael, and AES (optional).

- Wireless Network Adapter options include WPA information element, WPA two-phase authentication, TKIP, Michael, and AES (optional).

- Wireless Client Programs options include WPA client program (Windows XP SP1) and WPA-compliant configuration tool for wireless network adapter (Windows 2000).

## BEST PRACTICE

### Compatibility Issues

On certain wireless chip sets you might run into compatibility issues. Check with the manufacturer of your wireless network card before applying the new WPA client program.

### Authentication

WPA requires that 802.1x authentication be in place. This can be accomplished through the RADIUS (EAP-TLS) method. This is configured through the Windows Server 2003 Internet Authentication Server. In smaller organizations a preshared key can be used.

### Key Management

WPA requires the rekeying of both unicast and global encryption keys. Temporal Key Integrity Protocol (TKIP) is used to change the unicast encryption key for every frame and also synchronizes the changes between the AP and the wireless client.

### Temporal Key Integrity Protocol (TKIP)

TKIP is a replacement for WEP. It provides a new encryption algorithm that is stronger than WEP. TKIP uses the calculation facilities that are already present of existing wireless devices to perform the encryption operations. To be in compliance with the WPA standard TKIP is required.

### Michael

WPA uses a new data integrity method called Michael. WEP relies upon a 32-bit integrity check value (ICV) to proved data integrity assurance. This method can be captured and manipulated with cryptanalysis tools to update the ICV without the client knowing about it.

Michael specifies an algorithm that calculates an 8-byte message integrity code (MIC) using facilities available on existing wireless devices. This MIC is located between the data portion of the 802.11 frame and the ICV. Both the MIC and the ICV are encrypted along with the data frame. Michael also implements a new frame counter to prevent replay protection.

### Advanced Encryption Standard (AES)

WPA calls for AES to encrypt the traffic between the AP and wireless clients. AES is optional as a replacement to your current WEP encryption. This is because manufacturers need to update their firmware and drivers. This might not be feasible in all cases.

### Mixing WEP and WPA Wireless Clients

During the transition to a fully WPA-compliant environment it might be necessary to support pre-existing WEP clients. This is supported by the wireless AP after it has been upgraded. The AP determines which encryption method is being requested by the client. The WEP clients won't take advantage of the dynamic global encryption keys because they cannot support them.

# Maximizing Wireless Security Through Tunneling

In some cases it might not be feasible to have all the components compliant with your security planning, such as older pre-existing equipment that doesn't support 802.1x, RADIUS, or WPA. You also might not have control over portions of the WLAN to which your clients are connecting.

In these cases the best method for securing your network traffic would be a Virtual Private Network (VPN).

## While You're Away

Public Access Points are popping up everywhere. It might be in your local coffee shop or book-store. This convenience allows remote users and administrators access to their networks from almost anywhere. This convenience also creates challenges for the IT administrators.

Lack of WEP on the public access points means you're exposing your wireless traffic. This makes the use of VPN that much more important.

## VPN Pass-through Is Important

Not all firewalls allow VPN pass-through. Make sure that the firewall at that location is allowing VPN authentication and tunnels.

If the wireless client is in a public access point, have the user check with the FAQ section of that provider's Web site or call their technical support phone number.

# Maintaining Knowledge of Your Wireless Networks

By constantly reviewing the updates to IEEE standards and the application of new patches to wireless networks you can stay on top of your security.

Monitoring sites such as `wardriving.com` can keep you aware of whether or not your access points are on that list.

# Keeping Track of People, Places, and Things

Make sure you are keeping track of security events such as failed login attempts. Although these might just be indications of users forgetting their passwords, it also could be signs of a break-in attempt. By being alert to such indicators you can keep your users happy and attackers frustrated.

Ensure that firewall logging is also being monitored. You can learn quite a bit from unsuccessful as well as successful traffic. Usage patterns and attacks can be traced just through periodic review of your logs.

Occasional access point discovery can make your job easier. By using tools such as Network Stumbler and utilities that come with the wireless card you can discover rouge access points. You can also find out whether your desired signal levels are being maintained in each region of WLAN coverage.

# Wireless Networking–Related IEEE Standards

By knowing which standards are still in draft and which ones are approved you can make educated buying decisions. Make sure that you check with the IEEE Web site (`http://standards.ieee.org/wireless/`) regularly. Here are some of the standards that might have an affect on your future WLAN architecture:

- 802.11e—Quality of Service. The purpose of this standard is to enhance the current 802.11 Medium Access Control (MAC) to improve and manage Quality of Service and provide classes of service. The applications that could benefit from this standard include transport of voice, audio, and video over 802.11 wireless networks, video conferencing, and media stream distribution.

- 802.11f—Access Point Interoperability. This standard calls for recommended practices for Inter-Access Point Protocol (IAPP), which provides the necessary capabilities to achieve multivendor AP interoperability across a distributed system.

- 802.11h—Interference. This standard relates to the 802.11a (5GHz) range. It calls for network management and control extensions to allow for spectrum and transmit power management. This would enable regulatory acceptance of 802.11 5GHz products.

- 802.11i—Security. This standard proposes enhancing the Medium Access Control layer to enhance security and authentication mechanisms. 802.11x is a portion of this standard.

# Other Resources

Using the wealth of information that's available from the many vendors of wireless products, as well as software vendors such as Microsoft, is invaluable. There are many newsgroups focused on wireless security as well.

Communicating with other administrators who have implemented a similar wireless environment such as your company's can be very helpful. User groups such as the Bay Area Wireless User Group provide great suggestions as to product configurations and modifications.

Some useful Web sites include the following:

- IEEE 802.11 (http://grouper.ieee.org/groups/802/11/)
- Wi-Fi Alliance (http://www.wi-fi.org/)
- War Driving (http://www.wardriving.com)
- WLAN Monitoring (http://www.airdefense.net)
- Network Stumbler (http://www.netstumbler.com)

# Summary

The key to a successful implementation of secured wireless technologies is to begin with the end in mind. Never use a wireless LAN without some type of encryption, and be mindful of the type of encryption you plan to use. The standard WEP encryption should be the minimum level of encryption considered with even higher levels of encryption like 802.1x as the recommended norm.

When planning a wireless LAN implementation, an RF site survey can validate the number of access points needed to achieve the appropriate coverage in the facilities being used. Look at end user requirements such as the ability to roam throughout the office while maintaining a signal versus the expectation of a static position of users working wireless from just an office or conference room. These are important factors when determining access point positioning and overlap coverage.

Because Windows Server 2003 has built-in 802.1x encrypted wireless support, it requires the client system to be running Windows XP Service Pack 1 or later. The existing system configurations become important in the implementation of a secured wireless environment. An organization has the choice of lowering security to the lowest common denominator, and thus increasing security risk; or the organization has the ability to require all client systems to meet a minimum system configuration standard to raise the level of supported wireless security on the network.

Lastly, creating wireless access policies and enforcing the policies becomes extremely important. Keep your network secure by keeping everyone informed of the security risks of setting up their own rogue access points. Perform periodic network audits by walking around with your laptop or pocket PC scanning for networks. Double-check each of the access points to ensure that they are configured and working correctly.

By designing a secure network, and then monitoring and managing the secured infrastructure, an organization can improve its level of security support throughout the organization.

# 3

# Integrating Smartcard and Secured Access Technologies

**S**martcards and other security hardware have been around for several years. Most of the implementations of such devices have been at very large organizations, such as government agencies in the Unites States and in Europe. This mainly has been due to slow adoption and perceived difficulties in implementation.

Windows Server 2003 has made the deployment of such security devices much more straightforward. The incorporation of Group Policy templates, autoenrollment, and Windows XP's features as the certificate client has given the administrator much better tools with which to work.

# Maximizing Certificate Services Implementations

Creating a Public Key Infrastructure (PKI) environment takes quite a bit of time and planning to build and effort to maintain. Administrators often have to plan well beyond the current levels of hardware and software available to them at the time of implementation. If the company's PKI infrastructure was built on Windows 2000 the administrators may want to improve their environment with new functionality built in to Windows Server 2003.

With the advancements in Windows Server 2003's Certificate Services and Group Policies much of the administrator's time, planning, effort, and wishes will finally pay off. Creating and issuing certificates to computers and users has become much easier to deploy and ultimately to maintain and manage.

## Using Windows Server 2003 Updates

Administrators have at their disposal a very cost-effective platform to deploy a PKI infrastructure on Windows Server 2003. The new features that are available with this product are as follows:

- Cross Certification. The Certificate Services in Windows Server 2003 has demonstrated full compliance with the U.S. Federal Bridge Certificate Authority (FCBA) requirements. The FCBA is a nonhierarchical PKI architecture that permits heterogeneous PKIs from different U.S. government agencies to be cross-certified and interoperate between organizations. This feature creates a certificate trust path between participating domains.

- Flexible Certificate Templates. Windows Server 2003 supports both the Windows 2000 (version 1) and the new version 2 templates. Management of the templates is controlled through the new Certificate Templates MMC snap-in. This new tool enables administrators to control template properties (such as key size and renewal period), permit autoenrollment and autorenewal for both users and machines, set access control on certificate templates to determine which users or machines can enroll for certificates, and allow for specific Cryptographic Service Provider (CSP) use and key size.

- Certificate Autoenrollment. Administrators can specify the types of certificates a user or machine can automatically receive on logon. If the access controls permit, a Windows XP or Windows Server 2003 client can access the templates in Active Directory and enroll for their respective certificates.

- Autorenewal. Administrators can use the new templates to permit the autorenewal of a user or machine certificate. This removes the administrative overhead of managing certificate expiration.

- Role-based Administration. Windows Server 2003 makes it possible to enforce the separation of the many administrative roles for the CA and operating system. With different roles no single user can compromise the entire CA.

- Key Counting. The CA now supports key counting, where the CSP maintains a count of each use of the signing key. This feature provides additional audit information that can be used to track private key distribution.

- Key Archival. The CA now has the ability to archive the keys that are associated with the certificates it issues. These keys can now be recovered using the new key recovery agent certificate.

- Delta Certificate Revocation Lists (CRL). The CA can now provide delta CRLs that are in compliance with IETF RFC 2459. This reduces the CRL network traffic because the complete replication of the full CRL database is not required for a small number of certificate revocations.

- Event Auditing. Most events that occur on the CA server can be audited. This provides a useful logging and monitoring function. Examples of this are tracking role changes, key recovery, certificate issuance, and revocation of certificates.

## Choosing the CA Roles

Administrators have many choices in their enterprise security architecture. One of the choices related to PKI and smartcard secured access is the deployment of the CA roles within their organization:

- Enterprise Root CA

- Enterprise Subordinate CA

- Standalone Root CA

- Standalone Subordinate CA

> **The Server Does Not Have to Be a Domain Controller**
> Administrators can install an Enterprise CA on any domain member server. The server does not have to be a domain controller. This practice is especially important for security concerns and separating CA roles.

The most important CA role, as it relates to smartcard deployment, is the Enterprise Root CA. The Microsoft Windows Server 2003 Enterprise CA has the following characteristics:

- The Enterprise CA must be a member of a Windows Server 2003 Active Directory domain.

- The Enterprise Root CA certificate is automatically added to the Trusted Root Certification Authorities node for all users and computers in the domain.

> **For Administrators to Enable Support of Certificate Autoenrollment...**
> For administrators to enable support of certificate autoenrollment, the Enterprise CA must be installed on either a Windows Server 2003 Enterprise or Datacenter Edition server.

- User certificates can be issued that allow users to log on to the Active Directory domain using computer-stored certificates and/or certificates stored on smartcards.

- User certificates and the Certificate Revocation List (CRL) are stored in the domain's Active Directory.

- Unlike Standalone CAs, an Enterprise CA issues certificates via certificate templates that can be added and customized by the CA administrator.

> **Using the Web Enrollment Site to Obtain Certificates**
>
> Users and computers that are not domain members, or don't support autoenrollment, can use the Web enrollment site to obtain certificates.

- Unlike the Standalone CA, the Enterprise CA confirms the credentials of the user requesting a certificate.

- The Computer or User name (also known as the Subject) can be entered manually or automatically on the certificate.

The Enterprise CA is an ideal solution for a network with a Windows Server 2003 domain. All domain members can be assigned certificates via Group Policy–based certificate autoenrollment. You can limit the scope of autoenrollment by assigning permissions to the certificate template.

## Incorporating Smartcards

By using the security access philosophy of "Something you know, something you have, and something you are," information technology administrators can significantly increase their network security. The more you can do to keep people from impersonating valid log-in attempts, the more secure the data and network resources will become. To detail the best practices that lead to secured information system access, the three items are as follows:

- *Something you know.* This can either be a strong password, or in the case of a smartcard this would be the user's personal identification number (PIN).

- *Something you have.* This is any of several devices that contain a copy of the user's PKI certificate. Examples are smartcards and USB keys.

- *Something you are* (optional). This refers to some physically unique attribute of the user. Examples are DNA, fingerprints, facial features, or the iris of the user's eye.

### Securing Log-ins

End users in a less than secure environment can easily use someone else's username and password. This is especially open to attack when the impersonator is coming from a remote location. No one is watching the attacker sit at a remote terminal and access all the company's data.

By using a physical device such as a smartcard, secure ID, or other device, administrators can be more assured that users are actually who they say they are when they log-in.

The machines that are authenticated in Active Directory are usually known entities. This piece of information gives you a good idea of where the user is logging in from.

### Securing E-mail

Sending certified, or signed, e-mail in an application such as Outlook can be performed using smartcards. Using certificates stored on the smartcard to sign the end-user's e-mail enables the recipient to know that the sender is who he actually says he is. Certificates can also be used to make sure that only the intended recipient can open and read the e-mail sent.

### Securing Documents

Encrypted File System (EFS) can be employed to secure sensitive company data. This is especially critical for administrators who are tasked with protecting data on laptops and other portable devices.

Windows Server 2003 now supports EFS on offline folders and multiple user access. It is also harder for unauthorized recovery of EFS folders by third parties. EFS renders the data unreadable to anyone who is not granted access to that content.

### Securing Buildings

Smartcards can be incorporated into a company's identity badge that has a radio frequency identification (RFID) capability. Card readers can be installed on the exterior, or on critical access internal doors.

Maintaining an accurate record of smartcard holders and what level of access they have can be extremely useful. All entry accesses can be centrally logged and can be audited by the administrator or security personnel.

# Securing Certificate Services

Standalone and Enterprise Root servers contain the single copy of the company's private key. This component is essential in authenticating any and all access to the PKI-secured data and entry points.

Physical security and data security are both very important tasks in an administrator's role.

## Locking Down Servers

Microsoft provides very well-defined baseline security guidelines for locking down the operating system, IIS, and administrative access.

Change the local administrator and guest account names. Don't use the same administrator and guest account name on every server.

## Separating Server Roles

Placing more than a single role on a server makes an attacker's job easier. It then becomes possible to compromise several roles in the company's PKI infrastructure. Certificate Services storage and enrollment can be separated. The following list includes some of the tiers that can be physically placed on separate servers:

- Root CA Server
- Root Subordinates (Intermediate CA)
- Issuing CA Server

- Certificate Storage in Active Directory
- IIS

## Assigning Administrative Roles

Administrators need to work with senior executives to define the roles that will be assigned to personnel within the company when it comes to managing the PKI and smartcard system.

The persons entrusted with issuing smartcards within an organization are known as *enrollment agents*. Enrollment agents are typically members of the help desk, IT security, or company security staff. In locations where one of these personnel isn't readily available another trusted individual such as that location's supervisor or manager can be the enrollment agent.

Delegating the authority to issue smartcards has administrative as well as security benefits. Some of those benefits are listed here:

- Administrators can delegate this time-consuming process.
- Enrollment agents process all certificate and smartcard requests.
- Smartcard users can be stepped through the enrollment process.

There are also some disadvantages to delegating smartcard enrollment. Here are several points to consider:

- The trustworthiness of the enrollment agent could come into question.
- Overcoming concerns could require more personnel resources.
- Remote locations might not have an available enrollment agent full-time.
- An agent can perform only a limited number of smartcard enrollments per work day.

# Getting the Most Out of Smartcards

**Contact-less Smartcard Support**
Windows Server 2003 and Windows XP do not support the type of devices known as contact-less smartcards.

Any security measure that makes it harder for end-users to do their job is never accepted whole-heartedly. Administrators have to perform extensive planning and usability studies within their organizations.

## Choosing an Appropriate Smartcard

There are a variety of smartcards and USB tokens from which to choose. Smartcards that are used in a Windows Server 2003 environment run on the Microsoft Smartcard operating system. Smartcards and their readers must adhere to the ISO 7816 standard. To ensure compatibility you should always test the smartcard with the reader and confirm that USB ports will be available for token type devices.

Administrators have to plan for the usage requirements for the smartcards or USB tokens. The following list includes some considerations for the physical card or token:

- Hardware type (card or USB token)
- Memory requirements
- Company's intended lifetime of device
- Company's intended roles for device
- Reader hardware
- Physical location and availability of USB ports
- Device management software

## Memory Requirements

Smartcards and tokens use their memory to store the certificate of the user, the smartcard operating system, and additional applications. To use the smartcard in a Windows logon environment, you must be able to program the card to store the user's key pair, retrieve and store an associated public certificate, and perform public and private key operations on behalf of the user (enrollment agent).

Smartcards come in two common memory configurations—8KB and 32KB. To use the Microsoft Smartcard operating system, you need to specify the 32KB device.

The components that make up the memory storage requirements on a typical 32KB smartcard device are listed in Table 3.1

**Maximum Length of User's Logon Certificate**
The maximum length of the user's logon certificate is 1,024 bits due to fact that it is the largest certificate that will fit in the 2.5KB space provided on the smartcard.

**TABLE 3.1**
**Typical Smartcard Memory Use (32KB Device)**

| Content | Memory Used |
| --- | --- |
| Windows for Smartcards operating system | 15KB |
| Smartcard Vendor Applications | 8KB |
| Smartcard logon certificate | 2.5KB |
| Company Custom Applications (if any) | 1.5KB |
| Free Space | 5KB |

The memory configuration of the smartcard is ultimately up to the company and the administrator. Smartcards can be divided into public and private memory spaces. You can define separate

> ### Multiple Applications Must Use a Single Smartcard Logon Certificate
>
> Multiple applications, such as physical access and secure logons, must use a single smartcard logon certificate. Windows Server 2003 and Windows XP do not support the use of multiple certificates on a single smartcard device.

protected memory for the operating system, certificates, e-wallets, and other applications. This section of the card's memory can be allocated as Read Only.

The memory capacity on smartcards is increasing as vendor technology improves. This allows for more applications and certificates to be stored on the card or token. Multiple uses can be specified for the cards and the memory requirements that affect these applications should be taken into consideration when deciding to purchase such devices.

## Smartcard Roles

Administrators have three roles of smartcards at their disposal. When planning the company's smartcard deployment you need to determine the number and type of each card.

- Enrollment cards are issued to personnel who will be enrolling smartcards on behalf of other users. These cards have a special enrollment agent certificate that enables the card's user to act on behalf of the administrator.

- User cards can be permanently issued and point to a permanent certificate server

- User cards can also be temporary use cards that point to temporary certificates.

In better defining the user cards, the two types are as follows:

- Permanent cards are issued to the employees to be carried with them at all times. These cards contain the cardholder's credentials, certificates, data, and custom applications. Customization of the cards might include company logos and a photograph of the cardholder.

- Temporary cards are issued for limited-use and are issued to users such as guests, temporary employees, and employees who have forgotten their permanent cards.

## Smartcard Life Expectancy

Administrators must take into account a few factors when deciding on the type and durability of the smartcards or tokens. These considerations should be based on the normal wear and tear expected on the device and the length of end-user's usage.

When purchasing the smartcard device you should ask the vendor(s) for expected lifetime documentation for the device.

## Smartcard Reader

The physical device that the computer uses to interface with the smartcard is known as the "smartcard reader." The readers come in a few form factors, including USB, RS-232 serial port, and Personal Computer Memory Card International Association (PCMCIA) Type II slot.

The USB style token device is the simplest of the smartcard/reader combinations because it doesn't require a separate smartcard reader. One item to consider when choosing this type of device is the physical availability and access to open USB ports on the end-user's computer.

## Smartcard Management Tools

You need to evaluate the bundled software that comes with the smartcard or token device. The management software can enable you and the company's developers to customize the memory allocation and custom applications.

Some smartcard and token device manufacturers supply additional security management software as well. This is important when the deployment of smartcards is transitioning from pilot to production as well as maintaining the user's smartcard credentials on the devices.

Custom application development requires a robust application programming interface (API) from the smartcard vendor. This is especially important when combining multiple uses of the smartcard such as building access and secure logon and application access.

## Making Users Use Smartcards

By using group policies you can enforce user's behavior. The policies that affect smartcards are shown in Figure 3.1 and Figure 3.2.

**FIGURE 3.1**   Group policy smartcard enforcement.

Many company expenditures are underused, if used at all, because of increasing end-users perceived complexity. The smartcard is one device that can make the users' experience actually become easier.

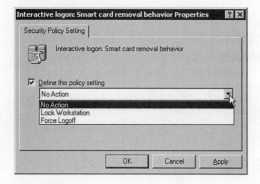

**FIGURE 3.2**   Group policy smartcard removal behavior.

Users will find that they don't have to memorize those hard-to-remember strong passwords. Administrators won't find yellow Post-it notes with the user's strong password stuck to the lower-corner of the user's monitor or under her keyboard.

## Providing Security Reports

More laws are passed every year that place companies and consultants at risk of not protecting users and client's data.

### To Take Advantage of Windows Server 2003 Auditing...

To take advantage of Windows Server 2003 auditing you need to enable Audit object access by using the Group Policy Object Editor and drilling down to Computer Configuration/Windows Settings/Security Settings/Local Policies/Audit Policy and double-clicking on Audit Object access.

By verifying who a user is and when and where he signed on to the system, it makes it easier to prove that person's identity and possibly his intentions.

Security and financial auditors need to be able to read reliable reports of not only hacking attempts but also normal day-to-day network usage and system access.

Administrators of Windows Server 2003–based CA servers can provide reporting on the following functions.

The CA audit log generates two types of events:

- Access check
- System events

CA-related system events are generated in seven key categories:

- Back up and restore the CA database
- Change CA configuration
- Change CA security settings
- Issue and manage certificate requests

- Revoke certificates and publish CRLs
- Store and retrieve archived keys
- Start and stop Certificate Services

Administrators can enable and configure CA event auditing by performing the following steps:

1. Log on to the server with an account with one of the following permissions: Domain Administrator, Certificate Authority Administrator, or Certificate Authority Auditor.

> **Auditing CA Events**
> Auditing CA events is only available on Windows Server 2003, Enterprise and Datacenter Editions.

2. Click on Start, Programs, Administrative Tools, Certification Authority.

3. In the console tree, right-click on the name of the CA on which you want to enable event monitoring and select Properties.

4. On the Auditing tab, click on the events to audit as shown in Figure 3.3.

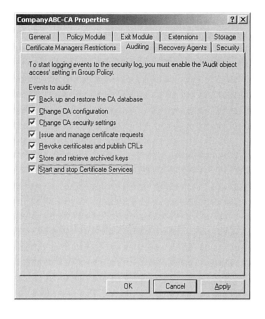

**FIGURE 3.3**    Enabling auditing on the Certification Authority.

# Tips and Tricks for Securing Access to the Network

Using certificates and smartcards to secure access to the network relies on several factors including practicing good firewall procedures, securing certificate authority servers, and tracking user access.

This section describes the benefits of a well-run smartcard enrollment and authentication strategy. These techniques are only as secure as the underlying practices that exist in the enterprise.

## Using Physical Security

As the old adage goes, keep honest people honest. Physical security is probably one of the most overlooked practices in a Windows-based network. Because of the friendly interface many administrators make the mistake of treating their Windows servers like any another desktop. Having the server's console invite you to sit down and see what you can change or peer into is just too tempting. This is especially likely when administrators walk away from the console while still logged in.

Lock your servers away. If a secure room isn't available, at least use a lockable server cabinet. If this isn't an option you can always remove the monitor, keyboard, and mouse. The server will still run and you can use Terminal Services to manage the server.

Keep backups in vaults. If the company doesn't have access to a storage vault, any off-site facility with reasonable physical security will do. Even if this means that you rotate backup sets at home.

## Keeping Security Rules Simple

If security measures are too hard to use or remember users won't use them. Using devices such as smartcards actually make the company's security policies easier to implement due to users not having to suffer through strong passwords.

If security measures are too hard to use or implement administrators won't want to roll them out. Microsoft and other vendors are making the securing of networks and user access more straightforward and easier to manage. Administrators are then able to create a more secure computing environment for their company and end-users.

## Covering Your Tracks

Some of the best practices that are relatively simple but effective involve the use of naming conventions, security roles, and client access control. When the simple processes are followed, it's easier to cover your tracks that make it more difficult for a hacker to gain access to your systems.

Don't advertise your systems. By using naming conventions that are somewhat cryptic, administrators can keep someone who is looking at the network from knowing which machine performs which role.

Don't broadcast your network vulnerabilities to outsiders by leaving nonessential system services running. Services such as file transfer protocol (FTP) are constantly polled by port scans. After someone knows which services are running they can then employ tools and bots to try and break into the system.

Another good practice is changing the port number that required services are running on. This method of security is best deployed when you can control the client's applications that are accessing the company's network based services.

# Creating a Single Sign-on Environment

Allowing access to the network and system resources by entering a single username and password is the holy grail of the network administrator. Using certificate services and smartcard devices can make this goal a reality.

The new Active Directory credential manager provides a secure store for user's X.509 certificates when used in conjunction with Windows XP credential management, which has three components; credential prompting user interface, stored user names and passwords, and a keyring to store PKI certificates. Together these infrastructure components form a single sign-on solution.

## Consolidating Directories

If feasible, a company can standardize on Windows Server 2003 Active Directory. Consolidate LDAP directories. Active Directory can become the single repository for the company's users, machines, log-in credentials, and contact information.

## Consolidating Applications

Security requirements on applications can be quite numerous. Inventory the current applications and their business purposes and security requirements. After administrators take the inventory of all the applications in the company some can be absorbed into other applications. Many applications are reliant on their underlying file system structure for their security. By reducing the number of applications and securing fewer network shares you can more easily allow and track access to those applications.

# Securing Access to Web Servers and Services

Using the smartcard to store the user's credentials to access any number of Web-based servers and services can greatly reduce the risk of impersonation. Ensuring the user is using two-factor authentication also allows for better tracking and auditing of network resource access.

## Locking the Doors

By locking down access to IIS 6.0 Microsoft has created a more secure by default design. The baseline security of the server enables you to decide which virtual doors to open to outside users of the Web-based applications.

Directory access is a primary concern with both Web and locally accessed file-based applications. Administrators must create the proper groups and grant those groups the appropriate level of access to the resources. Granting execute access to the appropriate directories where applications are contained is fundamental in securing the company's Web-based applications.

## Hiding the Keys

If the keys to the kingdom are hanging on a hook next to the front gate things are not very secure. Hackers know very well where applications are open. By moving things around a little bit it makes the opposition work a bit harder in compromising your network.

Moving ports can make port scanning less effective in finding which services are running on the network servers. All applications are listening on well-known TCP ports. Examples of common ports are as follows:

- 21 FTP
- 23 Telnet
- 25 SMTP
- 80 HTTP
- 110 POP3
- 443 SSL

## Requiring SSL

People who want to listen in to your network conversations can do this very easily. Now, what they get to listen to is up to you. Renumbering ports and encrypting the data going back and forth between the client and the server is a good way to keep people from eavesdropping.

# Protecting Certificate-based Services from Disaster

Bad things happen to good administrators. No matter what one does, hard drives go bad, power supplies burn out, and files get deleted. By keeping these inevitabilities in mind, you can protect yourself from accidental deletion and equipment failures.

## Building Fault Tolerance

No single point of failure is a common planning scheme among network administrators. If you have at least two of everything you can afford to lose one without user downtime. Administrators deploying a PKI environment with multiple tiers can deploy several layers of fault tolerance such as the following:

- Clustering essential roles in the CA infrastructure
- Hosting the CA servers in multiple locations

- Network load balancing of the CA enrollment servers

- Maintaining off-line copies of the CA certificates

## Planning Backup and Restoration

Administrators have the unenviable role of bringing lost data back from the netherworld or raising servers from the dead. By planning for failure you can create a disaster recovery plan of action and spare server parts and roles.

Tracking changes is important because restoring an old copy of a server can take the company back several weeks if not break the applications altogether.

Perform the following steps when backing up a Certificate Authority:

1. Log on to the system with at least Backup Operator or Certification Authority Administrator privileges.

2. Click Start, Programs, Administrative Tools and double-click Certification Authority.

3. In the console tree, right-click on the name of CA server that you want to back up.

4. Choose All Tasks/Back up CA as shown in Figure 3.4.

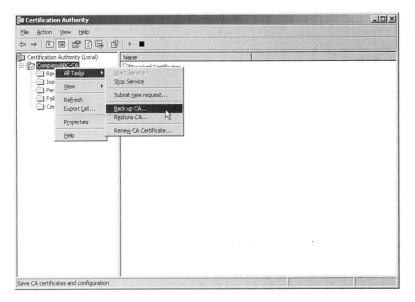

**FIGURE 3.4**
Backing up the Certification Authority.

# Integrating Smartcards with Personal Devices

Administrators can extend the security of their smartcard desktop enrollment and usage. Smartcards can replace the user's need to memorize passwords on Windows-based mobile devices as well. The same certificates stored on the smartcard to log on to the PC can be used to access the company's network and applications via Pocket PCs and Windows-based Smart Phones.

## Using Smartcards with a Pocket PC

Pocket PCs can be equipped with third-party smartcard readers to perform such tasks as Internet authentication or intranet security.

Pocket PCs use a certificate solution with smartcards based on the Windows CE Cryptographic Service Provider (CSP) for the specific brand/type of smartcard.

On a Pocket PC the CSP performs the following functions:

- Provides a CSP interface compatible with the Microsoft RSA provider.

- Uses the smartcard to save private keys securely.

- Uses the smartcard to perform private key operations such as key exchange and digital signing.

- Restricts access to private key operations with a user-supplied PIN.

- The Pocket PC can be used as an enrollment station by implementing the KP_CERTIFICATE property.

When used with smartcard enrollment the Pocket PC should extract the certificates stored on the smartcard. The Pocket PC saves them to the local system store for use by applications. The Certificate Management control panel applet can be used to perform these enrollment steps.

## Using Smartcards with Smart Phones

Mobile User Authentication of Global System for Mobile Communications (GSM) has, to date, been performed by a smartcard known as a Subscriber Identity Module (SIM) card. As of January 2000, there were more than 250 million smartcards being used in the mobile telephone industry.

Microsoft Smart Phones are based on the Windows CE operating system and will be able to take advantage of similar smartcard certificate management as the Pocket PC. Applications that use smartcards for certificate storage and computation will also work similarly to those on the Pocket PC.

# Summary

Smartcards have become an important component in the security strategy of organizations. Rather than relying on logon name and password, an organization that implements smartcards is leveraging two-factor authentication. Two-factor authentication that uses a combination of a logon/password sequence as well as the insertion of a physical smartcard device drastically improves network security in a Windows networking environment.

An important factor in setting up a secured smartcard environment is to start with a secured Certificate Authority setup. By minimizing access to the CA server, an organization can minimize the chance of unauthorized certificate creation and other key component factors in maintaining a secure authentication environment.

Smartcard administration such as issuing smartcards, managing smartcards, and applying the appropriate level of security for users also becomes a task for network administrators to manage. Fortunately with Group Policies built in to Windows Server 2003, the task of an administrator can be automated by specifying key security requirements for smartcard access.

# PART II

## Management and Administration Solutions

# 4

# Distributing Administration

The methods used to administer an IT organization can, in many ways, influence the success or failure of a company as a whole. Because the core of so many businesses relies heavily on IT resources, effective management of those resources through proper administration is of paramount importance. Windows Server 2003 provides the tools necessary to develop, deploy, and maintain administrative frameworks to meet the growing needs of IT organizations. Whether you have a small localized IT infrastructure or a large highly distributed environment, the administration of Windows Server 2003 can be easily customized to meet the specific needs of your organization.

This chapter will explore common administrative models and successful strategies developed to meet the needs of different IT organizations using Windows Server 2003. This chapter will guide the reader with tips and best practices on how to cost-effectively and securely distribute the administration of your IT resources.

# Choosing the Best Administrative Model for Your Organization

---

**It's a Lot Easier to Plan and Implement a Common Model in Early Active Directory Implementation Stages**

The selection of the administrative model for an organization should be done early on in the design and planning phase of the Active Directory migration and implementation process. Although you can change administrative models, it's a lot easier to plan and implement a common model in early Active Directory implementation stages.

---

Administrative models can help an IT organization begin to map out how IT resources and functions will be managed. Administrative models often follow a company's network architecture in terms of whether they are centralized, distributed, or a combination of the two. Many companies will find exceptions to this rule. Because administration in Windows Server 2003 environments can be granularly distributed, each model can be easily supported. This section will discuss centralized, distributed, and mixed administrative models.

## Centralized Administration

---

**Centralized Administration Can Be Maintained in a Distributed IT Environment**

In this case, network resources might be located at remote sites, but the administration and management of those systems are still administered at the local site. Even with distributed IT resources, you can still gain most of the benefits of a centralized architecture by localizing administration. As the need for hands-on administration grows at the remote sites, IT organizations begin adopting a distributed administration model.

---

With centralized administration, most if not all of the IT resources and functions are administered from a central location. This often means that all the critical servers and IT equipment are also located in one physical site. Having a completely centralized IT architecture provides the advantage of greater control of all the resources. There is also a cost savings when compared to distributed and mixed models in that operating costs are limited to maintaining a single site. This has become an increasingly attractive model to companies trying to save costs by consolidating their resources. The disadvantage to a completely centralized architecture may be the need to maintain an expensive wide area network (WAN) to provide high bandwidth to remote sites. If there are many users supported remotely, providing acceptable network performance characteristics might outweigh the cost of distributing the IT architecture. In such cases, IT resources will be located in the remote sites.

## Distributed Administration

In a distributed administration model, the administrative resources are physically located at both the local and remote site(s). In a Windows Server 2003 environment, there are varying levels of distributed administration. In a completely distributed administrative model, all administrative functions at the remote sites are managed and performed by IT staff in those same geographic locations. In this scenario, the company might gain better remote site performance by having onsite support for IT resources. Even in situations where all IT resources are kept in a central location, a distributed administration model might still apply. For organizations with a very large data center, various administrative roles can be distributed to different IT groups. For instance, one group might have administrative rights over DNS, but another group administers DHCP services. Obviously, with a completely distributed administration, an IT organization loses some of the benefits inherent to the central administration model.

To preserve those benefits, many companies adopt a centralized/delegated approach to distributing administration. In these scenarios, limited administrative functions are delegated to remote administrators, whereas the overall administration of the network is managed from the primary central site. When centralized and distributed administrative strategies are combined, the mixed model begins to emerge.

## Mixed Administration

The mixed model of administration will leverage the benefits from both centralized and distributed administration models. The mixed administration model benefits those companies that require distributed network architecture, but also want to maintain some level of central administration. Through granting permissions and rights for specific administrative functions to specific groups or users, the distribution of IT administration can be managed centrally. One example might be to have network security policies managed for the whole organization from the central site, but to have the user and computer account management administered at each remote site.

### BEST PRACTICE

**The Right Administrative Model**

Best practices in deploying the right model for your organization can be summed up as follows:

- **Centralize Whenever Possible:** You achieve the tightest control and cost savings when all your IT resources and staff are located in the same location.

- **Try to Maintain Centralized Administration:** When user population or specialized applications force the deployment of remote IT resources, try to maintain centralized administration by managing these systems remotely.

- **Delegate Administrative Tasks:** When you need an administrative presence at the remote sites, maintain central control and delegate specific administrative functions to remote IT staff.

- **Distribution of Administrative Tasks:** Distribute full remote administration only as a last resort because this is often the most expensive solution with the highest degree of inconsistency across the IT organization.

## Applying the Administrative Models

For most large size distributed organizations, adapting to a purely centralized or distributed administrative model is not practical. Finding the right combination of administrative strategies will be key in deploying a successful IT infrastructure. In making your administrative choices, you should design a strategy that balances between lowering cost and optimizing control (the centralized model) while meeting the needs of users and service level agreements (as in the distributed model).

# Using Role-based Administration for Optimal Delegation

When administrative functions are distributed or delegated to different groups or users, it helps to map out this distribution by first identifying those key responsibilities, and then to organize them into principal roles. This section will outline high-level IT administrative roles based on industry best practices. The following sections will detail how Windows Server 2003 can be used to delegate administrative control over the various IT functions.

Some of the roles outlined in this section can be combined depending on the size, structure, and service level agreements of the given IT organization. Small companies might have only one individual responsible for all administrative roles, whereas large companies might have several individuals responsible for a single role.

## The Operations Manager

The Operations Manager is responsible for the overall design of IT systems administration across the scope of the entire computing environment. Basically this is the top role that determines how administration will be distributed based on the size, architectural layout, geography, security requirements, and service level agreements of the company. The Operations Manager coordinates the efforts of all the other administrative roles.

## The Security Administrator

Security administration is an important role in any company's IT organization. An information system with a weak security foundation will inevitably experience a security breach. This administrative role covers many areas of IT administration. The key responsibility of the security administrator is to ensure the following:

- Data confidentiality. Data internal to the company should only be accessible to users who have authorization.

- Data integrity. The data available to authorized users should be accurate and free from tampering.

- Data availability. Users authorized to view data should be able to view it when they need it.

The security administration role requires delegated rights and permissions in order to implement, manage, and audit security controls and policies. This role also requires the administrative control to respond to security events.

## The Network Administrator

The network administration role is concerned with providing a reliable and consistent network infrastructure. The network infrastructure should meet or exceed service level agreements while at the same time optimize the company's assets. In addition to being responsible for network hardware configurations and performance, this role is often also responsible for network services such as DNS and DHCP.

When Active Directory is installed, Windows Server 2003 allows the responsibilities of the network administrative role to be further distributed through the use of built-in user groups. Though you can create your own groups for delegating rights and permissions, the following built-in groups can expedite the delegation of administrative control over the some network administrator functions:

- **Network Configuration Operators.** This group has the right to make TCP/IP setting changes on Domain Controllers within the domain.

- **DNSAdmins.** Installed with the DNS service, members of this group have administrative access to the DNS Server service.

- **DCHP Administrators.** This group is created when DHCP is installed on a server. Members of this group can administer all DCHP scopes configured on the server.

**BEST PRACTICE**

### Distributing Administrative Roles

It is best practice to distribute the role of the network administrator and the security administrator of the network to different individuals. The security administrator should have access to view and delete logs, as well as be authoritative over all modifications or changes to high-level security rights on the network.

By making the network administrator also the security administrator, there exists the potential for the network administrator to access sensitive information and then delete the logs that track the changes.

Although the network administrator might not have the intent to inappropriately access sensitive information, the fact that the network administrator could also change security privileges creates the potential for the network administrator to be blamed for security breaches. To minimize this risk, by simply providing another individual log deletion privileges, the network administrator can still complete all administrative tasks, and can limit her risk of being the target for unmanaged security information access and breeches.

## The Directory Service Administrator

A directory service enables users and applications to find network resources such as users, computers, services, and other information on the network. The directory service administration role is primarily concerned with the operation, management, and support of the enterprise directory.

The directory service administrator must have rights and permissions to distribute and replicate a directory across a network to provide increased performance and redundancy. It must also be able to enforce security to keep information safe from intruders.

The delegation of administering the Active Directory service in Windows Server 2003 is best performed by using Organizational Units (OUs) and the Delegation of Control Wizard discussed in the next section of this chapter.

# Leveraging the Delegation of Control Wizard

Delegating administration within Active Directory enables you to assign various levels of access and control to groups and users. Windows Server 2003 gives you the flexibility to grant control of a very focused access that might span the entire enterprise, or to grant entire control over a very limited scope of the directory. Delegating control also makes your network more secure by limiting the membership of the top level domain and enterprise administrator groups.

## Delegation Through Organizational Units

You can delegate control to any level of the domain tree by creating Organizational Units (OUs) and then delegating control of particular OUs to the groups or users that you have chosen. To determine what OUs to create, consider the structure of your organization.

> **It Is Important to Keep in Mind...**
> that although you have the capability to create multiple OUs in your directory, it might not be advisable to do so. You should only add an OU to a domain if a group needs special administrative control to a set Active Directory objects. Group Policies are covered in detail in Chapter 6, "Implementing Group Policies."

For example, you might want to grant administrative control of all users and computers that are associated with a particular department, like Sales, to a particular group or individual. The best way to accomplish this is to create an OU for Sales, place all Sales users and computers in that OU, and then delegate control of the Sales OU to your chosen Sales department admin or administrative group.

You can delegate administration of your Sales department with more granularity by nesting OUs. For example you could delegate control of computer accounts to one group, and delegate control of user accounts to another group by creating nested OUs under the Sales OU as shown in Figure 4.1.

## Delegating Simple Administrative Tasks

The Delegation of Control Wizard, as its name implies, enables you to delegate administrative control by using a wizard that guides you through the setup process. You can set varying levels of control using the wizard, even limiting the scope of the delegated control to a single operation.

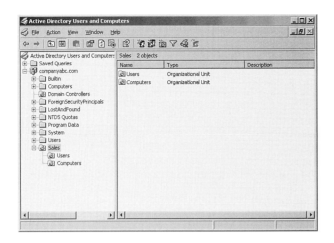

**FIGURE 4.1**
Nesting OUs for granular delegation.

For example, you might want to give a group the capability to do nothing more than reset passwords on user accounts in a particular OU. The process by which the wizard is used to accomplish this delegation is as follows:

1. In Active Directory Users and Computers, right-click the OU where you want to delegate permissions and choose Delegate Control.

2. Click Next at the Delegation of Control Wizard Welcome screen.

3. Click Add to select the group you want to grant access to.

4. Type in the name of the group and click OK.

5. Click Next to continue.

6. Under Delegate the Following Common Tasks, choose the appropriate permission; for this example choose Reset User Passwords and Force Password Change at Next Logon (see Figure 4.2). Then click Next.

7. Click Finish to finalize the changes.

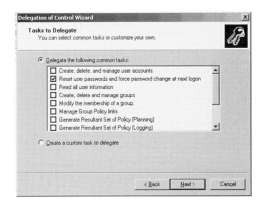

**FIGURE 4.2**    Choosing delegation of common task.

## Delegating Custom Tasks

In addition to enabling you to delegate common tasks like resetting user account passwords, the Delegation of Control Wizard provides an enormous variety of custom tasks for delegation. For example, you might want to grant the permission to create and remove computer accounts from a specific OU to a particular group. To perform this delegation, follow these steps to set the custom task:

1. In Active Directory Users and Computers, right-click the OU where you want to delegate permissions and choose Delegate Control.

2. Click Next at the Delegation of Control Wizard Welcome screen.

3. Click Add to select the group to which you want to give access.

4. Type in the name of the group and click OK.

5. Click Next to continue.

> **The Ability to Delegate Tasks with This Level of Granularity Can Be Useful**
>
> The ability to delegate tasks with this level of granularity can be useful in an automated desktop deployment scenario where adding the new desktop computer accounts to the domain is a scripted function following an automated image process. The script can leverage a user account that has the previous example's delegated permission, but with no other functional administrative access.

6. Select Create a Custom Task to Delegate and click Next.

7. Under Delegate Control Of, choose only the Following Objects in the Folder.

8. Check Computer Objects and then click Next.

9. Under Permissions, check Create All Child Objects and Delete All Child Objects as shown in Figure 4.3. Click Next.

10. Click Finish to finalize the changes.

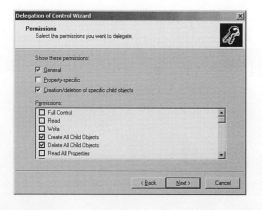

**FIGURE 4.3**    Setting Permissions for Custom Tasks.

## BEST PRACTICE

### Delegation of Administration

Keep in mind that when you use the Delegation of Control Wizard that you are altering the default security configuration of your Active Directory. Improper use of the wizard can create security vulnerabilities that might compromise service-level agreements and business policies. To get the most out of administrative delegation in a secure fashion, follow these best practices:

- Use the Delegation of Control Sparingly: Because you can allow permissions to inherit settings from parent containers, resist making duplicate delegations on child objects. A simpler administrative design is easier to manage.

- Testing the Intended Scope: After you make a change through the Delegation of Control Wizard, test to make sure that the change has the intended scope. Log into the domain as a user of the group granted access and make sure that the user has the permission to perform the delegated function. Also test that the user cannot perform additional functions, or perform the delegated function outside the scope of the delegation.

- Document Your Changes: Although the Delegation of Control Wizard is an easy tool to use to grant permissions, it does not generate reports on the changes you make. You should maintain a document that details what permissions have been granted to whom, and at what level.

If you need to see the permissions granted at a specific OU level, do the following:

1. In Active Directory Users and Computers, right-click the OU for which you want to review permissions and choose Properties.

2. Click on the Security tab and then click Advanced.

3. Under Permission Entries, double-click the group or user to whom you granted permissions.

4. You can view and edit the special permissions in the Permissions section, as shown in Figure 4.4.

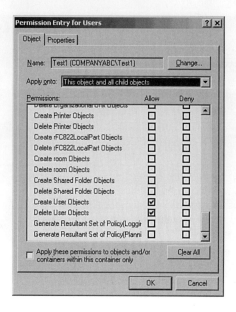

**FIGURE 4.4**    Viewing delegated permissions.

# Enhancing Administration with Functional Levels

You are probably familiar with the mixed and native modes of Active Directory in Microsoft Windows 2000. Mixed mode provides backward-compatibility with NT 4.0 environments where Backup Domain Controllers can exist and authenticate user logons. Promoting a Windows 2000 domain to Native mode eliminates the use of backup Domain Controllers and, in turn, provides additional Active Directory features such as Universal Groups.

> ## Common Misunderstanding
>
> There is a common misunderstanding that a native mode forest in Windows 2000 requires that *all* servers and workstations in the network are Windows 2000 or higher configurations and that an organization could not have Windows NT 4 servers or workstations, or Windows 9x workstations. This is a misunderstanding because a native mode forest in Windows 2000 only required that all domain controllers were Windows 2000. A native mode forest in Windows 2000 could have Windows NT 4 member servers, Windows NT4 workstations, and Windows 9x workstations in the domain and still function properly.

With Windows Server 2003, the concept of modes is augmented with the introduction of *functional levels*. Like Windows 2000 Active Directory modes, Functional levels provide levels of backward-compatibility for both Windows NT 4.0 and Windows 2000 domains. In Windows Server 2003, there are four domain functional levels and three forest functional levels. This section will provide an overview of the Windows functional levels and their implications on administrative design and management.

## Windows 2000 Mixed Domain Functional Level

The Windows 2000 Mixed Domain Functional level provides for backward-compatibility with a Windows 2000 Active Directory running in Mixed Mode. Installed at this level, Windows

Server 2003 domain controllers will be able to communicate with both Windows NT 4.0 and Windows 2000 domain controllers throughout the forest. At this level, Windows Server 2003 shares the same limitations present in the Windows 2000 mixed mode domain. Usually, this is a temporary level for most companies that are in the process of migrating to a native mode Active Directory.

## Windows 2000 Native Functional Level

The Windows 2000 native functional level is the initial operating level of Windows Server 2003 domain controllers installed into a Windows 2000 native mode domain. At this level there are no NT 4.0 domain controllers. All authentication is performed by Windows 2000 and Windows Server 2003 domain controllers.

## Windows Server 2003 Interim Functional Level

The Windows Server 2003 interim functional level is the initial operating level of Windows Server 2003 domain controllers installed into a Windows NT 4.0 domain. This level is provided primarily as a stepping stone during a migration from Windows NT 4.0 to Windows Server 2003. The interim functional level comes into play for those companies that have not upgraded to Windows 2000, but instead migrate directly to Windows Server 2003 Active Directory.

## Windows Server 2003 Functional Level

To gain the full functionality of a Windows Server 2003 Active Directory, the Windows Server 2003 functional level is the final goal for domain and forest functional levels. Functionality at this level enables many of the new features available to Windows Server 2003 such as renaming domains and domain controllers, schema deactivation, and cross-forest trusts. For you to promote your Active Directory to the full Windows Server 2003 Functional level, all domain controllers must be upgraded to Windows Server 2003. Individual domains can be promoted to the Windows Server 2003 functional level, but the forest can only be promoted to this functional level after all the domains in the forest are operating at this highest level.

You can use Active Directory Users and Computers or Active Directory Domains and Trusts to elevate domain functional levels. To raise the forest functional level, though, you must use the Active Directory Domains and Trusts tool. If you are ready to perform both operations, follow these steps:

1. Ensure that all domain controllers in the forest are upgraded to Windows Server 2003.

2. Open Active Directory Domains and Trusts from the Administrative Tools menu.

3. In the left scope pane, right-click on the domain name and then click the Raise Domain Functional Level.

4. In the box labeled Raise Domain Functional Level, shown in Figure 4.5, select Windows Server 2003 and then click Raise.

5. Click OK and then click OK again to complete the task.

6. Repeat steps 1 through 5 for all domains in the forest.

7. Perform the same steps on the forest root object, except this time choose Raise Forest Functional Level and follow the prompts.

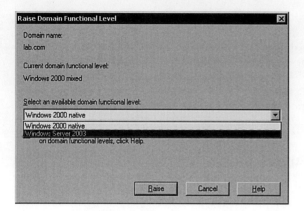

**FIGURE 4.5**
Raising the domain functional level.

## Domain Administrative Functionality

There are new administrative capabilities at each domain functional level that you should be aware of. In part, understanding the new capabilities help in the decision to elevate functional levels. It is also important to keep these capabilities in mind when deciding whether to grant or prevent access to these functions within your IT organization.

> **Raising Functional Levels Is a One-way Operation**
>
> Be sure you will not need to add Windows 2000 domains to your forest before performing this process. When the forest is Windows Server 2003 functional, this applies to child domains as well.

When you elevate your domain from a Windows 2000 mixed to a Windows 2000 Native functional level, you add the following administrative capabilities:

- SID History. This feature enables you to migrate security principles from one domain to another while preserving associated access control lists (ACLs).

- Converting Groups. This feature gives you the capability to change distribution groups and security groups.

- Nesting Groups. In mixed mode, you can nest distribution groups, but not security groups. Windows 2000 Native mode allows you full nesting of security groups.

- Universal Groups. Universal groups can contain accounts, global groups, and universal groups from any domain in the forest.

Elevating your domain from Windows 2000 Native functional level to Windows Server 2003 functional level gives you the capability to rename domain controllers within that domain.

## Forest Administrative Functionality

When you raise your forest functionality from Windows 2000 to Windows Server 2003, you enable the following administrative capabilities:

- Deactivation of schema objects. Although you cannot delete classes or attributes, you can deactivate them if they are no longer needed or if there was an error in the original definition.

- Forest trusts. With this functionality, you can link two disjoined Windows Server 2003 forests to form one-way or two-way transitive trust relationships. A two-way forest trust creates a transitive trust between every domain in both forests.

- Domain rename. Within a Windows Server 2003 native level forest, you have the ability to rename domains. This functionality also permits the restructuring of domains within the forest.

### The Senior Administrator Should Limit the Access of Who Can Raise the Functional Level of a Domain

Rather than leaving the privilege to all Domain Admins, the right should be blocked to all Domain Admins and assigned to specific administrators. Although it is unlikely an individual would maliciously raise the functional level of a domain and effectively cause non-compliant domain controllers to be dropped from the network, there is a very common possibility of an inexperienced administrator accidentally changing the functionality level, and thus creating authentication problems on the network.

### Be Very Careful in Designing Your Administrative Framework...

so that only individuals who understand and are responsible for the implications of forest-wide changes have access to make them.

The forestwide capabilities of Windows Server 2003 each have an enormous impact on the stability of your enterprise network.

# Managing Domain and Enterprise Administration

Perhaps the two most important administrative groups in the Windows Server 2003 Active Directory are the Domain and Enterprise Admins groups. Because of their importance, membership in these groups should be very limited. As has been detailed earlier in the chapter, it is very easy to delegate permission to varying degrees of access within the Active Directory structure. By delegating control, you are able to limit the membership of the Domain and Enterprise Admins to only those individuals who are responsible for making changes that affect the entire domain or forest.

This section provides an overview of the management of the domain and enterprise admins groups.

## Managing the Domain Admins Group

Members of the Domain Admins group have full control of the domain. By default, this group is a member of the Administrators group on all domain controllers, all domain workstations, and all domain member servers at the time they are joined to the domain. By default, the Administrator account is a member of this group.

Clearly a secure IT infrastructure will have a very limited Domain Admins group for each domain in the forest. This is easily accomplished when setting up a new domain from scratch. You simply identify those individuals (or services) who will have domainwide responsibility, and limit the membership of this group to those individuals. Domain group membership can be enforced via Group Policies, which will be discussed later in this chapter.

If you are upgrading a Windows NT or Windows 2000 domain to Windows Server 2003, it is important to review and validate the Domain Admins group membership before proceeding with the upgrade. One can often find built-in NT 4.0 domain local groups added to the Domain Admins, such as Account Operators. Depending on the membership of Account Operators, the integrity of the Domain Admins group could be compromised after the upgrade.

## BEST PRACTICE

### Domain Administration Rights

Rather than placing all administrators into the Domain Admin group, because Active Directory has granular security delegation capabilities, it is best practice to limit Domain Admin group membership.

Senior administrators can be placed in the Domain Admin group; however, they should have an administrative account and a separate day-to-day access account. The day-to-day access account should have the same access privileges as all other network users. This will limit the risk of the day-to-day user account being compromised and allowing full access to network resources.

When a situation requires domain admin access, the administrator can log in with his secondary account belonging to the Domain Admin group, perform the task, and log out. As a shortcut to this process, the individual could use the Run As feature of Windows 2000, Windows XP, and Windows Server 2003.

The Run As feature enables a user logged in with a primary user account to run a particular application or command from the security context of a secondary user account. To execute an application using the Run As feature, for example Active Directory Users and Computers, simply do the following:

1. Browse to Active Directory Users and Computers in Administrative Tools.

2. While holding down the Ctrl key, right-click the Active Directory Users and Computers.

3. Choose Run As.

4. In the Run As dialog box shown in Figure 4.6, check The Following User and provide an administrative account and password.

FIGURE 4.6 Using Run As to open an administrative application.

## Managing the Enterprise Admins Group

Members of the Enterprise Admins group have full control of all domains in the forest. By default, this group is a member of the Administrators group on all domain controllers in the forest. By default, the Administrator account is a member of this group. The Enterprise Admins group only appears in the forest root domain.

All of the precautions that apply to the Domain Admins group also apply to the Enterprise Admins group. In a forest that contains multiple domains, members of the Enterprise Admins have administrative control over Active Directory in every domain; hence the membership of this group should be even more limited.

### The Schema Is the Most Critical Component of Active Directory

Unauthorized access to the schema master domain controller for a forest can cause serious problems with the potential to corrupt the entire directory. Implementing a peer root domain segregates the keys to schema modification from the user base of the forest.

## BEST PRACTICE

### Limiting Administrative Access

Limit this group to a single user account, usually the default administrator account. An added layer of security can be accomplished by renaming the administrator account and using a complex password. The new name and password should only be known by those individuals responsible for making forestwide changes to Active Directory. Further, the account should only be used when such changes are warranted.

In addition to the earlier prescribed precautions, you can provide additional security to your Enterprise Admins group through your forest structure by creating a peer-root or placeholder domain. The peer-root and placeholder domain concepts are detailed in Chapter 10 "Advanced Active Directory Design," but essentially what these models provide is a separate domain that is unpopulated save the Enterprise and Schema Admins groups.

By placing these security principles in an empty root, membership of these groups will be protected from any other administrative accounts in the forest. For example, by default the only member of the Schema Admins group is the administrator account. Isolating the Schema Admins group in an otherwise empty root domain preserves and protects the membership of this group from domain level administrators.

# Developing Group Policies that Affect Administration

As mentioned earlier in the chapter, Active Directory group policy objects (GPOs) can be leveraged to manage and maintain a company's administration policies. This section will outline some industry best practices for controlling administrative delegation through GPOs. For more detailed information on using Group Policies, see Chapter 6.

---

**If You Are Enforcing Administrative Policies...**

that apply to member servers, computer accounts, or user accounts, create an OU structure to group these objects, and then link your GPOs to the appropriate OUs. If your policies are to apply domainwide, you should link the GPOs to the domain. More tips on linking GPOs to Active Directory containers can be found in Chapter 6.

---

## Linking Group Policies to the Appropriate Containers

Because policies that apply to administrative access within Active Directory are directly related to Domain Controllers, the scope of your group policy objects should be applied to the Domain Controllers container. You can edit the existing Default Domain Controllers policy or create additional GPOs and link them to the Domain Controllers container. You can also use the Default Domain Controller Security Settings snap-in.

## Enforcing a Complex Administrator Password via Group Policy

Many of the policy settings available for managing administration can be found by navigating through the GPO Editor to Computer Configuration\Windows Settings\Security Settings\ Local Policies\Security Options. For example, in Figure 4.7, a policy is set to rename the local administrator password, which could be a standard policy setting applied to all file servers in a particular domain.

## Restricting Administrative Group Memberships

To enforce group membership, like the static membership of the Domain Admins group, set a Restricted Groups policy. When a Restricted Groups policy is enforced, any current member of a restricted group that is not on the Members list is removed. Any user on the Members list who is not currently a member of the restricted group is added. To create a Restricted Groups policy, perform the following steps:

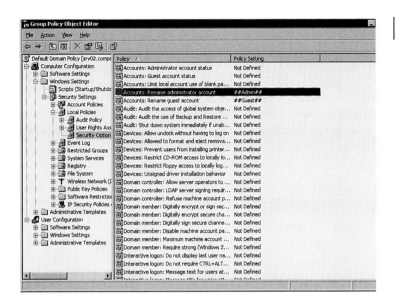

**FIGURE 4.7**
Enforcing Local Password Policy

1. In the Group Policy Editor, navigate to Computer Configuration\Windows Settings\Security Settings\Restricted Groups as shown in Figure 4.8.

2. Right-click Restricted Groups, and select Add Group. Type in the name of the group or click Browse for Group.

3. Click the Add button, and then type the names of the security principles that will belong to this group. Click OK.

4. Click OK again to finalize the process.

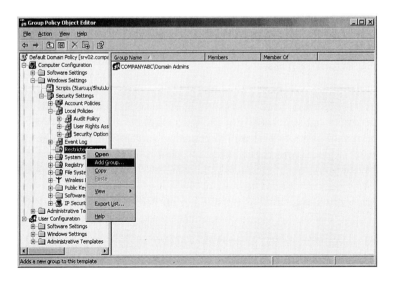

**FIGURE 4.8**
Creating a Restricted Groups policy.

## Delegating Rights with Group Policies

You can also use group policies to delegate rights not available in the Delegation of Control Wizard but required for some administrative tasks. These settings are found in the GPO Editor by navigating to Computer Configuration\Windows Settings\Security Settings\Local Policies. For example, standard user accounts do not by default have the right to log on to a Domain Controller locally. Although most maintenance tasks on Domain Controllers can be accomplished without a local logon, if a particular maintenance task requires a local logon, you could grant the right to a group by performing the following configuration on the Default Domain Controller GPO:

1. In the Group Policy Object Editor, navigate to Computer Configuration\Windows Settings\Security Settings\Local Policies\User Rights Assignments.

2. In the right-hand pane, double-click Allow Log On Locally.

> **Editing the Default Domain Controller Security Policy**
>
> The previous change can also be accomplished by editing the Default Domain Controller Security Policy.

3. Select the Define these Policy Settings box.

4. Click the Add User or Group button.

5. Type the Group name and click OK.

6. Click OK again to finalize the change.

# Testing Level of Administrative Access

It is always a recommended best practice to test changes that will affect Active Directory. Because administration has direct implications for network security, it is paramount that delegations of administration changes are made to withstand rigorous test procedures. This section will highlight some methods by which to ensure such delegations are made in a secure manner.

## Testing Changes in a Lab Environment

It is commonly understood that testing is a necessary stage in any IT deployment scenario. The test lab is an investment that can pay for itself many times over in reduced support and redeployment costs that arise from poorly tested solutions. You should always be sure to test your proposed design in an environment that simulates, as well as protects, your production environment. You can verify your design by devising and conducting tests that reflect the conditions of your production IT resources. Although this truism is usually incorporated into the deployment plans of large migrations, it is just as important to keep your testing environment in service post-deployment for ongoing testing of changes that affect security and administration in Active Directory.

The prototype lab environment should resemble the production environment insofar as primary components such as a Windows Server 2003 domain controller, file server, network equipment, and test workstations are represented. Lab components of course will vary depending on services in use and the complexity of the production architecture. The lab network should be isolated from the production network so as not to cause potential naming conflicts, replication errors, or database corruption. Though isolated, good lab environments will contain real data and applications. Data can be copied from live production servers, or data from tape can be restored into the testing environment.

> **When Testing Delegation of Control and Group Policy Results...**
> it is helpful to have the same security principles in both the test and production directories. You will get better results if group names and group memberships from both environments match.

It is important to keep your lab environment up to date with the latest patches and changes that are deployed in the production environment. If your lab domain computers are at a different revision level in service pack from the production domain computers, your test results might be inconsistent with the real world.

## Documenting Test Processes and Results

When testing modifications to the default administrative settings in the lab environment, it is important to document the processes by which the tests were conducted. If problems result in the production domain that did not manifest in the lab domain, you can return to your test procedures documentation to verify whether the correct steps were followed. Documenting the procedures and maintaining a database of the tests that have been performed will help you when similar tests are required at a later date.

As changes are implemented in the production environment, documentation should be maintained to precisely log when and what has been implemented. Although individual tests and directory modifications made at discreet times might prove successful, the combination of different changes made over time might have unexpected results. Also, the ramifications of some changes are not completely flushed out immediately. It might take days or weeks before a problem manifests itself. Keeping a log of the changes that have been made over time will expedite any troubleshooting should a conflict arise.

> **Carefully Documenting Test Procedures Is Extremely Important**
> Carefully documenting test procedures is extremely important if the testing is being carried out by a different group than the one responsible for implementing the changes. The documentation will serve as the step-by-step procedures used to replicate the test procedures in the production environment. If the documentation is not followed, the results of the production implementation might have different results than discovered in the test process.

## Group Policy Modeling

Windows Server 2003 provides tools for testing and troubleshooting your group policy changes. These are Group Policy Modeling (also referred to as Resultant Set of Policy Planning Mode) and Resultant Set of Policy. Although these tools are detailed in Chapter 6, it is important to highlight them here as tools to test and troubleshoot Delegation of Control and Group Policy settings.

Integrated into the Group Policy Management Console, Group Policy Modeling (also referred to as Resultant Set of Policy-Planning Mode) enables you to simulate a policy deployment that would be applied to users and computers before actually applying the policies. The Group Policy Modeling Wizard can be opened from the Group Policy Modeling container, the domain node, or from any OU. When the Group Policy Modeling Wizard is started from one of these containers, the wizard automatically passes the scope of management data to the wizard and pre-populates the User and Computer Selection page of the wizard.

After you run a simulation, an HTML report is generated that gives a summary that contains the GPOs and security group memberships. The simulation also generates a Settings report, shown in Figure 4.9, that shows the simulated Resultant Set of Policy given the policies that were chosen in the wizard. For more information on Group Policy modeling, turn to Chapter 6.

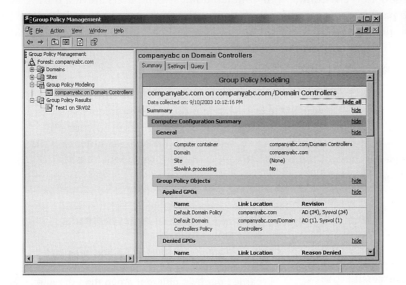

**FIGURE 4.9**
Simulating Policy assignment through Group Policy Modeling.

## Resultant Set of Policy (RSoP)

This feature enables you to determine the resultant set of policy that was applied to a given computer and (optionally) user that logged on to that computer. The data that is presented is similar to Group Policy Modeling data; however, unlike Group Policy Modeling, this data is not a simulation. It is the actual resultant set of policy data obtained from the target computer. Unlike Group Policy Modeling, the data from Group Policy Results is obtained from the client, and is not simulated on the DC. The client must be running Windows XP, Windows Server 2003 or later.

> **Group Policy Results Data**
>
> It is not possible to get Group Policy Results data for a Windows 2000 computer. However, with Group Policy Modeling, you can simulate the RSoP data.

Resultant Set of Policy is an ideal tool for documenting the Group Policy settings that affect administration in a Windows Server 2003 Active Directory as it generates easy-to-use HTML reports. The tool can also be used to troubleshoot access and permissions problems in environments where multiple GPOs and delegated permissions are assigned to various containers in the directory. For more information on RSoP, see Chapter 6.

# Auditing Administrative Activities

A key function in managing a centralized/delegated administrative model is proper monitoring of administrative activities. Not only does this give the Network Administrator role the ability to identify security breaches, but also it can provide an essential troubleshooting tool for the Directory Services administrator when permissions and access do not work as expected. To complete this chapter on distributing administration, this section will highlight what should be monitored in a securely distributed administration model. A more detailed account of monitoring is covered in Chapter 21, "Proactive Monitoring and Alerting."

## Audit Settings on Domain Controllers

Because most administrative delegation occurs in Active Directory, it is wise to monitor administrative activities on domain controllers. You can set the auditing policies for domain controllers by editing the Audit Policy component of the Domain Controller Security Settings as shown in Figure 4.10.

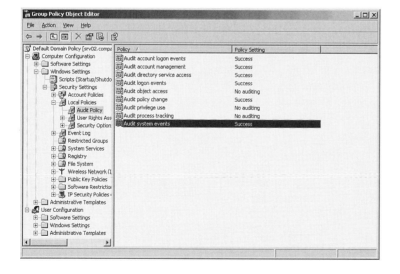

**FIGURE 4.10**
Editing the Audit Policy for Domain Controllers.

On domain controllers, auditing is turned off by default. By defining auditing settings for specific event categories, you can create an auditing policy that suits the security needs of your organization.

For each policy setting, you can specify whether to audit successes, audit failures, or not audit the event type at all. Success audits generate an audit entry when the specified type of event succeeds. Failure audits generate an audit entry when the specified type of event fails. To set this value to No Auditing, in the Properties dialog box for a policy setting, select the Define These Policy Settings check box and clear the Success and Failure check boxes.

## Collect and Archive Security Logs

An audit trail can contain information about changes that are made to your domain controllers or to Active Directory. If intruders gain administrator rights and permissions, or if delegated administrators abuse their rights and permissions, they can clear the security log, leaving you without a trail of their actions. If you use a tool that regularly collects and saves security log entries across your organization, even if intruders or administrators clear the local security log, you are more likely to be able to trace the actions of intruders or administrators. Microsoft Operations Manager is an example of such a tool.

### Audit Accounts Management Events

By auditing success events in the account management event category, you can verify changes that are made to account properties and group properties. Review these events with a keen eye to the administrative groups with the most control—the Domain and Enterprise Admins groups.

If you decide to audit failure events in the account management event category, you can see if unauthorized users or attackers are trying to change account properties or group properties. Although this can be helpful for intrusion detection, the increase in resources that is required and the possibility of a denial-of-service attack usually outweigh the benefits.

### Size the Security Log Appropriately

It is important that the size of the security log be configured appropriately, based on the number of events that your auditing policy settings generate. You can also set a retention period and method of retention for the security logs.

## Summary

By delegating administration you can allow distributed groups and users within your organization to play a role in the administration of network resources while at the same time maintaining a level central control. Delegation of administrative tasks and granting administrative rights and permissions helps protect your network resources by limiting membership in the domain and forestwide administrative groups. Windows Server 2003 provides easy wizard-based tools to aid in the planning, implementation, and troubleshooting of administrative policies.

# 5

## Managing User Rights and Permissions

**E**very user in an organization is an individual, with unique requirements necessary to perform his or her job. Many of those requirements involve IT resources. Part of a system administrator's job is making the appropriate IT resources available to each of these individual users. This is an easy task in a small company where each user's IT needs can be catered to individually. In an enterprise organization, the individual still needs IT resources, but his or her needs cannot be addressed one at a time. This is where solid directory services and efficient user management strategies play an important role. Understanding how to leverage the user management tools available in Windows Server 2003 Active Directory to manage user rights and permissions can greatly simplify the task of meeting the IT resource needs of the enterprise user community.

This chapter focuses on recommended Windows Server 2003 Active Directory administrative strategies for managing user rights and permissions. In addition to discussing such concepts as group policies, Intellimirror, and user profiles, this chapter will focus on recommendations for managing common types of users found in every organization.

# Leveraging Domain Local, Global, and Universal Groups

The first step in developing an efficient and secure design for managing user permissions to resources is understanding groups in Windows Server 2003. The concept of groups is nothing new to system administrators. As will be emphasized in later sections, it is far easier and more efficient to assign permissions and rights to groups rather than individual users. This section will explore the various types of groups available with Windows Server 2003 Active Directory, how and when to use a particular type over another, and general best practices for designing your group structure.

## Choosing the Appropriate Group Type

When a group is created in Active Directory, there are two decisions that need to be made. One decision concerns the scope of the group, which includes domain local, global, and universal. The other decision involves the group type: either security or distribution.

### Security Groups

Security groups are the primary types of group that administrators are used to managing. *Security groups* are used to assign permissions to resources for a collection of users. Like user objects in Active Directory, security group objects are each associated with a unique Security ID (SID). The uniqueness of the SID is used by Active Directory to apply security to resources in the domain. Because of this unique SID, you cannot simply delete group A, change the name of group B to A, and expect the renamed group to maintain the security settings of the original group A.

**Active Directory Permissions**
You cannot assign Active Directory permissions using a distribution group. Distribution groups are usually only found in environments with Exchange 2000.

### Distribution Groups
*Distribution groups* are group objects created so that group members can receive Simple Mail Transfer Protocol (SMTP) mail messages. Any application that can look for addresses in Active Directory (or perform LDAP lookups) can use this type of group object to send mail.

### Mail-enabled Groups

Understanding the difference between security and distribution groups is a fairly familiar concept to most administrators, especially those working with Microsoft networks. With Exchange 2000, though, comes the concept of a *mail-enabled* group that is a combination of the security and distribution group concepts. A mail-enabled group is essentially a security group that is referenced by an e-mail address and can receive SMTP messages sent to it. This functionality is only possible in an Exchange 2000 (or higher) environment. An Exchange 2000 implementation is directly integrated with Active Directory, and as such actually extends the attributes of AD objects to include e-mail addresses.

This tight integration with Active Directory makes Exchange 2000 an attractive mail service option to companies already benefiting from Active Directory deployments. Additionally, it greatly simplifies group management. A system administrator can now create a single group that can act as both a security principle and an e-mail address.

Additionally, once the functional level of a domain is in Windows 2000 Native or higher, distribution and security groups are interchangeable. As part of a migration path from an NT environment to Windows Server 2003, legacy distribution groups can be easily converted to security groups, thus allowing for a simpler group structure. To convert a distribution group to a security group (or visa versa), follow these steps:

1. Open Active Directory Users and Computers.

2. In the console tree, click the group that will be converted. Right-click, and then select Properties.

3. On the General Tab, under Group Type, select Security, as shown in Figure 5.1 Click OK to complete the change.

> **Windows 2000 Mixed Mode Functional Level**
>
> In a Windows 2000 mixed mode functional level, the alternate group type selection will be grayed out. After the functional level is elevated, changes to the group properties page will be available.

**FIGURE 5.1**    Changing a group type.

## Choosing the Appropriate Group Scope

There are four scopes to choose from when creating a group in Active Directory. Each scope serves a unique purpose, so it is important to understand the distinctions between them. The group scopes available are

- Machine local groups
- Domain local groups
- Global groups
- Universal groups

### Machine Local Groups

Machine local groups are by and large the default groups built into the operating system. Local groups can be created on a local workstation or server, but for the most part, in networked environments, the only local groups are installed with the operating system. These groups can be used to apply permissions to resources, but only on the local machine. The most commonly used local groups in Windows operating systems are Administrators, Users, and Power Users. Backup Operators is also a commonly used group for granting permissions to back up local resources on a machine.

> **Machine Local Groups Are Not Present on Domain Controllers in Active Directory**
>
> When a member server is promoted to a domain controller, the original machine local groups and users are removed and replaced with domain groups and users. Any permissions set using local groups would have to be re-created with domain groups.

Using machine local groups to assign permissions to resources in a domain environment is not recommended, though they can be useful for assigning particular rights on individual workstations.

### Domain Local Groups

Domain local groups are the next step up the ladder from machine local groups. Similar to local groups in Windows NT, Domain local groups are local in the sense that they can be used to assign permissions on resources local to the domain.

Although the domain local group can assign permissions on resources within its particular domain, it can contain members from anywhere in the Active Directory forest or even outside the forest if the external domains are trusted. Depending on the functional level of the domain, domain local groups can contain any of the following:

- User accounts
- Global groups
- Universal groups (in AD Native mode)
- Other Domain local groups (in AD Native mode)

### Global Groups

Similar to global groups in Windows NT, Active Directory global groups can contain the following types of objects:

- User accounts

- Other global groups from the same domain (in AD Native mode)

When creating groups in Active Directory, global groups are the default. This group scope is useful for sorting users into easily identifiable groupings and can be used for granting permissions to resources in any domain in the forest.

**BEST PRACTICE**

### Using Domain Local and Global Groups

As a best practice, use domain local groups to control access to resources and use global groups to organize users into similar groups of users. When you follow this design plan, global groups can then be added as members to domain local groups. This allows those members access to the appropriate resources while limiting the effect of replication on the network environment.

### Universal Groups

Introduced with Active Directory, and enhanced in Windows Server 2003, universal groups have the widest scope of all the group scopes. Universal groups can contain objects from any trusted domain, and can be used to apply permissions to any resource in the Active Directory forest.

When universal groups were introduced in Windows 2000, Microsoft made it possible to consolidate group membership across domain boundaries. Unfortunately, this functionality was limited by the fact that when the group membership of a universal group changed,

### Universal Security Groups

Universal security groups cannot be created unless the functional level of the domain is set to Windows 2000 Native.

the entire group membership would have to be replicated to every domain controller in the forest. System administrators would have to make prudent choices when creating and editing universal groups so as not to negatively affect replication traffic.

Windows Server 2003 enhances the functionality of universal groups in that replication of group membership is on a member-by-member basis rather than an entire group basis. This new functionality, called incremental universal group membership, drastically improves the replication impact on the network environment.

Although using universal groups is a feasible alternative to using global groups in Windows Server 2003 environments, it is still a best practice to reserve this group scope for situations where you need to group objects across domain boundaries.

# Using NTFS and AD Integrated File Shares

The second step in setting up an infrastructure where user rights and permissions can be managed is to properly configure the IT resources to which users will have access. Data and applications stored on the company network must be both secure and accessible to those who need it. Remember that a key role in systems administration is that of the security administrator, whose primary objective is to ensure the following:

- Data confidentiality. Data internal to the company should only be accessible to users who have authorization.

- Data integrity. The data available to authorized users should be accurate and free from tampering.

- Data availability. Users authorized to view data should be able to view it when they need it.

In Windows Server 2003, the cornerstone of ensuring security of shared company data is using NTFS formatted volumes with Active Directory integrated file shares. This section details the use of these features.

## Using NTFS to Set Permissions

Formatting Windows servers and workstations with the NTFS (New Technology File System) has been an industry standard for years. NTFS provides advanced features that are not found in any version of file allocation table (FAT). For example, NTFS guarantees volume consistency by using standard transaction logging and recovery techniques. If a system fails, NTFS uses its log file and checkpoint information to restore the consistency of the file system. NTFS also provides advanced features, such as file and folder encryption, disk quotas, and compression.

Most importantly, Active Directory and file and folder permissions rely on NTFS. There really is no centralized management of user rights and permissions without NTFS.

NTFS is used in Windows Server 2003 for file-level security in the operating system. Each file and folder on an NTFS formatted drive is marked by an Access Control Entry (ACE) that limits who can and cannot access the object. NTFS permissions control read, write, and several other types of access.

NTFS has been revised in Windows Server 2003 to secure, by default, critical operating system files and directories to disallow their unauthorized use. Additionally, Windows Server 2003 does not by default grant full control to the Everyone group when creating file shares.

Changing permissions on files or folders is a simple process. Remember when changing permissions to take into account that permissions on subdirectories are inherited from their parent directories. For example, to add a group to the Access Control List (ACL) of a particular folder, perform the following steps:

1. Right-click the folder for which the security will be applied and choose Sharing and Security.

2. Select the Security tab.

3. Check the Advanced button.

4. Uncheck the Allow Inheritable Permissions from the Parent to Propagate box.

5. Click Remove when prompted about the application of parent permissions.

6. In the Advanced dialog box, use the Add buttons to give access to the group who needs access to the folder.

7. Check the Replace Permission Entries on All Child Objects box, shown in Figure 5.2, and click OK.

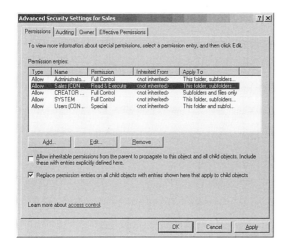

**FIGURE 5.2**    Changing NTFS permissions.

8. When prompted about replacing security on child objects, click Yes to replace child object security and continue.

9. Click OK to close the property page.

## Setting NTFS Permissions

As file resources are added to the enterprise, managing permissions can become an increasing chore. The administrator's job in securing data while providing appropriate access is simplified greatly if you adhere to the following:

1. Assign object permissions to groups of users rather than individual users whenever possible. Even if a group only includes one user, this will remove organizational dependence on one particular account and make alterations much simpler if a person leaves the organization.

2. Design group permissions so that you have a minimum of duplication. If a set of users need permissions X, Y, and Z, do not create groups with permutations of the three permissions but rather three separate groups. If all of the users need these permissions then only one group is needed. The ultimate goal is to keep the number of groups to a minimum.

3. Manage permissions globally from the ACL window. Right-clicking on objects will open their Security Permissions window. Use the Advanced button to allow or deny permission to one aspect of an object rather than the whole object.

4. Allow inheritance as much as possible. Inheritance is the default; specifying that children do not inherit specific permissions from their parents will make Active Directory harder to manage.

## Using Active Directory Integrated Shares

With Windows Server 2003, you have the capability to create, view, and manage permissions on any shared resource. A shared resource includes files, folders, printers, or any server resource made available, or published, to users.

Active Directory Shared Folders give you a tool for viewing a list of users connected over the network to a server share and the capability to disconnect one or all of them. Shared folders also give you the capability to see what shared files are opened by remote users and close one or all of the files.

To publish an Active Directory shared folder, follow these steps:

1. Open Active Directory Users and Computers.

2. In the console tree, right-click the folder into which you want to create a shared folder.

3. Point to New, and then click Shared Folder.

4. Type the name of the folder and the network path as shown in Figure 5.3

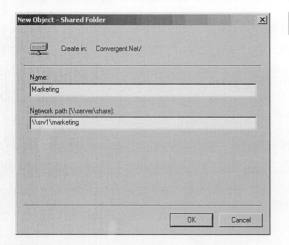

**FIGURE 5.3**  Publishing a shared folder in Active Directory.

Before there were NTFS permission settings, permissions were set at the share level. Although you still have the capability to set permission at the share level, it is preferable to use NTFS-level security. Setting NTFS permissions is the best practice because it inherently secures subdirectories. Share-level security does not protect subdirectories easily.

> **Share-level Security**
>
> Configure share-level security to be open to all domain users, but then set stricter security on the NTFS level. This allows primary security to be administered by NTFS permissions without share level security vulnerabilities.

## Using Allow/Deny Permissions

There are some special points to consider when setting up permissions on files, folders, resources, or shares. The concept of enabling a permission is fairly self explanatory. For example, if the Read permission is Allowed for a user or group on a particular file or folder, that user or group will be able to read the contents of the file or folder. If inheritance is set, that read permission will flow down the directory structure from where it was assigned.

The Deny permission is often a trickier concept to comprehend. As a result, access problems can be caused inadvertently by the misuse or misunderstanding of how this permission setting works.

When permissions are set on a parent container, for example a parent level folder in a shared folder tree, groups or users are granted a certain level of permissions. By doing this, the Access Control Entry (ACE) for that folder restricts access to those individuals defined as members of the groups listed in the ACE. The restriction *implicitly* denies access to users not defined in the ACE. In this scenario, there is no need for an *explicit* Deny permission setting.

Deny settings are only used to override an allowed permission that is already set. This situation might occur when allowed permissions are inherited from a parent folder setting. Even this situation might not require explicitly making a Deny setting, as you can break the chain of inheritance and start a new ACE on the subfolder in question by replacing the inherited settings that exclude the group or user you want to exclude.

Deny permission settings on parent level folders can also be overridden in this fashion. Inherited Deny permissions do not prevent access to a subfolder if that subfolder has an explicit Allow permission entry.

> **Explicit Permissions Take Precedence**
>
> Explicit permissions take precedence over inherited permissions, even inherited deny permissions.

> **Never Deny the Everyone Group Access to an Object**
>
> Never deny the Everyone group access to an object; the Everyone group also includes Administrators. Instead, exclude the Everyone group from the ACE in question.

# Assigning User Rights and Privileges

In addition to granting users permission to resources, Windows Server 2003 introduces the concept of user rights or *privileges*. Privileges are similar to permissions in that they involve controlling access. Where permissions involve access to objects such as files, folders, and printers, privileges grant access to operating system functionality.

The exact list of available rights that you can configure depends on the operating system to which a user will be assigned rights. Some common examples of controllable privileges in Windows Server 2003 and Windows XP are the capability to back up files and directories, log on through Terminal Services, and create a pagefile.

For a complete list of configurable user rights or privileges, open the local policy editor for the operating system on which you want to grant or restrict access. You can also view user rights and privileges through the Group Policy Editor.

Granting user rights is a fairly straightforward process. You have to choose whether rights will be granted at the workstation level via the Local Policy Editor, or at the domain level via the Group Policy Editor. Assigning rights locally will only affect users of that particular workstation. Assigning rights using a domain Group Policy will affect all users or computers in the particular Active Directory container to which the group policy object is linked. Using the Group Policy Editor will be covered in the following section, "Using Group Policy to Administer Rights and Permissions."

To assign a particular privilege, for example to grant the ability to load device drivers to the Power Users group on a local workstation, perform the following steps:

> **Assign User Rights to Group Accounts Rather Than Individual User Accounts**
>
> As is the case with assigning permissions, it is always a advisable to assign user rights to group accounts rather than individual user accounts.

1. Type **secpol.msc** at the Run line, and click OK.

2. Expand Local Policies, and then expand User Rights Assignments.

3. In the right pane, double-click Load and Unload Device Drivers, as shown in Figure 5.4.

4. Click Add User or Group.

5. Type **Power Users** in the dialog box, and click OK.

6. Click OK again to complete the configuration.

> **User Privileges Override File and Directory Permissions**
>
> Whether you are troubleshooting an access control issue, or you are designing an access control solution, it is important to keep in mind that user privileges override file and directory permissions.

Some privileges can override permissions set on an object. For example, a user logged on to a domain account as a member of the Backup Operators group has the right to perform backup operations for all domain servers. However, this requires the capability to read all files on those servers, even files on which their owners have set permissions that explicitly deny access to all users, including members of the Backup Operators group. A user right—in this case, the right to perform a backup—takes precedence over all file and directory permissions.

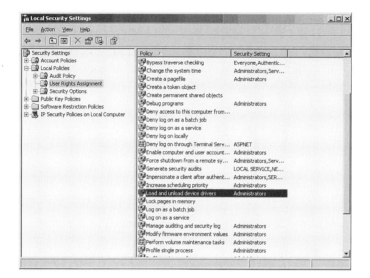

**FIGURE 5.4**
Managing user rights.

# Using Group Policy to Administer Rights and Permissions

To manage user rights and permissions on a larger scale than simply at the server or workstation level, administrators of Windows Server 2003 Active Directory networks can leverage group policies. Group policies enable directory-based change and configuration management of users and computers. This section focuses on the particular functionality of group policy for access management. For a more comprehensive approach to group policies turn to Chapter 6, "Implementing Group Policies."

## Assigning Rights with Group Policy

Previous sections demonstrated using the Local Policy Editor to manage user rights and privileges; you can assign these same user rights and privileges through the Group Policy Editor. The benefit of using group policies to assign user rights is that a larger scope of users or computers can be managed from a single configuration.

Assigning user rights with the Group Policy Editor is nearly identical to assigning rights with the Local Policy Editor. The exception is the process by which Group Policy Objects (GPOs) are linked to Active Directory container objects.

When you edit the local policy on a workstation or server to assign a particular user privilege, for example to grant the capability to perform backups and restores on a computer, then after the local policy is edited, the configuration is complete. When you make the same configuration at the domain level by creating or modifying a GPO, to enable the configuration, the administrator must also link that GPO to an Active Directory container, for example a particular Organizational Unit (OU). After the GPO is linked to an OU, the policy will apply to all computers contained in that OU. The process of linking a GPO to an AD container can be done in different ways. One way is to modify the properties of the target OU, and create or edit the GPO from that context.

To demonstrate this process in detail, the following example details the steps necessary to grant the capability to back up and restore files on all computers contained in the Sales OU to users contained in the local Power Users group of those computers.

1. In Active Directory Users and Computers, right-click on the Sales OU.

2. Choose Properties, and then click the Group Policy tab.

3. Click New, type a name for the GPO, and then click Close.

4. Click Edit to open the Group Policy Editor.

5. Navigate to Computer Configuration\Windows Settings\Security Settings\Local Policies\ User Rights Assignment.

### This Process Will Be Different

If the Group Policy Management Console is installed on the computer from which group policies are edited, this process will be different. See the section "Enhancing Manageability with GPMC," in Chapter 6 for more information on this new management utility.

6. Double-click Backup Files and Directories.

7. Check Define These Policy Settings as shown in Figure 5.5, and click Add User or Group.

8. Type in **Power Users**, and click OK to complete the configuration.

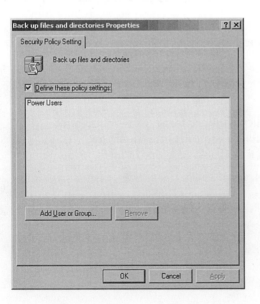

**FIGURE 5.5**    Defining policy settings for user rights.

Assigning user rights through group policies has the added security benefit of preventing changes to the configured settings at the local level. When there are conflicting settings between the local policy and a linked group policy, the group policy settings will override the local settings. Additionally, the local policy cannot be modified, even by a local administrator, if a group policy is in force.

**Manage User Rights Assignments through Group Policies**

For environments where a standard security policy is enforced for all workstations (or servers), manage user rights assignments through group policies. To provide flexibility in the environment, set the policies locally and allow local administrators to customize the user settings for particular computers.

## Granting Access to Files with Group Policy

Managing permissions for files and folders through group policies is similar to the process of editing the Access Control Entries (ACEs) on NTFS file folders and shares. Again, group policies can be used to enforce domain or OU-level security standards across a larger scope of computers. In the case of files and folders, you have the capability to replace the local ACEs on computers contained within the scope of the targeted AD container with ACE settings made in a GPO.

In addition to enforcing a security standard on common folder permissions across a broad target of computers, GPO permission settings can also be used to solve access problems that were not evident when initial permission settings were deployed locally.

For example, the default local permissions set on the folder, C:\Program Files, limits users to read and execute permissions on this folder and its subfolders in a standard Windows XP workstation. If at a later time a new application is installed on several workstations that create subfolders to which users will need the write permission for proper execution, there will be an access problem that could potentially span hundreds of workstations. The process of changing the local ACE of each workstation would be extremely tedious and time consuming. On the other hand, you can change the ACE through a group policy and fix the problem with just a few keystrokes.

The following example modifies permissions on a particular subfolder, C:\Program Files\HRApp, for all user workstations in the Human Resources OU:

1. Create or modify the GPO linked to the Human Resources OU.

2. Navigate to Computer Configuration\Windows Settings\Security Settings\File System.

3. Right-click File System and choose Add File.

4. In the Add File or Folders screen, type **C:\Program Files\HRApp**, as shown in Figure 5.6, and click OK.

**Programs Might Require Modified Permissions**

In some instances, programs might require modified permissions on only a single file in an otherwise tightly secured folder. This method of replacing permissions via group policy is granular enough to accommodate even single file ACE settings enabling you to maintain the most secure yet functional security policies.

**5.** On the Database Security screen, highlight the Users group, and then check the Write permission and click OK.

**6.** In the Add Object dialog box, choose Replace Existing Permissions and click OK.

**FIGURE 5.6**    Modifying User Permissions using Group Policy.

## Granting Access to Registry Settings with Group Policy

In addition to being able to modify file and folder permissions, you have the capability to modify security settings in the Registry using group policies.

As is the case with file permissions, the functional application of setting Registry permissions with group policies are twofold: you can establish security standards across a greater scope of user permissions on workstations or servers; and you can apply fixes to computers already deployed to a vast population of users.

Just as some software requires file permission modifications to run correctly, it is not uncommon to find similar requirements for specific Registry keys. Such requirements, though, might not show up when initial testing and configuration of the software is performed. If an application is deployed to several hundred workstations only to find that a particular functionality does not work with the standard user Registry permissions, it is possible to fix the problem by targeting the workstations with a GPO that addresses the particular Registry security setting.

For example, a company might discover after deploying 400 new workstations that standard users cannot change their default JPEG viewer from Internet Explorer to Photo Editor in Windows XP (or vice versa). The workstations will require modified permissions to the following Registry key: HKLM\SOFTWARE\Microsoft\Shared Tools\Graphic Filters. To modify these permissions through group policy, perform the following steps:

**1.** Modify or create a new GPO attached to domain.

**2.** In Group Policy Editor, navigate to Computer Configuration\Windows Settings\Security Settings\Registry.

**3.** Right-click Registry, and then choose Add key.

**4.** In the Select Registry Key dialog box, manually type the key **MACHINE\SOFTWARE\ Microsoft\Shared Tools\Graphic Filters**, and click OK.

5. Highlight Users, and click Advanced.

6. Highlight Users again, and click Edit, as shown in Figure 5.7.

7. Check Allow for Set Value, and then click OK three times.

8. Choose Replace Existing Permissions and click OK.

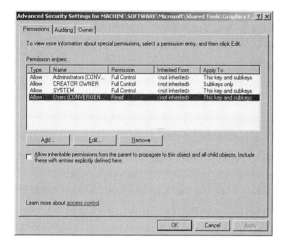

**FIGURE 5.7**    Editing Registry Permissions with Group Policy.

## Managing Groups with Group Policy

Because the most efficient way to manage access control to resources is by leveraging groups of various types, it is important to provide a means to manage group memberships across a wide scope of computer objects. To this end, group policies can be defined that limit or set the membership of groups across computer objects contained in the targeted AD container.

For example, you might want to limit the membership of the local Power Users group to the Engineering global group for computers contained in the Engineering OU of the domain. By enforcing such a policy, the local Power Users group cannot be modified at the local level to include any other members besides the Engineering global group.

To establish this restriction, perform the following steps:

1. Edit or create a GPO attached to the Engineering OU.

2. In the Group Policy Editor, navigate to the Computer Configuration\Windows Settings\Security Settings\Restricted Groups.

3. Right-click on Restricted Groups and choose Add Group.

4. Type Power Users in the dialog box.

5. Click the Add button for Members of this Group.

6. In the Add dialog box, type **Engineering** and click OK.

# Maximizing Security, Functionality, and Lowering Total Cost of Ownership (TCO) with User Profiles

Another facet of managing user rights and permissions involves user profiles. A user's profile is a collection of settings that configure the user's operating desktop experience. The user profile includes Internet Explorer settings, mapped drives, network printers, desktop settings, and even application-specific configurations. Managing a user's profile is similar to managing a user's privileges in that you can define in part what a user can and cannot do when logged in with a particular user account.

There are several types of user profiles available in Windows Server 2003 for you to manage. An understanding of the various types of profiles will enable you to better refine and manage user rights and permissions.

## Local and Roaming Profiles

Local profiles exist on a particular workstation or server's hard disk. A single user could have several local profiles, each with different configuration settings, on various machines to which the user has logged in. Local profiles are managed individually at the workstation or server on which they exist.

Roaming profiles, on the other hand, are stored on a server file share. These profiles are downloaded from the server to the local workstation or server when the user logs into the domain. When the user logs off, the profile is then pushed back up to the server.

> **Unless a User's Desktop and My Documents Folder Are Redirected to a Server Share...**
>
> they are included in a roaming user profile. Depending on the size of these folders, a user's logon/logoff time can be greatly affected.

Roaming user profiles have the advantage of providing a standard set of profile settings to users regardless of the machine at which she logs into. The disadvantage is that the time it takes to log on or log off will depend on the size of the roaming user profile in use. A best practice for implementing roaming user profiles is to also implement folder redirection. Folder redirection is detailed in Chapter 6 in the section "Increasing Fault Tolerance with Intellimirror."

## All Users and Default Profiles

Each Windows 2000, Windows XP, and Windows Server 2003 system includes Default and All Users Profiles. These profiles are helpful in setting up a user experience that will affect any user that logs into the system.

The All Users profile folder contains settings that will apply to all users logging into that system. You can use this folder to add desktop shortcuts or start menu items to the users' specific desktop settings in their local or roaming profile settings. The All Users profile are machine specific and will not modify a user's local or roaming profile settings.

The Default User profile is used whenever a user logs into a system for the first time. To manage how local profiles are configured on a system, configure the default user profile. You can configure the default user profile by configuring a local user profile, and then copying that configured profile to the default profile folder.

To create a default profile, follow these steps:

1. Log on to a workstation with a standard local or domain user account, with the same level of access a standard user will have. For this example, use an account called test1.

2. Configure the profile the way you want it. Create desktop settings, Internet settings, or whatever is necessary for a standard user.

3. Log off the workstation. The profile is then saved to the c:\documents and settings\test1 directory.

4. Log in with an Administrator account.

5. Double-click the System applet in Control Panel.

6. Select the Advanced tab, and then click the Settings button in the User Profile section.

7. Select the correct profile and click the Copy To button.

8. In the Copy To window, enter the path to the default user directory, C:\documents and settings\default user, and then click OK to complete the task.

> **Default Profile Will Not Apply**
>
> If a user's account is configured to use a roaming or mandatory profile, the default profile will not apply settings to that user's desktop settings.

## Mandatory Profiles

A mandatory profile is the same as a roaming profile except that changes made to the profile settings are not saved to the server upon logoff. These profiles are commonly used in classrooms or publicly shared workstations to strictly manage the profile settings. To change a profile to a mandatory profile, configure the profile to the preferred specification, and then log off the account. Next, with an Administrator account, locate the profile folder and rename the corresponding Ntuser.dat file to Ntuser.man.

## Temporary Profiles

Temporary profiles occur when the server authenticating the login for a user with a roaming profile cannot locate the profile folder on the server. When this happens, the machine attempts to load a cached copy of the user's profile from the local machine. If the user has never logged into the system before and no cached copy of the profile can be located, a temporary profile is created using the Default profile on the system. This temporary profile will become the user's roaming user profile when the user logs off and the profile is copied up to the server.

# Managing Rights and Permissions for Specific User Types

Regardless of the best efforts of CEOs to create a corporate environment in which every company associate feels like an equal, system administrators know that special groups of users require special management considerations. It follows, therefore, that different strategies for managing user rights and permissions should be adopted to meet the special requirements that some users have. This section will explore some of these strategies as they apply to common user types found in every organization.

## Managing Highly Managed Users

Highly managed users might be defined as users who have a very limited set of applications they must run on their workstation to perform their job function. These users typically have a lower level of computer skills than engineers and developers. As such, it is a best practice to limit these users so that it is difficult, if not impossible, for them to make configuration changes to the system that will cause it to work less efficiently or not at all. At the same time, you must be aware of any particular permissions that these users might require in order for their specific applications to run correctly in a limited environment.

## BEST PRACTICE

### Managing Highly Managed Users

- Enforce roaming user profiles. This is especially applicable if the user does not have a specified workstation. This way, the user always logs on to the same desktop environment regardless of the workstation.

- Limit NTFS permissions on the workstation to Read and Execute for this group and enable Folder Redirection. If the user is unable to write to the hard drive, there is less chance for files to be lost or corrupted. The user can still save files to specified server shares. Enabling Folder Redirection on the My Documents folder will save any files to the redirected server share.

- Limit the icons on the desktop and items in the start folder. This can be done using profiles and group policies. Limiting what a user can click on in the desktop environment to job-specific applications will greatly reduce the possibility of configuration settings being changed inadvertently.

- Prevent software installation. The software that the users require should already be present on the workstation.

- Restrict Internet Explorer. Limiting what users can do, and more importantly where users can go, with an Internet browser will greatly improve the stability of the workstation.

## Managing Mobile Users

Many companies have employees who either frequently travel or are located away from the typical office environment. These mobile users are unique because they usually log on to the company network through a portable computer from different locations over a slow-link dial-up modem connection. Though mobile users differ, both the slow-link connection and lack of local access should be used as the defining qualities for this type of network client.

### Managing Mobile User Rights

Some best practices for managing mobile user rights and permissions include the following:

- Enable users to log in with Power User rights. Because mobile users have less access to IT support, providing Power User membership for these users will enable them to satisfy many IT needs themselves. For example, the right to create local printers is granted to Power Users by default; this ability is important to the traveling user.

- Enable software installation. It is often hard to distribute software to mobile users. Providing software on transportable media and elevating the user permissions to install software will keep the mobile computers up to date with software and patches. You can enable the Group Policy setting, Always Install with Elevated Privileges, to accomplish this task.

- Grant more control over Network Connections. Because mobile users might need to change how they connect to the office depending on their location, enable access to modify network connections. Group policy settings for network connections can be found by navigating in the Group Policy Editor to User Configuration\Administrative Templates\Network\Network Connections.

- Enable Backup and Restore privileges. If the mobile users are rarely at the office to sync up important files to the network, it is advisable to grant these users the capability to do full system backups and restores.

## Managing Administrators for Flexibility and Security

In many companies, the administrators' workstations have no controls in place at all. The accounts the administrators use to log on to the network give them access to control every aspect of the workstation, as well as the servers. Because these accounts have so much power over the network, it is recommended that policies be in place to protect that power.

The following list provides best practices for safeguarding the administrator account privileges:

> **For More Information...**
> about managing delegating administration, see Chapter 4, "Distributing Administration."

- Provide administrators with standard user accounts. Instead of allowing system administrators to log in with administrative access for day-to-day functions like checking e-mail and editing documentation, create an additional account that has standard security settings. This prevents administrators from making accidental systemwide configuration changes. This also prevents the account's elevated privileges from getting into the hands of malicious users.

- Use the Run As feature. The Run As feature of Windows 2000 and Windows Server 2003 can be used from an administrator workstation or any network client to elevate privileges temporarily to perform administrative functions. For example, while logged in to a work-station with a user account that has standard user privileges, you can run Active Directory Users and Computers using the Run As command to execute the utility from an adminis-trative account.

■ Use password-protected screensavers. Enforce password-protected screensavers with a short timeout interval on administrator workstations. This protects the workstation from mali-cious users taking advantage of the administrator's credentials should the administrator be temporarily away from the machine. This setting can be made either through the local policy of the administrator or through Group Policy. This particular setting is found by navigating to User Configuration\Administrative Templates\Control Panel\Display\ Password Protect the Screen Saver.

## Summary

Clearly, Windows Server 2003 provides many ways in which the permissions and rights of users can be managed. By leveraging the various group types available, you can develop efficient methods for assigning the appropriate privileges to the users who require them. Windows Server 2003 provides a simple approach to permissions assignment that allows for granular control of user access to IT resources. The powerful functionality of Group Policy extends your ability to maintain a high level of security for IT resources while at the same time deploying a variety of policies that can target the special access requirements of particular types of users.

# 6

# Implementing Group Policies

Group Policy has existed in Windows products for many server versions. However, with Windows Server 2000 and now Windows Server 2003, Group Policy has become a major part of the operating system. Group Policy is used to deliver a standard set of security, controls, rules, and options to a user. In addition, it can be used to configure everything from login scripts and folder redirection to disabling Active Desktop and preventing users from installing software on their workstations.

## Leveraging Group Policies

Group Policy only applies to Windows 2000 Professional, Windows XP, Windows 2000 Server, and Windows Server 2003 server machines. Any machines running earlier versions of Windows, UNIX, or other operating systems will not receive Group Policy from Windows Server 2003. Machines receiving Group Policy settings also must be members of the domain.

There are two areas to which group policies can be applied. One is applied to computers and the other is applied to users.

## Using Computer Policies

Computer policies are applied upon boot of the machine, are in place before logon, and are independent of the user login credentials. They apply to the computer only, regardless of who will be logging in. Types of Group Policies that are best applied in the computer policies are the following (not a complete list):

- Startup scripts.

- Security settings.

- Permission configuration on local files, Registry hives, or services on a workstation.

- Software installation can be pushed if they are in an MSI format using either the User or Computer policies. However, it is suggested that it be pushed via Computer Policies.

## Using User Policies

User policies are applied when the user logs in and occur after boot and during logon. They apply to the user regardless of what computer or server the user is logging into. They follow the user wherever the user goes in the domain.

Types of Group Policies that are best applied in the computer policies are as follows (also not a complete list):

- Login scripts

- Restrictions on user rights

- Folder redirection

## Understanding Group Policy Refresh Intervals

Group Policy is refreshed at regularly scheduled intervals after a computer has been booted and a user has logged in. By default, Group Policy is refreshed every 90 minutes on non-domain controllers (with a stagger interval of 30 minutes) and every five minutes on domain controllers.

Refresh intervals are configurable via Group Policy by going to the following areas in Group Policy and changing the refresh interval times:

- To change the interval for computer policies and DCs choose Computer Configuration, Administrative Templates, System, Group Policy.

- To change the interval for user policies, choose User Configuration, Administrative Templates, System, Group Policy.

Most changes made to existing Group Policy Objects (or GPOs) or new GPOs will be enforced when the refresh cycle runs. However, the following settings will be enforced only at login or upon boot, depending on the GPO configuration settings:

> **Computer Configuration Security Settings**
> Computer Configuration security settings are refreshed every 16 hours whether or not the settings have been changed.

- Software installation configured in the Computer Policies
- Software installation configured in the User Policies
- Folder Redirection setting configured in the User Policies.

# Group Policy Deployment

Group Policy usage and configuration can vary greatly with each individual implementation. How GP is implemented can depend on the organization's users, sites, corporate culture, and a myriad of other factors. However, there are basic best practices that apply no matter what the Group Policy implementation. The following sections describe the basic best practices and lessons that have been learned through multiple GP implementations in many different organizations.

## Less Is More

The primary thing to remember with Group Policy is that less is more. Group Policy is very useful and administrators new to it frequently apply a great many Group Policies, using Group Policy as the elixir for all administrative issues. However, it's important to remember that with each Group Policy Object that is implemented and with each new layer of Group Policy, a fraction of a second is added onto computer boot time and user login time. Additionally, the GPOs take up space in SYSVOL on domain controllers, causing replication traffic as well as adding complexity that can make troubleshooting more difficult.

## Knowing Resultant Set of Policies (RSoP)

The new Group Policy Management Console (GPMC) provides you with a handy tool for planning and testing Group Policy implementations prior to implementing them. Because Group Policy can cause tremendous impact on users, any Group Policy implementation should be tested using the RSoP tool in planning mode. See the sections entitled "Using Resultant Set of Policies (RSoP) in GPMC" and "Group Policy Modeling Using Resultant Set of Policy (RSoP)" for more information.

## Group Policy Order of Inheritance

Group Policy can be configured on many different levels and, by default, is implemented in a particular order. However, by using the Block Policy Inheritance, Enforcement, and Link Enabled conditions the default order of application can be changed. It's a good idea to use these conditions sparingly because they can add a great deal of complexity to troubleshooting problems with Group Policy application. See the sections titled "Understanding GP Inheritance and Application Order" and "Modifying Group Policy Inheritance" later in this chapter for more information.

## Knowing the Impact of Slow Link Detection

Slow link detection can change the Group Policy that a user receives, which can be a difficult thing to troubleshoot as an administrator. Understanding the importance of slow links can make troubleshooting a great deal easier for you if you have WAN links that may go up and down or work in an environment with bandwidth issues. See the section in this chapter entitled "Understanding the Effects of Slow Links on Group Policy" for more information.

## Delegating GP Management Rights

It is important to delegate the proper rights for administrators to manipulate Group Policy. For example, a very small group of users should be able to edit policies on the domain level, but it might be necessary to allow diverse groups of administrators to configure Group Policies lower down the AD tree-in areas in which they administer.

An administrator can delegate the following rights to other administrators:

- Create GPO
- Create WMI filters
- Permissions on WMI filters
- Permissions to read and edit an individual GPO
- Permissions on individual locations to which the GPO is linked (Called the *Scope of management* or *SOM*.)

Using the Group Policy Delegation Wizard makes it easy to give the right groups of administrators the rights they need to do their job, and continue to administer Windows Server 2003 in the most secure ways possible.

## Avoiding Cross-Domain Policy Assignments

Avoiding cross-domain policy assignments is a recommended best practice. The more local the policies are, the more quickly the computers boot up and the users can log on, as the users or machines don't have to go across domain lines to receive group policies from other domains. This is especially pertinent for remote users.

## Using Group Policy Naming Conventions

The impact of using Group Policy naming conventions cannot be understated. Naming conventions allow for easier troubleshooting and identification of policies and simplify managing Group Policies, especially in a large environment.

**BEST PRACTICE**

**Using the Proper Naming Conventions**

- Use common naming conventions for similar policies ("Site_Name Software Policy," or "OU_Name Default Policy") rather than a different naming convention for similar policies. For example, begin Group Policy names with the name of the OU or site to which it applies.
- Use descriptive naming for Group Policy objects. Don't use the default "New Group Policy" for any policy. If it's a software push policy, label it so.
- Use unique names. It is not recommended to name two group policies the same name—especially in different domains or forests.

## Understanding the Default Domain Policy

The default domain policy is the domain level policy that is installed (but not configured) when Windows 2003 is installed. It should not be renamed, removed, deleted, or moved up or down in the list of Group Policies that exist on the top level of the domain. Certain security settings will only function properly when implemented in the Default Domain Policy (see the following warning). It's also a good idea to lock down the capability to edit the Default Domain Policy to a small number of administrators because security settings and other domainwide policies are set at that level.

By understanding and using these generic best practices, you can provide his users with a more secure, faster running, and uniform application of Group Policies.

> **Account Policy Settings**
>
> Account Policy settings applied at the OU Level affect the local SAM database, not Active Directory accounts. The Account Policy settings must be applied on the Default Domain Policy to affect Active Directory accounts.

# Understanding GP Inheritance and Application Order

Understanding the order in which Group Policy is applied is essential to administering Group Policy successfully. Without a clear understanding, Group Policy implementation and troubleshooting can be very difficult, even with the tools provided by Microsoft to help out with those very things.

## Group Policy Inheritance

To maximize the inheritance feature of Group Policy, keep the following in mind:

- Isolate the servers in their own OU. Create descriptive Server OUs and place all the non–domain-controller servers in those OUs under a common Server OU. If software pushes are applied through Group Policy on the domain level or on a level above the server's OU and do not have the Enforcement option checked, the server's OU can be configured with Block Policy Inheritance checked. As a result, the servers won't receive software pushes applied at levels above their OU.

- Use Block Policy Inheritance and Enforcement sparingly to make troubleshooting Group Policy less complex.

## Understanding the Order in Which Group Policies Are Applied

As stated previously, Group Policy objects are applied in a specific order. Computers and users whose accounts are lower in the Directory tree can inherit Policies applied at different levels within the Active Directory tree. Group Policy is applied in the following order throughout the AD tree:

- Local Security Policy is applied first.

- Site GPOs are applied next.

- Domain GPOs is applied next.

- OU GPOs is applied next.

- Nested OU GPOs and on down are applied next until the OU at which the computer or user is a member is reached.

If a setting in a Group Policy Object is set to Not Configured in a policy higher up, the existing setting remains. However, if there are conflicts in configuration, the last Group Policy Object to be applied prevails. For example, if a conflict exists in a Site GPO and in an OU GPO, the settings configured in the OU GPO will "win."

If multiple GPOs are applied to a specific AD Object such as a site or OU, they are applied in reverse of the order they are listed. The last GPO is applied first, and therefore if conflicts exist, settings in higher GPOs override those in lower ones. For example, if a Contacts OU has the following three Group Policies applied to it and they appear in this order (as shown in Figure 6.1) the policies will be applied from the bottom up:

- Contacts Default Group Policy

- Contacts Software Policy

- Contacts Temporary Policy

The Contacts Temporary Policy will be applied first. The Contacts Software Policy will apply next, and finally the Contacts Default Group Policy will be applied. Any settings in the Contacts Default Group Policy will override the settings configured in the two policies below, and the settings in the Contacts Software Policy will override any settings in the Contacts Temporary Policy.

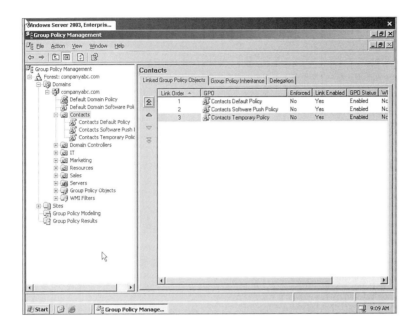

**FIGURE 6.1**
Group policy object order.

## Modifying Group Policy Inheritance

The Block Inheritance and Enforcement and Link Enabled features allow control over the default inheritance rules.

GPOs can be configured to use the Enforcement feature. This setting does not allow the parent organizational unit to be overridden by the settings of the child OU if conflicts exist. Additionally, it nullified the effects of Block Policy Inheritance if that functionality is applied on sub-GPOs.

GPOs can also be set to Block Policy Inheritance. This feature prevents the AD object that has the GPO applied to it from inheriting GPOs from its parent organizational unit, site, or domain (unless the parent GPO had Enforcement enabled as described previously).

Finally, the option exists that allows for the disabling of a Group Policy Object, also known as the GPO's Link Enabled status. By right-clicking on the Group Policy in the Group Policy Management Console and unchecking Link Enabled, you can disable the policy and render it unused until the time it is re-enabled. In Figure 6.2 the Contacts Temporary Policy Link Enabled state is disabled.

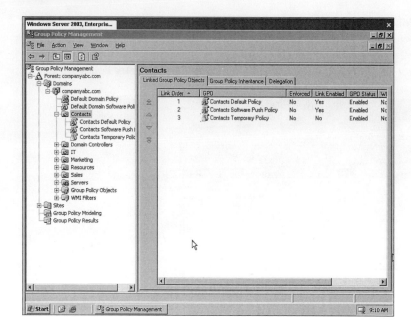

**FIGURE 6.2**
Disabling link enabled status.

## Configuring Group Policy Loopback

Loopback allows Group Policy to be applied to the user logging in based on the location of the computer object, not the location of the user object in AD. Loopback applies a Group Policy based on the computer the user is using, not the user whom is logging into the computer. An example of a good use of the loopback option concerns Terminal Services. If you need to apply specific permissions to everyone who logs into a particular Terminal Server, regardless of his or her user group policies, loopback in replace mode will accomplish this objective by ignoring all user GPOs. Loopback also provides a merge mode that merges the GPOs that apply to the user and computer but gives precedence to the computer GPO's, overriding any conflicting user GPOs.

# Understanding the Effects of Slow Links on Group Policy

A slow link is the speed it takes for a packet to get from one site to another. If the time the packet takes to reach the other site exceeds Microsoft's preconfigured slow link threshold, the link is determined to be slow.

## What Is the Effect of a Slow Link on a Site?

Microsoft Windows Server 2003 has a default determination of what constitutes a slow link between sites and automatically changes what Group Policies are provided to a user on the receiving end of a slow link. Security policies and administrative templates are always loaded, no matter what the link speed. However, group policies such as Login scripts, software pushes, and folder redirection are not pushed to the user who is accessing GP via a slow link. This can be problematic for sites that don't have local domain controllers and receive authentication across a slow WAN link.

If you have unreliable or saturated bandwidth you might want to change the configuration of what is considered a slow link in the site or disable slow link detection completely.

## Determining Slow Link Speed

By default, a slow link has an average ping time of greater than 32ms using 2048 byte packets, or a time greater than 500Kbps. Microsoft uses the following formula to convert ping times to Kbps. The formula is as follows:

```
16,000 / ping = Kbps
```

Therefore, the default value of a 32ms ping times equals the following when the formula is applied:

```
16,000 / 32ms = 500Kbps
```

To determine whether a site has a slow link, perform a ping from that location to the nearest DC it would use to authenticate and obtain its Group Policy. Use the following format for the ping command to make sure the test packet is a 2048KB packet:

```
ping –l 2048 servername (where servername is the closest domain controller)
```

The time it takes to return the ping will show if the link is more than 500Kpbs and is thus a slow link and subject to the slow link restrictions.

## Configuring a Unique Slow Link Speed

To override Microsoft's default definition of a slow link, change slow link behavior, or otherwise change slow link configuration, go to the following areas in Group Policy:

- Computer Configuration, Administrative Templates, System, Group Policy, Group Policy Slow Link Detection Properties. (Set to 0 to disable slow link detection or set a unique slow link time period.)

- User Configuration, Administrative Templates, System, Group Policy, Group Policy Slow Link Detection. (Set to 0 to disable slow link detection or set a unique slow link time period.)

Group Policy also allows for changing the behavior of processes such as scripts, folder redirection, software installation, and security when slow links are in effect. These can be changed by choosing Computer Configuration, Administrative Templates, System, Group Policy and editing the Policy Processing Group Policies.

# Using Tools to Make Things Go Faster

You can take specific steps to make Group Policy application faster for users as well as make it easier on system administrators to administer the Group Policies. This section covers some ways to make using Group Policies easier and faster.

## Linking Group Policies

If a Group Policy will be applied to many different locations, you should create the policy once and assign the permissions, and then link the policy to the other locations rather than creating the policy multiple times. Linking the policies achieves the following objectives:

- Creates fewer group policies in SYSVOL. This allows for quicker domain controller promotion and less replication traffic.

- A single point of change for the GPO. If the GPO is changed, the change is applied to all the locations where the GPO is linked.

- A single point of change for permissions. When permissions are configured or changed in one location on a linked GPO, the permissions are applied universally to each place where the GPO is linked.

## Configuring the Group Policy Snap-in

When a site administrator opens the GPMC or the Group Policy through ADUC the domain controller that is used to make Group Policy changes and will process the changes is, by default, only the one that holds the FSMO role of PDC Emulator Operations Master. Although this was configured to help eliminate replication problems, this can cause frustration and delays for remote administrators making changes to Group Policy under their control by having to wait for the changes to replicate from the remote PDC Emulator DC. To force the GPMC and Group Policy snap-in to use the most available domain controller, enable the following Group Policy:

User Configuration, Administrative Templates, System, Group Policy, Group Policy Domain Controller Selection.

Choose Use Any Available Domain Controller or Inherit From Active Directory Snap-ins to use the DC to which the open snap-in is connected. The default that points to the PDC Emulator is the choice to Use the Primary Domain Controller. Figure 6.3 shows the domain controller selection of Inherit from Active Directory Snap-ins.

## Disabling Configuration Settings

To speed up login and boot times for users, it is recommended that if the entire User Configuration or Computer Configuration section is not being used in a GPO, the unused section should be disabled for the GPO. This expedites the user logon time or the computer boot time, as the disabled sections aren't parsed upon boot or login.

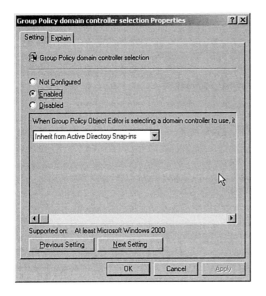

**FIGURE 6.3**    Configuring domain controller selection.

To disable configuration settings using Active Directory Users and Computers:

1. Click on a Group Policy.

2. Click Properties.

3. Go to the General Tab.

4. Click on one of the boxes, either Disable Computer Configuration Settings or Disable User Configuration Settings, whichever section is not being utilized.

To disable configuration settings using the GPMC:

1. Click on the Group Policy in GPMC.

2. Click on the Details tab.

3. Click on the drop-down box at the bottom of the Details tab.

4. Choose Computer Configuration Settings Disabled or User Configuration Settings Disabled, depending on which portion needs to be disabled.

## Viewing Group Policy Using the Show Configured Policies Only Setting

Searching through Administrative Templates for a particular Group Policy that is configured can be very time consuming. However, ADUC and the GPMC can be configured easily to show only the Administrative Templates objects that are configured. It removes from the view any policies or policy folders that don't have policies configured within them, making it much easier and faster to find a specific configured policy. Figure 6.4 shows what a GPO looks like when viewed using the Show Configured Policies Only.

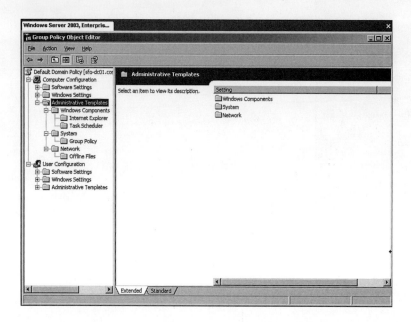

**FIGURE 6.4**
Standard group policy object screen.

To view only the configured policies while using ADUC or the GMPC:

1. Open ADUC or GPMC.

2. Edit a Group Policy to view.

3. Click on the Computer Configuration/Administrative Template or User Configuration/Administrative Template.

4. Right-click on the Administrative Templates section and choose View, Filtering.

5. Select the Only Show Configured Policy Settings option as shown in Figure 6.5.

## Deleting Orphaned Group Policies

When a Group Policy object is deleted, you have two choices: whether to just delete the link or delete the entire policy. Each option carries certain consequences.

If the Group Policy object should be removed from being applied at that location but it is or will still be applied elsewhere, choose to remove just the link. This leaves it in the available Group Policy list for future use. If the GPO will not be used elsewhere or ever again, delete the object permanently. This removes the policy from SYSVOL permanently and removes it from Active Directory.

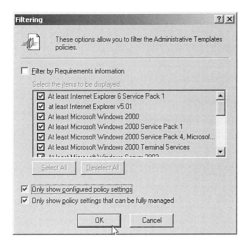

**FIGURE 6.5** Selecting the configured policy settings option in GPMC.

If the policy won't ever be used again and the policy isn't fully deleted, this results in the Group Policy being left unused in the SYSVOL area on each domain controller. This adds unnecessarily to the time it takes to create a new domain controller, and increases replication time and storage space on the domain controller.

If you are using ADUC to access Group Policy, Windows 2003 presents you with two choices when trying to delete a Group Policy: Remove the Link From the List or Remove the Link and Delete the Group Policy Object Permanently.

If you are using the GPMC, delete the link by right-clicking on the Group Policy object under the object to which it is applied. A pop-up box appears that asks, "Do you want to delete this link? This will not delete the GPO itself," thereby leaving the GPO available for linking elsewhere. To delete the link, click OK in the box.

To fully delete the GPO, click on the folder in GPMC entitled Group Policy Objects. Right-click the GPO and choose Delete. A pop-up box appears asking "Do you want to delete this GPO and all links to it in the domain? This will not delete links in other domains." To complete the deletion, click OK.

> **Be Sure to Check...**
> whether the GPO is linked elsewhere in the domain before deleting the object completely. This can be done through the GPMC and ADUC.

# Automating Software Installations

A major benefit of Group Policy is the ability to push software packages to computers and users via Group Policy. Although other applications (such as SMS) might provide a better method for distributing software (because they are probably more sophisticated and have better reporting capabilities,) Group Policy can be used to push software. An added bonus is that it comes free with the default installation of Windows Server 2003.

## Best Practices for Software Installs

As with many aspects of Group Policy, the choices and configuration methods of deployment are numerous. However, no matter which software package is being pushed, some basic best practices apply and can help make software deployment easier and less troublesome:

- Software packages must be in the format of an .msi package. Any format other than an .msi cannot be pushed using Group Policy. Third-party applications can help you create customized .msi packages to deploy any type of software as well as software with customized installation choices. Also, many software packages (such as Microsoft Office) come with default .msi packages with default configuration choices available.

- Configure software pushes at the highest levels possible. If the push is going out to more than a few OUs, the software should be pushed from the domain level. If the push is going out to only a few OUs or if there are multiple packages, the software should be pushed from the OU level.

- Configure software pushes to the Computer Configuration rather than the User Configuration. The option to install software can be configured on both the Computer and User policies. However, consider configuring software installation on computer policies if the users log on to more than one computer or use roaming profiles. If software is installed using the User Policies, the software will install on each separate workstation or server that the user logs into, causing the user to be annoyed at the long login times as well as cause problems with licensing.

  However, if multiple users use the same workstation and are assigned to receive the same software via user policies, Windows 2003 will not reinstall the package wholly when each new user logs in. The application's core files will only be installed once and the information about the application will be stored in the Application Data folder in the user profile or in the user's HKEY_USER Registry hive. This will eliminate long login times for users of the same workstation.

- Use DFS for multiple-site software installation MSI location. Using DFS ensures that software installations are installed at the closest source for installation. By inputting a DFS path as the source path, the software installation can be configured at the domain level and users in different sites will use the closest and most available source. The software push will not have to be configured with a different Group Policy Object with a different installation path for each site.

- Force after-hours automatic reboots if possible. Use a remote shutdown command (such as the DOS shutdown command or VBScript) to force computers that are to receive a software push to install software after the users have left for the day.

  Doing this achieves the following:

  *Increases user productivity.* The users won't have to wait for the software to load when they turn on their computer in the morning.

  *Decreases network bandwidth use.* By pushing the software after hours, the software pushes are using bandwidth when it is least used.

  *Alleviates user annoyance by minimizing startup/logon times.*

- Know the implications of using the Authenticated Users group to push software. Despite its name, Authenticated Users actually includes both users and computers. At the default domain level, every computer would receive the push if the group is not removed or the servers or computers are not segregated in an OU with Block Policy Inheritance enabled.

### Determining Whether a Push Was Successful

Without additional software it is not possible from a single centralized location to determine whether a software package was pushed successfully. All evidence of software pushes is seen locally on the client machines. On the local machines, there are three areas to check to determine whether a software installation was successful:

- MSI Installer events and Application Management events are written into the Application event logs.

- While the machine is booting and the software is installing, the Installing Managed Software dialog box will appear before the user is presented with the logon screen. Upon subsequent reboots the message does not appear.

- On the local machine, view Add/Remove Programs to see whether the software package is listed.

# Enhancing Manageability with Group Policy Management Console

The Group Policy Management Console (GPMC) is the new tool used for configuring and using Group Policy with Windows 2003. After it is installed, the choice to use AD Users and Computers to access and configure Group Policy is removed from the local computer.

The GPMC must be installed on Windows Server 2003 or Windows XP. The GPMC.msi package can be downloaded from the http://www.microsoft.com/downloads Web site. Search for "GPMC.msi" and download the tools. Once installed, it can be found by choosing Start, All Programs, Administrative Tools, Group Policy Management.

**Group Policy Tab**

If the Group Policy tab is accessed via ADUC, you are presented with a tab that says, "You have installed the Group Policy Snap-in so this tab is no longer used" and an Open button that opens the GPMC directly.

**GPMC**

The GPMC can be used to manage Windows 2000 Group Policy as well, but must be run on a Windows XP machine.

The GPMC provides many useful features; some of the most useful will be covered in the following section.

## GPO Operations: Backup, Restore, Copy, and Import

A crucial improvement in Group Policy is the ability to back up (or export) the data to a file. Then you can restore the Group Policy data into the same location. Note that the backup only backs up data specific to that GP itself. Other Active Directory Objects that can be linked to GPOs such as individual WMI filters (although the WMI links are backed up and restored) and IP Security policies are not backed up, due to complications with restores. Note also that performing a restore actually restores the original GUID of the GPO. This is useful when replacing a misconfigured GPO or especially one that was deleted.

The importing functionality allows for the importation of exported GPO data into a different location than the one from which it was exported, even to one with which no trust exists. Imports can be done in different domains, across forests, or within the same domain. This is most useful to move a GPO from a test lab into production without having to manually create what was done in the test lab, or, conversely, to update a test lab with the most current GPOs in production.

Copying GPOs is a very useful tool, as well. If you have configured a complex GP on a certain OU and want to duplicate the GPO(s) on other OUs, you need only copy the GPO and a new GPO is automatically created with the copy process. This new GPO can then be placed in the new location. You don't need to re-create the GPOs manually. This is quicker and also eliminates the possibilities of mistakes. Note however, that the data isn't saved to a file as it is in the backup or export of the GPO data. Trusts must be in effect for cross-domain or forest copies, or the Stored User Names and Passwords utility can be used if no trust exists. Note that copying a GPO requires creation of GPO rights in the target area as well as read access to the source GPO.

## Migrating Tables

During a cross-domain or cross-forest restore or copy operation, it might not be the best method to import all the exact configuration settings that exist in the backed up GPO to the new area. For this purpose, migration tables are useful. A migration table can be used to convert values from a *source* to values that apply in the new target location or *destination*. The source and destination mappings can be changed to accommodate any differences in configuration between the two.

> **Security Principles Must Already Exist**
> When using a migration table, the security principles being specified in the destination areas of the mapping table must already exist in order to import the backed up GPO.

## Supporting Group Policy Management Across Forests

The GPMC enables you to easily view and configure Group Policy in multiple forests and domains. The default view shows multiple forests, and you can configure which forests and domains to view and administer from the GPMC. It is not possible to link a GPO from a domain in a forest to another domain in another forest. However, it is possible to configure Group Policies to reference servers in another forest.

By default, a forest can only be managed if a two-way trust exists between it and the forest of the administrator. You can configure it to work with only a one-way trust or no trust at all by choosing View, Options, clicking the General tab, and un-checking Enable Trust Delegation.

If you are supporting Group Policy in a forest with which you don't have a trust, you will need to use the Stored User Names and Password tool to access the other forest. Find the Stored User Names and Password tool by choosing Start, Control Panel, User Accounts, Advanced, Manage Passwords in Windows XP or Start, Control Panel, Stored User Names & Passwords in Windows Server 2003. When the Stored User Names and Password tool appears, you will see a screen similar Figure 6.6.

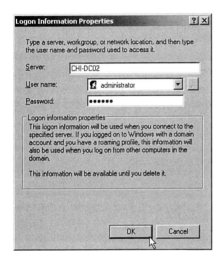

**FIGURE 6.6**  Stored user names and password tools screen.

## HTML Reporting Functionality and the Settings Tab

The Settings tab is a very useful area in the GPMC. You can use it to view the HTML reports on the GPO. These HTML reports state what is configured in the individual GPO. It provides an area to see all the settings, allows for looking easily at the descriptions (the "explain" sections) of the selected objects, and lets you condense and expand the details of the report by clicking on Show All. Additionally, the reports can be saved or printed.

## Linking WMI Filters

Linking WMI Filters enables you to apply group policies and establish their scopes based on attributes of target computers. You can do this by using the WMI filters to query the WMI settings of the target computers for true/false and apply group policies based on the true/false WMI queries. A "false" on the target computer results in the GPO not being applied. Conversely, a "positive" results in the application of the GPO.

Because WMI filters are separate from GPOs, they must be linked to GPOs in the GPO Scope tab to function properly. Only one WMI filter can be applied to each GPO. Additionally, WMI filters will only work on Windows XP and later workstations, not Windows 2000 or before, or non–Microsoft operating systems.

### Searching the GPMC for Group Policies

The GPMC enables you to search for specific group policies or data within the GPOs. Data such as permissions, GPO name, linked WMI filters, user configuration contents (what is configured), computer configuration contents, and GPO GUID can be searched for using the granular searching functionality in the GPMC.

# Using Resultant Set of Policies in GPMC

Resultant Set of Policies (RSoP) is part of the GPMC that provides a GUI interface that enables you to test a policy implementation prior to rolling it out in production and also enables you to view what policies a user or computer is actually receiving.

### Group Policy Modeling Using Resultant Set of Policy

RSoP Planning mode enables you to simulate the deployment of a specified Group Policy, check the results, change, and then test the deployment again. This is very helpful in a lab environment where you can create and test a new set of policies. After RSoP shows that the GPO is correct, you can then use the backup functionality to back up the GPO configuration and import it into production.

To run RSoP in simulation mode, right-click on Group Policy Modeling in the forest that will be simulated, and choose Group Policy Modeling Wizard. The wizard allows for inputting the possibility of slow links, Loopback configuration, and WMI filters as well as other configuration choices. Each modeling is presented in its own report as a sub-node under the Group Policy Modeling Node.

### Using RSoP Logging Mode to Discover Applied Policies

RSoP in logging mode enables you to view what exact policies a user or computer might be receiving. It shows in a readable format what polices are enforced, where conflicts exist, and what different policies are being applied to the user/computer. It can be run either on the local computer or on a remote computer by choosing the proper options in the wizard. To run RSoP in logging mode, right-click on Group Policy Results in the GPMC, and then click on the Group Policy Modeling Wizard selection and follow the wizard that appears.

# Maximizing Security with Group Policy

Group Policy is an excellent method to increase security in an organization. It can be used for everything from setting domain level security policies that apply to every user and computer (such as password length, complexity, and lock-out values) to applying security measures to specific groups of specialized users with specific needs.

For example, you might be managing a group of users who need to be highly managed. They need to have a very secure environment implemented on their workstations and logins, an environment that they cannot get around—environments where they cannot edit the Registry, add software, change permissions, stop or start services, or view the event logs. Applying a specific, highly secure Group Policy object to that group would accomplish this.

Additionally, the same policy could be applied easily using a template across various OUs and groups of users. If you are managing a group whose members need a great many rights and the capability to manipulate their workstations—such as the ability to install software, change settings, edit the Registry, and change drivers—applying more permissive Group Policies to that group could accomplish that as well.

## Predefined Security Templates

Microsoft provides predefined security templates for Group Policy, based on the type of users and environment needed (secure workstations and servers or highly secure workstations and servers). These templates can be imported into Group Policy objects where they can then either be implemented as-is, or changed, as the environment requires. However they are used, they are a great security starting point with which to obtain a base level of security. The templates can be used to configure settings such as account policies, event log settings, local policies, system service settings, Registry permissions, and file and folder permissions.

The following list describes the security templates that can be added after installation:

- Secure. There are two secure templates, one for workstations and one for domain controllers. The workstation is called Securews.inf and the domain controller is called Securedc.inf.

- Highly Secure. The highly secure template (hisecws.inf and hisecdc.inf) goes beyond the secure template and applies even more restrictive and secure policy configurations. It is also available for both domain controllers and workstations.

- System Root Security. This template (Rootsec.inf) provides a default set of secure root permissions for a root C drive. It is useful if the permissions have been changed and need to be returned to a secure default setting. With regard to child objects, it only propagates the security changes to child objects that inherit permissions; it does not overwrite explicit permissions on child objects.

- Compatible. This template (Compatws.inf) should only be applied to workstations. It changes the security settings for members of the users group by configuring a basic set of Registry and file permissions that allows most Microsoft software to function properly but securely. It also removes any members of the Power Users group.

## Required Default Domain Group Policy Settings

As stated earlier, Account Policy settings applied at the OU Level affect the local SAM database, not Active Directory accounts. The Account Policy settings must be applied on the Default

Domain Policy to affect Active Directory accounts. The Account Policy settings that must be configured in the Default Domain Policy to affect the accounts in AD are located in the following areas in the Group Policy:

- Password Policy

- Account Lockout Policy

- Kerberos Policy

## Restricted Groups: Assigning Local Groups Through GP

Restricted Groups can be used to set the membership of local groups such as Administrators and Power Users on servers and workstations. However, this cannot be applied to domain controllers because they don't have local groups. Restricted Groups can be useful in extremely secure environments where the addition of users to local groups on workstations or servers would be problematic or if group membership were accidentally changed. Assigning local groups would automatically remove the incorrect group membership and replace it with the membership specified in Group Policy.

For example, you can create an OU that is used only to replace local workstation administrative group membership that was changed. You would create a local group, and if the workstation were discovered to have incorrect group membership, the workstation would be moved to the OU. The next time the workstation was rebooted, the incorrect group membership would be removed and the proper group added. The computer could then be moved back to the proper location.

To create a Restricted Group:

1. Edit Group Policy.

2. Choose Computer Configuration, Windows Settings, Security Settings, Restricted Groups.

3. Right-click on Restricted Groups and select Add Group.

4. Click Browse.

5. Type the name of the group and click OK.

6. Click OK again on the Add Group dialog box.

7. On the top section labeled Members of This Group click the Add button.

8. Click Browse.

9. Type in or browse for the desired users or groups that should be members of the new local Restricted Group. After adding members to the group, the dialog box will look similar to Figure 6.7.

10. Click OK to finish and close the dialog box.

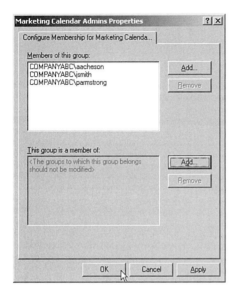

FIGURE 6.7  Members added to a restricted group.

# Increasing Fault Tolerance with Intellimirror

Intellimirror is a primary method for providing redundancy of user data reducing the probability of data loss in the event of a hardware failure. You can use it by enabling folder redirection, which redirects some critical folders off the local hard drive and to a networked (and backed up) file share. You can also enable roaming profiles, which allow customized user settings such as desktop settings and files to follow the user around no matter where the user logs in. Both are configured via Group Policy.

## Using Folder Redirection

Folder redirection configures the user's folders—such as My Documents, the desktop, application data, and the Start menu—to be redirected to another location, such as a server. This allows for critical data that is frequently located in these areas to be located on both the local desktop and the server. Because the redirected folders are automatically made available offline, if the file server is offline, the user can still access the data. Also, if the data is on a server, it can be easily backed up.

This is very useful for mobile users who need their data backed up and available while offline. However, if the user has a great deal of data, the synchronization can slow down log out/log on speeds, depending on when the synchronization is set to occur.

It is a best practice to configure the folder redirection using UNC paths as shown in Figure 6.8. You can also choose the option to redirect to the Home directory to configure the user's My Documents to automatically redirect to a personal drive already established on a server. This option is available only for Windows XP and Server 2003, although it can be configured using a more manual fashion on Windows 2000 machines.

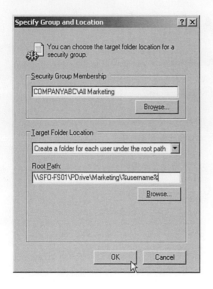

**FIGURE 6.8**  Setting up folder redirection in group policy.

## Using Roaming Profiles

Roaming profiles enable users to access their data, including redirected folders, wherever they log in. Items such as data on their desktop, application configuration, printers, and display options follow the users wherever they log on. The roaming profiles are stored on the local workstation(s) where the user logs in and also in a central repository on a server that can be accessed from any location from which the user might log in. This increases user productivity by giving users the tools and data they need, no matter where they are logging in. However, it does leave a copy of the user data, including offline files if configured, in every location where the user has logged on.

### Local Administrators Can Gain Access

Although the leftover roaming profiles left on the workstations and offline files are protected by ACLs, local administrators can gain access to the files on the local workstation. This should be a consideration when deciding whether to use the roaming profiles and offline files/folder redirection.

# Leveraging Other Useful Tools for Managing Group Policies

Microsoft provides additional tools for managing group policies and the File Replication Service, above and beyond ADUC and GPMC. Some are loaded automatically with Windows 2003 Server and others can be found on the Microsoft Web site or with the Windows 2003 Resource kit.

## Using the GPupdate Tool

The GPUpdate utility comes with Windows 2003 and replaces Windows 2000 Server secedit/ refreshpolicy command line utility. When run, it refreshes the Computer Policy or User Policy, both locally and AD-based, including security settings. This eliminates the need to have the user reboot or log out/in to receive the new policy changes immediately. The syntax is as follows:

```
Gpupdate [/target:{computer ¦ user}] [/force] [/wait:Value] [/logoff] [/boot]
```

For more information on the syntax commands, type the following at the command prompt to access help.

```
Gpudate /?
```

## Using the GPresult Tool

GPresult is a free utility from Microsoft that comes with the Server Resource Kit. It's a small program that has to be installed before use. It must be run via a command line on the machine that is being investigated. The GPresult.exe tool will discover where the computer and the logged in user are receiving their Group Policy and what policies are applied to them. Although a great deal of the information output by the gpresult.exe tool is available in other areas and using other tools, it is convenient to have it all displayed in one place.

## Using the GPmonitor.exe Tool

GPmonitor.exe is the Group Policy Monitor tool. It is used to gather information collected during GP refresh intervals and send the data to a specified central location. There, the tool can be used to analyze the data, as well. The gpmonitor.exe is available in the Windows Server 2003 Deployment Kit.

## Using the GPOTool Tool

The GPOTool should be used for troubleshooting Group Policy issues in domains with more than one domain controller or across domains. The tool scours all the domain controllers in a domain or across domains and checks for consistency between the group policies located in the SYSVOL share on each domain controller and reports on what it finds. It also checks the validity of the group policies on all domain controllers, checks on object replication, and displays detailed information about the GPOs. The GPOTool.exe is available with the Microsoft Windows 2000 Server Resource Kit and is also available for downloading on Microsoft's Web site.

## Using the FRSDiag.exe Tool

FRS replication is the replication service that is used to replicate Group Policy Objects between domain controllers. It can be very difficult to troubleshoot, due in no small part to the troubleshooting tools that were available for use up to this time. However, Microsoft now has an excellent new tool called FRSDiag that provides a GUI interface through which an you run tests easily to analyze FRS replication. You can choose to look at single or multiple domain controllers at a time, check their event logs for errors, run NTFRSUTL options, run REPADMIN /showreps and REPADMIN /showconn, and run many other of the previously available FRS tools. However, the results are much clearer and easier to understand when output to the GUI interface. When the tool is configured to output the results to a screen, it lists any DCs with failures in red and any successes in green. The output can also be put into cab files. FRSDiag.exe can be downloaded from http://www.microsoft.com/downloads.

A highly useful test available within FRSDiag is the Canary File Tracer. The Canary File Tracer can be configured to check the SYSVOL\domain name\policies directory (or any directory specified in the Share Root text area) for the correct number of folders or files. For example, if domain controllers cannot replicate Group Policies successfully and have a different number of policy folders present in their SYSVOL\domain_name\policies folder, this tool will, in minutes, check the number of folders on each domain controller across the domain to see if they match across the domain controllers and output this data to the screen. It even tells how many policies above or below the target number the domain controller is off by. To do this, follow these steps:

1. On the main screen, in the Target Server area, choose all the domain controllers in the domain.

2. In File Output, choose None.

3. Choose Tools, Canary File Tracer.

4. In the share root area, type the following: **domain_name\policies\\*.\***

5. In the Expected Number of Hits box, type the number of folders in the policies container (for example, 135).

6. Click the Go button.

> **.Net Framework v. 1.1 must be installed**
> This tool also works for Windows 2000 servers; however, the .NET Framework v. 1.1 must be installed for it to function.

The Canary File Tracer will then output the data to the screen, showing the results of the tests. Obviously, the Canary File Tracer can be used to troubleshoot other issues and search for other files and folders as well. It's not just limited to the search capabilities listed previously.

Figure 6.9 shows the configuration options for the Canary File Tracer.

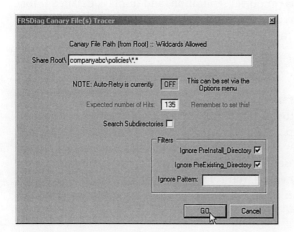

**FIGURE 6.9**
The Canary File Tracer configuration.

## Using the Sonar.exe Tool

Sonar.exe can be downloaded from `http://www.microsoft.com/downloads`. It provides a GUI interface that enables you to check the FRS replication health of all domain controllers in the domain, which can help with troubleshooting Group Policy replication problems. Sonar can be configured to poll the domain controllers at different intervals for FRS health and will output the results such as backlogged files waiting to be replicated, down FRS services, and other error states to the GUI screen. Sonar is also a useful tool for monitoring DFS health because it uses FRS as well.

# Using Administrative Templates

Administrative templates are installed by default in Group Policies. They are changes to the Registry of Windows 2000 and XP machines. In the Registry, the changes are stored in the \HKEY_LOCAL_MACHINE (HKLM) hive for computer policies and HKEY_CURRENT_USER (HKCU) hive for user policies and then in the following hives under HKLM or HKCU:

\SOFTWARE\POLICIES

\SOFTWARE\MICROSOFT\WINDOWS\CURRENTVERSION\POLICIES

By default, standard users do not have the rights to change Registry entries in these keys and change the Group Policy behavior because the keys are protected by ACLs.

You don't have to be limited by the default installed Administrative Templates. Microsoft provides additional templates to enhance the choices available for use with Group Policy, and custom Administration Templates can be written and imported to add custom keys and Group Policy options.

## Understanding Polices Versus Preference

Both preferences and Policies are controlled through the Registry. Preferences are changes to the Registry that the user has control over and are not found in the Registry keys listed previously. These are options, such as wallpaper or screensavers. Policies are changes to the Registry in the keys listed previously which are protected by ACLs. Although Group Policy can overrule preferences, the basic user would normally have access to change the Registry settings through the operating system or an application. The Policy does not overwrite the preference keys, and if the policy is removed, the preferences will return. The preference settings remain in effect until they are removed or changed via the Registry.

It is a good idea to use policies rather than preferences when you want to control a certain aspect of an application or want something the user accesses to remain static. You can disable users from being able to change the appearance, configuration, or functionality of the item. For those items, using Administrative Templates is your best answer.

## Using Microsoft Add-on GP Templates

Microsoft provides additional Administrative Templates for use with Microsoft Office—usually as part of the Office Resource Kits. Installing these administrative templates provides you with many more Group Policy options for each Microsoft Office product.

## Customizing Administrative Group Policy Templates

Beyond using the custom and default templates, it is possible for you to create your own customized Administrative template to enforce a Registry change. The changes appear in the Group Policy GUI format and can be configured through the GPMC or ADUC the way normal Group Policy would be configured. Customized templates can be very useful in a highly customized environment or one where the default choices are not sufficient.

To best determine how to write a custom template, you must first consider what you are trying to control or change. You must also discover whether the Registry change is in the User or Computer hive area and then also note the actual Registry path and Registry value. After you have determined these items, coding a new basic administrative template is not too complex.

Administrative templates vary from the very basic to the extremely complex (look at the common.adm that is installed with Windows 2003). However, they can be extremely useful tools with which to customize any environment using Group Policy. Read Microsoft's white paper entitled "Implementing Registry-Based Group Policy for Applications" for detailed instructions on how to build a custom Administrative Template.

# Finding Additional Resources About Group Policy

There are many additional sources for information about Group Policy, not just in technical manuals.

## Microsoft Group Policy Web Site

Microsoft provides a Web page with links to sources of information about Group Policy on the Group Policy TechNet Page at

http://www.microsoft.com/technet/treeview/default.asp?url=/technet/prodtechnol/
windowsserver2003/management/gp/default.asp

Any updated information about Group Policy will be there, including white papers, best practices, and other technical reference documents.

## Group Policy White Papers

The white papers that Microsoft provides about Group Policy are numerous and very helpful. There are white papers about all sorts of topics such as the following:

■ Designing scenario-based Group Policy implementations. In these white papers entitled "Designing Custom Desktop Management Scenarios," best practices for designing Group Policy implementations for specific groups of users are discussed. The user groups are as follows: kiosk users, lightly managed desktops, mobile users, application stations, task stations. The white paper gives actual recommendations of what GPs to implement depending on the group of users, as well as discusses Intellimirroring scenarios in detail for each group of users.

■ More detailed documents about the GPMC, including step-by-step documents on how to use the GPMC. Look for the white paper titled "Group Policy Administration with the Group Policy Management Console."

■ "Troubleshooting Group Policy" an excellent white paper to help with troubleshooting Group Policy issues.

## Summary

Windows Server 2003 builds on the functionality of Group Policy management technologies developed in Windows 2000. Window Server 2003 introduces powerful new change and configuration management features that provide greater flexibility and precision for managing users and computers in increasingly complex enterprise environments.

# 7

# Managing Desktops

**M**anaging desktops can be simplified using some of the tools and services available in Windows Server 2003 and XP Workstation Professional. However, desktop administrators still need to understand the different aspects of desktop administration, including maintenance tasks and administrative functions. Windows Server 2003 provides administrators the capability to select the appropriate method of administration to reduce or automate repetitive tasks and to provide task scalability to reduce the overall number of workstation visits or issues.

This chapter covers administrative tools and concepts that can be used to ensure data redundancy and facilitate the data restore process. Different scenarios to deploy images of and manage Microsoft Windows XP Professional desktops are discussed. Securing the desktop and deploying security patches are discussed as well. Also, remote administration and remote application installation are detailed in this chapter.

# Automating Backup of Desktop Data

Knowledge workers' workdays revolve around data, their data. If something happens to prevent them from accessing their data or their data is lost and not quickly available, it quickly can become what the system administrator's day revolves around. Two tools to help effectively manage user data and provide some level of redundancy are Shadow Copy of Shared Folders and Intellimirror's folder redirection component of Group Policy. These tools are designed to keep data off of the desktop and on network shares that can easily be backed up and allow users the capability to perform their own data restores when needed.

## Shadow Copy of Shared Folders

The VSS application Volume Shadow Copy Restore provides users with the capability to recover previous versions of data mistakenly deleted, updated, or corrupted. Shadow copies provide instant, point-in-time copies of a specified volume at a scheduled time. Data is then backed up from the shadow volume as opposed to from the original volume; this allows the original volume to continue to accept changes, allowing users to continue working and accessing data while the backup is in process.

> **The Shadow Copy Feature**
>
> The Shadow Copy feature can be enabled only on NTFS volumes; it cannot be enabled on FAT formatted volumes.

One of the nicest features of Shadow Copy Restore is the capability of the end user to restore his own data lost through accidental deletion, unwanted saved changes, or corruption. The bonus here is that once Shadow Copy Restore is configured and users are trained to restore their own data, you can enjoy fewer technical support calls.

To give the end user this capability, install the shadow copies of Shared Folders client pack on the desktop. Upon installation of the Shadow Copies of Shared Folders client software a Previous Versions tab, shown in Figure 7.1, is added to the Properties dialog box of files and folders on network shares. Users access shadow copies via Windows Explorer by selecting one of three options from the Previous Versions tab: View, Copy, or Restore.

> **Not to be Considered an Alternative**
>
> Shadow copies are not to be considered an alternative to regularly scheduled backups. Shadow copies are intended only to aid in the restoration of file-related accidents caused by human error such as accidental deletion, editing, or corruption of data.

Viewing the properties of files and folders, using the Previous Versions tab, users are presented with a read-only, point in time, history of the folder or file. Users can view content of past versions of a file or folder and then copy or restore the chosen version.

### Setting Up Shadow Copies Client

A default feature to Windows Server 2003, Windows XP requires that Twcli32.msi be run from the Windows Server 2003 server. The application plug-in can be found at %windir%\System32\ clients\Twclient\x86\Twcli32.msi. You can install Twcli32.msi manually from a Windows Server 2003 server to a small group of desktops, or use the software distribution component of Group Policy for larger deployments.

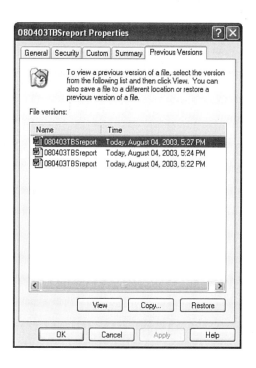

**FIGURE 7.1**    Accessing shadow copy files.

## Recovery of Files and Folders

Three general scenarios in which the end user might find the need to use the Previous Versions tab includes accidental file deletion (most common), accidental file replacement, or file corruption. The Volume Shadow Copy feature enables the user to easily recover from any of these scenarios without having to call the administrator for support.

## Recovering Deleted Files

To take advantage of the Volume Shadow Copy feature, perform the following steps to recover a deleted file:

1. In Windows Explorer navigate to the folder in which the deleted file had been stored.

2. Right-click in the blank space of the folder displayed in the right-hand pane of Explorer; select Properties and then select the Previous Versions tab.

### The Client Must Be Running...

Windows XP, Windows 2000 Service Pack 3 (SP3) or later, or Windows 98 in order to support the Shadow Copy client. The client software does not support Windows Me or Windows NT 4.0. The Previous Versions client, which provides the same functionality as the Shadow Copy client, can only be installed on Windows XP Professional.

### Volume Shadow Copy Service Stores Up to 64 Versions of a Share

The Volume Shadow Copy service stores up to 64 versions of a share, depending on disk space. When the service creates the 65th shadow copy (or if you've used all the disk space allotted for shadow copies), the service deletes the oldest shadow copy to make space for the newest shadow copy.

3. Select the version of the folder that contains a copy of the file before it was deleted, and then click View.

4. Select the file that will be recovered.

5. Drag and drop, or cut and paste, the shadow copy to the desktop or folder on the end user's local machine.

### Recovering Overwritten or Corrupted Files

Recovering an overwritten or corrupted file is easier than recovering a deleted file. To recover an overwritten or corrupted file perform the following steps:

1. In Windows Explorer navigate to the folder in which the deleted file had been stored.

2. Right-click on the overwritten or corrupted file; select Properties and then select the Previous Versions tab.

3. To view the old version, click View. To copy the old version to another location, click Copy. To replace the current version with the older version, click Restore.

### Recovering Folders

To recover a folder, perform the following steps:

1. In Windows Explorer, navigate to the folder that will be recovered.

2. Right-click in blank space of the folder displayed in the right-hand pane of Explorer; select Properties and then select the Previous Versions tab.

3. Choose either Copy or Restore.

4. Choosing Restore enables the user to recover everything in that folder as well as all subfolders. Selecting Restore will not delete any files.

## Folder Redirection

Folder redirection is a feature of Intellimirror that can be used to redirect certain folders on the network client's desktop to network locations. There are five special folders located under Documents and Settings: Application Data, Desktop, My Documents, My Pictures, and Start Menu.

The benefits of folder redirection that exist to both user and administrator include the following:

- User data is always available even when users access data from multiple computers on the network.

- Data stored on the network share can be scheduled for routine backups that require no action from the user.

- Data is safe in the event of local machine system or hard drive failure.

- Disk quotas can be set through Group Policy limiting the space used by user data.

- Having all users redirect their personal data to the network allows for easier administration of the backup and recovery of user data.

By default in Windows XP redirected folders are automatically made available offline. The benefit here is, as the name states, files stored on the network are available when the computer is offline. This is most beneficial to mobile computer users who need to access their data while on the road. It also benefits the desktop users in the event that the network or server that hosts the data is no longer available.

To override the default behavior of redirected folders automatically being made available offline, which is not recommended because it can prevent users from accessing their data, you can enable the policy Do Not Automatically Make Redirected Folders Available Offline. This setting is found in the Group Policy Editor under User Configuration, Administrative Templates, Network, Offline Files.

**Decreasing the Logon and Logoff Times of Users**

Folder redirection when used in conjunction with roaming user profiles has the added benefits of decreasing the logon and logoff times of users and a realized performance gain over low-speed network connections because only the data that user accesses is transferred.

The following are some basic rules of thumb to guide the system administrator when using folder redirection:

- *Allow the system to create the folders for each user.* Set the correct permissions on the root folder and the system will create the folder for you with the correct permissions. If you create the folders yourself, the folders will not have the correct permissions.

- *Use fully qualified (UNC) paths incorporating %username%.* For example, use \\server\ share\%username%. Although paths like C:\foldername can be used, the path might not exist on all your target networking clients, and redirection would fail.

- *Enable client-side caching.* This is important for users with portable computers.

- *Have My Pictures follow My Documents.* This is the default behavior; leave as is unless there is a good reason to change.

When organizing user data on the file server(s) by group, time can be saved by redirecting data via Group Policy. For example, within Group Policy, User Configuration, Windows Settings, Folder Redirection, My Documents on the Target tab, shown in Figure 7.2, you can set the users' My Documents folder to redirect to a specified directory by group membership. Again, use the UNC path incorporating the %username% to let the system create the folder.

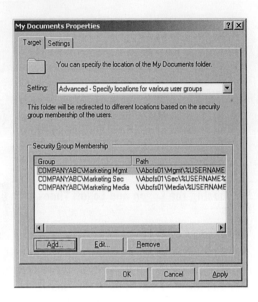

**FIGURE 7.2** Redirecting My Documents via Group Policy.

# Accelerating Deployments with Workstation Images

When considering deployment options for medium-to-large desktop deployments, you will find automated installations to be faster, easier, less expensive, and more consistent than manual installations. Windows Server 2003 and Windows XP provide several automated installation methods for automated operating system deployment. The following sections discuss unattended installations, Sysprep Installations, and RIS installations.

## Unattended Installation

The unattended installation is an optimal deployment method when the goal is to perform a large number of installations while keeping user involvement to a minimum. Preparing for an unattended installation begins with creating the answer file that contains answers to the installation questions that are prompted by Windows Setup.

Creating an answer file can be done using a text editor or by using Setup Manager (Setupmgr.exe). Building an answer file with a text editor (Notepad) is faster and easier than Setup Manager, but is more prone to user error. Setup Manager will prompt for answers and build an answer file based on the responses.

## BEST PRACTICE

### Answer Files

A best practice for building an answer file is to start with Setup Manager, and then use Notepad to add custom settings. When customizing the answer file refer to the Answer File Settings Worksheet (ACIUI_5.doc) for the listing of valid sections, entries and values. The AFSW can be found on the Windows Server 2003 Deployment Kit companion CD.

After creating the answer file, a distribution share can be created on a server that the destination computers can access, which contains installations files, device drivers, and any other files required for the custom installation. A distribution share is not required for unattended installations using the operating system CD-ROM.

> **Unattended Installation Files**
> Unattended installation files are now located in the ref.chm file located in the deploy.cab file. In Windows 2000 the unattended installation information was found in unattended.doc.

To perform a clean unattended installation from the operating system CD-ROM, perform the following steps:

1. Confirm the computer is connected to the network.

2. The unattended answer file must be renamed to Winnt.sif and copied to floppy disk.

3. In BIOS, set CD-ROM as the first startup device.

4. Add a [DATA] section to Winnt.sif with the following entries:

   ```
   MSDosInitiated=0
   UnattendedInstall=Yes
   ```

5. Add an [Unattended] section to Winnt.sif with the following entries:

   ```
   OemPreinstall=No
   UnattendSwitch=Yes
   ```

To perform a clean unattended installation with MS-DOS startup disk perform the following steps:

1. Confirm the computer is connected to the network.

   MS-DOS contains device drivers to connect to network or load drivers for CD or DVD drive.

2. In BIOS, set floppy disk as the first startup device.

3. If you are installing from a distribution share, set permissions to allow proper access to the distribution share.

4. The answer file is saved on an MS-DOS startup disk or distribution share.

## Using the Systems Preparation Tool (Sysprep) for Server Images

The Systems Preparation Tool (Sysprep) is the optimal tool when performing image-based installations with the identical operating system and software configuration on multiple computers as quickly as possible. Sysprep allows for hardware and software differences among computers, minimizes end-user interaction, and reduces the number of images needed.

There are four modes of operation for Sysprep in Windows XP:

- Audit—Used for verification of hardware and software installation while running in Factory mode.

- Factory—Allows for customization of software installation, driver updates, Registry updates, and .INI files such as Sysprep.inf. Use the `sysprep -factory` command to start in this mode.

- Reseal—This is run after Sysprep has run in factory mode and is ready for delivery to the end user. Use the `sysprep -reseal` command to start in this mode.

- Clean—Cleans the critical device database, a Registry listing of devices and services that have to start for Windows XP to boot successfully. Use the `sysprep -clean` command to start in this mode.

When preparing the master installation always start with a clean installation of the operating system and any software applications needed. Be sure to create the master installation on drive C. Also, confirm that the HAL on the master computer is compatible with the HAL of the destination computers.

A typical scenario for creating a master image would be to first run `sysprep -factory` on a clean installation creating your base master image. By rebooting the system in Factory Mode you can then install any software, drivers, or configuration changes required. When all installation and configuration has been completed run `Sysprep -reseal` to remove machine-specific information such as the SID, computer name, and so on. The system is now ready to be imaged and deployed en masse to multiple workstations, which requires using a third-party tool.

Some of the advantages of the Sysprep utility include the following:

- Master image can be copied to CD-ROM, duplicated, and then distributed for installation, thus reducing load on network.

- Enables the implementation of a standard desktop image containing a standard desktop, policies, and restrictions throughout the organization.

- Does not perform plug and play enumeration thus reducing installation time.

## Deploying Server Images with Remote Installation Service

Windows Server 2003 includes a server and workstation imaging and deployment product called Remote Installation Service (RIS). RIS can be used to store multiple images on a RIS Server, which can then be downloaded over a network connection to the client computer. RIS is very handy, but before desktops are deployed using this product, some testing and planning should be performed.

Installing RIS is a fairly simple process but planning your RIS deployment begins with the installation of RIS itself. As a best practice install RIS and RIS images on separate physical disks than the operating system to improve imaging performance.

Planning how the RIS server will be used can help ensure a successful implementation. Considerations for RIS include deciding how many systems the RIS server should deliver installation images to simultaneously.

Upon initial configuration, consider what the appropriate number of RIS servers will be for the environment. A small, nonrouted, LAN environment, for example, would require only a single RIS server to service all requests up to any network bandwidth or server resource limitations that might exist. In a routed environment set the DHCP forwarding option to allow routers to forward client requests to the RIS servers. Do not use RIS over low-speed links. Offices located on the WAN over a slow link will require their own RIS server. Use the settings that are available when prestaging the client machine to direct the client to be serviced by the RIS server that is in closest proximity on the network to it.

Another consideration during the initial configuration is that restricting installation options increases the number of successful operating systems that can be completed without assistance from the administrator. The default is one installation option and one operating system option to the user.

RIS client computers must support remote boot either with a boot-up disk or using Pre-Boot eXecution Environment (PXE) on compatible systems. Follow best practices for Network Security on any network that includes PXE-enabled computers. Because RIS servers will try to deliver the image to clients as fast as the network can handle, limit RIS server access to LAN clients to avoid having the RIS server saturate WAN links while imaging client computers. Storage is always a big concern for imaging servers and third-party imaging software stores each image in a separate file, which can take up a lot of storage space. Although many times these image files compress fairly well, RIS stores images in their native file formats and replaces duplicate files with file pointers or links to save storage space.

Also, during this process the first installation image will be created. This image is based on a clean OS installation of the particular operating system version. For example, a Windows XP Professional CD could be used for the first image on a Windows Server 2003 RIS server.

Advantages of RIS include the following:

- Enables standardized Windows XP Professional Installations

- Customizes and controls the end-user installation using Group Policy to configure specific choices for the end-user setup wizard.

> **Use Remote Boot Floppy Generator**
> Use Remote Boot floppy Generator (Rbfg.exe) to create remote boot disks for client computers that are not PXE-based. Rbfg.exe can be found on the RIS server at \\*RISServerName*\RemoteInstall\Admin\i386\Rbfg.exe.

- No physical media required for client computers using PXE technology. Non–PXE-based clients will require a boot floppy.

- Image size is not limited by capacity of physical media.

# Creating Windows XP Images

If RIS or a third-party imaging software will be used to deploy Windows XP desktop images, some steps must be followed to ensure that an image is created as problem-free as possible. The goals of deploying a new desktop image or the goals of creating standard builds and deploying using desktop imaging software might be very different between organizations but the following sections will cover steps that should be used for image creation regardless of the project goals.

## Installing Desktop Software

Unless a RIS image will be created only using the Setup Manager Wizard and the installation media for a vanilla installation, Windows XP and any additional updates and applications must be installed on a workstation. First the operating system must be installed and patched to the latest service pack and post service pack release. This will help ensure operating system reliability and security by raising the installation to the latest build and locking down known vulnerabilities.

After the OS is updated Microsoft and third-party applications should be installed and updated to the latest patch level. If necessary, open the applications to verify that all the installation steps have been completed such as registering, customizing, or activating the software.

## Standardizing the Desktop

After the operating system and application software have been successfully installed and configured, the desktop settings can be customized to meet the particular deployment needs. Things that might be performed during this phase are the enabling or configuring of Windows XP programs such as Remote Desktop, Remote Assistance, or Automatic Update. If roaming user profiles are not used in the organization, the desktop settings such as desktop look and feel and including screen resolution and desktop shortcuts and start menu options should be configured. After the desktop has been configured as desired, the administrator account can copy the user profile used to create the settings to the C:\Documents and Settings\Default User folder, assuming that the XP installation is on the C drive.

## The Little Things

Many times after you prepare desktop images there are a bunch of annoying things that are discovered after the image has been deployed to the enterprise. Things like leftover mapped drives or local printers or application install points that only exist in the imaging lab remain in the Registry and cause confusion when an application needs to be updated or uninstalled. Something as small as leaving a window open upon logging off of the workstation before the user profile is updated to the default user profile can prove to be very annoying or look unprofessional after image deployment. To avoid the little things that might have the end users, clients, or management view your image deployment as a failure, deploy the images to a few pilot users who will be meticulous enough to alert you of these issues before the entire user base has to experience it themselves.

# Automating Software Installation

Deploying applications using the software installation services of group policy requires that the applications are packaged using a Windows Installer Package file (*.MSI). When deploying applications to users, the package can be assigned to a user or the pack can be published. When deploying applications to computers, the application can be assigned.

Assigned applications will be installed automatically when the policy is applied to the computer or user. For users, published applications will be listed in the Control Panel Add/Remove Programs applet. If a user has an application published to her, the user only needs to open the Add/Remove Programs applet and double-click on the application for it to be automatically installed. Depending on how you configure the application when defining the application deployment properties in group policy, the application can be deployed using elevated privileges and can be customized using Transform files, which are used to specify installation criteria normally answered during a manual installation. Below is a step-by-step scenario for creating a software push assigned to a group of user computers:

To create a software push via group policy, perform the following steps:

> **For This Scenario...**
> it is assumed that a separate Software Distribution GPO and a security group, with all of the computers receiving the push as members, have been created.

1. From Active Directory Users and Computers, right-click the OU.

2. Select Properties.

3. Click the Group Policy tab.

4. Highlight the Software Distribution GPO and click Edit to open. As a best practice, create a separate GPO to administer each software package to be pushed.

5. Expand Computer Configuration, Software Settings.

6. Right-click Software Installation and select New, Package.

7. Browse to \\*server*\\*share*\ and select the folder and MSI package. You can't browse over a local or mapped drive, you have to use the UNC path.

8. From the Deploy Software window, select Advanced.

9. From the General tab, name the package.

10. From the Security tab, select Advanced.

11. Uncheck Allow Inheritable Permissions and click Copy. Then click OK.

12. Click Add.

13. Add the Security Group created for this push as shown in Figure 7.3.

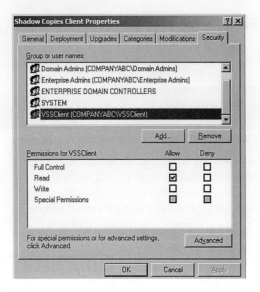

**FIGURE 7.3**   Adding a security group to a software installation package.

### Why Select Advanced?

This selection lets you modify a push before it is saved and applied. Because Authenticated Users is applied to a push by default, if the push was applied before you removed it, some computers might get the push that shouldn't.

### Why Remove the Authenticated Users Group?

Strangely enough, Authenticated Users actually includes both users and computers. As such, any computer that can read a push policy will get the push applied. Because Authenticated Users includes all computers in an OU, every computer would receive the push if the group were not removed.

### Why Create a Separate Software Distribution GPO?

The separate GPO allows for the capability to block the policy from certain OUs, like the Domain Controllers OU, to prevent software packages meant for your desktops from being applied inadvertently to your domain controllers.

14. Confirm the security group has Read permissions (default).

15. Highlight the Authenticated Users group.

16. Click Remove.

17. Click OK to exit the Properties box.

18. Close Active Directory Users and Computers.

When the computers with membership in the security group have been re-booted, the software package will be installed during logon.

## Slow Link Detection

Group Policy uses a built-in mechanism called *Slow Link Detection*, which causes some policies, software pushes being one of them, not to be applied if the link between the workstation and the domain controller does not meet certain minimum requirements.

By default, a slow link is defined as an average ping time of greater than 32ms using 2048 byte packets. To manually test whether a workstation is on a slow link, open a command prompt from that machine and type **ping –l 2048 *serverDC*** (where *serverDC* is your closest domain controller).

Rather than displaying ping times in Group Policy, Microsoft uses a formula to convert ping times to a Kbps rating. That formula is

```
16,000 / ping (ms) = Kbps
```

If the ping times are slower than 32ms you should lower the value of the Group Policy Slow Link Detection policy. Use the formula to figure out the required value.

For more details on slow link detection, see the section titled "Slow Link Detection" in Chapter 6, "Implementing Group Policies."

# Ensuring a Secured Managed Configuration

Most desktop management strategies have some form of security assessment and implementation involved. There are two typical areas of security; one is patch management, and the other is general desktop security policies. As an organization implements desktop management policies and practices, security planning and implementation should be reviewed and determined if they need to be applied at the time of policy rollout.

## Decreasing Vulnerabilities Through Security Patches

Before Software Update Service (SUS) 1.0 there was Windows Update service, which was ultimately managed by the end-user and required elevated rights to run. To avoid this scenario most administrators chose to disable Windows Update Service and create, then re-create, images that include the latest patches as they came out. As most of you know or could guess this takes a lot of time and energy.

With the introduction of SUS there is now a free patch management solution provided by Microsoft. Using the Automatic Update client installed with Windows XP Service Pack 1 or later (also installed with Windows 2000 SP3 or later), the automatic update client allows redirection to the SUS server. There are two ways that the redirection can be applied, either the hard way by specifically modifying the desktop Registry, or the easy way, through the use of an Active Directory group policy.

Some of the best practice recommendations in the use of the Software Update Server include the following:

- Configure Group Policy so that it points clients to SUS server

- Configure IIS on the SUS server to log client connections

> **Requires IE5.5 or Later**
> The SUS administration page requires IE5.5 or later, however because IE5.5 is not available through Windows Update, most organizations use IE6 or later. Local Admin rights to SUS server is required to view SUS admin page.

## Maximizing Security on the Desktop

Most organizations have groups or individual network clients who work with or require access to highly confidential data. Such users can be found working in the Human Resources or Payroll departments of the company. Executives in the company also fall under this category. Because these users are privileged to very sensitive information, it is important for you to secure the network accounts used to access this information as well as the means by which this data is accessed.

Because there is probably sensitive data stored on servers that are, in turn, accessed by privileged network clients, you should secure that data as it passes from server to client. Most data is not protected when it travels across the network, so employees, supporting staff members, or visitors might be able to plug into the network and copy data for later analysis. They can also mount network-level attacks against other computers. Windows Internet Protocol Security (IPSec) is a key component in securing data as it travels between two computers. IPSec is a powerful defense against internal, private network, and external attacks because it encrypts data packets as they travel on the wire.

You can create and modify IPSec policies using the IP Security Policy Management snap-in available in the Microsoft Management Console. IPSec policies can then be assigned to the Group Policy Object of a site, domain, or organizational unit. If sensitive data is located on a server, assign the predefined Secure Server policy to the server so that it always requires secure communication. Then assign the predefined Client (Respond Only) policy to the network clients that will communicate with the secure server. This policy ensures that when the network client is communicating with the secure server, the communication is always encrypted. The network client can communicate normally (unsecured) with other network servers.

To assign the Client (Respond Only) IPSec policy in the Group Policy Object, perform the following steps:

1. Navigate to IP Security Policies on Active Directory under Computer Configuration/Windows Settings/Security Settings.

2. In the Details pane, click Client (Respond Only).

3. Select Action, Assign.

Though it might be okay for high-security network clients to communicate normally (unsecured) with other servers within the organization that do not contain sensitive data, there might be a need to limit that client's ability to communicate outside the organization. There are many settings available within Group Policy to prevent a user from modifying or creating new network connections. For example, a Group Policy setting can be applied to prohibit connecting a remote access connection.

To enable Group Policy settings related to network connections in the Group Policy Editor, navigate to User Configuration/Administrative Templates/Network/Network Connections. Figure 7.4 displays the settings one can enable in this category.

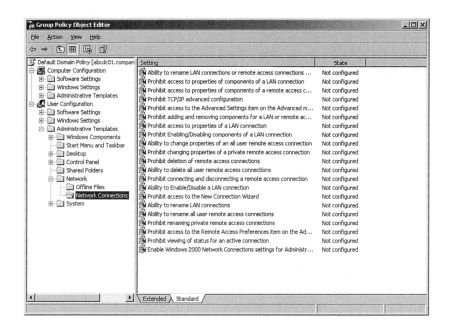

**FIGURE 7.4**
Group Policy
settings to restrict
network connec-
tions.

If the secure network clients save sensitive data to their local workstations, additional security can be provided to this data through the Encrypting File System (EFS). Because EFS is integrated with the file system, it is easy to manage and difficult to attack. Moreover, after a user has specified that a file be encrypted, the actual process of data encryption and decryption is completely transparent to the user.

To encrypt a file or folder, follow these steps:

1. In Windows Explorer, right-click the file or folder that you want to encrypt and then click Properties.

2. On the General tab, click Advanced.

3. Check the Encrypt Contents to Secure Data box.

To encrypt and decrypt files, a user must have a file encryption certificate. If the file encryption certificate is lost or damaged, access to the files is lost. Data recovery is possible through the use of a recovery agent. A user account of a trusted individual can be designated as a recovery agent so that a business can retrieve files in the event of a lost or damaged file encryption certificate or to recover data from an employee who has left the company.

One of the many advantages of using Windows Server 2003 domains is that you can configure a domain EFS recovery policy. In a default Windows Server 2003 installation, when the first domain controller (DC) is set up, the domain administrator is the specified recovery agent for the domain. The domain administrator can log on to the first DC in the domain and then change the recovery policy for the domain.

To create additional recovery agents, the user accounts must have a file recovery certificate. If available, a certificate can be requested from an enterprise Certificate Authority (CA) that can provide certificates for your domain. However, EFS does not require a CA to issue certificates, and EFS can generate its own certificates to users and to default recovery agent accounts.

To create an EFS recovery policy for a domain, follow these steps:

1. In Active Directory Users and Computers, right-click the domain whose policy you want to change and then click Properties.

2. Click the Group Policy tab.

3. Right-click the default domain policy and then click Edit.

4. Navigate to the Encrypting File System under Computer Configuration/Windows Settings/Security Settings/Public Key Policies.

5. Right-click Encrypting File System and then click Create Data Recovery Agent to create a certificate to use as the EFS recovery certificate.

# Managing Systems and Configurations

When an organization starts planning the management of its desktop systems, the initial thought is simply the management of office desktop and laptop systems. However, there are typically five different types of systems where user sessions and connections need to be managed. They include the following:

- Managing desktops remotely

- Managing multi-user desktops

- Managing mobile computers

- Managing public or kiosk workstations

- Managing administrator workstations

## Managing Desktops Remotely

For administrative tasks to be performed on workstations such as installing new hardware or configuring user profile settings that are not configured using group policy settings, you can use the tools provided with Windows Server 2003 and Windows XP. Remote Desktop can not only be used to install software remotely, but also it can be used to configure just about everything that could be performed from the local console. The only limitation is that the BIOS settings cannot be controlled so if a remote reboot is performed, and the BIOS is configured to first boot from a floppy disk, if a disk is in the drive the system might never restart and a visit to the workstation will be required.

Starting with Windows Server 2003 and Windows XP the Computer Management console can be used to perform several system-related software and hardware tasks remotely. New features include adding new hardware by scanning for hardware changes or adding local user accounts or local shares or manipulating system services. This tool is very flexible for remote administration.

## Managing Multiuser Desktops

The multiuser desktop is commonly used in public access situations where the desktop experiences high traffic and must be flexible for some customization, but should remain reliable and unbreakable. Keep the following items in mind when managing multiuser desktops:

- Some level of modification to the desktop must be allowed to the users while maintaining a high level of security. Users should not have access to hardware or connection settings.

- Enable users to modify Internet Explorer and the desktop, run needed applications, and configure some Control Panel options.

- Restrict users via group policy from using the command prompt or the run command, accessing network settings, accessing Add/Remove programs, or running executables from disk, CD, or the Internet.

- Set up roaming profiles so that the user's desktop settings follow him regardless of the workstation in use. Remove local copies of roaming profiles when the user logs off to preserve disk space. The user profile will synchronize with the network before it is removed so they will be available if the user logs on again. If a profile is not available, a new local profile will be created based on the default user profile. Computers can easily be replaced because all settings are on the network profile.

- To conserve disk space, applications should be server-based when possible. Configure shares that store applications for automatic caching so application files are cached at the workstation. You can also enforce disk quota limits through Group Policy. To do this in the Group Policy Editor, navigate to Computer Configuration/Administrative Templates/System/Disk Quotas.

- Use folder redirection to save My Documents and Application data on server shares. Use Group policy to prevent users from storing data locally.

## Managing Mobile Computers

Many companies have employees who either frequently travel or are located away from the typical office environment. These mobile users differ from desktop users in that they often log on to the network through a portable computer over a slow-link dial-up modem connection. A good management strategy for this type of user should take into account the lack of local access and connecting to the network over slow-link connection.

Because mobile users spend a majority, if not all, of their time away from the local office they will often find themselves in the unique position of having to provide their own computer support. As this is the case, mobile users often require more privileges than the standard office user. To do this, apply a separate Group Policy Object to your mobile clients that would enable users to perform software and local printer installs while at the same time restricting them from critical system files that might disable their system.

Whether or not the mobile user is connected to the network mobile users will expect to have access to their critical data. Intellimirror simplifies management of the mobile user in that it enables users to work on network files when they are not connected to the network and to have the offline version and the network version synchronize upon the next time the user connects to the network. Although Offline Files is a default feature of Windows XP, you still need to select the network files and folders that will be made available offline.

**Set Offline Files to Synchronize**

Set Offline Files to synchronize when users log on and to periodically synchronize in the background.

Another key management concern regarding the mobile user is software installation. It is not recommended to assign or publish software to mobile users who are rarely in the office. If they periodically work in the office, one can set the Group Policy slow-link detection to the default in the user interface so that software will install when the user is connected directly to the local area network (LAN).

One can verify or adjust the connection speed for Group Policy settings in the Group Policy slow-link detection setting. To do this in the Group Policy Object Editor, navigate to Computer Configuration/Administrative Templates/System/Group Policy or User Configuration/Administrative Templates/System/Group Policy.

Mobile users should not, for the most part, be running served applications. Typically, the mobile users' portable computers should have all the core software installed before they have to work outside the office. If users require additional software after they are in the field and cannot return to the office to have it installed, it might make sense to copy your software packages to CD to be installed locally by the mobile users with elevated privileges.

## Managing Public or Kiosk Workstations

The public or kiosk workstation exists in the public environment and generally is used to provide access to one or a limited set of applications. You should implement a highly managed configuration that restricts the user from performing any data management, software installs, or system configuration.

Another aspect of the kiosk workstation is that users should not be logging on with username and password; it is better to create a user account that automatically logs on when the computer starts. All users will use this one account to allow access to the applications provided for their use. The application that is being accessed should also be loaded automatically when the computer starts up.

The user should not be able to access Windows Explorer or the command prompt because these can be used to access the system directly. The application itself should be examined to confirm that it does not allow users a backdoor to any part of the system.

Characteristics of the policies associated with locking down the Kiosk workstation include the following:

- Desktops have a limited set of applications that the user can run. You can limit, through Group Policy, which applications the user can execute. To do this in the Group Policy Editor, navigate to User Configuration/Administrative Templates and expand the Start menu and taskbar.

- Desktops have no Start menu and might have limited desktop icons. You need to hide Network Neighborhood and other icons that normally appear on the desktop. As shown in Figure 7.5, many options are available for limiting the Start menu and taskbar.

- Users cannot install software. The software the users require is already installed on their computers.

- Users cannot access the hard disk, floppy drives, or CD-ROM. Again, you will find these policy settings under User Configuration/Administrative Templates.

- All data (if any) is stored on the network. You can implement folder redirection to satisfy this requirement.

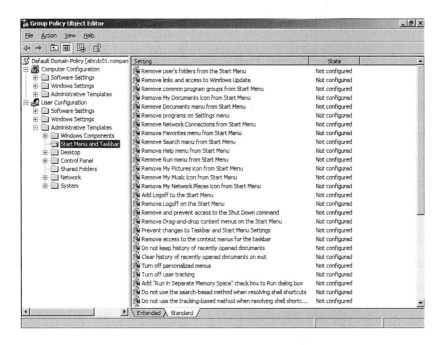

**FIGURE 7.5**
Group Policy options for limiting the Start menu and taskbar of a managed work-station.

## Managing Administrator Workstations

In many companies, the administrators' workstations have no controls in place at all. The accounts the administrators use to log on to the network give them access to control every aspect of the workstation, as well as the servers. Because these accounts have so much power over the network, it is recommended that policies be in place to protect that power. This section suggests some recommendations in the proper configuration and use of the administrator workstation.

To make changes in Active Directory, perform system maintenance, run backups and restores, and install software, administrators require a logon account that gives them elevated privileges. At the same time, administrators also perform normal network activity such as reading e-mail, writing documents, and setting schedules. For this reason, administrators should have two or more accounts. They should have an account that behaves as a normal network client account with the same privileges and subject to the same Group Policies as most normal users or power users. This account would then be used as the standard logon for the administrator workstation. Administrators should then have other accounts for workstation administration and network or domain administration that remain secure in virtue of not being used during the day-to-day network client work. Even administrators can inadvertently make damaging changes to a workstation or server configuration if they are logged in with Domain Admin privileges all the time.

> **Before Installing the Administration Tool Pack**
>
> Administration workstations should be at XP Service Pack 1 and have the QFE Q3289357 installed before installing the Administration Tool Pack.

To perform many of the tasks required of an administrator the Windows Server 2003 Administration Tool Pack should be installed from the Windows Server 2003 CD. These tools are packaged as adminpak.msi.

The Run As feature can be used from any administrator workstation or any network client to elevate privileges temporarily to perform administrative functions. For example, while logged in to a workstation with a user account that has standard user privileges, you can run Active Directory Users and Computers using the Run As command to execute the utility from an administrative account.

To run an application with the Run As command, do the following:

1. While holding down the Shift key on the keyboard, right-click the application you want to run.

2. Click Run As.

3. In the Run As Other User dialog box, type the username, password, and domain name of the administrative account.

You should also enforce a password-protected screensaver with a short timeout interval on administrator workstations. This protects the workstation from malicious users taking advantage of the administrator's credentials should the administrator be temporarily away from the machine.

To specify a particular screensaver with password protection and timeout in a Group Policy, do the following:

1. In the Group Policy Object Editor, navigate to User Configuration/Administrative Templates/Control Panel/Display.

**2.** Enable the following settings: Screen Saver Executable Name, Password Protect the Screen Saver, and Screen Saver Timeout.

Finally, when dealing with a large organization with distributed administration, it is a good idea to delegate authority for network clients to administrator groups based on geographical location. Some organizations make the mistake of creating a global administrators group populated with every administrator in the company. Just because an administrator in the Santa Clara office requires administrative rights over the network clients in his office does not mean that he should also get administrative rights over network clients in Papua, New Guinea. Keeping administrators organized also protects the network clients from receiving improper Group Policy assignments.

## BEST PRACTICE

### Managing an Administrator Workstation
The following are best practices for managing an administrator workstation

- Log on as a user with normal or restricted permission and use RunAs to operate the various MMC snap-ins.
- Use password-protected screensavers
- Keep administrative groups organized by administrative responsibilities

# Leveraging Useful Tools for Managing Desktops

The key to successful management and deployment of desktops is the administrator's ability to automate and simplify repetitive tasks. Microsoft has provided several tools that help to simplify otherwise manual administrative steps. The following section addresses some available resource kit tools that ease the deployment of workstations.

## Floplock

Floplock.exe is a utility, first introduced back in the NT 4.0 days, that puts a Discretionary Access Control List (DACL) on the floppy drive, providing the capability to lock the drive to all users except for Administrators and Power Users.

To install the FloppyLocker Service, run the Inetserv.exe utility. From a command prompt type

```
Instsrv FloppyLocker C:\{data path}\floplock.exe
```

After installation, use the services applet to configure the FloppyLocker service. Pick the account that the service should start up under and provide the correct password for the account. Administrator would be the obvious choice.

To remove the FloppyLocker service, type the following:

```
Instsrv FloppyLocker remove
```

The FloppyLocker Service can be a useful security feature in both the administrator workstation and kiosk workstation scenarios discussed previously in this chapter.

## Netdom

Netdom.exe is another resource kit utility that was first introduced in the NT 4.0 days that has many uses. It is most commonly used in a scripted installation to join a client computer to the domain. The correct syntax is

```
netdom join <ComputerName> /domain:<DomainName> /userd:<UserName> /passwordd:
<UserNamePassword>
```

Using * in place of <UserNamePassword> will prompt the user for password.

## Con2prt

Another old-school utility that is still useful today is Con2prt.exe, a command-line utility used to both connect and disconnect connections to network printers. Con2prt.exe is a useful tool for adding network printers while performing a scripted or automated XP desktop deployment.

From the command prompt type

- **CON2PRT /f**—Deletes all existing printer connections.
- **CON2PRT /C \\printserver\share printer**—Connects to specified printer.
- **CON2PRT /CD \\printserver\share printer**—Connects to specified printer and sets it as default printer.

## User State Migration Tool (USMT)

The User State Migration Tool (USMT) provides the same functionality as the Files and Settings Transfer Wizard but on a larger scale for migrating multiple users.

USMT is driven by a shared set of customized .INF files designed to manage the user's environment and needs.

USMT consists of two executable files: ScanState.exe and LoadState.exe, and four migration rule information files: Migapp.inf, Migsys.inf, Miguser.inf, and Sysfiles.inf. These files can be found on the Windows XP CD-ROM in the Valueadd\Msft\Usmt folder.

To migrate user data you need to first modify the .INF files to identify which file types, folders, or specific files you wish to migrate. To then gather the specific data run ScanState.exe. ScanState.exe gathers the specified data and copies it to a specified location where it can later be retrieved. Use Loadstate.exe, via script, to then add the user data to the new location, for example a newly imaged XP workstation.

# Summary

When it comes to desktop management in a Windows Server 2003 Active Directory environment, Microsoft has provided several administrative tools and options to simplify and scale these tasks. Using the Windows Server 2003 tools along with the services included with Windows XP Professional gives administrators several options for desktop management that can completely remove the need to physically visit a workstation for anything other that deploying the initial workstation image.

# 8

# Administering Windows Server 2003 Remotely

There are several methods by which system administrators can manage the IT environment's server resources. Though it is possible to manage each server locally, managing these resources remotely can greatly improve productivity. Remote administration reduces the administrative overhead required to manage servers in any size IT organization because it provides the flexibility for administrators to be centrally located while managing distributed server resources.

Windows Server 2003 provides the tools necessary for administrators to perform a vast array of management functions on remotely located servers. Server application and operating system upgrades can be performed remotely, as well as domain controller promotion/demotion and disk defragmentation.

This chapter describes the tools available for administrators to manage Windows Server 2003 servers remotely and provides best practices for leveraging remote administration features.

# Using Remote Desktop for Administration

Remote Desktop for Administration is one mode of the Terminal Services built into Windows Server 2003. Terminal Services can be enabled in one of two ways:

- Terminal Server mode. This is the Application Server mode that was available in Windows 2000 Server.
- Remote Desktop for Administration. This is an enhancement of the Remote Administration mode of Windows 2000 Server.

This second Terminal Services mode is used to administer Windows Server 2003 servers remotely. Remote Desktop for Administration provides remote access to the graphical interface–based tools available in the Windows environment. Remotely managing servers with Remote Desktop for Administration does not affect server performance or application compatibility.

Unlike the other terminal service mode, no terminal server Client Access Licenses (CALs) are required to use Remote Desktop for Administration. Windows Server 2003 provides two remote administrative sessions, for collaborative purposes, and a console session.

## Enhancements to Remote Administration with Remote Desktop Connection

By taking advantage of the new Terminal Services client, known as the Remote Desktop Connection (RDC), remote administration is enhanced in Windows Server 2003 in several ways.

The RDC supports a wide selection of hardware devices, so servers can be managed remotely from several different types of client hardware. The RDC is supported on the following hardware types:

- 16-bit Windows-based computers running Windows for Workgroups with TCP/IP.
- 32-bit Windows-based computers running every Windows OS from Windows 95 to Windows Server 2003.
- Windows CE-based handheld devices.
- Windows CE-based terminals, or thin clients.

The RDC allows for automatic restoration of interrupted network connections. This is key for remote administration. In the event that an administrator is disconnected in the middle of a mission-critical operation, the RDC will reconnect the session without losing the administrator's place in the operation.

The RDC supports a great deal of customization for the look and feel of a remote session. Providing high color, audio, and full screen sessions, the RDC allows you to control the graphic options and connection speed. This is an important feature because as you connect remotely to servers over a slow WAN link you will want to throttle the bandwidth usage for those particular sessions.

One of the biggest improvements to the RDC involves client resource redirection, which is available to Windows Server 2003 and Windows XP. You now have the capability to access local drives, network drives, and printers through the remote connection. Cut and paste, as well as large file transfers, can be accomplished between the client and server in a remote administration session.

Finally, in addition to the two remote sessions available for remote administration, Windows Server 2003 allows a console mode that enables you to connect to the "real" console of the server. Now administrative functions, such as some software installations that previously required local interaction, can be performed remotely.

## Enabling Remote Desktop for Administration

Enabling Remote Desktop for Administration is a simple procedure. Unlike Windows 2000, the Remote Desktop for Administration feature is now a separately configurable component from Terminal Services and has some new flexibility options previously unavailable.

The Remote Desktop for Administration feature is actually installed by default in Windows Server 2003, but it is installed in a disabled status for security reasons. To enable the feature with a default Start menu configuration, perform the following steps:

> **The default level of encryption for remote sessions**
>
> The default level of encryption for remote sessions is bidirectional 128-bit. Some older terminal service clients might not support 128-bit encryption.

1. From the Control Panel, double-click the System icon.

2. Choose the Remote tab.

3. On the bottom of the screen, click the check box to Allow Users to Connect Remotely to your computer, as shown in Figure 8.1.

4. Click OK to complete the configuration.

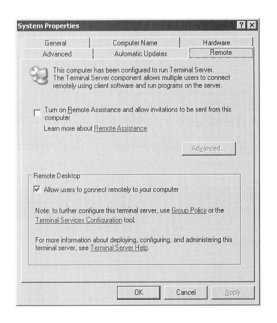

**FIGURE 8.1**   Enabling Remote Desktop for Administration.

If the Windows Server 2003 will be accessed remotely from a terminal server client that does not support high encryption, the encryption level of the remote session can be set to Client Compatible. This encryption level will provide the highest level of encryption to the remote session supported by the client. To change the default encryption level on the server to Client Compatible, follow these steps:

1. Open Terminal Services Configuration from All Programs\Administrative Tools.

2. In the right pane, under the Connection column, right-click RDP-Tcp, and choose Properties.

3. Set the encryption level to Client Compatible, as shown in Figure 8.2, and click OK to complete the configuration.

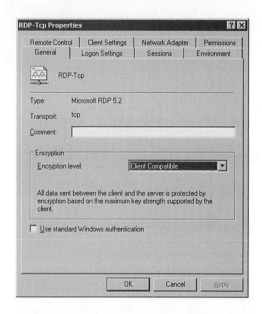

**FIGURE 8.2**    Setting the encryption level for Remote Administration.

## Best Practices for Remote Desktop for Administration

Understanding the following aspects of remote administration will enable system administrators to make the best use of the new Remote Desktop for Administration features in Windows Server 2003:

### Use the Console Mode

With the new console mode of connection available in Windows Server 2003, you can interact with the remote server as if you are directly at the physical server. This enables you to see pop-ups and messages that might only appear at the console.

### Configure Disconnect and Reset Timeouts

By default, disconnect and reset timeouts are not set. This has the potential to lock you out of remote sessions if there are two remote sessions that are active but in a disconnected state. On the flip side, when configuring the timeouts, allow enough time so that accidental disconnections can be resumed without resetting the session. By default, when a connection is broken, the session goes into a disconnected state and continues to execute whatever process it is running at that time. If the

> **Preventing Eavesdropping**
>
> For security purposes, when you are using the console mode of remote administration, the physical console of the server is automatically locked to prevent eavesdropping.

session is configured to reset when the connection breaks, all processes running in that session will be abruptly stopped.  Disconnect and reset timeouts can be configured using the Terminal Services Configuration Administrative tool.

### Coordinate Remote Administration

With Windows Server 2003, administrators are able to collaborate through multiple remote sessions. This feature has potential problems, though, if two administrators are unknowingly connected remotely to the same server. For instance, server data might be lost if two administrators attempt to perform disk defragmentation from two remote sessions at the same time.

### Distinguish Terminal Services from Remote Administration

Although administrators have the capability to install software through a Remote Desktop for Administration session, Terminal Services running in Terminal Server mode provides better installation and environment settings for office applications. For general desktop and remote application access functionality, use a dedicated Terminal Server solution.

# Taking Advantage of Windows Server 2003 Administration Tools

Another method for remote administration of servers from a client desktop computer is available by installing the Windows Server 2003 Administration Tools Pack on a workstation running Windows XP Professional Workstation. The primary target of administration for the Administration Tools Pack is the remote management of Active Directory. The Windows Server 2003 Administration Tools Pack includes Microsoft Management Console (MMC) snap-ins, Active Directory administrative tools, and other tools that are used to manage computers running Windows Server 2003.

## Installing the Admin Pack

The Windows Server 2003 Administration Tools Pack is included in the i386 folder on the Windows Server 2003 installation media. Once installed, you can run administrative tasks remotely on Active Directory using the Active Directory tools that are automatically installed on domain controllers. The tools only install on a computer running Microsoft XP Professional with Service Pack 1 applied to the operating system.

Installing the administrative tools requires local administrative access on the workstation. Running the tools requires the following:

- Administrative privileges in Active Directory.

- Network access to a domain controller in a Windows Server 2003 domain.

- Domain membership of the Windows XP Professional workstation in the Windows Server 2003 domain.

To install Windows Server 2003 Administrative Tools on a local Microsoft XP workstation, follow these steps:

> **Not Mutually Compatible**
>
> The Administration Tools Pack for Windows Server 2003 and Windows 2000 are not mutually compatible. To administer Windows 2000 domains, use the Windows 2000 Tools. To administer Windows Server 2003 domains, use the Windows Server 2003 tools.
>
> Although the Windows Server 2003 Administration Tools Pack can be used to manage 64-bit Windows Server 2003 servers, it cannot be installed on a computer running a 64-bit version of the operating system.

1. Insert the Windows Server 2003 CD-ROM and browse to the i386 folder.

2. Double-click Adminpak.msi.

3. Click Next, and then click Finish.

When installing the Windows Server 2003 Administration Tools on a Windows XP workstation, it is a best practice to also install the Windows Server 2003 help files. On a Windows XP workstation, by default, there is only the Windows XP help. If the workstation is intended to be an administrator's remote console, the Windows Server 2003 help files should be locally available.

Again, installing the Windows Server 2003 help files can only be installed on Windows Server 2003 servers and Windows XP Professional SP1 workstations.

The Windows Server 2003 help files can be installed on an XP workstation from either the installation media or over the wire from a Windows Server 2003 server. To install the help files from the install media, perform the following steps on the workstation:

1. Click Start, and then click Help and Support.

2. In Help and Support Center, click the Options button.

3. Under Options, click Install and Share Windows Help.

4. Choose Install Help Content from a CD or Disk Image.

5. Browse to the CD, and click the Find button.

6. Click the Install button.

# Using Convenience Consoles

To ease delegation of administrative functions, the Windows Server 2003 Administration Tools Pack includes Convenience Consoles that group specific tools into functional groups. The administrative tools in the Tools Pack can be roughly classified into four categories:

- System Administration
- Network Administration
- Storage Management
- Directory Services Administration

Basically, the Convenience Consoles are customized MMCs that contain tools and MMC snap-ins that fall into related groups. The MMCs are included in the installation and appear in the Administrative Tools program group of the XP Workstation. The consoles can be published to administrative workstations for administrators who have been delegated permissions in the given category. There are three Convenience Consoles included in the Tools Pack:

- Active Directory Management. This console includes Active Directory Users and Computers, Active Directory Sites and Services, Active Directory Domains and Trusts, and DNS. The file associated with this console is ADMgmt.msc.

- Public Key Management. This console includes Certification Authorities, Certificate Templates, Certificates for Current User, and Certificates for Local Computer. The file associated with this console is PKMgmt.msc

- IP Address Management. This console contains the DHCP, DNS, and WINS management tools. The file associated with this console is IPAddrMgmt.msc.

# Customizing Administration Consoles

The convenience provided in the administration consoles might be a good start for some IT organizations wanting to delegate administrative tasks. Most companies, though, will want further customization to the consoles, or will want to create completely new consoles to meet the delegation needs of the organization.

For example, the Active Directory Management Convenience console can be customized to include the Group Policy Management Console (GPMC) and remove the DNS snap-in. Organizations might create a Storage Management console that includes Windows Clustering, Network Load Balancing Clusters, and Remote Storage snap-ins.

If a custom console is created in an effort to delegate administration, the console should be configured so that it cannot be modified once it has been deployed to delegated administrators. To lock down the properties of a custom console, perform the following steps:

1. Click Start, click Run, type **mmc *path\filename.msc* /a**, and then click OK.

2. On the File menu, click Options.

3. In Console mode, choose User Mode—Limited Access, Single Window.

4. Select the Do Not Save Changes to This Console check box, as shown in Figure 8.3, and click OK.

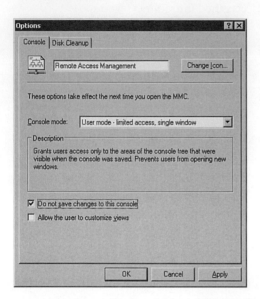

**FIGURE 8.3**   Locking down a custom console.

5. When the custom console is closed, choose Yes to save changes.

# Using Out-Of-Band Remote Administration Tools for Emergency Administration

All the methods for remote access to Windows Server 2003 servers discussed so far in this chapter rely on what are considered *in-band* connections. In-band connections typically involve connecting to the server directly through a network connection, and then using Terminal Service or Remote Desktop to manage the server with tools provided by Windows Server 2003. In-band connections are used with servers that are functioning normally. *Out-of-band* connections, on the other hand, refer to connections to a server that do not rely on a network connection, or a fully functioning server. Out-of-band remote administration is made available in Windows Server 2003 Emergency Management Services (EMS) to enable you to connect to and repair servers that are unavailable by in-band methods of connection.

## Emergency Management Service (EMS)

Emergency Management Service (EMS) is a new feature available in Windows Server 2003 that enables you to manage servers remotely that are not available through the normal (network) connections. With EMS and appropriate server hardware equipped with supporting firmware, you can manage a server without the need for a keyboard, mouse, local monitor, or video adapter. EMS uses text-mode communication only, which provides flexibility as to the means by which servers are remotely accessed. These methods include serial connections, terminal concentrators, and terminal emulators.

With the proper hardware and EMS configuration, out-of-band support is provided to the server's kernel components, the loader, setup, Recovery Console, and Stop errors. When the server is up and running, EMS provides a text-mode management console called Special Administration Console (SAC), which will be discussed later in this section.

If the server hardware supports it, EMS can be installed with the Windows Server 2003 operating system. By enabling firmware console redirection in the system's BIOS before installing the OS, EMS will be self-configured on installation. To enable EMS after the operating system is installed, you can use the bootcfg.exe command with the /EMS switch in the command console. For example, the following command enables EMS to use COM1 with a baud rate of 19200 on the first boot entry ID:

```
Bootcfg.exe /EMS ON /PORT COM1 /BAUD 19200 /ID 1
```

**BEST PRACTICE**

### bootcfg.exe Syntax

The syntax for the bootcfg.exe /EMS command is illustrated as follows:

```
BOOTCFG /EMS value [/S system [/U user [/P [password]]]]
[/PORT port] [/BAUD baudrate] [/ID bootid]
```

Parameter List:

| /EMSs | Value | On, Off, or Edit |
|---|---|---|
| /S | computer | Specifies a remote computer |
| /U | Domain\user | Specifies user context |
| /P | password | Password for the user account |
| /PORT | port | Specifies the COM port to be used for redirection. Valid ports are COM1, COM2, COM3, COM4, BIOSSET(EMS uses BIOS settings). |
| /BAUD | baudrate | Valid baudrates are 9600, 19200, 57600, 115200. |
| /ID | Bootid | Specifies the boot entry ID to add the EMS option. This is required when the EMS value is set to ON or OFF. |

## Configuring the Serial Connection for EMS

As indicated in the previous section, for EMS to manage Windows Server 2003, properly designed hardware must be integrated and configured on the server. The server motherboard should support Serial Port Console Redirection (SPCR). If it does not, the SPCR table will have to be configured manually. The server firmware should also be able to release control of the serial port to Windows Server 2003 once the operating system is started in order to take advantage of

> **Terminal Conventions Supported by EMS**
>
> The terminal conventions supported by EMS in Windows Server 2003 are VT100, VT100+, and VT-UTF8. Using the same terminal conventions in the server firmware, service processor, and client terminal ensures a consistent environment for managing servers in all states of operation (or failure).

most EMS functionality. Additional hardware, such as a service processor that is independent of the main server processor, will enhance EMS functionality. If the server hardware includes a service processor, console redirection should be available. The firmware must also use the same terminal conventions as EMS.

The serial port is the most common out-of-band hardware interface because it provides multiple methods of remote access, such as terminal concentrators and modems. By default, EMS uses the first serial port (COM 1 at 3F8). It is important to verify that the motherboard serial ports are enabled, and that no other device is using that resource. EMS and the Windows debugger cannot share the same COM port.

The actual configuration of the serial port will depend on the firmware settings available for a server. Some computers will enable user configuration, whereas others might simply have an Enabled/Disabled setting. Best practices for hardware configuration with EMS are as follows:

- Enable the appropriate port and maintain the default setting. Because EMS works with COM1 at 3F8 automatically in most cases, this should be the target configuration.

- Configure the port to use the highest baud rate available to the hardware. This will provide the best performance and reduce slow text-mode processes.

- Use a null modem cable with the serial port connection.

- Select hardware and firmware that support VT-UTF8. This terminal environment provides the best compatibility with EMS. Sending the proper command escape sequences are more difficult in a telnet session using VT100 and V100+.

## Special Administration Console (SAC)

The Special Administration Console (SAC) is the primary EMS command line environment available to Windows Server 2003. The SAC is different from the typical command line environment, and provides functionality intended for out-of-band management scenarios.

When EMS is enabled, SAC is available as long as the Windows Server 2003 kernel is running. SAC provides commands to perform the following management tasks:

- Restart or shut down the server.

- View and end active processes.

- View and set server IP address.

- Generate a stop error to create a memory dump.

- Start and access command prompts.

Because SAC enables you to access the command prompt, any text-based utilities usable in a Telnet session are available (provided there are system resources to run them). For example, the common communications accessory, HyperTerminal, can be used to access SAC on an EMS enabled server, as shown in Figure 8.4.

**FIGURE 8.4**  Using HyperTerminal to access the SAC command line.

SAC includes command shell utilities, such as dir, and text-based console programs, such as bootcfg.exe. Access to the command prompt requires a user logon with a local or domain account.

If SAC fails or becomes unavailable, !Special Administration Console (!SAC) is enabled. The !SAC is an auxiliary console environment hosted by Windows Server 2003 that has a subset of the features available with SAC. With !SAC, you can redirect Stop error message text and restart the server.

# Using and Configuring Remote Assistance

Remote Assistance is a feature that was introduced in Windows XP that enables a user on one computer to remotely view and even take control of the desktop environment of another user's computer. The interaction between the two computers is initiated either through an invitation or through an offer of assistance from one user to the other. For organizations that have deployed Windows XP in their desktop environment, Remote Assistance is a valuable tool for help desk departments. Many service calls that once required a visit to the end user to resolve a problem can now be resolved interactively through a Remote Assistance session.

Carrying the functionality forward, the Remote Assistance tool is also available to Windows Server 2003. Whereas Remote Assistance is a valuable tool for the help desk in a desktop environment, it becomes a valuable collaborative tool for system administrators in the server environment. Using Remote Assistance, an administrator of one server can request or offer remote assistance to an administrator of another server. The two administrators can then collaboratively resolve server configuration issues in real time through the same GUI on the server in question without having to be physically at the server.

This section describes how to configure and use the Remote Assistance tool to carry out collaborative remote administrative sessions on Windows Server 2003 servers.

## Requirements for Remote Assistance

To take advantage of Remote Assistance, both machines engaging in a collaborative session must be running either the Windows XP or Windows Server 2003 operating system. Additionally, both machines must be connected via a common network. What makes Remote Assistance so flexible is that the common network can be the Internet.

If the collaborative session is initiated by one administrator sending an invitation to the other administrator, the computer sending the invitation must be able to transfer a file. The file can be transferred through e-mail, or automatically through the Help and Support Center, which uses Outlook Express or Windows Messenger. The file can also be saved and transferred by any other means of transferring a file.

If the collaborative session is initiated by an offer to assist, thus bypassing the invitation, then both computers must be in the same domain or be members of two trusting domains. Additional configurations are necessary for a machine to accept Remote Assistance offers, which will be discussed later in the section.

To use Remote Assistance in Windows Server 2003, it must be enabled. For security purposes, it is disabled by default. To enable Remote Assistance, perform the following steps:

1. Open the System applet in the Control Panel.

2. Go to the Remote tab, and click the check box to Turn on Remote Assistance and Allow Invitations to be Sent from This Computer.

3. Click the Advanced tab, and enable the Remote Control feature and the invitation expiration, as shown in Figure 8.5.

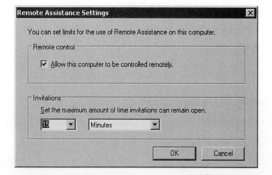

**FIGURE 8.5**   Configuring Remote Assistance.

## Sending a Remote Assistance Invitation

This section steps through the process by which a collaborative session is initiated through an invitation for Remote Assistance. The invitation can be sent in one of three ways:

- *Using Windows Messenger.* Windows Messenger is the preferred method for sending the invitation for assistance because it provides additional ways for the two machines to find each other over the Internet. If the two computers are on separate networks, separated by firewalls, and/or use Network Address Translation (NAT), this is the method to use.

- *Sending an e-mail.* Remote Assistance uses Simple Mail Advanced Programming Interface (MAPI) to help compose the invitation. The inviter or "Novice" sends an e-mail to the invitee or "Expert" with an attachment. When the Expert opens the attachment, he is prompted for a password, providing that the Novice specified a password, and the process continues.

> **Remote Assistance**
>
> If an e-mail client has not yet been configured, Remote Assistance attempts to help the Novice configure it. To change the e-mail client that Remote Assistance uses, in Control Panel, double-click Internet Options, and on the Programs tab, change the e-mail setting to the appropriate e-mail client. Some e-mail clients that do not support Simple MAPI will not appear as an option in the Internet Options Control Panel program.

- *Saving and transferring a file.* This method is used if there is no compatible MAPI client installed, or if other prerequisites are not available. This option enables the Novice to save the same file that would be created and attached to an e-mail automatically to be saved to her local drive or to a network share. The file can be transferred on a network share, a floppy disk, or other means. When the Expert receives the file, he can double-click it to open the invitation and start the Remote Assistance session.

To invite another administrator for Remote Assistance by sending a file, perform the following steps:

1. Open Help and Support Center by clicking Start and then clicking Help and Support.

2. Under Ask for Assistance click Invite a Friend to Connect to Your Computer with Remote Assistance.

3. Click Invite Someone to Help You.

4. Click Save Invitation as a File.

5. Specify the Inviter's name, and an expiration time for the invitation, then click Continue.

6. Type in a password that will unlock the invitation, retype the password for confirmation, and click Save Invitation.

7. Select a location accessible to the Expert to save the file.

8. When the Expert receives the invitation, the Expert is prompted for the password. After supplying this password, the Expert can initiate the Remote Assistance session.

9. After the Expert initiates the session, the Novice's computer verifies the password that the Expert entered.

10. The Novice's computer also checks to make sure that the invitation that the Expert used is a valid invitation and that the invitation is still open.

11. If the invitation is open and the password is correct, the Novice receives a notification stating that the Expert wants to start the session now and the Novice is prompted to start the Remote Assistance session.

12. If the Novice chooses to start the session, the Remote Assistance Novice chat dialog box will open on the Novice's computer, as shown in Figure 8.6, and the Remote Assistance Expert console opens on the Expert's computer. At this point, the Expert can see everything on the Novice computer, in real time.

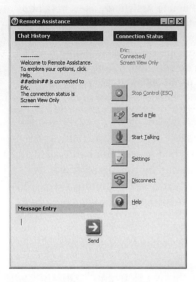

**FIGURE 8.6**  Establishing a Remote Assistance session.

**After the Expert Takes Control**

After the Expert takes control, the Remote Assistance session responds to both users' inputs. As a result, the mouse might behave erratically if both the Expert and Novice are attempting to control the session. If the Novice stops control, the Remote Assistance session continues and the Expert can still see the Novice's desktop.

13. The Expert can request to take control of the Novice's computer at this point by clicking the Take Control button on the Expert console. This sends a message to the Novice's computer notifying the Novice that the Expert is requesting to take control of the computer.

14. When the collaborative session is complete, the session can be ended by the Novice or Expert by clicking the Disconnect button.

# Securing and Monitoring Remote Administration

Remote administration of servers is a valuable tool for distributed IT organizations. It is important, though, when enabling remote administration features in Windows Server 2003, to maintain a high level of security for the server resources. Windows Server 2003 installs but disables remote access features by default for security purposes. When enabling these features, ensure that only administrators with the proper credentials will be able to remotely gain access to the server. This section provides tips on securing and monitoring remote administration.

# Securing Remote Administration

The security implications of enabling remote administration are fairly obvious. With remote administration features enabled, users who log on remotely can perform tasks as if they were sitting right in front of the server. Depending on the role the server plays in the organization, unauthorized access to a server can jeopardize a company's entire business. For this reason, it is important to protect the server from unauthorized access. Part I of this book, "Security Solutions," provides detailed approaches to securing Windows Server 2003. The following checklist points out key items to keep in mind for servers with remote administration features enabled:

- Depending on the topological location of the server, firewall technologies can be used to protect the server. Some servers, such as VPN and Web servers, are more prone to attack due to their topological proximity to the Internet. As such, firewalls should be deployed and properly configured to filter network traffic to and from such servers.

- Enable IPSec. IPSec policies provide both the strength and flexibility to protect communications between private network computers, domains, sites, remote sites, extranets, and dial-up clients. It can even be used to block receipt or transmission of specific traffic types. With an Active Directory domain, IPSec policies can be enforced using Group Policy.

- Require all users who make remote connections to use strong passwords. The role that passwords play in securing an organization's network is often underestimated and overlooked. Passwords provide the first line of defense against unauthorized access to the server. Password-cracking tools continue to improve, and the computers that are used to crack passwords are more powerful than ever.

- Limit the users who can log on to the server remotely. You can leverage security templates, or group policies to limit whom can connect to a server through Terminal Services. The setting Allow Logon through Terminal Services can be found in the Group Policy Editor by navigating to Computer Configuration\Windows Settings\Security Settings\Local Policies\User Rights Assignment.

- Always password-protect Remote Assistance. A Remote Assistance invitation that has no password associated with it might be intercepted by an attacker, giving him the capability to remotely interact with a server. For this reason, it is also important to set an expiration time on the invitation.

# Monitoring Remote Administration

Proper auditing practices go hand-in-hand with any good security policy. The Terminal Services Manager tool can be used to view and interact with remote connections in real time, but this is only helpful to view a server's current status. It is important to maintain and review the security logs of servers, as well as set up the proper items to monitor for events that occur when you are not actively watching for remote connections.

Auditing policies can be enforced on a server-by-server basis by applying security templates through the Security Configuration and Analysis MMC snap-in. In an Active Directory environment, auditing policies can be applied by group policy, as shown in Figure 8.7.

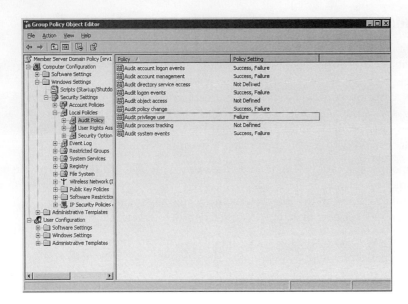

**FIGURE 8.7**
Setting up an audit policy
in group policy.

For servers enabled for remote administration, it is important to audit the success and failure of logon events, account management, policy changes, and system events. Also, failure of privileged use events should logged.

# Delegating Remote Administration

Perhaps the easiest way to control who has access to log on remotely to a server is to modify the built-in Remote Desktop Users group. By default, the security settings on Windows Server 2003 servers limits remote access to administrators and the Remote Desktop Users group.

To extend this security by limiting what a user can do after a remote session has been established to a server, you can delegate administration in Windows Server 2003. By delegating administration, a wide range of administrative tasks can be assigned to the appropriate users and groups. You can assign basic administrative tasks to regular server admin groups, and leave domainwide and forestwide administration to members of the Domain Admins and Enterprise Admins groups.

You can delegate administration by using either the Delegation of Control Wizard or the Authorization Manager MMC snap-in. The Delegation of Control wizard walks you through a series of steps to execute the process. The Authorization Manager provides a bit more flexibility, but with a lot more complexity. The Delegation of Control Wizard is detailed in Chapter 4, "Distributing Administration."

# Administering IIS in Windows Server 2003 Remotely

There are three different options available in Windows Server 2003 to manage Web services provided by Internet Information Services remotely: using the Internet Information Services (IIS) Manager, using Terminal Services, and using the Remote Administration (HTML) tool. Choosing the correct option depends on the type of administration necessary, the network connection, and the type of client machine from which the administrator is working. This section describes the different remote administration options for Web server administrators and defines the scenarios in which each method is appropriate.

## Using Internet Information Services Manager (IIS)

Internet Information Services Manager is the default tool by which Web services are administered on a Web server. In addition to managing the Web services on a local server, this administrative tool can be configured to connect to other servers running IIS. It is important to keep in mind that the IIS Manager should be used to remotely connect to Web servers available on the intranet, not on the Internet.

Windows Server 2003 provides a completely reworked version of IIS: version 6. Although there are many new features available in IIS 6.0, the manager tool installed with the Web service supports the management of down-level versions of IIS. So, in addition to providing remote administrative functionality to servers running IIS 6.0, the IIS Manager also can remotely connect to and manage Web servers running IIS 5.1 and 5.0.

To use the Internet Information Services Manager to manage a Web server remotely, follow these steps:

1. On the IIS 6.0-based server, click Start, point to Administrative Tools, and then click Internet Information Services Manager.

2. Click on the Action menu, and choose Connect.

3. In the Computer Name box, type the computer name of the remote Web server, and then click OK. It is also possible to enter the IP address of the Web server, as shown in Figure 8.8.

4. The remote computer is displayed under Internet Information Services (IIS) in the tree pane.

> **It Might Not Be Possible to Connect to an IIS Computer**
>
> If TCP/IP and a name resolution server such as Windows Internet Naming Service (WINS) are not available, it might not be possible to connect to an IIS computer by using the computer name.

**FIGURE 8.8** Remotely managing an IIS server.

## Using Terminal Services

If Remote Desktop for Administration is enabled on the Web server, you can connect to and administer IIS using the RDP client. Just as the previous method of connecting to a Web server with IIS Manager provided down-level support to Web servers that are not running IIS 6.0, the terminal service method of remote administration provides an up-level mode of administration. So, the client workstation from which the remote connection is made can administer IIS 6.0 from any operating system that supports the terminal service client. In addition to using Windows Server 2003, the client machine can be Windows 98, NT 4.0, XP, or 2000.

To remotely administer an IIS server with terminal services, simply follow these steps:

1. On a computer on which the Terminal Services client is installed, start the Terminal Services client.

2. Connect to the remote IIS-based computer.

3. From the Terminal Services Client window, administer IIS as if logged on to the computer locally. For example, click Start, point to Administrative Tools, and then click Internet Information Services Manager to start the Internet Information Services Manager.

## Using the Remote Administration (HTML) Tool

To manage Web servers through a Web browser, you can configure and use the Remote Administration (HTML) tool. Though this tool does not offer the full feature set of the Internet Information Services Manager, you can perform most Web and FTP site management tasks with the added flexibility of accessing your servers from the Web.

The Remote Administration (HTML) Tool provided with Windows Server 2003 IIS is not backwards compatible. In other words, it cannot be used to manage IIS 5.0 or 5.1; it will only work with IIS 6.0.

The HTML tool is not enabled by default when IIS 6.0 is installed. Also, depending on how IIS was installed on the server, the HTML tool might need to be added before it can be used. To add the HTML tool to an existing IIS server, perform the following steps:

1. From the Control Panel, run Add or Remove Programs.

2. Choose Add/Remove Windows Components.

3. Navigate to Application Server\Internet Information Services\World Wide Web Services and then choose Remote HTML Administration. Click the OK button three times for dialog prompts and then click Next.

4. Insert the Windows Server 2003 installation media when prompted.

5. When the installation completes, click Finish.

After the HTML tool is installed, the remote administration functionality must be enabled in Internet Information Services Manager. To maintain a high level of security for the Web server, it is important to restrict remote access to the server to a select IP address or group of IP addresses from which the server can be remotely administered. In the following example, a Web server will be enabled for remote administration, but will be configured so that only a computer with an IP address of 192.168.20.20 will be able to remotely administer IIS for that server. To enable the HTML remote administration tool, perform the following steps:

1. Click Start, point to Administrative Tools, and then click Internet Information Services Manager.

2. Expand *ServerName*, where *ServerName* is the name of the Web server, and then expand Web Sites.

3. Right-click Administration and then click Properties.

4. Under Web Site Identification, record the numbers that are displayed in the TCP Port box and SSL Port boxes. The defaults are 8099 and 8098.

5. Click the Directory Security tab, and then click the Edit button under IP address and domain name restrictions.

6. In the IP Address and Domain Name Restriction dialog box that appears, click Denied Access, and then click Add.

7. The Grant Access On dialog box appears. Under Type, click Single computer.

8. Type the IP address, in this example, 192.168.20.20 as shown in Figure 8.9, and then click OK.

9. Click OK again to complete the configuration, and close Internet Information Services Manager.

**Opening Remote Administration**
Although it is possible to open remote administration of Web servers and Web sites to all computers, it is advisable for security purposes to grant access to only a select group of computers.

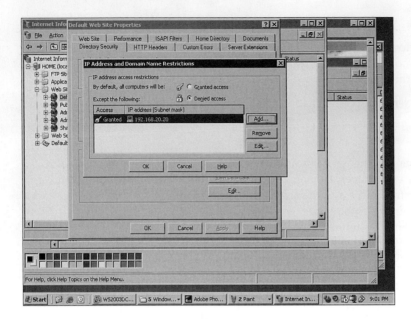

**FIGURE 8.9**
Securing Remote
Administration of IIS.

After the Remote Tool is installed, and the Web server is enabled for remote administration, perform the following steps to remotely administer the Web server:

1. Start Microsoft Internet Explorer, and then type the host name of the Web server, followed by the port number that was recorded earlier in the SSL Port box, and then click Go.

   For example, if the Web server is on an intranet, and the SSL port number is 8098, type the following URL: **https://ServerName:8098** (where *ServerName* is the name of the Web server).

2. At the prompt, enter a username and password for the Web server. The Remote Administration Tool is then displayed in the browser window.

3. From this point, there are several links and options to choose from in administering the Web server. Choose one that is appropriate for the task at hand and continue to remotely manage the server.

# Summary

Windows Server 2003 provides a wealth of options that enable administrators the flexibility necessary to manage servers in a distributed IT environment through remote administration tools and techniques. Although some tools are really just enhancements of technologies introduced in earlier operating systems, there are many new features that make Windows Server 2003 a compelling alternative and worthwhile investment in terms of both manageability and security. Administrators can now remotely attach to servers without a network connection, keyboard, mouse, or video adapter to troubleshoot and bring the server back online without making expensive and timely visits to the server's physical location.

# 9

# Maintenance Practices and Procedures

**A**fter the network operating system is installed and users are able to use the network on a daily basis, the job of the network administrator is not over. Although Windows 2003 is a very stable and resilient operating system, it won't perform ongoing maintenance and ongoing support on its own. To maintain a reliable network system, proper maintenance must be conducted. This will keep the environment stable and proactively prevent system failures. Potential problems with an Active Directory environment can be greatly mitigated through regular maintenance practices covered in this chapter. By proactively identifying and fixing inconsistencies in the Active Directory, you can avoid a downed network and a restore from tape later.

This chapter will explore best practices in system maintenance and provide step-by-step recommendations what can be done to implement an effectively maintained environment. The processes described in this chapter will help you improve the stability of your network and allow for more proactive support in managing the network.

# Maintenance Is Not As Interesting as Implementing New Technology

Although maintaining a network is not as interesting as implementing new technologies, finding out that the Active Directory is corrupted and that backups weren't working properly can lead to a very interesting few days of manual recovery.

### Ensuring That Maintenance Tasks Are Completed Regularly

Ensuring that maintenance tasks are completed regularly is critical to the stability of a network. When possible, distribute maintenance tasks throughout your IT staff in the areas of their expertise. This way there are qualified personnel doing the maintenance tasks and they don't feel as though their entire job is maintenance. Ensure that the people performing the maintenance tasks are following the written procedures to the letter. Have them sign off on the task on a checklist so that both employee and management can be sure the task was completed.

# What to Do Every Day

IT professionals know better than anyone that the moment they walk in the door there will be dozens of people vying for their attention. Everyone needs something done and they all need it done now. Although you want to be helpful and attentive, it's critical not to forget that there are daily tasks that need to be done to ensure the stability of the network.

## Read the Logs

The Event Viewer is the first thing you should monitor and review. The event logs keep track of critical events that can be telltale signs of system problems, and you should be in the habit of checking the event logs each and every day. This is especially critical if any changes have been made in the environment. The Event Viewer will usually spot potential problems before users do. Investigating each and every critical event in the Event Viewer before they become problems can result in proactive problem resolution. Eventually you will reach a point where some events are expected and can safely ignore those events. Any new issues should always be researched.

## Checking on System Resources

Being aware of the available resources on all systems serves several purposes. Not only can reviewing resources potentially identify short-term problems, but it also allows a network administrator to do educated resource planning. Part of maintaining a network is to know when to add servers and when to consolidate servers. There are several key items to examine daily:

- Available hard drive space. Ensure that there is sufficient space on the server system drives. Running low on available disk space will result in a noticeable reduction in system performance. In some instances it can cause the system to crash. If data is stored on separate drives, monitor the data drives as well.

  Running out of space on log drives can lead to a server crash because most applications that maintain log files halt the application service when the log files are full.

- Available system memory. If the system is running low on memory, a network administrator can expect a reduction of performance. When a server runs low on memory, the network administrator should consider adding more memory or examining the system more closely to determine if a particular application might warrant its own server. This is also a great way to spot memory leaks in an application.

- CPU utilization. This is much easier to monitor if you use a log of the performance counters. This allows you to spot anomalies in CPU usage. This can be a warning sign of upcoming system problems. This information can assist you in conducting capacity planning by determining what resources are required to add processing capability in a server or add an additional server.

Checking these items daily is a good start on the path to effective system maintenance. Logging the counter information on a long-term basis can help you conduct trending on a server to improve ongoing planning. This type of monitoring is covered more in depth in Chapter 21, "Proactive Monitoring and Alerting."

## Verify the Backups

Regular backups are vital to the recoverability of Windows 2003 and Active Directory. One of the most important maintenance tasks you can perform is to ensure that the backups are running properly. Most people think that this means checking the logs on the backup server and making sure there are no errors. Often, this is a task that is handled by the personnel that takes care of the backup systems. Server administrators should request a copy of the

### Any Event in the Event Viewer

For any event in the Event Viewer there will be a link that often leads to further insight on the issue and possibly a specific resolution.

For more information, go to the Help and Support Center at http://go.microsoft.com/fwlink/events.asp. Other helpful locations include Microsoft TechNet support at http://www.microsoft.com/technet, or Microsoft Support at http://support.microsoft.com.

Another resource for information on events is to perform a search on the Event ID on a search engine and possibly find useful information from someone who has encountered the same problem in the past.

Although it might seem redundant to check multiple resources for information, commonly the problem resolution is noted in one site that is not noted in another site. So using multiple resources can frequently identify problems that might otherwise not be found from other resources.

### If You See That Something Is Amiss

If you see that something is amiss with system resources, don't just take it at face value. Although it is easy to look at a drive that holds the logs and determine that the drive is full and just delete files, you might want to investigate why the tape backup software is not deleting log files after a successful backup. If the backup software is supposed to be clearing log files after the system is successfully backed up, could the system possibly not be backed up successfully? Another question to ask is whether the drive demand has been growing at a steady rate or did the capacity demand go from 10MB per day to 1GB per day? Sudden changes in system resource usage are sometimes related to failures in other subsystems or even viruses. Always get to the bottom of odd changes to identify the root cause rather than simply creating a short-term fix.

backup logs and review them as well to ensure they are working. This is a great time to compare the logs to your server's directory structure to ensure that no important directories are being missed.

Check to ensure that the backups are doing everything they are supposed to be doing. It's not unusual for a backup job to stop a particular service before the backup occurs and restart it afterward. If you are using these kinds of functions it's important to make sure they are doing what they are supposed to. If your backup software clears log files after they are backed up, ensure that this is happening. This can prevent annoying outages later due to drives becoming full.

Starting in Windows 2000, Microsoft added the concept of the System State. The System State contains information such as the system boot files, the system Registry, disk quota information, File Replication Service information, as well as databases for COM+ Class Registration, Certificate Services, Terminal Services, and Clustering. Even the event logs and context indexing catalogs are contained in the System State. On domain controllers, the System State also contains the Active Directory database. As such it is critical to ensure that the System State is being backed up on each Windows 2000 and 2003 server in the enterprise if you are to have the capability to recover Active Directory.

### Try Adding Flags

If your backup jobs do additional tasks such as launching batches before or after a job, try adding flags to the batches to make it easier to see that they were done. Something as simple as:

```
Net stop "Service A"
Echo Prebackup batch "Stop Service A"
ran on %date%
at %time% successfully >> batchre-
sults.txt
```

### Or something as fancy as:

```
mapisend -u "Default" -p "password" -r
Administrator
-s "Stopping Service A" -m " Prebackup
batch "Stop
Service A" ran on %date% at %time%
successfully "
```

will give you a single place to look to see that the batch jobs ran successfully.

# What to Do Every Week

In addition to the tasks that should be performed daily there are other tasks that should be performed once a week. You should consider doing weekly tasks on the same day of the week. If a task is done on Monday one week and Friday the next week, 10 days go by without doing the maintenance tasks. A slip of a few days can lead to longer slips in scheduled maintenance leading to the possibility of bigger problems occurring.

## Check for System Updates

Microsoft regularly releases system updates and hotfixes to address myriad bugs and issues. These updates are critical to the security and stability of your system.

Although updates are released on a semiregular basis, you should not blindly download and install each and every patch that is released. Patch management is a critical factor in system maintenance. Always download and test a new patch in a lab environment. This gives you an opportunity to test the new patch with applications to see if the patch or update causes anything on the system to stop working. When stability of a patch seems likely, apply it to the server during a maintenance window. Make sure you have a recent backup just in case. The following tasks should be performed when performing patch management:

- Check for new patches. This can be done easily via the Windows Update feature in Windows 2003 or by visiting the Web at `http://www.microsoft.com/windowsupdate`.

- Determine which servers the patch is applicable to. This process can be simplified through the use of the Microsoft Baseline Security Analyzer tool. It checks the services and applications running on a server and compares this information to an XML file maintained by Microsoft that references which patches are applicable to which services and operating systems.

- Download the patch and install it on a test server in the lab. This test server should be representative of the type of server this patch is applicable to.

- Test the applications on the server with the new patch in place. Pay attention to potential changes in performance, memory usage, and so on.

- If the patch tests out okay, pick a maintenance window in which to install the patch.

- Perform a system state backup of the server before applying the patch, just in case.

- Apply the patch and reboot if necessary.

### Better Confidence in Windows 2003

Windows 2003 has proven to have an extremely low rate of regularly released patches and updates. Unlike previous versions of Windows that had dozens of patches and updates released soon after the product introduction, Microsoft Windows 2003 has had virtually no updates required soon after release. This level of clean code provides better confidence that Windows 2003 will require less maintenance than previous versions of Windows.

### Hardware Availability

If availability of hardware in the test lab is a concern, consider using Virtual Machine technology from companies like VMWare or Microsoft. This enables you to maintain images of each type of server in your environment all on a single box. When you want to test a patch for SQL you simply "boot" the SQL Virtual Machine (configured just like your machine in production) and test the patch. Then launch your Exchange server and test and appropriate patches For Exchange. You can even test interaction between virtual systems after patch application to ensure that they won't break things in production. This will allow you to have a single system in the lab to test multiple systems and it's a whole lot faster than rebuilding the test system each time you need to test a new application.

Proper patch management is one of the most important maintenance tasks there is. Being up to date with the latest security fixes greatly reduces the chances of you being affected by hackers, worms, and viruses.

## BEST PRACTICE

### Keeping Up with Patches

Historically, some of the worst worms and viruses have taken advantage of vulnerabilities that were posted and fixed months prior to the release of the worm or virus. The SQL_Slammer Virus, for example, that wreaked havoc on thousands of SQL servers, exploited a security hole that had been posted and patched several months previously. Servers that were affected hadn't downloaded and installed the patch. The failure to keep up with patch maintenance resulted in an exciting weekend for a large number of system administrators.

## Verify Active Directory Replication

The Windows 2003 support tools provide a lot of useful applications for monitoring the health of the Active Directory. These tools are located on the Windows Server 2003 CD in the /Support/Tools directory. One of the key things to verify with these tools is that Active Directory replication is occurring properly.

In environments that are fairly "static," it is easy to miss a problem in Active Directory replication. You could easily go weeks without noticing that a user in a remote location with a local DC doesn't appear in your view of Users and Computers. Failures in replication of Active Directory can lead to myriad problems so it is critical to verify successful replication.

The tool Replmon.exe is very useful in verifying replication success. Consult this tool weekly to verify replication between all domain controllers.

## Audit Administrative Group Membership

System administrators are frequently on the alert against hackers and other forms of unauthorized user access. In an effort to control system access, many administrators have taken advantage of the granular approach to security rights offered by Active Directory. This results in less of a need for people to be Domain Administrator, Schema Administrator, or Enterprise Administrator. As such, companies are making efforts to keep the number of people in these groups as low as possible. Invariably, someone feels they need to be in one of these groups in order to accomplish a particular task. Sometimes they are placed in one of these groups for a specific task and then they are not removed. To control these types of rights and reduce the chances of accidental changes to the system it is very useful to audit these high level administrative groups weekly and ensure that there are no surprises in the membership. It's a great way to catch accounts that only needed temporary rights and it's a great way to spot hackers that have added their accounts into these groups. Take a look at the local administrators group on your member servers as well. You might be surprised what you find that you did not expect.

## Perform a Test Restore

As mentioned previously, successful backups of Windows 2003 and Active Directory are critical to the maintenance of the networking environment. Verifying successful backups daily is a great way to ensure there is a healthy copy of the network backup. Even more important than backups are restores. As many surprised administrators find, when they really need to restore from tape and the backup is corrupt or not accessible, the importance of being able to success-fully restore from tape is most apparent. Reading the backup logs is a good start but it's critical that a test restore is performed weekly to ensure that the backup tapes are actually viable. Pick a tape randomly from the past week and restore some random files. Uncheck the Restore to Original Location option and place the files in a temporary directory. Try to choose files that can be opened to verify their integrity. Restore the files and then open each of them. If any of the files fails to restore or are corrupted when you restore them, alert the backup group immedi-ately, or if you are the person in charge of backups, review your backup procedures and test the process until a successful backup can be achieved.

## Examining the Size of the Active Directory Database

Once a week, the size of the NTDS.DIT file should be checked. Compare the size of it to the size it was the previous week. After a few weeks you should have a good feel for "normal" growth of the file. If its size changes drastically for no apparent reason (such as migration of objects from another environment, recent hiring of a large number of employees, replication with a new LDAP source) this should flag to you that something out of the ordinary is going on and you should determine the cause immediately.

## Examine the DHCP Scopes

Make sure that the DHCP scopes for the network have enough available addresses to cover any anticipated growth. Because allocating additional network addresses might involve multiple individuals or groups of individuals, it is important to be able to predict when you will run out of addresses for a particular network and request additional resources in time.

# What to Do Every Month

There are some additional tasks that should be performed monthly to ensure a stable Active Directory.

## Active Directory Database Integrity Check

To make sure that potential problems don't get away from you it is useful to regularly check the integrity of the Active Directory database. This is performed via the NTDSUTIL application.

---

**Maintenance Tasks**

Some maintenance tasks, such as an integrity check or defragmentation of the Active Directory database, require that the server be rebooted into Directory Services Recovery mode. This means that the domain controller will not be available. Ensure that you are aware of this during your mainte-nance windows and that other domain controllers are available to service logon requests. Pay special attention when holders of the FSMO roles are receiving maintenance. Don't plan on Forest prepping your domain at the same time you are going to defragment the NTDS.DIT on the Schema Master.

### Database Integrity Check

To run the integrity check on the database, simply boot the server into directory services restore mode and run the NTDSUTIL command from a command prompt. Type **files** and then type **integrity**. After the completion of the test, simply type **quit**. This will alert you to any corruption in the Active Directory database. Interesting to note is that this function actually calls a separate program called esentutl.exe. It is not recommended that the esentutl.exe application be run on its own. Instead let the integrity check called within NTDSUTIL do it for you.

## Performing a Scandisk

Disk integrity is probably the single greatest cause of server failure. Files can become corrupted, disk sectors can go bad, or any number of things can cause disk integrity problems. By regularly running Scandisk, you can identify and usually repair file corruptions. Similarly, Scandisk can detect bad sectors on the physical disk and mark them as unusable. This reduces the chances of system failures due to corrupted drivers or system files. Scandisk has improved significantly over the years and is now several times faster than it was in the Windows NT 4.0 days.

## BEST PRACTICE

### Schedule the Scandisk

Due to disk locking, Scandisk will not be able to scan the system disk from within the operating system. You will need to tell it to schedule the Scandisk for the next reboot. Pay careful attention to messages that come up during the Scandisk process.

## Reboot the System

All server administrators love to brag about how long their systems have been up and running. After years of abuse from Unix administrators, Windows 2003 administrators can finally feel good about the stability of their platform. This fact not withstanding, it is still a good practice to reboot the system monthly. This allows system resources to be recaptured, it ensures that logs are committed to disk and gives you an opportunity to make any hardware changes that might have been inspired by your daily system monitoring.

## Defragment the System

Defragmenting the system and data disk can result in significant improvements in overall performance. By ensuring that data is read sequentially instead of randomly across the disk you are able to take full advantage of the throughput of your drive subsystem. This also results in significant improvements in backup performance.

### Defragmenting the Disk

Defragmenting the disk is one of those tasks that you can accomplish more quickly the more often you run them. Don't be surprised if the first time you run Defragment it takes a fair amount of time. If you run it monthly it will become a fairly quick process.

Be aware that running the defragmentation will noticeably affect disk performance during the time that it is being run. The defragmentation process is very disk-intensive. Make sure you don't run this while users are accessing the system heavily.

## Check WINS for Corruptions

Most environments have not yet reached the point of finally eliminating WINS from their environment. Legacy operating systems like Windows NT 4.0 and Windows 9x still require WINS for finding remote resources quickly. WINS, unfortunately, has a tendency to become corrupted. Once a month, open the WINS manager and display all records (all owners). Sort this alphabetically. Entries that begin with unreadable entries can safely be removed. This will help to reduce WINS-related issues with inability to find resources on the network.

Consistency checking is network- and resource-intensive for the WINS server computer. For this reason, run WINS consistency checks during times of low traffic, such as at night, on weekends, or during planned maintenance windows.

# Consolidating Servers as a Maintenance Task

Many maintenance tasks are performed on each server. Thus it stands to reason that reducing the number of servers will reduce the amount of necessary maintenance tasks. Similarly, older platforms often have more issues that must be dealt with manually and they are more prone to errors and failures. There are several technologies that can be leveraged to reduce the server count in the network.

## Windows System Resource Manager

Windows System Resource Manager (WSRM) is an application that allows you to enforce resource allocation for a particular application. Memory and CPU usage can be given limits that the application is not allowed to surpass. In this way you can partition a server to handle multiple applications without concern of a single application taking up all the available system resources. This can be exceptionally helpful with systems that usually see a low load. By consolidating these small servers into a single larger server you can ensure that no one application will monopolize the server resources allowing them to coexist in harmony. Although Windows System Resource Manager (WSRM) is included in the retail versions of Windows Server 2003 and Enterprise Edition, it can be downloaded from Microsoft at `http://www.microsoft.com/ windowsserver2003/downloads/wsrm.mspx`.

## Virtual Servers

Virtual machine technology is an excellent way to eliminate multiple legacy servers and consolidate them into a single server. This reduces the server count and in turn reduces the "per server" maintenance tasks. The side benefit is that you can eliminate legacy hardware and run the legacy applications on newer more supported hardware. A single server could literally run Windows 2003, Windows 2000, Windows NT 4.0, Windows 9x, and flavors of Unix/Linux all at the same time.

Virtual servers talk to each other in the same manner real servers do. This means that applications that traditionally couldn't run on the same server system can now share hardware but still perform in their original manner. Mail servers and antivirus gateways are a common example of applications that traditionally had to be run and maintained separately. Through Virtual Machine technology they can share the same physical hardware.

This type of consolidation also makes it much easier to standardize on a single hardware platform. Reducing the number of platforms to support also helps to reduce the overall maintenance load. Hardware freed up in this manner can be redeployed into a lab environment for testing patches or new maintenance procedures.

# Backup Tips and Tricks

One of the most common maintenance tasks is performing system backups of the servers on your network. Backups are also the single most important maintenance task in the enterprise. Backups can often be a frustrating task but there are ways to make the process smoother and faster.

## Improving Performance With a Dedicated Backup VLAN

In a perfect world there would be no users accessing data during the backups. Bandwidth would be unlimited and you wouldn't need things like routers or Access Control Lists to prevent traffic from spilling all over the network. Often, due to constraints in the network, it is necessary to put servers into separate networks. This often results in traffic having to cross switch backplanes, switch trunks, or even routers. One way to avoid this situation is to implement a dedicated network for the backups. By adding an additional NIC to each server and addressing it out of an address space unknown to the production network you are able to segment all backup traffic. This also enables users to access data without affecting the bandwidth available to the backup system. If you're using a chassis switch, all the NICs for the backup network should attach to the same card. This maximizes available bandwidth because network traffic does not have to cross the backplane.

**Additional NIC**

If the network is still supporting WINS, ensure that the additional NIC is not registering itself in WINS. This could result in an unreachable address being resolved by a client that was trying to reach the server. Similarly, the NIC for the backup network should not be dynamically registering itself in DNS.

Also consider running the backup server with a network interface card, or NIC, that is faster than the NICs in the target servers. Remote backups rarely take full advantage of the available bandwidth on a system due to the spooling of large numbers of small files. The backup server, on the other hand, can handle multiple conversations at once and spool data to multiple backup devices.

**Profiling Your Backup Network**

In switched 100MB networks, experiment with duplex settings on the switch and the servers. Very often, older hardware will perform its backups as much as twice as fast when forced to half duplex. Although this is counter-intuitive where full duplex should be twice as fast as half duplex, many older hardware adapters or network adapter drivers are not optimized at full duplex, therefore multiple retries for information transmission makes improperly configured network set systems run slower than expected.

## Spool to Disk and Later to Tape

In some backup situations the window of opportunity to perform a backup can be very small. Databases are often stopped during their backup and need to be back up and running as soon as possible. One of the simplest ways to get the database backed up quickly is to first back up to disk and later spool it off to tape. The fastest tape technologies on the market still can't keep up with a good disk. Many enterprise-level backups first run a job that uses a large SAN or NAS as the media and then runs a secondary job that writes the data from the SAN or NAS to tape. Because the database is only stopped for the fast disk copy the tape system has the rest of the day to commit the data to tape.

A less expensive variation on that theme is to have the server perform a local backup to another locally attached disk. The tape-based backup simply backs up this local backup file. It requires a two-step restore but the reduced impact on the database often makes this worth while.

**Just Basic Old Disk**

Although SAN and NAS are excellent technologies for spooling data to disk before spooling to tape, less expensive technologies like JBOD (Just Basic Old Disk) are also very viable choices.

The additional benefit to spooling to disk first is that statistically most restores are last night's data. By performing the restore from disk instead of tape the system can be brought back into a usable state much more quickly. In addition to the backup and restore processes being faster, the step of verifying the contents of the backup is often 10 times faster.

## Grandfather, Father, Son Strategies and Changers

Almost every administrator is familiar with the daily task of swapping tapes. Keeping a large array of labeled tapes, carefully placing them in order, and determining which tape needs to be moved into the fireproof safe is a managed process. Deciding which tape needs to go offsite, determining how to put the tapes that came back from storage back into rotation--these are all familiar and tedious tasks. Many companies have grown past this method and moved into the world of tape changers. Tape changers range from a single drive unit with a six-tape cartridge to backup devices that are literally the size of a conference room. These can have dozens and dozens of drives with rack after rack of tapes. Multiple robots perform a veritable ballet as they scan tapes with their barcode readers, pluck them from their homes and place them into drives. They carefully record which slot holds which tape for which job. They know when to place a tape into a mail slot to be picked up for storage. They take over a tremendous amount of work for backups.

These changers all have one thing in common. They use software that allows them to make dynamic decisions about tape management. It's a common occurrence for a system administrator to come in Monday morning and find their backup server asking for a second tape. Imagine the horror of finding out that your mail server crashed at 2 a.m. on Monday morning and the backup server has been asking for a second tape since Friday night. Through the use of tape changer hardware, you can create a group of tapes known as a scratch pool that the system can use if it runs out of space. This greatly reduces the possibility of a job not finishing on time for lack of tapes.

The concept of GFS (Grandfather, Father, Son) is commonly used with changers to simplify tape rotation management. The GFS strategy is a method of maintaining backups on a daily, weekly, and monthly basis. GFS backup schemes are based on a seven-day weekly schedule, beginning any day of the week. A full backup is performed at least once a week. Most organizations do the full backup on Friday night. All other days, full, partial, or no backups are performed. The daily backups are the Son. The last full backup in the week (the weekly backup) is the Father. The last full backup of the month (the monthly backup) is the Grandfather.

### Service Level Agreements

If offsite storage services are being used, don't forget to include their Service Level Agreements (SLA) in your own. If the offsite storage vendor only offers four-hour service response to pull and return a stored tape, you must factor that into your own SLA.

By default, you can re-use daily media after six days. Weekly media can be overwritten after five weeks have passed since it was last written to. Monthly media are saved throughout the year. These can and should be taken off-site for storage. You can change any of these media rotation defaults to suit your particular environment.

The primary purpose of the GFS scheme is to suggest a minimum standard and consistent interval at which to rotate and retire the media.

## Use the Appropriate Agents

Backup software often comes with specialized agents. These agents might deal with connectivity to proprietary systems, file compression, performance enhancements, or file locking. Agents that deal with proprietary systems like SQL or Exchange are absolutely critical to the backup and restore of these systems. Failure to use these agents will often leave you with backups that cannot restore the system to a usable state. Agents that deal with compression are mostly used in situations where there is limited bandwidth between the backup server and the remote server. By compressing the data, the total amount of data to be removed is reduced. This results in a faster transfer. The tradeoff is an increased CPU load on the server performing the encryption. To ensure a complete backup of data files the use of an Open File agent is very important. Without such an agent, files might get skipped during the backup. This could be an unfortunate situation if one of these files needs to be restored. Finally, agents that are built for accelerating backups can be very helpful in situations where large numbers of small files are being backed up. Due to the constant seeking of individual files, the disk subsystem is often underused in this situation. These acceleration agents prepackage the files into larger chunks to better use the disk subsystem.

## What to Include and Exclude in a Backup

Always be aware of the files on your system and make intelligent decisions about what files will be backed up. As stated earlier, the System State of a Windows 2003 system is critical for the ability to restore data. Other files can safely be excluded. The swap file, for example, will not get backed up properly and is not required for a system restore. Often you will overlook the fact that data is getting backed up twice. If you are backing up an application like Exchange with a dedicated agent there is probably no need to try to back up the .edb files at a file level. Similarly if a network is using DFS it is not necessary to back up each replica of the data. If DFS data needs to be restored you can simply re-create the replica and allow File Replication Services to re-create the information. In the meantime users will be accessing another replica anyway.

By examining the logs from the backups you can determine which files are always locked in use and can't be backed up. Based on this information you can determine if they need an agent or if this data can safely be skipped.

> **Hardware Compression Is More Efficient**
>
> Hardware compression at the tape device is almost always more efficient than software compression. Greater throughput can be had by allowing the server to spool data without pausing to compress it locally. If network connectivity is slow, it can be a worthwhile tradeoff to compress locally in order to reduce the traffic on the network

> **NTFS-level Flagging**
>
> Be aware of any NTFS-level flagging performed by your backup software. Some backup packages modify an NTFS field on the file to indicate that the file has been backed up. Other technologies such as DFS can see this change and believe that the file was modified and that it needs to be replicated. This can result in a large and unintended load on the network.
>
> Newer versions of tape backup software will not flag the file as being accessed and can minimize the unnecessary replication of files.

> **Bootstrap Portion of ASR**
>
> Microsoft wrote the bootstrap portion of ASR to be extensible. This means that third-party backup solutions can leverage this functionality to provide their own bare metal restore.
>
> If your third-party backup solution does not support ASR it might be a good idea to create an ASR backup via the built-in NTBackup utility that comes with Windows Server 2003 after you have the server configured with its applications. This will give you a head start if you need to do a ground-up restore later.

# Making Automated System Recovery Work for You

Windows 2003 offers an extremely helpful technology called Automated System Recovery, or ASR. The goal of ASR is to accelerate and simplify the process of a *bare metal restore* where you are restoring a system to new hardware from a recent backup.

ASR utilizes a precreated disk containing key information about recovering the system as well as special "bootstrap" code written into the setup executable on the Windows 2003 CD. This allows the CD to boot and read the recovery information from the recovery disk. The system then loads just enough of the operating system to access the backup software and device and performs the restore.

## BEST PRACTICE

### Saving Time on Restores

The clever administrator knows which systems need to run 24/7 and which systems can be taken down regularly. By taking down the non-24/7 systems regularly and creating a ghost image (or similar product) of your system drive you can create a bootable CD that will allow you to easily re-create the system drive. This is an extremely fast process. It's not unusual to be able to restore a system to brand new hardware and have the operating system and applications up and running in less than 20 minutes. Then you have the backup/restore agent available to restore data from tape. If you implement this type of a solution, be sure to update the ghost image and burn a bootable CD on a regular basis. Having a readily available image will allow for proactive planning for system recovery.

# Leveraging Scripting for Maintenance Practices

As mentioned earlier in this chapter, it is critical that maintenance tasks be carried out regularly and consistently. Traditionally, the bane of consistency has been human interaction. People get distracted. People get interrupted. Scripting basic maintenance tasks is an excellent way to ensure that the maintenance procedures are followed in exactly the same way each and every time.

These scripts can be as simple as a batch file that clears out a temp directory:

```
C:
 Cd temp
 Del *.* /s /y
```

Or the scripts can be as complex as a Visual Basic script that parses a text file to create mail enabled contacts regularly:

```
Set RootDSE = GetObject("LDAP://RootDSE")
DomainName = RootDSE.Get("RootDomainNamingContext")

Set oConnection = CreateObject("ADODB.Connection")
oConnection.Provider = "ADsDSOObject"
oConnection.Open "DS Query"
Set oCommand = CreateObject("ADODB.Command")
Set oCommand.ActiveConnection = oConnection
oCommand.Properties("searchscope") = 2
```

```
Set objContainer = GetObject("LDAP://OU=Contacts," + DomainName)
'Set objContainer = GetObject("LDAP://OU=Scripts,OU=Test," + DomainName)

Set FSO = CreateObject("Scripting.FileSystemObject")
Set ContactList = FSO.OpenTextFile("Contacts.csv",1,False)

on error resume next

Do While NOT ContactList.AtEndOfStream
  Line = ContactList.ReadLine
  Data = Split(Line,",")
'  LastName = Data(0)
'  FirstName = Data(1)
'  DisplayName = Data(2)
'  LogonName = Data(3)

  DisplayName = Data(1)
  LogonName = Data(2)
  EMail = Data(3)

  oCommand.CommandText = "Select ADsPath,cn From 'LDAP://" &
➥ DomainName & "' Where DisplayName='" + DisplayName + "'"
  Set rs = oCommand.Execute
  If rs.EOF Then

    wscript.echo DisplayName

    Set oContact = objContainer.Create("contact", "CN=" & LogonName)
    oContact.DisplayName = DisplayName
    oContact.SetInfo

    Set oRecip = oContact
    oRecip.MailEnable EMail
    oRecip.Mail = Right(EMail, Len(EMail) - 5)
    oRecip.SetInfo

    Set oContact = Nothing
    Set oRecip = Nothing
    Line = Null
    Data = Null
    LastName = Null
    FirstName = Null
    DisplayName = Null
    LogonName = Null
```

```
    If Err.Number <> 0 Then
      wscript.echo vbTab + "Error occured"
      Err.Clear
    Else
      wscript.echo vbTab + "Contact created"
    End If
  End If
  Set rs = Nothing
Loop

ContactList.Close
Set ContactList = Nothing
Set FSO = Nothing
Set RootDSE = Nothing
```

## Taking Advantage of Command Line Interfaces

One of the great things about Windows 2003 is that almost anything that can be done from a graphical user interface can also be done from the command line. This drastically simplifies the automation of maintenance tasks.

Rather than manually deleting a group of users at the end of the week based on a hire/fire list, you can automate this process. You can write a script using a simple Net User command: `"Net User username /DELETE"`. That's the same as opening Computer Management, highlighting the user, and pressing Delete.

You don't even have to be an experienced scripter to take advantage of command-line tricks. Take your list of users you want to delete and import them into Microsoft Excel. Add a cell to the left of the usernames. In the first cell type **Net User**. Copy that value down through the last username. Now add a cell to the right or the usernames and type **/delete**. Copy that down as well. You will notice that the format looks similar to `Net User username /DELETE`. Now export it back into a test file. Call it "deleteusers.bat". Run the batch file to bulk delete the names of several user accounts.

If you want to back up the WINS database each week as part of your maintenance, you could open the MMC, add the WINS snap-in, and highlight your server. Then choose Action, Backup Database, select a directory, and click OK.

Or you could have a prebuilt script using a quick Net Stop `wins` command. Type **xcopy wins.mdb** to move a copy of the WINS database to a location of your choice. Then follow up the process with a Net Start "wins" and run the whole process with a single command. Better yet, you can schedule the task to run weekly and never have to touch it. You can even have it e-mail you to let you know that it ran successfully.

Leverage the command-line version of common tools to automate and schedule tasks that don't require human interaction. Now don't go crazy and schedule a defragmentation of your Exchange databases each week and trust that the services will be running when you get in on

Monday. Something that important requires human interaction to react to any problems that arise. But simple batch tasks like importing users from a foreign mail system nightly or resetting passwords for test users on your training systems could easily be scripted and scheduled by taking advantage of command-line interfaces to common GUI tools.

## Customizing the MMC View

One way to speed and simplify maintenance tasks is to create a customized MMC view that contains the interfaces for the subsystems that you will access for your tasks. If you are in charge of checking DHCP scope availability and WINS integrity, you can create an MMC view with just those snap-ins. This makes it very easy to complete your tasks as you can simply go from the top down and go from task to task. This will help you save time and effort.

## Ensuring Consistency with Checklists

This chapter has covered a large number of recommended maintenance tasks. It has also talked about strategies to take the human factor out of the equation in order to ensure consistent maintenance practices. Creating checklists is absolutely vital to ensuring that tasks are completed regularly. A checklist should exist for each and every server in your environment. This checklist should be located next to the server and it should be regularly audited by someone other than the person doing the maintenance.

By having an easy-to-follow list of tasks with a signoff you can ensure that tasks are being completed. If problems arise the checklist can be critical to determining exactly what was done to a system, when it was done, and by whom.

**BEST PRACTICE**

### Make the Checklists Easy to Follow

Make the checklists easy to follow. Put dates on each page with a heading at the top for Daily, Weekly, or Monthly. Don't forget that weeklies and monthlies are in addition to the daily and/or weekly. If weeklies will occur on Fridays, put a note at the bottom of the Friday daily reminding them to also do the weekly, which should be the next page. Include space for the technician to include any details that might have come up as a result of the check. For example an entry for "Check available space on the C:\ drive" should have a spot for the technician to initial that it was done, a spot to enter the amount of free space, and a place to enter comments like "Free space has been at 2.1GB each day for the past two weeks. Today it is only 1.1GB. Something has changed." This way if the technician fails to alert the appropriate group it can still be caught during the audits of the checklists.

# Why Five-9s Might Be a Bad Idea

A lot of companies seem obsessed with the concept of 99.999% uptime, or *Five-9s*. This suggests that the system will be down roughly five minutes per year. This means that you have five minutes per year to install patches, run system maintenance, install upgrades, replace failed hardware, and reboot the system. That's a heck of a trick. The only way you can manage this kind of uptime is to eliminate a few tasks. Many administrators do not bother with any patch installations citing a company expectation that servers are to run 24 hours a day, 7 days a week. However over time, a server that has not been patched, updated, or maintained faces the risk of having a security flaw exploited by a virus or worm, or a lack of hardware or operating system maintenance can cause a system to fail due to system errors.

Although a good portion of downtime can be eliminated by technologies such as clustering or load balancing, ask yourself if it's worth the expense just to avoid a little planned downtime. Maintenance of a clustered server adds several levels of complexity to the equation and you want to avoid unnecessary complexity.

## BEST PRACTICE

### What Does Clustering Actually Accomplish?

Some companies try to eliminate maintenance windows through technologies like clustering. A *cluster* consists of two or more servers that are providing a specific service and share a common source of data. By performing maintenance, such as an application patch, on the passive node first, there is no interruption in service. By failing the service over to the upgraded node, the unpatched node becomes the passive node and then the active node can then be patched. This is fine for patch management but it doesn't address data integrity. If you never take the cluster down to perform an integrity check of the shared data, you are still vulnerable to a failure due to corruption of the data. One could argue that by mirroring the data and then "breaking" the mirror, an integrity check could be performed offline. Although this is true, if inconsistencies are found in the data, the cluster would still have to be taken down to fix the inconsistency.

## The Importance of Maintenance Windows

The secret to system uptime is to correctly define it as planned uptime. This means that the system can be down for predetermined amounts of time on a specific maintenance schedule. This also means that employees can plan for these events. A four-hour block once a month is pretty standard for a maintenance window. This gives you plenty of time to test patches, plan capacity changes, and let those developers know that their plan to replicate the code safe across the VPN falls right in the middle of your firewall reboots long before you get to the actual event.

It is critical to have managers agree to the concept of a maintenance window. If you cannot make them understand the value of planned downtime they will often first have to feel the sting of unplanned downtime. Make sure managers understand that things like security patches, capacity upgrades, and directory integrity are key factors in the stability of the network and therefore in the productivity of employees.

## Maintenance in a High Availability Environment

If you are operating under Service Level Agreements that do not allow for extended maintenance windows, you must be clever in the ways that you perform maintenance. Technologies like clustering and load balancing can avoid some of the downtimes associated with maintenance but at the cost of complexity and resources.

If you support a Web farm, you likely have a large number of servers that are providing the same service. By removing a Web server from a load-balancing group you can bring the server offline without affecting the end users. This assumes that you have an N+1 environment where you can take away a server without affecting the capacity of the load-balanced group. This will allow you to update patches and perform other intrusive system maintenance tasks without service interruption. You would then return the system to the farm and add it back to the load-balanced group. You would then repeat the task for the remaining systems in the group one at a time.

A similar situation can exist in an IT environment for file servers. If the files must be accessible at all times, you would normally not be able to take a file server down for maintenance. By using a technology like Distributed File System, you can abstract the file structure such that the end users are connecting to a virtual server that is comprised of links to real servers and real file shares. By doing this, you could migrate data and shares from one server to another and free up the original server of its file sharing responsibilities. This would allow you to perform the intrusive system maintenance tasks that would require reboots or extended downtime. When those tasks are completed the data could be migrated back to the system and the links redirected back to the original shares on that server. This would allow you to maintain the file servers without interruption to the end users. By using replicas of the shared data on multiple systems you wouldn't even have to perform the migration of data. Users connecting to a DFS share that was no longer available on the primary server would simply connect to a replica on a secondary server.

Database maintenance is where the whole process becomes a lot trickier. Technologies exist to mount the mirror of a database to run maintenance while the other instance of the database stores the logs so that they can be later committed to the offline database to make it current. This process is beyond the scope of this chapter and is covered in Chapter 22 "Creating a Fault-Tolerant Environment." Suffice it to say that the process is much easier and cheaper if you can enforce a maintenance window for any and all databases.

# Automating Updates

Microsoft provides a free server utility application called Software Update Service that helps with automating updates on servers and desktop systems. This product is designed to supplement the Windows Update Service by allowing you to cache updates and patches locally and authorize their local machine to update from this source. This not only reduces bandwidth consumption but it allows you a greater degree of control about when a patch can be installed. This is available as a standalone product or as a plug in to Systems Management Server 2.0.

## Software Update Service Tuning: Using NTFS Permissions and Machine Groups

By default a patch can only be "globally" allowed or disallowed. This means that after you authorize a given patch, any and all systems that attach to the SUS system will apply the patch. An easy way to add a level of filtering is to create groups of machine accounts for particular types of servers. You might create a "SQL Servers" group and add the SQL servers to it. Then you could take advantage of NTFS permissions on a patch file and only allow SQL Servers to apply the patch. This would prevent Web Servers from installing SQL patches unnecessarily. This process requires that you perform a bit of research on the intent of each patch being released by Microsoft but that process should already be occurring in the test lab. After a patch is deemed stable for the network you would assign the group permissions and then authorize the update.

## Using SUS with Systems Management Server

The Software Update Service is also available as an add-in for SMS 2.0. This version has greatly enhanced functionality. Instead of being limited to Windows 200x systems and Windows XP it extends support back to Windows NT 4.0 SP4. It also leverages the SMS environment to integrate logging and reporting as well as throttled replication. Perhaps the greatest benefit is the ability to leverage the system profiling performed by SMS. You could literally authorize a patch for any system running SQL 7.0 SP2 that also has a Web Server running but doesn't have FTP running. This allows for tremendous control of patch distribution and an amazing degree of reporting and auditing.

## Enabling SUS with Group Policy Objects

Although usage of SUS can be configured in a manual manner, a clever administrator can take advantage of Group Policy Objects (GPOs) to configure systems to use the SUS server. You shouldn't limit yourself to using SUS only on servers. SUS is an excellent way to ensure that desktops are kept up-to-date on patches and security fixes as well. To configure a GPO to point clients to an SUS server follow these steps:

1. Download the WUAU.adm template from Microsoft.

2. Click Start, and then click Run.

3. Type **GPEDIT.msc** to load the Group Policy snap-in.

4. Under Computer Configuration, right-click Administrative Templates.

5. Click Add/Remove Templates, and then click Add.

6. Enter the name of the Automatic Updates ADM file: %windir%\inf\WUAU.adm.

7. Click Open, and then click Close to load the wuau.adm file.

In the GPO editor choose Computer Configuration, Administrative Templates, Windows Components, Windows Update. There are two options that need to be configured:

- Configure Automatic Updates
- Specify Intranet Microsoft Update Service Location

By setting these two parameters you can configure hosts to contact a specified SUS server for their updates.

# Summary

This chapter has touched on a large number of concepts. You learned that the key to keeping your systems up is taking them down to perform regular maintenance and to apply security and application patches that have been tested in the lab. You learned that you need to have regular maintenance windows to ensure that you have time to perform needed upgrades and updates. You learned that by having these regularly scheduled windows you are able to accurately set expectation for management and the end-user community about the availability of the systems. This in turn enables you to post strong uptime numbers. By having management buy in on Service Level Agreements, you are able to justify your maintenance tasks and the manpower needed to accomplish them.

You saw that most maintenance tasks can be automated. Scripting can't replace a qualified technical resource for performing maintenance and for observing the effects on the system but they do allow you to remove the potential for human error and ensure that procedures are carried out exactly the same way every time. You saw that common GUI interfaces you use daily for tasks can often be accessed from a command line and be used in automated scripts.

Careful choices of files that get backed up and the usage of clever backup technologies can greatly simplify the task of backing up and restoring data.

By keeping checklists of tasks performed you are able to accurately audit the history of a system and spot trends in resource usage. This enables you to plan for the future rather than always exist in a reactive mode. By performing these tasks on a regular schedule, you become intimately familiar with your systems and can easy spot potential problems. These are the marks of a professional IT organization.

# PART III

## Design and Implementation Solutions

# 10

# Advanced Active Directory Design

Implementing Active Directory is a fairly straightforward task. Just install Windows 2003, tell the Configure Your Computer Wizard that you want to be a domain controller and vòila! You have Active Directory. Although technically this is true, if administrators were to do this, they'd quickly find themselves unhappy with the environment they created. There is no single best way to implement Active Directory. A properly designed Active Directory takes into account the business requirements, the technical requirements, and the political requirements of a company and designs a structure that will support the current environment and allow for flexibility of growth. A design should never be complex simply for the sake of being complex. A wise administrator realizes that there is beauty in simplicity and that unneeded complexity only adds more work down the road.

This chapter examines some of the typical and atypical needs of companies and will show how Active Directory can be tailored to support those needs. The goal is to start simple and add complexity if and only if the situation requires it. Topics such as forest design, domain design, LDAP integration, site design, and domain controller placement will be discussed showing the pros and cons of various decisions to give administrators greater insight into planning their own Active Directory environments.

The safest rule for Active Directory design is to first gather all the major players in the company and get them to agree to a list of goals for the implementation. After you have reached a consensus from everyone on the core goals they can serve as a focal point for decisions. When there is dissention among the ranks on a decision, you can always go back to the core goals for the project and see which decision supports those goals.

# Implementations Small and Large

There are many decision points that are common to both large and small environments that are moving to Active Directory. The simplest one to start with is determining if one is happy with the current domain design. A move to Active Directory is a perfect opportunity to change the basic architecture of a network if the administrator is unhappy with the current one. If multiple resource domains were created out of necessity to delegate control to various administrative groups, those domains could be brought back into a single domain due to the ability to delegate administrative tasks within Active Directory. Environments with multiple trusts can be simplified by using transitive trusts within a single forest. Another key factor is the stability of the current environment. It is difficult to consider an in-place upgrade of an NT domain to Active Directory if the domain is unstable. The creation of a pristine forest would allow an administrator to move user and computer objects into Active Directory and leave behind a corrupted SAM database. The following sections will offer suggestions for designs for several different scenarios.

## Single Domain In-Place Upgrade

The simplest situation to design an Active Directory for is one in which the company is moving from a single NT domain. All user accounts and computer accounts exist in a single NT 4.0 domain, for example, CompanyABC. CompanyABC is a prime candidate for a single forest/single domain model. By performing an in-place upgrade on the domain all the objects are moved to Active Directory with their native SID in tact. This means that resources will not have to have new ACLs (Access Control Lists) applied to them. Resources such as users and computers could be placed into organizational units if there was a need to manage different groups of objects in different manners. For example, computer and user objects that were located in a separate physical location that had their own administrator might be placed into a specific OU so that administrative control of that OU could be delegated to that administrator. To delegate access in this manner, click Start, All Programs, Administrative Tools, Active Directory Users and Computers.

Within the Active Directory Users and Computers tool, expand the domain and right-click the OU that will have its administration delegated to another user or group. Choose Delegate Control and the Delegation of Control Wizard will start. Click Next and then add the user or group that will receive administrative control. Click Next and check the appropriate rights to be granted to the user or group over the OU. Click Next and then Finish and the rights will be applied.

Optionally, CompanyABC could have chosen to create a pristine Active Directory forest and migrate all the user and computer objects into the new domain. This would have the advantage of being a completely clean environment without the possibility of corrupt information from the prior domain moving forward.

To perform this type of an upgrade, the new forest would be built with a NetBIOS name other then CompanyABC. This would prevent name conflicts with the existing domain. A trust relationship would be established between the old and new domains. The new domain would have to be in Native Mode for the administrator to be able to use the Active Directory Migration Tool to move the objects. Promoting a domain to Native Mode is performed within the Active Directory Domains and Trusts menu. Choose Start, All Programs, Administrative Tools, Active Directory Domains and Trusts.

Right-click the domain in question and select Raise Domain Functional Level. Choose Windows Server 2003 as the functional level. Having this domain in Native Mode would not be an issue because there would be no NT 4.0 Backup Domain Controllers in a pristine Active Directory domain.

Using ADMT would allow you to migrate over the users, groups, and computers within the NT 4.0 domain. ADMT 2.0, which comes with Windows 2003, offers significant improvements over the version that shipped with Windows 2000. By placing an agent on the NT 4.0 domain, ADMT 2.0 is able to migrate the user's passwords along with their account information. This greatly simplifies the ability to perform a secure and transparent migration. ADMT will even rejoin the workstations to the new domain and remotely reboot them.

Users that are migrated in this way will have accounts with multiple SIDs. This is to ensure that their old and new identities still exist. This enables them to still access legacy resources that have not yet been migrated to the Active Directory domain. User accounts will have their friendly name listed from the old domain. This is to say that if connectivity to the old NT 4.0 domain is lost, the SID lookup of a user will fail. For example, resources that were ACLed to CompanyABC\habbate would show up as something like ?Account Unknown(S-1-5-32-547). Administrators should use GetSID and SubinACL to flip the SID listed in the ACLs to reflect the SID provided by Active Directory.

> **Numerous Tools Available**
>
> There are numerous tools available to modify SID information in NT 4.0. Domain SIDs can be forged using these tools. An environment that supports SID history from migrated accounts is susceptible to Elevation of Rights attacks from forged SID information placed in the SID History field of an account.

## Multiple Domains—Child

In NT 4.0, domains were viewed as security partitions. This is much less the case in Active Directory. Multiple domain models address basically two functions. Password policies can only be set at a domain level. If a company wants to enforce industry best practice security settings on account behavior and needs to support developers who need to never have to change passwords, multiple domains could accomplish this. The second issue that multiple domains address is political. Administrators who used to be domain administrators want to remain domain administrators. Although they could be granted full control over an OU and even block administration from above, many groups will insist that they have their own domain.

When a company decides on a multiple domain model, the biggest question that comes up is one of naming. Most administrators assume that AD domain naming must map directly to DNS domain structures. This actually isn't the case. Although it makes management easier and troubleshooting simpler, it is not an Active Directory requirement.

One primary consideration for a multiple domain model is integration with LDAP. If a company needs to support recursive LDAP queries, Active Directory must be configured with Child domains with a common parent. So CompanyABC might have CompanyABC.com as a parent domain that is nearly empty with only domain controllers in that domain with NA.CompanyABC.com, EU.CompanyABC.com, and AP.CompanyABC.com below it. These domains would serve North America, Europe, and Asia/Pacific, respectively. By having a parent domain anchoring them, they would be able to pass LDAP queries up and down the tree to find the information they need. They could each control their own DNS zones with forwarders back to DNS in CompanyABC.com while CompanyABC.com would hold the NS records that delegate control to each of the subdomains. Important to note is that all four domains share the same schema. A clever administrator would note that domain administrators of the child domains have no ability to modify the schema. This allows a corporate headquarters to maintain top level control of the forest and still give remote offices full control of their domains.

## Multiple Domains—Discontinuous

Another way to implement multiple domains is to make their namespace discontinuous. For example, AD.NA.CompanyABC.com, AD.EU.CompanyABC.com, and AD.AP.CompanyABC.com would be three distinct domains that have discontinuous namespace. Even if there were a CompanyABC.com domain that anchored the forest, the three domains would not be child domains. This situation can arise when a company is trying to match Active Directory to an existing DNS hierarchy. Although this is perfectly acceptable from an Active Directory point of view, it is important to point out that this will break recursive LDAP lookups. If a query made against a Domain Controller in AD.AP.CompanyABC.com and the answer lives on a Domain Controller in AD.NA.CompanyABC.com, the answer will not be found. The LDAP query would have to ask each domain individually. Global Catalog queries would still be able to span the discontinuous domain. So although multiple domains are more administrative effort than a single domain, they do have their applications. Table 10.1 lists some advantages and disadvantages of implementing multiple domains.

**TABLE 10.1**

**Advantages and Disadvantages of Multiple Domains**

| Advantages | Disadvantages |
|---|---|
| Defined security boundaries for settings such as password requirements. | Increased administrative overhead from managing a number of domains. |
| Reduce domain controller database size. | Increased Global Catalog (GC) size. |
| Reduced File Replication System traffic. | Moving users from one domain to another is more administrative effort than moving them from one Organizational Unit (OU) to another. |

**TABLE 10.1**

**Continued**

| Advantages | Disadvantages |
|---|---|
| Reduced domain network traffic due to fewer changes that need to be replicated. | Increased GC replication due to increased number of domains. |
| Group policies, security, and delegation only have to be defined once. | Group policies, security, and delegation have to be defined in each domain. |
| Smaller impact if a domain suffers a failure. | Added cost of multiple domain controllers for each domain. |

## Consolidating Domains

Many companies are taking advantage of the capability to delegate administrative powers over an OU to replace legacy resource domains. This is to say that they are collapsing resource domains back into the account domain. The account domain is the logical domain to upgrade in place to Active Directory to avoid the need for SID history and to avoid having to modify ACLs on resources to eliminate the legacy SID information. The goal for this type of consolidation is to try to reduce the overall number of domains that are supported. This feeds back into the previous decision of single domain versus multiple domains. Although a company might have literally hundreds of resource domains and a few account domains, the resource domains can be collapsed back into the account domains, which are in turn collapsed into a simpler structure of either a single or a small number of child or discontinuous domains.

ADMT 2.0 offers numerous features that make domain consolidation simple. Perhaps the best feature is the capability to move users and only the groups to which users belong. This is a great way to eliminate unused groups. Member servers can be moved to another domain and be rebooted remotely so that no human interaction is required. Service accounts can also be migrated via ADMT so that if a server had services that were running under accounts from a resource domain, that account can be moved into the new domain and the service reconfigured automatically to run under the migrated account.

Migrating domain controllers is a slightly trickier task. The two most popular methods are to either retire the domain controller or to upgrade it to Windows 200x. If the domain controller did not host shares or applications that need to be migrated, it should simply be retired and the hardware redeployed. If the system holds resources that are still needed, an upgrade to Windows 200x allows you to use the DCPROMO utility to demote the server to a member server. Now ADMT can be used to migrate the server to the new domain.

**Always Get a Good System Backup First**

Although Microsoft doesn't provide any tools or utilities that can convert an NT 4.0 domain controller to a member server, numerous third-party software developers do. Products like uPromote can be run on a BDC or a PDC to make it an NT 4.0 member server. Although these utilities have been around for several years and used with good results, care should be taken in using them. Always get a good system backup first.

## Understanding Multiple Forests

One of the most unusual Active Directory designs is the use of multiple forests. Multiple forests in Windows 2000 were extremely restrictive in their ability to share resources between forests. The best way to think of a multiple forest design is to look at a forest that is anchored by a domain called CompanyABC.com that is built in a lab and think about its connectivity to Microsoft's internal Active Directory environment. CompanyABC.com has no ability to add Microsoft accounts to its ACLs and the reverse is true as well. CompanyABC.com administrators, although Schema Administrators, can't touch Microsoft's schema. Exchange servers in CompanyABC.com can't provide e-mail address information for Microsoft's users. For all intents and purposes, they are completely disparate and disconnected networks. Now place those two networks on the same LAN. Nothing changes; they are still completely disparate. Although at first this might seem somewhat useless, it does offer some characteristics that might be required by a company. The greatest offering of the multiple forest design is that each forest has its own schema. Schema administrators in one forest can't affect the schema in the other forest. This is a perfect situation for developers who are working on Active Directory applications in a development environment. If these developers needed access to the corporate forest, they would need separate accounts in the corporate forest. They would attach to the resources they need and be prompted for their login information in the target domain.

Windows 2003 has extended the functionality of forests by creating the concept of cross-forest trusts. Not unlike domain trusts of NT 4.0, this allows environments that were completely independent to share resources without sharing a common schema. This concept will be explained in greater detail in the section "Using Cross Forest Trusts Effectively" later in this chapter.

## Using a Placeholder Root Domain

Layered on top of the domain options discussed previously is the concept of the Placeholder Root Domain. A Placeholder Root Domain is the first domain created in a forest. It is built with a neutral name and it contains only domain controllers. As the anchor of the forest, it holds the schema along with the Enterprise Administrators group and the Schema Administrators group. The user domain would be built as a peer domain or a new domain tree in an existing forest. An example is the single domain model with CompanyABC.com being an in-place upgrade; the Placeholder Root would be built first to establish the forest and the CompanyABC NT 4.0 domain would be upgraded to CompanyABC.com as a new tree in the existing forest. This offers two very compelling benefits:

- *Forest Name Neutrality*. By giving the forest a generic name like Corp.root the forest is not tied to the identity of the company. If the company later wanted to rename or rebrand itself, it would be able to do so without having to rebuild the forest or live with the legacy name. Although renaming a domain is a fairly straightforward task, there is no mechanism to rename a forest.

- *Schema Isolation*. By placing the Schema Administrators group in a separate domain, administrators in the account domain have no capability to modify the schema. To perform schema modifications an administrator would have to log out of the normal use domain and log into the Corp.root domain. Because the Corp.root account would have no access to file shares or e-mail, the administrator would have no reason to stay logged in as the Schema Administrator account beyond the task of the schema modification. This drastically reduces the exposure of the Schema Administrator account. As viruses and Trojan Horses become more mature their most likely target in corporate environments will be the Active Directory schema. By preventing Domain Administrators from being to modify the schema the risk of accidental or malicious modification to the schema is greatly reduced.

A Placeholder Root Domain can be added to any of the scenarios mentioned here. The placeholder root gets built first to anchor the forest and an in-place upgrade would upgrade the domain as a domain in an existing forest.

> **For Redundancy...**
> it is recommended that the Placeholder Root Domain consist of three domain controllers. These domain controllers should be located at different physical locations if possible. Two should be configured as Global Catalog (GC) servers. The Domain Controller holding the Infrastructure Master FSMO role should not be configured as a GC.

# Configuring and Reconfiguring Domains and Organizational Units

Although it might seem that domains and OUs are fairly permanent objects, the truth of the matter is that objects can be moved pretty freely within a forest. Although this freedom is very valuable it should not be used as a crutch for a poor initial design. Moving objects around can drastically affect application of Group Policy Objects as well as make it difficult for other administrators to find objects that have been relocated. Moving objects to another domain could result in those objects no longer having a local domain controller and an increase in WAN traffic would result.

## Moving Objects Between Domains

In an environment with multiple domains there will invariably be situations in which you need or want to move objects from one domain to another. This might be due to domain consolidation or reorganization within the company. Windows 2003 provides a tool for this function called MoveTree. MoveTree.exe is a command-line utility that enables you to move Active Directory objects such as organizational units, users, or groups between domains in a single forest. Although MoveTree can move Active Directory objects between domains, not all objects can be moved in this manner. Potentially, there might be associated data such as profiles or login scripts that are not moved. Computer objects are not moved during a MoveTree operation; they require the use of the Active Directory Migration Tool (ADMT). Not unlike ADMT, MoveTree requires that the target domain be in Native mode.

When objects are moved via MoveTree, they are first copied to the Lost and Found container in the source domain and then they are moved to the destination domain. A file named MoveTree.log tracks all objects that are moved. This file also contains all error messages that are recorded during the move. Objects that cannot be moved to the target domain remain in an orphan container in the Lost and Found container of the source domain. Domain global and local groups cannot be moved during a MoveTree operation. However, group memberships remain intact so that security is not compromised.

Usage of the MoveTree utility is as follows:

```
MoveTree /start /s Server1 /d Server2 /sdn OU=SourceOU,DC=Dom1 /ddn OU=DestOU,DC=Dom2
/u Dom1\administrator /p *
```

The source and destination servers must be the RID masters for each domain. Otherwise an error will be logged stating "`ERROR: 0x2012 The requested operation could not be performed because the directory service is not the master for that type of operation.`"

In the case of moving organizational units to another domain, you should be aware that although the GPO link moves with the OU and continues to function, the GPO is actually linked to the source domain. This can result in a degradation of performance. It is strongly recommended that the GPO either be re-created or exported via the Group Policy Management Console and imported into the target domain.

## Moving Objects Between Organizational Units

Moving objects between Organizational Units is a simple way to keep a domain organized. Administrators are the only people in the network who can see OU structures, so administrators can build and modify OU structures without concern for how it will look to end users. Moving an object from one OU to another is as simple as right-clicking the object in Users and Computers and choosing Move. This will prompt you for the destination OU or container. Multiple objects can be moved at the same time.

Because OUs are often used to delegate control of objects and for the application of GPOs, you should be aware of the implications of moving objects. Objects that had explicit permissions assigned directly to them will retain those permissions after the move. Permissions that were inherited from the previous container or OU will no longer affect the object. The object will inherit permissions set on the new OU or container.

# Sites and the New Knowledge Consistency Checker

The Knowledge Consistency Checker and the Inter-Site Topology generator work together to determine the most efficient way to replicate information across the forest and within sites. These programs determine replication paths for both Active Directory replications and file replication. When a forest is upgraded to the Windows Server 2003 functional level, the new Windows Server 2003 spanning tree algorithm is enabled. This updated algorithm allows for improvements in both efficiency and scalability. For example, Windows 2000 spanning tree algorithm allowed one domain to contain up to 300 sites. The new Windows Server 2003 algorithm allows one domain to have up to 3,000 sites. The Windows Server 2003 algorithm uses a randomized selection process for bridgehead server selection via the inter-site topology generator. This process allows for more evenly distributed bridgehead replication workload among domain controllers in a site. The result is improved efficiency that only gets better as additional domain controllers are added to a site. The default behavior is for this randomized selection process to occur only when new connection objects are created in a site. Optionally, a Windows Resource Kit tool, called adlb.exe, can be run to redistribute the load each time changes occur in the topology or when the number of domain controllers in the site changes. In addition, adlb.exe can stagger the replication schedules so that the outbound replication load for each server is spread out more evenly across time.

## Summarizing Sites

In Active Directory, a site is a group of computers that are connected by 10MB or faster connections. The easiest way to look at this is any LAN separated by a WAN link is more often than not a site. Sites and subnets are used by Active Directory to find the "closest" object of a particular type. This could be a printer, a DFS replica or a domain controller. In some environments, it is not necessary to follow the strict definition of sites. If a site will never have a domain controller it will always be adopted by another domain controller. As such, by summarizing sites you can ensure that certain locations are serviced by a particular domain controller. As the number of domains and sites grows it is harder and harder for the Knowledge Consistency Checker (KCC) to maintain the topology. By reducing the number of sites you can lower the load on the KCC and leverage it longer as the environment grows.

As an example, let's say that CompanyABC has 40 small sites in Japan and 50 small sites in the United States. Each site consists of a single subnet. The largest office in Japan is in Tokyo. It has a pair of domain controllers. The largest site in the U.S. is in San Jose. It has two domain controllers as well. The two choices would be to either create 90 sites, 90 subnets, and 90 site links or create two sites, 90 subnets, and two site links.

If all 90 sites were defined, the KCC would process site link costs for all 90 site links to determine which Domain Controllers should adopt which sites. DNS would hold site records for all 90 sites to list _gc, _ldap, and _kerberos SRV records. If the Domain Controllers in Tokyo happened to be busy when the KCC was processing links, sites in Japan could be adopted by the DCs in San Jose and WAN traffic would increase as authentication, login scripts, and GPO application happened across the WAN.

If, on the other hand, the sites were summarized into only two sites, each holding the appropriate subnets, the KCC would perform much less work and sites could not be adopted by the wrong domain controllers as they would have local domain controllers. The DNS structure would be greatly simplified and administrative tasks would be reduced.

### Simplification of Site Management via Site Summarization Could Backfire

The simplification of site management via site summarization could backfire if you plan to implement distributed technologies that are based on Active Directory sites. SMS 2003 is an example of this. If each location were to get its own distribution server, which was previously managed by SMS Sites in SMS 2.0, and if the sites were summarized into two sites, there would be a very good chance that client machines would go to the wrong distribution server; their local site would not exist in SMS 2003. SMS 2003 eliminates its own Site database and leverages the Sites and Subnets area of Active Directory.

## Site Adoption

Site adoption occurs when a site is defined and it contains no domain controllers. Messages will appear in the event viewer such as "Site 'siteB' does not have any Domain Controllers for domain 'CompanyABC'. Domain Controllers in site 'closest_site' have been automatically selected to cover site 'siteB' for domain 'CompanyABC' based on configured Directory Server replication costs.". At the same time, the _sites records in DNS will populate with the new site and records pointing to the DCs in the site that adopted the site in question.

The Directory Server replication cost refers to the cost associated with the site links traversed to get from one site to another. These values default to a cost of 100 but can be manually configured to further control site adoption. This can be especially useful with multihub and spoke replication topologies where you want everyone's second choice of DCs to be a particular site.

To set the cost on a site link follow these steps:

1. Choose Start, All Programs, Administrative Tools, Active Directory Sites and Services.

2. Expand Sites.

3. Expand Intersite Transports.

4. Click IP and right-click the site link in the right column.

5. Select Properties.

The cost of the site link and the replication schedule can be modified here.

## Controlling Site Authentication Using DNS

Another way to control authentication for a particular site via a specific domain controller or group of domain controllers is through DNS. By maintaining DNS manually, specific records can be placed in _dc/_sites/_site in question/_tcp for the following:

- _kerberos SRV

- _ldap SRV

**Use Manual Control of DNS as a Last Resort**

Although disabling dynamic updates to DNS gives you greater control over DNS it also results in greatly increased administration of DNS. You should use manual control of DNS as a last resort to control authentication choices of hosts.

This forces the hosts in the site to always use a particular DC as their first choice for authentication. This can be useful if local DCs are to be dedicated to an application that places a very high load on the DC for either authentication or LDAP queries. To enable manual control of DNS, simply disable dynamic updates on the DNS zone. If the DNS is Windows 2003 DNS this can be accomplished by the following:

1. Choose Start, All Programs, Administrative Tools, DNS.

2. Expand the DNS server.

3. Expand Forward Lookup Zones.

4. Right-click the zone for which dynamics updates are to be disabled and click Properties.

5. In the drop-down menu for Dynamic Updates, change the dynamic updates option to None.

6. Click OK to finish and close the Properties dialog.

# Using Cross-Forest Trusts Effectively

Windows 2003 introduced two new concepts in the use of forests; cross-forest authorization and cross-forest authentication. Cross-forest authentication allows users secure access to resources in another forest. This feature enables users to securely access resources in other forests, using either NTLM or Kerberos. This allows access without sacrificing single sign-on or the benefits of having a single user ID and password maintained in the user's home forest. Cross-forest authorization allows you to select users and groups from trusted forests for use in local groups or ACLs. This is a similar concept to domain trusts that were used in NT 4.0 domains. This feature retains the forest's role as a security partition while still allowing trust between forests. It allows the trusting forest to enforce restrictions on what security identifiers (SIDs) will be accepted when users from trusted forests attempt to access protected resources.

To create a cross forest trust, perform the following steps:

1. Choose Start, All Programs, Administrative Tools, Active Directory Domains and Trusts.

2. Right-click the domain for which you want to establish the trust and select Properties.

3. Click the Trusts tab and click New Trust. This will launch the New Trust Wizard. Click Next.

4. At the prompt shown in Figure 10.1, type the name of the domain, forest, or Kerberos realm for this trust. Because this will be a forest trust, enter a fully qualified domain name (FQDN) and click Next.

5. Select the appropriate trust type, in this case, Trust with a Windows Domain. Click Next.

6. When prompted with the screen shown in Figure 10.2, select the direction for the trust and click Next.

7. Choose whether to create the trust on one or both sides. Click Next. This will depend on your rights in the other forest.

**Caution Should Be Exercised in the Use of Cross-Forest Trusts**

Although the capability to restrict usage of cross-forest authorization reduces exposure to potential elevation of rights attacks through SID history from a trusted forest, the potential for intrusion is not eliminated. Administrators don't have complete knowledge of security practices of administrators of other forests. Caution should be exercised in the use of cross-forest trusts.

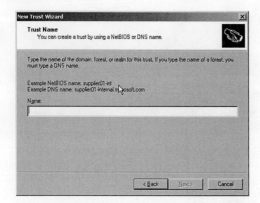

**FIGURE 10.1**    Enter the trust name.

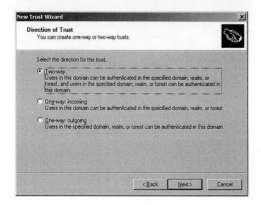

**FIGURE 10.2**    Choosing the trust direction.

8.  Choose domainwide or selective authentication when prompted with a screen similar to the one shown in Figure 10.3. Click Next. This will determine if some or all resources will be made available.

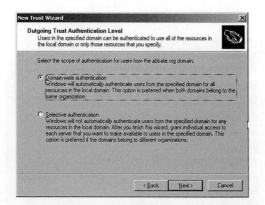

**FIGURE 10.3**    Setting the authentication level.

9. Input the appropriate trust passwords. Click Next.

10. This completes the trust creation. Click Next, Next, confirm the trust, Next, Next, and then Finish.

## Account/Resource Forests

With the ability to now support trusts between forests, many previously unavailable Active Directory architectures become available. Forests can be built to support a single Active Directory–aware application. Schema changes to that application would be independent of the schema supporting the account forest. Resource forests could be brought up to allow developers or QA groups to work in environments that look identical to production without the fear of changes to the schema affecting production users.

## Company Acquisition

Back in the days of NT 4.0 domains, company mergers or acquisitions were fairly easy to handle from a domain point of view. With the simple creation of a trust, resources could be ACLed with user information from the other company. When Windows 2000 and Active Directory came along, this scenario became a lot more challenging. Now with Windows 2003 and the support for cross-forest trusts, the fairly simple days of granting access to a resource via a trust have returned.

Although a cross-forest trust should not be considered a long-term solution for company acquisition or mergers, it is an excellent tool to get immediate access to resources. Companies in this situation should look back to their original Active Directory design and make determinations as to how best to integrate the new resources; either as a new domain in the forest or collapsing them into a single domain potentially as an OU. If the requirements of the partner are sufficient to warrant a separate forest, the trust could be maintained long term.

# Interforest Synchronization

Having the capability to connect forests via trusts makes an administrator realize that there were things that were taken for granted in a single forest model. Address lists for Exchange don't automatically list all the users in the other forests. Applications that fed their own databases from Active Directory won't automatically know about the objects in the other forest either. Additional tools will be needed to keep these multiple directories in sync.

## Using GALSync to Do Directory Synchronizations

The new version of Microsoft Metadirectory Services, 3.0, now called Microsoft Identity Integration Server, contains a simplified method for keeping the Global Address Lists of multiple forests in sync. GALSync replicates e-mail–specific attributes of user objects and distribution groups between forests to maintain a homogenized view of mail users from multiple forests.

## Microsoft Identity Information Services

Microsoft Identity Information Services offers significant flexibility in replicating identity data between forests. Any attributes on any objects in the Active Directory can be replicated to another forest or most any other foreign directory.

# Active Directory Migration Tool Best Practices

Active Directory Migration Tool (ADMT) is a simple and free way to move objects into an Active Directory. ADMT enables you to move users into a new domain without breaking access to their files in the old domain. ADMT can automate the process of moving multiple computer objects into a new domain. ADMT will even go as far as to remotely reboot the computers if you want. Depending on the situation in which it is used, there are many tricks to making ADMT work its best and many security implications that must be understood.

## Using ADMT to Migrate Resources

ADMT version 2.0 offers the capability to migrate passwords along with the users. This feature was unavailable in version 1.0. To migrate the password, you must also set up the Password Export Server. Follow these steps:

1. Create a key that encrypts the password list.

2. Run ADMT.exe from the command line using the key option. The syntax for this command is `ADMT.exe key Source_Domain_Name folder: [Password]`.

3. Set the value of the AllowPasswordExport Registry entry (located in HKLM\SYSTEM\CurrentControlSet\Control\Lsa on the PES) to 1. You can disable a PES from supporting password migration by setting the value to 0.

4. Add the Everyone group to the Pre-Windows 2000 Compatible Access group on the target domain. This will prevent ADMT from logging an Access Denied error.

5. In the Active Directory Users and Computers snap-in, verify that permissions on the PES server object are set to allow the Pre-Windows 2000 Compatible Access group to Read All Properties on the following object:

   `CN=Server,CN=System,DC=<domain_name>`

6. If you are running ADMT on a server running Windows Server 2003, add ANONYMOUS LOGON to the Pre-Windows 2000 Compatible Access group on the target domain to prevent an Access Denied error.

This will allow the migrate password option in ADMT 2.0 to work properly.

Next you should install the pwdmig.exe password migrator.

After those are in place, the ADMT itself can be run. Simply select the wizard for the type of migration desired.

The Active Directory Migration Tool is covered in more depth in Chapter 14, "Migrating from Windows NT 4.0."

## Implications of SID History

SID History is a field stored in a user's account that references previous identities. SID History is a field used by the ADMT to allow newly migrated users to access previously accessible resources. In addition to the primary SID for an account, all previous SIDs for that account are stored as well.

When a user attempts to access a resource the system checks Access Control Lists on the resource and compares this to the SID value on the account trying to access the resource. If the SID has been granted access, the account will be able to use the resource. This is the standard behavior of Windows. SID history complicates this process slightly in that both the primary SID and the SID history are checked to see if they have rights. A clever administrator could use this feature to elevate their rights from a separate domain. ADMT checks to see if a SID already exists before it will migrate an account. If a domain were disconnected from the other domains and Global Catalogs, ADMT would not know that a SID was a duplicate. By creating accounts in an NT 4.0 domain an administrator could modify the domain SID prefix on the domain and generate accounts until a SID matched the SID of an administrator in another domain. NT 4.0 generates SIDs sequentially. This account could then be migrated into the administrator's domain via ADMT. The domain could then be reconnected to the rest of the forest and the newly migrated account would have a SID History entry that matched an administrator in another domain. This migrated account would have the same administrative privileges as the real administrator whose account was essentially cloned.

## Cleaning Up SID History

If a user object is moved via ADMT it keeps a History of previous SIDs. Administrators can protect their networks by not allowing accounts with SID history to access resources. Because many legitimate accounts will be migrated and have a SID history, it is necessary to be able to remove the SID history from the accounts after their old resources have new ACLs applied to them that reference the primary account SID. Microsoft offers a Visual Basic Script that is designed to do just this.

## Improvements in ADMT 2.0

Windows Server 2003 shipped with version 2.0 of the ADMT. This version offered several improvements over the version that came with Windows 2000. Perhaps the single most useful improvement is the ability to migrate the user's password along with the user object. This prevents confusion or insecurity by not requiring the user to learn a new password or resetting all passwords to be the same value. This function involves setting a permission on a Registry key on the PDC in the source domain and running an agent that gathers the passwords to move along with the account.

# Using Microsoft Metadirectory Services Effectively

When Active Directory designs encompass multiple forests or when the design has to account for mergers and acquisitions, the Microsoft Metadirectory Services (MMS) tool can be invaluable in keeping directories in synch. MMS, now called Microsoft Identity Integration Server 2003 (MIIS 2003), enables you to integrate and manage identity information across multiple directories. These directories can be different systems or platforms. MIIS 2003 adds functionality to Active Directory by providing enhanced interoperability capabilities. These capabilities include integration with a various identity repositories, synchronizing identity information across multiple systems, managing changes of identity information by automatically detecting updates and passing the changes across systems as well as managing passwords. Prudent use of MMS enables you to keep an entire enterprise of various directories in sync by managing them through a single authoritative source.

## Features of Microsoft Identity Integration Server

Microsoft Identity Integration Server 2003 (MIIS) was built with four primary features in mind; centralization of identity information, managing identity information, managing changes to identity information, and broad connectivity.

### Centralization of Identity Information

In most companies, identity information is stored in various data sources. This can and usually does result in the duplication of identity information. Data stored in incompatible formats requires you to have access to multiple connected data sources, often with multiple clients.

To solve these issues, MIIS 2003 can do the following:

- Combine the data for a specific object in the metadirectory, creating a single entry that contains all or some subset of the identity information from each separate data source.

- Present a single, unified view of some or all of the attributes from the separate data sources even if the connected data sources are incompatible.

- Provide a single authoritative location from which administrators, users, or even applications can read or manage the identity information for a given object.

### Managing Identity Information

Disparate directories usually contain dissimilar identity information on the same person or resource. Invariably, the group that owns and manages the data in a specific data source believes that its data is accurate and authoritative compared to similar data that is owned and managed by another group. In these cases, identity data owners are often opposed to relinquishing control of the data.

To solve the issues resulting from conflicting identity information, MIIS 2003 can do the following:

- Manage the flow of data between identity information stores to resolve conflicts in identity data throughout the enterprise.

- Determine what identity data should be imported from each data source.

- Create rules to determine which identity data store contains the authoritative value for a specific attribute in the metadirectory and pass that authoritative value to other data stores.

## Managing Changes to Identity Information

An organization's identity data is often located in different data sources. As such, a change made to data in one source is not automatically made in the other data sources. Propagating the change throughout the enterprise often requires you to manually update the data in each information store. Failure to properly manage identity data can cause the data to become disorganized and out of synch across the enterprise.

To solve issues resulting from changes to identity data, MIIS 2003 can do the following:

- Determine when a change to identity data has occurred anywhere in the enterprise.

- Automatically propagate changes in identity data to all appropriate data sources.

- Ensure that enterprisewide updates to identity data are appropriate based on their authoritative source.

## Broad Connectivity

MIIS 2003 excels in the area of connectivity capabilities. MIIS 2003 ships with connectivity to most Network Operating Systems, e-mail systems, popular databases, directories, applications, and even flat-files.

MIIS 2003 ships with the "Management Agents" required to integrate with many various types of repositories, including the following:

- Microsoft Windows NT

- Active Directory

- Active Directory in Application Mode

- Novell eDirectory

- SunONE/iPlanet Directory

- X.500 systems

- Lotus Notes and Domino

- Microsoft Exchange 5.5

- PeopleSoft

- SAP

- ERP

- Telephone switches

- XML- and DSML-based systems

- Microsoft SQL Server

- Oracle

- IBM DB2

- Informix

- Sybase

- OLE/DB-based systems

- DSMLv2

- LDIF

- CSV

- Delimited or fixed width flat files

# Domain Controller Placement

One of the biggest questions in an Active Directory design session is on the placement of Domain Controllers. In NT 4.0 domain controllers were often used as a Band-Aid for poor network performance. By placing local backup domain controllers at every site, users were assured of having authentication and login scripts available in case of a WAN failure. Maintenance and management of remote domain controllers quickly became a major issue for large companies.

In Windows Server 2003 there have been great improvements in replication traffic, replication topologies, and the reduction of single master operations over NT 4.0. As such, many companies take the upgrade to Active Directory as an opportunity to reduce the number of domain controllers in the environment as well as to centralize them to reduce administrative costs.

## Replication Traffic Migrating from Windows NT 4.0 Versus Authentication Traffic

One of the most popular arguments in favor of domain controllers at each location is that of authentication traffic across the WAN. Most network administrators cringe at the thought of users authenticating across the WAN instead of locally. In reality, user authentication is only a few KB of data per authentication. Although domain controllers might not be local, login script locations can be.

In large companies, domain controllers can spend a lot of bandwidth replicating changes to objects that occur in other parts of the network. Users, on the other hand, rarely authenticate more then once per day. As such, it is not uncommon to see replication traffic take up more bandwidth then authentication traffic. Many companies have found that domain controllers placed in smaller sites that were intended to reduce bandwidth usage actually increased it. Removing those domain controllers freed up precious bandwidth.

A simple test is to enable monitoring on a WAN connection of a remote office and temporarily unplug its domain controllers. Their site will be adopted and another set of DCs will handle its authentication. Place a replica of login scripts on its local file server and make sure the users in that site point to that location for their scripts. If login scripts reference a DFS share, this will be unnecessary. Monitor the WAN connection for a day and compare it to the same day of the week from the previous week. This will provide the objective data needed to make a decision about the cut off point for the size of office that should maintain local domain controllers.

## Determining the Value of Local Domain Controllers

One of the most important considerations when looking at removing domain controllers from a site is determining exactly what the benefits are of having a local domain controller. Although being able to authenticate seems like a requirement for a site, if there are no resources locally that would be accessed via a local authentication, there is only minimal benefit. If all resources are remote and the domain controllers are also located remotely, a failure of the WAN would make local domain controllers pointless. If an office has local resources, most users could still access the resources via locally cached credentials if there was a WAN failure and no local domain controllers. These types of scenarios must be considered to determine if local domain controllers would add value to a site.

## Spending on WAN Connectivity Versus Domain Controllers

In many situations WAN traffic is more about replication than it is about authentication. But it is still important that client computers are able to reach domain controllers. If there is a WAN failure and there are no local domain controllers, users will only be able to reach resources for which they have cached credentials. But if there are local domain controllers, the users in the location are still limited to accessing only the local resources. In this type of situation it is often better to spend your budget on redundant network connections as opposed to spending the money on additional domain controllers. The redundant WAN links will not only ensure the users within a site will be able to authenticate properly with an available domain controller, but it will improve the users' connectivity to resources throughout the enterprise.

Many companies have literally removed all domain controllers from all remote sites and placed a much lower number of domain controllers in a central location. In this way, all the domain controllers are centrally located and centrally managed. Additional domain controllers are placed in a recovery site with connectivity between the two primary locations. Remote sites are given WAN connections to both locations for redundancy. The result has been improved overall performance and reliability along with a significant reduction in costs for managing the remote systems.

# Global Catalog Placement

Paralleling the question of where to place the domain controllers is the question of which domain controllers should be the main global catalog servers. The typical rule of thumb is that each site that has domain controllers should have at least one Global Catalog.

## What Does the Global Catalog Do?

A global catalog is a kind of index for Active Directory. Every directory object in the entire enterprise is represented in the global catalog, but only a subset of the properties of each object is stored in the catalog. The properties stored for each object are those most likely to be used as search attributes, such as the user's first or last name. You can specify storing additional object attributes in the catalog if desired. Having the global catalog store only a subset of an object's attributes in Active Directory improves the performance of search queries against Active Directory.

## GC Replication Traffic Versus Lookup Traffic

Any changes in Active Directory will show up on the Global Catalog servers when Active Directory replication occurs. Because this is only a subset of the entire Active Directory, replication traffic will be relatively light. This load will increase with the number of domains because Global Catalogs contain objects from all domains in the forest. As such, Global Catalog placement in a forest with a low number of domains can benefit from mirroring Domain Controller placement.

## Determining the Impact of Global Catalog Failure

When a user authenticates against an Active Directory domain controller, the domain controller must be able to contact a global catalog to determine if the user is a member of any universal groups. If a domain controller fails to contact a global catalog, the user's logon will fail. As such, if a domain controller is going to be placed in a remote site in order to ensure local access to local resources in an office where many users might not have locally caches credentials, it is important to make the domain controller a global catalog as well.

For extremely large sites, this additional global catalog traffic might be excessive if it must be placed on every domain controller in the enterprise to protect logons for remote sites. Optionally, you can disable this requirement for contacting a global catalog in order to authenticate a user successfully. Doing the following disables this function:

> **Only Use This Feature If It Is Unavoidable**
> You should only use this feature if it is unavoidable to have local domain controllers that are not global catalogs. If this key is enabled and a user is a member of a universal group, if that universal group is denied access to a resource, the user might still be able to access the resource. This is because the key turns off enumeration of universal groups so the universal group SID will not be added to the user's token.

1. From the run command, launch Registry Editor (Regedt32.exe).

2. Drill down to the following key in the Registry:

   HKEY_LOCAL_MACHINE\System\ CurrentControlSet\Control\Lsa

3. On the Edit menu, click Add Key, and then add the Registry key IgnoreGCFailures. After adding the Registry key, the Registry Editor screen will look similar to Figure 10.4.

4. Exit the Registry Editor.

5. Restart the domain controller.

This will enable sites with local Domain Controllers that are not Global Catalogs to still authenticate users if a Global Catalog server is not available.

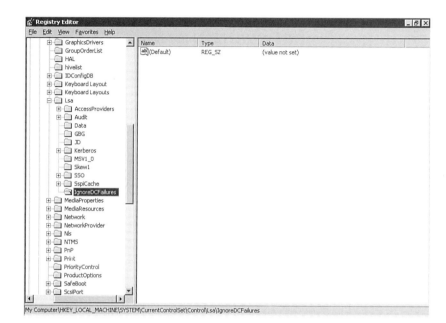

**FIGURE 10.4**
Adding the Registry key.

# Taking Advantage of Replication Improvements

Windows Server 2003 allows an Active Directory Architect more freedom in the placement of domain controllers across the enterprise. This is because Windows Server 2003 has improved the behavior of replication. At the most basic level, Windows Server 2003 has changed the model for replication. Windows 2000 Active Directory replicated changes object by object. Windows 2003 Active Directory takes this concept one step further by replicating changes attribute by attribute. The net result is an overall reduction in replication traffic.

## Benefits of Multi-Master Replication

One of the biggest differences between Active Directory and NT 4.0 is the introduction of multi-master domain controllers. This is to say that domain controllers all contain read/write copies of the account data. In NT 4.0, only the Primary domain controller was able to write to the SAM database. This meant that all Backup Domain Controllers had to get their SAM updates directly from the PDC. This hub and spoke replication resulted in large amounts of traffic, much of which had multiple conversations going across the same WAN connection. In Windows 2000 and 2003 Active Directory, domain controllers are able to determine their own replication topology and create meshed replication paths to make replication as efficient as possible. Rather then have all DCs in a site talk to the same DC for replication, a bridgehead server can replicate with a remote server and then replicate the same information locally among other domain controllers in the same site. This results in a significant decrease in domain controller replication traffic.

# Active Directory Functional Levels

Windows Server 2003 introduces a new concept called Active Directory Functional Levels. These levels occur at both a domain and forest level. Domain level functionality levels include the following:

- Windows 2000 mixed (default)—Allowing Windows NT 4.0, Windows 2000, and Windows Server 2003 domain controllers

- Windows 2000 native—Allowing Windows 2000 and Windows Server 2003 family domain controllers

- Windows Server 2003 interim—Allowing Windows NT 4.0 and Windows Server 2003 domain controllers

- Windows Server 2003—Allowing only Windows Server 2003 domain controllers

Forest level functionality levels include the following:

- Windows 2000 (default)—Allowing Windows NT 4.0, Windows 2000, and Windows Server 2003 domain controllers

- Windows Server 2003 interim—Allowing Windows NT 4.0 and Windows Server 2003 domain controllers

- Windows Server 2003—Allowing only Windows Server 2003 domain controllers

Some advantages of going to the Windows 2003 functionality level at the domain level are the capability to rename domain controllers without demoting them, support for time stamping of object logons, user passwords on InetOrgPerson objects, group nesting, and the capability to convert security groups to distribution groups.

At the forest level, Windows 2003 functionality level offers improvements in Global Catalog replication, the capability to deactivate schema classes, support for forest trusts, the capability to rename a domain, and improved Active Directory replication.

To raise the functionality level of a domain, follow these steps:

1. Open Active Directory Domains and Trusts.

2. In the console tree, right-click the domain for which you want to raise functionality, and then click Raise Domain Functional Level.

3. In Select an available domain functional level, do one of the following:

- Click Windows 2000 Native as shown in Figure 10.5, and then click Raise to raise the domain functional level to Windows 2000 native.

- Click Windows Server 2003, and then click Raise to raise domain functional level to Windows Server 2003.

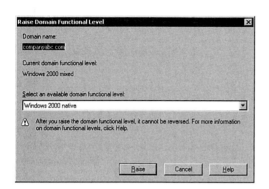

**FIGURE 10.5**    Raising domain functional level.

To raise the functionality level of a forest:

1. Open Active Directory Domains and Trusts.

2. In the console tree, right-click Active Directory Domains and Trusts and then click Raise Forest Functional Level.

3. In Select an Available Forest Functional Level, click Windows Server 2003, and then click Raise.

# Summary

This chapter has touched on many of the important design decisions that must be made to build a stable and scalable Active Directory. It has shown that companies have multiple options available to them and it has shown the importance of keeping the design as simple as possible. Each variation on the design offers additional flexibility but always at a cost of complexity. Complexity equals added management which increases cost of ownership. You must carefully weigh the costs of a design before embarking on a design that might prove difficult to manage.

You've seen that Windows 2003 has further improved in the area of Active Directory in terms of replication, security, and interoperability with foreign forests. These improvements make more complex designs more scalable and easier to support.

This chapter has touched on the benefits of Microsoft Identity Information Server and how it is able to tie multiple directories together to allow companies to better leverage their data stores.

New capabilities such as renaming domain controllers without demotion and renaming a domain give you powerful new tools for the management and rearchitecting of existing forests and domains.

You've also seen that the old philosophy of placing domain controllers at every location just isn't necessary anymore. Often times, investing the budget in WAN connectivity and redundancy will pay larger dividends.

Careful planning of the Active Directory is the easiest way to avoid problems down the road. A well thought out Active Directory is easy to scale and is flexible enough to accept change. Always take the opportunity to design a network the right way the first time. Be flexible in allowing changes but only if they meet a legitimate business need. Never let a change go undocumented. The original design should be a living document that captures the current state of the enterprise. As a map, it will be invaluable in assisting with any troubleshooting that might occur in the future.

# 11

# Implementing Microsoft Windows Server 2003

**W**ith each successive operating system release, Microsoft has traditionally made the installation process more intuitive and easier to perform. In keeping with that tradition, Windows Server 2003 is one of the easiest operating systems to install. Given some adequate hardware and install media, even novice system administrators will be able to build a Windows Server 2003 server with little effort. So, why dedicate a chapter to the subject? Well, in addition to making the install process a simple one, Microsoft has added a variety of ways to install its operating system that provides solutions to a myriad of real world business needs. It is important for the system administrator to be aware of the options available in order to streamline the process for deploying Windows Server 2003.

So, instead of simply providing instructions for installing Windows Server 2003 from the standard installation CD media, this chapter will cover more advanced deployment methods such as automation, customizing installs, licensing, and other best practices.

# Best Practices for Successful Server Deployments

This first section will detail some tried and true methods used to ensure a successful server deployment. Although this chapter is focused on installing Windows Server 2003, many of the tips provided here can serve as guidelines for any server installation in an enterprise environment.

Essentially, a successful server deployment strategy relies on three major components: planning, testing, and the actual execution or install.

## Planning the Deployment

Installing Windows Server 2003 is a fairly easy process, but without a solid plan, administrators might find themselves performing this easy process more than a few times before they get it right. Because there are so many options available when building a server, it is important to plan the installation process beforehand. A good server installation plan includes the following items:

- Verifying hardware requirements.

- Choosing to do a new install or an upgrade.

- Determining the server type.

- Gathering necessary information.

The first step in planning the installation involves verifying the intended target hardware meets the minimum system requirements. Keep in mind that in addition to minimum system requirements, there are recommended system requirements. It is always a best practice to stick with recommended (or better) hardware for servers. Table 11.1 lists the system recommendations for Windows Server 2003 Standard and Enterprise Editions.

**TABLE 11.1**

**System Requirements**

| Requirement | Standard Server | Enterprise Server |
|---|---|---|
| Minimum CPU Speed | 133MHz | 133MHz for x86-based computer<br>733MHz for Itanium-based computer |
| Recommended CPU Speed | 550MHz | 733MHz |
| Minimum RAM | 128MB | 128MB |
| Recommended RAM | 256MB | 256MB |
| Maximum RAM | 4GB | 32GB for x86-based computer<br>64GB for Itanium-based computer |
| Multiprocessor Support | Up to 4 | Up to 8 |
| Disk Space for Setup | 1.5GB | 1.5GB for x86-based computer<br>2.0GB for Itanium-based computer |

The next step in the planning process is deciding whether to do a clean install or an upgrade. Installing the server from scratch has the benefits of starting with a clean system from which change control can be tightly tracked. You can also take advantage of new hardware with a new installation. Even if the hardware is not new, the operating system will usually be installed on a freshly formatted hard drive, which has the benefit of removing old or possibly corrupt software.

Performing an upgrade also has advantages though. By performing an upgrade, existing users, settings, groups, rights, and permissions are kept intact. Depending on the requirements of the installation, preserving these settings might be mandatory and re-creating them on a new server would be an additional burden. Upgrading servers to Windows Server 2003 has its own requirements. These requirements can be found in Part IV, "Migration and Integration Solutions."

> ### Back Up the Existing Server
> If the install will be an upgrade, it is important to back up the existing server. This will provide a fallback plan if the installation fails. It is also important to verify that a backup can be restored.

> ### Creating a Domain Controller
> As with Windows 2000, creating a domain controller is accomplished through the promotion of a member server through the DCPromo tool.

The next planning requirement involves choosing the type of server to install. The new (or upgraded) server can be a domain controller, a member server, or a standalone server. Domain controllers play a role in a new or existing domain, whereas the standalone server is not joined to a domain.

Finally, there are pieces of information that the Windows Server 2003 setup process requires during the installation process that should be determined beforehand. These include the following:

- *Computer name.* Each computer on a network must have a unique name. It is valuable to follow a naming convention that limits server names to 15 characters or less. The characters should match Internet standards, which includes the letters A–Z (upper, and lowercase), the numbers 0–9, and the hyphen (-).

- *Workgroup or domain name.* If the server will be joined to the domain as part of the installation process, provide the domain name; otherwise, the server can be joined at a later time.

- *Network information.* When the server is installed, network information must be supplied in order for it to communicate with other machines on the network. If the TCP/IP protocol is installed, the server should be given a static or dynamic IP address.

## Testing the Deployment

Whenever possible, it is important to run through the deployment in a lab environment on non-critical systems. The test lab is an investment that can pay for itself many times over in reduced support and redeployment costs that arise from poorly tested solutions. Always be sure to test the server deployment in an environment that simulates, as well as protects, the production environment. Verify the functionality of the test server by devising and conducting tests that reflect the conditions of the production IT infrastructure.

The following is a list of stages that can be used as a general roadmap for your predeployment testing process. These steps can apply to a large-scale multiserver implementation, just as they can be applied to evaluating application compatibility with Windows Server 2003:

- Create a test plan that describes the scope, objectives, and methodology of the proposed change to the environment.

- Design test cases that describe how to conduct tests.

- Conduct the test and evaluate the results.

- Document test results.

- Escalate problems to the appropriate groups for resolution.

Throughout the testing stage, the following types of risks to the production environment might be identified and resolved before any business critical systems are affected:

- Hardware or software incompatibilities

- Design flaws

- Performance issues

- Interoperability difficulties

- Limited knowledge of new technologies

- Operational or deployment inefficiencies

## Executing the Deployment

Because most administrators planning to deploy Windows Server 2003 have installed Microsoft server operating systems in the past, it should not be necessary to do a step-by-step instruction here because the setup process has changed very little with this latest OS. Instead, this section will highlight some of the new options, and provide best practices for executing the setup process.

As with previous Windows operating systems, the first step in installing Windows Server 2003 involves creating and formatting the partitions. With Windows Server 2003, there are two additional options added to the familiar FAT or NTFS formatting options, as shown in Figure 11.1.

These two new options enable the administrator to do a quick format as opposed to a true full partition format. It is important to realize that a quick format, which can take up to 25 times faster to complete than a normal format, is only a high-level format of the disk. This means that the format is using tracks that a previous format has defined. Use this option only if the target system did not previously contain confidential information.

**FIGURE 11.1**
Options for formatting the Windows Server 2003 partition.

The recommended file system to use for Windows Server 2003 is NTFS. NTFS provides support for volumes as large as 16 terabytes (minus 4KB), with maximum file sizes of 16TB (minus 64KB). NTFS also provides file security, disk compression, encryption, and fault-tolerant disk configurations. The only scenarios in which the server should be installed on a FAT partition are the following:

- If the Windows Server 2003 system will be a dual-boot system with an operating system that does not support NTFS (such as Windows 95) is required.

- If the ability to boot to the server with a floppy disk (such as a DOS or Windows 95 boot disk) and access the files on the partition is required.

The remainder of the Windows Server 2003 setup process will be pretty familiar. The installer will be prompted for computer name, administrator password, date and time settings, and networking information. If the deployment process was well planned, these pieces of information should be readily available during the actual installation.

The only other piece of the install puzzle that might be new to you is the licensing and activation process. This topic will be covered in the next section.

# Licensing and Activating Windows Server 2003

As with earlier versions of Microsoft operating systems, the installation of a Windows Server 2003 server requires a product license key. The product key that is entered as part of the server installation depends on the type of license purchased. Depending on the type of license purchased, there might also be a process by which the operating system software must be activated in order to continue working past a grace period. This section will provide some help in determining licensing modes and activating Windows Server 2003.

## Providing a Product Key

For those who have installed a Windows 2000 server product, the product key is a familiar concept. Usually found on a label stuck to the back of retail CD media, the product key is a unique combination of numbers and letters that is used during the product installation to "unlock" or open the product.

There are two types of keys that can be used during the installation process:

■ *Retail Media Activation Key*. If the operating system software is purchased by a retail source, each key is unique to that specific installation of Windows Server 2003. Using this type of key will require the installer to activate the product after each installation.

■ *Volume Licensing Activation Key*. If the operating system is purchased as part of a Microsoft volume licensing program (such as Open, Select, or Subscription), a single key can be used to unlock all installations. Using this method also satisfies the activation requirement.

## Choosing a Licensing Mode

As with Windows NT and 2000, Windows Server 2003 can be licensed in either a Per Server or Per Device mode.

Choosing Per Server mode essentially means that the server will need to have enough client access licenses (CALs) purchased to support the maximum number of concurrent client connections to the server. If the number of concurrent connections exceeds the number of configured CALs, clients might be denied access to the server's resources. Choose Per Server mode for small organizations that only have a single server. This mode also makes sense for Web and Remote Access Service (RAS) servers where the maximum number of concurrent connections is configured. By setting the maximum number of concurrent connections, the licensing mode can be maintained.

**Choose Per Server**
If it is not clear which licensing mode to choose at the time of installation, choose Per Server. The licensing mode can be changed at a later time from Per Server to Per Device, but cannot be changed from Per Device to Per Server.

Choosing Per Device mode, on the other hand, means that a CAL is required for each client machine that accesses any licensed server. In this scenario, the licensed client machines are allowed to access any server within a Windows network. This is the common licensing mode because most companies have more than one server. A CAL is more costly than a Per Server license, but the client license buys access to an unlimited number of servers.

## Activating Windows Server 2003

If you install Windows Server 2003 from a retail media source, the operating system will need to be activated. Product activation takes place after the operating system is installed. The activation process can be initiated by either clicking the icon in the system tray that looks like a pair of keys, or by choosing Activate Windows from the Programs folder.

Windows Server 2003 can be activated over the Internet or by telephone. To activate over the Internet, select that option, and then click Next. An option to register the product with Microsoft is then provided. This step is optional and not required to activate the product. If the installer chooses to register at this time, the Collecting Registration Data screen will appear, as shown in Figure 11.2.

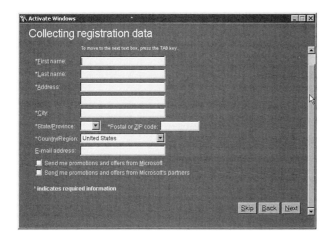

**FIGURE 11.2**
Windows registration data collection screen.

Fill out the required information and then click Next to continue. After connectivity to the Internet is verified, a window confirming the product activation is displayed. Click OK to finalize the process.

To activate Windows Server 2003 by telephone, select the option that reads: Yes, I Want to Telephone a Customer Service Representative to Activate Windows. Click Next to continue.

The wizard then generates a new installation and the Activate Windows screen shown in Figure 11.3 appears.

Providing a location exposes a phone number to call. After the customer representative is reached by phone, provide her with the new installation ID on the screen. The representative will then give a confirmation ID that can be entered in step 4. Entering the confirmation ID concludes the activation process.

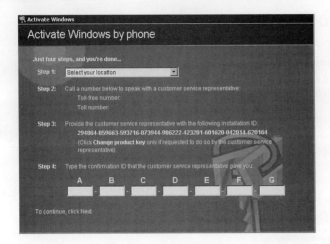

# Automating Deployment with Remote Installation Service

For those who have worked with Windows 2000 networks, Remote Installation Service (RIS) is a familiar Windows component used for creating and deploying on-demand desktop images. Though the desktop deployment features are still included, Windows Server 2003 now extends the functionality of RIS to include the ability to create on-demand server images for all versions of Windows 2000 and 32-bit versions of the Windows Server 2003 operating system.

> **RIS Is Not Included**
>
> RIS is not included in the Windows Server 2003, Web Edition operating system.

The primary benefits of using RIS for building Windows Server 2003 servers include the following:

- Rapid deployment of multiple servers. If an enterprise needs to deploy multiple servers that have similar hardware and software specifications, RIS can accelerate the deployment process that used to involve a manual install of one server at a time.

- Rapid recovery of mission critical servers. If a server is lost due to disaster, a RIS image of that lost server can be used to quickly build a replacement.

- Standardization of servers. For a company that manages many servers, having standard RIS server images in line with company policies and specifications takes the guesswork out of server configurations deployed across the enterprise.

## System Requirements for RIS

To take advantage of RIS, there are certain hardware and software system requirements that must be met. The following list describes the hardware requirements for building a RIS server:

- The server hardware must meet minimum requirements for the product version of the Windows Server 2003 family that is being imaged. For example, if you are installing Windows Server 2003, Enterprise Edition, your computer must meet the minimum requirements for this product.

- A minimum of 4GB of disk space is required for the RIS server folder tree. Because RIS images take up a great deal of space, it is recommended to dedicate an entire partition to the RIS folder tree.

- A 10 or 100Mb/sec Windows-compatible network adapter that supports TCP/IP (100Mb/sec recommended) is required. A RIS server cannot be a multihomed computer; that is, it can contain only one network adapter.

For the machine that will serve as the template, in other words, the machine from which an image will be taken, there are a couple of hardware requirements as well:

- As with the RIS server, this computer must meet the minimum requirements for the operating system that is to be installed.

- A Pre-Boot eXecution Environment (PXE) DHCP–based boot ROM version 1.00 or greater is required.

> **To Obtain a List of Network Adapters that RIS Supports...**
> run the Rbfg.exe utility that is installed with Remote Installation Service. This file can be found in \\server-name\reminst\admin\ i386\rbfg.exe.

The networking environment in which you install a RIS server must meet a few requirements as well. These requirements are listed here:

- There must be a DHCP server in the environment to assign addresses to machines being imaged. DHCP is also used to identify which RIS servers are available on the network.

- A DNS server is necessary in order to locate the directory service that will authenticate the client machines.

- Active Directory is required to set security parameters around the RIS process. Specifically, AD will restrict or control which RIS servers will respond to specific client requests for operating systems.

Finally, some additional considerations that are more software-based are needed when planning to use RIS. These include the following:

- RIS cannot be installed on the same partition as the system volume or boot volume.

- The volume on which RIS is installed must be formatted with NTFS.

- RIS does not support Encrypting File System (EFS).

- A Distributed File System (DFS) share cannot be used as a target for a RIS image. RIS can be installed, though, on a server running DFS.

Although there seems to be a rather long list of prerequisites to using RIS, most Windows Server 2003 environments will have all of the elements mentioned previously present already. As such, most companies would be able to add this service to their infrastructure quite easily with a single additional server with a good size data partition.

## Creating a Remote Installation Preparation Wizard (RIPrep) Image

There are two types of operating system images that can be used with RIS. The first type is a flat image, which is similar to using a CD install, only the installation files are located on a RIS server. The benefit of using a flat image type is that RIS supports flat images for all Windows 2000, XP, and Windows Server 2003 editions, including 64-bit editions.

> **Riprep Images Cannot Be Used for 64-Bit Versions of Windows Server 2003**
>
> RIPrep images cannot be used for 64-bit versions of Windows Server 2003 and cannot be used to create images of Windows 2000 if Internet Information Server (IIS) is installed.

The second type of RIS image is a Remote Installation Preparation Wizard (RIPrep) image. The RIPrep image type enables you to add application installations and other customizations to the image. RIPrep also uses the Plug and Play feature; therefore computers targeted with these images do not have to be exactly the same, though they do need to share the same Hardware Abstraction Layer (HAL). Because of this flexibility to customize the image, the RIPrep image has the most practical utility for most companies.

The remainder of this section will detail the process by which a RIPrep image is created. To install a RIPrep image of a Windows Server 2003, perform the following steps:

1. Install Windows Server 2003 on a computer that you will use to create the installation image. The operating system can be installed using either Remote Installation Services (RIS) or the product CD. Using RIS to do the install is the recommended practice.

2. Install any additional applications and modify the local configuration settings of the source Windows Server 2003 computer.

3. From the Run line, type the Universal Naming Convention (UNC) path of the RIPrep utility on the RIS server, for example: \\**Servername\RIS\reminst\Riprep.exe**, and then click OK.

4. Click Next at the Remote Installation Preparation Wizard welcome screen.

5. Type the name of the server to which the image will be copied, and then click Next. By default, this is the RIS server you typed in step 3.

> **Multiple Profiles on the Source Machine**
>
> At this point, a screen might appear indicating multiple profiles on the source machine, or services that are still running that should be stopped. See Figure 11.4 for an example of this screen. It is recommended to stop these services before proceeding.

6. Type the name of the folder to which to which the image will be copied, and then click Next.

7. Type the friendly description and the Help text, and then click Next. This information is displayed by the Client Installation Wizard when RIS clients request network services.

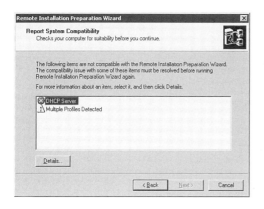

**FIGURE 11.4**
Running the RIPrep utility.

8. Click Next two more times to initiate the replication of the source machine image to the RIS server.

## Securing Server Images

RIS in Windows Server 2003 provides functionality for securing the imaging process of servers and desktops. RIS has an authorization feature that will prevent unauthorized RIS servers from making images available on an Active Directory network.

RIS can be used to specify which RIS servers can accept and process requests, and which RIS servers can only service clients on the network. Before a RIS server can accept requests, it must be authorized to run in Active Directory. To authorize a RIS server in Active Directory, run RISETUP –Check.

### Installer Must Be An Administrator

To run the RIPrep utility, the installer must be an administrator on the source machine and have permission to write to the RIS server data folder.

When the replication process completes, the source server will shut down.

When the source server starts up again, it will run a mini-setup.

### RISETUP Utility

The RISETUP utility must be run in the security context of an Enterprise Administrator to authorize a RIS server in Active Directory.

RIS also offers the capability to individually secure particular images. Using this feature allows flexibility on who is able to install the various images from the RIS server. For example, to limit access to install a Windows Server 2003 image from a RIS server to the Domain Admins group, the Authenticated Users group should be removed from the permissions on that particular image.

## Making the Most of the RIS Deployment Tool

RIS is a valuable deployment tool for companies that use it correctly. To gain the efficiency, security, and disaster recovery benefits of using RIS, consider the following best practices in designing and maintaining an enterprise RIS solution:

- Use the security features of RIS. Take advantage of both authorizing RIS servers in Active Directory and restricting access to RIPrep images. The PXE architecture on which RIS relies is inherently insecure. Without the RIS safeguards in place, there is little stopping a malicious user with a PXE-enabled network card from pulling images from a RIS server on the network. This is especially important with server images. Likewise, an intruder could set up a rogue RIS server that can interfere with a company's deployment plans.

- Install RIS servers appropriate to your network topology. For a small company located in a single subnet, a single RIS server can serve all PXE-related deployment needs. For distributed companies with sites connected over slow links, it makes sense to include RIS servers at the remote sites. Do not use RIS to deploy images over slow links.

- Install RIS on a physical disk separate from the disk that houses the operating system. Giving RIS its own physical hard drive will ensure optimal performance.

- Choose to create RIPrep images over RISetup flat images if capturing application installation and customizations in the image is desired. RIPrep can accommodate some differences in the hardware because it utilizes Plug and Play. Using RISetup with a scripted install can enable you to install to hardware that have different HALs.

- If your servers do not use PXE-enabled network cards, create boot disks using the rbfg.exe utility. The boot disks can be customized to access your RIS server images.

# Using Sysprep for Servers to Maximize Consistency

Another method of creating images for the deployment of Windows Server 2003 involves using the System Preparation tool or Sysprep. Sysprep is very similar to RIPrep in that it is an image preparation tool. Unlike RIPrep, though, Sysprep does not take advantage of RIS server management or deployment. Sysprep is used for standalone image preparation. After a Sysprep image is created from a template system, one of several third-party applications can be used to capture the image to a file for redeployment to other systems.

Sysprep was introduced with Windows 2000 with a purely command line interface intended for desktop image creation. Many updates were made to Sysprep when Windows XP was introduced, including a wizard-based setup manager, but it was still primarily a tool designed for preparing images for desktops. With Windows Server 2003, Microsoft has made Sysprep a supportable method for preparing server-based disk images.

## How Sysprep Works

As mentioned earlier, Sysprep is very similar to RIPrep. For example, both image types can include applications that might have already been installed on the image system, and the images can be customized before and after deployment of the image. Also, both image types require the same HAL for target systems. It follows from these similarities that the steps necessary to prepare a Sysprep server image are similar to creating a RIPrep server image. The following steps outline the process:

1. A template system is prepared by installing the operating system, installing applications, and customizing settings according to company specifications.

2. Sysprep is run on the computer, which then powers off.

> **HAL**
>
> HAL must be the same on the source and target systems for Sysprep to function. This is especially true when it comes to ACPI and non-ACPI computers. ACPI images cannot be deployed on non-ACPI systems, and non-ACPI images cannot be installed on ACPI systems.

3. Using a third-party tool, an image of the Sysprepped system is copied to a file server.

4. A new system is booted using a third-party tool, and the image is installed.

5. The new system is started and a mini-setup runs. The mini-setup is a pared down version of the full Windows setup.

6. The new system reboots and is ready to go.

There are some key differences between this process and the RIPrep process of which deployment administrators should be aware:

- Sysprep images cannot be deployed or managed with a RIS server. There are several third-party tools that can be used to capture the image. Xcopy can even be used to copy the system to a network share.

- Because RIS is not involved, Active Directory is not required. Sysprep can be used to create Windows Server 2003 images in an environment that does not have AD.

- A mini-setup is run when the newly imaged system is powered on. The mini-setup only prompts for information necessary to make the installation unique again, such as computer name, network configuration, or domain membership. The mini-setup can be completely automated by creating an .inf answer file. With RIPrep, there is a longer setup process for RIS imaged systems.

## Taking Advantage of New Sysprep Features

In addition to enabling Sysprep to support server images, Microsoft has further enhanced the tool for Windows Server 2003.

The new Sysprep can image a fully configured server with Internet Information Server (IIS) installed. For companies that support several Web servers, this would be a key deployment option.

Sysprep has a new mode of operation called Factory. By running Sysprep with a `-factory` switch, updated or out-of-the box drivers will be picked up by the image before the system is fully set up.

In conjunction with the Factory mode of operation, Sysprep can include an answer file, winbom.ini, that goes beyond driver installation and can actually gather and install applications from a network share at install time. This feature enables you to use a smaller image for deployment, with applications installing automatically from the network.

> **winbom.ini, Not sysprep.inf**
>
> The answer file for running Sysprep in factory mode is winbom.ini, not sysprep.inf. Setup Manager can be used to create either of these files.

Finally, the -PnP switch commonly used with Windows 2000 systems is no longer necessary. Because the Plug and Play functionality in Windows XP and Windows Server 2003 is dramatically improved, getting an image to work on systems with different hardware components is a lot easier.

# Customizing Setup Using Unattend and Setup Manager

> **Answer File Name**
>
> Although the answer file for Setup is commonly called Unattend.txt, for a network preinstallation the filename can be whatever you choose. For a CD-based Setup, the answer file must be named Winnt.sif.

Another tried and true method for automating the deployment of Windows operating systems is the use of the unattend.txt answer file. An answer file is simply a text file that answers the questions one would normally have to enter manually during the installation process. In this way, unattend.txt is like sysprep.inf. The unattend.txt is the answer file for the setup.exe file of Windows operating systems, including Windows Server 2003.

## Taking Advantage of Setup Manager Enhancements

Unattend.txt can be created and modified by using a text editor, or by using Setup Manager. Setup Manager is also the tool used to create sysprep.inf files and RIS-based answer files. The Setup Manager tool can be found on the Windows Server 2003 CD in the Support\tools\deploy.cab file.

The Setup Manager that ships with Windows Server 2003 has been enhanced with a cleaner GUI that helps you build answer files easier and faster than previous versions.

One primary improvement in Setup Manager for Windows Server 2003 is the ability to encrypt the local administrator password. With this feature, an unattend.txt file can be placed on a network share, with little concern for giving away the administrator password on all the machines that were used to install them. The password is fully encrypted, which prevents those machines from having a publicly available administrator password.

Because unattend.txt is just a text file, it is easy to modify to meet different requirements. This is very helpful when automating installs to different hardware platforms.

## Fully Automating Installs Using Unattend.txt

There are a variety of configurable options that can be included in an answer file. To build a fully automated install of Windows Server 2003 using an unattend.txt answer file, the following sections of the file must be completed:

- [GUIUnattended]—This section must include the completed AdminPassword and Timezone entries.

- [Identification]—This section requires either JoinWorkgroup or JoinDomain.

- [LicenseFilePrintData]—This section requires the AutoMode entry that handles Per User or Per Server licensing. It also requires the AutoUsers entry if Per Server licensing is chosen.

- [Networking]—This section is required if you want to configure networking as part of the install. If static TCP/IP addresses are to be used, this is a section that will likely be modified with a text editor on a per server basis.

- [Unattended]—This section requires the unattendmode value be set to FullyUnattended. This section also requires a TargetPath for the installation.

- [Userdata]—This section requires ComputerName and FullName. If ComputerName is set to *, a random name will be generated based on the specified Organization name.

Because it is a wizard-based tool, Setup Manager is easy to use to create an answer file for a fully automated installation of Windows Server 2003. The wizard will prompt for entries necessary to automate an install from a specified distribution point. The first two sections shown in Figure 11.5 outline the requirements for a fully automated installation.

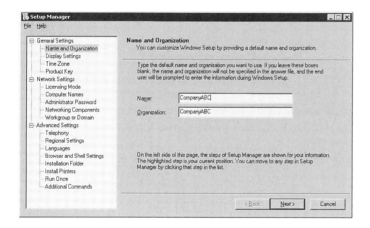

**FIGURE 11.5**
Creating a Unattend.txt with Setup Manager.

# Creating Custom Bootable CDs for Rapid Deployment

Another method for automating server installations of Windows Server 2003 is by building custom bootable CDs. By combining some of the other methods described in the previous sections, you are able to distribute via CD or DVD media a fully automated customized installation of the operating system.

The benefit of doing a CD-based install is the same as doing an unattended install except there is not the requirement for a network share to play the role of a centralized deployment point. You have the capability to customize the install so that it will work on different hardware platforms. It will also allow for the execution of scripts or installations through the GUIRunOnce parameters or cmdlines.txt

## Tools Needed for Creating Custom Install CDs

There are several third-party tools available that can be used to build the custom CD for a server install. You can leverage the answer files created with System Manager, and then use a third-party tool to capture the prepared image. The prepared image and answer files can then be copied to CD or DVD. Third-party tools can then be used to make the CD bootable, and autostart the customized installation.

Additionally, the tools required to create a bootable ISO image, which is the image that would be copied to a CD, are available in Windows Preinstallation Environment, or WinPE for short.

## Leveraging WinPE

WinPE is a bare bones operating system, based on the Windows XP kernel, that provides the functionality required to automate Windows Setup. In essence, WinPE replaces the MS-DOS and Windows 95 boot environments administrators are familiar with using to make their bootable CDs in the past. WinPE has the advantage of being able to access NTFS file systems and network environments, and supports all mass storage devices that use Windows 2000, XP, or Windows Server 2003 drivers.

> **Leveraging WinPE**
>
> A big advantage of leveraging WinPE is the creation of automated multi-partition server installations.

WinPE is designed to be hardware-independent. The idea here is that a WinPE CD will boot on any system and then perform a scripted install. To do this, the first step would be to prepare the system volume on the new hardware. The Diskpart and Format tools that seasoned administrators will be familiar with are also included in WinPE. Diskpart is extremely valuable for server installs because it enables you to script a multipartitioned installation on the target hardware. The Format utility, which is also scriptable, allows for a fast format of the drives. After these two steps have completed, the scripted install proceeds from the CD media in this case, but can also reference a RIS server or other network share for the source files.

# Optimizing Standard Server Configurations

After the operating system is installed, Windows Server 2003 can begin to take on the responsibilities for which it was designed. To get the most out of the new server, though, it is a best practice to confirm that everything is operating as expected. Running through a post-deployment checklist to make sure performance and security settings are in place will ensure the new system can reliably support its intended functionality. This section provides common recommendations for confirming and configuring optimal baseline settings in Windows Server 2003.

## Optimize Performance Settings

After setup has completed, log in to the new server with an administrator account, and perform the following routines to confirm the system is performing at an expected level:

- *Review events in the Event Viewer.* Pay special attention to the System log in Event Viewer to determine if there were any errors associated with the installation, or if any startup services failed to start.

- *Set the Event Viewer log size and wrap setting.* Set the log sizes appropriately depending on the type and severity of events logged. For example, increase the Security log if you will need to view a large number of security events. Also, set an overwrite setting that meets with security requirements. The default setting is for the log to overwrite when the maximum log size is reached.

- *Adjust Server Optimization.* Adjust the server optimization setting to correspond with the role the new server will play in the organization. Server roles are discussed in the section, "Customizing Servers with Setup Wizards," later in this chapter.

To configure memory-related settings in Windows Server 2003, perform the following steps:

1. Open Network Connections from the Control Panel.

2. Right-click Local Area Connection, and choose Properties.

3. Under This Connection Uses the Following Items:, double-click File and Printer Sharing for Microsoft Networks.

4. Under Optimization, notice that Maximize Data Throughput for File is selected. To turn this option off to reduce paging activity, click Maximize Data Throughput for Network. Some of the setting options that need to be reviewed and updated include the following:

   - *Verify Network settings.* The quickest way to do this is to open a command prompt, and type **ipconfig /all**. Make sure the IP, DNS, WINS, and default gateway information is correct.

   - *Verify full computer name.* The quickest way to perform this check is to open a command prompt, and type **net config rdr**. Compare the full computer name to the Active Directory name and make sure they match.

   - *Set the pagefile size.* Set the size and placement of the pagefile based on the memory size and server usage. It is recommended that the same value be set for both the minimum and maximum pagefile size. This keeps the file size static.

   - *Set the options for how the operating system behaves in the event of an unexpected stop.* For example, to configure Windows Server 2003 to send an alert to an administrator in the event of an unexpected stop, perform the following:

     1. Open System from the Control Panel.

     2. On the Advanced tab, under Startup and Recovery, click Settings.

     3. Under System Failure, check the box next to Send an Administrative Alert, as shown in Figure 11.6.

     4. Click OK twice, to finalize the setting.

   - *Configure for Remote Administration.* If the server will be managed remotely, specify settings for making the server available for remote administration. Remote administration is detailed in Chapter 8, "Administering Windows Server 2003 Remotely."

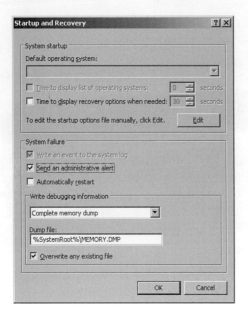

**FIGURE 11.6**   Setting System Failure parameters.

## Optimize Security Settings

In addition to basic performance settings, it is important to verify the proper security settings are in place after a new server is deployed in the IT environment. The security settings enforced on a particular server will depend on the role that server plays in the environment and on company security policies. Security solutions are detailed in Part I "Microsoft Exchange Server 2003 Overview" of this book. The following are recommendations that can apply to any server implementation:

- Change the local administrator account name. This account can also be disabled. In either case, it will make it a bit more difficult for the server to be compromised. The guest account should also be renamed or disabled.

- Review open network ports. Use either the netstat command or an external port scanner to determine if any unnecessary ports are open. Because an open port is a potential access point for an attacker, close any open ports that are not needed for the server to perform properly.

- Set up auditing, and install virus scanning software. Auditing security events help track changes made to the system and help to prevent unwanted changes to the new server. The importance of protecting the server from a virus attack goes without saying.

## Begin Routine Operations

Finally, after the server is configured to the desired specification, it is important to set up a backup routine and install the Recovery Console. Backups can be performed using the

NTBackup utility provided with Windows Server 2003, or any number of third-party tools might be employed. It is also a good practice to simulate recovery procedures from time to time to confirm that the backups are really working.

To install the Recovery Console as a Startup Option for Windows Server 2003, perform the following steps:

1. Insert the Setup CD into the CD drive.

2. From the Run line, type **X:\i386\winnt32.exe /cmdcons** and then click OK (where *X* is the CD-ROM drive letter).

3. Click Yes, and then when the install is complete, click OK to finish.

> **The Recovery Console**
> The Recovery Console can also be started from the Windows Server 2003 CD in the event that the server will no longer start. The Recovery Console cannot be installed on Itanium-based systems.

# Customizing Servers with Setup Wizards

As with Windows 2000, Windows Server 2003 takes some of the manual step out of customizing the server to perform common roles within the organization. By using the Configure Your Server Wizard, and the Manage Your Server utility, you can add/remove and customize a Windows Server 2003 server based on previously defined roles. This section will describe how to customize a server to support common roles in a Windows network environment.

## Configuring Server Roles

Windows Server 2003 provides several roles for which the server can be configured with the Configure Your Server Wizard. Although the roles available through the wizard are mostly the same as were available in the Windows 2000 server family, the GUI interface looks a bit different. Figure 11.7 displays the list of server roles available in Windows Server 2003.

The wizard automatically starts when you log in for the first time after the setup process is complete, and the wizard can be started from the Administrative Tools program group.

When a particular role is chosen in the Configure Your Server Wizard, the appropriate files and services are installed to satisfy that role. For example, if an administrator chooses to configure the Application Server role, the wizard will install IIS, as well as COM+ and ASP.NET, automatically. The wizard will then offer to install FrontPage extensions and enable ASP.NET.

Of course, you still have the capability to install these services and components individually through the Add or Remove Components applet in the Control Panel. The wizard simply streamlines the process. The Configure Your Server Wizard can also be used to remove roles from a previously configured server.

After the Configure Your Server Wizard completes (depending on the role installed, this often includes a reboot), the Manage Your Server utility will automatically start allowing the administrator to further customize the server based on the new role(s) installed.

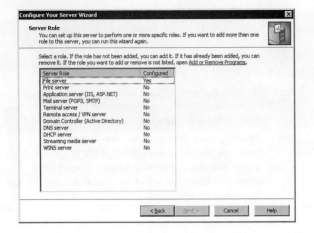

**FIGURE 11.7** Configuring server roles.

There are a few important items to be aware of when assigning server roles to Windows Server 2003:

- When installing the Terminal Server role, you must ensure that there is a licensing server available on the Windows network to handle Terminal Server licensing. If there is no Terminal Server licensing server available on the network, the new Terminal Server will stop accepting connections after 120 days.

- The Domain Controller role cannot be installed on a server that is a Certification Authority (CA). If the server is already a CA, the Domain Controller role is not an available option in the Configure Your Server Wizard.

- If the DNS server role will be installed, it is important to choose a unique registered domain name if the DNS server will store records for computers that exist on the Internet. DNS configuration is detailed in Chapter 13, " Infrastructure Integration (DNS, DHCP, Domain Controllers)."

## Managing Servers

When the Configure Your Server Wizard completes, the Manage Your Server utility launches automatically. This utility can also be found under the Administrative Tools program group. The Manage Your Server utility will display all the roles configured for the particular server. For each role, the utility will provide a list of specific actions appropriate for administering the functionality available to that role.

For example, if the server is configured with a Domain Controller role, the Manage Your Server utility will present options for executing the following management tools:

- Active Directory Users and Computers

- Active Directory Domains and Trusts

- Active Directory Sites and Services

If a particular role requires additional configuration, the Manage Your Server utility also provides a link to a help file that includes next steps. For example, for the File Server role, the next steps include information for configuring EFS, setting disk quotas, or installing the indexing service.

# Controlling the Back-end with the Windows Registry

Because much of this chapter has been devoted to customizations related to installing the Windows Server 2003 operating system, it seems appropriate to end with a discussion of that component through which Windows operating systems can be customized to the greatest degree. That component is of course the Registry. The Windows Registry has been around since Windows 95. It is the database containing hardware, operating system, policy, file association, application, and user configuration.

Rather than going into a detailed account of the Registry's architecture, this section focuses on best practices for using the Registry to secure and maintain the newly installed Windows Server 2003 server.

## The Registry Editor

In earlier versions of Windows, Registry editing was conducted through two different but similar tools: Regedit.exe and Regedt32.exe. Each tool could do some of the tasks involved in making Registry configuration changes, but one could not be used to the exclusion of the other. With Windows XP and Windows Server 2003, Microsoft has consolidated the features of the two tools into a single Registry Editor that has the look and feel of the old Regedit.exe but includes the security and remote access features of Regedt32.exe. Interestingly, both commands still exist in Windows Server 2003, but they each launch the same utility.

## Protecting the Registry

It is important when a new Windows Server 2003 server is built to verify that it meets or exceeds the security policies for the company. Because the Registry is a critical component of a server's capacity to perform, securing the server's Registry should be a part of that process.

The default security for the Windows Server 2003 Registry has improved over earlier Windows operating systems. There are sections of the Registry that are even locked down for administrators. For example, the HKEY_LOCAL_MACHINE\SAM and HKEY_LOCAL_MACHINE\SECURITY keys allow only read and write DAC access to administrators.

Some best practices for protecting the Registry include the following:

- *Audit the Registry*. An audit log of changes made to the Registry can be a crucial tool in troubleshooting, as well as uncovering security breaches. Auditing can be enabled either through group policy or local security settings.

- *Prevent Remote Access.* In some cases, it might be wise to limit or prevent remote access to a server's Registry. To do this, simply change the permissions on the following key: HKEY_LOCAL_MACHINE\SYSTEM\CurrentControlSet\Control\SecurePipeServers\winreg.

- *Include the Registry in backups.* As part of a disaster recovery procedure, in addition to backing up files and folders, always back up a server's Registry. Using the built-in backup utility, NTBACKUP.EXE, the Registry can be backed up by simply including the System State Data option.

## Maintaining the Registry

Though Windows Server 2003 automatically performs maintenance on the Registry, there are some tools and best practices related to the Registry that help improve performance:

- *Manage the Registry size.* In earlier Windows operating systems, administrators had the option to limit the size of the Registry. Because Windows Server 2003 manages the Registry in the computer cache rather than in paged, pooled memory, administrators no longer need to specify a Registry size. It is recommended, though, to provide an adequate amount of free space on the system partition. There should always be 25% free space at all times.

- *Use the Windows Installer Cleanup Utility (MSICUU.EXE).* This utility is installed with the Windows Server 2003 Support Tools. It can be used to remove Registry entries from applications installed with Windows Installer. This tool is useful in repairing a server's Registry after a failed or corrupted Windows Installer installation.

- *Use Windows Installer Zapper (MSIZAP.EXE).* This is the command-line version of MSICUU.EXE, which includes more features than the GUI version. For instance, MSIZAP can remove folders in addition to Registry entries. It can also be used to change access control list (ACL) permissions and remove rollback information.

# Summary

As this chapter demonstrates, Although the installation of Windows Server 2003 can be a simple process, there are many customization and automation features available to administrators. Proper planning and testing are key to a successful implementation. After these steps have been accomplished, the speed, reliability, and security of the installation process will enable organizations to rapidly deploy and maintain new Windows servers in small or global IT environments.

# 12

# Implementing Microsoft Active Directory

Even though many organizations can benefit from features present in Windows Server 2003 as member servers in an existing directory structure, the true defining characteristic of a Windows Server 2003 network is Active Directory. Active Directory is Microsoft's directory service that also provides a platform for the integration of many Microsoft and third-party technologies.

Active Directory is a familiar technology for those administrators who have worked in a Windows 2000 environment. The Windows Server 2003 implementation of Active Directory is an improvement on the Windows 2000 model through added and enhanced features. This chapter focuses on leveraging these enhancements and provides best practices for implementing a Windows Server 2003 Active Directory.

# Taking Advantage of Functional Levels

Many of the items discussed in this chapter are new Windows Server 2003 features that are only available when domain controllers are operating in Windows Server 2003 functional modes. In essence, to get some of the new features available to Active Directory, all domain controllers must be running Windows Server 2003.

The functional levels of Windows Server 2003 are similar to the mixed and native modes of Windows 2000 Active Directory. They provide for backward-compatibility to earlier operating systems and a migration path to the newest operating system. This section will explain the various domain and forest functional levels and point out which new features are available at each level.

## Windows 2000 Mixed Domain Functional Level

The Windows 2000 Mixed Domain Functional level provides for backwards-compatibility with a Windows 2000 Active Directory running in Mixed mode. Installed at this level, Windows Server 2003 domain controllers will be able to communicate with both Windows NT 4.0 and Windows 2000 domain controllers throughout the forest. At this level, Windows Server 2003 shares the same limitations present in the Windows 2000 Mixed mode domain.

Windows Server 2003 servers in the Mixed mode domain and forest levels can take advantage of installing Active Directory from Media. This feature will be discussed in the next section.

## Windows 2000 Native Functional Level

The Windows 2000 Native Functional Level is the initial operating level of Windows Server 2003 domain controllers installed into a Windows 2000 Native mode domain. At this level there are no NT 4.0 domain controllers. All authentication is performed by Windows 2000 and Windows Server 2003 domain controllers.

At this level, Active Directory can use Universal Groups and Windows Server 2003 domain controllers can cache Universal Groups. These features are discussed in following sections.

## Windows Server 2003 Interim Functional Level

The Windows Server 2003 Interim Functional Level is the initial operating level of Windows Server 2003 domain controllers installed into a Windows NT 4.0 domain. This level is provided primarily as a stepping stone during a migration from Windows NT 4.0 to Windows Server 2003. The Interim Functional level comes into play for those companies that have not upgraded to Windows 2000, but instead migrate directly to Windows Server 2003 Active Directory.

## Windows Server 2003 Functional Level

To gain the full functionality of a Windows Server 2003 Active Directory, the Windows Server 2003 Functional Level is the final goal for domain and forest functional levels. Functionality at this level enables many of the new features available to Windows Server 2003, such as renaming domains and domain controllers, schema deactivation, and cross-forest trusts. In order for you to promote your Active Directory to the full Windows Server 2003 Functional level, all domain controllers must be upgraded to Windows Server 2003. Individual domains can be promoted to the Windows Server 2003 functional level, but the forest can only be promoted to this functional level after all the domains in the forest are operating at this highest level.

At this level, Active Directory can benefit from all the new Windows Server 2003 features, including domain rename, cross-forest trusts, schema deletes, partial global catalog synchronization, and linked-value replication. All these new Active Directory features are discussed in the following sections.

# Improving Domain Controller Installation

Those who have installed Active Directory in a Windows 2000 environment realize that the process by which Active Directory is implemented is unique from the installation of the server operating system. A member server becomes a domain controller in an Active Directory domain through the use of the DCPromo utility, or the Active Directory Installation Wizard, after the operating system is installed. A domain controller provides network users and computers with the Active Directory directory service, which stores and replicates directory data and manages user interactions with the domain, including user logon processes, authentication, and directory searches. Every domain must contain at least one domain controller. This section provides information on how to use the DCPromo utility to build Windows Server 2003 domain controllers in new and existing directory service environments.

## Promoting a Member Server

When executed, the DCPromo utility enables you to promote a Windows Server 2003 member server to a domain controller. It also allows a domain controller to be demoted back to a member server.

The common tasks you can perform in promoting a member server to a domain controller are as follows:

- Creating a new forest (also creating a new domain). In this scenario, the server will be the first domain controller created for Active Directory.

- Creating a new tree in an existing forest. This scenario comes into play when creating a peer root Active Directory forest.

- Creating a child domain. A child domain creates a domain boundary within a forest while maintaining a contiguous namespace.

- Creating an additional domain controller in an existing domain. This is a common strategy for fault tolerance and load balancing.

Each of these domain controller roles has unique installation considerations depending on the overall Active Directory design for the organization(s). For design tips, see Chapter 10, "Advanced Active Directory Design." For any of these installation paths, though, keep the following in mind:

- The partition on which the server operating system is installed must be formatted with the NTFS file system.

- If DNS is not present or available, DCPromo will prompt the user with the option to have it configured automatically. Verify that DNS is installed and configured correctly before promoting the server.

## BEST PRACTICE

**Install and Configure the DNS Infrastructure Before the Domain Controller Promotion**

Although DNS can be installed as part of the DCPromo process, it is a best practice to install and configure the DNS infrastructure before performing the domain controller promotion. This will ensure the naming system is working properly before Active Directory depends on the DNS infrastructure. Also in many environments, Windows DNS is integrated with an existing Unix-based DNS. Having DNS implemented and validated ensures successful cross-integration between Windows and non-Windows DNS prior to the implementation of Active Directory.

- In any Active Directory installation that involves a domain controller that is not the first domain controller in the forest, there must be some method by which the server being promoted can transfer Active Directory information. In addition to transferring this information over the network, Windows Server 2003 allows Active Directory to be transferred from a backup copied to media. This feature is detailed later in this chapter.

- Verify that the installer has the proper level of administrative access to perform the operation. Creating a new domain in a new forest, the administrator need only have the local administrator level permission on the server. To create a new tree in an existing forest, the installer must be a member of the Enterprise Admins group or the Domain Admins group of the root domain. To create a child domain, the installer must be a member of the Enterprise Admins group or the Domain Admins group of the parent domain. To create an additional domain controller in an existing domain, the installer needs to be a member of the Domain Admins group of the existing domain.

## Demoting a Domain Controller

The ability to demote a domain controller to a member server was first made available with Windows 2000. This useful feature can still be leveraged in a Windows Server 2003 environment by using the DCPromo utility. Performing a domain controller demotion is a simple task, but it can have some far-reaching consequences if particular considerations are not taken into account.

To demote a domain controller, follow these steps:

1. On a domain controller, click Start, and then click Run.

2. In the Open box, type **dcpromo** to open the Active Directory Installation Wizard, and then click Next.

> **Before Performing a Domain Controller Demotion...**
>
> Before performing a domain controller demotion, make sure that the server is not the last global catalog server in the domain, and also that it does not contain any operation master roles.

3. On the Remove Active Directory page, click Next, and then continue to follow the wizard.

It is important to verify that there will still be a global catalog server available for users before the demotion of a domain controller is completed. If you choose to demote a global catalog server, the DCPromo process will prompt the user with a warning.

> **FSMO Roles Can be Transferred by Using NTDSUtil.exe**
>
> Flexible Single-Master Operations (FSMO) roles can be transferred by using the NTDSUtil.exe command line utility.

Also, if the server to be demoted holds any operation master roles, those roles should be transferred to another domain controller before a demotion takes place.

If the domain controller being demoted is the last domain controller in a domain, that Active Directory domain will be completely removed from the forest. Further, if this is the last domain controller in the forest, the demotion will also delete the forest. To delete a domain or forest using DCPromo, click the check box indicating this is the last domain controller in the domain as shown in Figure 12.1.

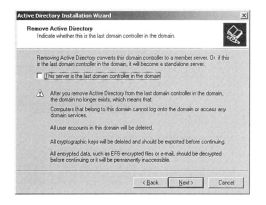

**FIGURE 12.1**    Deleting a domain with DCPromo.

## Creating Replicas from Media

Traditionally when a domain controller is added to an existing forest or domain, the Active Directory information that gets installed during the process is transferred over the network from an existing domain controller. This transfer presents a potential bottleneck, especially for building

> **Any Encrypted Files in a Domain Should Be Decrypted Before Deleting a Domain**
>
> Deleting a domain deletes all user accounts. Computers will no longer be able to log in and access domain resources. Also, any encrypted files in a domain should be decrypted before deleting a domain.

new domain controllers in remote sites connected by a slow WAN connection. One option for avoiding the bottleneck is to build the new domain controller locally, and then ship it to the remote location where only updates will be transferred over the WAN. Windows Server 2003 provides a new method to alleviate the bottleneck by enabling you to install Active Directory (and a global catalog server) from a backup copied to removable media.

The process of creating a domain controller from backup is fairly simple. By using the NTBackup utility provided with the operating system, a system-state backup can be performed on an existing domain controller. The backup is then copied to removable media such as a CD or tape. The media is then shipped to the remote location where the new domain controller is being built.

On the remote system, you run DCPromo with an /adv switch, which will activate the option to install the Active Directory database from media, as shown in Figure 12.2.

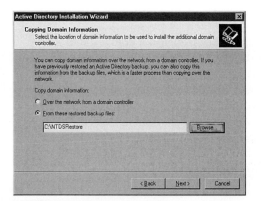

**FIGURE 12.2**    DCPromo from media.

> **Use an Up-to-Date Backup**
>
> When installing Active Directory from media, it is important to use an up-to-date backup. If the backed up copy of the global catalog information is older than the tombstone date for objects in Active Directory (by default, 30 days), this type of DCPromo will fail.

After the DCPromo process completes on the remote system, only incremental changes to the Active Directory database are transferred over the WAN.

# Getting the Most Out of Global Catalog Servers

A global catalog server is a domain controller that contains a copy of every Active Directory object in a forest. By default, the first domain controller installed in a forest is a global catalog server. The global catalog contains a full copy of every Active Directory object in its host domain, and a partial copy of every object in other domains in the forest. The partial copies include the most commonly queried attributes of objects. The attribute set that global catalogs will store is defined in the Active Directory schema, which can be modified if needed.

The role of the global catalog server is to perform the following primary tasks:

- Find objects anywhere in the forest. When users search for people or printers from the Start menu, the queries are sent directly to a global catalog.

- Authenticate User Principle Names (UPNs). When an authenticating domain controller does not have information about a user that is logging on with a UPN, (for example, user1@companyabc.com), it sends a request to a global catalog to complete the logon request.

- Contain Universal Group membership. Unlike global group memberships, which are stored in each domain, universal group memberships are only stored in global catalogs.

Windows Server 2003 has new features on how global catalog information is stored that will affect decisions on where to place a global catalog server in a distributed organization. The next section provides best practices for group catalog placement and customization based on the new features in Windows Server 2003.

## Global Catalog Placement

Conceivably, every domain controller can contain a copy of the global catalog. Because global catalog information must be replicated to every global catalog server in the forest, making every domain controller a global catalog server can significantly affect network performance. On the other hand, having too few GCs available to users can affect user logons and access tokens.

**Uses More Network Resources**

Network traffic related to global catalog queries generally uses more network resources than normal directory replication traffic.

For a single site environment, a single global catalog is sufficient. It is a best practice to have at least a second GC in a single site for fault tolerance.

It is also a best practice to place a GC in a remote site connected by an unreliable or slow connection. In this scenario, fault tolerance for user authentication is achieved at the price of a network performance hit.

If users at the remote site are members of a Windows 2000 native mode domain, they get their universal group membership information from a global catalog server. If the GC is not located in the same site, logon requests will have to be routed over the WAN to find a GC. Windows Server 2003 domain controllers can alleviate this problem with Universal Group Caching.

## Universal Group Caching

Due to the network performance issues related to locating GCs at remote sites, Microsoft has added a feature in Windows Server 2003 that enables domain controllers to cache and store Universal Group membership without containing (and replicating) a global catalog.

When enabled, the domain controller will query a global catalog for universal group membership when a user logs on once, and then cache that information indefinitely. The next time that
user logs on, the domain controller will refer to its local cache instead of querying the global
catalog server. The universal group membership information that is cached is periodically
refreshed (by default, every eight hours).

The benefits of universal group caching can be summarized as follows:

- *Faster logon times.* The domain controller can use its cached copy of universal group
  memberships instead of querying a global catalog server.

- *Greater bandwidth utilization.* Fewer domain controllers will be replicating the entire global
  catalog of Active Directory objects.

- *Better hardware utilization.* Potentially, fewer servers would be required to support Active
  Directory. At the very least, existing domain controllers could perform additional roles in
  the organization if they are not tasked with global catalog storage and replication.

Enabling universal group caching on a domain controller is accomplished by using Active
Directory Sites and Services. To enable universal group caching, perform the following steps:

1. Open Active Directory Sites and Services.

2. In the console tree, click the site in which you want to enable universal group membership caching.

3. In the details pane, right-click NTDS Site Settings, and then click Properties.

4. Select the Enable Universal Group Membership Caching check box, as shown in
   Figure 12.3.

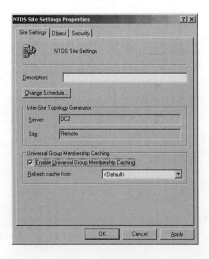

**FIGURE 12.3**   Enabling universal group
membership caching.

5. In Refresh Cache From, click a site from which this site will refresh its cache, or accept
   <Default> to refresh the cache from the nearest site that has a global catalog.

## Customizing the Global Catalog

As was indicated earlier, the global catalog contains only a partial list of attributes about objects not present in the host domain. Although the attributes that are included represent those items queried for most of the time (for example, a user's first name, last name, and e-mail address), there might be occasions for adding attributes to be replicated and available for users or applications to query against.

Adding attributes to the global catalog can improve query performance. When considering whether to add attributes to the global catalog, keep the following in mind:

- Added attributes can affect network bandwidth utilization. The more data there is to replicate, the more bandwidth will be used.

- Consider both the size of the attribute and the frequency with which it is updated. A small attribute will not take that much network traffic to replicate, but if it is an attribute that is updated often, it can potentially create more network traffic than a large attribute that rarely changes.

- Consider that global catalog information consumes disk space as well as network bandwidth.

- When a new attribute is added to the global catalog for Windows 2000 domain controllers, a forestwide synchronization occurs that will replicate the entire global catalog to all DCs. If the GC/DCs are Windows Server 2003 servers, only the added attribute is replicated.

To add attributes to the global catalog, you must use the Active Directory Schema snap-in.

To add an attribute to the global catalog, for example to add the primary mobile phone attribute, perform the following steps:

1. Open the Active Directory Schema snap-in.

2. In the console tree, click Attributes.

3. In the Details pane, scroll down the list and right-click on Mobile, and then click Properties.

4. Select the Replicate This Attribute to the Global Catalog check box shown in Figure 12.4.

5. Click OK to finish.

> **Modifying the Schema Is an Advanced Operation**
>
> The Active Directory Schema snap-in must be installed before it can be used. Only members of the Schema Admins group have the capability to modify the schema. Modifying the schema is an advanced operation best performed by experienced programmers and system administrators.

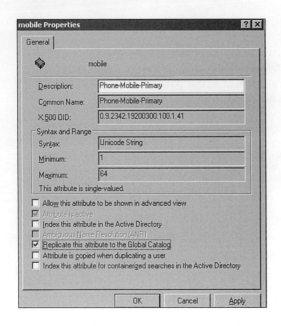

**FIGURE 12.4**    Adding an attribute to the global catalog.

# Maximizing Flexible Single Master Operation (FSMO) Roles

In Windows Server 2003, as with Windows 2000, domain controllers support multimaster replication. In essence, all domain controllers in these environments are peers distributing Active Directory access throughout an organization. This distribution also provides redundancy by eliminating the single point of failure present in the single master domain model of Windows NT.

Although domain controllers distribute most of the functionality available in managing an Active Directory forest, there are five unique functions that require the use of a single server to support because these particular functions are impractical to distribute. For each of these functions, there is only one domain controller that is the operation master.

There are two forestwide Flexible Single Master Operation (FSMO) roles that must appear in any forest. Also, there are three domainwide roles that must appear in any domain. The FSMO roles are outlined as follows:

- Schema Master—The server that contains this forestwide role contains the only writable copy of the schema in the forest.

- Domain Naming Master—This forestwide role is responsible for the addition or removal of domains within the forest.

- PDC Emulator—This domain FSMO role is responsible for authenticating pre-Windows 2000 client computers within the domain. It is also responsible for synchronizing the time on all domain controllers in the domain.

- RID Master—The server supporting this domain wide role allocates sequences of relative IDs (RIDs) to each of the various domain controllers in its domain. Whenever a domain controller creates a user, group, or computer object, it assigns the object a unique security ID (SID). The SID consists of a *domain* SID, which is the same for all SIDs created in the domain, and a RID, which is unique for each SID created in the domain. The RID Master is also responsible for moving Active Directory objects between domains.

- Infrastructure Master—The infrastructure master is responsible for updating references from objects in its domain to objects in other domains. The infrastructure master compares its data with that of a global catalog. It then requests updates from the global catalog and replicates that information to other domain controllers in its domain.

## Proper Placement of Operation Master Roles

Because each Operation Master role can only reside on a single domain controller, it is important to understand the ramifications of each role in order to determine its proper placement with a forest or domain. Changes in Windows Server 2003 also affect some placement restrictions present in Windows 2000 forests. This section provides some best practices for FSMO role assignments.

Firstly, the Infrastructure Master role should be assigned to a domain controller that is not a global catalog server. This is true even in single domain models because there is always the possibility that new domains will be added to the forest. In a multidomain model, if the Infrastructure Master has a local copy of the global catalog, it will never find data that is out of date, and therefore never replicate new information about other domains to the other domain controllers in its own domain.

Placement of the PDC Emulator domain controller might affect logon times in some organizations. Even for companies that no longer support pre-Windows 2000 clients on the network, the PDC Emulator gets preferential treatment with regards to password change replication. If a password was recently changed, that change takes time to replicate to every domain controller in the domain. If a logon authentication fails at another domain controller due to a bad password, that domain controller will forward the authentication request to the PDC emulator before rejecting the logon attempt.

Also, the PDC Emulator should get special consideration when setting up time synchronization. This FSMO role is responsible for the synchronization of time for all domain controllers in its domain. The PDC Emulator in the parent domain in a forest should be synchronized with an external time source.

Finally, there is a limitation of Windows 2000 functional level forests that requires the Domain Naming master role resides on a domain controller that is also a global catalog server. In a Windows Server 2003 functional level, this limitation is removed, so this forestwide role can exist on a DC that is not a GC.

## Moving Operation Master Roles

There might be occasion to move particular FSMO roles between servers after Active Directory is installed and distributed across several domain controllers. Also, in cases of disaster recovery or demotion of domain controllers serving these roles, it might become necessary to move FSMO roles. This section explains how to transfer the roles.

In cases where the FSMO role merely needs to be transferred between two functioning domain controllers, a GUI interface or the NTDSUtil command-line tool can be used. In disaster recovery situations where the operation master is lost, the FSMO roles must be seized using the NTDSUtil command line tool.

Transfer of the Schema Master role is performed by using the Active Directory Schema snap-in. This snap-in must be installed and executed by a member of the Schema Admins group in the forest. See the section "Using the Active Directory Schema Snap-in" for instructions on how to install the snap-in. To transfer the Schema Master role, perform the following steps:

1. Open the Active Directory Schema snap-in.

2. In the console tree, right-click Active Directory Schema and then click Change Domain Controller.

3. Click Specify Name and type the name of the domain controller that you want to hold the schema master role.

4. In the console tree, right-click Active Directory Schema, and then click Operations Master.

5. Click Change.

---

**Change the Focus of Active Directory Users and Computers**

To transfer a role to another domain controller, change the focus of Active Directory Users and Computers to the target domain controller. To do this, right-click Active Directory Users and Computers, click Connect to Domain Controller, and then click the target domain controller.

---

**Seizing FSMO Roles**

Do not seize FSMO roles if they can be transferred instead. Seizing the RID master is a drastic step that should be considered only if the current operations master will never be available again.

---

Transferring the Domain Naming master role is a similar procedure performed using Active Directory Domains and Trusts. Transferring the PDC Emulator, RID Master, or Infrastructure Master roles can all be performed using Active Directory Users and Computers.

In cases where the operation master is lost and cannot be recovered, the NTDSUtil command line tool can be used to seize the role from a functioning domain controller.

To seize the RID master role, for example, follow these steps:

1. Open a command prompt.

2. Type **ntdsutil** and press Enter.

3. At the ntdsutil command prompt, type **roles** and press Enter.

4. At the fsmo maintenance command prompt, type **connections** and press Enter.

> **The Operation Master Role**
> The *servername* is the domain controller that will seize the operation master role.

5. At the server connections command prompt, type **connect to server server-name** and press Enter.

6. At the server connections prompt, type **quit** and press Enter.

7. At the fsmo maintenance command prompt, type **seize RID master**, and after seizing the role, type **quit** (or just **q**) and press Enter until you've exited the ntdsutil tool.

8. Type **exit** to close the command prompt window.

# Expanding the Enterprise by Interconnecting Forests and Domains

The concept of a domain trust is familiar to system administrators in Windows NT and Windows 2000 environments. Windows Server 2003 introduces the concept of a forest trust. Domain trusts—and now forest-level trusts—provide a useful path through which autonomous organizations can share data and resources. Some scenarios that demonstrate the usefulness of establishing trusts are as follows:

- *Companies undergoing a merger.* When two companies are in the process of a merger, they might require a method by which to share network resources while maintaining their individual administrative models.

- *Companies with different Active Directory schema requirements.* A company could have different forests within their organization linked by a trust yet operate under different schemas and replication topologies.

- *Isolating a DMZ.* For increased security, a DMZ might be placed in a forest independent yet linked to the production forest by a trust relationship.

- *Separate companies requiring collaboration and sharing of resources.* Trust relationship can be set up for links to suppliers, customers, and other partner businesses.

In a Windows 2000 forest, if users in one forest need access to resources in another forest, you can create an external trust relationship between individual domains within each forest. External trusts can be one-way or two-way and are nontransitive, and therefore, limit the ability for trust paths to extend to other domains.

For Windows Server 2003 functional forests, disjoined forests can be joined together to form a one-way or two-way, transitive trust relationship. A two-way forest trust is used to form a transitive trust relationship between every domain in both forests.

Forest trusts benefit a company by reducing the number of external trusts that might be required to share resources cross-forest. They provide the ability to authenticate user principle names (UPNs) cross-forest. And they still enable companies to maintain autonomous administrative models in each forest.

## Configuring Forest Trusts

A forest trust can only be created between the forest root domain of one Windows Server 2003 forest and the forest root domain of another Windows Server 2003 forest. Both forests need to be operating in Windows Server 2003 functional level. Creating a forest trust between two Windows Server 2003 forests provides a one-way or two-way transitive trust relationship between every domain residing within each forest.

A one-way forest trust between two forests enables members of the trusted forest to use resources located in the trusting forest. The trust, therefore, only functions in one direction. For example, when a one-way forest trust is created between forest A (the trusted forest) and forest B (the trusting forest), members of forest A can access resources located in forest B, but members of forest B cannot access resources located in forest A using the same trust.

A two-way forest trust, on the other hand, enables members from either forest to use resources located in the other forest. Domains in each respective forest trust domains in the other forest implicitly. For example, when a two-way forest trust is established between forest A and forest B, members of forest A can access resources located in forest B, and members of forest B can access resources in forest A, using the same trust.

When creating a forest trust, be sure that DNS is configured properly. If there is a root DNS server that can be made the root DNS server for both of the forest DNS namespaces, make it the root server by ensuring that the root zone contains delegations for each of the DNS namespaces. Because this will probably not be the case, configure DNS secondary zones in each DNS namespace to route queries for names in the other namespace. Another alternative, if the DNS servers are both Windows Server 2003, is to configure conditional forwarders in each DNS namespace to route queries for names in the other namespace. For more information on Windows Server 2003 DNS, see Chapter 13, "Infrastructure Integration."

> **If Forest Trust Is Not an Available Option**
>
> If, at this point, forest trust is not an available option, it is likely that the forest functional level has not yet been raised to Windows Server 2003.

To create a two-way forest trust, open Active Directory Domains and Trusts and follow these steps:

1. In the console tree, right-click the domain node for the forest root domain, and then click Properties.

2. On the Trust tab, click New Trust, and then click Next.

3. On the Trust Name page, type the DNS name of another forest, and then click Next.

4. On the Trust Type page, click Forest Trust, and then click Next.

5. On the Direction of Trust page, click Two-way as shown in Figure 12.5

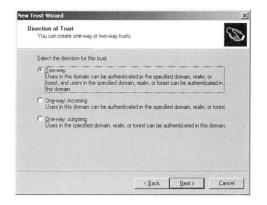

**FIGURE 12.5**   Creating a two-way forest trust.

6. On the Sides of Trust page, select This Side Only, and click Next.

7. On the Outgoing Trust Authentication Level, choose Forest-wide. (Authentication levels will be discussed in the *Authentication Firewall* section of this chapter).

8. Provide a password for the Trust, and click Next.

9. Click Next to complete the configuration.

## Granting Cross-Forest Rights

After a forest trust has been established, it is an easy process for you to grant rights and permissions to resources on one side of the trust to users on the other side. The object picker is updated, enabling you to see objects in the root domain of the trusted forest.

To assign permissions to a particular folder to the Domain Admins group in a domain in another forest, perform the following steps:

> **You Cannot Browse the Entire Trusted Forest**
>
> For security, performance, and privacy reasons, you cannot browse the entire trusted forest. You will need to know the names of the security principles in order to grant rights and permissions.

1. Right-click on the folder, choose Properties, and go to the Security Tab.

2. Click Add, and then in the Object Picker, click Locations.

3. Select the forest root domain of the trusted forest.

4. Type **Domain Admins**, and click Check Names.

5. Select the appropriate Domain Admins group and click OK to complete the configuration.

## Authentication Firewall

When a forest trust is created, you have the option to allow full authentication between every domain in each of the forests. This might be appropriate if both forests belong to the same company. If the trusting forests belong to two independent companies, it is likely that a selective authentication will be configured for the trust. The concept of selective authentication is also referred to as authentication firewall.

Authentication firewall is automatically set up during trust creation if Selective Authentication is chosen on the Authentication Level page of the wizard. To impose an authentication firewall after a trust is established, simply go the Authentication tab of the Properties sheet of the existing trust, as shown in Figure 12.6.

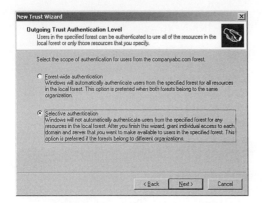

**FIGURE 12.6** Setting the Authentication firewall.

After Authentication firewall is configured, only users or groups from cross-forest that are assigned the extended right Allow to Authenticate will be able to authenticate.

To specify that only members of the domain admins group from a trusted forest domain can authenticate in a particular domain in the home forest, perform the following steps:

1. In Active Directory Users and Computers, right-click on the domain controller in the domain that will be the authenticating DC, choose Properties, and go to the Security tab.

2. Click on the Add button, and then click Location.

3. Select the trusted forest and click OK.

4. Type **Domain Admins**, and click Check Names.

5. Set permissions and set the Allowed to Authenticate permission; then click OK to complete the configuration.

# Enhancing Flexibility with Renaming Domains

Another new feature with Windows Server 2003 Active Directory is the ability to rename domains or move domains to different locations within an existing forest. Domain rename supports the ability to change the NetBIOS domain name, or the Active Directory namespace (companyabc.com for example).

The procedure to rename a domain is not a simple switch, and depending on the size of the organization, can require considerable downtime to complete. For these reasons, renaming domains should be planned out accordingly.

The best practices surrounding domain renames really boils down to understanding the limitations, meeting a list of prerequisites, following a six-step process, and providing the downtime necessary to complete the procedure. This section will help you to plan and navigate this process.

## Understanding the Limitations

The domain rename process will not work in every scenario. It is important to know what cannot be done before planning a big rename weekend. The following is a list of restrictions for domain rename:

- Identity of the forest root domain cannot be changed. Although the forest root domain can be renamed, it cannot be moved to another location in the forest as other domains can. The forest root remains the forest root.

- Domains cannot be dropped or added during the process. There are other methods to accomplish this task, so this is not a big limitation. The key point here is that after the domain rename process is completed there should be the same number of domains in the forest as there were at the outset.

- Two domains in the forest cannot swap names in a single process. Essentially, one domain cannot give up its name to another production domain in the forest in a single restructuring process.

- A forest-prepped domain cannot be renamed. If the schema has been updated with an Exchange 2000 installation, it cannot be modified by the domain rename process.

## Meeting the Prerequisites

After the constraints of the domain rename process are understood, you can begin to establish these prerequisites for carrying out the procedure:

- The forest must be in Windows Server 2003 functional mode. The process does not work with Windows 2000 domain controllers. All DCs in the forest must be running Windows Server 2003, and the forest must be elevated to Windows Server 2003 functional mode.

- DNS must be prepared. If the domain rename process involves renaming the DNS name-space, a DNS zone must be created to include the new namespace. This is not necessary for renaming the NETBIOS domain.

- The process cannot run on a DC. A member Windows Server 2003 server must be used as the "console" for the operation. Because domain controllers will be reconfigured and rebooted during the process, a DC cannot perform the actual operation.

- Temporary trusts might need to be created. If domain rename is being used as a reorganization tool with which domains will be moved around within the forest, temporary trusts must be created for any domain and its future parent domain.

## The Domain Rename Process

After the limitations are understood and the prerequisites have been met, the actual domain rename process is fairly simple. It is important to keep in mind, though, that depending on the size of the organization this process might require a great deal of network downtime.

> **Steps for the Domain Rename Process**
>
> Remember that all steps for the Domain Rename process must be performed from a single member Windows Server 2003 server.

### Step 1: Generate Current Forest Description

The tool used to perform the domain rename process is rendom.exe, which can be found in the Valueadd\Msft\Mgmt\Domren folder of the installation CD. The first step is to run rendom with the /list switch, which generates an XML file that lists the domain-naming information for a domain. A sample domainlist.xml file is shown in Figure 12.7.

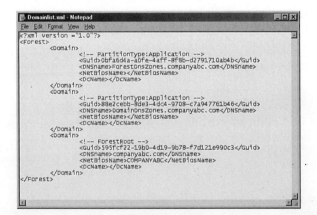

**FIGURE 12.7**
Forest description XML document.

### Step 2: Modify the XML File

In this step, open the XML file generated from step 1 in a text editor, and modify domain-naming information. For example if companyabc.com is being changed to organizationA.org, a simple find and replace operation can be used to change all references from one domain name to the other. Further, any changes to DNS and NetBIOS names should be changed as well.

### Step 3: Upload the Modified File

After the XML file is updated, run the rendom command with the /upload switch. This uploads the new information to every domain controller in the forest.

### Step 4: Prepare Domain Controllers

Because every domain controller must participate in the update process, it is important to verify that each DC has received the update file and is ready for the migration. Run the rendom command with the /prepare switch. The prepare function will fail if it cannot contact every DC in the forest, in which case this process must be restarted. This step will ensure a successful migration to the new structure.

### Step 5: Execute the Rename Procedure

After step 4 completes successfully, run rendom with the /execute switch. No changes to the production environment take place until this command is run. When executed, all domain controllers execute the change and automatically reboot. After the DCs reboot, every worksta-

tion and member server in the forest must also be rebooted to get the change. It might be necessary to reboot workstations and member servers twice to ensure all services receive the domain name changes.

> **Manually Rejoined to the New Domains**
> Windows NT clients will need to be manually rejoined to the new domains because they do not support automatic rejoin functionality.

### Step 6: Cleanup Tasks

The final step in the domain rename process is to run rendom with the /clean switch which removes temporary files from the domain controllers and returns the domain to a normal operating state.

Also, each domain controller will need to have its primary DNS suffix changed via the netdom command-line utility. To perform this procedure, execute the following commands on each domain controller:

1. Open a command prompt window.

2. Type **netdom computername oldservername /add:Newservername**.

3. Type **netdom computername oldservername /makeprimary:Newservername**.

4. Restart the server.

5. Type **netdom computername Newsservername /remove:oldservername**.

Replace *oldservername* and *newservername* with the full DNS name of the old and new server, for example srv1.companyabc and srv1.organizationA.com.

# Managing the Active Directory Schema

The schema is to the Active Directory what the Registry is to the Windows operating system. The schema is a database of definitions for all object types within the directory structure, which determines how all Active Directory objects can and are configured. Just as care is extended to managing and modifying the Windows Registry, extreme care should be extended to the administration of the schema. Changes to the schema affect the entire Active Directory environment. As such, the schema is not a database that should be modified casually. If modifications will be made, either for troubleshooting or development purposes, it is important to test these modifications in a test lab environment before implementing them in production.

The next section discusses the tools used to manage the schema and a new feature in Windows Server 2003 that allows for schema attribute deletes.

## Using Active Directory Service Interfaces (ADSI) Edit

One method for viewing and modifying the Active Directory schema is by using the Active Directory Service Interfaces (ADSI) Edit utility. The ADSIEdit utility provides a GUI interface similar to Active Directory Users and Computers, but with a much lower level view of Active Directory objects.

ADSI Edit is installed with the Support Tools available on the installation media in the Tools/Support folder. Once installed, ADSI Edit can be accessed through the MMC snap-in, or by executing adsiedit.msc from the run line.

Although ADSI Edit provides a method for modifying Active Directory objects, the tool is best used as a method for troubleshooting or gaining detailed configuration information about a particular Active Directory implementation. When changes to Active Directory fail to work through the normal administration tools, such as Active Directory Users and Computers and Active Directory Sites and Services, ADSI Edit can be used as a last resort to repair the AD database.

For example, as was discussed in an earlier section of this chapter, DCPromo can be used to promote a member server to a domain controller and demote a domain controller to a member server. If a DCPromo demotion process fails, it might become necessary to delete the specific domain controller object from Active Directory by using the ADSI Edit utility.

## Using the Active Directory Schema Snap-in

The easiest way to view and modify the Active Directory schema is by using the Active Directory schema snap-in. Unlike other Active Directory snap-ins that are installed by default with the Windows Server 2003 Administration Tools, the Schema snap-in must be activated by running the following command at a command prompt: **regsvr32 schmmgmt.dll.** After the program is registered on the computer, the snap-in can be access by adding it to an MMC session.

When executed, the Schema snap-in provides a GUI interface that lists both Active Directory classes and attributes, as shown in Figure 12.8

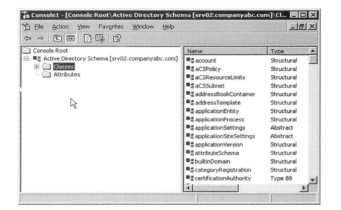

**FIGURE 12.8**
Viewing schema classes and attributes.

In the schema, an object class represents a category of directory objects, such as users, printers, or application programs, that share a set of common characteristics. The definition for each object class contains a list of the schema attributes that can be used to describe instances of the class. For example, the Computer class has attributes such as Network Address, Operating System, and Machine Role.

The Schema snap-in provides a low-level view of the classes and associated attributes in Active Directory providing schema administrators to view and modify individual characteristics of Active Directory objects.

> **The Schema Admins Group**
>
> By default, only members of the Schema Admins group have the capability to write to the schema. Also, by default only the administrator account of the root domain of a forest is a member of the Schema Admins group.

## Schema Deactivation

In Windows 2000, as with Windows Server 2003, it is possible to extend the schema with new classes and attributes. Installing Exchange 2000, for example, extends to the schema to almost double its original size. But after classes and attributes were added to the schema, it was not possible to remove them. Although it is still the case that added classes and attributes cannot be deleted, with Windows Server 2003, schema administrators now have the capability to deactivate and redefine classes and attributes.

> **Classes, Attributes, and the Forest Functional Level**
>
> Classes and attributes added to the base schema can be deactivated without raising the forest functional level. However, they can be redefined only in forests with the forest functional level set to Windows Server 2003.

To deactivate an attribute, for example to deactivate an attribute called BuildingName, perform the following steps:

1. Open the Active Directory Schema snap-in.

2. In the console tree, click Active Directory Schema.

3. In the console tree, double-click Attributes.

4. In the Details pane, right-click the BuildingName attribute, and then click Properties.

5. On the General tab, clear the Attribute Is Active check box, as shown in Figure 12.9.

6. Click Yes at the warning dialog.

7. Click OK to close the attribute properties sheet.

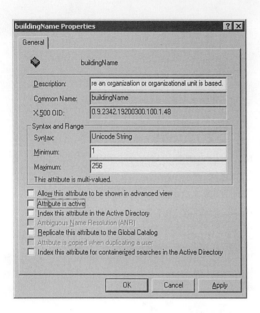

**FIGURE 12.9** Deactivating a schema attribute.

# Improving Replication with Application Partitions

Another new feature available in Windows Server 2003 is the concept of Application Partitions. This feature provides the ability to store data in Active Directory, taking advantage of Active Directory replication, without replicating that data to every domain controller in the forest.

Active Directory allows the creation of a new type of naming context (NC), or partition, called application partitions. This NC can contain a hierarchy of any type of objects except security principals (users, groups, and computers), and can be configured to replicate to any set of domain controllers in the forest, not necessarily all in the same domain.

This means that dynamic data from network services such as Remote Access Service (RAS), RADIUS, and Dynamic Host Configuration Protocol (DHCP) can reside in a directory so that applications can access them uniformly with one access methodology. Developers will be able to use this feature to write application data to dedicated application directory partitions rather than to a domain partition.

Most importantly, Windows Server 2003 uses application partitions to hold Active Directory Integrated DNS zones. For every domain in a forest, a separate application partition is created and is used to store all records that exist in each AD-integrated zone. Because the application partition is not included as part of the global catalog, DNS entries are no longer included as part of global catalog replication.

## Creating Application Partitions

Application partitions can be created using either the ADSIedit GUI interface, or by using the NTDSUtil command-line interface.

To create an application directory partition named "test" on a domain controller named DC1 in the companyabc.com domain, perform the following steps:

1. Open a command prompt.

2. Type **ntdsutil**, and press Enter.

3. At the ntdsutil command prompt, type **domain management**, and press Enter.

4. At the domain management command prompt, type **connection**, and press Enter.

5. At the connection command prompt, type **connect to server DC1**, and press Enter.

6. At the connection command prompt, type **quit**, and press Enter.

7. At the domain management command prompt, type **create nc dc=test,dc=companyabc, dc=com DC1**, and press Enter.

## Creating a Replica

After an application partition has been established, it is possible to add replicas of that partition to other domain controllers. Adding a replica initiates the replication process so that the application partition is available, for redundancy or data access, on any domain controller that is configured with a replica.

To add a replica, use the same NTDSUtil procedure used to create the application partition in the previous example. This time, add the replica to a domain controller named DC2 with the following command:

```
add nc replica dc=test,dc=companyabc,dc=com DC2
```

## Managing Replication

When changes are made in a particular application partition on a particular domain controller, those changes are replicated to other domain controllers containing a replica of that partition. The domain controller on which the change is made notifies its replication partners, and the replication is initiated. Windows Server 2003 enables you to control this replication process by setting the amount of time a domain controller will wait to send out the change notification to its first and subsequent replication partners.

Continuing with the previous examples, to configure DC1 to wait 10 minutes before notifying DC2 of a change to the test application partition, use the NTDSUtil command line interface, and type the following command at the domain management prompt:

```
set nc replicate notification delay dc=test,dc=companyabc,dc=com 600.
```

# Summary

As this chapter illustrates, there are several new features available to Active Directory with Windows Server 2003. Although many of the new features rely on a certain functional level of the Windows Server 2003 network, some features can be realized with only a single Windows Server 2003 domain controller running in a Windows 2000 functional mode (for example universal group caching). After the functional level of the forest is elevated to Windows Server 2003 mode, many of the barriers that once existed in Windows 2000 networks are broken, allowing administrators greater management and design flexibility than was ever possible before.

# 13

---

# Establishing
# a Solid
# Infrastructure
# Foundation

**W**hen implementing or migrating to a
new Windows Server 2003 environment,
the architects of the network frequently
focus on the Active Directory model. As
found through experience in the field, the
infrastructure of the network that includes
DNS, DHCP, and domain controllers sets the
proper foundation for a solid AD implementation. The functionality of core network
services is critical in a networking environment, and a good deal of thought should be
put into their design, administration, and
functional requirements. This chapter drills
down into the key aspects of the networking services and the best practice design and
configuration information for optimizing
the success of the network configuration.

# Focusing on the Windows Server 2003 Infrastructure Components

Although an enterprise network has many functional layers, this chapter focuses on three key components that are critical to the functionality of a Windows Server 2003 environment. These three aspects—network addressing, name resolution, and directory integration—provide for the base-level functionality expected of any modern enterprise network and provide the backbone for the Windows Server 2003 infrastructure.

## Network Addressing as the Infrastructure Foundation

The first critical component of a network is *addressing*, or allowing clients to assume a logical place in a network so that packets of information can be forwarded to and from the clients. This component was historically accomplished by proprietary network protocols, one for each network operating system (NOS). This gave NOS designers a great deal of flexibility in tailoring the communications components of their network to their specific design needs but made it difficult to exchange information between networks.

The Transmission Control Protocol/Internet Protocol (TCP/IP) was designed to interoperate between different varieties of networks, allowing them to speak a common "language," of sorts. The rise of this protocol coincided with the widespread adoption of the Internet itself, and it was this popularity and ubiquitous use of this protocol that led Microsoft to choose it as *the* standard protocol for Windows 2000. Windows Server 2003 continues to use TCP/IP as the default network protocol, expanding its place within the Microsoft NOS world.

TCP/IP requires that each node on a network be addressed by a unique IP address, such as 10.23.151.20. Each IP address must be assigned to every node on a network, either manually or by automatic methods. The automatic addressing component is the place where the DHCP service comes in with Windows Server 2003.

DHCP provides the automation of the critical TCP/IP addressing in Windows Server 2003 and makes administration of a network more palatable. You can find more details on DHCP in the section on "The Dynamic Host Configuration Protocol (DHCP) In Depth" later in this chapter.

## Simplifying Address Look-up with Name Resolution

The second critical aspect in networks is name resolution. Because humans understand the concept of names better than they do IP addresses, the need arises to translate those sets of numbers into common names.

Windows Server 2003 supports two types of name resolution. The first type, the domain name system (DNS), translates IP addresses into fully qualified domain name (FQDN) addresses, which allows them to be addressed in an Active Directory or Internet DNS structure.

The second type of name resolution, mapping legacy Microsoft NetBIOS names into IP addresses, is provided by WINS. Although it is technically possible (and ideal) to create a Windows Server environment free of NetBIOS name resolution, the truth is that divorcing a network from WINS dependency is very difficult, so it will remain an active part of network services in most organizations, at least for a few more years. You can find more information on WINS in the "Continuing Usage of Windows Internet Naming Service (WINS)" section later in this chapter.

## Centralizing Address Information with Directory Integration

The final important service that is supplied by a functional enterprise network is directory placement and lookup capability. Having a centralized directory that controls access to resources and provides for centralized administration is a vital function in modern networks.

Active Directory is the directory service that is provided with Windows Server 2003 and is built into many of the operating system components. The servers that handle the login requests and password changes and contain directory information are the domain controllers and global catalog domain controllers, which will be explained in more detail in the "The Active Directory Global Catalog" section later in this chapter.

Subsequently, domain controller and global catalog placement is a critical piece of a Windows Server 2003 environment. Special considerations must be made regarding this concept because access to directory lookup and registration is key for client functionality on a network.

## Network Services Changes in Windows Server 2003

Windows Server 2003's implementation of Active Directory expands upon the advanced feature set that Windows 2000 DNS introduced. Several key functional improvements were added, but the overall design and functionality changes have not been significant enough to change any Windows 2000 design decisions that were previously made regarding DNS. The following sections describe the functionality introduced in Windows 2000 DNS that has been carried over to Windows Server 2003 DNS and helps to distinguish it from other DNS implementations.

### Active Directory–Integrated Zones

The most dramatic change in Windows 2000's DNS implementation was the concept of directory-integrated DNS zones, known as AD-integrated zones. These zones were stored in Active Directory, as opposed to in a text file as in standard DNS. When the Active Directory was replicated, the DNS zone was replicated as well. This also allowed for secure updates, using Kerberos authentication, as well as the concept of multimaster DNS, in which no one server is the master server and all DNS servers contain a writeable copy of the zone.

Windows Server 2003 uses AD-integrated zones, but with one major change to the design. Instead of storing the zone information in Active Directory, it is instead stored in the application partition to reduce replication overhead. You can find more information on this concept in the following sections.

### Dynamic Updates

As previously mentioned, dynamic updates, using Dynamic DNS (DDNS), allow clients to automatically register and unregister their own host records as they are connected to the network. This concept was a new feature with Windows 2000 DNS and is carried over to Windows Server 2003.

### Unicode Character Support

Introduced in Windows 2000 and supported in Windows Server 2003, Unicode support of extended character sets enables DNS to store records written in Unicode, or essentially multiple character sets from many different languages. This functionality essentially allows DNS servers to use and perform lookups on records that are written with nonstandard characters, such as underscores, foreign letters, and so on.

## BEST PRACTICE

### Make Any DNS Implementation Compliant

Although Microsoft DNS supports Unicode characters, it is best practice that you make any DNS implementation compliant with the standard DNS character set so that you can support zone transfers to and from non-Unicode–compliant DNS implementations such as Unix BIND servers. This includes a–z, A–Z, 0–9, and the hyphen (-) character.

### DNS Changes in Windows Server 2003

In addition to the changes in Windows 2000 DNS, the Windows Server 2003 improvements help to further establish DNS as a reliable, robust name-resolution strategy for Microsoft and non-Microsoft environments. An overall knowledge of the increased functionality and the structural changes will help you to further understand the capabilities of DNS in Windows Server 2003. Some of the major changes in DNS in Windows Server 2003 that also solve several problem in Windows 2000 DNS are summarized in the following points:

- *DNS Stored in Application Partition.* Perhaps the most significant change in Windows Server 2003's DNS, Active Directory–integrated zones are now stored in the application partition of the AD. For every domain in a forest, a separate application partition is created and is used to store all records that exist in each AD-integrated zone. Because the application partition is not included as part of the global catalog, DNS entries are no longer included as part of global catalog replication.

  Previously, in Windows 2000, all AD-integrated zones were stored as global catalog objects and replicated to all global catalog servers in an entire forest. Many times, this information was not applicable across the entire forest, and unnecessary replication traffic was created. Subsequently, the application partition concept was enacted, and replication loads are now reduced, while important zone information is delegated to areas of the network where they are needed.

- *Automatic Creation of DNS Zones.* The Configure a DNS Server Wizard, as demonstrated in "Installing DNS Using the Configure Your Server Wizard" section later in this chapter, allows for the automatic creation of a DNS zone through a step-by-step wizard. This feature greatly eases the process of creating a zone, especially for Active Directory. You can invoke the wizard by right-clicking on the server name in the DNS MMC and choosing Configure a DNS Server.

- *No "Island" Problem.* Windows 2000 previously had a well-documented issue that was known as the "island" problem, which was manifested by a DNS server that pointed to itself as a DNS server. If the IP address of that server changed, the DNS server updated its own entry in DNS, but then other DNS servers within the domain were unable to successfully retrieve updates from the original server because they were requesting from the old IP address. This effectively left the original DNS server in an "island" by itself, hence the term.

  Windows Server 2003 DNS first changes its host records on a sufficient number of other authoritative servers within DNS so that the IP changes made will be successfully replicated, thus eliminating this "island" problem. As a result, it is no longer necessary to point a root DNS server to another DNS server for updates, as was previously recommended as a method of resolving this issue.

- *Forest Root Zone for _msdcs Moved to Separate Zone.* In Active Directory, all client logons and lookups are directed to local domain controllers and global catalog servers through references to the SRV records in DNS. These SRV records were stored in a subdomain to an Active Directory domain that was known as the _msdcs subdomain.

  In Windows Server 2003, _msdcs has been relocated to become a separate zone in DNS, as shown in Figure 13.1. This zone, stored in the application partition, is replicated to every domain controller that is a DNS server. This listing of SRV records was moved mainly to satisfy the requirements of remote sites. In Windows 2000, these remote sites had to replicate the entire DNS database locally to access the _msdcs records, which led to increased replication time and reduced responsiveness. If you delegate the SRV records to their own zone, only this specific zone can be designated for replication to remote site DNS servers, saving replication throughput and increasing the response time for clients.

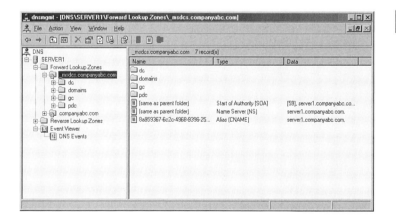

**FIGURE 13.1**
The _msdcs zone in Windows 2003 DNS.

# DNS in an Active Directory Environment

DNS is inseparable from Active Directory. In fact, the two are often confused for one another because of the similarities in their logical structures.

Active Directory uses a hierarchical LDAP-compliant structure that was designed to map into the DNS hierarchy, hence the similarities. In addition, Active Directory uses DNS for all internal lookups, from client logins to global catalog lookups. Subsequently, strong consideration into how DNS integrates with Active Directory is required for those considering deploying or upgrading AD.

## Impact of DNS on Active Directory

As any Windows 2000 administrator can attest, problems with DNS can spell disaster for an Active Directory environment. Because all servers and clients are constantly performing lookups on one another, a break in name-resolution service can severely affect Active Directory activity.

For this and other reasons, installing a redundant DNS infrastructure in any Active Directory implementation is strongly recommended. Even smaller environments should consider duplication of the primary DNS zone, and nearly as much emphasis as is put into protecting the global catalog AD index should be put into protecting DNS.

Security considerations for the DNS database should not be taken for granted. Secure updates to AD-integrated zones are highly recommended, and keeping DHCP servers off a domain controller can also help to secure DNS. In addition, limiting administrative access to DNS will help to mitigate problems with unauthorized "monkeying around" with DNS.

## Active Directory in Non-Microsoft DNS Implementations

Active Directory was specifically written to be able to co-exist and, in fact, use a non-Microsoft DNS implementation as long as that implementation supports active updates and SRV records. For example, AD will function in all versions of Unix BIND 8.1.2 or later. With this point in mind, however, it is still recommended that an organization with a significant investment in Microsoft technologies consider hosting Active Directory DNS on Windows Server 2003 systems because functionality enhancements provide for the best fit in these situations.

For environments that use older versions of DNS or are not able (or willing) to host Active Directory clients directly in their databases, Active Directory DNS can simply be delegated to a separate zone in which it can be authoritative. The Windows Server 2003 systems can simply set up forwarders to the foreign DNS implementations to provide for resolution of resources in the original zone.

## Using Secondary Zones in an AD Environment

Certain situations in Active Directory require the use of secondary zones to handle specific name resolution. For example, in peer-root domain models, where two separate trees form different namespaces within the same forest, secondaries of each DNS root are required to maintain proper forestwide synchronization.

Because each tree in a peer-root model is composed of independent domains that might not have security privileges in the other domains, a mechanism will need to be in place to allow lookups to occur between the two trees. The creation of secondary zones in each DNS environment will provide a solution to this scenario, as illustrated in Figure 13.2.

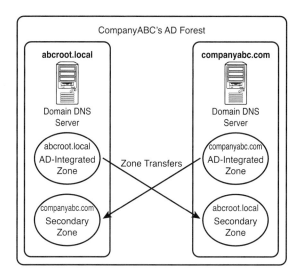

**FIGURE 13.2**
Peer-root domain DNS secondary zones.

## Specifying SRV Records and Site Resolution in DNS

All Active Directory clients use DNS for any type of domain-based lookups. Logins, for example, require lookups into the Active Directory for specific SRV records that indicate the location of domain controllers and global catalog servers. Windows Server 2003, as previously mentioned, divides the location of the SRV records into a separate zone, which is replicated to all domain controllers that have DNS installed on them.

Subdomains for each site are created in this zone; they indicate which resource is available in those specific sites. In a nutshell, if an SRV record in the specific site subdomain is incorrect, or another server from a different site is listed, all clients in that site are forced to authenticate in other sites. This concept is important because a common problem is that when Active Directory sites are created before they are populated with servers, an SRV record from the hub location is added to that site subdomain in DNS. When a new server is added to those sites, their SRV records join the other SRV records that were placed there when the site was created. These records are not automatically deleted, and they consequently direct clients to servers across slow WAN links, often making login times very slow.

In addition to the site containers, the root of these containers contains a list of all domain controllers in a specific domain, as shown in Figure 13.3. These lists are used for name resolution when a particular site server does not respond. If a site domain controller is down, clients randomly choose a domain controller in this site. It is therefore important to make sure that the only entries in this location are servers in fast-connected hub sites. Proper grooming of these SRV records and placement of servers into their proper site subdomains will do wonders for client login times.

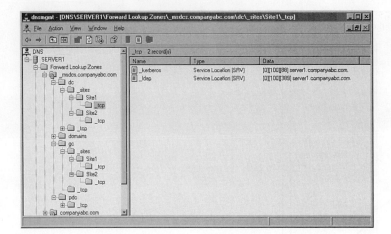

**FIGURE 13.3**
Site-level SRV records.

# The Domain Name System (DNS) In Depth

Name resolution is a key component in any network operating system (NOS) implementation. The capability of any one resource to locate other resources is the centerpiece of a functional network. Consequently, the name-resolution strategy chosen for a particular NOS must be robust and reliable, and it must conform to industry standards.

Windows Server 2003 uses the domain name system (DNS) as its primary method of name resolution, and DNS is a vital component of any Active Directory implementations of Windows Server 2003. Windows Server 2003's DNS implementation was designed to be compliant with the key Request for Comments (RFCs) that define the nature of a DNS. This makes it particularly beneficial for network infrastructures because it allows Windows Server 2003 to interoperate with external name-resolution environments.

This chapter details the key components of DNS in general and provides an overview of Windows Server 2003's specific implementation of DNS. A particular emphasis is placed on the role of DNS in Active Directory and the way it fits in standard and nonstandard configurations. Step-by-step instructions outline how to install and configure specific DNS components on Windows Server 2003. In addition, troubleshooting DNS issues and specific Active Directory design scenarios helps to give a hands-on approach to your understanding of DNS.

## The Need for DNS

As network infrastructure experts have found, a solid DNS design and implementation is critical to the successful lookup, views, and replication of DNS information across the Active Directory environment.

Although Microsoft developed its own implementation of DNS in Windows NT 4.0, it was based on the RFC standards on which DNS was founded. With the introduction of Windows 2000, Microsoft adopted DNS as *the* name-resolution strategy for Microsoft products. Older, legacy name resolution systems such as WINS are slowly being phased out. Since that time, the DNS implementation used by Microsoft has evolved to include a number of key benefits that distinguish it from standard DNS implementations, such as those in other DNS implementations—for example, Unix BIND. To understand these improvements, however, you first need a basic understanding of DNS functionality.

Microsoft very clearly heard from the marketplace how the DNS used for Active Directory needed to have better compatibility with the DNS used throughout the industry. Besides providing various options for AD integration into existing DNS environments, with Windows Server 2003 Microsoft now supports the InetOrgPerson attribute that further extends Microsoft's DNS compatibility for more common LDAP lookup and DNS integration compatibility.

## Framework for DNS

DNS structure is closely linked to the development of the Internet and often is confused with the Internet itself. The structure of DNS is highly useful, and the fact that it has thrived for so long is a tribute to its functionality. A closer examination of what constitutes DNS and how it is logically structured is important in understanding the bigger picture of how DNS fits in Windows Server 2003.

## Understanding the DNS Namespace

The bounded area that is defined by the DNS name is known as the *DNS namespace*. microsoft.com is a namespace, as is marketing.companyabc.com. Namespaces can be either public or private. Public namespaces are published on the Internet and are defined by a set of standards. All the .com, .net, .org, and like namespaces are external, or public. An internal namespace is not published to the Internet but is also not restricted by extension name. In other words, an internal, unpublished namespace can occupy any conceivable namespace, such as dnsname.internal or companyabc.root. Internal namespaces are most often used with Active Directory because they give increased security to a namespace. Because such namespaces are not published, they cannot be directly accessed from the Internet.

> **Microsoft DNS**
>
> Despite common misperception, Microsoft DNS does not have to be at the root of all organizational DNS structures. In fact, in most network environments that already have an extensive Unix-based DNS, Windows Active Directory frequently subordinates to Unix-based DNS servers. This minimizes the initial requirement of replacing all Unix DNS servers with Windows DNS servers, or more likely, to minimize the political infighting that might occur between Unix-DNS proponents and Windows-DNS proponents. If the existing DNS is Unix-based, the existing environment remains intact and the Active Directory DNS seamlessly ties in as a secondary.

# Installing DNS Using the Configure Your Server Wizard

Although there are various ways to install and configure DNS, the most straightforward and complete process involves invoking the Configure Your Server Wizard and subsequent Configure a DNS Server Wizard. The process detailed in this section illustrates the installation of a standard zone. Multiple variations of the installation are possible, but this particular scenario is illustrated to show the basics of DNS installation.

| |
|---|
| **If DNS Is Installed...** |
| If DNS is already installed on a server but not configured, start the procedure from step 7. |

| |
|---|
| **Running the Configure Your Server Wizard** |
| When you're running the Configure Your Server Wizard, as noted in step 3, and you select the typical configuration, the networking components for DNS and Active Directory Domain Controller will be installed automatically at this point. If you select the custom configuration in the Configure Your Server Wizard, you need to follow steps 4 through 21. |

Installation of DNS on Windows Server 2003 is straightforward, and no reboot is necessary. To install and configure the DNS service on a Windows Server 2003 computer, follow these steps:

1. Choose Start, All Programs, Administrative Tools, Configure Your Server Wizard.

2. Click Next on the Welcome screen.

3. Make sure that the listed prerequisites have been satisfied and click Next to continue. The Configure Your Server Wizard will then perform a network test.

4. Select the DNS Server Component and click Next. (If you are installing Active Directory with DNS, you need to select Domain Controller as well, although this procedure is not outlined here.)

5. Verify that the options to Install DNS Server and Run the Configure a DNS Server Wizard to Configure DNS are selected and click Next.

6. After DNS is installed, you might be prompted for your Windows Server 2003 CD. If so, insert it and click OK when prompted.

7. The Configure a DNS Server Wizard is then started automatically, as illustrated in Figure 13.4. (Or, if DNS is already installed, install it manually by choosing Start, Run and typing **dnswiz.exe**.)

8. On the Welcome screen for the Configure a DNS Server Wizard, click Next to continue.

9. Select Create Forward and Reverse Lookup Zones (Recommended for Large Networks) and click Next.

10. Select Yes, Create a Forward Lookup Zone Now (Recommended) and click Next.

**FIGURE 13.4** The Configure a DNS Server Wizard.

11. Select the type of zone to be created—in this case, choose Primary Zone—and click Next. If the server is a domain controller, the Store the Zone in Active Directory check box is available.

12. Type the name of the zone in the Zone Name box and click Next.

13. At this point, you can create a new zone text file or import one from an existing zone file. In this case, choose Create a New File with This File Name and accept the default. Click Next to continue.

14. The subsequent screen allows a zone to either accept or decline dynamic updates. In this case, enable dynamic updates by selecting the Allow Both Nonsecure and Secure Dynamic Updates radio button and clicking Next.

15. The next screen allows for the creation of a reverse lookup zone. Here, select Yes, Create a Reverse Lookup Zone and click Next.

## BEST PRACTICE

### When Enabling Dynamic Updates to Be Accepted by Your DNS Server

When enabling dynamic updates to be accepted by your DNS server, be sure you know the sources of dynamic updated information. If the sources are not reliable, you can potentially receive corrupt or invalid information from a dynamic update.

16. Select Primary Zone and click Next.

17. Type in the network ID of the reverse lookup zone and click Next. (The network ID is typically the first set of octets from an IP address in the zone. If a class C IP range of 10.1.1.0/24 is in use on a network, you would enter the values 10.1.1, as illustrated in Figure 13.5.)

18. Again, you are offered the option to create a new zone file or to use an existing file. In this case, choose Create a New File with This File Name and click Next to continue.

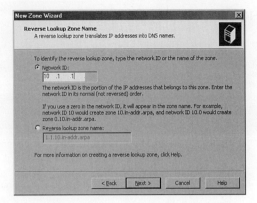

**FIGURE 13.5**    Reverse lookup zone creation.

### You Might See a Pop-up Dialog Box

Depending on your network connectivity, you might see a pop-up dialog box between the two clicks to finish your DNS changes in step 21. If you are not connected to a LAN, you will see an error dialog box regarding searching for root hints. Although the dialog box notes the root hint error, if you click OK, DNS will still be configured successfully, so this is just an information note.

19. Again, you are presented the option for dynamic updates. In this case, select Allow Both Nonsecure and Secure Dynamic Updates and click Next to continue.

20. The next screen deals with the setup of forwarders, which will be described in more detail in the "DNS Zones" section later in this chapter. In this example, choose No, It Should Not Forward Queries and click Next to continue.

21. The final window, shown in Figure 13.6, displays a summary of the changes that will be made and the zones that will be added to the DNS database. Click Finish twice to finalize the changes and create the zones.

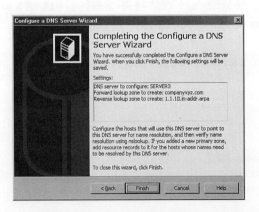

**FIGURE 13.6**    The final steps of the Configure a DNS Server Wizard.

# Configuring DNS to Point to Itself

DNS is installed immediately upon the closing of the Configure a DNS Server Wizard. One subtask that you should accomplish after the installation is configuring the DNS server in the TCP/IP settings to point to itself for DNS resolution, unless you have a specific reason not to do so. To accomplish this task, perform the following steps:

1. Choose Start, Control Panel, Network Connections.

2. While in Network Connections, right-click *<Local Area Connection>* (where *Local Area Connection* is the particular network adapter that is to be used on the network where DNS is implemented) and select Properties.

3. Double-click Internet Protocol (TCP/IP).

4. In the DNS Server boxes, make sure that Use the Following DNS Server Addresses is selected and then type the IP address of the DNS server into the Preferred DNS Server box.

5. If you have a hub DNS server, you can enter it into the Alternate DNS Server box.

6. Click OK and then OK again to complete the changes.

If you have installed DNS on a domain controller, all the Active Directory–integrated zones that exist in your domain DNS will subsequently be automatically transmitted to your new DNS installation. If, however, the zones in a domain are standard, or the new server is a new DNS structure, further configuration of zones will be required.

> **Configure a DNS Server to Point to Itself**
>
> Previous recommendations for Windows 2000 stipulated that a root DNS server point to another DNS server as the primary name server. This recommendation was made in response to what is known as the "island" problem in Windows DNS. Administrators will take heart in the fact that Windows Server 2003 no longer is subject to this problem, and it is now recommended that you configure a DNS server to point to itself in most cases as mentioned in an earlier section on "Configuring DNS to Point to Itself."

# Using Resource Records in a Windows 2003 Environment

In the DNS hierarchy, objects are identified through the use of resource records (RRs). These records are used for basic lookups of users and resources within the specified domain and are unique for the domain in which they are located. Because DNS is not a flat namespace, however, multiple, identical RRs can exist at different levels in a DNS hierarchy. The distributed nature of the DNS hierarchy allows such levels.

Several key resource records exist in most DNS implementations, especially in those associated with Windows Server 2003 Active Directory. A general familiarity with these specific types of RRs is required to gain a better understanding of DNS.

## Start of Authority (SOA) Records in DNS

The Start of Authority (SOA) record in a DNS database indicates which server is authoritative for that particular zone. The server referenced by the SOA records is subsequently the server that is assumed to be the best source of information about a particular zone and is in charge of processing zone updates. The SOA record contains information such as the Time to Live (TTL) interval, the contact person responsible for DNS, and other critical information, as illustrated in Figure 13.7.

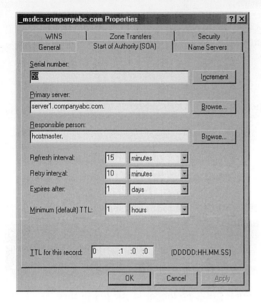

**FIGURE 13.7**   A sample SOA record.

An SOA record is automatically created when DNS is installed for Active Directory in Windows Server 2003 and is populated with the default TTL, primary server, and other pertinent information for the zone. After installation, however, these values can be modified to fit the specific needs of an organization.

## DNS Host (A) Records

The most common type of RR in DNS is the *host record*, also known as an *A record*. This type of RR simply contains the name of the host and its corresponding IP address, as illustrated in Figure 13.8.

The vast majority of RRs in DNS are A records because they are used to identify the IP addresses of most resources within a domain.

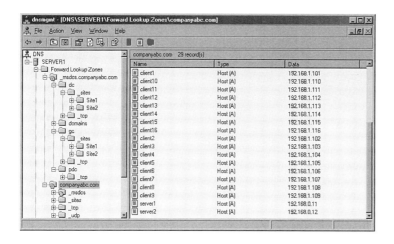

**FIGURE 13.8**
Sample host records.

## Name Server (NS) Records

Name Server (NS) records identify which computers in a DNS database are the name servers, essentially the DNS servers for a particular zone. Although there can be only one SOA record for a zone, there can be multiple NS records for the zone, which indicate to clients which machines are available to run DNS queries against.

> **Name Server Records**
>
> Name Server records, or NS records, do not actually contain the IP information of a particular resource. In fact, in most cases only A records contain this information. NS records and other similar records simply point to a server's A record. For example, an NS record will simply point to server1.companyabc.com, which will then direct the query to the server1 A record in the companyabc.com zone.

## Service (SRV) Records for Added DNS Information

Service (SRV) records are RRs that indicate which resources perform a particular service. Domain controllers in Active Directory are referenced by SRV records that define specific services, such as the global catalog, LDAP, and Kerberos. SRV records are a relatively new addition to DNS, and did not exist in the original implementation of the standard. Each SRV record contains information about a particular functionality that a resource provides. For example, an LDAP server can add an SRV record indicating that it can handle LDAP requests for a particular zone.

> **Unix BIND Servers, Version 8.1.2 or Later Is Recommended for Unix BIND Servers**
>
> Because SRV records are a relatively new addition to DNS, they are not supported by several down-level DNS implementations, such as Unix BIND 4.1.x and NT 4.0 DNS. It is therefore critical that the DNS environment that is used for Windows Server 2003 Active Directory have the capability to create SRV records. For Unix BIND servers, version 8.1.2 or later is recommended.

SRV records can be very useful for Active Directory because domain controllers can advertise that they handle global catalog requests, as illustrated in Figure 13.9.

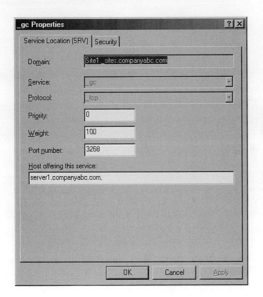

## Mail Exchanger (MX) Records Defining E-mail Routing

A Mail Exchanger (MX) record indicates which resources are available for SMTP mail reception. MX records can be set on a domain basis so that mail sent to a particular domain will be forwarded to the server or servers indicated by the MX record. For example, if an MX record is set for the domain companyabc.com, all mail sent to user@companyabc.com will be automatically directed to the server indicated by the MX record.

## Pointer (PTR) Records for Reverse DNS Queries

Reverse queries to DNS are accomplished through the use of Pointer (PTR) records. In other words, if a user wants to look up the name of a resource that is associated with a specific IP address, he would do a reverse lookup using that IP address. A DNS server would reply using a PTR record that would indicate the name associated with that IP address. PTR records are most commonly found in reverse lookup zones.

## Canonical Name (CNAME) Records for Alias Information

A Canonical Name (CNAME) record represents a server alias, or essentially allows any one of a number of servers to be referred to by multiple names in DNS. The record essentially redirects queries made to it to the A record for that particular host. CNAME records are useful when migrating servers and for situations in which friendly names, such as mail.companyabc.com, are required to point to more complex, server-naming conventions such as sfoexch01.companyabc.com.

## Other DNS Records that Store Information

Other, less common forms of records that might exist in DNS have specific purposes, and there might be cause to create them. The following is a sample list but is by no means exhaustive:

- AAAA—Maps a standard IP address into a 128-bit IPv6 address, as indicated in Figure 13.10. This type of record will become more prevalent as IPv6 is adopted.

- ISDN—Maps a specific DNS name to an ISDN telephone number.

- KEY—Stores a public key used for encryption for a particular domain.

- RP—Specifies the Responsible Person for a domain.

- WKS—Designates a particular Well Known Service.

- MB—Indicates which host contains a specific mailbox.

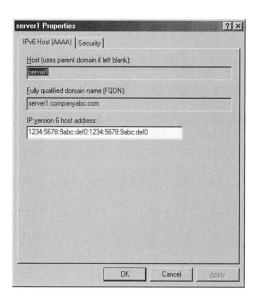

**FIGURE 13.10**    AAAA resource record.

# Establishing and Implementing DNS Zones

A *zone* in DNS is a portion of a DNS namespace that is controlled by a particular DNS server or group of servers. The zone is the primary delegation mechanism in DNS and is used to establish boundaries over which a particular server can resolve requests. Any server that hosts a particular zone is said to be "authoritative" for that zone, with the exception of stub zones, which are defined later in the chapter in the section on "stub zones." Figure 13.11 illustrates how different portions of the DNS namespace can be divided into zones, each of which can be hosted on a DNS server or group of servers.

It is important to understand that any section or subsection of DNS can exist within a single zone. For example, an organization might

**Caching-only Server**

A server that is installed with DNS but does not have any zones configured is known as a *caching-only server.* Establishing a caching-only server can be useful in some branch office situations because it can help to alleviate large amounts of client query traffic across the network and eliminate the need to replicate entire DNS zones to remote locations.

decide to place an entire namespace of a domain, subdomains, and sub-subdomains into a single zone. Or specific sections of that namespace can be divided up into separate zones. In fact, the entire Internet namespace can be envisioned as a single namespace with . as the root, which is divided into a multitude of different zones.

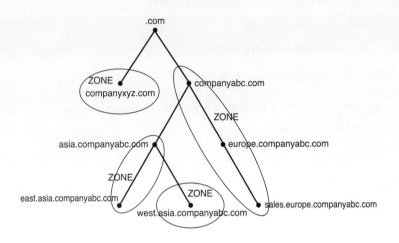

**FIGURE 13.11**
DNS zones.

## Forward Lookup Zones

A *forward lookup zone* is created to do, as the name suggests, forward lookups to the DNS database. In other words, this type of zone resolves names to IP addresses and resource information. For example, if a user wants to reach Server1 and queries for its IP address through a forward lookup zone, DNS returns 10.0.0.11, the IP address for that resource.

## Reverse Lookup Zones

### CNAME Records

There is nothing to stop the assignment of multiple RRs to a single resource. In fact, this practice is common and useful in many situations. It might be practical to have a server respond to more than one name in specific circumstances. This type of functionality is normally accomplished through the creation of CNAME records, which create aliases for a particular resource.

A *reverse lookup zone* performs the exact opposite operation as a forward lookup zone. IP addresses are matched up with a common name in a reverse lookup zone. This is similar to knowing someone's phone number but not knowing the name associated with it. Reverse lookup zones must be manually created, and do not always exist in every implementation. Reverse lookup zones are primarily populated with PTR records, which serve to point the reverse lookup query to the appropriate name.

## Primary Zones

In traditional (non-Active Directory–integrated) DNS, a single server serves as the master DNS server for a zone, and all changes made to that particular zone are done on that particular server. A single DNS server can host multiple zones, and can be primary for one and secondary for another. If a zone is primary, however, all requested changes for that particular zone must be done on the server that holds the master copy of the zone.

Creating a new primary zone manually is a fairly straightforward process. The following procedure outlines the creation of a standard zone for the `companyabc.com` DNS namespace:

1. Open the DNS MMC snap-in by choosing Start, Administrative Tools, DNS.

2. Navigate to DNS\\<*Servername*>\\Forward Lookup Zones.

3. Right-click Forward Lookup Zones and choose New Zone.

4. Click Next on the Welcome screen.

5. Select Primary Zone from the list of zone types available and click Next to continue.

6. Type in the name of the primary zone to be created and click Next.

7. Because you're creating a new zone file, as opposed to importing an existing zone file, select Create a New File with This File Name and click Next.

8. Determine whether dynamic updates will be allowed in this zone. If not, select Do Not Allow Dynamic Updates and click Next to continue.

9. Click Finish on the Summary page to create the zone.

## Secondary Zones

A *secondary zone* is established to provide redundancy and load balancing for the primary zone. Each copy of the DNS database is read-only, however, because all recordkeeping is done on the primary zone copy. A single DNS server can contain several zones that are primary and several that are secondary. The zone creation process is similar to the one outlined in the preceding section on primary zones, but with the difference being that the zone is transferred from an existing primary server.

## Stub Zones

The concept of *stub zones* is new in Microsoft DNS. A stub zone is essentially a zone that contains no information about the members in a domain but simply serves to forward queries to a list of designated name servers for different domains. A stub zone subsequently contains only NS, SOA, and glue records. Glue records are essentially A records that work in conjunction with a particular NS record to resolve the IP address of a particular name server. A server that hosts a stub zone for a namespace is not authoritative for that zone.

As illustrated in Figure 13.12, the stub zone effectively serves as a placeholder for a zone that is authoritative on another server. It allows a server to forward queries that are made to a specific zone to the list of name servers in that zone.

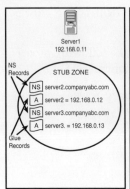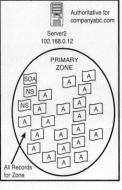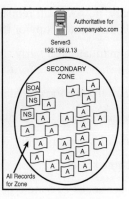

**FIGURE 13.12**
Stub zones in Windows 2003.

You can easily create a stub zone in Windows Server 2003 after it is determined that a stub zone is required. The following procedure details the steps involved with the creation of a stub zone:

1. Open the DNS MMC snap-in by choosing Start, Administrative Tools, DNS.

### AD Zone Replication Scope Steps

In the AD Zone Replication Scope steps, you will have three options: 1) to all DNS servers in the forest, 2) to all DNS servers in the AD domain, and 3) to all DCs in the AD domain. If you have a single domain and a single forest, your best choice is to select option 1 and replicate throughout your forest. If you are in charge of only a single domain in your organization, you should choose option 2 to replicate across DNS servers in your own domain. If DNS is not integrated to Active Directory, choosing option 3 will replicate just to the domain controllers in your domain.

2. Navigate to DNS\\<Servername>\\Forward Lookup Zones.

3. Right-click Forward Lookup Zones and choose New Zone.

4. Click Next on the Welcome screen.

5. Select Stub Zone from the list of zone types and click Next to continue.

6. Type in the name of the zone that will be created and click Next to continue.

7. Select Create a New File with This File Name and accept the defaults, unless you are migrating from an existing zone file. Then click Next to continue.

8. Type in the IP address of the server or servers from which the zone records will be copied. Click Add for each server entered, as shown in Figure 13.13, and then click Next to continue.

9. Click Finish on the Summary page to create the zone.

The newly created stub zone will hold only the SOA, NS, and glue records for the domain at which it is pointed.

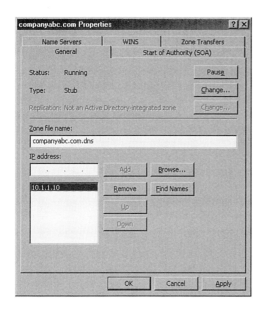

**FIGURE 13.13**    A newly created stub zone.

# Creating Zone Transfers in DNS

Copying the DNS database from one server to another is accomplished through a process known as a *zone transfer*. Zone transfers are required for any zone that has more than one name server responsible for the contents of that zone. The mechanism for zone transfers varies, however, depending on the version of DNS and whether the zone is Active Directory–integrated.

DNS servers can be configured to notify other DNS servers of changes to a zone and begin a zone transfer on a scheduled basis. To set up a server to send zone transfers to another server from a forward lookup zone, follow these steps:

1. Open the DNS MMC snap-in by choosing Start, Administrative Tools, DNS.

2. Navigate to DNS\<*Servername*>\Forward Lookup Zones.

3. Right-click the name of the zone and choose Properties.

4. Choose the Zone Transfers tab.

5. Check Allow Zone Transfers and select Only to the Following Servers.

6. Type in the IP address of the server that will receive the update, as shown in Figure 13.14.

7. Click OK to save the changes.

> **Only to Servers Listed**
>
> In addition to specifically defining recipients of zone transfers by IP address, you can select the Only to Servers Listed on the Name Servers Tab radio button as well, assuming that the recipient server or servers are listed under the Name Servers tab.

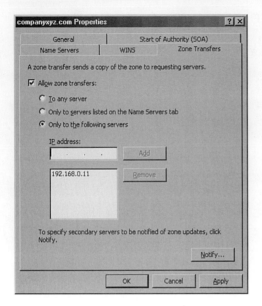

**FIGURE 13.14**   Setting up zone transfers.

## Full Zone Transfer

The standard method for zone transfers, which transfers the entire contents of a DNS zone to other servers, is known as asynchronous zone transfer (AXFR) or full zone transfer. This type of zone transfer copies every item in the DNS database to a separate server, regardless of whether the server already has some of the items in the database. Older implementations of DNS used AXFR exclusively, and it is still used for specific purposes today.

## Incremental Zone Transfer (IXFR)

An incremental zone transfer (IXFR) is a process by which all incremental changes to a DNS database are replicated to another DNS server. This saves bandwidth over AXFR replication changes because only the *delta*, or changes made to the database since the last zone transfer, are replicated.

IXFR zone transfers are accomplished by referencing an index number that is referenced on the SOA of the DNS server that holds the primary zone. This number is incremented upon each change to a zone. If the server requesting the zone transfer has an index number of 45, for example, and the primary zone server has an index number of 55, only those changes made during the period of time between 45 and 55 will be incrementally sent to the requesting server via an IXFR transfer. However, if the difference in index numbers is too great, the information on the requesting server is assumed to be stale, and a full AXFR transfer will be initiated. For example, if a requesting server has an index of 25, and the primary zone server's index is 55, an AXFR zone transfer will be initiated, as illustrated in Figure 13.15.

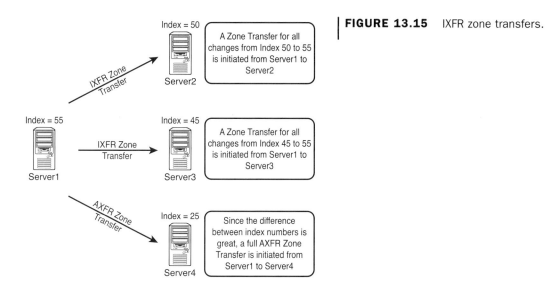

**FIGURE 13.15**    IXFR zone transfers.

# Understanding the Importance of DNS Queries

The primary function of DNS is to provide name resolution for requesting clients, so the query mechanism is subsequently one of the most important elements in the system. Two types of queries are commonly made to a DNS database: recursive and iterative.

## Recursive Queries

Recursive queries are most often performed by resolvers, or clients that need to have a specific name resolved by a DNS server. Recursive queries are also accomplished by a DNS server if forwarders are configured to be used on a particular name server. A recursive query essentially asks whether a particular record can be resolved by a particular name server. The response to a recursive query is either negative or positive. A common recursive query scenario is illustrated in Figure 13.16.

## Iterative Queries

Iterative queries ask a DNS server to either resolve the query or make a "best guess" referral to a DNS server that might contain more accurate information about where the query can be resolved. Another iterative query is then performed to the referred server and so on until a result, positive or negative, is obtained.

In the example shown in Figure 13.16, Client1 in CompanyABC opens a Web browser and attempts to browse to the Web site for www.microsoft.com. A recursive query is initiated to the default name server; in this case, Server1 is contacted. Because Server1 is authoritative only for the companyabc.com namespace, and no entries exist for microsoft.com, the query is sent to an "upstream" DNS server that is listed in the root hints of the DNS server. That server, Server2, is not authoritative for microsoft.com but sends a referral back to Server1 for Server3, which is a name server for the .com namespace. Server3 knows that Server4 handles name-resolution requests for microsoft.com and sends that information back to Server1. A final iterative query is then sent from Server1 to Server4, and Server4 successfully resolves www to the proper IP address. Server1, with this information in hand, returns Client1's original recursive query with the proper IP address and Client1's browser successfully resolves www.microsoft.com.

This type of functionality lies at the heart of the distributed nature of DNS and allows DNS lookups to function as efficiently as they do.

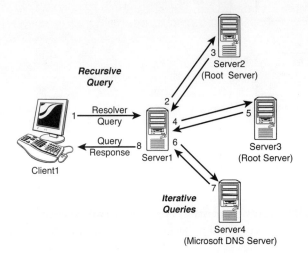

**FIGURE 13.16**
Recursive and iterative queries.

# Other DNS Components

Several other key components lie at the heart of DNS and are necessary for it to function properly. In addition, you need to fully understand the functionality of several key components of DNS that are used heavily by Microsoft DNS.

## Dynamic DNS (DDNS)

Older versions of DNS relied on administrators manually updating all the records within a DNS database. Every time a resource was added or information about a resource was changed, the DNS database was updated, normally via a simple text editor, to reflect the changes. Dynamic DNS was developed as a direct response to the increasing administrative overhead that was required to keep DNS databases functional and up to date. With Dynamic DNS, clients can automatically update their own records in DNS, depending on the security settings of the zone.

It is important to note that only Windows 2000/XP and later clients support dynamic updates and that down-level (NT/9x) clients must have DHCP configured properly in order for them to be updated in DNS.

# Time to Live (TTL)

The Time to Live (TTL) value for a server is the amount of time (in seconds) that a resolver or name server will keep a cached DNS request before requesting it again from the original name server. This value helps to keep the information in the DNS database relevant. Setting TTL levels is essentially a balancing act between the need for updated information and the need to reduce DNS query traffic across the network.

In the example from the "Iterative Queries" section, if Client1 already requested the IP of www.microsoft.com, and the information was returned to the DNS server that showed the IP address, it would make sense that that IP address would not change often and could therefore be cached for future queries. The next time another client requests the same information, the local DNS server will give that client the IP address it received from the original Client1 query as long as the TTL has not expired. This helps to reduce network traffic and improve DNS query response time.

The TTL for a response is set by the name server that successfully resolves a query. In other words, you might have different TTLs set for items in a cache, based on where they were resolved and the TTL for the particular zone they originated from.

The TTL setting for a zone is modified via the SOA record. The procedure for doing this in Windows Server 2003 is as follows:

1. Open the DNS MMC snap-in by choosing Start, Administrative Tools, DNS.

2. Navigate to DNS\<Servername>\Forward Lookup Zones\<Zonename>.

3. Find the SOA record for the zone and double-click it.

4. Modify the Minimum (Default) TTL entry to match the TTL you want, as shown in Figure 13.17.

5. Click OK to accept the changes.

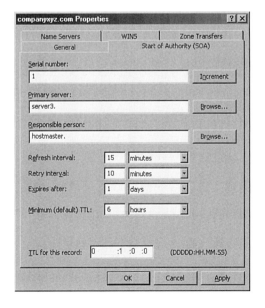

**FIGURE 13.17**   Changing the TTL.

## Secure Updates

One of the main problems with a Dynamic DNS implementation lies with the security of the update mechanism. If no security is enforced, nothing will prevent malicious users from updating a record for a server, for example, to redirect it to their own IP address. For this reason, dynamic updates are, by default, turned off on new standard zones that are created in Windows Server 2003. However, with AD-integrated DNS zones, a mechanism exists that will allow clients to perform *secure dynamic updates*. Secure updates use Kerberos to authenticate users and ensure that only those clients that created a record can subsequently update the same record.

If you're using DHCP to provide secure updates, one important caveat is that DHCP servers should not be located on the domain controller because of specific issues in regards to secure updates. The reason for this recommendation is that all DHCP servers are placed in a group known as DNSUpdateProxy. Members of this group do not take ownership of items that are published in DNS. This group was created because DHCP servers often dynamically publish updates for clients automatically, and the clients would need to modify their entries themselves. Subsequently, the first client to access a newly created entry would take ownership of that entry. Because domain controllers create sensitive SRV records and the like, it is not wise to use a domain controller as a member of this group, and it is subsequently not wise to have DHCP on domain controllers for this reason.

# DNS Maintenance, Updates, and Scavenging

DNS RRs often become stale, or no longer relevant, as computers are disconnected from the network or IP addresses are changed without first notifying the DNS server. The process of *scavenging* those records removes them from a database after their original owners do not update them. Scavenging is not turned on, by default, but you can enable this feature in Windows Server 2003 by following these steps:

1. Open the DNS MMC snap-in by Start, Administrative Tools, DNS.

2. Right-click the server name and choose Properties.

3. Select the Advanced tab.

4. Check the Enable Automatic Scavenging of Stale Records box.

5. Select a scavenging period, as shown in Figure 13.18, and click OK to save your changes.

Scavenging makes a DNS database cleaner, but aggressive scavenging can also remove valid entries. It is therefore wise, if you're using scavenging, to strike a balance between a clean database and a valid one.

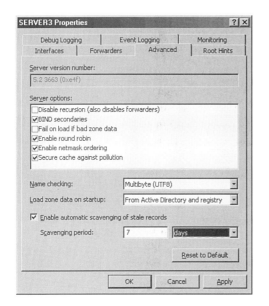

**FIGURE 13.18**   Turning on scavenging.

## Root Hints

By default, a DNS installation includes a listing of Internet-level name servers that can be used for name resolution of the .com, .net, .uk, and like domain names on the Internet. When a DNS server cannot resolve a query locally in its cache or in local zones, it consults the Root Hints list, which indicates which servers to begin iterative queries with.

The Hints file should be updated on a regular basis to ensure that the servers listed are still relevant. This file is located in \%systemroot%\system32\DNS\cache.dns and can be updated on the Internet at the following address:

```
ftp://ftp.rs.internic.net/domain/named.cache
```

## Forwarders

*Forwarders* are name servers that handle all iterative queries for a name server. In other words, if a server cannot answer a query from a client resolver, servers that have forwarders simply forward the request to an upstream forwarder that will do the iterative queries to the Internet root name servers. Forwarders are used often in situations in which an organization uses the DNS servers of an ISP to handle all name-resolution traffic. Another common situation occurs when Active Directory's DNS servers handle all internal AD DNS resolution but forward outbound DNS requests to another DNS environment within an organization, such as a legacy Unix BIND server.

In conditional forwarding, queries that are made to a specific domain or set of domains are sent to a specifically defined forwarder DNS server. This type of scenario is normally used to define routes that internal domain resolution traffic will follow. For example, if an organization controls the companyabc.com domain namespace and the companyxyz.com namespace, it might want queries between domains to be resolved on local DNS servers, as opposed to being sent out to the Internet just to be sent back again so that they are resolved internally.

Forward-only servers are never meant to do iterative queries, but rather to forward all requests that cannot be answered locally to a forwarder or set of forwarders. If those forwarders do not respond, a failure message is generated.

If you plan to use forwarders in a Windows Server 2003 DNS environment, you can establish them by following these steps:

1. Open the DNS MMC snap-in by choosing Start, Administrative Tools, DNS.

2. Right-click the server name and choose Properties.

3. Select the Forwarders tab.

4. In the DNS Domain box, determine whether conditional forwarders will be established. If so, add them by clicking the New button.

5. Add the IP address of the forwarders into the Selected Domain's Forwarder IP Address List box, as shown in Figure 13.19.

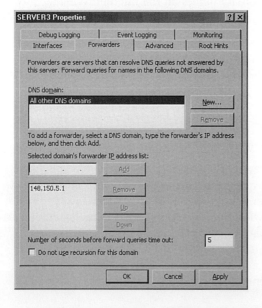

**FIGURE 13.19**   Setting up forwarders.

6. If this server will be configured only to forward, and to otherwise fail if forwarding does not work, check the Do Not Use Recursion for This Domain box.

7. Click OK to save the changes.

## Using WINS for Lookups

In environments with a significant investment in WINS lookups, the WINS database can be used in conjunction with DNS to provide DNS name resolution. If a DNS query has exhausted all DNS methods of resolving a name, a WINS server can be queried to provide for resolution. This method creates several WINS RRs in DNS that are established to support this approach.

To enable WINS to assist with DNS lookups, follow these steps:

1. Open the DNS MMC snap-in by choosing Start, Administrative Tools, DNS.

2. Navigate to DNS\<Servername>\Forward Lookup Zones.

3. Right-click the zone in question and choose Properties.

4. Choose the WINS tab.

5. Check the Use WINS Forward Lookup box.

6. Enter the IP address of the WINS Server(s), click Add, and then click OK to save the changes.

# Troubleshooting DNS

Much has been written about the complexity of DNS, and even more misconceptions have been written about it. In truth, however, DNS structure is logical, so you can easily troubleshoot it, if you use the proper tools and techniques. A good grasp of these tools and their functionality is a must for proper name-resolution troubleshooting with DNS.

## Using the DNS Event Viewer to Diagnose Problems

As any good administrator knows, the Event Viewer is the first place to look for any type of troubleshooting. Windows Server 2003 makes it even more straightforward to use because DNS Events compiled from the Event Viewer are immediately accessible from the DNS MMC console. Parsing this set of logs can help you to troubleshoot DNS replication issues and query problems.

For more advanced Event Log diagnosis, you can turn on Debug Logging on a per-server basis. It is recommended that you turn on this functionality only as required, however, because log files can fill up fast with debugging turned on. To enable Debug Logging, follow these steps:

1. Open the DNS MMC snap-in by choosing Start, Administrative Tools, DNS.

2. Right-click on the server name and choose Properties.

3. Select the Debug Logging tab.

4. Check the Log Packets for Debugging box.

5. Configure any additional settings as required and click OK.

It is recommended that you turn off these settings after the troubleshooting is complete.

## Using Performance Monitor to Monitor DNS

Performance Monitor is a built-in, often-overlooked utility that allows for a great deal of insight into issues in a network. In regards to DNS, many critical DNS counters can be monitored relating to queries, zone transfers, memory use, and other important factors.

## Client-Side Cache and HOST Resolution Problems

Windows 2000 and later clients have a built-in client cache for name resolution that caches all information retrieved from name servers. When requesting lookups, the client resolver parses this cache first, before contacting the name server. Items remain in this cache until the TTL expires, the machine is rebooted, or the cache is flushed. In cases where erroneous information has been entered into the client cache, you can flush it by typing **ipconfig /flushdns** at the command prompt.

By default, all clients have a file named HOSTS that provides for a simple line-by line resolution of names to IP addresses. This file is normally located in \%systemroot%\system32\drivers\etc. Problems can occur when these manual entries conflict with DNS, and it is therefore wise to ensure that there are not conflicts with this HOSTS file and the DNS database when troubleshooting.

## Using the NSLOOKUP Command-Line Utility

The NSLOOKUP command-line utility is perhaps the most useful tool for DNS client troubleshooting. Its functionality is basic, but the information that you obtain can do wonders for helping you to understand DNS problems. NSLOOKUP, in its most basic operation, contacts the default DNS server of a client and attempts to resolve a name that is input. For example, to test a lookup on www.companyabc.com, type **nslookup www.companyabc.com** at the command prompt. Different query types can be also input into NSLOOKUP. For example, you can create simple queries to view the MX and SOA records associated with a specific domain by following these steps, which are illustrated in Figure 13.20:

1. Open a command prompt instance by choosing Start, All Programs, Accessories, Command Prompt.

2. Type **nslookup** and press Enter.

3. Type **set query=mx** and press Enter.

4. Type *<domainname>* and press Enter.

5. Type **set query=soa** and press Enter.

6. Type *<domainname>* and press Enter.

NSLOOKUP's functionality is not limited to these simple lookups. Performing an nslookup /? lists the many functions it is capable of. NSLOOKUP is a tool of choice for many name-resolution problems and is a must in any troubleshooter's arsenal.

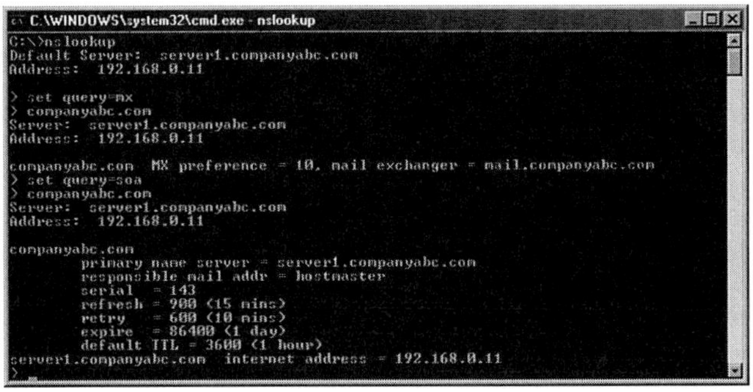

**FIGURE 13.20**
NSLOOKUP on an MX record.

## Using the IPCONFIG Command-Line Utility

Another important tool for DNS resolution problems is the IPCONFIG utility, the same utility used for common TCP/IP issues. There are several key functions that IPCONFIG offers in regards to DNS. These functions can be invoked from the command prompt with the right flag, detailed as follows:

- ipconfig /flushdns—If you experience problems with the client-side cache, the cache itself can be "flushed" through the invocation of the flushdns flag. This removes all previously cached queries that a client might be storing and is particularly useful if a server name has just changed IP addresses and particular clients have trouble connecting to it.

- ipconfig /registerdns—The registerdns flag forces the client to dynamically re-register itself in DNS, if the particular zone supports dynamic updates.

> **These Three Flags**
>
> These three flags, as well as a few others, are available only in Windows 2000 or later clients. Previous clients such as NT 4.0 were limited to more basic functionality with IPCONFIG, and other clients such as Win9x clients used a different utility known as WINIPCFG. As with any utility, you can unearth more advanced functionality by invoking the utility with a ? flag (ipconfig /?).

- ipconfig /displaydns—An interesting but not well-known flag is displaydns. This flag displays the contents of the client-side cache and is useful for troubleshooting specific issues with individual records.

## Using the TRACERT Command-Line Utility

The TRACERT utility is a valuable resource that gives you an idea of the path that a DNS query takes when being sent over a network. By directing TRACERT at www.microsoft.com, for example, you can get an idea of how many routers and DNS servers the packet is crossing. The way that TRACERT works is simple but actually quite interesting. A DNS query that has a TTL of 1 is sent out. Because all routers are supposed to drop the TTL by 1 on each packet that they process, this means that the first router will refuse to forward the packet and send that refusal back to the originator. The originating machine then increments the TTL by 1 and resends the packet. This time the packet will make it past the first router and get refused by the second. This process continues until the destination is met, as illustrated in Figure 13.21. Needless to say, using this command-line utility is a simple yet effective way of viewing the path that a DNS query takes as it crosses the Internet.

**FIGURE 13.21**
Sample TRACERT results.

## Using the DNSCMD Command-Line Utility

The DNSCMD utility is essentially a command-line version of the MMC DNS console. Installed as part of the Windows Server 2003 Support tools, this utility enables you to create zones, modify records, and perform other vital administrative functions. To install the support tools, run the support tools setup from the Windows Server 2003 CD (located in the \support\tools directory). You can view the full functionality of this utility by typing **DNSCMD /?** at the command line, as illustrated in Figure 13.22.

**FIGURE 13.22**
DNSCMD command-line options.

# The Dynamic Host Configuration Protocol (DHCP) In Depth

The day-to-day operations of TCP/IP can be complex because clients must be able to receive and update their network information on a regular basis to keep in step with changes to a network. Each object in a TCP/IP environment requires a unique address that defines its location and provides for a means of routing network packets from place to place. This address, the IP address, must be assigned to each client in a network, to allow the clients to communicate using TCP/IP. In the past, most IP addresses were manually distributed as new clients were added to a network. This required a large amount of administrative overhead to maintain, and often resulted in problems in configuration caused by simple typographical errors and basic human error.

An automatic method for distributing IP addresses to clients was subsequently sought because the administrative advantages of such a system were obvious. The search for such a system led to the predecessors of DHCP: RARP and BOOTP.

## The DHCP Client Service

The server portion of DHCP is only half of the equation in a DHCP transaction. The request for an IP address comes from a specific interface known as the *DHCP client*. The client is installed with TCP/IP in Windows 2000 and higher clients and can be installed as an additional component in down-level clients.

The DHCP client, as previously mentioned, handles the communications with the DHCP Server service, in terms of handling IP requests and updates. Each iteration of the Windows client includes a different DHCP client, and there are slight variations in the functionality of each client; however, the overall function—to apply for and receive an IP address from a DHCP server—remains the same in each Windows client.

## Automatic Private IP Addressing (APIPA)

The Client/Server service has been updated in Windows 2000 clients and later, enabling it to automatically assign itself an IP address if no server is available; it does so through a process called Automatic Private IP Addressing (APIPA). APIPA clients automatically assign themselves an IP address in the 169.254.0.0/16 range in this situation, which allows them to have basic TCP/IP connectivity in small networks.

APIPA might be problematic in larger networks because it forces clients to assign themselves addresses in a range that is normally not part of a local company subnet. If a DHCP server is down, clients that are attempting to renew a lease with the server will fail and automatically assign themselves an APIPA address. When the server comes back online, they will not immediately re-register themselves and will effectively be cut off from the network. Subsequently, Microsoft supplies a Registry key that will disable APIPA in this situation. The key to be created is

```
HKLM\SYSTEM\CurrentControlSet\Services\Tcpip\Parameters\Interfaces\<AdapterName>\IPAutoconfiguration
Enabled:REG_DWORD=0
```

You can create this key by following these steps on the client:

1. Open Registry Editor (choose Start, Run and then enter **regedit**).

2. Navigate to HKEY_LOCAL_MACHINE\SYSTEM\CurrentControlSet\Services\Tcpip\ Parameters\Interfaces\<*AdapterName*> (where *AdapterName* is the name of the network adapter in question).

3. Right-click on the <*AdapterName*> key and choose New, DWORD Value.

> **APIPA**
>
> APIPA can also be effectively disabled in Windows XP clients through an alternative IP configuration, which allows for the designation of a static IP address if a DHCP is unavailable.

4. Enter IPAutoconfigurationEnabled to rename the DWORD Value.

5. Double-click the new value and ensure that 0 is entered as the value data.

6. Click OK and close the Registry Editor.

## DHCP Relay Agents

Because DHCP clients use network broadcasts to seek out DHCP servers, it is important that this traffic is routed properly on a network with multiple subnets. Effectively, this means that there must be some type of agent to detect DHCP broadcast packets and forward them to the appropriate DHCP server, if it is located on another network. For Cisco routers, for example, this takes the form of an ip-helper entry in the router configuration that designates the destination IP address for broadcast packets to be forwarded to. If this entry is not used, a Windows server running the Routing and Remote Access service must be configured as a DHCP relay agent, as illustrated in Figure 13.23.

> **Include the Network Architecture Team in Any Discussions on DHCP Design**
>
> In most real-world implementations of DHCP, the routers between network segments are configured to forward client DHCP broadcast packets directly to the DHCP server. In large organizations, it is therefore important to include the network architecture team in any discussions on DHCP design.

## DHCP and Dynamic DNS

Using the DNS Service in Windows Server 2003, clients can automatically register themselves in the DNS database through a mechanism called Dynamic DNS (DDNS).

DHCP in Windows Server 2003 integrates directly with DDNS to provide for automatic registration of clients into DNS. By default, all Windows 2000 or later clients will perform this function by themselves, but DHCP can be configured to allow for the Server service to update the Dynamic DNS record for the client. This option can be turned on and off at the server level, through the DHCP Manager MMC.

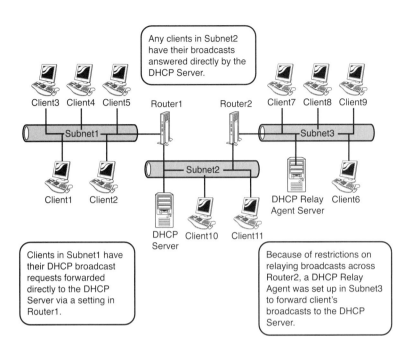

**FIGURE 13.23**
DHCP broadcast
packet routing.

Any clients in Subnet2 have their broadcasts answered directly by the DHCP Server.

Clients in Subnet1 have their DHCP broadcast requests forwarded directly to the DHCP Server via a setting in Router1.

Because of restrictions on relaying broadcasts across Router2, a DHCP Relay Agent was set up in Subnet3 to forward client's broadcasts to the DHCP Server.

# DHCP Changes in Windows Server 2003

As previously discussed, two improvements have been made to the functionality of DHCP in Windows Server 2003. These improvements allow for an increased level of functionality beyond the major improvements made in Windows 2000, but do not significantly change any design decisions that might have been made in Windows 2000 DHCP.

## DHCP Database Backup and Restore Automation

The process of backing up all DHCP settings and restoring them onto the same (or a different) server has been streamlined in Windows Server 2003. No longer do you need to export Registry keys and manually move databases between servers to migrate DHCP because the Backup and Restore process can be accomplished directly from the MMC. The process for backing up and restoring a DHCP database is as follows:

**DHCP Backup and Restore**

The DHCP Backup and Restore process is extremely useful in migrating existing DHCP server configurations, scopes, and up-to-date lease information to new DHCP servers. However, because down-level (pre–Windows Server 2003) DHCP servers do not support automatic Backup and Restore, you will need to migrate from these servers by exporting and re-importing the DHCP Registry and manually moving the database files.

1. Open the DHCP Manager by choosing Start, All Programs, Administrative Tools, DHCP.

2. Right-click the server name and choose Backup, as illustrated in Figure 13.24.

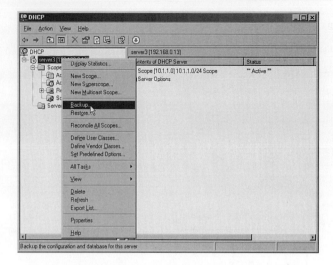

**FIGURE 13.24**
Backing up a DHCP database.

3. Specify a location for the backup file and click OK. The backup files will then be saved into the location you chose.

4. If you plan to use a new server as the destination for the restore, move the backup files and subdirectories created to the new server and run the restore procedure as outlined here.

5. Open the DHCP Manager again by choosing Start, All Programs, Administrative Tools, DHCP.

6. Right-click the server name and choose Restore.

7. When you see a dialog box asking whether the service can be stopped and restarted, click Yes to continue. The service will be restarted, and the entire database and Registry will be restored.

## DHCP in the Windows XP Client

The DHCP client that is included in the Windows Server 2003 client equivalent, Windows XP, can have a static IP address assigned to clients when a DHCP server is unavailable. This static IP address takes the place of the APIPA address that would normally be configured in these cases.

This type of functionality would normally be used on mobile laptop computers that connect to different networks. When a user is at work, for example, his laptop would receive a DHCP address. When the user is at home, however, his laptop would use the backup static IP address defined in the network settings. To configure this functionality on a Windows XP client, perform the following steps:

1. Choose Start, Control Panel.

2. Double-click Network Connections.

3. Right-click the adapter in question and choose Properties.

4. Select TCP/IP and choose Properties.

5. Select the Alternate Configuration tab.

6. Enter the appropriate Static IP Information and click OK.

7. Click the Close button to shut down the property page.

# Installing DHCP and Creating New Scopes

DHCP installation has always been a straightforward process. In Windows Server 2003, installation has been even more streamlined through the use of the Configure Your Server Wizard. This wizard installs the DHCP Server service and automatically invokes the New Scope Wizard, which can be used to establish and configure DHCP scopes. To establish a Windows Server 2003 system as a DHCP server, follow these steps:

1. Choose Start, All Programs, Administrative Tools, Configure Your Server Wizard.

2. Click Next at the Welcome screen.

3. Verify the preliminary steps and click Next to continue. A network test will be completed at this point.

4. Select DHCP Server and click Next.

5. Verify the options on the next screen, as illustrated in Figure 13.25, and click Next.

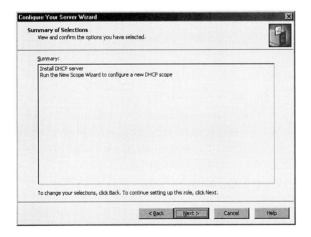

**FIGURE 13.25**
Verifying options for DHCP install.

6. At this point, the New Scope Wizard will be invoked and the process of configuring a scope will begin. Click Next to continue.

7. Type a name for the scope and enter a description. The names should be descriptive, such as 10.1.1.0/24 Scope. Click Next to continue.

8. Enter the range in which the scope will distribute IP addresses. In addition, type in a subnet mask for the subnet in question, as illustrated in Figure 13.26. Click Next to continue.

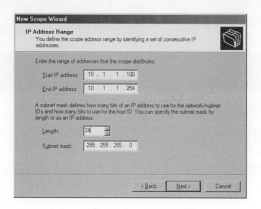

**FIGURE 13.26**  Defining the address in the New Scope Wizard.

9. Enter any exclusion ranges, if necessary. This range will identify any addresses that fall in the scope range that will not be used for the client leases. Click Next when finished.

10. Enter a duration time for the lease. This information will indicate how often clients must renew their DHCP leases. Click Next to continue.

11. At the next screen, you can add DHCP options to the scope. In this example, configure a gateway, a WINS server, and a DNS server as options for the scope, so choose Yes, I Want to Configure These Options Now and click Next.

12. Enter the IP address of the default gateway to be used on this subnet and click Next.

13. Enter the necessary information into the DNS server information fields and click Next when finished.

14. Enter the WINS server information on the next screen and click Next when finished.

---

**DHCP Can Potentially "Steal" Valid Clients**

Because DHCP can potentially "steal" valid clients from a production network, it is recommended that all tests using DHCP be conducted in a lab environment. In addition, testing in production will be difficult because the Authorization component of DHCP will also make it impossible to enable scopes on a Windows Server 2003 DHCP server, as described in the "DHCP Authorization" section later in this chapter.

---

15. Select whether the scope will be activated immediately or later. In this case, because the server has not been authorized, choose to activate later. After the change, click Next to continue.

16. Click Finish to close the wizard.

17. The Configure Your Server Wizard then indicates that the server has successfully become a DHCP server, as indicated in Figure 13.27. Click Finish to close the wizard.

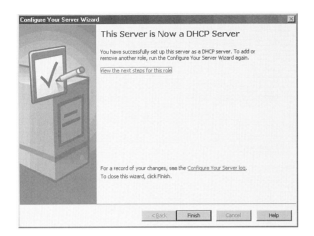

**FIGURE 13.27**
Completion of the Configure Your Server Wizard for DHCP.

# Creating DHCP Redundancy

The importance of DHCP cannot be understated. Downtime for DHCP translates into hordes of angry users who can no longer access the network. Consequently, it is extremely important to build redundancy into the DHCP environment and provide for disaster recovery procedures in the event of total DHCP failure.

Unfortunately, the DHCP service has no method of dynamically working in tandem with another DHCP server to synchronize client leases and scope information. However, using a few tricks, you can configure a failover DHCP environment that will provide for redundancy in the case of server failure or outage. Three specific options will provide for redundancy, and the pros and cons of each should be matched to the requirements of your organization.

## The 50/50 Failover Approach for DHCP Fault Tolerance

The 50/50 failover approach effectively uses two DHCP servers that each handle an equal amount of client traffic on a subnet. Each DHCP server is configured with similar scopes, but each must have a different IP range to avoid IP addressing conflicts.

Figure 13.28 illustrates the 50/50 failover approach. As indicated in the diagram, the network has 200 clients defined by 192.168.1.0/24. Each DHCP server contains a scope to cover the entire specific client subnet. Server1's scope is configured with exclusions for all IPs except for the range of 192.168.1.1–192.168.1.125. Server2's scope is configured with exclusions for the first half and a client lease range of 192.168.1.126–192.168.1.254.

Upon requesting a client IP address, the first server to respond to a request will be accepted, thus roughly balancing the load between the two servers.

The advantage to this approach is that a degree of redundancy is built into the DHCP environment without the need for extra IP address ranges reserved for clients. However, several caveats must be considered before implementing this approach.

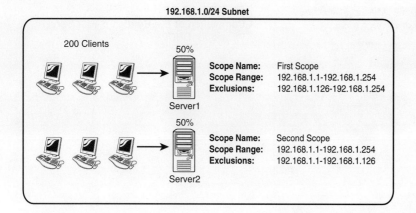

**FIGURE 13.28**
The 50/50 failover
approach.

First and foremost, it is theoretically possible that one server is located closer to the majority of the clients, and therefore more clients would be directed to that particular server. This could theoretically cause the DHCP server to run out of client leases, making it ineffectual for redundancy. For this reason, it is preferable to consider other methods of failover for DHCP, if available.

Another important consideration whenever configuring DHCP servers in this method is that an exclusion range must be established for the range that exists on the other server so that when a client from the other server attempts to renew the lease, it is not refused a new lease. This situation could potentially occur if the exclusion is not established because the client and server would have trouble negotiating if the client was using an IP address out of the range that exists in the scope. Consequently, if the range exists, but an exclusion is established, the server will simply assign a new address in the backup range.

## The 80/20 Failover Approach to DHCP Fault Tolerance

The 80/20 failover approach is similar to the 50/50 approach, except that the effective scope range on the server designated as the backup DHCP server contains only 20% of the available client IP range. In most cases, this server that holds 20% would be located across the network on a remote subnet, so it would not primarily be responsible for client leases. The server with 80% of the range would be physically located closer to the actual server, thus accepting the majority of the clients by responding to their requests faster, as illustrated in Figure 13.29.

In the event of Server1's failure, Server2 would respond to client requests until Server1 could be re-established in the network.

The downside to this approach is that if Server1 is down for too long of a period of time, it would eventually run out of potential leases for clients, and client renewal would fail. It is therefore important to establish a disaster recovery plan for the server with 80% of the scopes so that downtime is minimized.

Just as with the 50/50 approach, it is important to establish exclusion ranges for the other DHCP server's range, as described in the previous sections.

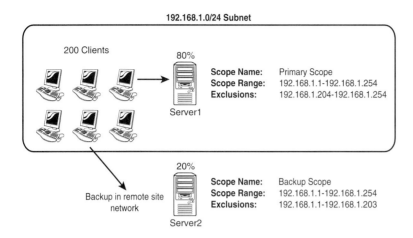

**FIGURE 13.29**
The 80/20 failover
approach.

## The 100/100 Failover Approach to DHCP Fault Tolerance

The 100/100 failover approach in Windows Server 2003 DHCP is the most effective means of achieving high availability out of a DHCP environment. However, several big "gotchas" must be worked out before this type of redundancy can be implemented.

The 100/100 failover approach in its simplest form consists of two servers running DHCP, with each servicing the same subnets in an organization. The scopes on each server, however, contain different, equivalent size ranges for clients that are each large enough to handle all clients in a specific subnet.

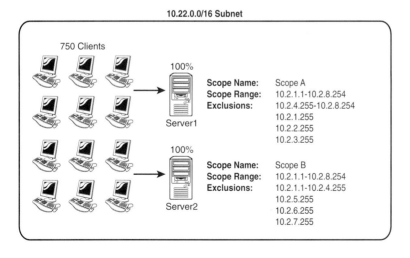

**FIGURE 13.30**
The 100/100 failover
approach.

In Figure 13.30, the 10.2.0.0/16 subnet has a total of 750 clients. This subnet is serviced by two DHCP servers, each of which has a scope for the subnet. Each server has a scope with addresses from 10.2.1.1 through 10.2.8.254. The scope on Server1 excludes all IP addresses except those in the range of 10.2.1.1 through 10.2.4.254. The scope on Server2 excludes all IP addresses except those in the range from 10.2.5.1 through 10.2.8.254. Each effective range is subsequently large enough to handle 1,000 clients, more than enough for every machine on the network.

If one of the DHCP servers experiences an interruption in service, and it no longer responds, the second server will take over, responding to clients and allowing them to change their IP addresses to the IPs available in the separate range.

The advantages to this design are obvious. In the event of a single server failure, the second server will immediately issue new IP addresses for clients that previously used the failed server. Because both servers run constantly, the failover is instantaneous. In addition, the failed DHCP server could theoretically remain out of service for the entire lease duration because the second server will be able to pick up all the slack from the failed server.

The main caveat to this approach is that a large number of IP addresses must be available for clients, more than twice the number that would normally be available. This might prove difficult, if not impossible, in many networks that have a limited IP range to work with. However, in organizations with a larger IP range, such as those offered by private network configurations (10.x.x.x and so on), this type of configuration is ideal.

You must ensure that both ranges include the scopes from the other servers, to prevent the types of problems described in the preceding examples.

## BEST PRACTICE

### Segment Available IP Addresses

If your organization uses a private IP addressing scheme such as 10.x.x.x or 192.168.x.x, it is always wise to segment available IP addresses on specific subnets to include several times more potential IP addresses than are currently required in a network. This not only ensures effective DHCP failover strategies, but it also allows for robust network growth, without the need for an IP addressing overhaul.

## Standby Scopes Approach

A Standby DHCP server is simply a server with DHCP installed, configured with scopes, but not turned on. The scopes must be configured in different ranges, as in the previous examples, but they normally lie dormant until they are needed. The advantage to this approach lies in the fact that the DHCP service can be installed on a server that will not normally be using additional resources for DHCP. If there is a problem, you simply need to activate the dormant scopes. An automated tool or script can be used to perform this function, if desired.

## Clustering DHCP Servers

The final redundancy option with DHCP is to deploy a clustered server set to run DHCP. In this option, if a single server goes down, the second server in a cluster will take over DHCP operations. This option requires a greater investment in hardware and should be considered only in specific cases in which it is necessary.

# Advanced DHCP Concepts

DHCP has been an unassuming network service as of late. The simplicity of the protocol is another reason for its success because it is not cursed by a high degree of administrative complexity. However, greater control over a DHCP environment can be achieved through the understanding of some advanced concepts regarding its use. Some of these concepts are new to Windows Server 2003, and some were introduced in Windows 2000. These improvements can help you to gain control over a DHCP environment, and provide for more security and ease of use.

## DHCP Superscopes

A DHCP Superscope is used for environments in which multiple network subnets encompass a single scope environment. In these cases, a Superscope can be created to contain multiple scopes. The individual scopes are subsequently dependent on the master Superscope. If it is turned off, they will also be deactivated. Figure 13.31 illustrates a sample DHCP Superscope.

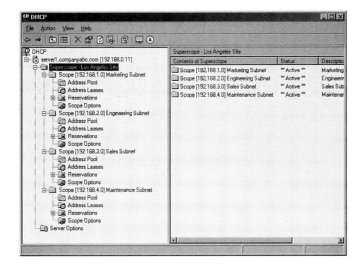

**FIGURE 13.31**
A DHCP Superscope.

## DHCP Multicast Scopes

A Multicast scope is created to allow clients to be assigned multicast IP addresses. A multicast IP address is one in which destination hosts can each have the same IP address, which is useful in one-to-many forms of communications such as Webcasts and videoconferencing sessions.

## DHCP Administrative Delegation

It is never wise to hand over full administrative privileges to individuals who need to perform only a specific network function. If a small group of administrators needs control over the DHCP environment, Windows Server 2003 makes it easy to delegate administrative capabilities to them through the inclusion of a group called DHCP Administrators. Adding users or, prefer-ably, groups to this Security Group will enable those users to administer the DHCP servers in an environment.

## Netsh Command-Line Utility

Windows Server 2003 has made great strides in allowing virtually all administrative functions to be performed through the command line. This not only helps those users who are used to command-line administration, such as that in Unix operating systems, but also allows for the execution of scripts and batch files, which can automate administrative processes.

The Netsh command-line utility is one such utility that effectively enables you to accomplish virtually all DHCP tasks that can be run through the MMC GUI interface. For a full listing of potential functions with Netsh, run `netsh /?` from the command line, as illustrated in Figure 13.32.

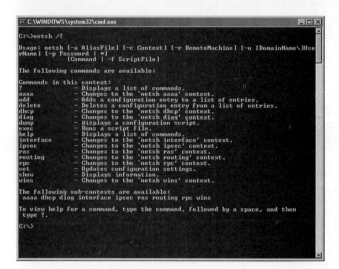

**FIGURE 13.32**
Netsh command-line options.

# Optimizing DHCP Through Proper Maintenance

The DHCP database is stored in the dhcp.mdb file, located in \%systemroot%\system32\dhcp. This database is structured using Microsoft JET database technology, the same technology used for Exchange Server, Active Directory, and many other databases in the Microsoft world.

As any administrator who has worked with JET databases will attest, frequent maintenance of the DHCP database is required to keep it functioning properly and to groom it for defragmenta-tion and recovery of whitespace. By default, DHCP is configured to perform online maintenance to the database, but only during intervals in which it is not being used for client requests. For busy, large DHCP servers, there might never be downtime, so it is therefore important to run offline maintenance against the dhcp.mdb file on a quarterly to semi-annual basis.

You can run maintenance against the dhcp.mdb DHCP database file by using the `jetpack` utility in Windows Server 2003. From the command line, enter the following commands, illustrated in Figure 13.33, to stop the DHCP Server service, compact the database, and restart the service:

- `cd %systemroot%\system32\dhcp`

- `net stop dhcpserver`

- `jetpack dhcp.mdb tmp.mdb`

- `net start dhcpserver`

**FIGURE 13.33**
DHCP database maintenance.

**BEST PRACTICE**

**Maintenance Schedules**

A maintenance schedule for DHCP and all other Microsoft JET-based databases should be established, in addition to any other maintenance schedules that might be in effect. Such a schedule will help to keep these network service environments in top shape. Using redundant servers that will take over while the database is down can also minimize downtime from this maintenance.

# Securing a DHCP Implementation

The DHCP protocol is effectively insecure. There is no way to determine whether a request from a client is legitimate or is malicious. Users who have evil intentions can conduct denial-of-service attacks against the DHCP server by simply requesting all available IP addresses in a range, effectively disallowing legitimate users from being granted IP addresses. For this and other reasons, it is important to keep wire security as a high priority. Although this point might seem obvious, keeping potential intruders physically off a network is a must, not only for DHCP but also for other network services prone to denial-of-service attacks. This includes auditing the security of wireless networks, such as 802.11b, which can (and often do) provide unrestricted access to malicious users.

In addition to physical and wire security, you should examine several security considerations and mechanisms, to provide for a better understanding of the vulnerabilities and capabilities of DHCP.

# DHCP Authorization

DHCP in and of itself is an unauthenticated service, which means that anyone can establish a DHCP server on a network and start to accept clients and assign them erroneous addresses or redirect them for malicious purposes. Consequently, since Windows 2000, it has become necessary to authorize a DHCP server that is running in an Active Directory domain. After the DHCP server is authorized by the proper domain administrative authority, that server can then accept client leases.

The downside to this approach is that a Windows NT 4.0 server could still be added, unauthenticated, to a network. In this situation, it would become necessary to pull out a network analyzer to determine the location of rogue DHCP servers.

Authorization of a Windows Server 2003 DHCP server is straightforward and can be accomplished by following these steps:

1. Open the DHCP Manager by choosing Start, All Programs, Administrative Tools, DHCP.

2. Right-click the server name and choose Authorize, as illustrated in Figure 13.34.

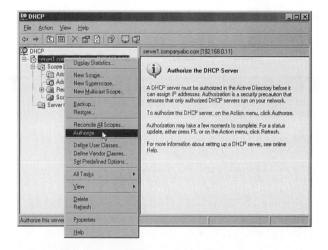

**FIGURE 13.34**
Authorizing a DHCP server.

3. In a few minutes, the DHCP should be authorized, and the scopes can be activated.

# DHCP and Domain Controller Security

If at all possible, the DHCP service should not be run on an Active Directory domain controller because the security of the SRV records generated is diminished. The reasons for this are as follows.

DNS entries in an Active Directory–integrated DNS zone are secure, which means that only the client that originally created the record can subsequently update that same record. This can cause problems with the DHCP server automatically updating client records, however, because the client no longer performs this function and cannot have security applied to a record.

DHCP in Windows Server 2003 overcomes this limitation by placing all DHCP servers in a special group in Active Directory, called DNSUpdateProxy. Members of this group do not have any security applied to objects that they create in the DNS database. The theory is that the first client to "touch" the record will then take over security for that record.

The problem with this concept is that the records created by DHCP servers possess no immediate security and are consequently subject to takeover by hostile clients. Because domain controllers are responsible for publishing SRV DNS records, which indicate the location of domain controllers, Kerberos servers, and the like, this leaves a gaping security hole that users could exploit. Consequently, it is preferable to keep DHCP off domain controllers. If this cannot be avoided, it is recommended that you not place the DHCP server into the DNSUpdateProxy group to avoid the security problems associated with it.

# Continuing Usage of Windows Internet Naming Service (WINS)

The Windows Internet Naming Service (WINS) has a long history in Microsoft networks. Because early Microsoft networks were primarily broadcast-based using protocols such as NetBEUI to identify local computers, and there is a need to maintain backwards compatibility for earlier operating systems, Microsoft continues to support WINS.

## Legacy Microsoft NetBIOS Resolution

WINS is effectively a simple database of NetBIOS names and their corresponding IP addresses. Some additional information, such as domain name, server type, and so on, can be determined as well, from the 16th byte in a NetBIOS name stored in WINS.

WINS is considered legacy in the Microsoft world because NetBIOS resolution is being phased out in favor of the domain name system (DNS) form of name resolution. However, it is difficult to divorce WINS from modern networks because of the reliance on WINS by down-level (pre-Windows 2000) clients, legacy applications, and even some Microsoft services such as DFS that use WINS by default. Consequently, you might need to keep using WINS in Windows networks, unless you can definitively prove that it is no longer necessary.

## Integrating WINS and DNS

DNS can use the WINS database to provide for quasi-DNS resolution of WINS clients. This means that if a request is sent to a DNS server to resolve `client1.companyabc.com`, for example, it is possible for that DNS server to use the WINS database to resolve requests for any zones where the WINS forward lookup is configured. If Client1 does not exist in the DNS database but exists in the WINS database instead, the DNS server will return the IP address that it obtained from WINS and attach the `companyabc.com` suffix to the record, as illustrated in Figure 13.35.

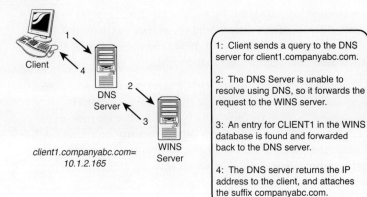

**FIGURE 13.35**
WINS integration with DNS.

1: Client sends a query to the DNS server for client1.companyabc.com.

2: The DNS Server is unable to resolve using DNS, so it forwards the request to the WINS server.

3: An entry for CLIENT1 in the WINS database is found and forwarded back to the DNS server.

4: The DNS server returns the IP address to the client, and attaches the suffix companyabc.com.

Client

DNS Server

WINS Server

client1.companyabc.com= 10.1.2.165

This functionality must be enabled on the DNS server because it is not configured by default. To enable WINS resolution on a DNS server, follow these steps:

1. On a server running DNS, open the DNS MMC snap-in by choosing Start, Administrative Tools, DNS.

2. Navigate to DNS\\<Servername>\\Forward Lookup Zones.

3. Right-click the zone in question and choose Properties.

4. Choose the WINS tab.

5. Check the Use WINS Forward Lookup box.

6. Enter the IP address of the WINS server(s) and click OK to save the changes, as illustrated in Figure 13.36.

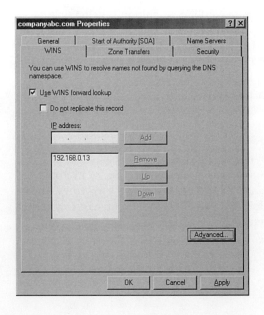

**FIGURE 13.36** Configuring WINS resolution in DNS.

## Changes in Windows Server 2003 WINS

Although =the overall function of WINS has not changed significantly in Windows Server 2003, some additions to the management tools allow for increased functionality and capabilities:

- *Advanced search capabilities for WINS databases.* Previous implementations of WINS had simplistic search capabilities that were limited to simple keyword searches of NetBIOS records in the database. The search engine for WINS has been updated in Windows Server 2003 to support more advanced search parameters, thus giving administrators more flexibility in searching for specific records.

- *WINS pull record filtering and replication partner acceptance.* Instead of entire transfers of all records on other servers, replication can be limited to only those records owned by a specific server, thus excluding extraneous records from littering a WINS database.

In addition to these advances in Windows Server 2003, Windows 2000 introduced enhancements to WINS, such as an updated database engine, persistent connections, manual tombstoning, and other improvements.

# Installing and Configuring WINS

As with many services in Windows Server 2003, the installation and configuration process of a WINS server is streamlined through the Configure Your Server Wizard. This wizard automatically installs all necessary services and databases and configures other settings pertinent to a particular service. Although other methods of installation still exist, this method is the preferred approach in Windows Server 2003.

## WINS Installation

To install WINS on a server using the Configure Your Server Wizard, follow these steps:

1. Choose Start, All Programs, Administrative Tools, Configure Your Server Wizard.

2. Click Next at the Welcome screen.

3. Verify the preliminary steps and click Next to continue. A network test will then be performed.

4. Select WINS Server from the list of Server Roles and click Next to continue.

5. On the Summary page, click Next to continue.

6. If you are prompted for the Windows Server 2003 Media, insert it and click Next to continue.

7. Click Finish on the final wizard page to finish setup, as illustrated in Figure 13.37.

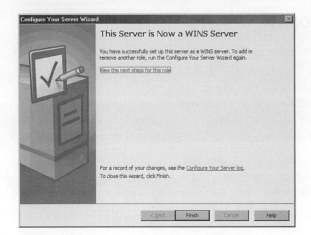

**FIGURE 13.37**
WINS server installation.

## Configuring Push/Pull Partners

If a WINS server in an environment is the sole WINS server for that network, no additional configuration is required other than ensuring that clients will be pointing to the WINS server in their IP configuration. However, if additional WINS servers are established in an environment, exchanging database information between the multiple servers will become necessary. You establish this type of replication topology through the designation of push/pull partners.

A *push partner* for a particular WINS server is another WINS server that serves as the destination for WINS changes to be "pushed" to. A *pull partner* is a WINS server from which changes are "pulled." In a nutshell, if Server1 has Server2 configured as a push partner, Server2 must have Server1 configured as a pull partner, and vice versa.

A WINS push/pull topology should roughly map to an organization's network topology. For example, if an organization is composed of two main offices that serve as network hubs, and several branch offices, each with its own WINS servers, the WINS push/pull topology could look something like Figure 13.38.

## WINS Replication

WINS replicates database changes on a set schedule, which can be modified on a per connection basis. Just as with any network communications, the replication schedule should be modified to fit the particular needs of an organization. If a WAN link is saturated with traffic, it might be wise to throttle back the WINS replication schedule. However, if a link between push/pull partners is robust, a shorter schedule can be established. To change the default schedule of 30 minutes, follow these steps:

1. Open the WINS Manager by choosing Start, All Programs, Administrative Tools, WINS.

2. Choose the Replication Partners folder.

3. Right-click Push/Pull Partner and choose Properties.

4. Change the Replication interval time to the desired length, as indicated in Figure 13.39, and click OK to save the settings.

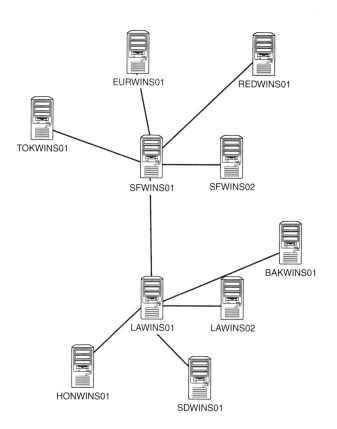

**FIGURE 13.38**
Sample WINS push/pull topology.

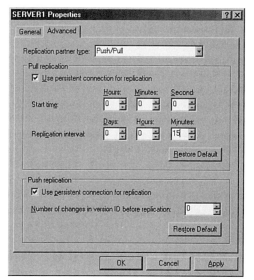

**FIGURE 13.39**     WINS replication settings.

The page shown in Figure 13.39 can also be used to change other push/pull partner settings, such as replication partner types, persistent connections, and other pertinent replication information.

## NetBIOS Client Resolution and the LMHOSTS File

A Windows client does not immediately resort to a WINS server to determine the IP address of a NetBIOS name. This knowledge is essential in the troubleshooting of name resolution on a Windows client. Instead, a client first contacts a local NetBIOS cache for resolution. If an IP address changes, this cache might report the old address, impeding troubleshooting. To flush this cache, run nbtstat -R (with uppercase R) at the command line.

In addition to the local cache, clients always parse an LMHOSTS file, if one exists, before contacting a WINS server. If the LMHOSTS file contains erroneous information, it will impede proper name resolution. Always check to see whether this file is populated (it is usually located in \%systemroot%\winnt\system32\drivers\etc on clients) before beginning to troubleshoot the WINS server.

# WINS Planning, Migrating, and Maintenance

As previously mentioned, WINS is necessary in most production environments because the over-riding dependencies on NetBIOS that were built into Windows have not entirely been shaken out. In fresh installations of Windows Server 2003, you do not need to install WINS, but for older, upgraded environments, you should still plan on WINS being around for a few years.

Now that you have this knowledge, you can properly design an upgraded Windows Server 2003 environment.

## Designing a WINS Environment

There are two key factors to consider when designing a WINS environment. The first factor is accessibility. Having a local, fast connection to a WINS server will aid in the processing of client requests. Because WINS has low overhead for servers, it is consequently a good idea to include at least one WINS server in all locations with more than 5–10 users. In smaller environments, WINS can be installed as part of a local file server whereas in larger environments, dedicated multiple utility servers running WINS are recommended.

The replication topology you establish should normally follow the lines of a network infrastructure, as previously mentioned. If a network uses a hub and spoke design, WINS should follow the same basic topology.

## Upgrading a WINS Environment

The WINS service itself is one of the more straightforward services to migrate to a separate set of servers as part of an upgrade to Windows Server 2003. A simple upgrade of the existing WINS server will do the trick for many environments; however, migrating to a separate server or set of servers might be beneficial if you're changing topology or hardware.

Migration of an existing WINS environment is most easily accomplished through the procedure described in this section. This procedure allows for the migration of an entire WINS database to a new set of servers, but without affecting any clients or changing WINS server settings. Figure 13.40 illustrates a WINS migration using this procedure.

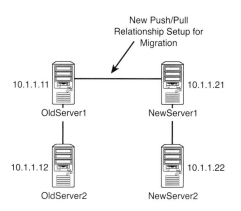

New Push/Pull
Relationship Setup for
Migration

**FIGURE 13.40**     WINS migration procedure, step 1.

In Figure 13.40, the existing servers, OldServer1 and OldServer2, handle WINS traffic for the entire network of fictional CompanyABC. They are configured with IP addresses 10.1.1.11 and 10.1.1.12, which are configured in all clients' IP settings as Primary and Secondary WINS, respectively. OldServer1 and OldServer2 are configured as push/pull partners.

The new servers, NewServer1 and NewServer2, are added to the network with the WINS service installed and configured as push/pull partners for each other. Their initial IP addresses are 10.1.1.21 and 10.1.1.22. OldServer1 and NewServer1 are then connected as push/pull partners for the network. Because the servers are connected this way, all database information from the old WINS database is replicated to the new servers, as illustrated in step 1 shown in Figure 13.40.

After the entire WINS database is replicated to the new servers, the old servers are shut down (on a weekend or evening to minimize impact), and NewServer1 and NewServer2 are immediately reconfigured to take the IP addresses of the old servers, as illustrated in step 2 shown in Figure 13.41.

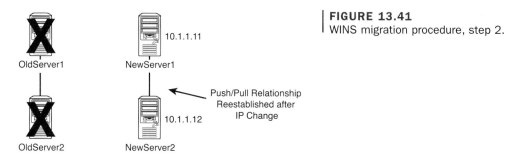

**FIGURE 13.41**
WINS migration procedure, step 2.

The push/pull partner relationship between NewServer1 and NewServer2 is then re-established because the IP addresses of the servers changed. The entire downtime of the WINS environment can be measured in mere minutes, and the old database is migrated intact. In addition, because the new servers assume the old IP addresses, no client settings need to be reconfigured.

There are a few caveats with this approach, however. If the IP addresses cannot be changed, WINS servers must be changed on the client side. If you're using DHCP, you can do this by leaving all old and new servers up in an environment until the WINS change can be automatically updated through DHCP. Effectively, however, WINS migrations can be made very straightforward through this technique, and they can be modified to fit any WINS topology.

## WINS Database Maintenance

Just like the DHCP database, the WINS database is based on the Microsoft JET database technology and is consequently subject to the need for regular maintenance. Scheduling maintenance for each WINS database is recommended on a quarterly or semi-annual basis. The WINS database file, wins.mdb, is stored in the \%systemroot%\system32\wins directory. You can run maintenance against the database by entering the following commands at the command line:

- `cd %systemroot%\system32\wins`

- `net stop wins`

- `jetpack wins.mdb tmp.mdb`

- `net start wins`

# Global Catalog Domain Controllers (GC/DCs) Placement

The placement of domain controllers in Windows Server 2003 is the critical factor to improve the communication response time from an Active Directory query. Without prompt response from a domain controller, a user might have to wait several seconds to several minutes to merely log on to the network, or it could take a similar length of time to even view the list of e-mail recipients the user wants to send a message to.

This section deals with specific server placement issues for Active Directory domain controllers and global catalog servers.

## The Active Directory Global Catalog

The global catalog in Active Directory is an index of all objects in an Active Directory forest. All domain controllers in Windows Server 2003's Active Directory are not by default global catalog servers, so they must be established as such through the following procedure:

1. Open Active Directory Sites and Services.

2. Navigate to Sites\<SiteName>\Servers\<ServerName>.

3. Right-click NTDS Settings and select Properties.

4. Check the Global Catalog box, as indicated in Figure 13.42.

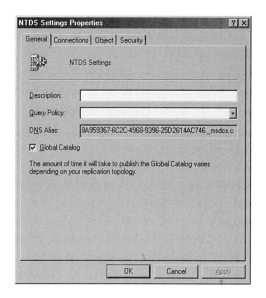

FIGURE 13.42    Making a domain controller into a global catalog server.

# The Need to Strategically Place GCs and DCs

It is important to understand that global catalog objects must be physically located close to all objects in a network that require prompt login times and fast connectivity. Because a global catalog entry is parsed for universal group membership every time a user logs in, this effectively means that this information must be close at hand. This can be accomplished by placing GC/DCs on the same WAN site or by using a process new to Windows Server 2003 called universal group caching.

## Universal Group Caching

*Universal group caching* is a process by which an Active Directory site caches all universal group membership locally so that the next time clients log in, information is more quickly provided to the clients and they are able to log in faster.

Universal group caching is more effective than placing a GC/DC server locally because only those universal groups that are relevant to a local site's members are replicated and are cached on the local domain controller. The downside to this approach, however, is that the first login for clients will still be longer than if a local GC/DC were provided, and the cache eventually expires, requiring another sync with a GC/DC.

You can set up universal group caching on a site level as follows:

1. Open Active Directory Sites and Services.

2. Navigate to Sites\\<Site Name>.

3. In the right-hand pane, right-click NTDS Site Settings and choose Properties.

4. Check the Enable Universal Group Membership Caching box, as illustrated in Figure 13.43.

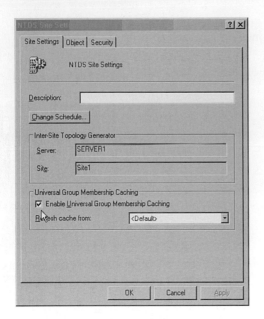

**FIGURE 13.43**　Enabling universal group caching.

## Global Catalog/Domain Controller Placement

As you learned in the preceding sections, you must make decisions regarding the most efficient placement of DCs and GC/DCs in an environment. Decisions on placement of GC/DCs and universal group caching sites must be made with an eye toward determining how important fast logins are for users in a site compared to higher replication throughput. However, for many Windows Server 2003 environments, the following rules apply:

- Sites with fewer than 50 users—Use a single DC configured with universal group caching
- Sites with 50–100 users—Use two DCs configured for universal group caching
- Sites with 100–200 users—Use a single GC server and single DC server
- Sites with 200+ users—Alternate adding additional DCs and GC/DCs for every 100 users

The recommendations listed here are generalized and should not be construed as relevant to every environment. However, these general guidelines should help you to size an Active Directory environment for domain controller placement.

# Summary

Although often overlooked, the services of DNS, DHCP, and WINS are some of the most critical components of a functional Windows Server 2003 environment. In addition, global catalog domain controller placement and related issues are integral to the functionality of an Active Directory environment. Consequently, it is important to properly plan, implement, and support the infrastructure environment to ensure high availability, reliability, and resilience that is expected of the foundation for the network infrastructure.

# PART IV

---

# Migration and Integration Solutions

# 14

# Migrating from Windows NT 4.0

**W**hen organizations begin a migration to Windows Server 2003, even though they have completed a detailed plan, each implementation task has been carefully considered. Often many unforeseen factors can arise that can have adverse effects on the migration, disrupting the flow of the progress and productivity of the migration project.

This chapter focuses on best practices and tips that can assist administrators with a migration by identifying common mistakes and best practices to avoid unforeseen issues. Some of these issues may include improper network designs, problemsome network communication links, improperly configured systems, or errors in site to site replication.

Besides avoiding these issues, other key factors covered in the chapter are the various migration strategies and best practices to avoid downtime and streamline the migration process.

# Migrating to a Scalable Windows 2003 Server Environment

When planning a migration to Windows Server 2003, one of the key components is to design and implement a new Windows 2003 Active Directory infrastructure and forest that is scalable and flexible enough to meet an organization's existing and future business needs.

To meet this goal, it is important for organizations to understand the current Windows NT 4.0 environment beyond their basic Windows NT operating systems. Knowing and understanding all existing hardware and third-party applications in use can assist an organization in avoiding setbacks and disruptions when planning and migrating to Windows Server 2003 and Active Directory.

Understanding these components and how they can affect a migration and Windows Server 2003 will assist administrators and planners in ensuring that a new Active Directory infrastructure is fully functional and scalable to an organization's future plans and needs.

## Planning for Future Hardware Needs

Before planning a migration, it is important to know whether existing hardware currently in use in the network environment can support the various editions of Windows Server 2003 that will be implemented as part of the migration.

### Planning Hardware Upgrades

Plan hardware upgrades according to server roles and installed applications that might require additional memory or faster processor speeds to ensure optimal server performance. Combine your software and hardware inventory to plan and deploy a scalable optimal performing server hardware environment.

Begin planning your migration by assessing future hardware needs and conducting a detailed inventory of all existing server hardware that will be migrated to a new Windows 2003 Server family platform.

Begin by creating a detailed and documented hardware inventory to assist in identifying existing server hardware. The inventory can be used to identify server hardware that does not meet the Microsoft Windows Server 2003 family minimum hardware requirements.

Review the requirements in Table 14.1 to determine if your Windows NT 4.0 installations meet the minimum Microsoft hardware requirements for installing Windows Server 2003.

**TABLE 14.1**

**Windows Server 2003 Minimum Requirements**

| Windows Server 2003 | Processor and Speed Minimum | RAM | Required Disk Space for Installation |
|---|---|---|---|
| Web Edition | 133MHz | 128MB | 1.5GB |
| Standard Edition | 133MHz | 128MB | 1.5GB |
| Enterprise Edition | 133MHz | 128MB | 1.5 GB |
| Data Center Edition | 400MHz | 512MB | 1.5 GB |

## Using the System Compatibility Checker

Another method to determine hardware compatibility is by using the Compatibility Check Tool available on the Windows Server 2003 installation CD-ROM. This tool can be run directly from the Windows Setup on the installation CD-ROM and does not require administrators to install Windows Server 2003.

You can use the autorun feature built into your server systems to launch the Windows Server 2003 setup screen, which will enable you to navigate to the Compatibility Check Tool. If your server hardware does not support the autorun feature, or it has been disabled in the server bios, the compatibility check utility can be run from the command prompt or Windows run option. To run the compatibility check tool, at the prompt type: **D:\I386\winnt32/checkupgradeonly** (where D: represents the CD-ROM drive letter of the server you are checking).

> **Software Compatibility List**
>
> You can also review the Windows Server 2003 Family hardware and software compatibility list on the Microsoft Web site.

> **Processor Compatibility**
>
> Windows 2003 Server might not upgrade Windows NT systems with multiple Pentium Pro or Pentium II processors correctly. Windows Server 2003 setup and the Compatibility Check will identify if dual processors and multiple processor servers will only run with one processor after the upgrade is complete. More information on the subject can be found on the Microsoft System Requirements Web site at www.microsoft.com/windowsserver2003.

## Supporting Third-Party Software Applications

One key component to a successful migration is identifying all applications currently installed and present in the existing Windows NT 4.0 environment. By identifying all applications in use as well as specific applications that might no longer be in use, administrators can have a full understanding of the application migration requirements they might be challenged with. Knowing what applications are to be migrated and what the specific requirements are for compatibility with Windows Server 2003 will assist you in avoiding any issues with application functionality after applications are migrated to Windows Server 2003 and Active Directory.

One challenge in identifying these applications is the method you should use to accomplish this large task. Organizations with Microsoft Systems Management Server (SMS) can produce a detailed inventory of applications using the collection of data obtained through the software inventory component of SMS.

> **Application Compatibility Tool Kit**
>
> Download the Application Compatibility Tool Kit from the Microsoft Windows Server 2003 Web site at http://www.Microsoft.com/windowsserver2003/compatible/appcompat.mspx.

For organizations that do not have Systems Management Server (SMS), another method to inventory software in a Windows NT 4.0 environment is to use the tools provided in the Application Compatibility Tool Kit for Windows Server 2003.

## Using the Compatibility Tool Kit Analyzer

The Application Compatibility Tool Kit (ACT) is a deployment tool provided by Microsoft to assist IT staff in identifying and testing applications for compatibility with Windows Server 2003. There are three components to the ACT:

- *Microsoft Application Compatibility Analyzer* is a tool used to remotely gather all installed programs within a Windows NT network. This tool automatically creates an inventory of all installed programs without requiring a management tool such as SMS.

- *Windows Application Verifier* can be used to identify compatibility issues with existing and new application to be installed on Windows Server 2003.

- *Compatibility Administrator* is a complete tool that can determine the necessary fixes required for application support with Windows Server 2003. The compatibility administrator can also be used to create packages of fixes stored in a database that can then be distributed to application servers or computers on the network.

## Migrating to a Flexible Active Directory Forest

**Logging Tips**

Use the command line tool Collector.exe to inventory systems applications and write information to a log file. By default, the Collector tool writes information and places the log file on the system desktop in which the tool is being run. Use the `-o` switch to specify an alternative location to write the collectors logs; for example, `Collector.exe -o c:\AppInfo\Collect.log`.

**Advance Active Directory Design**

To better understand options that can be applied to your Active Directory design, review Chapter 10, "Advanced Active Directory Design."

After the discovery of hardware and software has been completed and documented, the next step is to design and implement a scalable Windows 2003 Active Directory environment. By designing and implementing a Forest Root that is scalable, organizations can leverage the flexibility and migrations options when migrating to Windows Server 2003.

You can begin understanding how to implement scalability into a migration and Active Directory by understanding the different migration paths available when upgrading from Windows NT 4.0.

The first option is an in-place domain upgrade. This method is the most restrictive of the three methods; however, it is best used for organizations that want to maintain the existing domain model.

The second option is a domain migration; this method is best implemented by organizations that want to migrate all existing domain objects to a single newly created Active Directory domain.

The most effective and flexible method is a domain consolidation. When performing a domain consolidation, a newly created Active Directory Root is implemented and connected to the existing NT domain using domain trust.

This option provides the most migration flexibility and a broader range of migration options. By leveraging all the functionality available in the first two migration paths a domain consolidation is ideal for organizations that want to implement change and maintain certain existing domain configurations (see Figure 14.1).

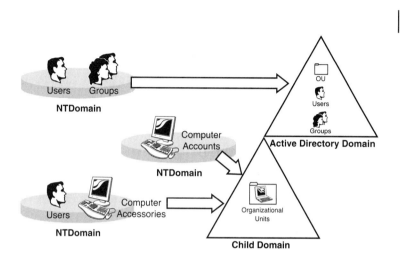

**FIGURE 14.1**
Consolidating Windows NT domains.

# Fallback Plans and Failover Procedures

When planning a migration, how to migrate is not always the most import component to consider. Sometimes understanding the best approach and tasks involved to recover from a failed migration can be just as important as the migration tasks themselves.

The following sections review common areas to consider and tips that can allow administrators the capability to undo tasks in certain migration scenarios.

> **Test All Migration Scenarios**
>
> It is best practice to test all migration scenarios in an isolated lab environment prior to attempting a live migration.

## Simple Methods to Recovering the SAM Database

When performing an in-place upgrade of a Windows NT 4.0 domain, or even when migrating domains, corruption of SAM databases or unrecoverable failures of the Windows NT Primary Domain Controller (PDC) and Backup Domain Controllers (BDCs) can occur. These cases require a full recovery of the original source domain's SAM database.

One method to recovering the original NT source domain is to create a backup Domain Controller that can be isolated from the production domain for recovery purposes in case of an unrecoverable failure.

Installing an additional Windows NT Back Up Domain Controller on the source domain creates a copy of the SAM database, which can then be pulled of the network and shut down. To recover the SAM database in case of a failure, the recovery server can simply be turned on and promoted to the domain's new primary domain controller, providing a complete copy of the original SAM database.

## Recovering from Failed Account Migrations

When migrating accounts such as desktops and user accounts, one challenge administrators face is how to recover if a migration were to fail. The simplest method is to understand and leverage the options available with the Active Directory Migration Tool (ADMT).

Using the Active Directory Migration Tool to migrate accounts enables you to preserve the original account in a disabled state within the source domain, while at the same time creating a new account in the new Active Directory target domain. In the case of a failed migration, administrators can simply enable the original account, providing immediate access to network resources for the user account that failed to migrate. Review the options and settings available for account migration in Figure 14.2 to determine the best method for migrating accounts based on the migration's specific requirements.

**FIGURE 14.2** ADMT user migration options.

# Tips to Minimize Network Downtime

As with most day-to-day administrative tasks, avoiding network downtime is a priority when migrating to Windows Server 2003 and Active Directory. Avoiding end user disruption and network downtime can be accomplished by carefully planning, documenting, and testing the method in which a migration is performed as well as implementing an effective failover plan.

To address network downtime, review the Windows Server 2003 Active Directory design and functionality available with Windows Server 2003.

## Avoiding Downtime Through Server Redundancy

One simple method you can use to leverage Windows Server 2003 functionality and redundancy is to implement redundant domain controllers and global catalog servers in a new active directory domain. You can rely on the secondary server to support the domain in the case of a domain controller failure.

Installing an additional domain controller to support redundancy on the Active Directory domain during a migration, even if the domain controller is temporary, can be the difference between an immediate recovery and a complete domain restore.

Domain Functional roles can be seized at any point of failure by the secondary domain controller to restore immediately domain functionality and user authentication.

## Configuring Redundant Global Catalogs

By installing an additional domain controller, you can also configure this system easily to provide additional redundancy by replicating the Active Directory Global Catalog. Configuring this option on a second domain controller will dynamically create a complete redundant copy of the domain's global catalog on the additional domain controller.

To configure this option on an additional domain controller, perform the following steps:

1. Begin by selecting Start, All Programs, Administrative Tools.

2. From the Administrative Tools program group, select Active Directory Sites and Services.

3. Select the Sites folder and navigate down to the server that you would like to configure as a Global Catalog server by choosing Sites, Default First Site Name, Servers, Server Name, NTDS Settings.

4. From the File menu, select Action and click Properties. This will open the Properties page on the server you want to configure.

5. Place a check in the Global Catalog check box as shown in Figure 14.3.

> **For More Information**
>
> This option can be created as a temporary solution or added into the Active Directory Design. For more information regarding design considerations, review Chapter 10.

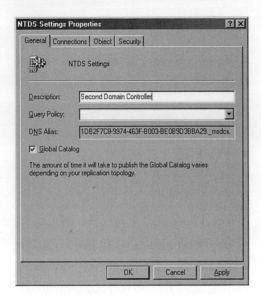

**FIGURE 14.3**  Global catalog server configuration.

# Planning and Implementing Name Resolution When Migrating

During a migration or while maintaining coexistence during a domain consolidation, it is important to maintain effective and proper name resolution between the source Windows NT 4.0 domain and the destination Active Directory domain.

Planning and managing effective name resolution ensures that server-to-server communications and client server communication are not disrupted. Another area of importance is ensuring third-party applications that are dependent on server name resolution continue to function properly. Review the different name resolution options in the following section to meet your organization's migration requirements.

## Understanding Name Resolution with Windows 2003

The solution for managing this task is best determined by understanding the different method in which each of the Microsoft Windows operating systems perform name resolution when querying a host name lookup.

The Windows NT Server 4.0 operating system along with many legacy applications rely primarily on the Windows Internet Naming Services (WINS) built into Windows NT 4.0. When a Windows NT Server requests a host name lookup, NetBIOS name resolution is used to query the domain's WINS. This is the primary means of resolving host names to network addresses with Windows NT 4.0 unless other methods of name resolution are configured to override this method. This method also works with Windows 95, Windows 98, and Windows NT client desktops.

Unlike Windows NT 4.0, Windows Server 2003 and Active Directory rely on the Domain Naming System (DNS) standard as their primary method of name resolutions. This functionality is mandatory and required for the installation of Active Directory. When implementing Windows Server 2003, this becomes the primary method of host name resolution for Windows Server 2003 and Active Directory.

To maintain effective server-to-server and client-server communications when migrating to Windows Server 2003, it is important to consider and design which domain will be responsible for providing name resolution and how name resolution will be affected when the source domain is decommissioned.

## Implementing WINS in a Mixed Mode Environment

When integrating Windows Server 2003 and Windows NT Server environments, domain controllers must be able to communicate via their NetBIOS name as well as Fully Qualified Domain Name (FQDN). To implement effective name resolution, it is often a good decision to migrate the Windows NT 4.0 primary WINS services to the newly created destination Active Directory Domain. By migrating WINS services to the destination Active Directory domain, name resolution can be maintained during the migration as well as during the decommissioning of the source Windows NT domain and servers.

**Implementing a New Installation of WINS Services in the Destination Domain**

Implementing a new installation of WINS Services in the destination domain requires reconfiguring the TCP/IP WINS properties for all servers and clients in the source domain.

Disable the source domain's WINS Service using the services Control Panel. Maintain one installation of WINS as a means of redundancy in case a problem were to appear requiring a fallback to the original WINS server.

## Installing WINS

To install WINS on the Windows 2003 Server platform, open the Control Panel and perform the following steps:

1. From the Windows 2003 Server, select Start, Control Panel, Add Remove Programs.

2. Select Add/Remove Windows Components.

3. Select Network Services and click the Details tab.

**Incorporating the Installation and Configuration of Windows 2003 WINS into the Migration Project Plan**

Incorporate the installation and configuration of Windows 2003 WINS into the migration project plan. Installing and configuring the service when building the domain controller to replicate information can allow the service to function properly for a period of time prior to beginning to migrate domain users and resources.

4. Select the Windows Internet Naming Services (WINS) and click OK. This installs WINS on the server. Management of the WINS can be completed through the Windows Administrative tools.

# Decommissioning Windows 2003 Internet Naming Services

After all domain users and resources have been migrated to the destination Active Directory domain, you can begin to decommission unneeded WINS services previously required for coexistence with the Windows NT 4.0 source domain.

To begin, review the current state of the Windows Server 2003 domain controller's Domain Name Systems logs in the server event viewer to identify any potential DNS name resolution issues. Address and resolve any errors prior to removing the WINS service.

To decommission WINS in an Active Directory environment, changes must take place on the Windows clients as well as all servers in the domain. In every scenario, servers and workstations must be modified to remove old WINS entries from the TCP/IP properties of the system and optimize configurations.

### Changing Windows 2003 Server WINS TCP/IP Properties

Best practice is to start with the modifications of network servers, choosing a server that has little to no impact on the network. Modify the TCP/IP properties of the server and test access to network resources. Then continue modifying WINS TCP/IP properties on the remaining servers in your network.

### Best Practices for Modifying Workstation WINS Properties

Modifying workstation TCP/IP properties can be much more difficult if an organization has not implemented Dynamic Host Configuration Protocol (DHCP) to distribute network addresses to client workstations.

If your organization is using DHCP, you can modify and remove WINS server entries in the client TCP/IP configuration by modifying the DHCP scope at the server level. This modification can be made at any time with little to no impact on the end user community.

**Testing Name Resolution**

Modify a workstation's TCP/IP properties and test name resolution prior to implementing an enterprisewide DHCP configuration change.

Test all server-to-server communications and applications requiring name resolution to ensure that functionality will not be affected when decommissioning WINS services.

Use the Services Control Panel to stop the WINS Service and test name resolution functionality before removing the WINS service and database.

### Removing Windows 2003 WINS Services

After all WINS-dependant areas have been addressed, it is now time to uninstall WINS service from the Windows 2003 Server. To complete this task, follow these steps:

1. Open the Control Panel of the server and open the Add/Remove Programs tool.

2. Select the Add/Remove Windows Components and choose Networking Services from the Selections dialog box.

3. Click the Details button to review the networking services options and deselect the WINS component.

4. Select Finish and close Add/Remove Programs to complete the removal of WINS services.

# Planning and Upgrading File Systems and Disk Partitions

Often when Windows NT 4.0 Servers where installed without hardware fault-tolerant equipment such as RAID controllers, the Windows NT 4.0 disk manager was used to create volume sets, mirrored sets, stripe sets, and stripe sets with parity. Because the Windows Server 2003 operating system does not support Windows NT 4.0 disk manager configurations, you must modify software-based disk configurations before performing an in-place upgrade of a Windows NT Server to Windows Server 2003. Perform the following tasks for each server that meets this configuration before continuing to upgrade any Windows NT server to Windows Server 2003.

## Mirrored Volumes

If Windows NT 4.0 disk administrator was used to create a mirrored set for redundancy prior to upgrading to Windows Server 2003, the Windows NT 4.0 mirrored set must be broken to install Windows Server 2003 successfully.

> **Perform a Backup of Server Information and Data**
>
> Before performing any disk maintenance or disk reconfiguration, perform a backup of server information and data.

## Volume Sets, Striped Sets, and Striped Sets with Parity

If you are performing an in-place upgrade of a server that has been configured using Windows NT 4.0 volume sets, stripe sets, or stripe sets with parity, the sets must be deleted and new fault-tolerant drive configurations will need to be configured before an upgrade to Windows Server 2003 can be completed successfully.

> **Don't Delete All the Data from the Volume**
>
> Performing the task of deleting a volume set, stripe set, or stripe set with parity will delete all the data from the volume.
>
> Back up all server data prior to deleting any type of volume or stripe sets.

Because any upgrade from Windows NT 4.0 to Windows Server 2003 using volume sets, stripe sets, or stripe sets with parity requires a reconfiguration of hardware, you should build a new Windows NT 4.0 domain controller, promote this system to the domain's primary domain controller, and conduct the in-place upgrade on the new system.

> **Manually Synchronize All Domain Controllers in the Domain**
>
> When promoting a new Windows NT primary domain controller, it is good practice to manually synchronize all domain controllers in the domain.
>
> Allow enough time for synchronization to occur and validate this by reviewing the domain controller's system event logs.

By adding this new domain controller to the source domain without unsupported volume and stripe set disk configurations, you can conduct the in-place upgrade without being required to take any domain controllers offline during the upgrade.

When the new domain controller is promoted to become a Windows NT 4.0 primary domain controller, the old server will become a backup domain controller and a copy of the Windows NT 4.0 SAM database and its information will remain intact.

# Avoiding Failures and Disruptions During Server Upgrades

Commonly overlooked server hardware and operating system service packs can cause unrecoverable failures and lengthy downtime when upgrading servers. Understanding the hardware being used for upgrading and installing the proper service packs for compatibility will help you perform the migration and prepare for any physical failures or migration tasks that need to be repeated.

## Planning for Failed Hardware

Whether upgrading existing server hardware to Windows Server 2003 or installing new server hardware, failures of physical hardware components can affect a migration timeline and schedule.

With a detailed hardware inventory, you can plan and purchase spare components such as hard drives, memory, and RAID controllers to ease recovery in case of a hardware failure. This is often a good practice especially when network availability is a priority. This can also be beneficial when upgrades are being performed on server hardware that has been in production for any length of time.

## Windows NT Upgrade Paths and Service Packs

When preparing a network for upgrade, you must plan to upgrade all Windows NT Server operating systems, taking into account the operating system version. With many organizations supporting various versions of the Windows NT 4.0 Server operating system, you must determine whether the existing installations of Windows NT 4.0 meet the minimum Microsoft requirements for upgrading as well as minimum Service Pack revisions required for an upgrade to Windows Server 2003.

### Windows NT Upgrade Paths

Not all Windows NT 4.0 server operating system platforms can be upgraded to just any Windows 2003 Server family platform. To understand the different upgrade paths and options available, look at Table 14.2. This will assist you in planning the best approach to implement your design and design needs.

## TABLE 14.2

**Microsoft Supported Upgrade Paths**

|  | Standard Edition | Enterprise Edition | Datacenter Edition | Web Edition |
|---|---|---|---|---|
| Windows NT 4.0 Server | X | X |  |  |
| Windows NT 4.0 Terminal Server Edition | X | X |  |  |
| Windows NT 4.0 Enterprise Edition |  | X |  |  |

### Meeting Windows NT Service Pack Requirements

The Windows NT 4.0 Server upgrade paths are only supported by Windows NT 4.0 Service Pack 5 or later. It is always best to install the latest service pack and allow time to evaluate the service pack installation by reviewing server logs and server performance before upgrading.

Conduct a detailed review of all servers being upgraded in the migration plan. Determine any required service pack installations needed and schedule a service pack upgrade for any existing Windows NT 4.0 servers not meeting the minimum requirements. As a good practice, allow these systems to run long enough to evaluate their performance and stability to ensure that they are not experiencing any issues prior to performing any upgrades to Windows Server 2003.

> **Installing a Clean Copy of Windows Server 2003**
>
> Whenever upgrading existing Windows NT Servers, Microsoft recommends installing a clean copy of Windows Server 2003 as a best practice whenever possible.
>
> Further information about service packs requirements and server upgrade paths can be found at `http://www.microsoft.com/ windowsserver2003/evaluation/ whyupgrade/supportedpaths.mspx`.

# Keeping Windows Servers Current with Windows Updates

After the Windows Server 2003 operating system is in production and functional. One challenge often overlooked in previous versions of Windows was maintaining server drivers to optimize performance. The time and effort required in the past to maintain servers with updates is no longer a factor with Windows Server 2003. Using the Windows Update services built into the Windows 2003 server operating systems has simplified the task of updating service packs, security fixes, critical updates, and Microsoft signed drivers.

# Finalizing Server Upgrades with Windows Update

After the upgrade or installation of Windows Server 2003 is complete, use Windows Update to install any required Windows updates and driver library updates to ensure server performance and optimal security.

Windows Update can only be run on server systems connected to the Internet with the proper TCP/IP properties configured to support Internet access.

To use Windows Update services to install the latest service packs, hot fixes, and security update, complete the following steps:

1. From the Start menu, select All Programs, Windows Update. This will launch the Windows Update service and connect the server being updated to the Microsoft Windows Update Web site.

2. Accept the Windows Update upgrade as required if you're prompted.

3. Select Scan for Updates; this will automatically scan the server system for any required updates.

4. Select the updates to be installed and finalize the server installation by selecting Install Now.

> **Restart the Server and Review Server Logs**
> After completing a Windows Update, it always good practice to restart the server and review server logs to validate server health and functionality.

# Supporting Windows Clients During Coexistence

While planning and implementing a migration, it important to review and determine the support requirements for domain clients. Ensuring effective Windows client network authentication and access to domain objects should be considered as important as upgrading domain servers.

When installing Windows Server 2003, the Windows Setup Manager prompts you that the Windows Server 2003 operating system does not support certain Windows clients. This is by design, because the Windows Server 2003 upgrades NTLM authentication from version 1 to NTLM version 2, thus disabling the ability for older Windows 95, Windows 98, and Windows NT 4.0 clients to access network resources without additional software to support connectivity to Active Directory.

There are two methods by which support for these clients can be enabled: installing the Active Directory Client and enabling support for NTLM V1 through the local server policies on the Windows 2003 domain controllers.

In addition to supporting legacy clients on the domain, another area to consider is authentication performance for existing clients during coexistence and domain controller upgrades.

## Load Balancing Domain Authentication

As Windows Server 2003 domain controllers are implemented into a Windows NT domain, the first domain controller to be upgraded takes on the role of PDC emulator. Once upgraded, this single domain controller is now responsible for providing domain services to all domain controllers as well as the domain authentication to all existing Windows 2000 and Windows XP client systems accessing the domain.

Organizations with large numbers of Windows 2000 and Windows XP clients, as well as legacy clients such as Windows NT and Windows 98, can experience PDC locator overload in this configuration. PDC overload can affect performance of the PDC emulator and prevent proper network authentication to client systems as well as replication of network changes.

> **Avoiding PDC Emulator Overload**
>
> To avoid PDC emulator overload, install and configure additional Windows 2003 domain controllers and configure each to emulate Windows NT 4.0 domain services.

Also, upgrading client computers during a migration without adding additional domain controllers can affect PDC performance and load balancing.

## Configuring PDC Emulation on Windows 2003 Domain Controllers

To configure a Windows Server 2003 domain controller to emulate Windows NT domain controllers, change the Registry of the domain controller to the following settings:

1. Edit the Windows Registry on the server to be upgraded by selecting Start, Run. Type **regedit** and select OK.

2. Edit the Registry key by selecting HKEY_LOCAL_MACHINE \SYSTEM CurrentControlSet\Services\Netlogon\ Parameters.

3. Add the REG DWORD "NT4Emulator" to the Registry key and add the REG DWORD value 0x1.

> **After the Server Upgrade Is Complete...**
>
> modify the server Registry and configure the Windows 2003 Server to perform Windows NT domain PDC emulation before running the Active Directory Installation Wizard.

> **Modifying the Registry Setting**
>
> Modifying the Registry setting will also modify the method in which the new Domain controller performs Domain Name System Lookups. After the Registry setting is in place, Windows Server 2003 domain controllers use the Windows NT 4.0–compatible Locator process to performed Domain Name Systems lookups.
>
> After all client upgrades are complete, modify the Registry setting on each domain controller to reverse the Registry setting change and enable the Windows Active Directory Internet Protocol Locator Process.

## Supporting Windows 95, 98, and NT 4.0 Client Systems

Before upgrading to Windows Server 2003, client support and compatibility with Active Directory must be considered for legacy

Windows clients. The Windows Server 2003 family of operating systems do not support Windows 95, Windows 98, or Windows NT 4.0 client systems and will not authenticate these clients to the domain after the presence of Windows NT domain controllers are eliminated.

To enable the ability for these client systems to authenticate and access domain resources, additional client software must be installed or domain controller configurations completed to support authentication. Review the methods by which support can be enabled for these clients and the specific features that each method provides. Determine which method best meets your migration needs and test the configuration in a lab environment before implementing.

### Active Directory Client Extensions

The most common method of enabling support for client systems running nonsupport versions of Windows is to install the Microsoft Active Directory Client software.

Available for free download from Microsoft, the Active Directory Client installs the Active Directory extensions enabling support for Windows 95, Windows 98, and Windows NT Service Pack 6a systems in a Windows 2003 Active Directory environment.

By installing the Active Directory Client extensions, client support is enabled in the following areas:

- *NTLM version 2 Authentication.* Support for improved authentication using NTLM version 2.

- *Site Awareness Support.* This functionary allows client systems to authenticate to the domain, logging onto the most available and physically closest Windows 2003 domain controller to the client system. Also, client systems can now change the password on any Active Directory domain controller in the domain.

- *Active Directory Service Interfaces (ADSI).* ADSI support provides client scripting ability often used to manage and retrieve information in Active Directory.

- *Distributed File Systems Support DFS fault tolerance.* This function enables support for access Distributed File System (DFS) shares configured on the Windows 2003 Active Directory domain.

- *Active Directory Windows Address Book (WAB) property pages.* Enabling WAB support allows clients authenticated to the domain to search active directory for user object retrieving information, such as addresses and phone numbers.

### Enabling Client Support Without Active Directory Extensions

**Download the Windows NT 4.0 SP6a Active Directory Client Extensions**

The Windows NT 4.0 SP6a Active Directory Client Extensions can be downloaded from the Microsoft Web site at `http://www.microsoft.com/ntworkstation/downloads/Other/adclient.asp`.

One other method of enabling support for legacy clients is to use the local domain controller policy on the Windows Server 2003 domain controller. When organizations want to support legacy clients in an Active Directory environment, authentication can be accomplished through configuration changes to the local domain controller policy by doing the following:

1. You can enable support by relaxing the NTLM version settings and modifying the Digitally Sign Communication Settings of the default policy as shown in Figure 14.4.

2. To modify the local server policy, open the Administrator Tools and click the Domain Controller Policy Management Console.

3. Expand the Local Policies and select Security Options in the left pane of the Policy Management Console.

4. Modify the following settings as shown in Figure 14.4:

   ■ Microsoft Network Server: Digitally Sign Communication (always)—Modify the setting to Disable.

   ■ Microsoft Network Server: Digitally Sign Communication (if Client Agrees)—Modify the setting to Enable.

   ■ Network Security: LAN Manager Authentication Level—Modify the setting to Send NM & NTLM—Use NTLM Version Session Security if Negotiated.

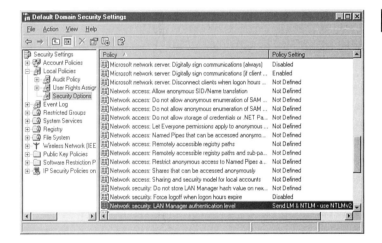

**FIGURE 14.4**
Local domain controller security policy.

# Implementing and Securing Password Migrations

The Active Directory Migration Tool is a comprehensive tool for migrating user accounts, computer accounts, and groups. One area this tool does not complete without additional configuration is the migration of user passwords to the new Active Directory domain. This feature is important when organizations require users to maintain passwords for access to the source domain as well as migrating service accounts to active directory.

Implementing a secure Password Export Server (PES) into the migration design enables you to focus on migration tasks without spending excessive time supporting user password changes when migrating accounts. Also, with the password migration utility, single sign-on requirements can be maintained and supported by preserving Windows NT 4.0 account user passwords in the newly migrated Active Directory domain.

## Setting Up an ADMT Password Migration Server

To migrate passwords, select or install a backup domain controller in the source Windows NT 4.0 domain to act as the Secure Password Export server. This server will communicate with the Active Directory Migration Tool (ADMT) Server in the Target Domain. To provide secure password migrations and ensure no issues with the installation of the Password DLL, a Password Export server should be added to the network during the migration process.

### Enhancing Security on your Password Server

Password migrations are sensitive and information about user's password are being sent over the network and are stored on the password server.

Enabling security and encryption on the Password Export server and Active Direction Migration Tool server in the target domain is a good practice. Ensure that the following requirements are met before installing the Password Export Server and migrating with ADMT:

- Install 128 Bit Encryption Service Pack 6a on the Password Export server

- Install 128 Bit Encryption on the ADMT server

- Create an encryption key to install on the Password Export server

### Using an Encryption Key on the Password Export Server

The Password server encryption key is a key created on the ADMT server and is required to complete the installation of the Password Export Server. The encryption key can be created and stored in one or both of the following methods, by copying to the local floppy disk drive for transport to the password export server or by storing the encryption key in a folder on the local hard drive.

To create the Password Encryption key, begin by opening a command dialog box on the ADMT server in the target domain and do the following:

> **Storing the Key**
>
> Regardless of which methods are used to store the password encryption key, it must reside on the local server hard drive. Mapped network drives and shares cannot be used for this purpose and will prevent the installation of the Password Export server.

1. From the command line type the following to create a PES encryption key and create a password: **ADMT.exe key Source Domain Name Folder: [Password]**

   (For example, C:\ADMT.exe DunePoint A: Zip&Harley123)

2. After the encryption key has been created, copy the key to a floppy disk and insert the disk into the floppy drive of the PES server.

3. On the PES server, run the Password Migration installation from D:\I386\ADMT\ PWDMIG.exe where D: represents the drive of the CD-ROM. Type in the password and complete the setup process.

4. To enable password migrations the AllowPasswordExport Registry key value on the Password Export server must be set. Open the Registry editor on the PES server by typing **regedit** from the run command dialog box. Open the HKLM\SYSTEM\CurrentControlSet\ Control\Lsa key in the Registry. Modify the Registry key to allow password migrations by adding the value of 1 to the key. This enables password migration on the source domain's backup domain controller.

> **For Maximum Security**
>
> For maximum security when migrating passwords, always disable the Registry entry functionality for migrating password on the PES. Use the Registry value of 0 to disable password migrations when not being used.

### Configuring Permissions to Enable Password Migrations

After the installation of the PES is complete, the next step is to set domain permission to allow password migrations between the target domain and source domain. Perform the following steps:

1. Add the Everyone group to the Pre-Windows 2000 Compatible Access group in the target domain. This must be completed using the command line by typing the following: **NET LOCALGROUP "Pre-Windows 2000 Compatible Access" Everyone /ADD**.

2. Add anonymous access to domain controllers in the target domain. From the ADMT domain controller, open the group policy editor and choose Default Domain Controllers Policy, Computer Configuration, Windows Settings, Security Settings, Local Policies, Security Options, Additional Restrictions for Anonymous Connections.

3. Ensure that Rely on Default Permissions or Not Defined is set. This setting must be present to allow password migration to complete.

4. Add Anonymous Logon user to the Pre-Windows 2000 Compatible Access group using the command line by typing the following: **NET LOCALGROUP "Pre-Windows 2000 Compatible Access" Anonymous Logon /ADD**.

> **Test Migration**
>
> Perform a test migration to ensure that proper rights have been configured and password migration functionality is present before performing migrations of domain users.
>
> Additional information about password migrations and password server installations can be located on the Windows Server 2003 CD under I386\ADMT\readme.doc.

# Addressing Permissions Issues When Migrating Desktops

Now that you understand migration concepts and options available using the Active Directory Migration Tool, let's focus on desktop migration and options that can be implemented to ease the client experience during the migration.

Using the Active Directory Migration Tool, domain member desktop systems can be migrated from the source Windows NT domain to the target domain with little to no need for user intervention. By preparing and understanding the requirements needed to migrate desktops, you can install the ADMT agent easily and remotely.

The following sections review the key elements involved with migrating a desktop and common permissions you need to avoid a failed migration.

## Knowing Desktop Migration Requirements

Before migrating desktops to Active Directory, the account being used to migrate will require administrative permission to the local desktop administrator group and domain administrator group. This is required to perform certain functions, including changing the domain membership of the desktop on the domain controller and installing the desktop migration agent on the local desktop.

## Local Desktop Permissions

A local group is a desktop system account that is strictly prohibited to the individual desktop and is used to grant permissions and rights to the local computer. The local administrative group is the most privileged of the local groups and allows members access to all function of the local desktop such as services, installing software, and access profiles.

Unlike domain and global groups, which are managed at the domain level by the domain network administrator, local groups can only be managed at the local desktop and require administrative privileges to be changed locally to grant an account membership to this group.

Local administrative groups can host memberships to local user accounts, local groups, domain user's accounts, domain groups, and global groups.

## Tips for Configuring Desktop Permission

Many times when migrating, the actual domain administrator account is used to perform all migration functions. Using this account, including adding it to the local administrative group of the desktop, can create network vulnerabilities and allow anyone with access to this account information on the local user's desktop.

# Creating Desktop Migration Accounts

As a best practice, creating a separate account to migrate the desktops systems allows you the capability to control access to the local systems by simply disabling and enabling the account for migration or administrative purposes.

Create a desktop migration account on the target domain. This account will require membership to the domain administrative groups on the source and target domains in order for the administrator to be able to perform these migration functions.

# Tips for Configuring Desktop Permissions

One thing that often stops administrators from creating and using a desktop migration account is the task of deploying the account to the local desktop administrator group. There are several tips and tricks that can be used to add the desktop migration account to the local desktop administrator group without requiring the administrator to visit each individual desktop system.

> ## Enhancing Security
>
> To enhance security, the desktop migration account can be disabled when not migrating desktops.
>
> Also the desktop administrative account password can be changed at any time without affecting any other domain administrator account functions.
>
> Most importantly, this account can later be leveraged for administrative purposes. By enabling the desktop account, you can perform tasks at the local desktop level without requiring the domain administrator account to be used.

## Leveraging the Domain Administrators Group

One way to create the proper administrative permission required for migrating desktops is to simply add the desktop migration account that resides in the source domain to the domain administrators group in the target domain. Using this method will allow the Active Directory Migration Tool to perform the required functions; however, this will not provide local administrative rights to the desktop after it has been migrated to the target domain.

## Using the Net Add User Command

The second method that can be leveraged to easily populate the desktop migration account to all domain desktops is to use the Net Add User command in the logon script in the Windows NT 4.0 source domain. By adding a single net add statement to the Windows NT 4.0 domain logon script, the desktop migration account can be added to the local administrators group on all desktops when users logon to the domain. Using this method will also leave the account membership intact even when the desktop has been migrated to active directory.

# Best Practices for Maintaining and Managing Coexistence

For most migration scenarios, it is unrealistic to think that the migration can be completed in a single upgrade. When this occurs, providing coexistence and functionality between Windows NT domains and Active Directory domains become a major component of the domain migration.

Because Windows Server 2003 is fully integrated with Windows NT security, networking and logon services, coexistence can be supported for a period of time with relative ease of management.

Understanding the migration time frame and logistics of how objects will be moved can better assist you in planning for domain coexistence. Knowing the key elements of the migration and implementing them into the migration plan can provide domain users a reliable level of service during the migration and avoid lengthy network disruptions.

## Consolidating Network Services

One major benefit to implementing coexistence with Windows Server 2003 is its compatibility with Windows NT domain services. When managing and maintaining coexistence, you can plan to migrate domain services such as Dynamic Host Configuration Protocol (DHCP), Domain Name Service (DNS), and Windows Internet Naming Services (WINS) to Windows Server 2003 as a first step. By migrating these services up front, the ability to take advantage of the features and performance of Windows Server 2003 even when providing functionality of these services to a Windows NT 4.0 domain is greatly enhanced.

Because Windows Server 2003 provides increased performance and availability, migrating and consolidating network services to the new Active Directory domain can actually improve domain performance and client server response. Also, moving these domain services and consolidating to Windows Server 2003 will effectively eliminate Windows NT 4.0 domain servers and provide an increased level of reliability to clients still residing on the Windows NT 4.0 domain.

## Using SID History to Maintain Access to Resources

As users are migrated to the new target domain, maintaining and managing coexistence to ensure uninterrupted access to user resources can be difficult. Backward compatibility to objects such as Windows NT 4.0 file shares and network resources not yet migrated can be accomplished by leveraging and implementing features available in the Active Directory Migration Tool.

With the Windows Server 2003 Active Directory Migration Tool, network administrators can now migrate user accounts while also migrating users' Windows NT 4.0 Secure Identifier (SID) information to maintain access to resources still residing in the source domain.

In Windows NT 4.0, all users, computers, and groups are associated with a unique domain SID. Windows NT 4.0 domains grant access to domain resources based on a user's SID information stored in the Access Control List (ACLs). These can be viewed as permissions pages for principles such a file shares and domain resources. These user SIDs can be appended to the new Active Directory Account using the Active Directory Migration Tool. This enables users to maintain privileged access to resources still residing in the Windows NT 4.0 domain.

## Migrating SID History

By choosing the option to migrate SID history, all account information of the domain user object in Windows NT 4.0 is migrated to the new account in Windows Server 2003 Active Directory domain. To migrate user SID history along with the domain user account, select Migrate User SIDs to Target Domain when using the Active Directory Migration Tool to migrate accounts as shown in Figure 14.5.

To migrate Windows NT 4.0 account SID history, select the Migrate SID History check box on the user migration options page of the Active Directory User Migration Wizard.

**FIGURE 14.5**    ADMT user SID history option page.

## Additional Tools for Managing Coexistence

There are many tools and third-party utilities to assist your organization when migrating to Windows Server 2003. One of the most common and effective tools is the Microsoft Active Directory Connector (ADC). The ADC allows organizations to synchronize Windows Server 2003 and Active Directory with the Microsoft Exchange Server directories. The ADC can be implemented and used to support coexistence between mail systems and active directory while user's accounts are being migrated.

> **For More Information**
>
> More information on the Active Directory Connector, directory synchronization, and additional tools can be found at www.microsoft.com/windowsserver2003/upgrading/nt4/tooldocs/default.mspx.

# Common Mistakes When Decommissioning Domains and Servers

As the migration of user objects and domain resources continues, administrators find that key design decisions have become clear and the implementation is well in progress. The remaining focus now turns to how and what is the most effective method to remove the Windows NT 4.0 source domain and domain servers. Questions often asked by network administrators when beginning to consider the removal of a Windows NT 4.0 domain or server are:

What are the best practices and order in which domain servers can be decommissioned?

How do I reduce risks that can affect the overall progress of the migration?

Key to decommissioning a Windows NT 4.0 source domain involves removing the Windows configuration that existed to support coexistence. The following sections describe common areas often overlooked, methods that ensure that domain communication and Windows 2003 performance is not compromised by residuals remaining from the migration, the methods in which to identify potential issues, and the tools used to resolve them.

## Decommissioning Windows NT 4.0 Domain Servers

When migration of network file and print services begin, administrators often focus on the migration of resources and not how this is directly related to decommissioning the servers on which services resided.

When domain servers are not directly upgraded to Windows Server 2003, roles must be migrated to the target domain, leaving servers in the source domain ready for removal. By understanding the best practices for migrating server roles, administrators can also systematically begin decommissioning server resources simultaneously, which would normally be removed at the end of the migration.

## Prioritizing Server Roles During a Migrations

During a migration, there are certain servers that can or should be migrated before or after others. The various server roles that should be prioritized during the migration process are as follows:

- Domain Services and Backup Domain Controllers (BDCs)—Leveraging Windows 2003 performance enhancements by moving key domain services such as DHCP and DNS improves client server communications immediately and eases administration during the migration. This also allows your organization to begin downgrading immediately the total amount of Windows NT 4.0 Domain BDCs and reducing replication requirements and network traffic when changes are made.

- File and Print Servers—When hardware requirements are met, it is sometimes more effective to upgrade file servers using an Inplace upgrade scenario to Windows Server 2003.

When this is not possible, migrating these files and print services can be done with relative ease allowing these larger capacity servers to be reallocated into the new active Directory Domain.

- Application and Web Services—With more organizations relying on Web services and server-based applications to support daily business needs, extensive testing and validation is required to ensure application compatibility and a successful migration. By migrating these services later rather than sooner, you have time to test and validate application upgrades and functionality before migrating.

- Migration Support Servers—Review the server roles that reside in the target domain that were used to support the migration such as the Active Directory Migration Tool and server services. Decommission these roles that were used for the migration.

- Primary Domain Controllers—At the very last point of the migration, the only system that should actually remain is the Windows NT 4.0 Primary Domain Controller. Remove this server and archive this system for a period of time acceptable to your organization. This system is the last remaining archive of the original Windows NT 4.0 domain state. Having this domain controller available can enables you to recover domain information if necessary at a later time.

## Removing Permissions

When establishing connectivity between domains for migration purposes and to support the migration tools, many configuration changes and group membership entries are created. These changes are just as important to review and remove after a migration is complete as they were to implement and provide functionality for the actual migration. By ensuring that permissions and group membership are removed after the migration is complete, ghost entries in Active Directory referencing Windows NT 4.0 administrative accounts are avoided and administrative cleanup requiring lengthy review and manual cleanup tasks at later time can be avoided.

Review the administrative changes created to support the migration and remove these accounts from the Active Directory administrative groups before removing the last Windows NT 4.0 server from the Active Directory domain.

## Using the Active Directory System Editor ADSI

The Active Directory Services Interface editor (ADSI Edit) is an Active Directory Service tool that gives you the capability to use an alternative editor to manage the Active Directory domain and schema objects. ADSI enables you to add, remove, and modify all directory objects viewing the schema from a low level perspective. This tool can be used with many of the same features provided in Active Directory Users and Computers but without the restrictions sometimes experienced when trying to delete directory objects.

**Using ADSI Edit Can Cause Irreversible Effects**

Using ADSI Edit can cause irreversible effects with no option to recover from mistakes. Before deleting objects using ADSI Edit, ensure that you understand the full repercussions and have backed up the Active Directory completely.

Use the ADSI editors to remove objects such as legacy server objects remaining from the Windows NT 4.0 source domain created during coexistence. ADSI editors can sometimes be the only option for removing these objects.

The ADSI editor can be installed from the Windows 2003 Server CD-ROM by installing the SupTools.msi installation package. To install ADSI Edit, install the installation file located in the D:\\SUPPORT\TOOLS directory where D: represents your system's CD-ROM drive.

# Summary

Migrating from Windows NT 4.0 to Windows Server 2003 can be as simple as inserting the Windows Server 2003 CD into the Windows NT 4.0 PDC and allowing for an automated upgrade. However, there are several things that can be done to validate and test for a successful migration in a test environment prior to doing the migration in a live production environment.

Leveraging tools available for compatibility and migration testing and creating tested fallback plans can minimize the risk and the potential failure of a migration to Windows 2003. Planning can also minimize risk, as well as testing and validating procedures and processing times during a prototype or lab test to clarify how long it will take to initiate the migration.

With security enhancements built into Windows Server 2003, the migration process takes on a whole new test of tasks that require security testing and validation before proceeding. Testing security processes can minimize migration failure caused by a Windows service not starting automatically, or access to necessary administrative accounts are blocked by policy or rule.

By leveraging best practices and lessons learned in the migration process, an organization can improve the success factors that lead to a successful migration to Windows Server 2003.

# 15

# Migrating from Windows 2000

**D**uring the life cycle of a migration, administrators are often focused on the details and tasks of planning a migration and performing the tasks required to migrate to Windows Server 2003. As more and more migrations to Windows Server 2003 are completed, organization has experienced unforeseen issues resulting from the state of the original Windows 2000 environment at the time of the migration.

In this chapter, you will learn to identify these areas and highlight the tasks, tips, and best practices involved with each. In addition, administrators and organizations will find other tasks and tips to assist in planning the migration, preparing Active Directory to be migrated, and preparing server hardware before a migration.

With preparation focused on the most import areas of a migration, just as important as the preparation tasks of the migration is the migration phase and the maintenance tasks involved with migrating to Windows Server 2003. This chapter focuses on the tips and tricks to help during the migration and the tasks to be performed after the migration to Windows 2003 is complete.

These planning considerations and hardware compatibility issues can be addressed to validate the migration strategy and ensure the migration path is the one that best fits your organization's needs.

# Preparing the Migration

As organizations plan and prepare to migrate to Windows Server 2003, one important consideration is the proactive tasks that can be completed prior to a migration to avoid issues when executing the migration task and concerns that might arise after the migration is complete.

To begin planning a migration, one of the first areas you can consider is planning and creating a maintenance schedule which will allow you to review each task and proactively identify concerns and address areas that can affect a migration and server upgrade to Windows 2003.

Review server roles, existing hardware, and the state of the Active Directory environment and adjust the migration strategy based on these findings. This ensures a successful migration and healthy Active Directory environment after the migration is complete.

The following section provides insight to addressing these areas. Utilities and tips for using them to prepare you and the Windows 2000 environment for a successful migration to Windows Server 2003.

## Preparing Windows 2000 Servers to Be Migrated

Begin by preparing the existing Windows 2000 servers and evaluating the readiness of the Windows 2000 environment. Create a server inventory and evaluate the existing Active Directory so your organization can plan server roles such as domain controllers and application servers based on the existing hardware being migrated.

You can also determine upgrade paths and hardware replacement needs, which can then be incorporated into the migration plan.

### Scripts to Inventory Hardware

Begin understanding your migration hardware needs by creating a detailed inventory of the existing Windows 2000 server hardware. Create a detailed inventory of the server hardware by manually inspecting servers, exporting hardware information using Microsoft Systems Management Server, and by using Microsoft Scripts which will query servers and report installed hardware.

> **Gather More Hardware Information...**
> You can download and use Windows scripts to collect, inventory, and enumerate hardware components such as memory and plug and play devices on servers belonging to the Windows 2000 domain.
>
> Go to the Microsoft scripting center at
> `http://www.microsoft.com/technet/`
> `treeview/default.asp?url=/technet/`
> `scriptcenter/Default.asp.`

By creating and using a documented list of server components, you can determine which servers will be incorporated into the new Windows 2003 environment and which servers require upgrades to meet the minimum hardware requirements recommended by Microsoft for installing Windows Server 2003.

## Checking Hardware Compatibility

To determine hardware compatibility, you can use the Compatibility Check Tool available from Microsoft. Located on the Windows Server 2003 installation CD-ROM, this tool can be run directly from the Windows 2003 CD-ROM.

The inventory tool can be accessed through the Windows setup screen when installing Windows Server. Use the compatibility check tool to identify noncompatible hardware and conflicts that might exist on servers to be upgraded when migrating.

**Compatibility Check Tool**

Using the Compatibility Check Tool does not require you to perform the installation of Windows Server 2003 when running.

To use the Compatibility Check Tool, run the tool on the server to be evaluated. To run this tool from a command prompt, insert the Windows 2003 installation CD-ROM. From the Run Command dialog box, use the following command to run the Compatibility Check Tool: **D:\setup /checkupgradeonly** (where D: represents the drive of the local server CD-ROM).

## Evaluating Server Hardware Life Expectancy

Another key consideration when evaluating hardware is server hardware life expectancy and the life cycle of the hardware components installed.

The hardware life cycle is the total amount of time you can expect server hardware to remain in production before performance, capacity, or failure can become a concern.

Often you can continue the hardware life cycle by adding memory and extending the total amount of drive space on a server. In addition to supplying additional memory and hardware drive space, often the replacement of older server drives can help avoid drive failures and lengthy recovery processes caused by server hard drive failures.

**Evaluate All Server Components**

Along with the server drive, it is a good practice to evaluate all server components to determine risks related to hardware failures. Review server history and identify existing servers that have failed in the past. Evaluate those servers that might pose any risk in the future once migrated to Windows 2003 before considering them as part of the migration.

## Service Packs and System Bios Updates

One of the final considerations is Microsoft Windows service packs and server hardware BIOS revision updates. As a best practice before migrating, it is always a good idea to install the latest Windows 2000 service packs and hardware BIOS updates to ensure compatibility and avoid complications when upgrading servers to Windows 2003.

In Windows 2003 mixed-mode environment scenarios, you should also address installing the latest Microsoft service packs, updates, and hot fixes on each Windows 2000 server you plan to keep in a mixed-mode environment after the migration of the domain is complete.

To install Windows critical updates and hot fixes without requiring multiple reboots during the installation, use the QCHAIN utility available from Microsoft for download. This utility is included with Windows 2000 service pack 4 and all post service pack 4 hot fixes. You can install multiple hot fixes using the QChain utility built into post SP3 hot fixes and updates.

To install multiple hot fixes and updates using the QChain utility, follow the example in Figure 15.1. In this example, three hot fixes will be installed from a folder called D:\Updates. To install multiple updates and fixes, begin by downloading the updates and placing them into a folder from where the fixes will be installed. Create a batch file using the following commands to install the updates using QChain as shown in Figure 15.1.

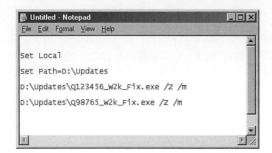

**FIGURE 15.1**   QChain update batch file.

Use the /z command switch so the server does not restart after the update has been installed. Use the command line switch /m to perform the installation in unattended mode. Additional information on using the QChain utility commands can be found at http://www.microsoft.com/downloads.

**Before Applying BIOS and Firmware Updates**

Before applying BIOS and firmware updates, it is a good practice to back up server data to avoid any possible loss of information.

When applying updates, read and follow installation instructions carefully.

In addition to service packs and updates, it is good practice to apply any server BIOS updates and firmware updates for devices such as array controllers and systems boards to leverage functionality and ensure compatibility with the Windows Server 2003 family of products. To find system BIOS updates and firmware updates for server hardware, see the server manufacturers Web site support section.

## Calculating Active Directory Hardware Requirement

As server hardware and compatibility requirements become clearer, additional considerations can be made to validate domain controller performance and hardware requirements when considering support for Microsoft's Active Directory.

Using the ADSIZER tool from Microsoft, you can input information to identify additional Active Directory–related hardware requirements to provide adequate Active Directory performance and support the future plans of the Windows 2003 Active Directory Environment.

Leveraging information included in the Active Directory, such as the total amount of users in and the directory site topology, the Active Directory Sizer Tool will validate the server hardware needs and total amount of server required to support a planned Active Directory design. Areas tested using the tool include hardware drive performance and server memory and total amount processors as well as areas regarding the total amount of domain controllers needed to support the future Active Directory infrastructure according to Microsoft standards.

The ADSIZER tool and additional information on this utility can be accessed on the Windows 2003 resource kit and by downloading the utility from the Microsoft Web site at `http://www.microsoft.com/downloads`.

### Determining Active Directory Health State

One of the last considerations to review before deciding which migration path to implement is to determine the overall state and health of the Active Directory environment. To do this, use common administrative tasks and tools available from Microsoft such as DCDiag.exe to maintain Active Directory.

To begin, review each domain controller's event viewer system and application logs, identify common replication issues and event errors related to Active Directory and domain controller replication.

Also, installing additional utilities like Netdiag and DCDiag from the Windows 2000 support tools and resource kit as well as leveraging built-in utilities will enable you to perform additional tests on the Windows 2000 Active Directory environment to ensure system state health before migrating.

> **Before Performing Any of the Tasks Listed in the Following Section**
> Back up all system state data before performing any of the tasks listed in the following section. Failure to back up information might result in the loss of Active Directory information.

Also, included in the preparation tasks should be the review and maintenance of the existing Windows 2000 Domain Name System (DNS). Because Active Directory is heavily dependent on DNS, you should review the state of DNS and perform any maintenance required before migrating to Windows Server 2003.

### Using Netdiag.exe

Often errors with replication and domain controller communication are not present in the domain controller server event logs; in this section you will apply the DCDiag and Netdiag utilities to identify Active Directory communication issues and issues related to replication.

Use the following commands, to run the Netdiag utility and parse information to a log for review:

To begin using the Netdiag utility, complete the steps listed here:

1. Download or install the Resource Kit from the Windows resource Kit CD-ROM.

2. Run the Netdiag utility from the installation path of the Windows Resource Kit:

   `C:\Programs Files\Resource Kit\Netdiag.exe`.

**For Additional Information and Netdiag Commands**
Additional information and Netdiag commands can be found by reviewing the Netdiag_d.htm files located in the resource kit installation path directory.

3. Using the following command to run the Netdiag utility and create a log file showing errors only for review:

```
Netdiag.exe /q /I /d:DomainName
```

### Using Replmon to Validate Replication

The replication monitor, installed with the Windows 2000 support tools, is a helpful GUI interface tool to assist in identifying and manually controlling replication of Active Directory.

To use the replication monitor, install the Windows support tools. It is best to install and run the replication monitor from a domain controller in the Forest Root Domain.

To install the Replication Monitor Utility and test Domain Controller replication, complete the following steps:

1. Install the Windows support tools from the Windows installation CD-ROM.

2. Open the Replmon utility by selecting Start, Programs, Support Tools, Replmon.

### Performing Offline Defrag of Active Directory

One task that can greatly improve Active Directory performance and prepare Active Directory to be migrated to Windows 2003 is performing an offline defragmentation of the Ntds.dit file.

Performing a defrag of the Ntds.dit file can reduce the overall size of the file by up to 40 percent. To defrag a database offline, perform the following steps:

1. Begin by backing up the Active Directory. Use the native Windows backup utility or third-party backup software to back up and validate the server System State data.

2. Restart the domain controller and, when rebooting, select the F8 command to boot the server into the directory service restore mode.

3. Log on to the directory service restore mode using the Directory Service Restore Mode administrator account and password configured when the server was installed. Press Enter twice to restart the server.

4. From Windows choose Start, Run and enter **command**. Click OK to continue. This will open a command window.

5. From the command window, Type **NTDSUtil** and press Enter.

**For the Following Steps...**
Document the information provided in the previous steps, and record the path information to be used in the following steps.

6. Type the command **files** and press Enter.

7. Type the command **info** and press Enter. Note the information displayed about the database size and log files.

8. Create a location on the server that has enough drive space to create a new Ntds.dit file.

9. From the command prompt enter the drive and path of the location where the new Ntds.dit file will be created; for example, E:\New (where E: represents the drive and \New represent the folder where the new Ntds.dit will be created).

   You must specify a drive and directory to place the new Ntds.dit file. If the path contains a space, you must use quotes around the pathname. This will create the new database in the path location created.

10. Type the **quit** command and **quit** again to exit the NTDS utility and continue.

11. Copy the new Ntds.dit to the location of the original Active Directory location recorded in step 7 of this procedure.

12. Once complete, restart the server and allow the domain controller to boot normally.

13. Review the server logs to identify errors and issues regarding the defragmentation of the Active Directory database.

### Verifying Domain Name System Functionality

Another area to validate when reviewing Active Directory health and functionality is the current Domain Name System or DNS services in the domain.

You can check DNS consistency and functionality using tools in the Windows resource kit.

To check the consistency of the existing DNS and validate DNS functionality, use the DNSLint.exe utility from the Windows support tools located on the Windows installation CD-ROM.

To test the Active Directory DNS, use the DNSLint.exe utility located in the C:\Program File\Support Tools directory to test the server DNS. Use the /ad switch to query DNS and test the record used by Active Directory to replicate information in the domain.

## Planning the Type of Upgrade

Now that the hardware requirements have been determined, you can focus on which migration path scenario and approach best fits your specific migration needs.

With server hardware identified and capacity of future requirements being considered, review the following bullets to determine the most effective migration path for your organization.

- Domain in-place upgrade—By far the simplest method to deploy Windows 2003. The option is often applied when hardware is current and the Active Directory infrastructure design is sufficient for the future needs of the organization. This allows administrators to easily perform in-place upgrades of the existing Windows 2000 Active Directory domain controllers by directly upgrading the existing domain.

- Migrate to Windows 2003—When migration processes dictate the need for a domain name change or the organization is consolidating domains, this option is often used. By creating a new domains and even a new forest, you can leverage the Active Directory Replication Monitor to migrate and consolidate domain objects to a new domain infrastructure.

# Windows Server 2003 Applications Compatibility

> **Validate and Verify**
>
> It is always a good practice to validate and verify application compatibility with the software manufacturer.
>
> Before upgrading, apply vendor application updates to ensure the compatibility and proper functionality after upgrading.
>
> Contact application vendor support to validate each application's compatibility with Windows 2003.

When migrating, one of the most important areas to validate is applications compatibility. Because existing Windows environments can consist of many different types of applications, you should leverage all resources available to confirm application compatibility with Windows Server 2003.

To provide the most effective results when testing applications, you can use the Application Compatibility Tool available with Windows 2003 as a first means of verification.

# Using the Application Compatibility Tool Kit

The Application Compatibility Tool Kit (ACT) is a deployment tool provided by Microsoft to assist IT staff in identifying and testing applications for compatibility with Windows Server 2003. There are three components to the ACT:

- *Application Compatibility Analyzer* is a tool used to gather remotely all installed programs within a Windows NT network. This tool automatically creates an inventory of all installed programs without requiring a management tool such as SMS.

> **Use the Command Line Tool Collector.exe To...**
>
> Inventory systems applications and write information to a log file. By default, the Collector tool writes information and places the log file on the system desktop in which the tool is being run. Use the `-o` switch to specify an alternative location to write the collector logs such as `Collector.exe -o c:\AppInfo\Collect.log`.

- *Application Verifier* can be used to identify compatibility issues with existing and new applications to be installed on Windows Server 2003.

- *Compatibility Administrator* is a complete tool that can determine the necessary fixes required for application support with Windows Server 2003. The compatibility administrator can also be used to create packages of fixes stored in a database that can then be distributed to application servers within Active Directory.

# Upgrading and Installing Windows Server 2003

In this section, you will review the specific requirement for installing and upgrading Windows 2000 servers to Windows 2003. In addition to hardware and software requirements, this section provides you with valuable tips and techniques when installing or performing installations and upgrading to Windows 2003.

## Upgrade Paths and Requirements

When upgrading server operating systems to Windows 2003, servers must meet the Microsoft minimum hardware and software requirements to install Windows 2003 successfully. In addition to hardware requirements, consideration must be made to decide which Windows 2003 Family product to update with. Review the Windows 2003 Upgrade paths in Table 15.2 to determine which Windows 2003 Server operating system can be used when upgrading a Windows 2000 Server version.

Table 15.1 lists the requirements you need to ensure that all servers being upgraded meet the minimum requirements to ensure that each server upgrade will complete successfully.

**TABLE 15.1**

**Windows 2000 System Requirements**

| Windows Server 2003 | Minimum Processor Speed | RAM | Required Disk Space for Installation |
|---|---|---|---|
| Web Edition | 133MHz | 128MB | 1.5GB |
| Standard Edition | 133MHz | 128MB | 1.5GB |
| Enterprise Edition | 133MHz | 128MB | 1.5GB |
| Datacenter Edition | 400MHz | 512MB | 1.5GB |

**TABLE 15.2**

**Windows 2003 Upgrade Paths**

| Windows 2000 Server Edition | Standard Edition | Enterprise Edition | Datacenter Edition | Web Edition | Small Business Edition |
|---|---|---|---|---|---|
| Standard | X | X | | | X |
| Advanced | | X | | | |
| Datacenter | | | X | | |

## Upgrading by Performing a Clean Installation

When the requirements allow it, a clean installation of Windows server 2003 can be the most effective manner to create new domain controllers and upgrade a domain to Windows 2003. Using this method enables you to implement new server hardware and a clean installation of Windows 2003 without requiring existing domain controllers to be upgraded.

> **Before Upgrading Any Server or Domain...**
> Perform a full backup of the existing domain and validate the backup in case a recovery is required.

By using the DCPROMO command to create a new domain controller in the Windows 2000 domain, you can then use the NTDSUTIL to seize the domain FSMO roles to the new Windows 2003 domain controller. To upgrade a domain to Windows 2003 without upgrading existing hardware, review the following steps.

1. Install Windows 2003 server on the new server hardware. You can choose to join the domain at this time or when the server installation and service pack update is complete.

> **Add the Permanent Address**
> To ensure proper communications and domain registration, add the permanent IP address of the server and DNS server for the domain during the installation of Windows 2003.

2. Install any related Windows 2003 service packs and updates.

3. If not completed during the installation, join the new server to the Windows 2000 domain by selecting the My Computer option and opening the Properties page.

4. Select the Computer Name tab and click Change button to join the domain.

5. Upgrade the server to be a domain controller by running the DCPROMO command. Select Start, Run and type **DCPROMO**. Click OK to upgrade the server to a domain controller.

6. On the Welcome to Active Directory Installation Wizard, select Next to continue.

7. On the Operating Systems Compatibly screen, note the information and review the Client Support section in this chapter before continuing.

8. On the Domain Controller Type screen, select Additional Domain Controller for an Existing Domain as shown in Figure 15.2.

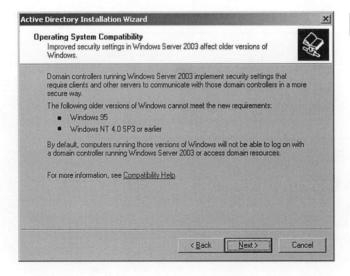

**FIGURE 15.2**
DCPROMO domain controller type.

9. On the Network Credentials screen, enter the administrator account name and password for the domain.

10. Verify the domain name the server is joining on the Additional Domain Controller screen and click Next to continue.

11. Verify the database and logs folder path and click Next.

12. Verify the serve Sysvol location and click Next to continue.

13. From the Directory Services Restore Mode dialog box, enter the password for the directory service administrator. This password is separate and not associated with the domain administrator account. When complete, select Next.

14. Review the Summary page to ensure the upgrade information is correct and select Next to begin installing Active Directory on the new domain controller.

After the server has been upgraded to a domain controller in the Windows 2000 domain, seize the domain FSMO roles to the new Windows 2003 domain controller to upgrade the domain. To use the NTDSUTIL, see the "Recovering from a Failed Upgrade" section in this chapter to complete the upgrade.

> **Seize the FSMO Roles Once in the Forest Root Domain**
>
> Seize the FSMO roles once in the forest root domain. For environments with child and sub domains, create a new domain controller and seize roles for each domain to replace the primary domain controller in multidomain environments.

After the new domain controller and any additional domain controller installations have been completed, you must migrate vital network services such as DNS and DHCP services to the new domain controllers.

To understand more about migrating network service to new Windows 2003 domain controllers, refer to the Migrating Network Services section of this chapter.

## Tips to Upgrading a Windows 2000 Domain

When upgrading a Windows 2000 domain, consideration should be given to the order in which each domain and domain controller will be upgraded. When Windows 2000 domains are upgraded to Windows 2003, the Windows Server 2003 operating systems add certain security principles and resources to the existing Windows 2000 domain. The following guide describes when to upgrade single and multidomain environments and how to replicate the proper Windows 2003 security information correctly when performing a domain upgrade.

> **Upgrading and Windows Client Support**
>
> When upgrading a Windows 2000 domain, all client support for Window NT 4.0 and Windows 95 clients without the Active Directory client software are lost. This is because the SMB server signing becomes enabled when a Windows 2000 domain is upgraded to Windows 2003. To enable support for legacy clients, review the "Client Support with Windows Server 2003" section in this chapter.

When upgrading to Windows Server 2003, the order in which servers are updated are important and can greatly affect the outcome of the domain upgrade. The following information will help in planning and understanding the best practices when upgrading.

> ### Remove the Windows 2000 Administration Tools Prior to Upgrading
>
> Before performing an upgrade of a Windows 2000 domain controller, Microsoft recommends removing the Windows 2000 administration tools prior to upgrading. The Windows 2003 administrative tools that leverage the Windows 2003 domain security principles can then be installed after the upgrade of the domain controller is complete.
>
> After any upgrade is complete successfully, review the server logs for errors related to server functionality.
>
> Complete the upgrade by installing any Microsoft updates for Windows 2003.

- *First Domain Controller Upgraded*—Begin your domain upgrade by performing an in-place upgrade of the domain controller possessing the domain naming master role in the forest root of the domain. This will create the default DNS program partition in the new Windows 2003 domain.

- *Second Domain Controller Upgraded*—Upgrade the primary domain controller in the root forest domain. This upgrade will add the security principles and the ACLs that Windows 2003 creates when the domain is migrated.

- *Upgrade Each Child Domain PDC*—In multidomain environments, upgrade the Primary domain controller in each child domain. Upgrading these servers will begin replication of domain-specific security principles.

# Migrating Network Services

During a migration from the source to target Windows 2003 domain, one decision you must make is when it is best to migrate domain-based service and when is it best to create new ones. Often failure to move these services correctly can cause connectivity issues between client systems and the domain resulting in failed logons. The following sections provide you with the information available to cleanly and easily move these services to avoid disruption in client server communications when migrating.

## Migrating Network Services

One benefit of the integration between Windows 2000 and Windows 2003 is the ability to migrate services between operating systems.

When upgrading domains, you can migrate network services to new Windows 2003 domain controllers. This section focuses on the three components of Windows 2000:

- Dynamic Host configuration Protocol (DHCP)
- Domain Name System (DNS)
- Group Policy Objects

Each of the following sections provide insight and best practices on when to migrate these services and the basic steps for moving the service and components to Windows 2003.

## Migrating Domain Name Systems Services

When addressing DNS there are two key areas to consider. First, what is the best method to cutover services from Windows 2000 to Windows 2003. You can decide which method to use depending on whether the cutover is used for a migration to a new Windows 2003 domain or the existing Windows 2000 domain is being upgraded.

When upgrading, you can use the built-in functionality of Active Directory Intergraded DNS Zones to establish DNS services on new Windows 2003 servers. When a domain controller is promoted to a domain controller, DNS can be installed as an Active Directory Integrated zone. This will dynamically replicate all zone information to the DNS server.

After replication of the zone is complete, you can then modify the DHCP Scope to implement the new DNS server into the domain.

When migrating to a new domain, DNS in the source domain can be configured to forward DNS lookup to the new DNS server in the target domain. Reverse lookup zones can be created for each to enable efficient DNS reverse lookups as well.

To configure DNS forwarding, open the DNS manager in the Windows 2000 domain and perform the following steps:

1. Select the forward lookup zone for the domain being migrated.

2. Sect the server where the forward lookup zone will be added. Right-click the selection and choose Properties.

3. Add the TCP/IP addresses of the Windows 2003 DNS server in the Forwarder Properties dialog box and click OK when complete.

To configure the reverse lookup, add the domain to the reverse lookup zone on both the source domain and target domain DNS Servers. This will enable reverse lookup for both domains.

## Migrating DHCP to Windows 2003

When existing Windows 2000 DHCP services are in place, you can migrate DHCP server configurations and databases from Windows 2000 to a new Windows 2003 domain controller. By migrating, you are free from the time required to configure services and ensure the scope is correct and identical before being moved. Also, client lease information is preserved, enabling a transparent migration of DHCP in the client environment.

To migrate the existing Windows 2000 DHCP services, use the DHCPExim.exe and Netsh.exe utilities located on the Windows Resource Kit. Begin by downloading the resources kit from Microsoft at `http://www.microsoft.com/downloads`.

Install the Windows 2003 Resource Kit and migrate the DHCP services by performing the following steps:

1.  Open a command prompt by choosing Start, Run and typing **command** in the dialog box. Select OK to open the command dialog.

2.  Export the DHCP server information by running the command DHCPExim.exe.

3.  From the DHCPEXIM Export to File dialog box enter the name and location where the information will be exported. Confirm the location shown in the dialog box and select OK to continue.

> **Wait to Be Prompted**
>
> When exporting, step 5 might take several minutes to complete. During this time no dialog box will be displayed indicating the progress of the export. Wait to be prompted before continuing.

4.  From the Export dialog, select the DHCP scope to be exported. This selection will migrate all DHCP settings for the scopes.

5.  Select the Disable the Elected Scopes on the Local Machine Before Export To option. This will disable the scopes being migrated to avoid any conflicts when the scope is imported to Windows 2003.

6.  At the This Operation Has Completed Successfully dialog box, select OK to complete the export operation.

7.  Move the exported file to the new Windows 2003 server where the DHCP service will be migrated.

8.  Begin the migration to the new Windows 2003 server by installing the DHCP service using the Add/Remove Programs tool in the server Control Panel.

9.  Open a command prompt on the Windows 2003 server by choosing Start, Run and typing **command** in the dialog box. Select OK to open the command dialog.

10. From the command prompt, enter the import command using the Netsh command: Netsh DHCP Server Import (Path to Export File) all.

The command will import the DHCP information and scope configuration to the new Windows 2003 server.

## Migrating GPOs

Unlike migrating from Windows NT, one major area often not considered to be migrated is Windows 2000 Group Policies or GPOs. Using the Windows 2003 Group Policy Management Console, you can use the copy function to move previously configured GPOs from Windows 2000 domains to Windows 2003 domains.

Using the copy functionality of the GPMC, GPOs can easily be copied or dragged to the desired new domain. To migrate GPOs using the Group Policy Management Console, download and install the GPMC.msi installation package from Microsoft at http://www.microsoft.com/downloads.

Once installed, open the Group Policy Manager and add the forest and domain to the GPMC to copy GPOs from the source domain to the new Windows 2003 destination domain as shown in Figure 15.3.

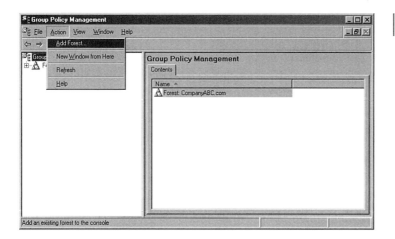

**FIGURE 15.3**
Adding a forest to the Group Policy Manager Console.

Begin migrating Windows 2000 GPOs by adding a forest trust between the source and target locations. If no forest trust will be used, you can leverage the Stored User Name and Password utility for authentication to the source domain along the GPMCs.

Open the GPMC on the Windows 2003 domain controller and add the forest and domain for the Windows 2000 source domain where the existing GPO will be copied from. Select the GPO object and drag it to the target Windows 2003 domain.

# Migrating Active Directory Objects

The Active Directory Migration Tool version 2 (ADMT v2) is an effective way of migrating users, groups, and computers from a Windows 2000 domain to a Windows 2003 domain. It is robust enough to migrate Active Directory objects, permissions, and settings, and fully supports a rollback procedure in the event of migration problems. ADMT v2 is composed of several components as detailed here:

- ADMT Migration Wizards—ADMT includes a series of wizards, each specifically designed to migrate specific components. Different wizards exist for migrating Users, Groups, Computers, Service Accounts, and Trusts.

- Low Client Impact—ADMT automatically installs a service on source clients, which negates the need to manually install client software for the migration. In addition, after the migration is complete, these services are automatically uninstalled.

- SID History and Security Migrated—Users will continue to maintain network access to file shares, applications, and other secured network services through migration of the SID History attributes to the new domain. This preserves the extensive security structure of the source domain.

- Test Migrations and Rollback Functionality—An extremely useful feature in ADMT v2 is the ability to run a mock migration scenario with each migration wizard. This will help to identify any issues that might exist prior to the actual migration work. In addition to this functionality, the most recently performed user, computer, or group migration can be undone, providing for rollback in the event of migration problems.

To begin, download the Active Directory Migration Tool from Microsoft and install the tool on a Windows 2003 domain controller in the target domain.

## Migrating Security and Distribution Groups

When migrating, it is often best to migrate domain groups before user account Objects. The reason for this suggestion is the fact that if users are migrated first, their group membership will not transfer over unless selected. However, if the groups are migrated prior to user objects and exist before domain users are migrated, they will automatically find their place in the group structure when migrated. To migrate groups using ADMT v2, use the Group Account Migration Wizard, as detailed in the following steps:

> **Testing the Migration**
>
> It is always a good practice to test any migration and review the results before actually migrating domain security principles. Testing the migration can be completed by selecting the Test the Migration Setting and Migrate Later from the Test or Make Changes page of the Group Migration Wizard.
>
> Open the Active Directory Migration Tool and launch the Group Migration Wizard from the Action menu to begin testing a group migration.

1. After you have completed testing your group migration, run the Group Migration Wizard. From the Action menu launch the Group Account Migration Wizard to begin the actual migration of Groups. At the Welcome screen, click Next to continue. Select the Migrate Now option from the Test or Make Changes Page and then click Next.

2. On the Domain Selection page, use the drop-down box to select the source domain and target domain for this migration. Select, Next to continue.

3. On the Group Selection page, enter the name or names of the groups in the source domain you want to migrate. Select the Add button to enter the group name and select Check Name to validate the group name. Click OK to add the group to the Group Selection page and select Next to continue migrating.

4. On the Organizational Unit selection page, select the target Organizational Unit for where the group will be migrated. Use the Browse button to view the Active Directory Tree and select the target domain and Organizational Unit that will host the migrated group. Click OK to finish the selection and then click Next to continue.

5. When migrating Windows Groups, options such as user rights and group membership can also be migrated. Review the group migration options on the Group options page and choose the selections that best fit your migration needs.

6. When migrating, a target domain that contains group names could conflict with your groups' migration.

7. Review the migration selection and ensure that the proper options have been checked. Select the Next option to continue migrating groups.

8. To complete the migration, the ADMT will need to authenticate to the source domain. Enter the username and password of an account with administrative rights on the source domain and select Next.

9. Use the Naming Conflicts page to configure actions ADMT should take to resolve conflicts with group names and group memberships.

10. Use the scroll bar to review the Migration Wizard task description. Ensure that all options you have selected are identified in the summary before clicking Finish to continue. The Migration Progress screen enables you to view the results of your group migration as well as selecting the View Log button to review the migration log details for any errors. Exit the migration log and click Close to complete the Group Account Migration Wizard.

## Migrating Users Accounts

The Active Directory Migration Tool version 2 (ADMT) also  enables  you to migrate user accounts with SID History, GUIDs, and passwords to the new Windows 2003 domain. This functionality fully enables Active Directory accounts the ability to access resources in the source domain during coexistence scenarios.

To migrate users, follow these steps:

1. Open the ADMT MMC Console and launch the User Migration Wizard from the Action menu to begin the migration of User Objects. At the Welcome screen, click Next to continue. Select the Migrate Now option from the Test or Make Changes page and then click Next.

2. The next screen offers the option to test the migration before actually migrating the account. This is recommended because you can evaluate the overall results before performing the migration process. Select Migrate Now and then click Next to continue.

3. Select the Source and Target domains and click Next to continue.

4. The following screen allows user accounts to be chosen for migration. Click the Add button and select the user accounts that will be migrated. After all user accounts have been selected, click Next to continue.

5. The next screen allows for a Target Organization Unit to be chosen for all created users. Choose the Organization Unit by clicking the Browse button. After the Organization Unit has been selected, click Next to continue.

6. The new password migration functionality of ADMT v2.0 is enabled through the following screens. Migrating passwords require additional configuration. Review the password migration requirements and click Next to continue.

7. On the Details screen select the options required for this user migration. For more information, click Help for an overview of each option.

8. Enter the administrator username, password, and source domain. Click Next to continue.

9.  There are several migration options presented as part of the next screen. As before, clicking Help will elaborate on some of these features; enter the options selected and click Next to continue.

10. At the next screen, any properties of the user object that should not be migrated should be specified here. Select the desired setting and click Next to continue.

11. Object Naming conflicts are a procedure for dealing with duplicate accounts when migrating. Select the appropriate options for duplicate accounts and click Next to continue.

12. Review the verification screen to determine if the settings chosen are correct before migrating. Verify each setting and select Next to begin migrating the account object.

13. The Migration Progress status box will display the migration process as it occurs, indicating the number of successful and unsuccessful accounts created. After the process is complete, review the log by clicking View Log and verify the results of the migration.

# FailOver Best Practices

When upgrading and migrating to Windows 2003, unforeseen failures can occur requiring administrators to recover the Windows 2000 domain. The following sections touch on several areas to assist in addressing failed upgrades and issues when migrating. Best practices describe how to proactively recover from any problems should they arise and how to roll back after one upgrade to a domain controller fails.

## Backing Up Active Directory

Whenever working with a domain controller and Active Directory, it is a good practice to back up the system state of the domain controller whether you are migrating, upgrading, or performing maintenance in preparation for a server upgrade.

To back up Windows Active Directory, back up the system state of the domain controller. In this scenario, you will learn how to back up the system state data using the Windows Backup Wizard from a command prompt on the Windows 2000 domain controller.

To begin the backup process, log on to the server with the domain administrator account.

Open the command prompt by selecting Start, Run and typing **command**. Click the OK button to open the command prompt and follow these steps:

1. From the command prompt, type **ntbackup** and press Enter. Select the Advance Mode option and select Backup Wizard (Advanced) to continue.

2. On the Backup Wizard screen select Next to continue.

3. On the selection screen, select Only Backup System State Data.

4. On the Where to Store Backup selection, choose File and select a backup location located on a different server than the domain controller being backed up.

5.  In the backup Media or File Name selection, enter the path and filename to be backed up to. Select Next to continue.

6.  This will launch the Completing the Backup Wizard screen; verify that the Prompt to Replace data is listed and click Next.

7.  Click Next on the remaining screen and click the Finish option to begin backing up system state data.

## Recovering from a Failed Upgrade

When upgrading domain controllers, especially a domain controller that holds the domain FSMO roles, it is important that you are prepared to recover these roles should the upgrade fail. Should the upgrade of the FSMO Role holder fail, you can seize these roles to another domain controller on the domain.

To recover from this scenario and still end up with the same results, you with a little time can seize the FSMO roles to an addition Windows 2000 domain controller. Install the failed server with the fresh installation of Windows 2003 and transfer the roles to the new Windows 2003 server. This process will work fine to recover the failed domain controller upgrade.

To seize and transfer FSMO roles between domain controllers, use the NTDSUtil Utility built into the Windows 2000 and Windows 2003 operating systems.

In the scenario, the FSMO Roles will be seized to an additional Windows 2000 domain controller restoring domain functionality. To finish seizing the roles, complete the following:

1.  Begin by opening a command prompt on the Domain Windows domain controller where the roles will be placed.

2.  From the command prompt, type **NTDSUTIL** and press Enter. This enables you to enter the NTDS utility mode on the domain controller.

3.  At the NTDSUTIL prompt type `roles` and press Enter to continue.

4.  Next type **Connections** and press Enter; this connects the NTDSUTIL to the specific domain controller.

5.  Next type **Connect to Server DC01@*CompanyABC*.com** (where DC01 represents the fully Qualified Domain Name of the domain controller that will house the roles). This connects to the specified server and prepares the authentication for the roles to be seized.

6.  Enter the command **quit** and press Enter. This command returns you to the FSMO Role maintenance screen.

7.  To begin seizing the roles to the new FSMO Role master, type the command **Seize Domain Naming Master** and press return. When prompted select OK to begin seizing the role.

8.  Repeat step 7 for the remaining four domain roles:

    ■  Seize Infrastructure Master

    ■  Seize PDC

> **When Seizing Roles in Child Domain...**
> When seizing roles in child domain, only seize the PDC, RID Master, and Schema Master roles.

- Seize RID Master
- Seize Schema Master

Once completed, verify each role's placement and review the server logs to determine if any issues have occurred as a result of seizing the roles.

## Planning and Avoiding Network Downtime

One of the biggest challenges you face when upgrading is avoiding network downtime if problems arise. This section provides some insight to common practices and simple tricks to ensure that domain authentication and name resolution are available quickly should a failure occur.

One of the very first areas to consider is redundancy of vital network services. These services are configured with Active Directory and can be redundant to avoid client/server communication issues should an upgrade of a domain controller fail.

> **To Export the DHCP Service Database and Configuration Information...**
> To export the DHCP service database and configuration information, see the "Migrating DHCP to Windows 2003" section in this chapter.

One of these services is the DNS service, which provides domain name resolution for the Active Directory domain begin upgraded. Before upgrading the domain controller with the primary Active Directory DNS services, you should install an additional Active Directory DNS server and allow replication to complete before upgrading.

One other major service is the DHCP service; you can easily export all DHCP server information to a stored network location to be recovered easily.

# Supporting Clients with Windows Server 2003

One of the first things you see when promoting a server to Windows 2003 is the warning regarding client support for Windows 95 and Windows 98 as shown in the Figure 15.4. This message dialog informs you at the time of upgrade that these client operating systems will no longer be available to authenticate to the domain after the upgrade is complete.

This screen informs you that these client operating systems will no longer be able to authenticate; this is because the NTLM version is upgraded during the upgrade of the Windows 2000 domain to Windows 2003.

## Understanding Windows 2003 Client Capability

To enable these client systems to authenticate and access domain resources, additional client software must be installed or domain controller configurations completed to support authentication.

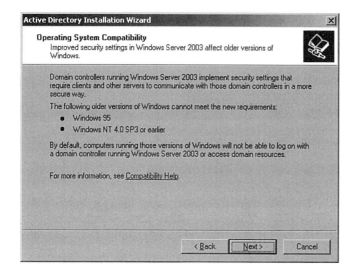

**FIGURE 15.4**
Operating system compatibility
notice.

The most common method of enabling support for client systems running non–support versions of Windows is to install the Microsoft Active Directory Client Software.

Available for free download from Microsoft, the Active Directory Client installs the Active Directory extensions enabling support for Windows 95, Windows 98, and Windows NT Service Pack 6a systems in a Windows 2003 Active Directory environment.

By installing the Active Directory Client extensions, client support is enabled in the following areas:

- *NTLM version 2 Authentication*—Support for improved authentication using NTLM version 2.

- *Site Awareness Support*—This functionary allows client systems to authenticate to the domain logging onto the most available and physically closest Windows 2003 domain controller to the client system. Also, client systems can now change passwords on any Active Directory domain controller in the domain.

- *Active Directory Service Interfaces (ADSI)*—ADSI support provides client scripting capability often used to manage and retrieve information in Active Directory.

- *Distributed File Systems Support DFS fault tolerance*—This function enables support for access Distributed File System (DFS) shares configured on the Windows 2003 Active Directory domain.

- *Active Directory Windows Address Book (WAB) property pages*—Enabling WAB support allows clients authenticated to the domain to search Active Directory for user object, retrieving information such as addresses and phone numbers.

## Enabling Legacy Client Support

There are two methods you can use to enable legacy client support; the first is to install the Active Directory client software on each Windows NT and Windows 9X client.

The other method is to relax the security setting on the local default domain security policy.

When software updates cannot be installed on legacy clients before an upgrade to Windows 2003, you can provide support for these clients by disabling the SMB service in the local domain controller Group Policy.

To disable SMB signing and enable support for legacy clients, open the local domain controller policy, you will see a screen similar to the one shown in Figure 15.5.

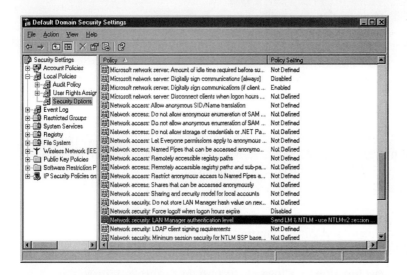

**FIGURE 15.5**
Default domain controller security settings screen.

To provide support for legacy clients, complete the following steps:

### When Domain Controllers Are Not in the Default Domain Controllers

If the domain controllers being modified are not located in the default domain controllers organizational unit container, the policy must link the organizational unit with the domain controller, which will authenticate where the legacy client resides.

1. Expand the Local Policies and select Security Options in the left pane of the Policy Management Console.

2. Modify the following settings:

   - Microsoft Network Server: Digitally Sign Communication (always)—Modify the setting to Disable

   - Microsoft Network Server: Digitally Sign Communication (if Client Agrees)—Modify the setting to Enable

■ Network Security: LAN Manager Authentication Level—Modify the setting to Send NM & NTLM—Use NTLM version session security if negotiated

# Decommissioning Windows 2000

One of the very last steps to be completed is the decommissioning of servers. After functionality and clients have been migrated to Windows 2003, you are still faced with the tasks of removing domains and domain servers no longer in use.

In some cases the removal of source domain controllers and servers leave undesired entries in Active Directory and server lists. The following sections provide insight and best practices for decommissioning source domains and domain servers as well as methods to perform clean-up tasks when the removed servers are still present in Active Directory.

## Decommissioning Windows 2000 Domains and Domain Controllers

When preparing domain controllers to be decommissioned, you should first focus on the connectivity that was required when the domain was functional and communicating with the Windows 2003 domain.

Review areas such as existing domain trusts and migration tools that were installed on the source domain that may still be needed once the domain is decommissioned. Be sure to break and remove any unneeded trusts before decommissioning the last domain controllers in the source domain.

As a migration comes to a close, additional domain controllers that are no longer needed can be demoted using the DCPROMO command. This will uninstall Active Directory from the domain controller and enable you to then remove the server from the source domain.

After the remaining areas such as trust have been broken, the remaining Windows 2000 domain controller can simply be turned off. This will not affect the new Windows 2003 domain and information regarding the source domain should be removed dynamically.

## Decommissioning Domain Member Servers

When domain servers are not directly upgraded to Windows Server 2003, roles must be migrated to the target domain, leaving servers in the source domain ready to effectively be removed. By understanding the best practices for migrating server roles, you can also systematically begin decommissioning server resources simultaneously, which would normally be removed at the end of the migration.

## Prioritizing Server Roles During a Migration

During a migration process, server roles need to be prioritized so that the migration process is done in a manner that supports dependencies between servers as they exist. The three server roles are as follows:

■ *File and Print Servers*—When hardware requirements are met, it is sometimes more effective to upgrade file servers using an in-place migration scenario to Windows Server 2003. When this is not possible, migrating these files and print services can be done with relative ease allowing these larger capacity servers to be reallocated into the new Active Directory domain.

### When the Source Domain Continues to Appear in the Server Browse List ...

When the source domain continues to appear in the server browse list after it has been decommissioned and turned off, use the Regedt32 to remove the information.

Run the Regedt32 from the Run command prompt and navigate the Registry to find the following:

HKEY_LOCAL_MACHINE\SYSTEM\ CurrentControlSet\Services\ LanmanWorkstation\ Parameters

Select the Other Domains value and the REG_MULTI_SZ data type, and expand the value.

If the domain name of the unneeded domain is present, remove the domain name and restart the server.

■ *Application and Web Services*—With more organizations relying on Web services and server-based applications to support daily business needs, extensive testing, and validations are required to ensure application compatibility and a successful migration. By migrating these services later rather than sooner, you can leverage time to complete detailed testing and validation of application upgrades and functionality before migrating.

■ *Migration Support Servers*—Before the migration becomes strictly focused on decommission of the remaining Windows servers, review the server roles that reside in the target domain that were used to support the migration. Decommission these roles such as the Active Directory Migration Tool and server services used for the migration.

## Removing Servers with ADSI Editor

As is often the case in Active Directory, a domain controller might have been removed from the forest without first being demoted. This might happen because of server failure or problems in the administrative process, but those servers will need to be removed from the directory before completing an upgrade to Windows 2003. Simply deleting the object out of Active Directory Sites and Services will not work. Instead, a low-level directory tool, ADSI-Edit, will need to be used to remove these servers.

The following process outlines how to install and use ADSI-Edit to remove these domain controllers:

1. Install ADSI-Edit from the Windows 2003 Support Tools.

2. Navigate to Configuration|CN=Configuration|CN=Sites|CN=SITENAME|CN = Servers|CN=SERVERNAME (Where SITENAME and SERVERNAME correspond to the location of the domain controller being removed).

3. Right-click on the CN=NTDS Settings and click Delete.

4. At the prompt, click Yes to delete the object.

5. Close ADSI Edit. This will allow the server to be deleted from the container using Active Directory Users and Computers.

# Raising Windows 2003 Functional Levels

When a migration or clean installation is completed, Windows Server 2003 does not immediately begin functioning at a native mode level. This is the case even when all domain controllers have been migrated to Windows 2003.

This section will focus on domain functionality with Windows 2003 and how and when it is best to raise functional levels to raise domain functional levels.

> **The Functionality of Mixed Mode Environments**
>
> When considering raising functional level in Windows 2003, you should understand the functionality of Mixed mode environments cannot be returned after the mode has been changed to native.

## Domain Functional Levels

Windows 2003 supports four functional levels. These levels allow Active Directory to include down level domain controllers during an upgrade process. Review the following information to understand the different functional levels before determining which is best for your organization:

- *Windows 2000 Mixed Mode Domain*—When Windows Server 2003 is installed into a Windows 2000 Active Directory forest that is running in Mixed mode, it essentially means that Windows 2003 domain controllers will be able to communicate with Windows NT and Windows 2000 domain controllers throughout the forest. This is the most limiting of the functional levels, however, because functionality such as Universal Groups, group nesting, and enhanced security is absent from the domain. This is typically a temporary level to run in, as it is seen more as a path towards eventual upgrade.

- *Windows 2000 Native Mode*—Installed into a Windows 2000 Active Directory that is running in Windows 2000 Native mode, Windows 2003 servers will run at a Windows 2000 functional level. Only Windows 2000 and Windows 2003 server domain controllers will be able to exist in this environment.

- *Interim Level*—Interim mode gives the Windows 2003 Active Directory the capability to interoperate with domains composed of Windows NT 4.0 domain controllers only. Although this is a confusing concept at first mention, the Windows 2003 Server Interim level does serve a purpose. In environments that seek to upgrade directly from NT 4.0 to Windows 2003 Active Directory, Interim mode allows 2003 servers to manage large groups more efficiently than if an existing Windows 2000 Active Directory exists. After all Windows NT domain controllers have been removed or upgraded, the functional levels can be raised.

- *Windows Server 2003 Functional Level*—The most functional of all of the various levels, Windows Server 2003 Functional Level allows for full functionality of the Windows 2003 Domains server family products.

## Raising Functional Levels

After each domain functional level has been raised, as well as the forest functional level, the Active Directory environment will be completely upgraded, and fully compliant with all of the Active Directory enhancements in Windows 2003. Functionality on this level opens up the environment to features such as schema deactivation, domain rename, domain controller rename, and cross-forest trusts.

After all domain controllers have been upgraded or replaced with Windows Server 2003, the domain and then the forest functional levels can be raised. To raise the domain functional level with Windows Server 2003, complete the following steps.

1. Ensure that all domain controllers in the forest are upgraded to Windows Server 2003.

2. Open Active Directory Domains and Trusts from the Administrative Tools.

3. In the left pane, right-click on Active Directory Domains and Trusts and the click Raise Domain Functional Level.

4. In the box labeled Select an Available Domain Functional Level, select Windows Server 2003, and then select Raise.

5. Click on OK, and then click OK again to complete the task.

6. Repeat the steps for all domains in the forest.

7. Perform the same steps on the forest root, except this time click Raise Forest Functional Level.

# Summary

There are two paths for migrating from Windows 2000 to Windows 2003. One is the easy path; the other is the hard path. In the end, the results are the same, so the easy path is recommended. By simply preparing for the migration from Windows 2000 to Windows 2003 and creating a fallback plan as a safety net, the administrators of the network can perform an in-place upgrade to Windows 2003 Active Directory relatively quickly.

Part of the insider solutions in the migration process involves pretesting and validating to minimize the risk of failure during the migration process. For organizations that want to prototype, test, and validate the migration process, there are several steps available. This includes doing hardware and software compatibility testing, preinstallation migration testing, and network validation testing prior to the migration process.

If successful, the actual migration process in a production environment only takes a couple hours one evening or weekend. After the migration process has been completed, the clean-up of Windows 2000 or Windows NT 4.0 objects will finalize the migration steps, and get the organization into a native Windows 2003 Active Directory configuration.

# 16

## Integration with Unix/LDAP-Based Systems

**B**eing the administrator of heterogeneous environments often requires compromise. You often have to use lowest-common-denominator protocols and tools. With a little research and an open mind, this doesn't always have to be the case.

There are many standards and tools that allow Microsoft Windows–based servers and Unix to interact with their various directory services. With the correct configuration, and in some cases scripting, systems on different platforms can work well together.

# Designing and Planning Platform Integration

Many of today's applications require a platform decision. With more and more lines of business applications written for the Windows platform, Unix platforms need to be able to access those applications. Creating a directory structure, sign-in process, and file sharing services are critical.

Creating a single-sign-on environment is the panacea that most if not all administrators of Unix/Windows environments strive for. With vendors having different versions of LDAP and various levels of RFC compliance, this can be pretty difficult. Synchronizing different versions of LDAP and Active Directory requires some in-depth analysis and planning.

A truly integrated environment is possible with today's tools. By putting aside any preconceptions about the other platform, whether Unix or Windows, administrators and network architects can make the two platforms work together in harmony.

## Taking Inventory

One key factor in making the Windows and Unix environments work together is finding out which versions of LDAP, Kerberos, NIS and other components they have in common. Different platform vendors have chosen to adopt at different levels and versions of these Internet standards.

Knowing the location of each of the services and how they interact is crucial to determining the placement of common servers and services.

Client operating systems and versions also play an important role in determining the required services.

## Creating an Integration/Migration Plan

Microsoft uses a pretty well thought out and tested methodology for projects called Microsoft Solutions Framework (MSF). A complex undertaking like integrating disparate platforms requires a well thought out road map. The following list describes the high-level steps in an undertaking such as integrating Windows with other LDAP based systems:

- *Evaluate* the current state of the company's directory structures.
- *Plan* what the new directory structure will provide.
- *Build* the lab and test account creation and user authentication.
- *Deploy* the directory solution into the production environment.
- *Operate* and manage the new directory solution. This step also provides feedback in evaluating future solutions.

Defining the company's business requirements should be part of an initial study. Administrative resources should always be considered. Your company might have to invest in either twice the number of administrators or administrators with twice the knowledge.

# Creating an Integrated Infrastructure

Before any servers or the services that they host can be integrated they have to be able to locate each other and to communicate. Creating a network infrastructure that all the involved platforms can work together on needs to be one of the first items on your agenda.

When it comes right down to it, most operating systems have more similarities than differences. They all need to store data, authenticate users, and store and locate resources both locally and on the network. Two of the services in common are Domain Name Services and Directories. By determining the versions that will work together you can create an integrated infrastructure.

## Finding the Common Ground

One of the key strengths of Active Directory on Windows Server 2003 is that it's based on several important industry standards. This conformity allows greater interoperability within a heterogeneous environment. The interaction between Active Directory and other vendor's products isn't always seamless, but it does provide the potential for information exchange in a multi-operating system environment. These common standards are ratified and published by the Internet Engineering Task Force (IETF) in the form of Request for Comments (RFC). Some of the standards and conventions that Active Directory is based on are listed in Table 16.1.

**TABLE 16.1**

**Partial List of Standards Used by Windows Server 2003 and Active Directory**

| Standard | Reference | Description |
| --- | --- | --- |
| DNS Service (SVR) Resource Records and Dynamic Updates (DDNS) | RFCs 2052, 2163 | Dynamic host name management and Service Resource Records |
| Dynamic Host Configuration Protocol (DHCP) | RFC 2131 | Network IP address management |
| Kerberos v5 | RFC 1510 | Certificate-based authentication |
| Lightweight Directory Access Protocol (LDAP)v3 | RFC 1777, RFC 2251 | Lightweight Directory Access Protocol and LDAP v3 |
| LDAP 'C' | RVC 1823 | Directory application programming interface (API) |
| LDAP Schema | RFCs 2247, 2252, 2256 | Directory schema |
| Simple Network Time Protocol (SNTP) | RFC 1769 | Distributed time service for networks |
| Simple Mail Transfer Protocol (SMTP) | RFC 821 | Message transfer |
| Transfer Control Protocol/Internet Protocol | RFCs 791, 793 | Network protocols |
| X.509 v3 Certificates | ISO X.509 | Authentication of Identities |

RFCs are guidelines for vendors to follow. They make your life easier by being able to reference which functionalities in various vendors' products might work together. It's important for the IT community to have some common ground on which to build their systems.

## Integrating Domain Name Services (DNS)

Windows Server 2003 and Active Directory are very dependent on the DNS service for all their operations. There are three primary roles that DNS performs with Active Directory. Those roles are outlined in the following list:

- *Name Resolution.* DNS maps the host names to IP addresses. This eliminates the need for WINS (Windows Internet Name Space), when Windows 2000 or newer clients are used.

- *Namespace Definition.* The DNS namespace maps to the Active Directory namespace. This simplifies the Windows Server namespace.

- *SRV (Service) Resource Records.* Used to locate physical components of the Active Directory. The DNS service provides a list of all the IP addresses to all the domain controllers.

A few of the LDAP-specific SRV resource records that are created in a Windows Server 2003 domain are as follows:

- **_ldap._tcp.<DNSDomainName>**　This record enables the client to locate the domain controller.

- **_ldap._tcp.<SiteName._sites.<DNSDomainName>**　This record enables the client to find the domain controller in a specific site.

- **_ldap._tcp.pdc._ms-dcs.<DNSDomainName>**　This record enables the client to find the primary domain controller (PDC) flexible single master object (FSMO) role of a mixed-mode domain.

- **_ldap._tcp.gc._msdcs.<DNSTreeName>**　This record enables the client to find a Global Catalog (GC) server.

- **_ldap._tcp.<SiteName>._sites.gc._msdcs.<DNSTreeName>**　This record enables the client to find the GC server in a specific site.

- **_ldap._tcp.<DomainGUID>.domains._mscds.<DNSTreeName>**　This record enables the client to find a domain controller based on its globally unique Identifier (GUID).

---

### GUID

A GUID is a 128-bit (8 byte) number that is generated automatically for referencing Active Directory objects.

---

### netlogon.dns

The netlogon.dns file contains all of the DNS SRV records that Active Directory uses to identify service resources in the domain. The entries in this file can be added manually to DNS servers that do not support Dynamic updates.

---

This is a partial list of the entries created when Active Directory is installed. A text file containing all the DNS resource records is called netlogon.dns and can be found in the %systemroot%\system32\config folder.

Active Directory can resolve names via DNS in a number of models. Four such scenarios are listed here:

- Active Directory Dynamic DNS performs all name resolution within the domain.

- A third-party (BIND) Dynamic DNS that supports SRV resource records performs all name resolution within the domain.

- Making the Active Directory DNS the master and allowing zone transfers between the BIND DNS Server and the Active Directory DNS.

> **BIND**
>
> BIND (Berkeley Internet Name Domain) DNS version 8.1.2 and later supports dynamic updates. Support for SRV resource records is also required, which was introduced in earlier versions of BIND DNS.

- Making the BIND DNS the master and allowing zone transfers between the Active Directory DNS and the BIND DNS.

## Heterogeneous Directory Services

Directory services store much of the information about the users and resources contained on a computer network. These services are analogous to phone books for users and computers to locate resources. Authentication credentials can also be stored in the directory. A few of the desired characteristics of a directory service are security, fast read access, and fault-tolerance.

Microsoft's Active Directory is based on LDAPv3. LDAP is a directory access protocol based on X.500 directory service. It's derived from the X.500 directory service Directory Access Protocol (DAP). DAP is a heavyweight protocol that operates over an Open Systems Interconnection (OSI) protocol and is used to operate very powerful computer systems. Unlike DAP, LDAP is designed to operate over TCP/IP and maintains most features of DAP without using its expensive resources.

Some Unix systems still use the Sun Network Information System (NIS). NIS automated the task of manually administrating users and hostname resolution. This was performed by creating a NIS master and having Unix clients receive a replica of the files created and modified by you. This system is easier to manage than individual user accounts in the /etc/password files and host names in the /etc/hosts files. This method of administrating user and host name management is being replaced by services such as LDAP.

# Integrating Directories Across Environments

There are several ways to integrate directories across multiple environments. Two of the most popular architectures are creating a master/slave model or a metadirectory model. When designing a master/slave model the architect must decide which directory service will be used to manage directory objects actively and which one will only receive published updates. In the metadirectory model a separate directory management product is introduced to act as the master directory. The existing directories receive published updates from the metadirectory.

## Integrating LDAP Directories with Active Directory

Active Directory's LDAP is based on v3 of the LDAP standard. Not all LDAP implementations are based on LDAP v3. This makes it somewhat challenging to integrate them.

The LDAP schema objects that are going to be synchronized must match exactly. To do this you must do some planning and decide which of the versions of LDAP schemas will be the standard for the integration. By extending the LDAP schema you enable synchronization of entries within the schema and ensure that they will match correctly.

Different tools are available for accessing (reading) and manipulating or editing the LDAP schema of Active Directory. Tools can be purchased from third parties, such as Softerra's LDAP Administrator, to manage multiple LDAP schemas on different platforms with one product. The native Windows Server 2003 tool to edit the Active Directory is an MMC snap-in named ADSI Edit.

### Configuring ADSI Edit Snap-in

To install the ADSI Edit snap-in into a new MMC console you need to perform the following steps:

1. Select Start, Run and type **mmc**. Then click OK.

2. In the Console window select File, Add/Remove Snap-in.

3. Select the Add button in the Add/Remove Snap-in dialog box.

4. In the Available Standalone Snap-ins pane choose Active Directory Schema. Choose Add and then Close.

5. The ADSI Edit snap-in should now appear in the Add/Remove Snap-in window; choose OK.

6. The MMC Console can now be saved by selecting File, Save As.

### Creating a Referral in Active Directory

The ADSI Edit MMC snap-in can be used to perform referrals to external naming contexts. This allows a limited coexistence for users and applications to access multiple directories during an integration/migration project. You create a referral by performing the following steps:

> **Connect To Option**
>
> It is also possible to connect to alternative domains or domain controllers through the Connect To option by typing or selecting the domain or server name in the Select or Type a Domain or Server field.

1. Open the ADSI Edit MMC snap-in console, right-click on ADSI Edit and choose the Connect To option, as shown in Figure 16.1.

2. In the Connection Settings dialog box, change the naming context to Configuration, as shown in Figure 16.2, and then click OK.

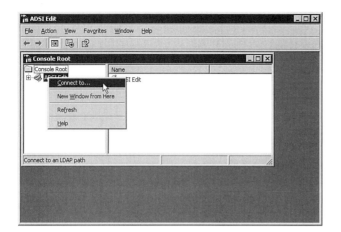

**FIGURE 16.1**
Connecting to a naming context.

**FIGURE 16.2**   Choosing a naming context.

3. Right-click on CN=Partitions and select New, Object, as shown in Figure 16.3.

4. In the Select Create Object dialog box, shown in Figure 16.4, the default class option is crossRef. Choose Next.

5. In the CN Attributes dialog box, shown in Figure 16.5, enter a common name for the LDAP directory to be referred to and choose Next.

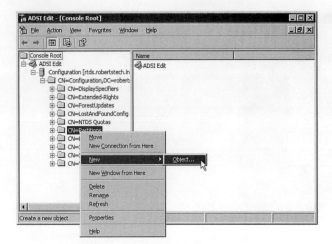

**FIGURE 16.3**
Creating a new object.

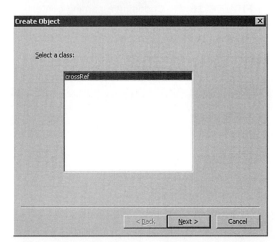

**FIGURE 16.4**    Selecting the object class.

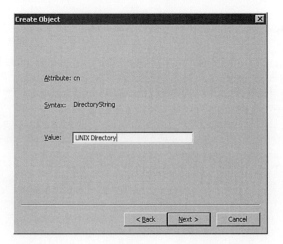

**FIGURE 16.5**    Entering a common name.

**6.** In the nCName (naming context name) attribute dialog box, shown in Figure 16.6, enter the naming context of the LDAP server, and choose Next.

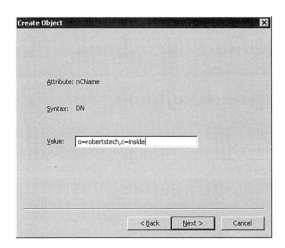

**FIGURE 16.6**    Entering the referenced naming context.

**7.** In the dnsRoot Attribute dialog box enter the fully qualified domain name of the LDAP server, shown in Figure 16.7, and choose Next.

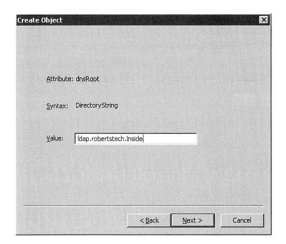

**FIGURE 16.7**    Entering the referred server.

**8.** The final dialog box enables you to choose More Attributes, such as an administrative description of this object. Choose Finish to add the referrer object to the CN=Partitions container.

## Integration Using Metadirectories

In larger environments where major investments have been made in large Unix or mainframe directory deployments, migration might not be an option. In cases such as these a metadirectory could be a desirable option to consider.

A *metadirectory* is used to consolidate disparate data from multiple directory structures. The metadirectory might consolidate a superset of data gathered from multiple disparate directories with different attributes, managed from different systems. A second option is a subset of data, while maintaining the company's common namespace alongside the namespace mappings to all of the connected systems, as well as key attributes, such as e-mail and public keys. Either approach works, and depends on your company's strategy for its directory usage.

Microsoft Identity Integration Server 2003 (MIIS) is an example of a LDAP metadirectory integration product. MIIS uses SQL Server 2000 (SP3 or later) to store the LDAP schema and synchronizes with multiple disparate LDAP schemas.

# Using Password Synchronization

One of the more laborious tasks of a network administrator or, in larger environments, the help desk, is assigning and changing passwords. This becomes especially challenging when multiple disparate platforms are involved.

To automate password synchronization the multiple platforms must be able to communicate such events as password expiration, resets, and lockouts. This process is usually best accomplished through scripting or automation programs.

## Synchronizing Passwords in Unix and NIS

You can use password synchronization to make it easier on users by only having to remember one username and password for both Windows and Unix systems. One way to accomplish this is to synchronize the passwords when one of them changes. Synchronization can either be one-way or two-way, depending on how the systems are configured.

Microsoft SFU 3.0 password synchronization runs as an extension of the Local Security Authority (LSA) service on Windows Server 2003. On the Unix platform a daemon called the single-sign-on (ssod) daemon and the pluggable authentication module (PAM) perform the synchronization processing. The Windows and Unix password information is encrypted when transported over the network.

Microsoft SFU 3.0 supports password synchronization between the Windows Server and the following flavors of Unix running NIS:

- Sun Microsystems Inc. Solaris version 7
- Hewlett-Packard HP-UX version 11

- IBM Corp. AIX version 4.3.3

- Red Hat Inc. Linux version 6.2 and later

To perform a test password synchronization you must ensure that SFU password synchronization is installed (not installed in default installation).

Prior to testing, you should configure DNS and test connectivity between the two systems. TCP port 6677 must be allowed by the firewall. The following steps can be taken to confirm that password synchronization is configured correctly:

1. Create a couple of test users on the Windows server with the following settings:

   a. Username "bsmith", password "bgrvfe"

   b. Username "rjones", password "mjunhy"

2. Open up the Services for Unix Administration mmc console and select Password Synchronization.

3. In the right pane, configure the Password Synchronization Default settings as shown in Figure 16.8.

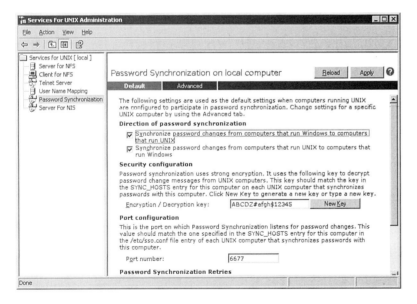

**FIGURE 16.8**
Password Synchronization default settings page.

4. Click on the Advanced tab and configure the Password Synchronization Advanced settings (inserting the name of the desired Unix server) as shown in Figure 16.9.

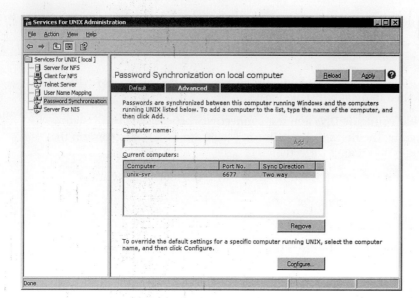

**FIGURE 16.9**
Password
Synchronization
Advanced settings
page.

5.  Click on the Configure button at the bottom of the Password Synchronization Advanced page and configure the settings as shown in Figure 16.10 and click Apply.

**FIGURE 16.10**    Configure Advanced
Password Synchronization.

On the Unix system (Red Hat Linux 7.3 in this test), you need to perform the following steps:

1.  Log in as root.

2.  In a console run the following commands:

    a.  `useradd bsmith`

    b.  `useradd rjones`

     **c.** `password bsmith (set bgtvfr as password)`

     **d.** `password rjones (set mjunhy as password)`

**3.** Copy the following files from the Microsoft SFU CD (located in the \unix\bin folder) to the Unix system: pam_sso.l52, sso.cfg, and ssod.l52.

**4.** In a console, change to the directory where the files in the previous step were downloaded and run the following commands:

     **a.** `cp ssod.l52 /user/bin/ssod`

     **b.** `chmod +x /user/bin/ssod`

     **c.** `cp sso.cfg /etc/sso.conf`

**5.** Edit the sso.conf file to specify the following:

     **a.** ENCRYPT_KEY=ABCDZ#efgh$12345 (This is the same value as entered in the Default page in the SFU Password Synchronization on the Windows computer).

     **b.** PORT_NUMBER=6677

     **c.** SYNC_HOSTS=(windows-dc, 6677, ABCDZ#efgh$12345) (Replace windows-dc with the name of the Windows host performing password synchronization).

     **d.** USE_NIS=0

     **e.** USE_SHADOW=1 (if applicable)

**8.** Copy pam_sso.l52 to the /lib/security directory with the file name of pam_sso.so.1.

**9.** Edit the /etc/pam.d/system-auth file to specify the following:

     **a.** password required /lib/security/pam_cracklib.so retry=3

     **b.** password required /lib/security/pam_sso.so.1

     **c.** Delete the line containing: password required /lib/security/pam_deny.co

**10.** Copy /etc/pam.d/password to the /etc/pam.d/ssod directory.

**11.** Run the /user/bin/ssod command.

The users will now be able to change their passwords on either Unix or Windows server and be able to log on to either platform with the same username and password.

## Synchronizing Passwords in LDAP

Password management involves quite a set of complexities. Different platforms employ methods for encrypted storage and transmission of passwords. This usually involves installing management agents on the host system to ensure that a common set of technologies are employed. There are several commercially available LDAP Gateway and Synchronization products available. Cost and complexity are often key factors to consider prior to deploying such a system.

Microsoft Identity Integration Server (MIIS) 2003 (formerly known as Microsoft Metadirectory Services) provides password management for the following platforms:

- Novell eDirectory 8.6.2 and 8.7

- Sun and Netscape Directory Servers (formerly iPlanet Directory Server)

- Lotus Notes Releases 4.6 and 5.0

- Active Directory

- Active Directory Application Mode

- Windows NT 4.0

Installing Microsoft Identity Integration Server 2003 requires some advanced planning and should first be deployed in a lab environment. MIIS Password Management requires installation and configuration of the following products:

- Microsoft Windows Server 2003, Enterprise Edition

- Microsoft SQL Server 2000, Enterprise Edition, Service Pack 3 (SP3) or later

- Microsoft Visual Studio .NET 2003

- Microsoft Identity Integration Server 2003, Enterprise Edition

MIIS Password Management uses the .NET framework to generate Web-based forms that administrators and help desk personnel and end users can use to set and change passwords. This requires the installation of IIS 6.0, Active Server Pages. If development debugging is desired FrontPage 2002 Server Extensions must also be installed.

# Centralizing the Management of Cross-Platform Resources

Over the past few years, Microsoft has been consolidating management resources for the various tools they have available. With the release of Windows 2000, the use of the Microsoft Management Console (MMC) has become the standard management interface used in the Microsoft tools. Windows Server 2003 continued to leverage the MMC for manageability; however for many of the non-Windows products covered in this chapter, you can also use native tools that might be more familiar to you for the administration and management of Unix, NetWare, or other environments.

## Using Telnet to Manage Unix and Windows

Windows Server 2003 has added access to many command line utilities that allow you to access the server via telnet on the Unix platform and perform many administrative tasks that were only available through the graphical user interface (GUI) previously.

## Using Microsoft Management Console (MMC)

The MMC gives you a unified view of the Active Directory and LDAP schema. By installing snap-ins to manage the components of the Active Directory, you can customize and delegate control of discrete functions.

There are a couple of essential tools that ship with Windows Server 2003. These tools are the Active Directory Services Interfaces (ADSI) Edit and Active Directory Schema snap-ins. Setting up an MMC console that allows you to manage and extend the LDAP schema is described in the following sections.

## Configuring Active Directory Schema Snap-in

To register the schmmgmt.dll either open a command window or from the Run dialog box, shown in Figure 16.11, type regsvr32.exe %systemroot$\system32\schmmgmt.dll. After the DLL is registered a message window appears as shown in Figure 16.12 that the registration succeeded.

> **Active Directory Schema MMC Snap-in**
>
> The Active Directory Schema MMC snap-in is disabled by default. Its DLL (schmmgmt.dll) must be registered before it can be installed.

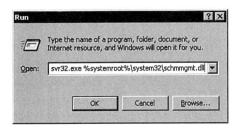

**FIGURE 16.11**   Registering the schmmgmt.dll.

**FIGURE 16.12**   Registration success.

To install the Active Directory Schema snap-in perform the following steps:

1. Select Start, Run and type in **mmc** and click OK.

2. In the new Console window select File, Add/Remove Snap-in.

3. Select the Add button in the Add/Remove Snap-in dialog box.

4. In the Available Standalone Snap-ins pane choose Active Directory Schema, and then choose Add, Close.

5. The Active Directory Schema snap-in should now be Add/Remove Snap-in window; choose OK.

6. Choose File, Save As and select a filename.

---

**MMC Console**

By default, the newly created MMC console will be saved in the Administrative Tools folder. Choosing the default folder enables you to find the newly created console easily.

---

The Active Directory Schema snap-in is now available for use in the MMC console. This will allow you to browse all classes and attributes.

To modify the schema, the Schema Operations Master needs to be selected and modifications allowed on this domain controller. To enable this configuration you must right-click on the Active Directory Schema and select Operations Master, as shown in Figure 16.13.

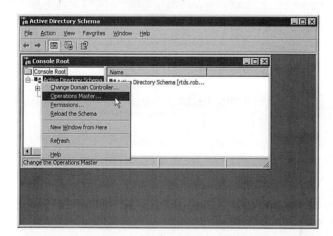

**FIGURE 16.13**
Selecting Operations Master.

# Accessing Unix from a Windows Perspective

For the two disparate systems to work together an important piece of the puzzle is securely sharing files. There are several possible ways to share files and folders between the two operating systems. The most prevalent method of sharing is emulating or hosting the native file sharing protocols of the other system.

## Accessing File Services

In the case of Unix file sharing to Windows, either the native NFS shares can be accessed or use Samba, which emulates the Windows Server Message Block (SMB) sharing. These two approaches are discussed in more detail in the following sections.

### Configuring Windows Client for NFS

The NFS Client that is included with SFU gives the Windows-based computer the ability to access Unix-based NFS resources. Once installed and configured the NFS client creates the ability to use UNC (\\servername\share) style mappings. To configure the NFS client on the Windows side perform the following:

1. On the Windows computer open Explorer and right-click on a directory to share and choose Sharing and Security.

2. On the NFS Sharing tab select Share This Folder, as shown in Figure 16.14.

**NFS**

By default, Server for NFS, Client for NFS or Gateway for NFS are not part of the Services for Unix installation.

**To Configure the NFS Services...**

To configure the NFS services you must ensure that the server for NFS is installed and started and that the client for NFS is installed.

**FIGURE 16.14**    NFS Sharing tab.

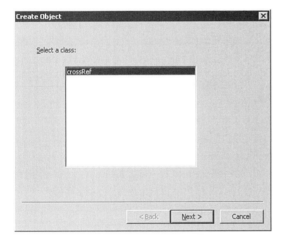

3. In the Share Name box type a name for the new share, and then choose Allow Anonymous Access.

4. Click on the Permissions button and allow and configure the access rights, as shown in Figure 16.15.

### Configuring Samba on Unix

Samba on Unix uses the /etc/samba/smb.conf as its configuration file. You need to edit this file to match your Windows environment to share files and printers. The following list shows some of the essential settings in the smb.conf file:

- `workgroup = <Windows Workgroup Name>`

- `server string = Brief Description of Server`

- `hosts allow = <single IP or subnets of allowed hosts>`

**Encrypted Samba Passwords Required**

Windows Server 2003, Windows 2000, and Windows NT 4.0 with Service Pack 3 or later require encrypted Samba passwords.

- comment = Description of the Share

- path = /home/share/

- valid users = usera userb userc

- public = no

- writable = yes

- printable = no

- create mask = 0765

- encrypt passwords = yes

- smb passwd file = /etc/samba/smbpasswd

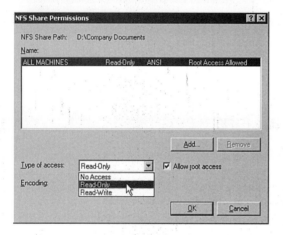

**FIGURE 16.15**  Setting NFS Share Permissions.

The following command creates a Samba password file and encrypts the contents:

```
cat /etc/passwd | mksmbpasswd.sh > /etc/samba/smbpasswd
```

**smb.conf Changes**

Any changes to the smb.conf file do not take effect until the Samba service is restarted.

The new file will only be populated by user accounts. The passwords need to be set using the following command:

```
smbpassword <username>
```

This section only covers some of the very basic configuration settings to allow Windows users to access Unix resources shared using Samba. The detailed settings for each version of Samba are given in that version's manual (man) pages.

## Accessing Print Services on Unix

On the Unix client the user can access Windows printer shares using Samba or with their native remote line printer (LPR) client. On the Windows Server 2003 platform you can use Print Services for Unix to enable the following:

- Act as a Line Printer Daemon (LPD)
- Remote Line Printer (LPR) client
- Send print jobs to Unix servers

By default Print Services for Unix is not installed. To install this service you must perform the following steps:

1. Click on Start, Control Panel, Add or Remove Programs and then select Add/Remove Windows Components.

2. Select Other Network File and Print Services and then Details.

3. Choose Print Services for Unix and then click OK.

# Accessing Windows from a Unix Perspective

With the adoption of Samba and the availability of mature file sharing utilities such as FTP and NFS, the lines have blurred where files are located on a computer network. Windows Server 2003 also exposes many command line tools for management that can be accessed via telnet from Unix-based clients.

> **Windows Server 2003 Must Be Run in Mixed Mode**
>
> For interoperation with utilities such as Samba, Windows Server 2003 must be run in Mixed mode. With the updated version of Samba (3.0.0 RC2 as of this writing), Windows Server 2003 can be run in Windows 2000 mode.

## Accessing Windows with Telnet

Unix system administration is predominantly command-line driven, with Telnet being one of the main tools of choice for this purpose. Windows Server 2003 has come a long way in providing command-line utilities, all of which are available through the Telnet server both natively and with Windows SFU.

An administrator telnetting to a Windows Server 2003 session can, for example, run command line scripting utilities such as adsutil.vbs, as shown in Figure 16.16.

> **Telnet Server on Windows 2003**
>
> The Telnet Server on Windows 2003 is disabled by default. You need to set the startup to Automatic and start the service.

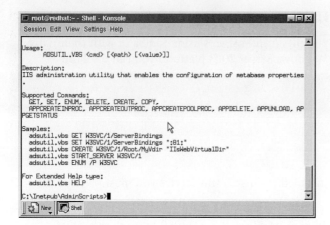

**FIGURE 16.16**
adsutil.vbs command line usage via
Telnet.

## Accessing Windows File Services

On a Unix-based system Samba uses the *smbclient* to access Windows-based shares. This is a command-line interface-based tool that has many functions besides just connecting to Windows shares. It can also be used for testing configurations, debugging, and automating administrative tasks when used in shell scripts.

There are many combinations of variables and command line options with the smbclient. The following are a few examples:

To list the resources in the domain (rtds is the domain controller and master browser):

```
$ smblicent -L rtds
```

To list the services on a single computer (rtws01), run this command:

```
$ smbclient -L rtws01
```

To connect to a share using username/password authentication:

```
$ smbclient //rtws01/shared -U username%password
```

These are just a few examples of the smbclient command. The Samba documentation concerning smbclient contains a complete reference.

## Accessing Windows Print Services

Samba allows the Unix/Linux user to print to a printer shared on a Windows system. This makes it convenient for you because you only have to set file and print sharing for Unix.

Many Unix variants, including Linux, use what is called the BSD printing system. With this system all the printers that will be used have an entry in the /etc/printcap file. This file describes printer capabilities used by the line printer daemon (lpd) and other programs that assist with printing.

Listing 16.1 shows a sample printcap.local file that shows a Hewlett-Packard LaserJet 4050 being shared on a Windows Server 2003 system named rtfnp.

**The Red Hat Linux /etc/printcap File**

In Red Hat Linux the /etc/printcap file is generated automatically and should not be edited. Any manual entries should be placed in the /etc/printcap.local file which is read by the /etc/printcap file.

**LISTING 16.1**  /etc/printcap.local

```
lp¦rtfnp-hplj4050:\
  :cm=HP 4050 on rtfnp:\
  :sd=/var/spool/lpd/rtfnp:\
  :af=/var/spool/lpd/rtfnp/acct:\
  :if=/user/local/samba/bin/smbprint:\
  :mx=0:\
  lp:=/dev/null:
```

This entry describes the server and printer as follows:

- In line 1, `lp` designates this as the default printer, `rtfnp-hplj4050` describes the name of the print server and the type of printer.
- In line 2, the `cm` keyword allows for a description of the printer share.
- In line 3, the `sd` keyword assigns the printer's spool directory.
- In line 4, the `af` keyword assigns the printer's accounting files.
- In line 5, the `if` keyword assigns the print filter (in this case the `smbprint` command to the shared printer).
- In line 6, the `mx` keyword sets the maximum file size to be printed. In this case it is set to zero, which allows any size file.
- In line 7, the `lp` keyword is set to `/dev/null` to discard error messages.

This example can be used to create as many printers as desired on the client's Unix-based system.

To set up Samba printing on the Unix client, perform the following steps:

1. Install the smbprint program (from the Samba source root directory):

   ```
   # cp examples/printing/smbprint /user/local/samba/bin
   ```

2. Create the printer's spool directory.

   ```
   # cd /var/spool/lpd
   # mkdir rtfnp
   # chown lp:lp rtfnp
   # chmod 700 rtfnp
   ```

3. Create the .config file.

```
# cd rtfnp
# >.config
# chown lp:lp .config
# chmod 600 .config
```

4. Insert the following information about the printer and how to connect with a text editor into the .config file:

```
server=rtfnp
service=hplj4050
password="<domain password>"
```

5. Restart the printer daemon:

```
# /etc/rc.d/init.d/lpd restart
```

Following this procedure you have created a default printer on the local system that will print to the hp 4050 share on the Windows Server 2003 system named rtfnp. To print a test page (/etc/hosts file) to the default printer you can use the following command:

```
# lpr /etc/hosts
```

## Using LPD/LPR

To print to a Windows-based printer from Unix using the LPR command, you must first set up Print Services for Unix on the Windows Server 2003 machine. This is accomplished by performing the following steps:

1. Select Start, Control Panel, Add or Remove Programs and then select Add/Remove Windows Components.

2. Select Other File and Print Services and then click on the Details button.

3. Choose the Print Services for Unix check box and then click on OK.

4. Select Next and then after the installation is complete choose Finish.

This procedure sets up what looks like a Unix server running the LPD service. The Unix system prints to this resource using the BSD printing system.

# Migrating Resources from One Platform to the Other

Maintaining multiple operating systems and various versions makes administration very difficult and time consuming. It should always be a goal to consolidate platforms onto a single operating system, if feasible. Window Server 2003 offers great promise in being able to consolidate many functions performed by Unix and other LDAP-based directory services.

## Hosting Directory Services

LDAP services can be hosted by multiple platforms simultaneously in an enterprise. This should only be used as a stopgap measure. The Windows Server 2003 LDAP schema can be extended to accommodate a range of client requests.

Synchronization between LDAP servers should be configured as a one-way transaction to the Active Directory. This enables you to consolidate and manage all the directory resources from a central location.

## Consolidating File Shares

File shares need to be consolidated for ease of management and security. To consolidate these resources you can methodically transition clients off the Unix file-sharing platform. NFS file shares can be hosted via Windows SFU-based NFS Server. Samba shares can be migrated to Windows-based DFS shares for fault-tolerance and load balancing.

## Consolidating Printers

Printer shares can be consolidated within the organization by transitioning them to the Windows Server 2003 print servers. Samba printer shares can be migrated and native LPD services can be hosted by Print Services for Unix.

# Summary

In the short term, products such as Samba, Windows Services for Unix, and Microsoft Identity Integration Server provide seamless integration between the disparate platforms. This situation is complex to implement and costly to manage.

The long-term goal should be to consolidate on a single platform. Windows Server 2003 is proving to be a stable and more secure platform than previous generations of Windows-based servers. This provides a compelling argument for administrators who are familiar with the Windows platform. Migrating to a single platform tends to reduce training, licensing, and administrative costs.

# 17

# Integrating Windows 2003 with Novell Networks

For many organizations with Novell Networks in their environments there seems to be one of two pretty common scenarios. The organization is looking to integrate Windows Active Directory more tightly with Novell eDirectory and NDS, or the organization is looking to eliminate Novell in place of a full Windows environment. This chapter will highlight the tips, tricks, and best practices to accomplish both a better integrated Microsoft/Novell environment, as well as ways to replace Novell networking with a Microsoft-centric environment.

# Leveraging Services for NetWare

Services for NetWare (SFNW) is a US$150 add-on available from Microsoft that provides a series of tools that help organizations integrate and migrate Novell and Microsoft networks. Surprisingly, very few organizations are even aware that the product exists; however, when working in a co-existence environment, or even considering migrating from NetWare to Windows, the SFNW can greatly assist an organization with the task.

SFNW provides organizations with the tools to integrate or migrate Novell users and resources to Windows environments. SFNW provides the following tools:

> **SFNW**
>
> To run SFNW on a Windows Server 2003 system, you must run version 3.5 or higher. SFNW v3.0 will only run on a Windows 2000 Server system

- Gateway Services for NetWare (GSNW)
- File and Print Services for NetWare (FPNW)
- Microsoft Directory Synchronization Services (MSDSS)
- File Migration Utility (FMU)

## Using Gateway Services for NetWare to Bridge Environments

Integration of a Windows environment with Novell network operating systems is simplified through the use of Gateway Services for NetWare (GSNW). Gateway Services for NetWare is an integration product that allows Windows Server 2003 systems to provide a bridge to Novell NetWare server resources. GSNW provides for the following functional elements:

- Windows client access to file and print services on NetWare servers
- NetWare client service access to Windows file and print servers

Specific scenarios for GSNW include the following:

- A Windows Server 2003 or Exchange server requires direct access to NetWare File or Print Services.

  One circumstance in which this service would be required is the extraction of NetWare accounts from a server or the source extraction of accounts from a NetWare-hosted messaging system such as GroupWise.

- A company is migrating desktop clients from a Novell-based network to a Microsoft Windows Server 2003 network.

  The Microsoft-based clients that have been migrated over and no longer belong to the Novell network but require access to NetWare resources can access the NetWare resources through GSNW.

> **Multiple Simultaneous Connections Are Not Supported**
>
> A Windows server can provide only a single gateway to one NetWare server at a time. Multiple simultaneous connections are not supported.

## Using File and Print Services for NetWare to Replace Servers

File and Print Services for NetWare is a back-end service that allows a Windows server to emulate a NetWare 3.12–compatible File and Print Server. NetWare clients can connect to the file and printer shares as if they were connecting to a Novell server. Novell clients use the same user interface to access file and printer resources running on an FPNW server. Essentially, FPNW allows an FPNW server to spoof an existing NetWare server after it has been retired, allowing you the time to gradually migrate desktops over to the Windows environment.

Specific scenarios for FPNW would include the following:

- A company needs to retire an aging Novell 3.12 server without having to make any network configuration changes to the NetWare desktop clients. The Windows Server 2003 running FPNW would be configured with the same File and Print Services as the Novell 3.12 server.

- A company is migrating from a Novell-based network to a Microsoft Windows Server 2003 network. During the migration, Novell-based clients that have not yet been migrated over to the Windows Server 2003 network can access the File and Print Services that have already been migrated over to Windows Server 2003 through FPNW.

## Using Microsoft Directory Synchronization Service to Integrate Directories

Microsoft Directory Synchronization Services (MSDSS) is a tool used for synchronization of directory information stored in the Active Directory and Novell Directory Services (NDS). MSDSS synchronizes directory information stored in Active Directory with all versions of NetWare; MSDSS supports a two-way synchronization with NDS and a one-way synchronization with Novell 3.x bindery services.

Because Active Directory does not support a container comparable to an NDS root organization and because Active Directory security differs from Novell, MSDSS, in migration mode only, creates a corresponding domain local security group in Active Directory for each NDS organizational unit (OU) and organization. MSDSS then maps each Novell OU or organization to the corresponding Active Directory domain local security group.

MSDSS provides a single point of administration; with a one-way synchronization, changes made to Active Directory will be propagated over to NDS during synchronization. Synchronization from Active Directory to NDS allows changes to object attributes, such as a user's middle name or address, to be propagated. In two-way synchronization mode, changes from NDS to Active Directory require a full synchronization of the object (all attributes of the user object).

One of the key benefits to MSDSS is password synchronization. Passwords can be administered in Active Directory and the changes propagated over to NDS during synchronization. Password synchronization allows users access to Windows Server 2003 and Novell NDS resources with the same logon credentials.

The MSDSS architecture is made up of the following three components. These components manage, map, read, and write changes that occur in Active Directory, NDS, and NetWare bindery services:

- The configuration of the synchronization parameters is handled by the session manager.

- An object mapper relates the objects to each other (class and attributes), namespace, rights, and permissions between the source and target directories.

- Changes to each directory are handled by a DirSync (read/write) provider. Lightweight Directory Access Protocol (LDAP) is used for Active Directory calls and NetWare NCP calls for NDS and NetWare binderies.

In addition to the core components of MSDSS, the session configuration settings (session database) are securely stored in Active Directory.

Specific scenarios for MSDSS would include the following:

- A company is migrating directly from Novell to a Windows Server 2003 network. All network services such as DNS, DHCP, and IIS services are running on a single server. MSDSS can be used to migrate all users and files over to Windows Server 2003 after all services have been migrated.

- A company is gradually migrating from Novell to a Windows Server 2003 network. The network services such as DNS, DHCP, and IIS are installed on multiple servers and sites. MSDSS can be used to migrate and synchronize AD and NDS directories during the migration.

### File Migration Utility (FMU)

The File Migration Utility is used to manage the migration of files from NetWare File and Print Servers to Windows Server 2003 systems automatically.

Integrated with MSDSS, FMU copies files while preserving the permissions and access control lists (ACLs) associated with each file. FMU copies the file permissions using a user-mapping file that matches an NDS user account with an Active Directory account. Through this mapping file created with MSDSS, files and the rights inherited or assigned in NetWare are calculated and maintained in the Windows network, preserving security and minimizing the time-consuming process of reassigning file rights and permissions. Without the mapping file, FMU will assign file permissions on all migrated files to the administrator.

## Creative Ways of Bridging the Gap Between Novell and Windows

Besides using a tool like SFNW, organizations have found other methods of bridging the gap between a Novell and Microsoft environment. The best solutions for choosing to integrate or cross support Novell and Windows environments is to determine what applications are desired to be shared.

If there is an equal split between applications that have to run on Windows and applications that have to run on Novell, then an organization has to create a tightly integrated multi-platform environment. However many organizations remain in a tightly integrated dual operating system environment when there are other options to address specific application access across platforms.

## Using a Dual-Client Approach to Access a Multi-Platform Environment

The most common method of multi-platform access and integration is to have both the Novell client and the Windows client installed on each client system. This dual client approach provides users the capability to access Novell servers and resources as well as Windows servers and resources. The simplicity for many organizations is that their client systems already support the dual client configuration, so there is no additional work to set up or configure the mixed environment.

To set up a dual client approach, an organization would typically download and install the Novell client from the Novell Web site. There are different versions of the Novell client, and while it typically makes no difference from a Microsoft network perspective which version of the Novell client is used, various Novell applications will not work without the correct version of the client software. Therefore it is best practice to use the latest version of the client to ensure compatibility with the latest Novell administration, management, and operational tools.

### Full Compatibility with Novell Directory Services

Microsoft provides a client for NetWare, however the Microsoft client is limited in its ability to access multiple Novell directory trees as well as limits the user the ability to run many of the Novell administrative tools. Therefore, most organizations use the Novell client to get full compatibility with Novell directory services, application services, and application compatibility.

## Taking Advantage of Windows Terminal Services in a Novell Environment

For many organizations that have effectively eliminated most of their Novell network infrastructure but are limited to a handful of legacy applications that are still running on Novell servers, there's a need for cross compatibility, but possibly not as important to continue to support a dual-client configuration. In these cases, one option an organization can consider is implementing Windows Terminal Services with the Novell client installed on the Terminal Server system. With a Terminal

### A Remote Client Does Not Need to Have the Novell Client Installed

By leveraging the application launch capabilities of Terminal Server, an organization can place an icon on a user's desktop that effectively launches a Terminal Server session to run a remote client session. A remote client does not need to have the Novell client installed; it just needs to have a Terminal Server client icon linked with the execution of the Novell-based application.

Server system, a single system running the Novell client can host dozens if not a couple hundred client application sessions without having any Novell client software on the client desktop and laptop systems.

When configuring a client for access to NetWare as well as to Microsoft Windows, the Novell client software provides the ability to log on to a Novell Bindery network, a NetWare eDirectory or NDS tree, a Windows NT domain, and a Windows Active Directory forest simultaneously. The default server, directories, and trees can be configured in the Properties window on the Network Properties page as shown in Figure 17.1.

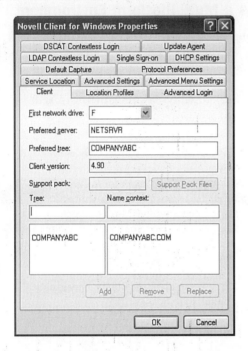

**FIGURE 17.1** Configuring the default properties for the Novell client.

By preconfiguring the property page options on the client configuration, default settings can be made relative to the network configuration desired. Many times the name services are different between the Novell and Microsoft environment, so a priority order needs to be created to access either the Novell or the Windows look-up tables. Additionally, logon scripts or drive mappings need to be resolved if multiple networks are accessed with similar default drive mappings or printer mappings across the different networks. In areas where configurations and access across multiple networks conflict, the properties option can be set to choose the settings desired.

## Using Web Services for Access to Microsoft Technologies

Another option to provide access to multiple platforms is to identify whether applications that are being used are Web services–enabled applications. Rather than trying to provide a 32-bit client access to applications, many times an application has a universal Web front-end that can be accessed with just a browser.

As an example, an organization that is heavily committed to Novell but needs to access possibly a corporate-hosted Exchange messaging environment might choose to use the Outlook Web Access for e-mail access rather than supporting and accessing Windows logon and network authentication. In a reverse scenario, if an organization has predominantly Microsoft-based applications yet needs to have support for a legacy Btrieve application, or a legacy NLM-based application, rather than supporting the dual-client approach, the organization could potentially use a browser version of the software that runs on Novell.

Web services and Web-enabled applications have become relatively common and greatly simplify the ability for an organization to implement multi-platform integrated configurations. Instead, of supporting a dual-client configuration, an application that might be on a cross-platform environment could be accessed using a more strategic view of application operation and configuration.

# Installing the Microsoft Services for NetWare Tool

To take advantage of the Microsoft Services for NetWare tool, the network administrators need to install Services for NetWare on a Windows 2000 or Windows 2003 server system. There are various versions of the Services for NetWare product. Services for NetWare 5.0 can be purchased for less than US$150; however, version 5.0 is not compatible with Windows 2003. With Services for NetWare Service Pack 2, there was support for Windows 2003 directory synchronization and server operation access.

## Preparing the Basic Configuration for Services for NetWare

Services for NetWare provides tools for gateway services, directory synchronization services, and file migration services. Each of the various tools has different system requirements as the tools affect different components in a Windows and NetWare environment. The basic configuration requirements for Services for NetWare are as follows:

- Pentium 133Mhz or faster
- 256MB Ram
- 130MB of available disk space
- CD-ROM, Network Adapter, and VGA Video

The actual system demands of the server system or systems supporting Services for NetWare depends on which of the modules will be used. As an example of varied system configuration:

- File Migrator—The file migrator tool in Services for NetWare does not necessarily need to run on a Windows 2000 or Windows 2003 server. It can actually run on a Windows XP workstation to transfer files from one server to another. The biggest area of performance for File Migrator is the performance of network speed because information is read and written across a network configuration.

- File and Print Services—The file and print services along with the gateway services utilities can greatly benefit from having a faster server (Pentium III 500Mhz or faster) with 512MB or RAM for a workstation class system, or 1GB of memory for a server class system to cache the reads and writes of the tool.

- Microsoft Directory Synchronization Service—MSDSS is probably the most processor and system performance–demanding tool in Services for NetWare. MSDSS requires the product run on a Windows Active Directory domain controller because it is doing direct synchronization between directories. Also because directory synchronization is frequently a real-time proce7ss, the faster the processing capability of the system, the faster it will process the directory requests. A fast system (potentially Pentium III 1Ghz or faster) with 1GB of RAM would be appropriate for an organization trying to synchronize hundreds if not thousands of objects.

## Installing the File and Print Services for NetWare

Because Services for NetWare is a series of tools, all the utilities do not need to be installed. Only those tools that will be used should be installed. On the first CD are the File and Print Services for NetWare (FPNW) tools as well as the Microsoft Directory Synchronization Service (MSDSS) tools for Windows 2000 and Windows 2003 networks. The second CD contains the tools and utilities for Windows NT 4.0 and Windows NT 3.51. This book only focuses on the first CD for Windows 2003.

From the first Services for NetWare CD, the installation process for File and Print Services for NetWare is as follows:

1. On the computer where the FPNW will be installed, insert the CD into the CD-ROM drive.

2. Add the network service by selecting Start, Settings, Network Connections and explore the Network Connections folder.

3. Right-click and choose Properties on the primary network adapter on the server where the FPNW will be installed.

4. Click on the Install button and choose Service, and then click on Add.

5. Click on Have Disk and choose the FPNW directory on the CD-ROM (such as D:\FPNW). File and Print Services for NetWare will appear on the Network Service option screen shown in Figure 17.2. Choose OK.

> **"Driver is Not Digitally Signed"**
> If you install FPNW v3.0 on a Windows Server 2003 system, the installation process will note. See insert.

6. When prompted to enter installation options, this is where you enter information about this system and how it will appear in a Novell network environment. For Directory for the SYS Volume, type in the physical path where normal Novell SYS utilities should be stored (such as E:\SYS).

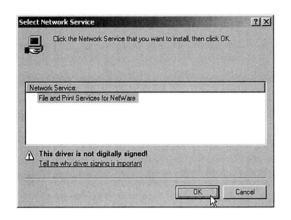

**FIGURE 17.2**  Installing FPNW on a Windows 2003 server.

7. For Server Name, this is the name that this server will publish when a Novell client tries to look for this server. This can be different than the Windows server name, so pick any name that is appropriate for this server in the Novell arena.

8. Enter the password for this server. Again, the information entered could be different than the Windows administrative password. This is the password that will be used as the Novell server "supervisor".

9. Choose one of the three tuning options for server performance. If uncertain, choose maximum performance. This can be changed later.

10. Click OK to select the settings and proceed with the installation. After the installation is complete, you will be prompted to restart the server. Restart the server to have the new Service for NetWare tools applied.

After File and Print Services for NetWare have been installed, Service Pack 2 or later of the Services for NetWare (v5.02 or later) needs to be applied for full Windows 2003 compatibility. To install the Service Pack for Services for NetWare, do the following:

1. Download the Service Pack from the Microsoft (http://www.microsoft.com) using the keyword search services for netware and in the downloads section, look for the latest service pack for Services for NetWare.

2. After the Service Pack has downloaded, run the Service Pack executable that will install the update on the Windows 2003 server.

3. Reboot the system as prompted to have Services for NetWare updated.

## Installing the Microsoft Directory Synchronization Service

Separate from the installation of the File and Print Services for NetWare (FPNW) is the installation of the Microsoft Directory Synchronization Service (MSDSS). This tool is not installed with the rest of the File and Print Services for NetWare tools because an organization might install FPNW on one server, whereas MSDSS will likely be installed only on a single server. Effectively, MSDSS does the synchronization between Active Directory and Novell NDS and eDirectory. MSDSS needs to be installed on a Windows domain controller to properly synchronize directory information between the two different network environments.

### Installing MSDSS

Installing MSDSS initiates an extension of the schema of the Active Directory forest. As with any schema update, the Active Directory should be backed up before performing a schema update. Also with a schema update, because the update will replicate directory changes to all Global Catalogs throughout the organization, the replication should be done at a time when a Global Catalog synchronization can take place without affecting the normal production environment.

To install MSDSS, follow these steps on a Windows 2003 domain controller:

1. On the domain controller computer where the MSDSS will be installed, insert the CD into the CD-ROM drive.

2. Go into the MSDSS directory on the CD-ROM (such as D:\msdss) and run the msdss.msi script package. This will launch the Installation Wizard.

3. Choose to install the Microsoft Directory Synchronization Service.

# Creating a Single Sign-on Environment

When logging in to multiple networks, one of the first things that is requested is the ability for a user to type in a logon name and password, and not have to be prompted to enter a logon and password for each additional network being accessed. The request is to have a single logon name and password that can be entered so that the user can access both Microsoft and Novell resources with an initial logon and password entry.

There are several ways that a single sign-on can be accomplished. The key to having an effective single sign-on process is to synchronize logon names and passwords between the multiple environments. When the logon names and passwords are identical, it's just a matter of having the logon process connect to each of the different systems.

## The Effectiveness of a Dual-Client Authentication Method of Access

One way that organizations try to accomplish a single sign-on process is to load both the Microsoft and Novell client software programs on the same system. With the same logon name and password, users think they have a fully integrated single sign-on process because they can access both a Microsoft and Novell network with a single logon.

Unfortunately a dual-client configuration does not provide manageability between the multiple logons. Effectively the single sign-on works until the user changes his or her password. Because the system was working on a dual-client architecture, changing the password on one operating system does not synchronize the password on the other network operating system. Each system will require a separate password change sequence.

So although the logon process with dual clients only requires a single logon and password entry when the logon names and passwords are identical, there is no manageability between the platforms. The user has to make password changes on each of the operating environments.

## Synchronizing Directories as a Method of Shared Logon

To effectively create a fully managed single sign-on environment, the logon names and passwords on the network systems need to be synchronized. There are many ways to try to accomplish this; however, the Microsoft Services for NetWare includes the Microsoft Directory Synchronization Service (MSDSS) tool that not only maintains a link between user accounts in Active Directory and NetWare, but also synchronizes user's passwords.

MSDSS enables users to change their passwords on the NetWare system and have the password automatically replicate to the Windows system. And the user can also change the password on the Windows systems and have the password updated on the NetWare system. This automated synchronization of user accounts and passwords across Windows and NetWare provides an easy way for an organization to maintain common logon and password information throughout a migration process.

# Synchronizing eDirectory/NDS with Active Directory

For organizations that have both a Windows Active Directory and a Novell eDirectory, or Novell Directory Service (NDS) environment, there are two primary methods of performing directory synchronization between the two directories. One method is using the Novell dirXML product, and the other method is using the Microsoft Directory Synchronization Service utility. With regard to synchronization of user accounts and passwords, both tools do the same job, and for the purpose of this book, the Microsoft solution will be the focus of this section. To configure and run the MSDSS utility, do the following:

1. Launch the MSDSS utility by choosing Start, Programs, Administrative Tools, Directory Synchronization.

2. Right-click on the MSDSS tool option and select New Session.

3. Click Next at the New Session Welcome screen.

**Use the Bindery Option**

Use the NDS option if Novell NetWare v4.x or later running NDS or eDirectory is used. Use the Bindery option if Novell NetWare v3.2 or lower bindery mode is running on the Novell network.

4. At the Synchronization and Migration Tasks screen, choose either Novell Directory Service (NDS) or Bindery for the type of service.

5. Dependent on the synchronization option, choose either a one way (from Active Directory to NDS/Bindery), a two-way (AD to NDS/Bindery and back), or a migration from NDS/Bindery to Active Directory. Click Next.

6. For the Active Directory container and domain controller, choose the AD container where objects will be synchronized to as well as the name of the domain controller that will be used to extract and synchronize information similar to the settings shown in Figure 17.3. Click Next.

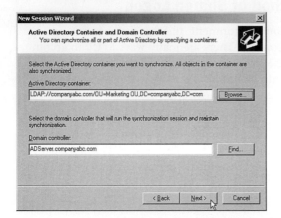

**FIGURE 17.3**    Setting server synchronization information settings.

7. For the NDS Container and Password, select the NDS container where AD information will be synchronized from and/or to the Novell directory. Enter in a logon name and password for a supervisor account on Novell to access the Novell directory. Click Next.

8. On the initial reverse synchronization screen, select the password option to either define passwords to be blank, same as the username, set to a random value (that can be viewed in the log file), or set to an organizational default. Click OK after making the password option, and then click Next to continue.

9. Click Finish to begin the synchronization/migration process.

## Best Practices Implementing MSDSS

MSDSS runs on a Windows 2000 or Windows 2003 domain controller and replicates user account and password information between the Active Directory environment and a Novell eDirectory or NDS environment. MSDSS is a Windows service that synchronizes user account information between Active Directory and NetWare. The following are best practices determined in the implementation of MSDSS in an enterprise environment:

- Ensure the Microsoft MSDSS server that is running on a Windows Active Directory domain controller and the Novell directory server are on the same network segment or have limited hops between each other.

- Because directory synchronization reads and writes information directly to the network directory, test the replication process between mirrored domain and directory services in a test lab environment before implementing MSDSS for the first time in a production environment.

- Monitor directory and password synchronization processing times to confirm the transactions are occurring fast enough for users to access network resources. If users get an authentication error, consider upgrading the MSDSS server to a faster system.

- Password characteristic policies (requiring upper/lowercase letters, numbers, or extended characters in the password, and password change times) should be similar on both the Microsoft and Novell environments to minimize inconsistencies in authorization and update processes.

## Identifying Limitations on Directory Synchronization

While directory synchronization can provide common logon names and passwords, MSDSS does not provide dual client support or any application-level linkage between multiple platform configurations. This means that if a Novell server is running IPX as a communication protocol and Windows is running TCP/IP, the MSDSS does not do protocol conversion. Likewise, if an application is running on a Novell server requiring the Service Advertising Protocol (SAP), because Windows servers commonly use NetBIOS for device advertising, a dual client protocol stack must be enabled to provide common communications.

MSDSS merely links the logon names and passwords between multiple environments. The following are areas that need to be considered separate of the logon and password synchronization process:

- Protocols like TCP/IP and IPX/SPX need to be supported by servers and clients.

- Applications that require communication standards for logon authentication might require a client component to be installed on the workstations or servers in the mixed environment.

- Applications that were written for Novell servers, such as Network Loadable Modules (NLMs) or Btrieve databases, need to be converted to support Windows.

- Login scripts, drive mappings, or other access systems compatible with one networking environment might not work across multiple environments, so those components will need to be tested for full compatibility.

- Backup utilities, antivirus applications, network management components, or system monitoring tools that work on one system will need to be purchased or re-licensed to support another network operating configuration.

## Backing Up and Restoring MSDSS Information

MSDSS configuration, tables, and system configurations are critical to the operations of the MSDSS synchronization tool. Microsoft provides a backup and restore utility that allows for the storage and recovery of MSDSS information. To back up MSDSS, do the following:

**1.** Select Start, Programs, Administrative Tools, MSDSS Backup & Restore Utility. You should see a screen similar to the one shown in Figure 17.4.

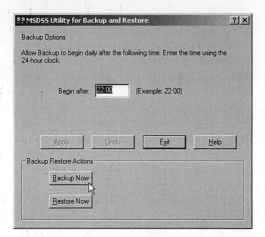

**FIGURE 17.4** Backing up MSDSS information.

**2.** Either click on Backup Now to back up the MSDSS session directory, or change the default time when the MSDSS information should be backed up.

**3.** If you choose to back up the session directory information you will be notified that the MSDSS service will need to be stopped. Choose Yes to continue.

**4.** Upon completion of the backup, you will be prompted that the MSDSS service will need to be restarted. Choose Yes to restart the MSDSS service.

At any time, if the MSDSS session directory information gets corrupt or behaves erratically, the MSDSS information can be restored. To restore MSDSS, do the following:

**1.** Select Start, Programs, Administrative Tools, MSDSS Backup & Restore Utility.

**2.** Click on Restore Now to restore the MSDSS session directory.

**3.** When notified that the MSDSS service will need to be stopped. Choose Yes to continue.

**4.** Upon completion of the restoration, you will be prompted that the MSDSS service will need to be restarted. Choose Yes to restart the MSDSS service.

# Replacing NetWare Servers with Windows Servers

A common process in a migration or partial migration from Novell NetWare to a Windows network environment involves the replacement of servers. Sometimes the server replacement is performed in entirety; sometimes the server replacement process is performed over an extended period of time. Regardless of the strategy chosen, the Services for NetWare tools provide options for the integration and migration process. The options are as follows:

- Enable a Windows server to simulate a Novell NetWare server.

- Set up a gateway to bridge a Windows share to link to a Novell server share.

- Migrate files from a Novell server to a Windows server.

## Enabling a Windows Server to Simulate a Novell NetWare Server

One method of replacing a Novell server with a Windows server is to physically replace the Novell server with a Microsoft Windows system. The problem is usually the situation where users who are mapped to the Novell server need to have their mappings changed to the new Windows server. This creates a chicken and egg scenario where the server cannot be replaced because each client system needs to be touched, but each client system cannot be reconfigured until the server data is migrated.

By using the File and Print Services for NetWare server replacement functionality, a Microsoft Windows server can take on the exact same server name, IP address, and drive and resource mapping as the old Novell server. Effectively, the Microsoft server responds not only as a Windows server, but also can respond to Novell MAP commands for sharing files, printers, and other network devices. One day, the server was running on Novell NetWare, and the next day a Windows server running Windows 2000 or Windows 2003 responds to the exact same Novell access commands.

Login scripts, drive mappings, configuration access files, file permissions, and all other information is migrated from the old to new server. The process in which this is done is as follows:

1. Install Windows 2000 or Windows 2003 on a new server. Give the server a new Windows server name.

2. Install File and Print Services for NetWare on the server as described in the "Installation of the File and Print Services for NetWare" section earlier in this chapter.

3. When choosing the Novell name, temporarily select a new NetWare server name for this system (this will be changed later to be the exact same name as the old Novell server, however it cannot be changed now because the names will conflict in the directory).

4. Use the file migration tool to migrate all volume information from the old Novell server to the new Windows server as described in the "Using the File Migration Wizard to Migrate Files" section later in this chapter.

5. After all files have been migrated, unplug the old Novell server from the network. Do not shut the server off, delete the server from the directory, or make any changes to the network. Simply unplug the network cable to remove the system (that way if you have any problems with the new Windows server, you can simply plug the old server back in without making any network changes).

6. Change the IP address of the new Windows server to be the same IP address as the old Novell server.

7. Change the File and Print Services for NetWare server name to be identical to the name of the old Novell server.

8. Reboot the Windows server to reconnect to the network that will then respond as if it were the old NetWare server.

## Bridging a Migration Gap Between Novell and Microsoft Environments

Another method of gaining access to Novell information during a migration to Windows is to set up the Gateway Services for NetWare (GSNW), which is part of the File and Print Services for NetWare installation tool. What GSNW does is allow a workstation that no longer has the Novell client installed to access a Novell NetWare shared resource by connecting through a Windows server. Instead of connecting directly from the client to the Novell server for file and print access, all file and printer components are redirected through a Windows server.

> ### The Windows Server Becomes a Bottleneck
> Because all traffic to a Novell server has to first go through a Windows server, the Windows server becomes a bottleneck if an extensive amount of traffic must be routed through the server. GSNW works fine for organizations with less than 25–50 connections, or for organizations that are using GSNW for a temporary cross-over server in a migration process. When more than 100 users have to access resources through a GSNW server for an extensive period of time, the performance might be degraded and should be tested before using GSNW for an extensive server reroute of information.

This minimizes the need for the client systems to have the Novell client installed, and a quick and easy way to share old legacy Novell file shares or printers without having to configure Novell workstation configurations. GSNW is installed on a Windows server and the Windows server has the Client for Novell installed and accesses the Novell resource, and then redistributes the shared access to Windows clients.

To install GSNW, perform the following steps:

1. After File and Print Services for NetWare has been installed on a Windows 2000 or Windows 2003 server, click on Start, Settings, Control Panel, and then double-click on GSNW.

2. Click on Settings, and then click on Enable Gateway.

3. Type in a username that will be the default access path from the Windows server to the Novell server. If the user account is in eDirectory or NDS, enter the username as *.username.organization-alunit.organization* format.

4. Enter in the password for the selected user account, again enter the same password into the Confirm Password box, and then click OK.

5. Type the Windows share name as you want this Novell network share to appear in Windows, click OK.

6. If you want to apply new permissions for Windows users to this share, click on Permissions and choose the Type of Access and the Access Through the Share information. Click OK to select the settings.

> **A Security Limitation for GSNW**
>
> Because all users route through the GSNW server using the same logon and password, usually a supervisor type password is used. However, this becomes a security limitation for GSNW because all users routing through GSNW will have the same access name and password to the Novell system, so permissions should be applied in step 6.

> **GSNW Will Not Work on the Same Server That Is Running MSDSS**
>
> GSNW will not work on the same server that is running MSDSS, so if directory synchronization will take place on a network, make sure it is also not going to be the GSNW server.

## Using the File Migration Wizard to Migrate Files

A utility that is installed with the MSDSS tool is the File Migration Utility. The File Migration Utility migrates files from one server to another, particularly from Novell servers to Windows servers while preserving filenames, file paths, access control lists (ACLs), and user and directory permission information. The File Migration Wizard simplifies the process of moving information from one server to another in an ability to migrate information without having to manually track file permissions or to rebuild configuration settings.

To run the File Migration Wizard, do the following:

1. Launch the File Migration Wizard by selecting Start, Programs, Administrative Tools, File Migration Utility.

> **Build a Brand New Microsoft Windows Server**
>
> A common practice for organizations replacing Novell servers with Microsoft Windows servers is to build a brand new Microsoft Windows server and then run the File Migration Wizard to extract information from a Novell server and replace the information onto a Windows server. Upon completion of the file migration, a drive mapping is changed in the network logon script remapping the user drive from a Novell volume to a Microsoft Windows share.

2. For Step 1 – Mappings, enter the name of a log file that will be used to record the server, drive, and configuration mappings. This is extremely helpful in creating a prototype test migration in a lab environment that can then be replicated in a production environment using the exact same settings. Choose Next to continue.

3. For Step 2 – Security Accounts, if not already logged on to Novell, click on the Log On to Novell button and enter in a valid account (typically the supervisor account) that has full access to the Novell server information. Click Next.

4. For Step 3 – Source and Target, choose the Novell server volume that is the source of information to be migrated, and select the Microsoft Windows share that is the target of the migrated information as shown in Figure 17.5. Choose Next to continue.

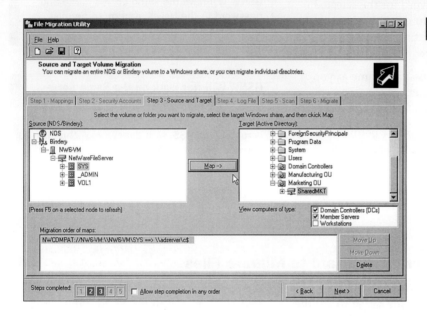

**FIGURE 17.5**
Selecting source and destination servers.

5. For Step 4 – Log Settings, choose to log the migration process. During a test migration during the prototype phase, select high log detail to view all migration change information. If after a test migration all processes are validated in the test, you can choose to log at a low or medium level to save disk space on the migration process. Click Next to continue.

6. Step 5 – Scan performs a test to validate whether there will be any failures during the migration process. The scan tests for available disk space, read and write permissions, matching account information, and proper configuration settings between the source and target servers. Click Next to continue.

7. Step 6 – Migrate performs the migration. If there were any errors in the test migration process, the errors will be reported and a warning will be displayed onscreen to prevent a migration process from occurring with undesired results. If the migration test phases are successful, the migration will proceed with a progress displayed similar to the one shown in Figure 17.6.

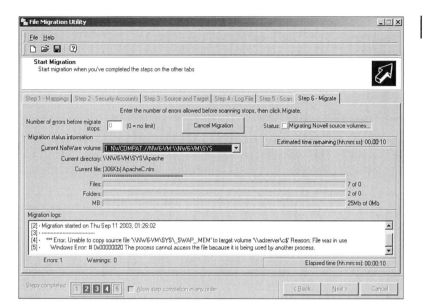

**FIGURE 17.6**
File migration process
proceeding as initiated.

# Summary

Integrating and migrating Novell networks and Windows networks might seem to be a challenging task; however, the Services for NetWare is a great resource for Windows to NetWare interconnectivity. An organization can choose to simply migrate files, including file permissions, from a Novell server to a Windows server all the way through, completely replacing the Novell server with a Windows server system.

For an organization that wants to create a single sign-on type environment, the Microsoft Directory Synchronization Service, or MSDSS, does the synchronization between Novell and Windows networks. MSDSS also includes the File Migration Wizard that migrates files, file properties, and file permissions from a Novell server to a Windows server.

The combination of all the tools included in Services for NetWare simplifies the task and the process of migrating or integrating Novell and Windows networks together.

# PART V

# Remote and Mobile User Solutions

# 18

# VPN and Dial-up Solutions

**A**s more and more companies become more and more dependent on computers for all business processes, users have an increased need to access corporate resources from locations other than the office. Traveling users, telecommuters, and business partners all benefit from being able to access corporate resources remotely.

This remote access to resources traditionally takes one of two forms—Virtual Private Networks (VPN) or direct dial-up access. VPNs often use the Internet for their connectivity and encrypt the flow of data to ensure that data is not intercepted and stolen or modified. Dial-up access refers to the classic modem access via the telephone network to corporate-owned modem pools.

Both methods are commonly used in the industry. Both methods also have some inherent insecurities and performance issues that must be addressed to optimize their use. This chapter gives you the information you need to build secure and scalable remote access solutions based on your specific needs.

# Choosing the Right VPN Solution

You have several choices when it comes to implementing VPNs. There are software-based VPNs such as those offered by Windows Server 2003. Point to Point Tunneling Protocol (PPTP) and Layer 2 Tunneling Protocol (L2TP) are both integrated into Routing and Remote Access Services. There are VPN products built into firewalls such as Checkpoint or Sonicwall. There are even dedicated hardware VPNs that run a specialized operating system such as those from Ravlin. Although each of these choices is viable, there are pros and cons to each which must be considered.

## Windows 2003 Routing and Remote Access Services

Windows Server 2003 offers several VPN choices through its Routing and Remote Access Services. These options include Point to Point Tunneling Protocol (PPTP), Layer 2 Tunneling Protocol (L2TP), and Point to Point Protocol over Ethernet (PPPoE). Like most Microsoft offerings, these VPN options are all tightly integrated with other Microsoft products. Microsoft has conveniently placed support for all of these VPN types into the client operating systems. This makes it very easy and economical for you to use Windows Server 2003 RRAS for VPN.

One of the drawbacks to using Windows Server 2003 RRAS for VPN is that although the Choose Your Role Wizard allows Windows Server 2003 to tailor itself for VPN use it is still an operating system that was built to fit many needs. Exposure to security vulnerabilities will be higher than with a device that is designed to do VPNs exclusively. It will be very important to administrators to ensure that a Windows Server 2003 RRAS system has been secured as much as possible. This chapter will cover such settings and recommendations.

Something of a hybrid solution is offered by companies such as Celestix. These hybrids are dedicated VPN systems that are based on a subset of Windows Server 2003. This gives them the advantages of the tight integration with Microsoft products without the exposure to security vulnerabilities that would be present in a full implementation of the operating system. Such devices leverage Active Directory for the storage of security account information and thus integrate well into Microsoft-oriented networks.

## Examining Firewall-based VPNs

Most of the major firewalls on the market today offer VPN functionality. Many of these firewall manufacturers have gone out of their way to create proprietary VPN systems to differentiate themselves from Microsoft offerings. Although some of the smaller firewall manufacturers offer PPTP and L2TP w/IPSec, most of the larger companies such as Checkpoint or Cisco have created their own implementations.

These proprietary VPN systems often tout improved security in the areas of authentication and data encryption. Higher bandwidth saturation as well as larger numbers of concurrent connections is often offered by these solutions. Although there is a lot to be said for improved performance and security, it usually comes at a price. These firewall-based VPNs usually require that an additional VPN client be purchased and installed onto each system that will be accessing the network via the VPN. This results in additional costs not only in the purchase of licenses but in the added management of installation of this client onto workstations. For companies with high security requirements, this is usually not a big issue. As the philosophy goes, there are three components involved with security: the overall security of the system, the convenience of using the system, and the cost of the system. To increase security, either cost will increase or convenience of use will decrease. If you reduce cost in an implementation, either security or usability will suffer. Making an environment easier to use will either cost more money or security will suffer. There is no perfect balance of these components. It is up to you to determine the requirements and design accordingly.

Pay careful attention to performance numbers and don't be swayed by impressive numbers. If VPN box #1 can saturate 10MB and VPN box #2 can saturate 100MB, box #2 seems a lot more impressive. If the company only has a T-1 to the Internet, both boxes are more than sufficient and there would be no reason to spend extra money for the added capacity of box #2 over box #1.

## Examining Hardware-based VPNs

The last class of VPN device is the dedicated hardware VPN. Manufacturers like Cisco or Ravlin offer devices that are designed to do nothing other than act as a consolidation point for VPNs. As the saying goes, let routers route, let firewalls firewall, and let the VPN system handle the VPN. Although in many cases it is advantageous to consolidate multiple functions into a single device, security usually takes the exact opposite approach. By separating tasks, not only are devices able to focus on what they are best at but a network gains multiple layers of security. Layered security is harder and more importantly, more time-consuming to defeat. Time is the bane of the hacker. The longer their attack takes, the more likely you are to see the attack and take appropriate measures. Never forget that computers don't know whether an access is legitimate. A VPN is a doorway into your network. Your job is to ensure that only appropriate users access it.

In the past, most dedicated VPN devices ran proprietary VPN protocols. Today most of these devices have moved toward standards-based VPNs with protocols like PPTP, IPSec, and IKE. This gives you greater flexibility in integrating multiple VPN devices. This is especially helpful when companies merge, acquire, or partner up.

## Deciding When to Make the Move from Software to Hardware

Small networks that don't have specific security requirements and that want to take advantage of VPN technologies are prime candidates for software-based VPNs. Windows Server 2003—with PPTP or L2TP w/IPSec on the back-end and the client running native VPN stacks from a Windows operating system—allows easy access to corporate resources.

Eventually companies outgrow this simple architecture. Because alternative operating systems need access to the resources, it is often helpful to abstract the VPN portion of the traffic. Site-to-site VPN technologies can be leveraged to allow normally unsupported operating systems to access a VPN as long as they are able to communicate via TCP/IP. An Apple computer or a Linux system can both ride a TCP/IP VPN tunnel into a network regardless of its ability to support PPTP if it is communicating through a PPTP capable site-to-site VPN device.

Site-to-site VPN devices are generally very secure, easy to install, and flexible in their protocol support. Rather than install client VPN software on all machines in a remote location and configure them all to connect to a single VPN device, local VPN gateways can be installed to allow traffic to route from site to site across the VPN. This enables a user to travel to any location with one of these VPN gateways and access the corporate network. In many companies, these types of VPNs have replaced traditional WAN connections. Because these VPNs leverage the Internet as their backbone, they are only as reliable as the Internet. The primary benefit of a site-to-site VPN over a traditional WAN connection is the cost. Local Internet connectivity is relatively inexpensive and this reduction in cost versus a long distance Frame Relay or ATM connection allows a site to purchase higher bandwidth than it would have normally been able to afford. The savings are often great enough to allow the site to also purchase a redundant Internet connection. This further improves the stability of the VPN and makes a compelling argument for replacing traditional WAN connections with site-to-site VPN connections.

# Best Practices for Securing L2TP

It is important to note that L2TP is, in and of itself, a tunneling protocol. By itself it offers no data encryption. L2TP is traditionally used with IPSec to add encryption to this IP tunnel. L2TP offers a feature that used to be unavailable with PPTP. This feature is the ability to place the VPN server behind a Network Address Translation device. This is to say that the L2TP VPN device does not require a routable IP address to be usable from the Internet. It merely requires that the appropriate UDP port be mapped to the firewall and the necessary protocols be passed to the L2TP server. These ports, configured in the Advanced TCP/IP Settings for the system network adapter shown in Figure 18.1, are specified:

- UDP source port of 500. This allows IKE traffic to be sent to the L2TP server.

- UDP source port of 1701. This allows IPSec traffic to be sent to the L2TP server.

- IP Protocol ID of 50. This allows IPSec ESP traffic to reach the L2TP server.

- IP Protocol ID of 51. This allows IPSec AH traffic to be sent to the L2TP server.

To secure the L2TP server itself, it is useful to treat the VPN server like a firewall. This is to say that all unessential services should be disabled. The POSIX subsystem should be disabled and the OS2 subsystem should be disabled as well. File securities should be audited to ensure that no users have access to any of the files. The High Security Workstation template from the Security Analysis and Configuration Tool is a great starting point.

To ensure that traffic passes through the VPN device it should be configured with at least two network cards that should be addressed on different networks. One NIC would connect to the production network and the other would normally connect to the DMZ network. This enables you to configure the two interfaces differently. TCP/IP filtering should be enabled on the DMZ interface of the L2TP device. Only the required ports and protocols should be accepted by the server. This greatly minimizes the attack profile of the server. Because this server is a gateway into the network, it should be treated as such and locked down as far as possible.

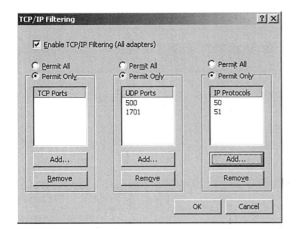

**FIGURE 18.1**  Port filtering for L2TP.

## Using L2TP in Parallel with a Firewall

It is a fairly common practice to install a VPN device in parallel with the firewall. This is to say that both the firewall and the VPN device have an interface that is connected directly to the Internet. Remote VPN users connect directly to the VPN device and their traffic does not pass through the firewall.

This configuration requires that the VPN device itself be well hardened and secured. Careful monitoring of the device will also help to ensure that it is not compromised. This configuration is often used in cases where the firewall is not able to correctly pass L2TP traffic to the VPN device.

One advantage of the VPN in parallel with the firewall is that it offloads traffic from the firewall, resulting in a smaller load on the firewall. Configuration of the VPN is also simpler as there is no configuration of the firewall necessary. This configuration can also reduce the number of licenses needed for the firewall because each VPN connection doesn't use up an outgoing session license.

If an L2TP device is going to be run in parallel with the firewall it is preferable for the device to be a dedicated VPN device with a dedicated operating system. If the L2TP device runs a full operating system, such as Windows Server 2003 RRAS, it is recommended you perform the following tasks:

- Disable all nonessential services

- Enable TCP/IP port filtering on the external facing NIC

- Allow only UDP ports 500 and 1701

- Allow only protocols 50 and 51

- Enable logging on the L2TP server

> ### Running the L2TP Device in Parallel
>
> To run the L2TP device in parallel with the firewall, it will be necessary to have at least two Network Interface Cards in the device. The port filtering should only be placed on the external interface.

- Require IPSec encryption
- Do not allow unencrypted passwords (PAP)
- Require MS-CHAP v2
- Allow EAP methods MD5, PEAP, and smartcard or other certificate

## Using L2TP in Series with a Firewall

If the firewall supports it, there are numerous security advantages to placing the L2TP VPN device in series with a firewall. The concept of layering security is a popular one and the philosophy works well with VPNs. In addition to being able to secure the local VPN device as was described in the previous section, "L2TP in Parallel with Firewall," having the firewall in series and ahead of the VPN device enables you to filter traffic at the firewall as well. In this way, before the VPN device could be attacked, the firewall would first have to be compromised. Anything that increases the time necessary to compromise a system increases the overall security of an environment.

Most Application Layer firewalls, Proxy Level firewalls, and Port Filtering firewalls will work very well with L2TP. L2TP can be passed through a firewall as well as be translated to an Internet host via Network Address Translation. This allows smaller companies with a single IP address to map L2TP services through a firewall back to an internal VPN device.

## L2TP Client Requirements

To make an L2TP/IPSec virtual private network (VPN) connection, you must first have an Internet connection. If a system tries to make a VPN connection before it has an Internet connection, it will likely experience a noticeable delay, perhaps 60 seconds, and then receive an error message stating that there was no response or that something is wrong with the modem or other communication device.

To use L2TP/IPSec connections, it is useful to understand how an L2TP/IPSec connection works. When a system starts the connection, an initial L2TP packet is sent to the server. This packet is requesting a connection. This packet causes the IPSec layer on the client computer to negotiate with the VPN device to set up an IPSec protected session. This protected session is also called a security association or simply an SA. Based on network speed and latency, the IPSec negotiations can take from a few seconds to several minutes. When an SA has been established, the L2TP session starts. When this session starts, the user will be prompted for a username and password. After the VPN device accepts the username and password, the session setup is completed.

Some common issues with the use of L2TP/IPSec connections include:

- An incorrect or missing certificate
- An incorrect or missing pre-shared key

- An incorrect or missing IPSec remote access policy

- Insufficient dial in rights for the user

- Use of Network Address Translation at the client side

Many small networks use a router or firewall with NAT functionality to share a single routable address among all the computers on the network. The original version of IPSec drops a connection that goes through a NAT because it detects the NAT's address-mapping as packet tampering. Home networks also frequently use an NAT. This blocks the use of L2TP/IPSec unless the client and VPN gateway both support the NAT Transparency standard for IPSec. NAT transparency is supported by Windows Server 2003.

## Leveraging Remote Access Policies

For a common policy, you must choose the following:

- An access method:

| VPN access |
| --- |
| Dial-up access |
| Wireless access |
| Ethernet |

- Whether to grant access permissions by user or by group

- Authentication methods

- Levels of allowed encryption (depending on the access method selected)

For a custom policy, you must configure the following:

- A set of policy conditions

- Whether remote access permission for the policy is granted or denied

- Remote access policy profile settings

# Best Practices for Securing PPTP

Point-to-Point Tunneling Protocol, or PPTP, is a common and popular form of VPN. It is simple to configure and supports situations where multiple clients will NAT through a single IP address to reach one or more VPN devices. Most any modern operating system has built-in support for PPTP, making it a very easy solution to implement.

PPTP encapsulates traffic on port 1723 through the use of GRE or Generic Routing Encapsulation. This basically means that a client establishes a tunnel via a single port that will allow traffic of any type and any port to travel through this tunnel. This gives PPTP client's full access into a network by routing traffic at the PPTP VPN device between the tunnel and the rest of the network.

In the past, PPTP got a bit of a bad reputation for its security. This was an issue with MS-CHAP v1 that allowed for the potential for a "man in the middle" attack. This issue was fixed in MS-CHAP v2. Similarly, the 14-character password limitation of MS-CHAP v1 was also fixed in v2.

## Using PPTP in Parallel with a Firewall

It is a fairly common practice to install a VPN device in parallel with the firewall. This is to say that both the firewall and the VPN device have an interface that is connected directly to the Internet. Remote VPN users connect directly to the VPN device and their traffic does not pass through the firewall. This is especially common for PPTP implementations due to the fact that PPTP traffic cannot normally be translated to an internal host via Network Address Translation. Without specific proxy type support for PPTP, the PPTP VPN device requires a routable IP address on the Internet in order to function correctly. Some modern firewalls allow a DMZ function where any undefined traffic will default to a particular device. This effectively places the device outside the firewalls and negates the normal protection provided by the firewall. If this method of passing traffic is employed it should be treated as though it was in parallel with the firewall as opposed to being connected in serial.

This parallel configuration requires that the VPN device itself be well hardened and secured. Careful monitoring of the device will also help to ensure that it is not compromised. Appropriate port filtering and security templates should be applied to the PPTP device where appropriate.

One advantage of the VPN in parallel with the firewall is that it offloads traffic from the firewall, resulting in a smaller load on the firewall. Configuration of the VPN is also simpler because there is no configuration of the firewall necessary. This configuration can also reduce the number of licenses needed for the firewall because each VPN connection doesn't use up an outgoing session license.

If a PPTP device is going to be run in parallel with the firewall, it is preferable for the device to be a dedicated VPN device with a dedicated operating system. If the PPTP device runs a full operating system, such as Windows Server 2003 RRAS, it is recommended you configure the following items on the Advanced TCP/IP Settings as shown in Figure 18.2 for the network adapter:

- Disable all nonessential services
- Enable TCP/IP Port filtering on the external facing NIC

- Allow only TCP port 1723

- Allow only protocol 47 (GRE)

- Enable logging on the PPTP server

- Do not allow unencrypted passwords (PAP)

- Require MS-CHAP v2

- Allow EAP methods MD5, PEAP, and smartcard or other certificate

> **Running the PPTP Device in Parallel**
>
> To run the PPTP device in parallel with the firewall, it will be necessary to have at least two Network Interface Cards in the device. The port filtering should only be placed on the external interface.

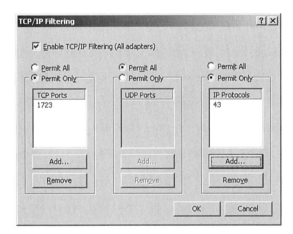

**FIGURE 18.2**    Port filtering for PPTP.

## Using PPTP in Series with a Firewall

If the firewall supports it, there are numerous security advantages to placing the PPTP VPN device in series with a firewall. The concept of layering security is a popular one and the philosophy works well with VPNs. In addition to being able to secure the local VPN device as was described in the previous section, "PPTP in Parallel with Firewall," having the firewall in series and ahead of the VPN device enables you to filter traffic at the firewall as well. In this way, before the VPN device could be attacked, the firewall would first have to be compromised. Anything that increases the time necessary to compromise a system increases the overall security of an environment.

Most modern Application Layer firewalls, Proxy Level firewalls and Port Filtering firewalls will work very well with PPTP. When supported, PPTP can be passed through a firewall as well as be translated to an Internet host via Network Address Translation. This allows smaller companies with a single IP address to map PPTP services through a firewall back to an internal VPN device.

## PPTP Client Requirements

To make a PPTP virtual private network (VPN) connection, you must first have an Internet connection. If a system tries to make a VPN connection before it has an Internet connection, it will likely experience a noticeable delay, perhaps 60 seconds, and then receive an error message stating that there was no response or that something is wrong with the modem or other communication device.

Some common issues with the use of PPTP connections include the following:

- An incorrect or missing account name
- An incorrect or missing password
- Insufficient level of encryption chosen
- An incorrect or missing PPTP remote access policy
- Insufficient dial-in rights for the user
- Blocking PPTP at the firewall at the client side
- Use of Network Address Translation at the server side

## Leveraging Remote Access Policies

For a common policy, you must choose the following:

- An access method:

| |
| --- |
| VPN access |
| Dial-up access |
| Wireless access |
| Ethernet |

- Whether to grant access permissions by user or by group.
- Authentication methods
- Levels of allowed encryption (depending on the access method selected)

For a custom policy, you must configure the following:

- A set of policy conditions
- Whether remote access permission for the policy is granted or denied
- Remote access policy profile settings

# Taking Advantage of Internet Authentication Service

Internet Authentication Service, or IAS, is the Windows Server 2003 implementation of Remote Authentication Dial-in User Service (RADIUS) server and proxy. As a RADIUS server, IAS supports centralized authentication, accounting, and authorization for multiple types of network access. These access types include VPN connections, wireless connections, switch authentication, and remote access dial-up connections. As a RADIUS proxy, IAS is able to forward switch authentication and accounting messages to other RADIUS servers. RADIUS is an Internet Engineering Task Force (IETF) standard that is designed to handle authentication, auditing, and accounting tasks for connectable devices.

**BEST PRACTICE**

### Installing and Using IAS

Always install and test each of your access servers using local authentication methods. Ensure that this works before making them RADIUS clients. This will make troubleshooting easier as the access server becomes a known good device.

After installing and configuring IAS, save the configuration by using the `netsh dump > file.txt` command. For more information, see the `Netsh /?` command. Save the IAS configuration with the `netsh dump > file.txt` command every time a change is made to make recovery simpler.

When configuring a Windows Server 2003 system running IAS or Routing and Remote Access that is a member of a Windows NT Server 4.0 resource domain, if your user account database is stored on a Windows Server 2003 domain controller in another domain, Lightweight Directory Access Protocol (LDAP) queries from the IAS server to the Windows Server 2003 domain controller will fail.

When administering an IAS server remotely, avoid sending sensitive or confidential data over the network in plaintext. This would include data such as passwords or shared secrets. The two recommended methods for remote administration of IAS servers are Terminal Services or IPSec encrypted traffic.

## Using Terminal Services to Access the IAS Server

When using Terminal Services, data is not actually sent between client and server. Only the user interface of the server (for example, the IAS console image and the operating system desktop) is sent to the Terminal Services client. This is called Remote Desktop Connection in Windows XP. The client sends keyboard and mouse input, which is processed locally by the server that has Terminal Services installed. When Terminal Service users log on, they can view only their individual client sessions, which are managed by the server and are independent of each other. This means that other Terminal Sessions don't have access to the traffic associated with other connection. Additionally, Remote Desktop Connection provides 128-bit encryption between the client and the server.

# Using IPSec to Encrypt Confidential Data

Like with any type of traffic, IPSec can be used to encrypt communication between the IAS server and the remote client computer that is being used to administer it. This ensures that none of the configuration information is being passed in clear text. To administer the server remotely, the Windows Server 2003 Administration Tools Pack must be installed on the client computer, and the IAS snap-in must be added to the Microsoft Management Console (MMC).

The IAS server provides authentication, authorization, and accounting for connection attempts to a corporate network. It is very important to protect the IAS server and RADIUS messages from unwanted internal and external intrusion. IAS is the key to accessing a corporate network and it is critical that only the appropriate people have access to those keys.

Always take standard precautions to secure an IAS server. Limit access to the system to only a limited number of members of the IT staff. Store the IAS server in a locked and controlled data center. Audit the security logs regularly and be sure to password-protect the system backups. This way the tapes can't be easily used to create a server that can impersonate the corporate IAS server.

Use the RunAs command to administer local IAS servers rather than logging in with an administrative-level account. You can use the RunAs command to perform administrative tasks when you are logged on as a member of a group that does not have the required administrative credentials.

Because the IAS system is the gatekeeper to remote access it is critical that access via the system is well logged. There are two types of logging offered by IAS—event logging and authentication logging.

Event logging can be used to record IAS events in the system event log. This is primarily used for auditing and troubleshooting connection attempts. This information goes directly into the Windows Server 2003 Event Viewer.

IAS is able to log user authentication and accounting information to log files in text or database format. Optionally it can log to a stored procedure in a SQL Server 2000 database. This type of logging is primarily used for connection trend analysis as well as for billing purposes. This type of data can also be useful as a security investigation tool, giving you another method of tracking down the activity of an unauthorized user.

With either type of logging, ensure that there is sufficient capacity to maintain the logs. In the case of auditing information, one would usually need at least a month of data to accurately perform bill back tasks to various departments. On the security tracking side, it is useful to have many months of data so that it will be possible to track the activities of a suspected hacker. Be sure to back up the log files regularly as they cannot be re-created if they are damaged or deleted.

You can optimize IAS authentication and authorization response times as well as reduce network traffic by installing IAS on a domain controller. Similar gains can be achieved by making the IAS system a Global Catalog as well. This is because when universal principal names (UPNs) or

Windows Server 2003 domains are used, IAS will use the global catalog to authenticate the users. Making the IAS a global catalog or at least having a global catalog on the same subnet as the IAS system will reduce the time needed to perform the authentication.

In a large RADIUS implementation where there is heavy authentication traffic, you can effectively load balance the RADIUS environment by doing the following:

- Install IAS as a RADIUS server on all domain controllers.

- Configure multiple IAS proxies to forward the authentication requests between the RADIUS servers and the access servers.

> ### IAS in Windows Server 2003
>
> IAS in Windows Server 2003, Standard Edition, supports a maximum of 50 RADIUS clients and a maximum of two remote RADIUS server groups. You can define a RADIUS client using either an IP address or a fully qualified domain name. You cannot define groups of RADIUS clients via IP address ranges. IAS in Windows Server 2003, Enterprise Edition, and Datacenter Edition, support an unlimited number of RADIUS clients and remote RADIUS server groups. Additionally, you can configure RADIUS clients via an IP address range. You should be sure to understand their needs before deciding on which version of Windows 2003 they will run.

- Configure the access servers to use the IAS proxies as RADIUS servers.

This is especially useful in large 802.1x implementations where wireless connections are using certificates to authenticate via IAS/RADIUS to gain access to an internal network.

# Using VPN for Wireless

With the recent popularity of wireless technologies like 802.11a, 802.11b, and 802.11g, there is increased concern with making the wireless connections as secure as wired connections. One of the simplest factors that helps secure wired connections is that all the network jacks are physically secured within the building. Access to one of these network ports requires access to the office itself. Given the nature of wireless technologies, the client needs only proximity to the access point. What this means is that clients outside the office could potentially gain access to the internal network. One of the most common ways to avoid this security issue is to place the wireless connection outside the internal network. Typically, the connection is placed in the DMZ or Demilitarized Zone. By placing the access point in the DMZ outside the firewall the connection becomes akin to the Internet connection. At this point, wireless connections, just like remote users, would logically connect via a VPN connection.

For companies that use a classic DMZ, which is to say that there is a "third leg" on the firewall that separates hosts from both the Internet and the internal network, access points should be placed in a separate DMZ. This prevents wireless clients from doing several potentially destructive things such as

- Attacking DMZ hosts from inside the DMZ itself

- Leaching Internet access

- Launching denial of service attacks from corporate owned IP ranges

- Sending SPAM from corporate owned IP ranges

- Performing denial of service attacks on the DMZ by binding multiple IP addresses and causing IP conflicts

- Sniffing traffic between the DMZ and internal hosts

# Deploying VPN and Dial-up Services

Deploying VPN and Dial-up services is a fairly straightforward task that most any administrator can handle. There are several factors that should be taken into consideration when designing a remote access system:

- Corporate security policies

- Number of simultaneous users

- Client support

- WAN connectivity

- Telco resources

- National versus worldwide access

- Quality of Service requirements

- User-to-port ratios

- Accounting requirements

- Logging requirements

## Leveraging the Microsoft Connection Manager

The Microsoft Connection Manager (CM) is a client dialer for connecting to network resources on a public network or to private networks over the Internet. CM sits on top of Dial-Up Networking (DUN) and simplifies the network access experience for end users. This dialer client can be preconfigured for the users by the Administrator by using the Connection Manager Administration Kit (CMAK).

The Connection Manager Administration Kit is a step-by-step wizard that creates custom service profiles and enables you to append applications. The Service Profile is a collection of connection information tailored to specific employees. This connection information is combined with applications and Connect Actions to create an Installation Package.

When installed, the Service Profile merges with the resident Connection Manager dialer to enable employees to easily connect to a public or private network. Through the use of the

CMAK, you can standardize and simplify the configuration of remote connectivity and improve the end users' connection experiences.

The CMAK can preconfigure any of a variety of items for each Service Profile within an Installation Package.

### Desktop and Tray Icons

CMAK supports the customization of both a desktop icon and a taskbar tray icon. The tray icon can be configured as an interface to additional applications distributed by the company.

### Animated Dialer Logon Screen

Support for animation in the dialer interface and keys for integration with the connection status enable you to communicate to the client with connection status or network status information.

### Phone Book

The Connection Manager Phone Book stores POP and RAS (dedicated line) access numbers with an easily navigable user interface. Employees can always have a local phone number for network access at their fingertips. Each phone number can also be configured as a PPTP connection, making encrypted connections transparent to the client.

### Interface Support for Multiple Service Types

Specification of multiple service types enables you to support different levels of services for different user types. This is especially useful in ensuring that VIP users receive priority connectivity.

### Connect Actions

Connect Actions are client events that are preconfigured by the administrator. These events are keyed upon the onset or termination of network secession and are used like login or logoff scripts.

### Automated Phone Book Updates

Automated updates of the client's resident POP/RAS phone book is a Connect Action. The update downloads new POP/RAS information (incrementally) upon termination of the logon session as needed. In this way, you can rest assured that each client will always have the latest version of a phone book and access to the latest local POPs.

### Auto-applications

Auto-applications are Connect Actions configured to automatically launch or close resident applications upon the start or termination of a connection. This enables you to facilitate the use of your services by launching a browser or other resident application (e-mail client) and closing that application upon termination of the connection.

### License Agreement

In an increasingly litigious society, it's necessary for you to insulate yourself from the legal and financial risks you might incur in the provision of virtual private networking services. Corporations need to inform employees of the responsibilities, duties, and obligations of the corporation regarding confidentiality of information. For this reason, and because you might want to append your own proprietary application to custom service profiles, the CMAK supports the appending and distribution of custom contracts to the client. In this manner, you can defer legal exposure to an informed client and protect your software investments.

### Connection Status

The CM interface can be configured to keep the client apprised of the connection status with specific terminology. This feature can be coupled with the animation support to keep each client informed of the connection status at all times.

### Support Phone Number

Quality of service and support is critical to employee productivity and subscriber satisfaction. The CMAK configures the CM interface with a support phone number at the logon screen.

### Custom Help File

The CMAK allows for the inclusion of a custom help file in the service profile. This custom help file can help reduce support costs through the inclusion of targeted frequently asked questions. In addition, this help file can let corporate customers make business policy regarding remote network use explicit to their employees. Custom help files reduce support costs by making clients more self-sufficient and can reduce the risk of inappropriate online behavior.

### Language Support

The CMAK also provides for the simple, efficient editing of service profiles. Service profiles can be easily created in multiple languages including English, French, German, Spanish, and Japanese.

### Automatic Password

You can use the CMAK to specify whether end-user passwords can be saved for Internet access or access to the corporate network. This facility can be enabled or disabled depending on your security policy. Forgetting passwords is a large support issue that can be addressed and reduced directly through this facility.

### Realm Name Prefix and Suffix

Many service providers require the appending of some very specific syntax to log on to their servers. Non-intuitive logon script results in end-user frustration and support calls. The CMAK tool enables you to preconfigure realm name (@companyabc.com) as well as the prefix or suffix extensions, facilitating the provision of basic Internet access and VPN services.

### Assign Encrypted Connections

Key to the provisioning of Virtual Private Networks is network security. One popular means of providing security is through encryption of the transmitted data. The CMAK enables you to associate with each POP phone number a PPTP configuration status.

### Append an Application

The CMAK enables network administrators to append applications to the custom Service Profile information during the creation of an Installation Package. This enables you to ensure that the clients at the receiving end have all the software and information they need to immediately engage in VPN activity.

### Edit Existing Service Profiles

To facilitate the creation of service profiles for different departments within an organization or subscriber base, with the CMAK, you can edit pre-existing service profiles so that you don't need to re-enter all data when making minor service profile changes.

The Connection Manager Administration Kit is installed as a Windows component in the Management and Monitoring Tools area.

## Leveraging Softmodems

As companies scale the number of supported users they often replace banks of modems with dedicated hardware such as routers with multiple asynchronous interface cards. This enables you to bring in T-1 lines and create 23 dial-up connections rather than bringing in hundreds of analog lines. This concept scales well but eventually even it becomes unrealistic. For companies that must support huge numbers of dial-up connections there are Softmodems.

A *Softmodem* is a device that enables you to connect a large circuit connection, like a T-3 or an OC-3, and create a very large number of dial-up connections. Rather than have dedicated circuitry for each modem device, a Softmodem leverages a central processor to effectively create multiple virtual modems. This technology is scalable well into the ISP class of service.

## Consolidating Lines with Larger Circuits

As companies grow past a few modems and a few analog lines connected to a RAS device it makes sense to compare prices and costs against aggregating those connections into a larger circuit.

Racks of modems take up valuable space in a corporate data center. Racks of modems can be replaced by routers with asynchronous cards and Telco circuits to save space and improve performance. Consolidated devices are often more reliable than common off-the-shelf modems.

Let's say, for example, that analog phone lines cost a company $40/month. Let's say a T-1 line in the same location costs $600/month. A T-1 line provides the equivalent of 23 analog phone lines. After the company breaks 15 analog lines, the T-1 line is less expensive. Lines 16–23 effectively become savings that would apply against any additional costs of the consolidation device versus the costs of the old style modems. In some cases, the consolidation device will be less expensive than the RAS device and the modems would have been.

These consolidation devices usually support RADIUS for authentication and auditing as well as SNMP for management and monitoring. Between the savings in monthly costs and the reduction in space used in the data center, these solutions can be very viable for companies with even modest RAS needs.

## Leveraging RADIUS

RADIUS, or Remote Authentication Dial-in User Service, is the de facto standard for authenticating and tracking remote access users. RADIUS is used for dial-up, VPN, and even wireless connections. Microsoft's IAS is its implementation of RADIUS.

A RADIUS remote access environment has three primary components: Users, Remote Access Servers, and the RADIUS server. Each user connection is a client of a Remote Access Server, which, in turn, is a client of the RADIUS server.

The user is the person who is trying to gain remote access to the corporate network from home or from the road. Usually, the user has a PPP or perhaps SLIP dialer that enables him to dial into a Remote Access Server at the corporate office and become a remote node on the network, with IP or IPX access to network resources.

The Remote Access Server (or RAS) is a device that does the following:

- Accepts remote connections such as SLIP or PPP dial-in calls, authenticates each user via the RADIUS or some other authentication server, and then routes or bridges that user onto the network.

- Accepts direct connections to the network through a firewall, authenticates the user via the RADIUS or other authentication server, and then grants network access to specific resources.

- Accepts VPN connections, authenticates the user via the RADIUS or some other authentication server, and routes that user onto the network.

- Forwards requests from another RAS device using Proxy Radius. This is similar to call-forwarding, where an external RAS service can direct all authentication and accounting transactions to a company's RADIUS server.

Because most RAS devices can handle multiple connections at once, a corporate network might include a single RAS or multiple RASes working in tandem to handle the traffic.

The RADIUS server is the device that accepts authentication requests from one or more Remote Access Servers, performs the authentication, and responds with the result. This result is either an accept or a reject. The RADIUS server also provides Accounting services that not only allow a network to handle "charge back" to departments that use the remote access system, but also provides for logging and auditing functions.

Typical installation of RADIUS will include a single RADIUS server to handle all the Remote Access Servers. An additional RADIUS could be added to increase redundancy. It is always preferable to not have a single point of failure in an enterprise RAS system. Some companies will have Remote Access Servers at multiple sites and could elect to have a separate RADIUS server at each site. If the various sites are sufficiently linked over a WAN of reasonable speed or over the Internet, a single RADIUS server can be used to handle multiple Remote Access Servers at multiple sites. This allows a single pair of RADIUS servers to be leveraged enterprisewide.

It is useful to understand the steps involved in a typical transaction in which a user is successfully authenticated via RADIUS:

1. A user dials in to a Remote Access Server and PPP negotiation begins.

2. The RAS device passes authentication information, specifically the username and password, to the RADIUS server.

3. If the RADIUS server is able to authenticate the user, it will issue an accept response to the RAS device. The RAS device will also send the profile information required by the RAS to set up the connection. This usually includes IP address, maximum connect time, hours for valid access, and the like.

4. If the RADIUS server is unable to authenticate the user, it issues a reject response to the RAS device, along with a message indicating the reason for denial of access.

5. With this information, the RAS device completes PPP negotiation with the user. If the RAS received an accept response, it can now enable the user to begin accessing the network. If the RAS device received a reject response, it terminates the user's connection. Optionally, the RAS device will display the reason for terminating the connection at the user's terminal.

In an authentication transaction, there is password information that is transmitted between the RADIUS server and the RAS device. The password information is encrypted via secret key that is entered at both the RAS device and the RADIUS server.

This password information originates from the user, usually as part of PPP negotiations. In a sense, the RAS device is just an intermediary device. It is easier to think of the authentication process as being a transaction between the user and the RADIUS server.

There are a few types of authentication transactions used between a remote access user and RAS that are supported by the Windows Server 2003 implementation of RADIUS:

- PAP (Password Authentication Protocol)
- CHAP (Challenge Handshake Authentication Protocol)
- EAP (Extensible Authentication Protocol)

Password Authentication Protocol is a fairly simple protocol. The user sends her password to the RADIUS server, and the RADIUS server validates it. This validation is performed either against RADIUS' own database or against Active Directory. One of the drawbacks to PAP is that the password is initially sent unencrypted. RAS encrypts the password before forwarding it to the RADIUS server and the RADIUS server decrypts it using a shared secret key. Ultimately, the RADIUS server has the password in clear text form and is able to make use of it directly for authentication.

Challenge Handshake Authentication Protocol is much more secure in that it never sends passwords in clear text over any communication link. With CHAP, the RAS device generates a random number (the challenge) and sends it to the user. The user's PPP client creates a digest, which is a one-way encryption, of the password concatenated with the challenge. This digest is sent to the RAS device. Because the digest is a one-way encryption, the RADIUS server cannot recover the password from the digest. It doesn't need to recover the password. Instead it can perform the identical digest operation using its own copy of the user's password stored in its database. If the two digests match, the user is authenticated successfully.

Extensible Authentication Protocol is an extension to the Point-to-Point Protocol (PPP). EAP supports arbitrary authentication methods using credential and information exchanges of arbitrary lengths. EAP was developed as a result of an increasing demand for authentication methods that leveraged third-party security devices and provide an industry-standard architecture to support additional authentication methods within PPP.

## Managing Remote Users with GPOs

One of the most compelling benefits of Active Directory was the ability to manage users and their computers via Group Policy Objects. System settings, services, applications, and many other items could be controlled on a per-user or per-computer basis. One of the classic issues faced by administrators was how to manage remote users so that they were not impacted by their relatively slow connection speed. Publishing full applications to remote users would be a very slow and intrusive process. Taking users and computers in and out of OUs would be nearly impossible to manage to try to reflect their status of local or remote. The easy solution to this issue is to take advantage of the fact that RRAS can hand out its own block of IP addresses. You can pretty safely assume that if a client machine has an IP address that is handed out by the RRAS system, that client is either dialed in or connecting via VPN. By creating a site within Active Directory that contains the subnets owned by the RRAS server, specific GPOs can be applied to that site that take into account the reduced bandwidth.

# Using Site-to-Site VPNs

After VPN use from a site scales past four or five users it is often beneficial to switch architectures from a *client-to-site* VPN to a *site-to-site* VPN. This means that instead of managing individual clients for VPN access, entire networks are connected via an encrypted VPN tunnel. This allows all resources on one side of the tunnel to reach all resources on the other side of the tunnel. This is a common way to replace dedicated WAN connections with less expensive connections. Both sites support local Internet access and a site-to-site VPN provides the secure connection between the two networks. Although the networks might be dozens of hops away from each other, the VPN tunnel makes them appear to be adjacent networks as shown in Figure 18.3.

## Using Windows Server 2003 RRAS for Site-to-Site VPNs

Windows Server 2003 Routing and Remote Access Services supports not only client-to-server VPNs but also site-to-site VPNs. By creating VPN interfaces in addition to having physical interfaces, RRAS is able to route IP traffic not only throughout the network but across VPN connections as well.

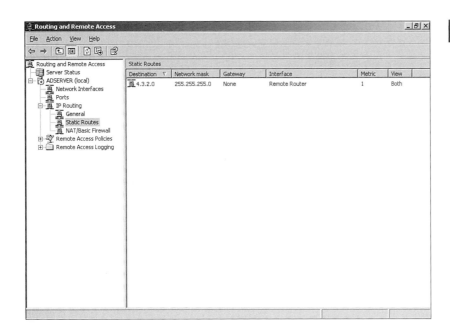

**FIGURE 18.3**
Remote network is one hop away.

To create a site-to-site VPN, do the following:

1. From within the Routing and Remote Access manager, right-click the Network Interfaces and choose to add a new Dial Demand Interface. This will launch the wizard.

2. Click Next and give the interface a name. This name should easily identify the site to which it is connecting (see Figure 18.4).

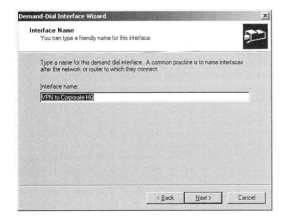

**FIGURE 18.4**    Configuring the interface name.

3. Choose the connection type and the VPN type. Then enter the IP address of the VPN device to which you are connecting. Click Next.

4. Check the box labeled Route IP packets, shown in Figure 18.5, on this interface.

5. Enter the subnets located on the opposite side of the VPN tunnel. This will be entered by the system as a static route through the VPN interface. Click Next.

6. Enter the dial-in credentials for the interface. This account must exist at the other side of the VPN. Click Next and then Finish and the VPN is complete.

# Using Load Balancing to Add Scalability and Resiliency

Both RAS and RADIUS services work well when load balanced. Because neither service is connection-specific, it doesn't matter which device is actually contacted so long as each of the devices provides the services needed. This is to say that a company could have multiple RAS devices that answer to a single identity. In the case of RAS devices, this could mean either a single phone number that is transferred to the next available line or a load-balanced IP address that contacts the RAS device with the lowest load. Similarly these RAS devices can be pointed to the load-balanced address of multiple RADIUS devices to ensure that connections can be validated.

Windows Server 2003 Enterprise and Datacenter editions have built-in support for load balancing. A less expensive solution for load balancing RAS devices for VPNs is to attach to the device via DNS name. By placing multiple records into DNS for the same name that resolve to each of the IP addresses, the connections can be *round-robined* to cause each successive request to reach a different RAS device.

# Summary

You have a number of options available to you when it comes to enabling remote access to corporate data. Modem banks, hardware and software VPNs, native clients, and third-party clients all work with various types and levels of authentication and encryption to allow secured access to data. By allowing access to users when they are outside the office, users are able to increase their productivity.

Technologies like wireless networking offer users amazing flexibility when it comes to accessing the network while away from their office. Conference rooms no longer have to fight over available LAN jacks and facilities that require flexibility in configuration are no longer limited by static wiring. But with this improvement in accessibility comes the potential for insecurity. By treating a wireless connection like a remote access user, you can offer the same level of security and functionality with a minimal increase in management. Not unlike the OSI model, by abstracting the wireless connection to look like a remote access user to the rest of the environment, the remainder of the remote access system is totally unchanged in order to support the wireless users. This philosophy can be used in many aspects of networking to further leverage existing technologies and resources.

This chapter has shown the importance of not only controlling access to a network but also the importance of being able to carefully audit that access. By tracking user access and connection time, a clever administrator will know when it is time to expand connectivity resources. This chapter has shown how connectivity technologies can be used to save money as demand for capacity increases.

You have learned in this chapter that there are many types of authentication available to you and that each type has its own strengths and weaknesses. This chapter has shown options for configuring firewalls to support various types of VPN traffic and has offered workarounds for use with firewalls that do not natively support VPN protocols.

This chapter has shown the differences between various VPN types and has shown which types are appropriate for different situations. This gives you the knowledge you need to support mixed environments.

This chapter has discussed various implementation options and shown how to automate client configuration for protocols that are present in various flavors of Windows. This greatly simplifies the implementation of Remote Access systems and helps you to keep their project costs low.

Remote Access systems can be one of the most valuable resources available to a company. By implementing flexible and resilient failure tolerant Remote Access systems, companies can have employees who are productive whether they are on the road, at home, or in the office. Remote Access systems are also a doorway into the corporate environment and should always be protected and monitored as such.

# 19

# Web Access to Windows Server 2003 Resources

**M**icrosoft has increasingly and quite seamlessly integrated the Internet, such as Web-based accessibility, into the core of Windows. Windows Server 2003 epitomizes this integration and offers a broad spectrum of features aimed at simplifying the way users access and publish information via a Web-like interface. Resources that were once inaccessible while either on the road or otherwise away from the office can now be accessed securely and reliably.

The wide adoption of Web-based functionality and accessibility to access file and print resources from anywhere, anytime has created some security challenges in the past for the Windows administrator. Ensuring that the underlying files and print resources aren't compromised has been quite a daunting challenge. This was, in part, due to many features being installed with the Everyone group enabled and Anonymous access by default. However, Windows Server 2003 is now more secure by default than its predecessors. As a result, you can focus on providing valuable services for your users rather than worrying about locking everything down.

# Best Practices for Publishing Web Shares to the Internet

Web shares, or virtual directories, can be very useful in publishing corporate information to users both inside and outside the company's network. By using the existing server or DFS (distributed file system) shares within the company, administrators and end users can publish content without the use of specialized Web editing tools.

Securing such shares requires you to pay special attention to both the underlying operating system and the method by which the end user is accessing the resources. Using both NTFS permissions and Web-based permissions to ensure the security of the Web shares is the best possible method because it provides a layered approach to securing the Web shares.

You should pay special attention to the root folder of each disk volume. By default Windows Server 2003 installs the Everyone group on the system volume. This is the volume where Windows Server 2003 is installed. By default this group has Read and Execute permissions on any new folders that are created on this volume. It's a best practice to remove this group to avoid leaving the entire directory structure vulnerable to attack.

## Protecting the Perimeter

Companies should always use a firewall plan and an intrusion detection system (IDS) to create a way to monitor traffic to and from their Web servers. It is called a firewall plan because it's not just a hardware or software product. A firewall plan involves multiple products and security planning, including what to do when there is a compromise in the company's security. Compromises will happen; what you do to reduce exposure is an essential part of the plan.

Part of the firewall plan can be virtual private network (VPN) access and some form of Internet authentication services such as the one provided by RADIUS. Both of these services are available on the Windows Server 2003 platform. The VPN approach should be used when accessing any enterprise resources from outside the firewall perimeter. As is discussed later in this chapter, in "Establishing Virtual Directory Permissions," authentication and document access can be provided by front-end Web servers that are placed between two firewalls in what is known as a demilitarized zone (DMZ).

## Protecting the Server Content

There are numerous best practices for protecting Web servers facing the Internet. Here are just a few ways to reduce the impact of a security breach:

- If you have the server resources, do not host the Internet Information Services (IIS) server on a domain controller or even a domain member if possible. The less participation the IIS server has with the domain the better (from a security standpoint).

- Enable only the services that the server will be hosting. Inadvertently forgetting that a service is on or not yet configured is probably the biggest security risk on an IIS server.

- Secure the NTFS permissions on the partition where the operating system is loaded. Remove nonessential groups and allow only administrators and designated groups access to the OS partition and its folders.

- Move the Web and FTP root directories to a partition other than where the operating system resides. This ensures that if a traversal of directories takes place the attackers do not have access to operating system or IIS functions.

## Following the HTTP Authentication Request

IIS authentication is the front line of defense in the access authorization process. When a user makes an HTTP request for a Web page several security-related steps take place. The sequence of events is as follows:

1. Is the request coming from an IP address, subnet, or domain name that has authorized access?

2. Is the user required to authenticate with a username and password or .NET Passport?

3. Do the IIS permissions allow the specific HTTP action the client is requesting?

4. If the virtual directory is located on another host, do the UNC share permissions allow access?

5. Finally, do the NTFS permissions allow the authenticated user or anonymous account access to the OS resource?

Following the order in which IIS allows access makes your troubleshooting efforts easier. By turning off or lessening levels of authentication you can determine which authentication method might be disallowing the delivery of the Web content to the end-user.

## Allowing Trusted Networks

Narrowing the field of possible vulnerabilities is one of your best tools in protecting Web-based content. By allowing only trusted IP addresses or disallowing known abusers to access the Web content you can keep your eyes on efficiency. To enable or disable IP addresses, IP ranges, or domains perform the following steps:

1. Open IIS Manager, and click on the desired server.

2. Right-click on the Web site you want to protect, and choose Properties.

3. Click on the Directory Security tab, and select Edit in the IP Address and Domain Name Restrictions section.

**4.** Initially the By Default, All Computers Will Be Granted Access radio button is selected. You now have two possible options:

- Choose the Granted Access radio button and then choose Add. This option enables you to Deny Access to individual IP addresses, Groups of computers (by subnet), or by Domain names.

- Choose the Denied Access radio button and then choose Add. This option gives you the ability to Allow Access to known trusted IP addresses, Groups of computers (by subnet), or trusted Domains.

The method by which you choose to limit access will most likely depend on whether the Web site will be used solely on an intranet, in which you should allow access by domain name. If the Web site is going to be accessed via the Internet as well, you might have to grant access to domains as well as front-end Web servers and known IP addresses or subnets of users.

## Creating the Virtual Directory

**IIS Administrator Needs to Allow Either Browse or Directory Browsing**

To allow content to be viewed that doesn't have an HTML formatted home page, the IIS administrator needs to allow either Browse or Directory Browsing. Otherwise an error page will appear instead of the desired folder contents.

To publish content to the company's intranet or to an SSL-secured Internet site, you need to create a Web site in IIS and then Virtual Directories under that Web root. These Virtual Directories can exist in the directory structure of the server that IIS is running on, or a UNC (Universal Naming Convention) path. These Virtual Directories can be created either from the IIS Management console or in the file system using Explorer.

### Creating a Virtual Directory with IIS Manager

To create a Virtual Directory in the Internet Information Services (IIS) Manager, perform the following steps:

**1.** Right-click on the Web site to which you want to publish.

**2.** Select New, Virtual Directory.

**3.** The Virtual Directory Creation Wizard opens; click Next.

**4.** Fill in the Virtual Directory Alias box. (This should be an abbreviated version of the directory or UNC that will be published.) Click Next.

**5.** Fill in the Path box (this can either be a folder located on the IIS server or a UNC path to a share). Click Next.

- If the Path box was filled in with a locally hosted folder the Virtual Directory Access Permissions page will be displayed. Choose the appropriate permissions and click Next.

- If the Path box was filled in with a UNC path, the Security Credentials page will be displayed. Either fill in the desired username and password of an individual user or select the check box stating Always Use the Authenticated User's Credentials When Validating Access to the Network Resource and click Next.

6. Finally, click Finish.

### Creating a Virtual Directory with Windows Explorer

You have the option of creating a Web site Virtual Directory through the Windows Explorer. This is an easy way to publish content quickly that resides on the IIS server without opening up the IIS Manager tool. To create a Web share, perform the following steps:

1. On the IIS server navigate to the desired drive and right-click on a folder to share, and then select Properties.

2. Click on the Web Sharing tab and select the desired Web site from the pull-down menu.

3. Select the Share This Folder radio button shown in Figure 19.1. The Edit Alias dialog box appears.

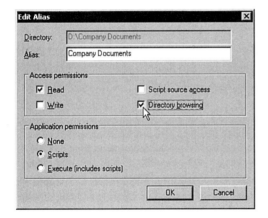

**FIGURE 19.1**   The Edit Alias dialog box.

4. Enter an abbreviated Alias for the Virtual Directory. Also select the appropriate Access Permissions and Application Permissions for this folder. Click OK twice.

## Establishing Virtual Directory Permissions

When creating either a new Web site or a virtual directory under that site, you must decide who will have access, and of which type to the published content. A preferred method of protecting the content is by first choosing the access rights to the content.

### Securing Virtual Directories Mapped to Local Directories

IIS Virtual Directories that reside on the local server are secured by both the underlying NTFS permissions and the permissions granted through IIS. To set the permissions on a locally hosted Virtual Directory perform the following steps in IIS Manager:

1. Right-click on the virtual directory to secure, and then select Properties.

2. On the Virtual Directory tab find the section called Local Path.

3. In the Local Path section, select the desired boxes that are associated with access permissions:

    ■ Script Source Success. Used with IIS features such as FrontPage and WebDAV to allow access to executable content as long as Read or Write, or both are enabled.

    ■ Read. Allows the browser to read content published within the virtual directory folders. If this box is checked without any others being checked it creates a read-only scenario.

    ■ Write. This option is desirable when publishing folders where contributors might post content such as a document repository or through IIS tools programs like FrontPage and WebDAV.

    ■ Directory Browsing. You should enable this feature when no home page document is present in the root folder of the virtual directory. This feature is useful when publishing a set of folders and documents that might normally reside on a file server in a legacy Windows environment.

### Securing Virtual Directories Mapped to Windows Shares

As described previously, virtual directories can point to UNC paths containing content hosted on other servers or workstations on the local area network. Shares can have their own permissions as well. It's a best practice to leave the share permission to Everyone Full Access. This method makes it much easier to track the applied permissions on folders and files within the enterprise.

Placing permissions on the folders and down to the files, if desired, allows for more granular management and auditing of file access. NTFS permissions enable you to discretely allow or deny any group or user permissions down to the file level. Authentication either directly from the Web site or passed through to the host of the UNC share will determine the permissions allowed to that user.

IIS 6.0 now allows you to use pass-through Web authentication to UNC share and NTFS permissions. Simply put, the Web server sends the authentication request on to the server or workstation that is hosting the virtual directory UNC resource and asks permission for access. The steps to allow this process to take place are as follows:

1. Open IIS Manager, select the server and click on Web Sites, and then the Web site that is hosting the virtual directory.

2. Right-click on the virtual directory to secure and click Properties.

3. Click on the Connect As button located next to the Network Directory box containing the UNC path.

4. In the Network Directory Security Credentials dialog box you can choose either of the following:

   - Choose a static User Name and Password to authenticate against the remote UNC share and NTFS permissions.

   - Use delegation to pass the Web user's username and password to the computer hosting the UNC share. To do this select the Always Use the Authenticated User's Credentials When Validating Access to the Network Resource check box. When this box is checked the User Name and Password boxes become grayed-out.

## Choosing Proper User Access Controls

Just as you set permissions on traditional file shares, you must also take this approach on directories and files exposed via IIS virtual directories. There are also several options related to Web content access as mentioned in the "Securing Virtual Directories Mapped to Local Directories" section earlier in this chapter.

As stated previously, there are several lines of defense—at the IIS level, at the share level, and at the file level. How you choose to secure their shared data depends quite a bit on their installed environment. Creating the IIS 6.0 virtual directories will definitely give you more tools and levels of authentication than ever before. To choose the proper authentication method you need to take the following steps:

1. Open IIS Manager, select the server, and double-click on Web Sites.

2. Right-click on the Web site that is hosting the virtual directory, and then choose Properties.

3. In the Web Site Properties dialog box, choose the Directory Security tab, and then choose Edit in the Authentication and Access Control section.

4. In the Authentication Methods dialog box you are presented with several choices, as shown in Figure 19.2. The options and their function are as follows:

   - Enable Anonymous Access, in which a default "IUSR_MachineName" User Name and Password are prefilled in. This option should only be used for nonsecure publishing of content, in which the user's identity is less important for tracking access.

   - In the Authenticated Access section you have the following choices:

     Integrated Windows Authentication—This option is checked by default and is the easiest to use in a Windows domain environment. Internet Explorer works well with this authentication method.

Digest Authentication for Windows Domain Servers—This method is best used to selectively grant access to users in select realms. This is much easier to do within strictly a Windows Server 2003 environment. In a mixed environment with both Windows 2000 and 2003 IIS sub-authentication must be installed and configured.

Basic Authentication (Password Is Sent in Clear Text)—This method should only be used when the client's credentials are being sent through SSL, VPN, or on an intranet that is secured. If you need to support browsers other than Internet Explorer they must use this method.

.NET Passport Authentication—If you choose this method, all other authentication methods are unavailable. This method should only be chosen if your Web sites are enabled to work with .NET Passport authentication from the Microsoft servers.

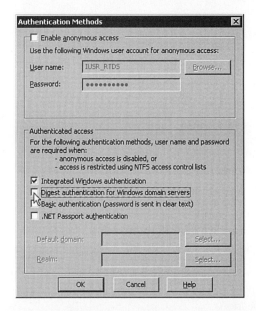

**FIGURE 19.2**    Authentication methods.

# Securing Access to Resources with SSL

You need to be constantly aware of risks associated with giving access to users outside the company. This is especially true with Web traffic that is traversing numerous unknown and possibly unsecure networks. Network packet analyzers are constantly looking for key words and phrases such as "username" or "password". Using Secure Sockets Layer (SSL) encryption you can make sure that authentication of the Web folders on their IIS servers is not being passed in the clear.

# Enabling SSL on a Web Server Directory

SSL can be applied to an entire Web site, directories (including virtual directories), or just certain files within the site. You can specify which sections of the Web site are secured using SSL through the Internet Information Services (IIS) Manager. This Microsoft Management Console (MMC) snap-in should also be used in conjunction with authentication methods and access control lists (ACLs) to ensure that access to those resources is as secure as possible.

> **SSL Requires an X.509 Digital Certificate**
>
> SSL requires an X.509 digital certificate that can be obtained either from a trusted certificate authority such as Verisign or from the company's public key infrastructure (PKI).

To assign a certificate to a Web site it must first be requested and then installed. The request can either be created to obtain a certificate from an external Trusted Certificate Authority (CA), or when used internally from a standalone root CA or Enterprise CA within the organization's PKI infrastructure. For example, to request and install a certificate from an internal Enterprise CA the following steps should be performed:

1. Open IIS Manager; expand the desired computer, Web sites, and the desired Web site to assign the certificate.

2. Right-click on the Web site and select Properties.

3. On the Directory Security tab, select Server Certificate located in the secure communications section.

4. The Web Server Certificate Wizard will open; click Next.

5. Choose the Create a New Certificate button and click Next.

6. Select the Prepare Request Now, But Send It Later button and click Next.

7. Type a "friendly" name in the dialog box and choose the desired Bit Length for the encryption key then click Next.

8. Type the company's legal name in the Organization box and the responsible department for either this site or the company's security department in the Organization Unit box, and then click Next.

9. Type the name of the computer hosting the Web site in the Common Name box. If the site will be accessed from the Internet be sure to fill in the fully qualified domain name, such as server.domain.com. Click Next.

> `The name on the security certificate is invalid or does not match the name of the site`
>
> The Common Name in step 9 is the name that the certificate is published with and is checked against for validity. If this name does not match the URL exactly the user will receive an error stating `The name on the security certificate is invalid or does not match the name of the site.`

10. Select a Country or Region from the first pull-down menu and type in the State/Province and City/Locality that will be embedded in the certificate; click Next.

**11.** Enter an easily remembered filename, including path, or browse for a desired location and enter the filename in that path. (This file is important and will be used in subsequent steps. Note its name and location.) Click Next.

**12.** The next screen is called the Request File Summary. If there are any errors, select the Back button and navigate to the page where the data was entered and correct it now. If everything looks correct click Next and then Finish.

After the certificate is requested it can be sent to an external trusted certificate authority. This is usually the case when the SSL secured content is going to be viewed by customers. If the SSL secured pages are going to be viewed internally or by users who can be instructed on how to install an internally generated certificate, the less costly option is to generate the certificate with the internal PKI services. To process the certificate request internally follow these steps:

**1.** Enter the URL of the company's IIS server that is hosting Certificate Services (for example, http://servername/certsrv).

**2.** If a sign-in dialog box appears, enter a username and password with sufficient privileges to generate the certificate and click OK.

**3.** On the initial Welcome page select Request a Certificate.

**4.** On the Request a Certificate page select Submit an Advanced Certificate Request.

**5.** On the Advanced Certificate Request page select Submit a Certificate Request By Using a Base 64-encoded CMC or PKCS #10 File, or Submit a Renewal Request By Using a Base-64-encoded PKCS #7 File.

**6.** On the Submit a Certificate Request or Renewal Request page, click on Browse for a File to Insert link, click on the Browse button and find the certificate request text file created in the previous section.

**7.** When the filename appears in the Full Path Name box click on the Read button. The Saved Request box will now be populated with the text that was contained in the certificate request.

**8.** Under the Certificate Template section use the pull down to select the Web Server selection and then click the Submit button.

**9.** On the Certificate Issued page, select the Download Certificate link. When prompted select Save and Select a Folder and Desired Filename to save the certificate. When the download is complete click Close and then close the browser window.

**10.** Open IIS Manager and navigate to the Web site for which the certificate was created.

**11.** Right-click on the Web site and select Properties.

**12.** Click on the Directory Security tab and select the Server Certificate button.

**13.** Click Next on the initial Server Certificate Wizard page.

**14.** Select Process the Pending Request and Install the Certificate, and then click Next.

**15.** Browse for the certificate file that was created in the previous steps and select it (this will be a filename ending in .cer). Click Next.

**16.** On the SSL Port page enter the desired SSL listening port for this Web site (443 is default). Click Next.

**17.** On the Certificate Summary page the information from the certificate response file is displayed. Ensure that the correct filename and corresponding information is displayed. If it's not, click on the Back button and choose the correct file. If the information is correct click Next, and then Finish.

After the certificate is installed on the site all three buttons under the Secure Communications section of the Directory Security tab become available for selection.

# Enabling and Securing Internet Printing

Internet Printing Protocol (IPP) is defined in the Internet engineering task force (IETF) request for comment (RFC) 2910. IPP is a useful tool that can simplify the publishing and management of printers within an enterprise. You can use this tool to expose printer shares to both their intranet Remote Procedure Call (RPC) and Internet (HTTP) users.

RPC offers more features and is the preferred method of connecting to printers in an intranet environment. If the user's Internet Explorer security is set Medium to High he will connect via HTTP. For the user to acquire a True-connect like a UNC share over RPC, his Internet Explorer security settings must be set to medium-low. Microsoft is focusing on more features on the RPC capabilities over the HTTP IPP feature set.

Standard Windows Server 2003 print server shares can be exposed via IPP through the use of a simple URL such as http://<servername>/printers. This enables users to connect and automatically configure printers and administrators to view and manage print queues from a single Web page per IPP-enabled print server.

## Installing and Configuring Internet Printing Protocol (IPP)

On a Windows Server 2003 with IIS 6.0, Internet Printing and Active Server Pages (required for Web-based printer management) are not installed by default. To install these required services you must perform the following steps:

**1.** Go to Control Panel, choose Add/Remove Programs, and then Add Remove Windows Components.

**2.** Open Application Server, Internet Information Services (IIS) and then select Internet Printing, as shown in Figure 19.3.

**3.** Finally, go to World Wide Web Service, select Active Server Pages, and then select OK.

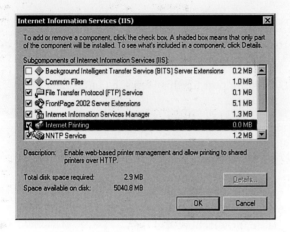

**FIGURE 19.3**
Installing Internet Printing Service.

With HTTP, the print server generates a .cab file that contains the required .inf and installation files and sends the .cab file to the client. On the client computer, the .cab file starts the Add Printer Wizard to complete the installation. A progress bar is displayed in the browser while the printer drivers are being installed.

### Securing Internet Printing

You must pay special attention to printers that you've shared to intranet and Internet users. Removing the Everyone group and allowing only authenticated domain users or defined security groups print access is a best practice. The security on the printer is set at the share level as follows:

1. Click on Start and then click Printers and Faxes.

2. Right-click on the desired printer and select Sharing.

3. On the Security tab, select the Everyone group and click the Remove button.

4. To select groups with Print, Manage Printers, Manage Documents, or Special Permissions access, click on the Add button and choose the appropriate Active Directory security groups. Then select the Desired Level of Access check box under the Allow column.

## Best Practices for Securing FTP Services

File Transfer Protocol (FTP) has been used effectively for many years on the Internet. This protocol is very efficient at serving up static documents for download or for anonymously posting material to a folder. With the ease of use comes widespread abuse. Many FTP sites are set up carelessly and left wide open for illegal trading of copyrighted files and hijacked storage space for hackers.

You should know what your FTP sites are going to used for in advance of implementation. Simple downloads can be accomplished safely by imposing a few basic rules. Creating a useful posting space for company employees, clients, or partners can be done quite easily, with some planning and the appropriate settings.

## Enabling FTP Services

On Windows Server 2003 and IIS 6.0 the FTP server service is not installed by default. This is due to IIS being locked down by default. Too many IIS servers were installed with FTP services left with the default TO allow Anonymous users read and write access. This is part of the overall plan of leave the service off unless it's going to be used.

To install FTP services you must perform the following steps:

1. Go to the Control Panel and choose Add/Remove Programs. Then choose Add/Remove Windows Components.

2. Next open the Application Server and then Internet Information Services (IIS).

3. Finally, choose File Transfer Protocol (FTP) Service, as shown in Figure 19.4, and then select OK.

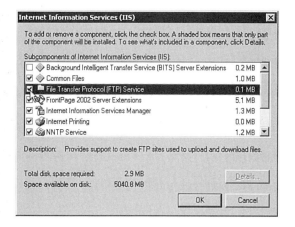

**FIGURE 19.4**
Installing FTP Services.

### Configuring Secure Anonymous FTP Access

In many scenarios documents and drivers are shared with the public from files stored on an FTP server. This can be done safely by locking down the folders with NTFS permissions on the published folder. In the case of public access like this, there should be a minimal number of entries in the permissions on those folders. The Anonymous alias should have read-only access and the group responsible for posting content should have read/write access.

### Configuring FTP Logging

FTP logging can be used to track access of the FTP site and for troubleshooting logon issues as well as other valuable statistics.

Choose W3C Extended Log File Format. This format has the most comprehensive list of available logging options.

Move the log file directory to the root of your IIS FTP server folder as a best practice. This will make it easier to find that log file if multiple sites are configured.

### Hardening Folder Permissions

When Anonymous is disabled, the permissions on the root folder that the FTP user is accessing grants or denies what that user can do. You should take special care in removing unnecessary users from that folder and propagating permissions to the subfolders.

### Configuring FTP Blind-Put Access

*Blind-put access* describes a method of hosting an FTP site where the user has only write access. Read access is left off at both the Home Directory and the folder being accessed.

### Enforcing Disk Quotas

> **Windows Server 2003 Enforces Disk Quotas**
>
> Windows Server 2003 enforces disk quotas by user only. To enforce quotas on a larger scale, commercially available products such as NTP Software's Quota & File Sentinel allows for management of disk quotas by groups and other criteria.

Administrators of IIS FTP servers should take advantage of the operating system storage features. Disk quotas have been available for some time now. One of the best applications of this functionality is to prevent users from filling up hard disk space. In the case of FTP, creating quotas on users of this service minimizes the danger of someone hijacking an account and using the FTP server as a storage point for illegally copied movies, MP3 files, and so on.

### Using Logon Time Restrictions

When used in conjunction with FTP services logon time restrictions can help reduce the exposure of the server during nonworking hours when no one is around to monitor the server.

### Restricting Access by IP Address or Range

One of the first items IIS checks is the permitted or excluded IP address range of the client requesting data. Protecting FTP from unwanted attack can be narrowed down that much more by limiting the range of allowed IP addresses.

### Auditing FTP Events

By monitoring the FTP logging constantly, you can see problems with failed logon attempts and other malicious behavior. By using tools such as Web Trends to analyze user traffic and folder usage, you can block IP addresses or domains that are constantly attempting to logon. You can also use the logging to see when valid users are having trouble opening their home directories or being locked out due to authentication problems.

### Enforcing Strong Passwords

Enforcing the use of strong passwords is one of the keys to securing FTP services. Windows Server 2003 allows you to enforce user's compliance with strong password requirements by enabling the Passwords Must Meet Complexity Requirements Policy. This option is located in the Local Security Policy (standalone server), or Group Policy (Domain member).

### Enabling Account Lockout and Account Lockout Threshold

FTP server accounts are very popular targets for password cracking programs that often use an exhaustive list of passwords in an attempt to guess the correct password. You can greatly reduce the success of such an attack by enabling the Password Policy settings in either the Local Security Policy or Group Policy. When an attacker tries repeatedly to log in with a valid username and bad password the account should be set to lock.

### FTP User Isolation

By limiting the FTP user to her home folder you create yet another barrier of protection for the underlying system. When the user logs on with her FTP username and password she is placed in her home directory and cannot traverse up the directory tree.

> **Only Newly Created Sites Have the Option of User Isolation Authentication**
>
> The Default FTP server cannot be placed in User Isolation mode. Only newly created sites have the option of User Isolation authentication.

# Accessing Resources with Terminal Services and Remote Desktops

With local drive mapping now available Windows Server 2003 Terminal Services is a great way to work with computers remotely. Remote Desktop allows access to documents and corporate applications that might not be available on the local machine.

## Allowing Remote Desktop Control

By default Remote Desktop is disabled on Windows XP and Windows Server 2003. You need to perform the following to enable Remote Desktop control:

> **The Domain Administrator Has Remote Desktop Access**
>
> By default (in a domain environment) the domain administrator has Remote Desktop access after this feature is enabled.

1. Right-click on My Computer and choose Properties.

2. Click on the Remote tab.

3. Click on the Allow Users to Connect Remotely to This Computer check box in the Remote Desktop section.

4. Click on the Select Remote Users to Add Authorized Users to Access This Computer.

## Securing Terminal Services

Terminal Services is one of the more popular remote control programs for Windows. It also has a pretty well-known port (3389) and therefore is well port scanned. It is a good practice to change this port to avoid unwanted Remote Desktop connections.

To change the port number that Terminal Services listens on, perform the following:

1. Run Regedt32.exe and navigate to the following key:

   LOCAL_MACHINE\System\CurrentControlSet\Control\Terminal Server\WinStations\ RDP-Tcp

2. In the Details pane find the PortNumber subkey and double-click on it.

> **Place the Port Number After the Server Name**
>
> The RDP or Terminal Services client must connect to the same port number that Terminal Services is now listening on. Place the port number after the server name (for example: server.domain.com:4555).

3. In the Base section of the window choose the Decimal radio button. The number now in the Value Data box, by default, will be 3389. Change this to any high port number that is not being used in the company for another service. Before closing the window change the Base value back to Hexadecimal, and then click OK.

4. For the listening port number to take effect, Terminal Services must be restarted. At the command prompt type **net stop termservice** and then **net start termservice**.

# Monitoring IIS Access Through Auditing and Logging

One of the most important factors in server security is awareness. Logging and auditing allow you to monitor suspicious activity as well as establish a normal baseline of user interaction with server resources.

The standard Windows Server 2003 installation doesn't have auditing turned on by default. One reason for this is that on a busy server over-auditing can fill up event logs and drag down system resources. You need to be selective in what you choose to audit.

IIS 6.0 does have logging turned on, but it might not be a suitable configuration for all cases. The default directory for log files is %winddowsroot%\system32\LogFiles. You might want to place your log files under a directory that better identifies the logs. Also, as mentioned earlier in this chapter, it's better to create the IIS data folders on a partition other than where the operating system resides.

## Auditing Security and Site Content

You should enable both successful and failed login attempts to the IIS server that is hosting the Web sites and FTP services. This can be both a good troubleshooting tool, when the sites are first established, and a security measure over time. You should watch your Security event logs for repeated failed logon attempts. This could point out an attack or simply a user who forgot his password and needs it to be reset.

### Enabling Security Auditing

On the Web server security auditing needs to be enabled and configured. There are two possible scenarios for enabling auditing. The first is on a standalone server that is not a member of the domain. The second is a member-server.

To enable or modify auditing policy settings on a standalone Web server follow these steps:

1. Click on Start, Administrative Tools and then choose Local Security Policy.

2. In the console tree, click Local Policies and then click Audit Policy.

3. In the Details pane, double-click on the desired event category.

4. On the Properties page for that event category select both Success and Failure and then click OK.

To enable or modify the auditing policy settings for an event category on a server that is a domain member perform the following steps:

> **Auditing Group Policy**
>
> Defining this Auditing Group Policy is performed on the domain controller.

1. Click on Start, Administrative Tools and then Active Directory Users and Computers.

2. Right-click on the desired domain, site, or organizational unit (OU) and click Properties.

3. On the Group Policy tab, select or create a Group Policy object to edit.

4. In the Group Policy Object Editor console tree expand Computer Configuration, Windows Settings, Security Settings, Local Policy, and then click Audit.

5. In the Details pane, double-click on the desired event category.

6. If the auditing policy has not been set for this event select Define These Policy Settings check box.,

7. Enable auditing by clicking either Success or Failure or both and then click OK.

### Enabling Web Site Content Auditing

Web server administrators need to be especially aware of content changes on their Web sites. Due to the fact that most Web sites, either intranet or Internet facing, contain mostly static pages or templates, content changes are usually planned events by specific users. Tracking any change attempts by un-authorized users is a good way to reduce attacks such as de-facing of the site where content is replaced by a hacker's slogan or undesired content.

Auditing of file or folder objects is defined on their perspective Property pages. Before auditing becomes active it must be enabled by the administrator or a designee that has Manage auditing and security log rights.

To enable object access auditing on a standalone server follow these steps:

1. Click on Start, Administrative Tools, and then click Local Security Policy.

2. Expand Local Policies and then click Audit Policy.

3. Right-click on Audit Object Access and select Properties.

4. Enable auditing by clicking either Success or Failure or both and then click OK.

To enable object access auditing on a domain member server perform the following steps:

1. Click on Start, Administrative Tools, and then Active Directory Users and Computers.

2. Right-click on the desired domain, site, or organizational unit (OU) and click Properties.

3. On the Group Policy tab, select or create a Group Policy object to edit.

4. In the Group Policy Object Editor console tree expand Windows Settings, Security Settings, Local Policy, and then Audit Policy.

5. Double-click on Audit Object Access.

6. Ensure that the Define These Policy Settings check box has been selected.

7. Enable auditing by clicking either Success or Failure or both, and then click OK.

Now that the object access policy has been enabled you can define the auditing policy settings for folders or files contained in the Web site. To apply or modify auditing policy settings perform the following steps:

1. Navigate in Windows Explorer to the desired folder within the Web site.

2. Right-click on the folder or file that you want to audit and then select Properties.

3. Select the Security tab.

4. Click on the Advanced button and then select the Auditing tab.

5. At this point you can either Add, Remove, or Edit Users or Groups that are being audited.

6. In the Apply Onto box, indicate what actions are to be audited.

7. In the Access box, indicate which actions are to be audited.

8. To stop auditing on this container, click Clear All.

9. If you want to audit subfolders as well as the current folder, ensure that the Apply These Auditing Entries to Objects and/or Containers Within This Container Only check box is cleared.

### Consolidating Log Files

Administrators who have to maintain numerous Web and FTP sites will find that writing the log files of each site to a central location becomes more convenient. One way to accomplish this is by enabling centralized binary logging. The steps to accomplish this are as follows:

1. At a command window, change to the following directory: c:\inetpub\AdminScripts\.

2. Type **cscript.exe adsutil.vbs SET W3SVC/CentralBinaryLoggingEnabled true.**

3. Press Enter. You will see the Windows Script Host version number and Microsoft copyright information followed by CentralBinaryLoggingEnabled: <BOOLEAN> True.

4. Stop the Web services by typing **net stop W3SVC** and then press Enter.

5. Start the Web services by typing **net start W3SVC** and then press Enter.

For detailed output of this procedure see Figure 19.5.

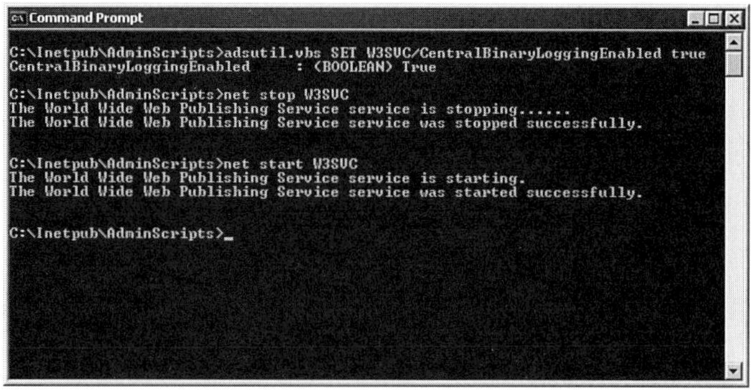

**FIGURE 19.5**
Consolidating log files using ADSI utilities.

This procedure will create a new file in the C:\windows\system32\logfiles\w3svc directory with the name format of rawyymmddhh.ibl. The .ibl extension stands for Internet binary log. This extension change ensures that text editors, by default, do not attempt to open these files.

You can use the Log Parsing Tool 2.1 that ships with the IIS 6.0 Resource Kit, or downloadable from Microsoft's Web site, to run queries against the .ibl files. The Microsoft script center Web site at http://www.microsoft.com/technet/scriptcenter/ has examples of how to use the Logfile Parsing Tool.

### Log File Definitions

As mentioned previously the W3C Extended Logging offers the most comprehensive list of events occurring on the IIS 6.0 Web and FTP servers. Tables 19.1 and 19.2 contain the field name definitions and descriptions of the log file content.

**TABLE 19.1**

**W3C Extended Logging Prefix Definitions**

| Prefix | Meaning |
| --- | --- |
| s- | Server actions |
| c- | Client actions |
| cs- | Client-to-server actions |
| sc- | Server-to-client actions |

**TABLE 19.2**

**W3C Extended Logging Field Definitions**

| Field | Appears As | Description |
|---|---|---|
| Date | date | Date that the activity occurred. |
| Time | time | Time that the activity occurred. |
| Client IP | c-ip | The IP address of the client accessing the server. |
| User Name | cs-username | The name of the authenticated user who accessed the server. (Anonymous users are represented by a hyphen.) |
| Service Name | s-sitename | The Internet service and instance number that was accessed by the client. |
| Server Name | s-computername | The name of the server that generated the log entry. |
| Server IP Address | s-ip | The IP address of the server on which the log entry was generated. |
| Server Port | s-port | The port number the client connected to. |
| Method | cs-method | The action the client was attempting to perform (such as **GET** or **PUT**). |
| URI Stem | cs-uri-stem | The resource access (such as default.asp). |
| URI Query | cs-uri-query | The query, if any, the client was attempting to perform. |
| Protocol Status | sc-status | The status of the action, in HTTP or FTP terms. |
| Win32 Status | sc-win32 status | The status of the action, in terms used by Microsoft Windows. |
| Bytes Sent | sc-bytes | The number of bytes sent by the server. |
| Bytes Received | cs-bytes | The number of bytes received by the server. |
| Time Taken | time-taken | The duration of time, in milliseconds, that the action consumed. |
| Protocol Version | cs-version | The protocol (HTTP, FTP) version used by the client (Example HTTP or HTTP 1.1). |
| Host | cs-host | Displays the contents of the host header that the client is requesting. |
| User Agent | Cs(user-Agent) | The browser being used by the client. |
| Cookie | cs (Cookie) | The content of the cookie sent or received, if any. |
| Referrer | cs (Referrer) | The previous site visited by the user that provided a link to the current site. |

# Using Windows Tools and Scripts to Manage IIS

You can use a variety of tools to manage your IIS 6.0 Web sites and permissions. Microsoft has provided many new tools for use at the command line and through scripting.

You can use IIS Manager to create, edit, or delete sites and properties. You can also use VBScript to perform those same tasks. If the task needs to be repeated several times, scripts are usually more efficient tools. If you want to see the status of the network or items such as disk space, the command line instruction might be faster.

## Using the GUI to Manage IIS

For simple one-time management requirements the IIS Manager MMC console works fine. If you need to set up a new FTP site quickly, creating or editing a script might take too long. A simple rule to follow is: if you have to do it more than twice automate it.

## Using Command-Line Administration

You often use the Windows command console to quickly find out status of a machine or the network. Examples of this are using ping to check the status of a network resource or running ipconfig to see what the IP addresses are associated with the network interfaces on the local machine.

Taking this logical approach one step further is the Windows Management Command Line (WMIC). This tool makes it easier for you to access WMI for quick tasks.

## Managing IIS with ADSI Utilities

To see items such as which servers are bound to which TCP port number on the current server, they might run a command line request such as the adsutil.vbs example shown in Figure 19.6.

**FIGURE 19.6**
Show server bindings using ADSI utilities.

## Using Windows Management Instrumentation (WMI)

In the past you could use WMI to passively monitor your network and servers. In the latest version of WMI you can also make changes to parameters of those networks and servers. There are two ways to use WMI to manage IIS. The first is via the Windows Scripting Host (WScript.exe) and the second with through the console, or command line with CScript.exe.

Windows Server 2003 has more than 6,000 managed resource properties that can monitored by WMI. Of these resources, more than 140 can be configured by WMI.

IIS 6.0 places some sample scripts in the Windows\System32 directory. These scripts are written in the Microsoft Visual Basic scripting language and use the IIS 6.0 WMI provider to access configuration information within the IIS metabase. The included scripts are as follows:

**Console-based Scripts Run with the CScript Engine**

Console-based scripts run with the CScript engine. To force the WScript.Echo lines to display in the Command Prompt window call your script preceding it with CScript //nologo.

- IISapp.vbs—List process IDs and application pool IDs for currently running worker processes.

- IISback.vbs—Back up or restore IIS 6.0 configuration.

- IISftp.vbs—Create, delete, start, stop, and list FTP sites.

- IISftpdr.vbs—Create, delete, or display virtual directories under a given root.

- IISconfg.vbs—Export and import IIS 6.0 configuration to an XML file.

- IISext.vbs—Configure Web service extensions.

- IISweb.vbs—Create, delete, start, stop, and list Web sites.

- IISvdir.vbs—Create and delete virtual directories, or display the virtual directories of a given root.

### Monitoring Hard Disk Space

One of the important duties of an IIS administrator is making sure that the drives don't fill up and crash the server. The following is a sample script to monitor hard disk utilization:

```
Const LOCAL_HARD_DISK = 3
strComputer = "servername"
Set objWMIService = GetObject("winmgmts:" _
& "{impersonationLevel=impersonate}!\\" & strComputer & "\root\cimv2")
Set colMonitoredDisks = objWMIService.ExecNotificationQuery _
("Select * from __instancemodificationevent within 30 where " _
& "TargetInstance isa 'Win32_LogicalDisk'")
i = 0
Do While i = 0
Set objDiskChange = colMonitoredDisks.NextEvent
If objDiskChange.TargetInstance.DriveType = LOCAL_HARD_DISK Then
If objDiskChange.TargetInstance.Size < 10000000000 Then
Wscript.Echo "Hard disk space is below 10000000000 bytes."
End If
End If
Loop
```

If the hard disk on the local machine drops below 10GB free then a dialog box pops up on the screen and says Hard disk space is below 10000000000 bytes. This is just a simple example using Windows Scripting and WMI to monitor computers on the network.

Obviously an IIS administrator wouldn't be standing at the console of the IIS server waiting to see if the hard disk space is running out. A more realistic scenario would be to have the preceding script monitoring the group of computers running IIS and FTP send an e-mail if the drive space dropped below a certain number of bytes free.

### Querying Log Files for Stop Errors

You need to know pertinent information when monitoring the health of your servers. Poring over hundreds or thousands of entries to find meaningful errors can be tedious. The following is a sample script to query the System event log on the local machine for stop errors that have the string SaveDump in them:

```
strComputer = "servername"
Set objWMIService = GetObject("winmgmts:" _
& "{impersonationLevel=impersonate}!\\" & strComputer & "\root\cimv2")
Set colLoggedEvents = objWMIService.ExecQuery _
("Select * from Win32_NTLogEvent Where Logfile = 'System'" _
& " and SourceName = 'SaveDump'")
For Each objEvent in colLoggedEvents
Wscript.Echo "Event date: " & objEvent.TimeGenerated
Wscript.Echo "Description: " & objEvent.Message
Next
```

This script is an example of how you might parse through very large log files and only extract the data that helps them troubleshoot hard errors on their servers.

# Summary

Creating alternative ways to access data stored in a Windows environment with tools such as Web folders, Internet Printing Protocol, and FTP services allows you great flexibility over where the data is stored and how it is accessed. By using some of the examples outlined in this chapter you will be able to give easier visibility and possibly more secure access to your company's data.

# 20

## Leveraging Thin Client Terminal Services

Long ago the world of computing was a centralized world. Giant mainframes and "dumb terminals" were the norm. Then came the personal computer. The PC revolutionized traditional thinking and put the power into the hands of the end users; decentralization was all the rage throughout the computing world.

Now things are coming full circle. Supporting thousands of individual desktops is a very tedious, complicated, and expensive task. With new versions of software being released constantly, operating system patches, virus definitions, end users who like to "experiment" with their PC, buggy code causing system crashes, and so on, now smaller IT staffs have an almost impossible task of keeping up. One method of combating these problems is to flash back to the past and move again toward centralized computing. You can now take back the power and manage a dozen servers instead of a thousand desktops. Using Microsoft Terminal Services is one way of doing this. In theory you could never have to manage applications on the end user's desktop again. By centralizing the applications and running them via Terminal Services you could significantly reduce the amount of time and money spent on maintaining end user desktops.

Using Terminal Services can also reduce hardware costs for an organization. Any computer capable of running Windows 95 or later is a candidate for being a client machine. Because all the computing is being done server side and the client device need only display a bitmap of what is occurring on the server the client-side hardware requirements are minimal. Alternatively a PC is not even needed. There are many manufacturers like Wyse, Neoware, and others that manufacture what are called Windows-based terminals. These devices have an extremely small footprint and are designed specifically for use in the server-based computing world. With Terminal Server there is now no need to upgrade client hardware to support newer applications. You no longer have to maintain or repair applications on individual desktops or fix individual client operating system problems. If a client manages to corrupt his client OS, you can simply re-image or reload the box with the base operating system and Terminal Services client and the user is back in business in minutes.

# Advantages of Using Terminal Services

You might think that Microsoft Terminal Services is only good for providing a convenient way for the system administrator to do some remote administration their server. Although it is a great built-in tool for administering servers remotely, Terminal Services running in Application mode can accomplish a good many more things than just remote administration. Some of the ways organizations leverage Terminal Services include the following:

- *Simplifies Help Desk duties.* Using the Terminal Services administrator snap-in, help desk employees can be given the ability to shadow terminal sessions. With this ability there is now no longer a need to go visit the end user or buy or configure some sort of helpdesk or remote control application to assist in troubleshooting an application or answer a "how do I" question. The help desk employee instead clicks on a session, chooses Remote Control, and can see everything the end user sees in real time and can interact with that user's desktop.

- *Reduces software installation and upgrade time dramatically.* Instead of upgrading 1,000 desktops with new software, you would just upgrade a dozen terminal servers instead. Maintaining a dozen servers is going to be a lot easier and more cost effective than maintaining 1,000 desktops.

- *Makes data protection easier.* Use GPOs and Folder redirection intelligently along with Terminal Services and you can guarantee the safety of your users' data. Because all the computing is being done server side you have total control of where data is being saved. You can now know for certain that data resides on file servers where it gets backed up versus local hard drives where data can easily be lost.

- *Easily deploys specialized applications.* Some organizations have an application or suite of applications that change revisions much too often, or perhaps a difficult application that might take 30 minutes just to install and configure. These types of applications are ideal for Terminal Server. You can now just maintain the applications on a team of servers instead of hundreds or even thousands of individual end user machines.

- *Consolidate and simplify IT for hub and spoke environments.* Rather than hire unnecessary IT staff for small locations, administrators can use Terminal Services to maintain PCs and applications. Using Terminal Services, a corporation can in essence become its own ASP and serve applications from a central location to those 20 remote offices. This greatly reduces the complexity and cost of supporting the remote offices.

## Performance Improvements in Terminal Services 2003

Microsoft's Terminal Services, now in its third generation, continues to evolve. A good number of improvements have been made based on the Windows 2000 platform. Significant enhancements include the following:

- *Greater support for low bandwidth connections.* Previous versions of Terminal Services did not fair well over low bandwidth connections. With Windows 2003 Microsoft promises marked improvements in low bandwidth performance.

- *Greater scalability.* At the Windows Server 2003 launch events Microsoft made claims of 2003 Terminal Services being able to support up to twice the number of users as the same hardware would with Windows 2000 Terminal Services. Although this seems a little aggressive to make this claim it must mean significant improvements have been made.

- *Easier to manage.* Terminal Services now takes greater advantage of Group Policies and remote management is now available through a comprehensive WMI provider.

- *Greater client feature set.* Terminal Services now supports true color, audio redirection, com port redirection, local and network drive redirection, smart card support, and time zone support.

## Scaling Terminal Services

As the number of terminal servers needed and the number of users accessing these terminal servers increase so does the complexity for you. Administrators now have to consider how to scale hardware, how to handle redundancy, availability, load balancing, printing, user data, profiles, and so on. Without proper planning and consideration, Terminal Services can quickly become a burden instead of a blessing.

There are two schools of thought regarding how to scale the hardware needed to support the end users. For example, look at a company that wants to support 1,000 concurrent users and will be deploying a single application that it knows a server with dual 2.0 GHz processors and 4GB of RAM will be able to support 100 concurrent user sessions. One school of thought is consolidation, meaning do as much as possible with as few machines as possible. For this scenario you could purchase three 8-way servers loaded with 16GB of RAM, each machine supporting 350 concurrent users per server. The other school of thought is to tackle the issue with a larger amount of less powerful machines. For example you could purchases 10 dual processor servers with 4GB of RAM, each machine supporting 100 concurrent users per server.

Although both approaches will meet the goal of supporting 1,000 concurrent users, let's look at the pros and cons of each school of thought. Using three 8-way servers, updating applications, applying patches, monitoring performance, and other maintenance tasks only have to be performed on three servers as opposed to 10. Although this might look attractive, using this approach puts a lot of eggs into one basket. If a server has a problem, be it loss of connectivity, a blue screen, a hardware failure, or something else that will cause a service outage, 350 users are now affected versus 100 if you go with more of the smaller hardware.

With the cost of hardware today it will be more cost-effective to purchase 10 dual-processor boxes versus three 8-processor boxes. Terminal Services does not scale linearly with the number of processors. Just because a dual processor machine can support 100 users that does not mean an 8-processor machine can support 400 users. In reality scaling really starts to fall off beyond a quad-processor machine so a lot of money can be saved by choosing the hardware wisely. Blade type servers can be quite cost-effective in this application.

Using the larger amount of smaller servers will allow for more flexibility for you as far as redundancy is concerned. Having a larger hardware pool allows for additional flexibility in terms of where applications are installed. A particular application might be unstable or a huge resource hog and as such you might want to quarantine it to its own set of servers. With the larger amount of hardware you could do this and still have enough resources to support the user community.

## Redundancy and Load Balancing

With Terminal Services out of the box load balancing is only available at the server level and not the application level and is accomplished using Microsoft Network Load Balancing or your favorite hardware/software-based solution such as those offered by F5, Cisco, and others. Unfortunately this means there are a few drawbacks of which you must be aware. Load balancing at the hardware level means that if you are publishing individual applications versus whole desktops then every server that is part of the load balancing pool must have the ability to serve up the particular application. This means that the application must exist on all the servers in the pool and be installed using the same path on each server.

Although at first this might not appear to be much of a hurdle, just make each server identical. Unfortunately, that is not always practical. As mentioned before, certain applications might need to be quarantined to a subset of servers, or for security reasons there might be multiple smaller farms of servers assigned to particular organizations within the company. So one large load balanced pool of identical servers might not be the solution. Instead some creative use of multiple load balancing pools might be in order.

For example you could break up your server farm into three distinct groups and create three load-balancing pools for it. Instead of one virtual address on the load balancer being associated with nine identical servers you might use three virtual addresses and associate them with three sets of three servers. Each smaller farm of three servers would be serving a different set of applications. For example, instead of the clients connecting to ts.companyabc.com they could have three separate connections defined that would connect to tsfinance.companyabc.com, tsengineering.companyabc.com, and tssales.companyabc.com. Each of which would be load balancing a team of three servers containing applications associated with finance, engineering, and sales.

Another drawback with the hardware-based load-balancing solution that Windows 2003 now addresses is that of reconnection. Prior to Windows 2003 if a user disconnects from a terminal server session and then attempts to reconnect to a hardware load balanced farm, the user might or might not attempt to connect back to the server where their disconnected session awaits them. Instead the user can end up having to start a brand new session instead of being able to continue working where she left off in the disconnected session. This leads to inconsistency, open files, wasted resources, and ultimately end user confusion and frustration.

# Keeping Users Connected with Session Directory

Windows 2003 now addresses this problem with Session Directory. Session Directory is a database that keeps track of sessions on terminal servers in a cluster and provides the information used at connection time to connect users to existing sessions. With session directory when a connection attempt is made to the cluster, the server that receives the request first checks with the session directory server to see if the user has an existing connection on another server.

If so the session directory informs the server of this and it directs the client to the appropriate server that contains the existing session. If the user does not have an existing session, then the session is launched from the server that received the initial request. In both cases after the connection is established the session directory is then updated. Session Directory is not enabled by default. You must perform the following steps to set up Session Directory properly:

1. A server must be identified as the session directory server. Any server in the domain will work. It is not required to even be running Terminal Services.

2. After you have chosen what server you want to be the session directory server, you must go into the services control panel and start the terminal server session directory service. It is highly recommended you also set this service to Automatic so that it will start after a server reboot.

3. After this has been done, open the Terminal Services Configuration MMC snap-in, go to server settings, and right-click session directory.

4. Here you would check Join Session Directory, and then identify the Session Directory Server by entering the name of the server that has been configured to run the service. See Figure 20.1.

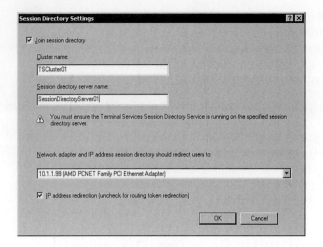

How you configure setting pertaining to Terminal Server IP Address Redirection depends on the load-balancing solution you use and how it is implemented.

5. If the load-balancing solution allows for the clients to attach directly the terminal server's IP address you should leave the IP address redirection box checked and select the proper network interface and IP address.

6. If the load-balancing solution does not allow for direct connection to the terminal server IP address and instead requires the client to attach to the virtual address to direct the request to the proper terminal server, terminal server clients and the load-balancing hardware must both support the use of routing tokens. This requires configuration and software support in the load-balancing device specifically for terminal servers and routing tokens. Uncheck the IP address redirection box and follow the documentation provided by your load balancing solution.

---

**Terminal Servers Requirements**

Terminal servers are required to be running Windows Server 2003, Enterprise Edition, or Windows Server 2003, Datacenter Edition, to participate in a Session Directory–enabled farm.

---

After completing these steps all servers will become members of the cluster and use the session directory. Note this can also be accomplished via a GPO and that would be a more efficient method of configuration as opposed to configuring each terminal server individually.

Although Session Directory does improve things over Windows 2000 Terminal Services it still might not provide the flexibility and effectiveness you want. So in most cases after an environment has outgrown the ability to use machine-based load balancing the company will turn to a third-party software provider like a Citrix, New Moon Systems, or Jetro Platforms to provide application-based load balancing. All of these products will allow for load balancing to be performed at the application level. This allows for dissimilar servers in the farm and the ability to take advantage of dissimilar hardware. Using one of these third-party tools you can configure the system to ensure the client always connects to a server capable of running the specified application with the most resources available at that particular point in time.

# Adding Redundancy to Session Directory

To avoid the Session Directory from becoming a single point of failure you can configure Session Directory to run as a clustered service using Microsoft's clustering technology. You create the cluster by following these steps:

1. Set Terminal Services Session Directory Server service to Automatic.

2. Ensure that the following resources are available in the server cluster configuration:

    ■ Physical Disk—In addition to the quorum disk, the cluster will require a shared disk for the shared data. This shared data disk must be able to failover to all nodes in the cluster that you want to be able to host the Terminal Services Session Directory database.

    ■ IP Address—A static IP address accessible from all the terminal servers that will be configured in the load balancing cluster.

    ■ Network Name—A name that is resolvable from all the terminal servers in the cluster. Kerberos is required for all communication between the terminal server and the Session Directory server. Make sure to select Enable Kerberos Authentication and DNS Registrations Must Succeed before bringing the network name resource online.

3. Select File, New, Resource. This will start a wizard. Enter the name and description, and set the resource type to Generic.

4. Click Next and accept the defaults.

5. Define your dependencies. Specify the Physical Disk and Network Name resources.

6. Define the Generic Service Parameters. Specify the service name, TSSDIS, in the Service Name box, and check the box next to Use Network Name for Computer Name.

7. Configure Registry Replication. Click Add and type System\ CurrentControlSet\Services\Tssdis\ Parameters.

8. Click Finish.

9. Bring the new service resource online.

> **Clustering the Session Directory Servers**
> You must be using Windows Server 2003 Enterprise or Datacenter edition to be able to cluster the Session Directory servers.

# Optimizing Terminal Service Performance

Out of the box there are a number of things you can do to improve the performance of your terminal servers. Many of the options will depend on the specific environment, applications, and expectations of the end users. Things like color depth, audio redirection, printer redirection, and encryption level all have an effect on the amount of CPU, memory, and bandwidth used per session. This, in turn has a direct correlation on the number of users that can effectively work per server and the performance of the connection over the network. It is up to you to evaluate the environment and modify the client connection settings or the server side connection settings to maximize performance.

As a general rule turn off all features that are not needed for the end user to complete his tasks. Server-side resources can also be optimized by the effective use of the terminal server connections. Limiting users to one session, limiting the number of sessions per terminal server, and logging off disconnected or idle sessions are all things you can do to conserve server-side resources and thus increase the overall performance of the system as a whole. It is also important to look at the application(s) being delivered via Terminal Services and tweak them for maximum performance. Microsoft Office is a great example of this. Turning off the Office Assistant, spell and grammar check as you type, automated windows, and things of that sort can greatly reduce the amount of network traffic and CPU consumed.

## Taking Advantage of Profile Redirection

You can use a few simple tools to help create a very consistent, efficient user environment for the terminal server users. With the use of Terminal Services profiles along with folder redirection to centralize user settings/data the terminal server administrator's users will enjoy a very consistent environment no matter which terminal server they connect to. Without the use of these tools a new profile will be created every time a user log's into a terminal server. For the end users this means setting up application preferences over and over again, potentially not knowing where they saved their work, and other inconsistencies that can lead to confusion for the end users.

To define a TS profile you go into your Active Directory Users and Computers snap-in, select a user account, and then click on the Terminal Services Profile tab. Then define the path to the profile storage area. Typically it's \\servername\sharedfolder\username. Alternatively, you can use a terminal server GPO to define the location of the profiles. To configure via GPO, edit Computer Configuration/Administrative Templates/Windows Components/Terminal Services/Set Path For TS Roaming Profiles and place the desired path there. It is very important to make sure the server that the profiles are stored on is robust, highly available, and has plenty of disk space to store all the profiles. Do not use the same path for Terminal Server profiles that has been defined for the regular roaming profiles if they are being used. Having the profile open and updated from multiple locations will cause strange behaviors and even data loss.

It is a good idea to use a GPO to define exclusions for the roaming profile. Things like temporary Internet files, temp files, history, and things of that sort can cause profiles to grow tremendously. By excluding these from the profile it will keep the profile size down and thus require less disk space and will speed up launch times because the time it takes to copy the profile from the central location to the terminal server does directly affect the amount of time it takes to open and close the application. To define the exclusions you will want to modify and enable the following GPO within the Group Policy editor: User Configuration/Administrative Templates/System/User Profiles/Exclude Directories in Roaming Profile.

The use of folder redirection with Terminal Services has a few benefits making it worthwhile. By redirecting folders instead of storing them in a profile and having them copied back and forth the amount of network traffic required to upload and download the profile is greatly reduced. For example if a user has 100MB worth of Word documents in his My Documents folder all that has to be brought over during launch thus causing a slow application launch and closing as it copies everything back.

> **Folder Redirection**
>
> If folder redirection is used, you will want to exclude those redirected folders from the roaming profile as well because it would be counter-productive to redirect the folder and then copy it to the local profile.

> **Use Folder Redirection Globally**
>
> Use folder redirection globally in your network and redirect everything (application data, desktop, My Documents, and Start menu) and now no matter if your users are running local applications from their desktop or applications via Terminal Services their experience and file locations are the same.

If you instead do folder redirection the data will always reside out on a server on the network and does not have to be copied back and forth. It is instead only accessed when necessary and now instead of copying over 100MB worth of profile it might be as small as 2–3MB. The use of folder redirection also ensures that user data is in a known central location making it very easy for you to back up. Use the GPO to remove cached copies of user profiles to help keep the application servers clean. The deletion of the profiles is not 100% so if you are worried about disk space, periodic house cleaning will be necessary because profiles will sometimes be left behind. Include a section to clean up profiles in a reboot script as a good practice.

## Leveraging Windows Resource Manager to Control Resources

New for Windows 2003 is the Windows Resource Manager. Although its use is not exclusive to Terminal Services it is a great tool to take advantage of. You can now limit the amount of CPU and memory an application can use. You can even go as far as to have separate settings based not only on an application but a user or group as well. Using Windows Resource Manager you can now provide a more consistent user experience, enforce a certain level of QoS, and be able to prevent things like a single rogue session from bringing all the other sessions on the server to a grinding halt.

Windows Resource Manager can also be used to provide tiered levels of performance for users. A Terminal Server that is dedicated to the engineering department might be underutilized so you might want to open it up to the sales group. By placing CPU limitations by both program and user, you can ensure that the sales users that utilize the Engineering Terminal Server can never use more then 10% of the system's capacity. This ensures that engineering jobs will still run with acceptable performance on the occasions that they are used.

# Managing Terminal Service Users with Group Policy

Windows Server 2003 now provides specific Terminal Services policies to assist you in managing
your terminal servers. These are but a handful of the group policies available and will need to be
used in conjunction with the other non–TS-specific policies.

Within Server 2003 there are both computer-specific and user-specific terminal server group
policies. These policies should be used to maximize the security and performance of your terminal servers. Computer-specific policies will affect the terminal server as a whole no matter who
logs into the system. As such care must be taken when applying these particular GPOs.

A simple way to manage the GPOs for your terminal servers is to create an OU for your terminal
servers and place the servers into that OU and then apply GPOs to it. One GPO that is very
important to apply is the Computer Configuration, Administrative Templates, System, Group
Policy, User Group Policy loop back processing mode (see Figure 20.2).

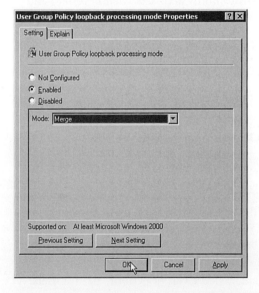

**FIGURE 20.2**   Enabling loopback processing
mode.

Enabling this GPO is very important if you have created a separate OU for your terminal servers
as mentioned previously and have defined the GPOs there. Otherwise the user context GPO
settings will not take effect. This means that there are going to be settings that you want to take

effect only when a user logs into the terminal server. To accomplish this you create your special set of GPO policies for the OU the terminal servers are in and apply the loopback processing to either merge or replace.

If you select Merge, then existing domain GPOs are merged with the special set created for the terminal servers. If Replace is selected then all the inherited GPO settings are ignored and only the set of GPOs defined for the terminal servers are applied. Some of the configuration options that are available for the GPO are as follows:

- Keep Alive Connections. This GPO is particularly useful when the clients are connecting via a WAN link or via the Internet. By enabling this GPO the terminal server will check the session state between it and the client instead of the default behavior, which more or less assumes the session state. The benefit realized by enabling keepalive connections is that if there is a network hiccup that causes a break in the network connection between the client and the server the session will be placed into a disconnected state. Should the client attempt to reconnect to the Terminal Server it will connect back to the existing session instead of being forced into a new session. This prevents the client's current work from sitting idle in a session it can no longer reconnect to without administrative intervention.

> **GPO**
> The shortest interval that can be configured is one minute. Realistically if the environment lends itself to needing configuration, some end user training will be needed. The server will inform the end user to wait one minute, or to default to the keepalive setting before attempting to reconnect. Otherwise this setting is effectively useless.

- Automatic Reconnection. Assuming the RDP client is version 5.2 or later this setting can be used with or in lieu of the keepalive connection setting. If automatic reconnection is enabled the client will attempt to reconnect to a broken session every five seconds for 20 attempts.

## BEST PRACTICE

### Test This Setting in Each Particular Environment

It will be wise to test this setting in each particular environment to verify the desired behavior is what occurs. Assuming the session will just pick back up where it was left off five seconds prior is not a good assumption. The connection speed, how the connection was broken, and so on, will affect whether the session is thrown into a disconnected state or remains active. If the session remains active a reconnect after five seconds really does no good because it results in a new connection instead of the user reconnecting back to their existing session and resuming their work.

- Restrict Terminal Services users to a single remote session. By enabling this GPO you can accomplish two major things. First is maximizing the performance of the terminal server. By not allowing the user to have multiple separate sessions running at any given time resources are preserved. *Zombie sessions*, those that are running in an active state with no user actually connected, or sitting idle in a disconnected state forever, are a waste of system resources and will have a direct effect on performance and scalability. By limiting the user to a single session, the zombie sessions can be avoided. Secondly by limiting the users to a single session end user confusion is greatly reduced. If the users have the potential to have multiple sessions they then have the potential over time to leave behind dozens of disconnected or active sessions, which in turn can leave applications running in those sessions that might end up causing all sorts of confusion or even data loss.

■ Client/Server data redirection section. For granularity these type settings are normally configured client-side but in an environment that is particular about security it might be wise to look at these GPOs. Within this section, things like clipboard, drive redirection, printer redirection, com port redirection, and LTP redirection can all be disabled to prevent the user from being able to upload, download, or print information from the terminal server application.

■ Encryption and Security section. Enables you to force an encryption level. This is useful not only for security but also for performance. If all the terminal server users are on the local LAN encryption might not be a huge concern for you and as such you can force the encryption level to low and save CPU cycles on the server. This helps with performance and the number of users per server. You can also force a prompt for the password during a connection. This is especially useful in a more secure environment where a user might have checked the Save Password option on her client, which means that any person that walks up to the machine and clicks the icon will now be able to successfully connect to the terminal server as this user and access that data. Instead now even if the Save Password option was checked, the terminal server will always ask for the password thus helping prevent unauthorized use.

■ Licensing section. By default the terminal server licensing server will hand out licenses to any computer that requests one. Now (as of this printing) that a TS CAL is required for any type of computer accessing the terminal server, managing your licenses becomes more critical than ever. Not doing so might create headaches for you as the help desk gets flooded with calls from end users who cannot connect to the terminal server due to running out of licenses. By using the License Server Security Group policy, you can define a group of computers that the licensing server is allowed to issue licenses to, preventing rogue systems on the network, in perhaps a QA or development environment, from taking away CAL's need for end user access.

■ Sessions section. This section is particularly useful for performance and even licensing reasons. You would use these settings to automatically log off disconnected sessions after a particular time frame. Disconnect active but idle connections for security reasons. There is also an option to log off the disconnected sessions or even active but idle sessions. This is particularly useful if the application being run is one with a limited number of licenses and a larger pool of users. By logging off idle sessions, instead of a license being used by a user who is off at lunch, that idle session is logged off and the license is made available to a new user.

User-specific settings are those settings applied to the users and not to the machine. As such by controlling via permissions what users or groups the GPO can be applied to you can control the behavior much more granularly than with the computer settings. Creative thinking here can go a long way in maximizing resources, performance, and security.

> **It Helps Avoid Confusion**
> You might find is a lot easier to define a particular application to run rather than publishing an entire desktop. It helps avoid confusion and makes it easier to secure the terminal server.

For example you could create two separate GPOs that modify the User Configuration settings differently. In this example the GPOs are called Finance and QA. For the Finance GPO you could define Start a Program on Connection and configure the financial package as that executable.

For security reasons you could also set the Remote Control of Terminal Server User Sessions to No Remote Control Allowed because this company has a policy that no one other than those in finance should be able to view finance information. Set the disconnected session to time out after 30 minutes and only allow reconnection from the original client to secure who is gaining access to the financial application and its data.

Conversely, the QA manager might want the administrator to define an application like a bug tracking package and would want to be able to view the QA engineer's session at any time without asking for permission in order to monitor his work. Perhaps also have the session automatically log off after 10 minutes of idle time because the department has a 20 concurrent user license for this particular application but has 40 engineers who might need to use it. By using Terminal Services and managing the sessions via the GPO it is now very possible to need only 20 licenses for 40 users and still allow all 40 users to work effectively.

# Keeping Terminal Service Secure

Because terminal servers will often be accessible via the Internet it is important to ensure that they are well secured. Whenever possible, take a layered approach to securing the devices.

## Adding Security via Firewall Settings for ASP Terminal Servers

When using Terminal Servers in an ASP environment or sometimes even in a corporate environment you will want to provide some protection for the servers by placing them behind a firewall. By default RDP communicates over TCP port 3389. If for some reason you would like to change the default port this can be done by modifying the following Registry key:

> **Use Registry Editor at Your Own Risk**
> If you use Registry Editor incorrectly, you could cause serious problems that might require you to reinstall your operating system. Microsoft cannot guarantee that you can solve problems that result from using Registry Editor incorrectly. Use Registry Editor at your own risk.

HKEY_LOCAL_MACHINE\System\CurrentControlSet\Control\Terminal Server\WinStations\ RDP-Tcp\PortNumber

> **Only RDP Clients Version 5.1 or Later**
>
> Only RDP clients version 5.1 or later are able to connect to a Terminal Server running on a nonstandard port. To make a connection to a server running on a nonstandard port you must follow the server name with a colon and the port number, for example, Terminalserver1.companyabc.com:1234

After modifying this key the server must be rebooted. A simple service restart does not do the trick.

Administrators will need to fully understand their firewall and its settings. A lot of firewalls are configured to close connections after a certain period of inactivity. Although in theory this is a great feature for a firewall, when you're trying to run a terminal server session through this firewall it is not. Prolonged periods of inactivity within the terminal session (if someone steps away to a meeting, goes on break, or takes a phone call, for example) mean no packets are passed back and forth between client and server. So what happens is the firewall closes the connection resulting in a lost session for the user. Worse yet, more times than not due to the way the session is broken the terminal server ends up leaving the session in an active state and the end user cannot connect back to it without assistance from you. In these cases you might attempt using the keepalive or reconfigure the firewall so it doesn't drop idle connections.

To properly configure Keepalive, modify the following Registry keys:

HKEY_LOCAL_MACHINE\SYSTEM\CurrentControlSet\Control\Terminal Server

DWORD "KeepAliveEnable" value should be set to 1

DWORD "KeepAliveInterval" value should be set to 1

HKEY_LOCAL_MACHINE\SYSTEM\CurrentControlSet\Services\Tcpip\Parameters

DWORD "KeepAliveInterval" value in milliseconds

DWORD "KeepAliveTime" value in milliseconds

DWORD "TcpMaxDataRetransmissions" numeric value

After setting these go into the Terminal Services Configuration Snap-In and under Sessions check the Override Users Settings box and chose Disconnect from Session.

## Building Terminal Services the Right Way

Special thought and care should go into building a terminal server that is being used for the deployment of applications or desktops to end users. You should approach this with the knowledge that the end user is now effectively sitting down at the console of the server and working. As such the proper planning and building of the terminal server is critical to providing a stable, secure, and easy to use Terminal Server.

Because the end user is in essence sitting in front of the server it is your task to not only build the server so that the end user can run the applications necessary to work, but also restrict as much as possible of what the end user can do yet still work. An improperly locked down terminal server can and will spell disaster for the end users. Whether done purposely or accidentally, system changes, installation of third-party applications, deletion of files, and so on can equal downtime for *all* the users of that terminal server while you attempt to repair the damage.

Take the time up front to plan and build a securely locked down terminal server and it will pay off down the road in fewer support issues and less server maintenance.

One of the goals of managing an Application Terminal Server is to simplify security. One easy way to accomplish this is to break the server into three discrete partitions that can be secured independently. An example of a multipartition configuration would be as follows:

- Use C: for the Operating System—4 gigs + pagefile space

- Assign D: for the applications—depends on how many apps you plan to install—use common sense

- Utilize E: for the temporary profiles—depends on how many concurrent users you have and if you do or do not use folder redirection and profile exclusions. If you do not use folder redirection or exclusions from the profile, the temporary profiles can grow to be very large. In the tens or even hundreds of megabytes. If you do use folder redirection and or exclusions profiles can be kept as small as a few hundred KB, generally growing no more than 2–4MB in size.

As you progress you will see that by breaking the server into three partitions you make things easier because the server has now been broken down into distinct categories that NTFS permissions can be applied to fairly easily without disrupting the functionality of the operating system or applications.

The C: drive will be for the operating system and system files only. By doing this, access to the C: partition can be locked down because there will be no user or application files here and thus no need for any accounts other then system and administrators to be able to write or even view the files.

The D: drive will be used as the target drive for application installations. It is advised that each application be installed into its own separate directory. For example install application A into D:\applicationA and application B into d:\applicationB not D:\program files\applicationA and d:\program files\applicationB. Different applications will require different file permissions to run correctly. If they are all installed into the same root directory it makes it a lot more tedious to secure with NTFS permissions.

That leaves the E: drive. This partition is set aside for the temp profiles terminal server creates during a session. Remember that even if you use roaming Terminal Server profiles, a local profile is always created for each session. By default Windows will place the users' profiles under C:\documents and settings\username. Because the goal here is to simplify securing the partitions you do no want to require any end user access to the C: partition and as such would rather have the profiles be created on the E: partition instead. To change the default behavior and move the profile location to the E: drive, the following steps must be performed.

1. Create a Documents and Settings Folder on the E: drive.

2. Modify this key to change where the local copy of the profiles is written. By default it is %systemdrive%\documents and settings.

3. Modify HKEY_LOCAL_MACHINE\SOFTWARE\Microsoft\Windows NT\CurrentVersion\ProfileList\ProfilesDirectory Reg_Sz to a value of *e:\Documents and Settings*

4. Reboot the server.

5. Copy over the Default and All Users profiles to the new location.

## Locking Down the Server with GPOs

Building the server with the three distinct partitions, installing applications into separate directories, and moving the location of the temporary profiles is a great foundation for building a great terminal server. This only the beginning.

Using GPOs you can effectively limit a lot of undesired activity on the terminal servers. Although GPOs cannot protect the terminal servers 100% they are a great tool to use to achieve your goal.

A simple way of managing the GPO(s) for your Terminal Servers is to create an OU for your terminal servers and place the servers into that OU, and create a group policy for them. In this example it is called Lockdown. In order to prevent the group policy from interfering with your ability to perform your duties on the box, you will want to modify permissions on the GPO so that the terminal server administrators, whomever they might be, have the Deny box checked next to Apply Group Policy. See Figure 20.3.

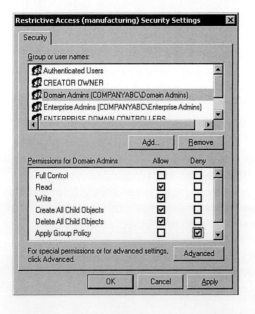

**FIGURE 20.3**   Setting Deny permission on the lockdown GPO.

This prevents the policy from being applied when you log in so you can still work. Remember that machine policies will still take effect, but most policies that would end up crippling you are user-based and as such won't be applied when you log into the server. Now you can safely modify settings in the lockdown GPO. What you do and don't do here really depends on your environment and the applications you're going to deploy. It is highly recommended that you configure a set of policies, test your environment, configure another set, and test again until you are completely satisfied.

## Locking Down Directory and File Permissions

Applying proper directory and file permissions is a very important step in locking down the terminal server. Although the GPOs do a great job of attempting to keep users from doing malicious or accidental harm to the system they are not enough. A good set of directory and file permissions are a crucial piece of the lockdown process. This is also the area that you need to take the most care. Restrictive directory and file permissions can end up causing undesirable side effects while running applications via Terminal Services. It is imperative you fully test to the best of your ability the functionality of all applications hosted via Terminal Services after every round of modifications to directory and file permissions.

> **The Office Resource Kit Has Templates You Can Add**
>
> If you're deploying Office, the Office Resource Kit has templates you can add to lock down and configure Office applications. Setting default file save locations, removing the Visual Basic editor, and much more can be done via GPO.

> **Policy Templates Will Be Too Restrictive**
>
> Although policy templates might work great for a standalone server with the role of a print server or a file server, they will be too restrictive for Terminal Services. Always fully test the environment after applying the templates.

# Leveraging Local Resources

With Microsoft 2003 Terminal Services Microsoft now provides a much more impressive list of redirected local resources to a terminal session. With 2003 Terminal Services and an RDP client version 5.1 or later, you now have the ability to provide the user not only access to local and network drives and printers, but also COM ports and audio redirection. Users can now again enjoy something as simple as a new mail notification sound all the way up to viewing a multi-media presentation all via a terminal server session.

Although audio redirection is nice and another step closer to making a terminal server session experience rival running the application locally a perhaps more useful addition to 2003 Terminal Services is COM port redirection. The most requested use of this is being able to synch a Palm Pilot to applications running via Terminal Services. Prior to 2003 Terminal Services an administrator was usually unable to deploy Outlook to a fair number of users because the users had to be able to sync to their Palm Pilot. This is no longer the case. Although audio and COM port redirection are nice, Windows 2003 Terminal Services have been really improved in the area of local and network drive and printer access. Windows 2003 Terminal Services can now automatically map all of a user's local and network drives and printers. The user now has full access to all their local and network drives and printers without you having to do anything in the background to set it up.

## Optimizing Local Printing

Ask any terminal server administrator the number one problem she has encountered while deploying Terminal Services and 9 out of 10 times you will hear about printing problems. By default when a client connects to the terminal server the terminal server will attempt to create all the printers that the client device is attached to into the terminal server session. Depending on the type and model of printer this might or might not work. The terminal server is only able to create printers for which it has drivers. By default the only printers that Terminal Services will be able to install are those listed in the ntprint.inf file and whose drivers are contained in the i386 directory. So, if a client device has a printer attached that uses a driver not listed in the .inf file that printer will not get created and the user will not be able to print to it.

To ensure the client device can print you have a few options. One option is to install the printer driver for the device onto the terminal server. Even though the printer is not really attached to the server you just go through the steps of installing the printer to lpt1 and then when complete you can now delete the newly installed printer and choose to leave the drivers behind. Now when the client connects the printer drivers are already installed onto the terminal server and the client will be able to print.

There are major drawbacks to using this method. A majority of manufacturer print drivers are not certified for use on terminal server and as such can cause various undesirable effects ranging from print spooler crashes to the infamous blue screen of death. Also in a large environment imagine trying to identify every single printer that will need to have a driver loaded onto every single terminal server; a daunting, potentially neverending task. A small modification to the previously mentioned method will result in a much more stable terminal server printing environment.

As previously mentioned, by default Terminal Services will be able to install all printers listed in the ntprint.inf file. What you can do is modify the ntprint.inf file to support the client printers. The basic steps are as follows. First identify the name of the printer driver from the client computer. Then the ntprint.inf must be modified by adding an entry to the Previous Names section that exactly matches the name of the client-side driver and then maps to a known stable printer driver that will print to the device. As you can see managing printers can potentially be a very big task for you and is probably the number one reason that people turn to the third-party manufacturers like Citrix, Newmoon, Jetro systems, and so on for their printing solutions. All of these manufactures provide what they call a unidriver. This is a single print driver that will allow printing to most any printer on the market. Although this is excellent for the stability of the terminal server, these unidrivers do lack in functionality and as such at times it will still be a requirement to install vendor drivers for the user to print properly.

## Leveraging Local and Network Drives

If enabled Windows 2003 Terminal Services now maps both local and network drives defined on the client into the terminal session. Now it becomes very simple for a user to be able to run applications on the terminal server yet still access files from their local machine. This feature can of course be disabled for security reasons. It is not always desirable to give the end user the capability to upload and download files to and from the terminal server. In fact in most cases one can argue strongly that it is counter-intuitive to what is trying to be accomplished by using centralized computing. That being said there will be many instances where Terminal Services is just being used either for remote access or a specialized application in a traditional decentralized computing environment and access to local resources will be a necessity.

> **Greater Performance Over Low Bandwidth Connections**
>
> Greater performance over low bandwidth connections will be achieved by not enabling client drive redirection. When at all possible keep user data on the local network and map drives via login scripts instead of redirecting the resources from the client.

# Summary

In this chapter you learned that Microsoft 2003 Server brings with it a much more feature rich and higher performing version of Terminal Services by providing true color support, audio support, local drive mapping, local printer redirection, better support for low bandwidth connections, greater scalability, session directory, and more.

You have also learned the importance of taking the time to properly build and deploy Terminal Services. All the way from partitioning drives, installing applications, applying file permissions, and leveraging group policies, to other aspects of Windows 2003 such as load balancing and clustering to provide high performance, highly available, and secure server-based computing solution for one's enterprise.

The Terminal Services functions in Windows Server 2003 give you a good indication of things to come from Microsoft. After seeing Terminal Services in Windows 2003 one can see a future where employees will be able to attach to airport kiosks to RDP into their office Terminal Servers, look at their e-mail, and synch that e-mail onto a PDA through a redirected port. Applications will talk to each other even though they are running on separate terminal servers. There is already talk of technologies to allow you to move live user sessions from one Terminal Server to another so that the server can be taken down for maintenance.

As the pendulum continues to swing back and forth between centralized and distributed computing, each cycle of the pendulum brings more and more functionality to the end user. Terminal Services continues to be a valuable and exciting technology that makes the end user experience better and your life easier.

# PART VI

## Business Continuity Solutions

# 21

# Proactive Monitoring and Alerting

**S**ystem management has been greatly improved in Windows 2003. Great strides have been made toward making Windows 2003 better able to monitor itself and alert administrators of problems. Almost all aspects of the operating system can be exposed to various monitoring systems. Service availability, resource usage, replication queues, and most anything else an administrator would care to know about can be monitored across the enterprise. Remote systems can all report to a central location so that the health of the entire network can be viewed from a single location. This chapter endeavors to give you an idea of what technologies are available for systemwide monitoring and offer insights into the different types of monitoring and how they can be used together to give a holistic view of the network. This chapter will also make recommendations on areas on which administrators should focus their monitoring as well as give examples of scripts that can be triggered by monitoring events to try to fix problems and alert the appropriate resources that an event has occurred.

# Leveraging Windows Management Instrumentation

Right out of the box, Windows 2003 has a number of items that give it excellent insight into its own operation. Event viewers, SNMP traps, and performance monitors have long been available to Windows systems to allow it to track its own health. Windows 2003 has made these and many other monitoring components available through a central mechanism called Windows Management Instrumentation, or WMI.

## Understanding WMI

WMI is Microsoft's implementation of WBEM, or Web-Based Enterprise Management. WBEM was designed to provide one method for accessing management data that originates from disparate sources. WBEM has been developed over the years by a consortium of companies that all shared a common vision for how monitoring should be implemented. The old methods of proprietary monitoring subsystems for each operating system or platform have made way for an open standard for monitoring, independent from platform or OS-specific APIs. Like most "open standards," various companies have created their own implementation but these exist as supersets of the original WBEM requirements and follow the standards of Common Information Model and Desktop Management Interface as set forth by the Distributed Management Task Force.

### Excellent Source for WMI Scripts

The Internet is an excellent source for finding commonly used WMI scripts. Rather than reinvent the wheel, you can check to see if another scripter has already created a script that does what you need.

## Uses for WMI

WMI enables you to query the system for events and cause those events to trigger actions. Actions can be as simple as adding entries to a log file or as complex as changing system parameters and rebooting a system. Windows 2003 ships with several built-in providers for accessing specific subsystems:

- Performance Monitor Provider—Provides access to Windows NT Performance Monitor data.

- Registry Provider—Provides access to system Registry data.

- Registry Event Provider—Sends events when changes occur to Registry keys, values, or trees.

- SNMP Provider—Provides access to events and data from SNMP devices.

- Windows NT Event Log Provider—Provides access to data and event notifications from the Windows NT Event Log.

- Win32 Provider—Provides access to data from the Win32 subsystem.

- WDM Provider—Provides access to data and events from device drivers that conform to the WMI interface.

- Shadow Copy Provider—Supplies management functions for the Windows Server 2003 Shared Folders feature.

- Storage Volume Provider—Enumerates all volumes known to the Windows Mount manager and manages volume drive letters, mount points, and storage quotas.

By using these providers, WMI can be leveraged to act on information captured from these sources. For example, Event notification could be used to detect hardware events or errors. The event could then be passed to the WMI for corrective action based on the specific event that occurred. For example, a Network Interface Card (NIC) detects the presence of an Ethernet signal and sends notification to a script that disables the Wireless Network Interface Card to eliminate the possibility of a wireless connection being used as an entry point to a wired network.

Similarly, the Event Log Provider could pass an event to a WMI script that watched for a specific Event ID and would trigger a restart of a service to fix a known bug. This can be especially useful with internal software that is still under development. If an application were known to have a memory leak, WMI could watch the process and restart a specific service when the process consumed over 256MB of memory, or some other threshold. At the same time the WMI script could alert a developer via e-mail and pass specific system parameters based on WMI queries that could help the developer troubleshoot the process.

> **There Are Additional Providers**
>
> There are additional providers above and beyond the ones included in Windows 2003. When adding services such as load balancing or clustering, check to see if specific WMI providers are available so that those functions can be accessed via WMI as well.

# Leveraging Scripts for Improved System Management

The WMI scripting API can be used for the multiple purposes:

- Enumeration—A WMI scripter can write scripts to enumerate processes running on a local system or settings on a device.

- Method execution—A WMI scripter can create scripts to initiate or shut down a specific process or application on a remote computer.

- Queries—Rather than enumerate, a WMI script could query a subsystem to determine if a specific process or device is running on a local or remote system.

- Event registration and reception—A WMI script would watch for specific events from the Windows NT Event Log on a local computer.

- Instance modification—WMI can be leveraged for modification of information. For example, workstations created with Sysprep could change their own names to their unique processor ID automatically via a WMI script upon their first boot.

- Local and remote access—WMI scripts can be targeted to operate on local resources as well as remote resources. This can be especially powerful in allowing one machine to monitor and potentially fix another.

Through combinations of these functions, you have amazing flexibility in creating complex scripts that can react to a number of situations and trigger events, alerts, or even other scripts. By chaining these scripts one can create fairly advanced logic for determining how a system should deal with its own triggers.

## Basic WMI Scripts

Here is an example of a basic script that will query a machine called Godzilla for its total physical memory:

```
strServer = "Godzilla"
Set wbemServices = GetObject("winmgmts:\\" & strServer)
Set wbemObjectSet = wbemServices.InstancesOf("Win32_LogicalMemoryConfiguration")

For Each wbemObject In wbemObjectSet
WScript.Echo "Physical Memory (kb): " & wbemObject.TotalPhysicalMemory
Next
```

By feeding this script a series of machine names, WMI could be used to perform a memory audit on a series of machines to see if they needed to be upgraded prior to an OS upgrade.

This script shows how to enable you to select targets for a script. This script queries the user for a target machine and a target application to terminate on the target machine:

```
do
SrvrName = inputbox("Enter the name of the system to kill an
➥application on.", "Input")
loop until SrvrName <> ""
do
target = inputbox("Enter the name of the program you wish to
➥kill. ", "Kill a Process")
loop until target <> ""
for each process in GetObject("winmgmts:{impersonationLevel=impersonate}!\\"&SrvrName&"
➥\root\cimv2").ExecQuery ("select * from Win32_Process where Name='" & target & "'")
process.terminate(0)
Next
wscript.echo "Program terminated."
```

> **Defaulting to the Local Machine**
> If a script uses a target [strServer =] of "." it is defaulting to the local machine. If a script is only dealing with a single remote system, the system name can be entered there.

A script like this could be handy for remote administration. If a user called the help desk and complained of a runaway process that they did not have rights to end, the help desk could run a script like this to end the process for the user. This would eliminate the need for a technician to be dispatched to the user's location.

# Building Services

By combining C++ or Visual Basic with WMI calls, services can be written to use WMI functions. This enables you to effectively run a script continuously without the system overhead of a script running over and over. A service of this type is created with the `Win32_BaseService.Create` parameter. It is recommended to run WMI services of this type under the System context. This prevents users from being able to simply stop the service.

---

### Use the AT Scheduler

To control services running under the system context it is necessary to access them via the system context. The easiest way to do this is to use the AT scheduler to launch a command window with an `/interactive` switch. Anything done from this command window will run under the SYSTEM context.

---

# Building Temporary Event Consumers

A *temporary event consumer* is created by a consuming application and ends when the application ends. In this way the subscriptions are only active when the consuming application is running. This is one way to reduce the CPU load on a system that is using WMI.

# Building Permanent Event Consumers

A permanent event consumer is a COM object that is able to receive a WMI event at all times. A permanent event consumer uses a set of persistent objects and filters to capture a WMI event. Not unlike with a temporary event consumer, a series of WMI objects and filters are set up that capture a WMI event. When an event occurs that matches a filter, WMI loads the permanent event consumer and notifies it about the event. Because a permanent consumer is implemented in the WMI repository and an executable file that is registered in WMI, delivery of an event also continues across reboot of the operating system while WMI is running.

A permanent event consumer continues to receive events until its registration is explicitly cancelled. A permanent event consumer is a combination of WMI classes, filters, and COM objects that reside on the system.

A logical event consumer is an instance of the permanent consumer class. The properties of a logical event consumer specify the actions to take when notified of an event, but do not define the event queries with which they are associated. When signaled, WMI automatically loads the COM object that represents the permanent event consumer into active memory. Typically, this occurs during startup or in response to a triggering event. After being activated, the permanent event consumer acts as a normal event consumer, but remains until specifically unloaded by the operating system.

---

### Be Sure to Test the Service and Watch for Memory Leaks

When creating permanent event consumers, be sure to test the service and watch for memory leaks. Some WMI classes are known to have memory leaks. If the memory consumption of svchost.exe increases continuously, this is a common sign of a WMI memory leak.

# Deciding What to Monitor

There is a plethora of parameters that you can monitor. Some are very useful; some are not. By limiting the monitored items to only those in which you are interested, there is less chance of missing important information due to the sheer volume of incoming data. Because different types of monitoring have access to different types of data, the following sections each end with the recommendations of specific items to monitor with that type of monitoring.

## Monitoring Hardware

Simple hardware monitoring such as pinging a device to see if it will respond is one way to determine if a machine is up and running. This essentially tests layers 1, 2, and 3 of the OSI model. The problem with this type of monitoring is it only tells you if the box itself is physically responding to ping. It does not tell you whether the machine has a particular service running or if that service is in fact running properly. Hardware monitoring is a good basis for other types of monitoring because it enables you to do things such as event correlation. If a number of machines stop responding to a particular query and a router is not responding to ping the software can safely assume that the reason the machines are unreachable is because the router itself is down. For this level of monitoring, basic hardware monitoring is fairly effective.

> **Ensure that All Interfaces Are Being Monitored**
>
> When monitoring a network with redundant connections it is critical to ensure that all interfaces are being monitored. If only the "far side" IP addresses are being monitored, a packet could be taking an alternative route to get there and a failed local interface could be missed.

Recommended monitoring points include the following:

- Local routers
- Remote routers
- ISP
- Switches
- VPN devices

## Port-Level Monitoring

Going beyond simple ping tests is an effective way to get more information about a system's health. Well-known services such as SMTP or POP3 can be monitored easily by querying the server on ports 25 or 110, respectively. This goes beyond the simple ping test by ensuring that port is available, which generally means that the application is running. This enables you to make a determination about whether or not a particular service is available. This can be especially effective in finding problems before users report them. One of the primary goals of monitoring is to proactively capture system problems before users discover them. Most monitoring packages on the market support the capability to monitor a system at a port level. By combining hardware-level monitoring with port-level monitoring a clever administrator can reduce the load on the monitoring system. If the link to a remote network is not responding to a physical ping test there is no reason for the software to continue processing port checks on machines on that network. This allows the system to perform event correlation to reduce the number of false positives and that in turn reduces the number of alerts being sent. This will result in less traffic on the network as well as reduce the "boy that cried wolf" effect.

> **The Netstat Command**
>
> An easy way to find the ports to monitor on a system is via the Netstat command. By identifying the ports that multiple users are connecting to, you can identify the ports that are important to the end users. Running Netstat -nao on a Windows Server 2003 system will list source IP addresses, destination addresses and the ports on which they are connecting. Additionally it will list process identifiers associated with each connection. These PIDs can be compared to the Task Manager to see what processes are connecting on which ports.

Some recommended monitoring points are as follows:

- Port 25 (SMTP)
- Port 110 (POP3)
- Port 80 (Web)
- Port 443 (Secure Web)
- Port 53 (DNS)
- Port 1723 (PPTP)
- Port 3389 (Remote Desktop Protocol)

## Service-Level Monitoring

Going one step further in the area of monitoring is the ability to query a service to see if it is running properly. Rather than simply see that port 25 is responding, a monitoring package can send an SMTP query to see if the server will respond with the correct hello. This enables you to ensure that an e-mail server, for example, is correctly receiving e-mail messages. Similarly, software packages

> **Identify Dependencies for All Services**
>
> When possible, identify dependencies for all services to help reduce redundant alerts. For example, in Exchange, if the System Attendant service is down, there is no point in checking the Information Store service. This would only generate a needless alert.

that perform service-level monitoring can query the operating system to see if a service is in the "running" state. Services that have failed or that have been stopped can be identified in this manner.

Because the services running will be very specific to the type of server in question it is recommended that you research the system to determine the specific services needed for the server to properly do its job. For example, on an Exchange server you might monitor the following:

- Microsoft Exchange IMAP4

- Microsoft Exchange Information Store

- Microsoft Exchange Management

- Microsoft Exchange MTA Stacks

- Microsoft Exchange POP3

- Microsoft Exchange Routing Engine

- Microsoft Exchange Site Replication Service

- Microsoft Exchange System Attendant

- Simple Mail Transfer Protocol

- World Wide Web Publishing Service

- Antivirus

- Antispam

## Application-Level Monitoring

Monitoring systems at the application level enables you to pull useful performance information from the system. Not only can you determine whether or not a service is running, but you can also determine how well it is running. Specific performance metrics such as SMTP queue sizes or mailbox sizes can be monitored to determine the health of the system. Databases can be monitored for critical things like available file locks, replication status, or even current user load. This type of monitoring allows thresholds to be used to determine when reactive measure should be taken to address a system problem. By layering several types of application-level monitoring, complex tests can be performed on the system. Rather than simply pinging a Web server to make sure it's running or querying it on port 80 or even checking to see if the World Wide Web publishing service is running, an application-level monitoring system can send a specific query to the Web server and determine whether the correct response was received. This level of monitoring gives you an impressive level of insights into the workings of the network.

This type of monitoring can be exceptionally useful in the area of capacity planning. By monitoring and logging application-level performance counters, you can use long-term system-usage tracking to determine when a resource will become insufficient.

Not unlike service-level monitoring, the key monitoring points of application-level monitoring will vary by application based on the role of the server. An Exchange server, for example, might be monitored for the following types of items:

- SMTP Queue growth

- MTA Queue growth

- MAPI transaction time, average

- Mailbox sizes

- NDR count

- Information Store size

- User load

- Concurrent connections

- Traffic on connectors to foreign mail systems

However, a SQL server might be more concerned with the following:

- Transaction response time

- Number of long running transactions

- Error log tracking

- Process blocks

- Page-level locks

- Table-level locks

- Exclusive locks

- Shared locks

- Log space

- Database space

- Cache hit rate

In any case, it is critical for the administrator who is implementing the monitoring solution to work very closely with the application owners to ensure that the important monitoring points are being captured, both from an alerting standpoint as well as from a capacity monitoring and planning standpoint.

**Application-Level Monitoring Solutions**

Most application-level monitoring solutions require the installation of a monitoring agent on the target system. This allows the monitored system to have greater knowledge of its applications but could potentially increase the CPU load on the monitored system.

## Performance Monitoring

Although a monitoring system is quite useful for spotting problems and outages it can also be used to measure and track the performance of the system. By identifying key performance

> **Performance Monitoring's Real Value**
>
> Although performance monitoring is useful for identifying problems with a system, its real value comes in long-term trend identification.

metrics such as memory usage or database transaction times you can not only be aware of outages but also see changes in system performance that would affect the end-user experience. By logging these performance metrics you also have the capability to see a long-term view of the performance of the system. Trends in system usage and trends in resource usage become extremely valuable when tracked over extended periods of time. This information can be used to predict when upgrades will be needed.

Some recommended monitoring points are as follows:

- CPU usage

- Available memory

- Available disk space

- Transaction rate

- Network utilization

- Disk I/O

## Monitoring Pitfalls

There are a lot of different types of monitoring packages on the market and there are pros and cons to each type. There are a few things you should be aware of when picking a monitoring package.

> **Resist the Temptation...**
>
> Resist the temptation to turn on monitoring for each and every subsystem available. Limit the scope of the monitoring to data points that will actually be used either for long term performance trending or for failure notification. Enabling too many monitoring points only serves to cloud the valid data and discourage you from addressing all of the data. Monitoring too many data points also imposes an unnecessarily harsh load on the system and reduces the scalability of the monitoring system.

A lot of monitoring packages use agents. This means that some piece of code needs to be installed on each machine that will be monitored. This introduces an unknown to the server. You should always baseline the performance of a server before adding a monitoring agent. In this way, any negative impact to the server's performance can be accurately measured. Also, be aware of packages that utilize protocols that are built into the operating system. Almost every monitoring package on the market supports Simple Network Management Protocol. SNMP is built into most Windows operating systems.

Unfortunately, the version built into older versions of Windows isn't terribly secure. It sends its traps in clear text. Although updates to SNMP are available and have been included in service packs, most administrators don't know to reinstall their latest service pack after loading SNMP on the system. Also, an administrator should never leave the default community strings! This is a huge security risk.

Other monitoring packages gather information about a Windows system through the use of NetBIOS calls. Although at first this seems like a good idea, keep in mind that if a legitimate monitoring system can gather vital information about a server via NetBIOS requests, so can any other system. Never enable NetBIOS for monitoring purposes on a system that is reachable from outside your network. This goes for DMZs and wireless networks alike.

# Determining What to Monitor and Alert Upon

Monitoring and alerting go hand in hand. The real value in system monitoring is being able to alert an administrator if something goes wrong. As such, it is important to determine what parameters should result in an alert being generated. As a general rule any outage in a nonredundant system should be alerted immediately. Any outage in a redundant system that would result in a single system remaining should be immediately alerted. Any security-related events should generate an alert.

Most monitoring and alerting systems today not only track the failures of systems, subsystems, and services but they can also detect these items coming back online. It is always worthwhile to trigger an event when a system comes back into an "up" state. This can mean the difference between coming in to the office at 4 a.m. and going back to sleep.

**Mail System Alerts**

Alerts regarding a mail system should not be sent via e-mail only. If this is the only choice, try to have more than one mail server available to relay the message. Similarly, alerts regarding an Internet connection should be sent via a pager that it not dependent on the Internet connection.

## Hardware Alerting

Although the knowledge that a computer is responding to a ping is of only limited value, the knowledge that a computer has stopped responding to ping is quite useful. Most network hardware places a high priority on ICMP traffic. It is unusual for a router or switch to fail to respond to ping due to excessive load. This means that hardware monitoring rarely results in false positives. As such, failures determined by hardware monitoring should always be alerted. These alerts should use event correlation so that the failure of a router generates an alert but the apparent failures of the upstream routers do not create additional alerts.

**E-Mail Is an Excellent Vehicle for Sending Alerts**

Always be aware if an alert method is dependent on the device that is being monitored. E-mail is an excellent vehicle for sending alerts but it becomes much less useful when it's e-mailing a pager to tell it that the Internet connection is down.

## Port-Level Alerting

It is not unusual for a port-level monitoring event to timeout before the system has properly responded. As such it is often necessary to set thresholds that report failures. Rather than having a port-level failure immediately trigger an alert it should be set to require multiple failures on consecutive cycles to generate an alert.

## Service-Level Alerting

Service-level monitoring looks to the operating system to determine if service is running. As such, service-level checks rarely produce false positives. Service failures reported via the operating system should immediately generate alerts. Services returning to a "running" state should also generate an alert. These types of "up and down" alerts are often used to determine system uptime.

## Application-Level Alerting

Application-level alerts are almost always generated by specific counters meeting specific thresholds. Because application parameters can spike under burst conditions it is necessary to set thresholds for how long a specific parameter must remain at a specific level before triggering an alert. By doing so, false positives can be greatly reduced.

As with application-level monitoring, you should work closely with the application owner to determine thresholds for alerting. The application owner will have a much better understanding of the application and will know how to spot abnormal behavior.

## Performance Alerting

Performance counters tend to fluctuate greatly during the operation of a system. As a result, point-in-time monitoring can very easily result in false positives. By setting thresholds for not only the value of a performance counter but also for how long the counter must remain above a threshold, an administrator can greatly reduce the number of false positives generated by the system.

> **Be Aware of Any Service-Level Agreements**
> Be aware of any service-level agreements when determining the thresholds for triggering a performance-based alert. If a system has an SLA requiring it to be back in service within one hour, using a threshold of more than 10 minutes would be ill-advised.

Administrators must depend on their familiarity with servers to determine the thresholds for alerting. Although a system might run fine at 75% utilization, if the system normally spikes to no more than 10% utilization, a sustained load of 20% might be enough to cause the administrator some concern. Avoid falling into the trap of only generating alerts if something is "pegged" at max utilization for an extended period of time. Any sustained and drastic change in system behavior is most likely a sign that something is wrong and the appropriate resources should be notified.

## Alerting Pitfalls

There are many ways to get an alert to the appropriate resource. It is to your advantage to use more than one method for each alert. The two most commonly used alerts are e-mail and pager. E-mail can be a very effective method but it is susceptible to failures in the e-mail system and the Internet connection. There is nothing more annoying than receiving two messages back to back stating "The Internet router is down!" and "The Internet router is back up!" Mail server failures can elicit the same response. Whenever possible, have the alert sent via a media that isn't a single point of failure. E-mail along with a pager that is dialed via a phone line is an excellent way to ensure that critical alerts reach their intended target.

If alerts are going to an onsite 24/7 resource, make sure that the staff is responding correctly to alerts by performing regular tests. Monitoring a "fake" server that can be used to trigger alerts is a good way to keep the monitoring staff on their toes. An onsite monitoring staff that ignore alerts or doesn't know how to react aren't benefiting anyone.

Don't just take the default values offered by the monitoring package. Some servers just don't behave in a normal fashion. Generate alerts on values that are outside the server's normal behavior. Don't always assume that a resource will hit 100% if there is a problem. Similarly, don't focus only on high utilization. If a server has been between 30%–40% utilization for the past year, a sustained 5% should be just as alarming as a sustained 75%. Both situations suggest that something bad has happened.

# Responding to Problems Automatically

Traditionally systems are monitored so that problems can be seen immediately and the appropriate administrator can be notified of the issue. The administrator would then go to the site where the system is located to perform the necessary maintenance task to return the system to usable state. Modern monitoring systems are able to not only alert administrators to problems but they are able to react to system events and process

> **Reactive Monitoring Systems Are No Replacement for Qualified Technical Resources**
>
> Although many monitoring systems are quite sophisticated, they are only as good as the administrator that configured their responses. Even then, reactive monitoring systems are no replacement for qualified technical resources.

commands to attempt to fix the problem on their own. In this way problems can be responded to automatically. Often simple fixes can be attempted by the system itself. If these fixes fail the problem can be escalated to an administrator who can handle the problem in person.

## Triggering External Scripts

One of the simplest ways to allow a system to repair itself in the event of simple problems is by triggering an external script. External scripts also enable the clever administrator to extend the abilities of the monitoring system. Rather than using static reactions to an event, any external script can call external programs to do more advanced tasks to determine who is the administrator on call and page them rather than statically paging the same person every time. External scripts enable an administrator to stack events such as triggering a pager, sending e-mails to multiple recipients, or simply trying to restart a series of services.

> **External Scripts Might Be Prevented**
>
> Some external scripts might be prevented by OS level security settings. The MAPISEND, for example, will not be allowed by default on Outlook 2000 SP-1 and higher. This is because the default security settings don't allow an external script to use a MAPI profile without user intervention. This behavior can be excluded for a system in the Exchange configuration. Always be aware of these types of limitations with scripts and test them before they get used in production.

External scripts often require additional programs to fully execute all the items an administrator would typically want to occur. One of the most useful things an administrator can do is to initiate a command line e-mail message. Programs like Mapisend.exe can be leveraged to send messages to different resources that indicate the situation that has occurred.

```
mapisend -u Outlook -p password -r recepient@companyxyz.com -s %hostname% is down -m
➥ "at %time% on %date%"
```

## Services Recovery and Notification

Windows 2003 has a built-in function that allows services to not only attempt to restart themselves, but also to alert the system in some way that a restart has occurred. By going into the Properties of a service and going to the Recovery tab there are options for what the system should do on first, second, and subsequent failures. There is also an option to determine when to reset the failure counter. The options are to Take No Action, Restart the Service, Run a Program, or Restart the System. Although restarting the service might seem very tempting, it is preferred to run an external program instead. This external program should restart the service but also it should alert you that the service has been restarted. If the monitoring system in use doesn't natively detect service failure, the program could send an SNMP trap, send a message to the your system, or trigger an e-mail to you to alert you that the event has occurred. This built-in functionality gives you great flexibility in integrating this built-in function to almost any type of monitoring system.

> **Append an Entry to a Log File**
>
> Have the program that restarts the service append an entry to a log file by passing an error message along with the %time% and %date% parameters to enable you to check a single file to determine when and how often a service is failing and restarting. This information, covering a long stretch of time, can be a very useful troubleshooting tool.

# Using Microsoft Operations Manager for Advanced Automation

Microsoft has made a huge push into the arena of enterprisewide system monitoring. Microsoft released Microsoft Operations Manager, or MOM, as a tool that integrates tightly in the monitoring and alerting process of Microsoft's technologies. The result is a monitoring application that supports hardware-level, port-level, service-level, and application-level monitoring. By having access to Microsoft's full source code for all Microsoft applications, the MOM developers were able to create management packs that could gather every last iota of useful information from an application and allow rules and thresholds to determine when to generate alerts or log useful information.

## Understanding MOM

MOM, as a comprehensive monitoring and alerting package, consists of data providers, event correlation, filters, rules, knowledge packs, and knowledge base integration that work together to not only monitor a system, but also to link the administrator to solutions for problems. Rather than just identify a problem, MOM is able to link the user to the Microsoft Knowledge Base to suggest solutions to the issue that has arisen. Similarly, MOM enables you to store problem resolution in a local knowledge base so that other site administrators can learn from the past experiences of their coworkers. Rather than reinvent the wheel each time, MOM helps companies pool together the "islands of knowledge" that exist at any company. By putting the resources into a central location, it is easier for administrators to draw from it.

## Benefits of MOM

MOM is oriented around three primary goals—managing, tuning, and securing Windows and Windows-based applications.

In the area of managing, MOM offers full-time monitoring of all aspects of the Windows server–based environment. It provides proactive alerting and responses by using built-in filters and logic to recognize events and conditions that can lead to failure in the future.

Like most monitoring applications, MOM collects long-term trending data about the performance of a system. MOM takes this concept one step further by providing suggestions for improving performance and enabling you to compare the results of performance adjustments to historical information. This addresses one of the fundamental issues with performance tuning, which is having a valid benchmark of the data that can be referenced historically to see if changes to the system are actually improving the performance of the system. MOM provides the empirical data needed to measure the effect of system tuning.

Windows 2000 and Windows 2003 provide excellent auditing capabilities. The problem is that this can produce an incredible amount of data that must be reviewed regularly by the system administrator. The sheer volume of data will limit the amount of attention an administrator can give to the data. This makes it nearly impossible to really review the security logs for subtle security problems. The natural tendency of the system administrator is to reduce the number of items being audited. Although this frees up time for the administrator, it reduces the amount of valuable data entering the system. Unlike an administrator, MOM will tirelessly monitor the logs on every server round the clock, correlating individual events to identify potential hacking attempts or security breeches. MOM can be an administrator's best friend because it is able to take on the tedious task of reviewing the event logs on all servers in the enterprise to determine if the conditions for a failure are present.

Statistics suggest that 40% of system outages are caused by application failure, including software bugs, applications-level errors, and interoperability problems. Another 40% of outages are attributed to Operator Errors, including configuration errors, entering data incorrectly, and failure to monitor. The other 20% are attributed to hardware failures, power failures, natural disasters, and so on.

As you can see, application-level errors and operator errors together account for 80% of system outages. As such, the greatest return on investment for system uptime is to focus on application failures and operator errors. Although the end users are very good at spotting and reporting system outages, it is greatly preferred to predict potential outages and fix them proactively.

In large companies, administrators tend to work in groups with other administrators who are knowledgeable in a specific area. By putting these specialists together in teams, systems can be effectively managed by these experts. The downside to this philosophy is that a company ends up creating isolated containers of knowledge. Groups that specialize in managing a specific application might not be knowledgeable about the operating system that it runs on. Similarly, applications that are dependent on other applications are usually managed by administrators who only understand their own application, not the applications upon which they are dependent. The result of this is that information outside a group's area of expertise is not well utilized. An Exchange support group might be getting error messages in the event log that reference data about the connection to a SAN. Without SAN knowledge, the Exchange group can't know if the log entries are problems or simply informative messages. This can make it very easy to ignore potential problems. MOM attempts to combat this type of issue by providing its own expertise and knowledge. MOM can correlate events with other events and predict the actual outcome. MOM draws information from each of the separate systems in the network and places it in a single location. Equally important, MOM stores this information long term. A busy administrator can easily miss key event log entries because they are overwritten by other events. MOM, on the other hand, reads each and every log diligently and reacts to events based on filters and logic. By storing these key events centrally over a long period of time, administrators are able to go back and look at historic events on a server. By having access to all the data centrally, MOM is able to act on the big picture rather than only be able to react to individual system problems.

Similarly, by having access to all the data and seeing the big picture, MOM is able to filter out false positives by understanding what errors are actually results of a "lowest common denominator" error. For example, if MOM knows that the local router interface is down, it knows not to report all objects known to be on the far side of that router as down as well. It knows that the service checks or application parameter checks on those systems are failing because the system is unreachable. This drastically reduces the number of false positives and reduces the load on the system.

The other area in which MOM really shines is in helping to secure the servers in the enterprise. MOM is able to monitor remote servers for the presence of security patches and hot fixes. Because MOM is tied in with the Microsoft Knowledge Base, it is able to determine what patches should be on a system based on the services it sees the system running.

Having a centralized view of a distributed environment makes managing the security of the environment much easier. By being able to monitor such a large number of events on a server and having access to a centralized knowledge base, MOM is able to perform a basic level of Intrusion Detection as well. MOM will recognize patterns in traffic and events on a server that most administrators will miss.

## Third-Party Monitoring and Alerting

There are many other third-party monitoring solutions on the market that provide various levels of monitoring, reporting, alerting, and trend analysis. Some of the more popular ones are

- HPOpenview
- Unicenter TNG

- Servers Alive

- What's Up? Gold

- BMC Patrol

- SiteScope

- MRTG

Aside from HPOpenview and BMC Patrol, most of these applications are meant for smaller networks and do not provide the depth of monitoring options that an administrator would get from something like MOM. For small environments, these applications do a good job of alerting administrators when monitored parameters surpass a particular threshold. But these applications are insufficient for providing the capability to support knowledge base links, local knowledge bases, or event correlation with other events to determine holistic situations.

## Improving Monitoring Via SMS

Most administrators view SMS as purely a tool for distributing software. Although it is very good at this task, a clever administrator can leverage the capabilities of SMS to further enhance their monitoring environment. Most monitoring packages deal exclusively with servers and network hardware. SMS, on the other hand, is focused mostly on desktops. Because licensing a monitoring package to monitor desktops is usually prohibitively expensive, SMS is a logical choice because it is already gathering information on all the desktops.

SMS software inventory reports are a great source of data to mine for potential intrusions into the network. Monitoring systems for unexpected software packages is a great way to catch viruses or Trojan horses that install themselves on a system. After all, one of the key points of monitoring is to improve network security. As any administrator will tell you, the greatest threat to his network's security is the end users. SMS is a great tool to keep tabs on end users' computers.

# Summary

This chapter touched on many aspects of monitoring and alerting. You learned that monitoring can come from many sources. ICMP ping checks, OS service statuses, port query responses, and detailed application interrogation can all supply an administrator with information about the status of a system. Monitoring systems can leverage existing standards like SNMP (Simple Network Management Protocol), WMI, or NetBIOS queries or they might require dedicated agents to be installed on the systems to be monitored.

Monitoring information can be useful in both a short term and long term sense. Short term monitoring can determine whether a service stops, whether a piece of hardware changes status, or whether a system stops responding to service requests. Performance counters can be queried for point-in-time information to see if they are within expected ranges. This information can also be useful from a long-term tracking standpoint. By tracking when services go from up to down an administrator can begin to accurately track system uptime. Performance counters can be used from a capacity-planning standpoint to predict when resources will become insufficient. Administrators can plot system resource consumption against the number of users supported to gain valuable insight into the actual capacity of the systems. By having this information, upgrades to the system can be accurately measured in terms of the increase in capacity.

This chapter has shown the various types of monitoring available on the market and has made suggestions about how to determine what parameters should be monitored on different types of servers.

This chapter has introduced the reader to the concepts of scripting. Scripting is an excellent way to extend the capabilities of a monitoring and alerting system by creating complex responses to simple inputs. Rather than just raise a flag when an error occurs, a script can attempt to fix the situation and alert multiple resources about the situation.

You also saw how dedicated monitoring and alerting applications like MOM take the concept to new heights. By centralizing monitoring results, MOM also centralizes the information and expertise. By applying its own knowledge of software applications, MOM is often better able to diagnose problems than the administrator is. MOM intelligently links the administrator to knowledge specific to the situation encountered. By offering knowledge packs for all Microsoft applications, MOM has a significant advantage over other monitoring systems.

# 22

# Creating a Fault-Tolerant Environment

**B**ecause more and more businesses rely on constant and uninterrupted access to their IT network resources, many technologies have been created to help ensure continuous uptime of servers and applications. Windows Server 2003 is inline with these new technologies to meet the demands of the modern business model that seeks to provide a fault-tolerant network environment where unexpected downtime is a thing of the past. By combining Windows Server 2003 technologies with the appropriate hardware and general best practices, IT organizations can realize both file-level and system-level fault tolerance to maintain a high level of availability for their business-critical applications and network services.

This chapter highlights the features available in Windows Server 2003 that target fault tolerance and provides best practices for their implementation of and application to the IT environment. On the file-system side, in addition to proper disk management and antivirus protection, Windows Server 2003 provides Distributed File System (DFS), Volume Shadow Copy (VSC), and Remote

Storage technologies. Related to system-level fault tolerance, Windows Server 2003 includes the Microsoft Cluster Service (MSCS) and Network Load Balancing (NLB) technologies to provide redundancy and failover capabilities.

# Optimizing Disk Management for Fault Tolerance

System administrators have long since relied on Redundant Arrays of Inexpensive Disks (RAID) technologies to provide levels of fault tolerance for their server disk resources. And though the technology is a familiar mainstay in server management, its importance should not be overlooked. There are a couple of ways to leverage RAID to optimize disk management in Windows Server 2003. The first is creating RAID disks using disk controller configuration utilities, and the second is creating the RAID disks using dynamic disk configuration from within the Windows Server 2003 operating system.

## Hardware-based RAID Solutions

Using two or more disks, different RAID-level arrays can be configured to provide fault tolerance that can withstand disk failures and still provide uninterrupted disk access. Hardware-based RAID is achieved when a separate RAID disk controller is used to configure and manage the disks participating in the RAID array. The RAID controller stores the information on the array configuration, including disk membership and status.

Implementing hardware-level RAID configured and stored on the disk controller is preferred over the software-level RAID configurable within Windows Server 2003 Disk Management because the Disk Management and synchronization processes in hardware-level RAID are offloaded to the RAID controller. With Disk Management and synchronization processes offloaded from the RAID controller, the operating system will perform better overall.

Another reason to provide hardware-level RAID as a best practice is that the configuration of the disks does not depend on the operating system. This gives administrators greater flexibility when it comes to recovering server systems and performing upgrades.

Because there are many hardware-based RAID solutions available, it is important to refer to the manufacturer's documentation on creating RAID arrays to understand the particular functions and peculiarities of the RAID disk controller in use.

## Using Dynamic Disk RAID Configurations

Windows Server 2003 supports two types of disks: basic and dynamic. Basic disks are backward-compatible, meaning that basic partitions can be accessed by previous Microsoft operating systems such as MS-DOS and Windows 95 when formatted using FAT; and when formatted using NTFS, Windows NT, Windows 2000, and Windows .NET Server 2003 can access them.

Dynamic disks are managed by the operating system and provide several configuration options, including software-based RAID sets and the capability to extend volumes across multiple disks. Though there are several configuration options, including spanned and stripped volumes, the only really fault tolerant dynamic disk configurations involve creating mirrored volumes (RAID 1) or RAID 5 volumes as described in the following list:

- Mirrored Volume (RAID 1). Mirrored volumes require two separate disks, and the space allocated on each disk must be equal. Mirrored sets duplicate data across both disks and can withstand a single disk failure. Because the mirrored volume is an exact replica of the first disk, the space capacity of a mirrored set is limited to half of the total allocated disk space.

- RAID 5 Volume. Software-based RAID 5 volumes require three or more disks and provide faster read/write disk access than a single disk. The space or volume provided on each disk of the RAID set must be equal. RAID 5 sets can withstand a single disk failure and can continue to provide access to data using only the remaining disks. This capability is achieved by reserving a small portion of each disk's allocated space to store data parity information that can be used to rebuild a failed disk or to continue to provide data access.

## Using the Disk Management MMC

Most disk-related administrative tasks can be performed using the Disk Management MMC snap-in. This tool is located in the Computer Management console, but the standalone snap-in can also be added in a separate Microsoft Management Console window. Disk Management is used to identify disks, define disk volumes, and format the volumes.

**New Feature in the Windows Server 2003 Disk Management Console**

A new feature in the Windows Server 2003 Disk Management console enables administrators to also manage disks on remote machines.

To use the Disk Manager to create a software-based RAID, the disks that will participate in the array must first be converted to dynamic disks. This is a simple process by which the administrator right-clicks on each disk in question and chooses Convert to Dynamic, as shown in Figure 22.1.

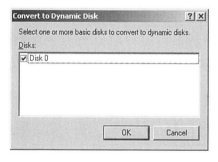

**FIGURE 22.1**   Convert basic disks to dynamic.

The system will require a reboot to complete if the system volume is being converted to Dynamic. After the disks are converted, perform the following steps to set up a Mirrored volume or RAID 1 of the system volume:

1. Click Start, All Programs, Administrative Tools, Computer Management.

2. In the left pane, if it is not already expanded, double-click Computer Management (local).

3. Click the plus sign next to Storage, and select Disk Management.

4. In the right pane, right-click the system volume and choose Add Mirror.

5. Choose the disk on which to create the mirror for the system volume and click Add Mirror.

6. The volumes on each disk start a synchronization process that might take a few minutes or longer, depending on the size of the system volume and the types of disks being used. When the mirrored volume's status changes from Re-synching to Healthy, select File, Exit in the Computer Management console to close the window.

## Using the Diskpart Command-Line Utility

Diskpart.exe is a flexible command-line disk management utility that performs most of the functions available to it with the Disk Management console. Using diskpart.exe, both basic volumes and dynamic volumes can be extended whereas the Disk Management can only extend dynamic volumes. The real value of using Diskpart.exe is that it can be run with a script to automate volume management. This is particularly useful when automating server builds across several servers that have the same characteristics. For more information on automatic server installations, refer to Chapter 11, "Implementing Windows Server 2003."

> **Extend a Basic Volume Using Diskpart.Exe**
> If you want to extend a basic volume using diskpart.exe, the unallocated disk space must be on the same disk as the original volume and must be contiguous with the volume you are extending. Otherwise, the command will fail.

The syntax for Diskpart.exe is as follows:

```
Diskpart.exe /s script
```

The script referenced by the utility is a text file that will include the specific instructions necessary for the desired function. For example, to extend a volume using unallocated space on the same disk, the associated script file would look like this:

```
Select Volume 2
Extend
Exit
```

# Maximizing Redundancy and Flexibility with Distributed File System

One method for creating low-cost failover and redundancy of file shares is leveraging Microsoft's Distributed File System (DFS). A feature introduced in Windows NT 4, DFS improves file share availability by providing a single unified namespace to access shared folders hosted across different servers. Because the same data can be synchronized through replication across multiple servers, there is no single point of failure for the access of the data.

Further, because a DFS root can support multiple targets physically distributed across a network, the network load for accessing particular file shares can be load-balanced rather than taxing a single server.

DFS also improves the users' experience for accessing files because the user needs to remember only a single server or domain name and share name to connect to a DFS-shared folder. Because domain-based DFS, available from Windows 2000, is published in Active Directory, the DFS namespace is always visible to users in the domain. Moreover, if a server hosting a particular share becomes unavailable, DFS will use the site and costing information in Active Directory to route the user to the next closest server.

Finally, because DFS uses NTFS and file sharing permissions, administrators can improve security of data by ensuring only authorized users have access to DFS shares.

The next section explains new DFS features available in Windows Server 2003 and provides best practices for deploying DFS in a Windows Server 2003 network environment.

## New DFS Features in Windows Server 2003

Administrators deploying DFS in Windows NT 4, or even in a Windows 2000 Active Directory, often found that the technology promised more than it could deliver. With Windows Server 2003, such problems have been worked out, startup and configuration times have been reduced, memory usage has been improved, and new features have been added.

### Closest Site Selection

One such enhancement deals with site costing, which exists in both Windows 2000 and Windows Server 2003. When a client accesses a DFS namespace, DFS will connect the client to a DFS root target in the client's site. In Windows 2000, if there are no available root targets in the client's site, the client will randomly connect to another DFS root target in any site.

With Windows Server 2003, if a root target is not available in the client's site, it will randomly look for a target in the next closest site, and so on. This feature, called Closest Site Selection, improves upon site costing by automatically connecting the client to the closest possible DFS target.

**Intersite Topology Generator (ISTG) Must Be Running**

For Closest Site Selection to work on link targets, Intersite Topology Generator (ISTG) must be running on Windows Server 2003. All domain controllers in a domain must be running Windows Server 2003 for Closest Site Selection to work on domain root targets.

To enable Closest Site Selection, use the DFSutil.exe command-line tool that is installed with the Windows Server 2003 support tools. The syntax for the command is as follows:

```
Dfsutil /root:\\servername>\dfsrootname /sitecosting /enable
```

### Multiple Roots per Server

With Windows 2000 DFS, administrators were limited to creating a single DFS root per server. With Windows Server 2003, a server can contain multiple DFS roots. This new feature provides an immediate server and namespace consolidation opportunity for existing Windows 2000 DFS deployments.

More importantly, Windows Server 2003 provides an opportunity to set up different DFS roots on a single server that each have unique security settings. For companies that want to delegate administration of different DFS roots to particular organizational groups, this can now be accomplished from a single server.

With Windows Server 2003 Enterprise or Datacenter Edition, server clusters can support the multiple DFS roots. Multiple DFS roots can exist in multiple resource groups and each group can be hosted on a different node in the cluster. Microsoft Cluster Service (MSCS) is discussed in a later section of this chapter.

### Administration Improvements

Windows Server 2003 provides a new DFS Microsoft Management Console (MMC) snap-in that eases the administration of the File Replication Service (FRS). Replication of DFS targets can now be configured via a wizard that includes a built-in topology generator as shown in Figure 22.2.

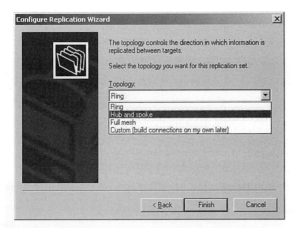

**FIGURE 22.2**.
Configuring DFS Replication topology.

---

## BEST PRACTICE

### Setting Up DFS

DFS is included with a default installation of Windows Server 2003. Setup begins with defining the DFS namespace. The namespace starts with a root that maps to one or more root targets. Below the root are links that map to their own targets, which refer to shared folders on separate servers.

DFS roots can be server-based or domain-based, but they must exist on NTFS volumes. A domain-based DFS root has the following format: \\*domainname*\*rootname*, as shown in Figure 22.3.

In Active Directory environments, use the domain-based DFS namespace. This type of namespace can include approximately 5,000 links. Multiple DFS targets can be created in the same domain to ensure availability.

For a single namespace that includes more than 5,000 links, use a standalone server-based DFS namespace. A single, standalone DFS namespace can support as many as 50,000 links. Configuration information for a server-based DFS is stored in the local Registry instead of Active Directory.

## BEST PRACTICE

Domain-based DFS leverages Active Directory for fault tolerance. For a single server implementation of DFS, high availability is achieved by using Microsoft Cluster Service (MSCS).

Many client types can access targets in a DFS namespace by default. These include Windows Server 2003 family, Windows XP Professional, Windows 2000 family, and Windows NT 4 with Service Pack 6a. Windows 95/98 will need to have the DFS client installed.

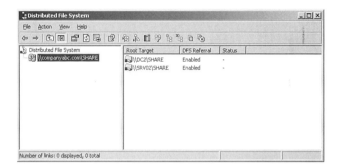

**FIGURE 22.3**
Setting up the DFS root.

## BEST PRACTICE

### DFS Replication

The following best practices for DFS replication can help ensure that replication occurs as expected. Because file replication is triggered by a file version change or last-saved or modified time stamp, a standard file share might generate many replication changes, which can saturate the network bandwidth. To avoid such scenarios, follow as many of these suggestions as possible:

- Start with an empty DFS root folder to keep from having to replicate any data at the root level. Also, this can simplify the restore process of a DFS root folder because it contains only links that are managed by DFS.

- Do not replicate DFS roots because the roots will try to replicate the data in the root folders plus the data contained within the link targets. Replication is not necessary if the links are already replicating. Because the roots will not replicate for redundancy, deploy domain DFS roots and add additional root targets.

- If possible, use DFS for read-only data. When data is being replicated, FRS always chooses the last-saved version of a file. If a group share is provided through a replicated DFS link and two employees are working on the same file, each on different replica targets, the last user who closes and saves the file will have his change(s) saved and replicated over the changes of other previous saved edits.

- Schedule replication to occur during nonpeak hours to reduce network congestion. For replicating links that contain frequently changing data, this might not be possible, so to provide data redundancy in the unified namespace, create only a single target for that link and deploy it on a cluster file share. This provides server-level redundancy for your file share data.

# BEST PRACTICE

- Back up at least one DFS link target and configure the backup to not update the archive bit. Changing the archive bit might trigger unnecessary replication.

- Thoroughly test server operating system antivirus programs to ensure that no adverse effects are caused by the scanning of files on a replicated DFS target.

- Verify that the drive that will contain the staging folder for a replication connection contains ample space to accept the amount of replicated data inbound and outbound to this server.

## DFS and Security

Although DFS in Windows Server 2003 enables delegation of administration for assigning permissions to DFS roots and links, it does not provide any additional security to the actual DFS root or link targets. What this means for administrators is that the permissions will need to be set on the NTFS shares manually to provide proper access to files and folders within DFS targets.

### Combining the Functionality of DFS with Software Distribution Via Active Directory Group Policies

When combining the functionality of DFS with software distribution via Active Directory Group Policies, it is important to appropriate NTFS permissions on those shares that contain the software installation packages. If Group Policies are used to push software to computer accounts from DFS shares, make sure those computer accounts have NTFS permission to the file shares.

Moreover, when multiple targets are involved, it is important for administrators to duplicate the NTFS permissions exactly for each additional target. Otherwise, administrators might inadvertently grant users elevated privileges or deny users access completely. To prevent this problem, administrators should create the target file share and configure the share and NTFS permissions manually at the shared folder level before defining the share as a DFS target.

# Simplifying Fault Tolerance with Volume Shadow Copy

When a user deletes a file from his workstation and needs to recover it, she can restore that file from the recycle bin (assuming the recycle bin has not been emptied). In a traditional networking environment, when that same user deletes a file on a network share, that file is gone. To restore the file, a call will be made to a help desk, an administrator will need to load a backup tape, and a restore process will ensue. This typical routine can consume a great deal of time and effort. Further, if the file in question is a business critical database, the company might experience cost impacting downtime waiting for the file to be restored.

Windows Server 2003 provides a solution to this downtime scenario with the Volume Shadow Copy Service (VSS). VSS is a new technology that provides file system–based fault tolerance that does not rely on the typical backup-restore routine. VSS is used to perform a point-in-time backup of an entire NTFS volume, including open files, to a local or remote disk. The process is completed in a very short period of time but is powerful enough to be used to restore an entire volume, if necessary. VSS can be scheduled to automatically back up a volume once, twice, or several times a day.

## Configuring Volume Shadow Copies

If shadow copies of a server's volume are created on a separate local disk, administrators can avoid having to restore data from a backup tape or library. Volume Shadow Copy is already installed and is automatically available using NTFS-formatted volumes.

To enable and configure shadow copies, follow these steps:

1. Log on to the desired server using an account with Local Administrator access.

2. Click Start, All Programs, Administrative Tools, Computer Management.

3. In the left pane, if it is not already expanded, double-click Computer Management (local).

4. Click the plus sign next to Storage.

5. Select Disk Management.

6. Right-click Disk Management, select All Tasks, and select Configure Shadow Copies.

7. On the Shadow Copies page, select a single volume for which you want to enable shadow copies and click Settings.

8. The Settings page enables you to choose an alternative volume to store the shadow copies. Select the desired volume for the shadow copy, as shown in Figure 22.4.

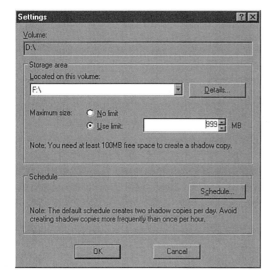

**FIGURE 22.4**    Selecting an alternative drive to store the shadow copies.

9. Configure the maximum amount of disk space that will be allocated to shadow copies.

10. The default schedule for shadow copies is twice a day at 7 a.m. and 12 p.m. If this does not meet the business requirements, click the Schedule button and configure a custom schedule.

11. Click OK to enable shadow copies on that volume and to return to the Shadow Copies page.

12. If necessary, select the next volume and enable shadow copying; otherwise, select the enabled volume and immediately create a shadow copy by clicking the Create Now button.

13. If necessary, select the next volume and immediately create a shadow copy by clicking the Create Now button.

14. After the shadow copies are created, click OK to close the Shadow Copies page, close the Computer Management console, and log off the server.

## Restoring Data from a Shadow Copy

The server administrator or a standard user who has been granted permissions can recover data using previously created shadow copies. The files stored in the shadow copy cannot be accessed directly, but they can be accessed by connecting the volume that has had a shadow copy created.

To recover data from a file share, follow these steps:

1. Log on to a Windows .NET Server 2003 system or Windows XP SP1 workstation with either Administrator rights or with a user account that has permissions to restore the files from the shadow copy.

2. Click Start, Run.

3. At the Run prompt, type \\*servername*\*sharename*, where *servername* represents the NetBIOS or fully qualified domain name of the server hosting the file share. The share must exist on a volume in which a shadow copy has already been created.

4. In the File and Folder Tasks window, select View Previous Versions, as shown in Figure 22.5.

5. When the window opens to the Previous Versions property page for the share, select the shadow copy from which you want to restore and click View.

6. An Explorer window then opens, displaying the contents of the share when the shadow copy was made. If you want to restore only a single file, locate the file, right-click it, and select Copy.

7. Close the Explorer window.

8. Close the Share Property pages by clicking OK at the bottom of the window.

9. Back in the actual file share window, browse to the original location of the file, right-click on a blank spot in the window, and select Paste.

10. Close the file share window.

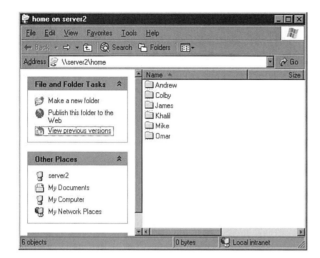

## BEST PRACTICE

### Using Volume Shadow Copy Service (VSS)

When considering the ease with which VSS can be used to recover files, administrators might be tempted to enable Volume Shadow Copies for every NTFS volume in the IT environment. Before attempting such an extensive plan, review the best practices surrounding the use of VSS:

- Do not use VSS on dual-boot machines. Shadow copies created within Windows Server 2003 can become corrupted when the machine is booted into an earlier Windows operating system.

- Mount points are not VSS protected. If the volume is using mount points, the mounted drive will not be part of the shadow copy.

- Set schedule options that reflect work patterns. Consider what times during the day files are most likely to change or be accessed to maintain a manageable set of previous versions for files.

- Select a volume on a separate disk for the shadow copy. Using a separate volume on another disk provides better performance and is recommended for heavily used file servers.

- Continue to perform regular backups. Shadow copies are not a replacement for performing regular backups. Use a backup utility in coordination with shadow copies as your best preparation for disaster recovery.

- Do not schedule more than one copy an hour. Shadow copies will consume disk space. There is also an upper limit of 64 copies per volume that can be stored before the oldest copy is deleted. If shadow copies are taken too often, this limit might be reached very quickly, and older copies could be lost at a rapid rate.

- Before deleting a volume, delete the shadow copy task. If you do not delete the task, VSS will continue to run and generate an Event ID: 7001 in the Event Log each time it fails.

# Optimizing Disk Utilization with Remote Storage

Another fault tolerance technique devised in Windows Server 2003 to protect the file system is *Remote Storage*. When it is installed and configured, Remote Storage has the ability to migrate eligible files from an NTFS volume to a library of magnetic or optical tapes, thus freeing up space on the production server's managed volume. The eligibility is determined in the configuration of Remote Storage based on certain criteria: the percentage of free space on the volume, the size of the files, and a time period over which the files have not been accessed.

**Not Available on Windows XP or the Standard and Web Editions of Windows Server 2003**

Remote Storage functionality is only available in Windows Server 2003 Enterprise and Datacenter editions. It is not available on Windows XP or the standard and Web editions of Windows Server 2003.

When Remote Storage migrates a file or folder, it is replaced on the volume with a file link called a *junction point*. Junction points take up very little room, which reduces the amount of used disk space but leaves a way for this data to be accessed later in the original location. When a junction point is accessed, it spawns the Remote Storage service to retrieve the file that was migrated to tape.

The next section explains how Remote Storage is configured and provides best practices for its use.

## Configuring Remote Storage

Remote Storage is not installed by default in Windows Server 2003, but is easily added from the install media through the familiar Add/Remove Windows Components section of the Add or Remove Programs applet. Once installed, the administrator must configure the backup device that will be used, allocate backup media, and then configure the settings Remote Storage will use to determine whether files should be migrated to the media.

**Remote Storage Supports All SCSI Class 4mm, 8mm, DLT, and Magneto-Optical Devices**

Remote Storage supports all SCSI class 4mm, 8mm, DLT, and magneto-optical devices that are supported by Removable Storage. Using Remote Storage with Exabyte 8200 tape libraries is not recommended. Remote Storage does not support QIC tape libraries or rewritable compact disc and DVD formats.

### Configuring the Backup Device

Ideally the backup device to be used in conjunction will be a tape library, so that file retrieval from junction points can occur automatically.

To enable a device, follow these steps:

1. Install the backup device or library on the Windows Server 2003 system. Use the backup device manufacturer's documentation to accomplish this process.

2. After the backup device is connected, boot up the server and log on using an account with Local Administrator access.

3. Click Start, All Programs, Administrative Tools, Computer Management.

4. In the left pane, if it is not already expanded, double-click Computer Management (local).

5. Click the plus sign next to Storage.

6. Click the plus sign next to Removable Storage.

7. Click the plus sign next to Libraries.

8. Right-click the library (backup device) and select Properties.

9. On the General tab of the Device Properties page, check the Enable Drive box, and click OK.

## Allocating Media for Remote Storage

After the backup device is configured, tape media needs to be allocated for Remote Storage usage. New, unused media inserted into the device is placed in the free media pool. Previously used media will be placed in the import, unrecognized, or backup media pools. Remote Storage uses the Remote Storage media pool, but will look in the free media pool if it does not find available media in Remote Storage.

> **Specify the Type**
>
> Remote Storage can support only a single tape or disk type for use as Remote Storage. Specify the type during the Remote Storage Setup Wizard process.

To inventory a backup device and allocate media for Remote Storage, follow these steps:

1. Locate the desired device, as outlined in the preceding section. Then right-click the device and choose Inventory.

2. After the device completes the inventory process, select the backup device in the left pane. The media will then be listed in the right pane.

3. Right-click the media listed in the right pane and select Properties.

4. On the Media tab of the Media Properties page, note the media pool membership in the Location section. Figure 22.6 shows media that are part of the Import\DLT media pool.

5. Click Cancel to close the Media Properties page.

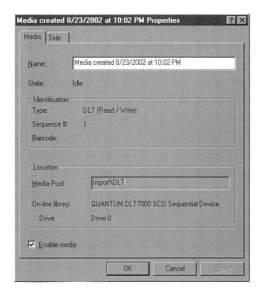

**FIGURE 22.6**   Removable media in the Import\DLT media pool.

**Configuring Remote Storage Settings**

After the backup device and media are properly configured and allocated, a volume can be managed by configuring Remote Storage settings. To configure a managed volume, follow these steps:

1. Click Start, All Programs, Administrative Tools, Remote Storage.

2. If this is the first time the Remote Storage console has been opened or no volumes on the server have been configured for Remote Storage management, the Remote Storage Wizard will begin. Click Next on the Welcome screen to continue.

3. On the Volume Management page, choose whether to manage all volumes or manage only selected volumes by selecting the appropriate radio button. In this example, select Manage Selected Volumes, and click Next.

4. Select the volume to manage and click Next.

5. On the Volume Settings page, enter the amount of free space for the managed volume.

6. On the same page, configure the minimum file size before it will be migrated by Remote Storage; then configure the number of days a file must remain unaccessed before Remote Storage will make it a possible candidate for migration, and then click Next.

   Figure 22.7 shows a volume setting that will migrate data to Remote Storage when a volume has 10% free space remaining, and the file that will be migrated must be larger than 12KB and must remain unaccessed for 120 days.

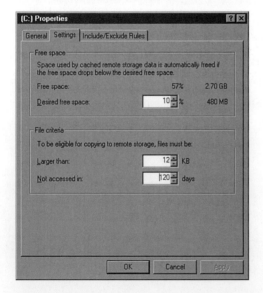

**FIGURE 22.7**   Setting typical Remote Storage volume settings.

7. On the Media Type page, choose the media type associated with the backup device enabled for Remote Storage to use. Choose a media type from the Media Types pull-down menu.

8. On the next page, you can configure a schedule to perform the file copy. The default is to run at 2 a.m. seven days a week. Click the Change Schedule button to configure a custom schedule or click Next to accept the default schedule.

9. Click Finish on the Completing the Remote Storage Wizard page to complete the process.

**BEST PRACTICE**

**Using Remote Storage**

Remote Storage is a powerful new feature of Windows Server 2003, but if used improperly it can make an administrator's job more difficult. When setting up a Remote Storage to provide volume-level fault tolerance, keep the following best practices in mind:

- Continue to perform backups. Remote Storage is not a replacement for running normal scheduled backups. It is also important to provide fault tolerance to Remote Storage itself by backing up the Remote Storage database. It is also a good practice to schedule Remote Storage migration activity to occur at a different time than normal scheduled backups, especially if both rely on the same backup tape library.

- Set antivirus software to scan files only on access. If antivirus programs are scanning volumes managed by Remote Storage on a regular schedule, any data previously migrated by Remote Storage might be requested and be migrated back to disk.

- Do not enable Remote Storage on DFS targets configured for replication. If a new target is added to a replicating DFS link, the entire contents of that DFS target folder will be read by the File Replication Service (FRS). This read operation is necessary to generate the staging files in preparation for synchronizing the target data, which again would cause migrated files to be restored back to the volume.

- Validate Remote Storage functionality. It is important to schedule validation of managed volumes on a regular basis. Validation ensures that all files on managed volumes point to the correct data in Remote Storage.

# Optimizing Clusters to Simplify Administrative Overhead

Microsoft Cluster Service (MSCS) is included with the Enterprise and Datacenter versions of Windows Server 2003. MSCS provides system fault tolerance through a process called failover. When a system fails or is unable to respond to client requests, the clustered services are taken offline and moved from the failed server to another available server, where they are brought online and begin responding to existing and new client requests.

**Cluster Support**

Windows Server 2003, Enterprise Edition supports clusters up to four nodes. Datacenter Edition supports up to eight nodes. A cluster cannot be made up of nodes running both Windows Server 2003, Enterprise Edition, and Windows Server 2003, Datacenter Edition.

MSCS is best used to provide fault tolerance to such resources as file shares, print queues, e-mail or database services, and back-end applications. Applications and other services defined and monitored by the cluster, in addition to cluster hardware, are called cluster resources.

## Choosing the Best Cluster Configuration Model

MSCS can be deployed in one of three different configuration models: single-quorum device cluster, single-node cluster, and majority node set cluster. Choosing the best model depends on the type of service that will be clustered and the type of fault tolerance intended.

### The Single-Quorum Device Cluster

The most common model adopted for clustering is the Single-Quorum Device Cluster. The defining characteristic of this model is that each node in the cluster is connected to a shared storage device that houses a single instance of the quorum, or cluster configuration, data.

This configuration is appropriately suited to providing fault tolerance to applications and services that access large amounts of mission-critical data. Examples would be file, messaging, and database servers. When the cluster encounters a problem on a cluster group containing a shared storage disk resource, the group is failed over to the next node with little or no noticeable disruption to the end user.

### The Single-Node Cluster

A single-node cluster, as its name suggests, utilizes only a single node. In addition to running solely on local disks, a single-node cluster has the ability to use shared storage. A single-node cluster is primarily created as a first step to creating a single-quorum cluster. Because only a single server with local resources is needed, single-node clusters are also beneficial for application development for testing cluster applications.

Because the single-node cluster only contains one node, there is no failover when the server goes down.

### The Majority Node Set Cluster

The Majority Node Set (MNS) cluster can use shared storage devices but it does not depend on the shared resource for configuration data as does the single-quorum cluster. Each node in an MNS cluster maintains a local copy of the quorum device data. As such, MNS clusters can be deployed across a WAN in a geographically distributed environment to provide fault tolerance to two distinct sites in an IT organization.

In situations where the cluster needs to failover across sites, the two sites need to be either bridged or a virtual private network (VPN) or Network Address Translation (NAT) must be installed and configured for proper recovery to occur. The latency between the cluster nodes for private communication must not exceed 500 milliseconds; otherwise, the cluster will go into a failed state.

For an MNS cluster to remain up and running, more than half of the nodes in the cluster must be operational. For example, in a four-node cluster, three nodes must be operational; a three-node cluster requires two operational nodes.

## Installing Microsoft Cluster Service

The Cluster Service is installed by default in Enterprise and Datacenter editions of the operating system. Both the GUI-based Cluster Administrator and the command-line Cluster.exe utility can be used to create and manage clusters. In any event, Microsoft recommends that the Manage Your Server and the Server Configuration Wizard not be used to configure cluster nodes.

## BEST PRACTICE

### Configuring Clusters

- Configure cluster disks as Basic. Partition and format all disks on the cluster storage device as NTFS before adding the first node to a cluster. Do not configure them as dynamic disks, and do not use spanned volumes (volume sets) or Remote Storage on the cluster disks.

- For clusters accessing a shared storage device, ensure that only the first node has access to the cluster disk. The cluster disks can become corrupted if more than one node has access to it. After the Cluster Service is running properly on one node, the other nodes can be installed and configured simultaneously.

- Use multiple network cards in cluster nodes. This allows one card to be dedicated to internal cluster (private network) communication, whereas the other can be used for client (public network) communication, or for mixed (both public and private) communication.

- Cluster certified applications. Be sure that both Microsoft and the software manufacturer certify that the applications are compatible with Cluster Services and will work on Windows Server 2003.

- Do not enable MSCS on a server with Network Load Balancing enabled. NLB can interfere with a server cluster's use of network adapters and Microsoft does not support this configuration.

To install the first node in the cluster using the Cluster Administrator, perform the following steps:

1. Shut down both the cluster nodes and shared storage devices.

2. Connect cables as required between the cluster nodes and shared storage devices.

3. Connect each node's NICs to a network switch or hub using appropriate network cables.

4. If a shared storage device is being used, power on the shared storage device and wait for bootup to complete.

5. Boot up the first node in the cluster. If a shared disk will be used, configure the adapter card's ID on each cluster node to a different number. For example, use ID 6 for node 1 and ID 7 for node 2.

6. Log on with an account that has Local Administrator privileges.

7. If server is not a member of a domain, add the server to the correct domain and reboot as necessary.

8. Configure each network card in the node with the correct network IP address information. Network cards that will be used only for private communication should have only an IP address and subnet mask configured. Default Gateway, DNS, and WINS servers should not be configured. Also, uncheck the Register This Connection's Address in DNS box, as shown in Figure 22.8, on the DNS tab of the Advanced TCP/IP Settings page. For network cards that will support public or mixed networks, configure all TCP/IP settings as they would normally be configured.

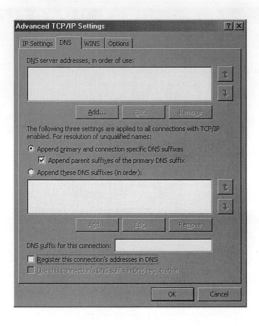

**FIGURE 22.8** TCP/IP DNS configuration settings.

9. Log on to the server using an account that has Local Administrator privileges.

10. Click Start, Administrative Tools, Cluster Administrator.

11. When the Cluster Administrator opens, choose Create New Cluster Action, and click OK.

12. Click Next on the New Server Cluster Wizard Welcome screen to continue.

13. Choose the correct domain from the Domain pull-down menu.

14. Type the cluster name in the Cluster Name text box and click Next to continue.

### Cluster Service Account

The Cluster Service account needs to be only a regular domain user, but specifying this account as the Cluster Service gives this account Local Administrator privileges on the cluster node and also delegates a few user rights, including the ability to act as a part of the operating system and add computers to the domain.

15. Type the name of the cluster node and click Next to continue. The wizard defaults to the local server, but clusters can be configured remotely. The cluster analyzer analyzes the node for functionality and cluster requirements. A detailed log containing any errors or warnings that can stop or limit the installation of the Cluster server is generated.

**16.** Review the log and make changes as necessary; then click Re-analyze or click Next to continue.

**17.** Enter the cluster IP address and click Next.

**18.** Enter the Cluster Service account name and password and choose the correct domain. Click Next to continue.

**19.** On the Proposed Cluster Configuration page, review the configuration and choose the correct quorum type by clicking the Quorum button, as shown in Figure 22.9.

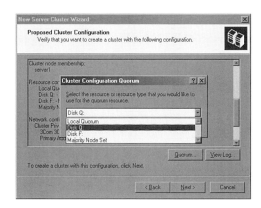

**FIGURE 22.9**   Choosing the cluster quorum configuration.

- To create an MNS cluster, click the Quorum button on the Proposed Cluster Configuration page, choose Majority Node Set, and click OK.

- If a SAN is connected to the cluster node, the Cluster Administrator will automatically choose the smallest basic NTFS volume on the shared storage device. Make sure the correct disk has been chosen and click OK.

- To configure a single node cluster with no shared storage, choose the Local Quorum resource and click OK.

**20.** Click Next to complete the cluster installation.

**21.** After the cluster is created, click Next and then Finish to close the New Server Cluster Wizard and return to the Cluster Administrator.

After the cluster is created on the first node, additional nodes can be added. To add a node to a cluster, perform the following steps:

**1.** Log on to the desired cluster node using an account that has Local Administrator privileges.

**2.** Click Start, Administrative Tools, Cluster Administrator.

**3.** When the Cluster Administrator opens, choose Add Nodes to a Cluster and type the name of the cluster in the Cluster Name text box. Click OK to continue.

**4.** When the Add Nodes Wizard appears, click Next to continue.

5. Type in the server name of the next node and click Add.

6. Repeat the preceding steps until all the additional nodes are in the Selected Computer text box. Click Next to continue. The cluster analyzer will then analyze the additional nodes for functionality and cluster requirements.

7. Review the log and make changes as necessary; then click Re-analyze or click Next to continue.

8. Enter the Cluster Service account password and click Next to continue.

9. Review the configuration on the Proposed Cluster Configuration page and click Next to configure the cluster. After this is finished, click Next and then Finish to complete the additional node installation.

10. Select File, Close to exit the Cluster Administrator.

## Configuring Failover and Failback

Although failover is configured automatically on clusters of two or more nodes, failback needs to be configured manually. *Failback* is designed to allow a preferred server, assuming it is available, to always run a cluster group. Failover functionality can be configured manually as well to set a threshold number of failovers after which the cluster group is changed to a failed state.

Creating a failover/failback process will automate server cluster functionality. To create a failover/failback process, perform the following steps:

1. Click Start, Administrative Tools, Cluster Administrator.

2. When the Cluster Administrator opens, choose Open Connection to Cluster and type the name of the cluster in the Cluster Name text box. Click OK to continue. If the local machine is part of the cluster, enter . (period) as the cluster name, and the program will connect to the cluster running on the local machine.

3. Right-click the appropriate cluster group and select Properties.

4. Select the Failover tab and set the maximum number of failovers allowed during a predefined period of time. When the number of failovers is exceeded within the Period interval, the Cluster Service will change the group to a failed state.

5. Select the Failback tab, choose the Allow Failback radio button, and set time options for allowing failback.

6. Click Next and then Finish to complete the failback configuration.

7. Select File, Close to exit the Cluster Administrator.

# Leveraging Network Load Balancing for Improved Availability

Another method used to provide fault tolerance to system services in Windows Server 2003 is through Microsoft's second clustering technology, Network Load Balancing (NLB). An NLB cluster works by distributing the network traffic targeted across a cluster of host servers each running the clustered service. The load weight to be handled by each host can be configured as necessary. Hosts can be added dynamically to the cluster to handle increased load. Additionally, Network Load Balancing can direct all traffic to a designated single host, called the default host. Network Load Balancing allows all the computers in the cluster to be addressed by the same set of cluster IP addresses (but also maintains their existing unique, dedicated IP addresses).

Whereas MSCS is intended primarily for clustering services with dynamic content such as database, e-mail, and file and print services, NLB is best used in clustering services that provide static content. Good candidates for NLB would be Terminal services, VPN, proxy services, Web server applications, and streaming media services.

## Choosing a Network Load Balancing Model

When an NLB cluster is created, a general port rule for the cluster is also created to define the type of network traffic that will be load-balanced. Additionally, the administrator will need to choose an operational mode, either unicast or multicast, for the cluster. Within the port rule, three types of filtering modes are available: Single Host, Disable Port Range, and Multiple Host. The combination of the operational mode with a filtering mode defines the NLB model for the cluster.

Most NLB clusters will leverage the unicast operational mode unless the functionality delivered by the cluster is specifically multicast services such as steaming media, Internet radio, or Internet training courses. NLB does not support a mixed unicast/multicast environment within a single cluster. Within each cluster, all network adapters in that cluster must be either multicast or unicast.

The filtering modes are defined as follows:

- *Single Host.* This filtering mode directs the specified network traffic to a single host. For example, in an IIS Web farm in which only one server contains the SSL certificate for a secure Web site, the single host port rule will direct port TCP 443 (SSL port) traffic to that particular server.

- *Disable Port Range.* This filtering mode specifies ports that the cluster will not listen on, dropping such packets without investigation. Disabling ports that do not need to be load balanced secures and enhances the performance of NLB clusters.

- *Multiple Host Range.* The default filtering mode allows network traffic to be handled by all the nodes in the cluster. Application requirements will then determine the multiple host affinity configuration.

There are three types of multiple host affinities:

- *None*. This affinity type can send a unique client's requests to all the servers in the cluster during the session. This can speed up server response times but is well suited only for serving static data to clients. This affinity type works well for general Web browsing and read-only file and FTP servers.

- *Class C*. This affinity type routes traffic from a particular class C address space to a single NLB cluster node. This mode is not used too often but can accommodate client sessions that do require stateful data. This affinity does not work well if all the client requests are proxied through a single firewall.

- *Single*. This affinity type is the most widely used. After the initial request is received by the cluster nodes from a particular client, that node will handle every request from that client until the session is completed. This affinity type can accommodate sessions that require stateful data.

## Creating a Network Load Balancing Cluster

The Network Load Balancing Manager is a new tool in Windows Server 2003 that is used for creating and managing NLB clusters. Administrators still have the ability to configure NLB clusters through the network interface card properties page, or through the NLB.EXE command-line utility, though the preferred method is through the NLB Manager. The NLB Manager also simplifies the process by which additional nodes are added to the cluster.

To create a cluster, perform the following steps:

1. Log on to the local console of a cluster node using an account with Local Administrator privileges.

2. Click Start, All Programs, Administrative Tools, Network Load Balancing Manager.

3. Choose Cluster, New.

4. Enter the cluster IP address and subnet mask of the new cluster.

5. Enter the fully qualified domain name for the cluster in the Full Internet Name text box.

6. Enter the mode of operation (unicast will meet most of your NLB application deployments).

7. Configure a remote control password to use the command-line utility NLB.exe to manage the NLB cluster remotely and click Next to continue.

8. Enter any additional IP addresses that will be load-balanced and click Next to continue.

9. Configure the appropriate port rules for each IP address in the cluster, being careful to set the correct affinity for the load-balanced applications.

10. After creating all the allowed port rules, create disabled port rules to reduce network overhead for the cluster nodes. Be sure to have a port rule for every possible port and click Next on the Port Rules page after all port rules have been created. Figure 22.10 shows a best practice port rule for an NLB Terminal server implementation.

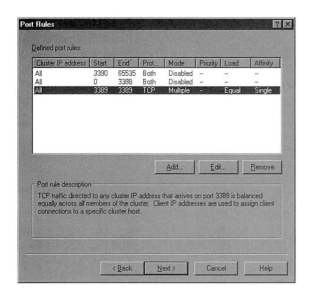

**FIGURE 22.10**
Port rule settings for NLB configuration.

11. On the Connect page, type the name of the server you want to add to the cluster in the Host text box and click Connect.

12. In the Interface Available window, select the NIC that will host the cluster IP address and click Next to continue.

13. On the Host Parameters page, set the cluster node priority. Each node requires a unique host priority, and because this is the first node in the cluster, leave the default of 1.

14. If the node will perform non–cluster-related network tasks in the same NIC, enter the dedicated IP address and subnet mask. The default is the IP address already bound on the network card.

15. For nodes that will join the cluster immediately following the cluster creation and after startup, leave the initial host state to Started. When maintenance is necessary, change the default state of a particular cluster node to Stopped or Suspended to keep the server from joining the cluster following a reboot.

16. After all the information is entered on the Host Parameters page, click Finish to create the cluster.

17. When the cluster is ready for release to the production environment, add the HOST or a record of the new cluster to the DNS domain table.

Use the Network Load Balancing Manager to add nodes to the existing cluster by performing the following steps:

1. Click Start, All Programs, Administrative Tools and right-click Network Load Balancing Manager.

2. Choose the Run-as option and specify an account that has Administrative permissions on the cluster.

3. Choose Cluster, Connect to Existing.

4. In the Host text box, type the IP address or name of the cluster and click Connect.

5. From the Clusters window, select the cluster and click Finish to connect.

6. In the right pane, right-click the cluster name and choose Add Host to Cluster, as shown in Figure 22.11.

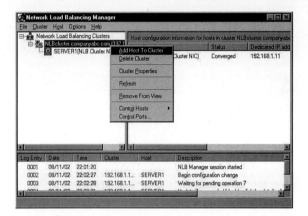

**FIGURE 22.11**
Choosing to add a host to the cluster.

7. On the Connect page, type the name of the server you want to add to the cluster in the Host text box and click Connect.

8. In the Interface Available window, select the NIC that will host the cluster IP address and click Next to continue.

9. On the Host Parameters page, set the cluster node priority. Each node requires a unique host priority, and because this is the first node in the cluster, leave the default of 1.

10. If the node will perform non-cluster–related network tasks in the same NIC, enter the dedicated IP address and subnet mask. The default is the IP address already bound on the network card.

11. For nodes that will join the cluster immediately following the cluster creation and after startup, leave the initial host state to Started. When maintenance is necessary, the default state of a particular cluster node can be changed to Stopped or Suspended to keep the server from joining the cluster following a reboot.

12. After all the information is entered in the Host Parameters page, click Finish to add the node to the cluster.

**BEST PRACTICE**

## Network Load Balancing

Keep the following best practices in mind when setting up an NLB solution:

- Use at least two network cards in each cluster host. Although it is not necessary, having more than one network adapter in a cluster host allows the administrator greater management flexibility. Using this configuration, one adapter is configured to participate in NLB, while the other can be used to access the computer for management or other purposes.

- Do not enable NLB remote control. The Network Load Balancing remote control option presents many security risks, including the possibility of data tampering, denial of service, and information disclosure. It is highly recommended that you do not enable remote control and instead use Network Load Balancing Manager.

- Set up all NLB hosts on the same subnet. No cluster interconnect is used by Network Load Balancing other than the subnet in which the cluster is located. To reduce the risk of switch flooding, the NLB nodes should be connected to an isolated switch or should be configured in a single VLAN if the switch and network support VLANs. For detailed information regarding VLAN configuration and avoiding switch flooding, refer to the network switch documentation.

- Properly secure NLB hosts. Although NLB is configured to filter traffic, this should not be the only means of protecting NLB host computers from network attacks. The Network Load Balancing subnet must be physically protected from intrusion by unauthorized computers and devices in order to avoid interference from unauthorized heartbeat packets. Moreover, applications that run on NLB clusters should also be protected according to application security best practices.

# Realizing Rapid Recovery Using Automated System Recovery (ASR)

Another new feature of Windows Server 2003 is Automated System Recovery (ASR). ASR is more a recovery feature than a fault-tolerance tool, although in an effort to increase server availability in the event of a disaster, ASR can be a valuable component to the overall solution.

The primary goal of ASR is to accelerate recovery time in the event of the loss of a server by bringing a nonbootable system to a state from which a backup and restore application can be executed. This includes configuring the physical storage to its original state, and installing the operating system with all the original settings.

## Improving the Disaster Recovery Process

Prior to Windows Server 2003, the process by which a lost server is rebuilt and recovered was a time-consuming ordeal. The old methods usually resembled the following process:

1. The administrator gets new hardware.

2. Windows is reinstalled from installation media.

   3. Physical storage is manually configured to match original system.

   4. Backup and restore application and drivers are installed.

   5. The original operating system is manually restored to restore settings.

   6. The server is rebooted, and services are manually adjusted.

   7. Data is restored.

With ASR, many of the steps in the old model are eliminated or automated. The new recovery method now proceeds as follows:

   1. The administrator gets new hardware.

   2. From the Windows CD, the administrator executes ASR (by pressing F2 on startup).

   3. The administrator inserts other media when prompted.

   4. Data is restored.

ASR is broken down into two parts: backup and restore. The backup portion is executed through the Automated System Recovery Preparation Wizard located in Backup. The Automated System Recovery Preparation Wizard backs up the System State data, system services, and all disks associated with the operating system components. It also creates a floppy disk, which contains information about the backup, the disk configurations (including basic and dynamic volumes), and how to accomplish a restore.

### A Full Data Backup

ASR is primarily involved with restoring the system; it does not back up data. Always include a full data backup in disaster recovery solutions.

The restore portion of ASR is initiated by pressing F2 during the text portion of Windows Server 2003 setup. When the ASR restore process is initiated, ASR reads the disk configurations from the floppy disk and restores all the disk signatures, volumes, and partitions on the disks required to start your computer. ASR then installs a simple installation of Windows and automatically starts to restore from backup using the backup ASR set created by the Automated System Recovery Preparation Wizard.

To take advantage of ASR in a disaster recovery solution, systems must meet a limited set of requirements:

   ■ Similar hardware. The restored server must have identical hardware to the original server with the exception of network cards, video cards, and hard drives.

   ■ Adequate disk space. Obviously, the restored server must have adequate disk space to restore all critical disks from the original server. Disk geometries must also be compatible.

   ■ ASR state file (asr.sif) must be accessible from a floppy. ASR requires a local floppy drive access. Remote or network recovery procedures do not work with ASR.

   ■ ASR supports FAT volumes of 2.1GB maximum. For volumes larger than 2.1GB, the volume should be formatted with NTFS.

## Using ASR to Recover Cluster Services

ASR can be used to recover a cluster node that is damaged because of corrupt or missing system files, cluster registry files, or hard disk failure. To prepare for an ASR recovery of clustered servers, run the Automated System Recovery Preparation Wizard on all nodes of the cluster and make sure that the cluster service is running when the Automated System Recovery backup is run. Make sure that one of the nodes on which the Automated System Recovery Preparation Wizard is run is listed as the owner of the quorum resource while the wizard is running.

In addition to having the ASR disk, recovering a damaged node in a cluster requires the Windows Server 2003 installation media, backup media containing data backup, and potentially the mass storage driver for the new hardware. With these in hand, perform the following steps to recover a damaged cluster node:

1. Insert the original operating system installation CD into the CD drive of the damaged cluster node.

2. Restart the computer. If prompted to press a key to start the computer from CD, press the appropriate key.

3. If there is a separate driver file for the mass storage device, press F6 when prompted to use the driver as part of setup.

> **Restoring a Disk Signature to a Damaged Cluster Disk**
>
> If you are restoring a disk signature to a damaged cluster disk, power down all other cluster nodes except the one on which you are performing the ASR restore. This cluster node must have exclusive rights to the damaged cluster disk.

4. Press F2 when prompted during the text-only mode section of Setup. This will generate a prompt for the ASR disk.

5. Follow the directions on the screen.

6. If there is a separate driver file for the mass storage device, press F6 (a second time) when prompted after the system reboots.

7. Follow the directions on the screen.

8. After all the restore steps have completed, the restored node can rejoin the cluster.

# Summary

As this chapter has demonstrated, there are many ways to add fault tolerance to network services and resources running on Windows Server 2003 servers. Moreover, each of the features discussed in this chapter is included with the installation of the operating system: no additional licensing fees for third-party software are required to add redundancy and increase availability to Windows Server 2003. Depending on the type of fault tolerance required in an organization's Service Level Agreements, there might be an increased investment in hardware. However, with server consolidation opportunities available with Windows Server 2003, organizations might find that they have freed up hardware that can be re-assigned to participate in fault tolerance solutions.

# PART VII

## Performance Optimization Solutions

# 23

# Tuning and Optimization Techniques

**P**erformance tuning and optimization is frequently overlooked by administrators in an era where hardware has become relatively inexpensive and the processing power of systems in many cases far exceeds the utilization demands of an organization. However in cost-cutting efforts, organizations are consolidating servers, sometimes consolidating five to 10 servers into a single server. In other cases, organizations are fine-tuning servers to optimize the performance of the systems in an effort to minimize server operation inefficiencies that frequently lead to premature server failures.

This chapter focuses on tips, tricks, and best practices to tune and optimize a Windows Server 2003 system and the Windows 2003 networking environment.

# Understanding of Capacity Analysis

Most capacity analysis works to minimize unknown or immeasurable variables, such as the number of gigabytes or terabytes of storage the system will need in the next few months or years to adequately size a system. The high number of unknown variables is largely because network environments, business policies, and personnel are constantly changing. As a result, capacity analysis is an art as much as it involves experience and insight.

If you've ever found yourself specifying configuration requirements for a new server or estimating whether your configuration will have enough power to sustain various workloads now and in the foreseeable future, proper capacity analysis can help in the design and configuration of an efficiently running network environment. These capacity-analysis processes help you weed out the unknowns and make decisions as accurately as possible. They do so by giving you a greater understanding of your Windows Server 2003 environment. This knowledge and understanding can then be used to reduce time and costs associated with supporting and designing an infrastructure. The result is that you gain more control over the environment, reduce maintenance and support costs, minimize fire-fighting, and make more efficient use of your time.

Business depends on network systems for a variety of different operations, such as performing transactions or providing security, so that the business functions as efficiently as possible. Systems that are underused are probably wasting money and are of little value. On the other hand, systems that are overworked or can't handle workloads prevent the business from completing tasks or transactions in a timely manner, can cause a loss of opportunity, and might keep the users from being productive. Either way, these systems are typically not much benefit to operating a business. To keep network systems well tuned for the given workloads, capacity analysis seeks a balance between the resources available and the workload required of the resources. The balance provides just the right amount of computing power for given and anticipated workloads.

This concept of balancing resources extends beyond the technical details of server configuration to include issues such as gauging the number of administrators that might be needed to maintain various systems in your environment. Many of these questions relate to capacity analysis, and the answers aren't readily known because they can't be predicted with complete accuracy.

Capacity analysis provides the processes to guide you through lessening the burden and dispelling some of the mysteries of estimating resource requirements. These processes include vendor guidelines, industry benchmarks, analysis of present system resource use, and more. Through these processes, you'll gain as much understanding as possible of the network environment and step away from the compartmentalized or limited understanding of the systems. In turn, you'll also gain more control over the systems and increase your chances of successfully maintaining the reliability, serviceability, and availability of your system.

To proactively manage your system, first establish systemwide policies and procedures that shape service levels and user expectations. After these policies and procedures are classified and defined, you can start characterizing system workloads, which will help gauge acceptable baseline performance values.

# Best Practice for Establishing Policy and Metric Baselines

If you first begin defining policies regarding desired service levels and objectives, the resulting procedures are more easily created and implemented. Essentially, policies and procedures define how the system is supposed to be used—establishing guidelines to help users understand that the system can't be used in any way they see fit. Many benefits are derived from these policies and procedures. For example, in an environment where policies and procedures are working successfully and where network performance becomes sluggish, it would be safer to assume that groups of people aren't playing a multiuser network game, that several individuals aren't sending enormous e-mail attachments to everyone in the global address list, or that a rogue Web or FTP server wasn't placed on the network.

Network performance is a combination of both individual uses of the system just as well as IT department optimization. Therefore, it's equally important to gain an understanding of user expectations and requirements through interviews, questionnaires, surveys, and more. Some examples of operational policies that can be implemented in a networking environment pertaining to end users could be the following:

- Only certain applications will be supported and allowed on the network.
- E-mail message size can't exceed 2MB.
- Beta software can be installed only on lab equipment (that is, not on client machines or servers in the production environment).
- All computing resources are for business use only (in other words, no gaming or personal use of computers is allowed).
- All home directories will be limited to 300MB per user.
- Users must request assistance through a managed helpdesk rather than try to apply patches, fixes, or conduct system repairs on their own.

Policies and procedures, however, aren't just for end users. They can also be established and applied to IT personnel. In this scenario, policies and procedures can serve as guidelines for technical issues, rules of engagement, or simply an internal set of rules. The following list provides some examples of policies and procedures that might be applied to the IT personnel:

- System backups must include System State data and should be completed by 5 a.m. each workday.
- Routine system maintenance should be performed only on Saturday mornings between 5 and 8 a.m.
- Basic technical support requests should be attended to within two business days.
- Priority technical support requests should be attended to within four hours of the request.

- Technical support staff should use Remote Desktop on client machines first before attempting to solve the problem locally.

- Any planned downtime for servers must be approved by the IT management at least one week in advance.

## Benchmark Baselines

If you've begun defining policies and procedures, you're already cutting down the number of immeasurable variables and amount of empirical data that challenge your decision-making process. The next step to prepare for capacity analysis is to begin gathering baseline performance values.

Baselines give you a starting point against which to compare results. For the most part, determining baseline performance levels involves working with hard numbers that represent the health of a system. On the other hand, a few variables coincide with the statistical representations such as workload characterization, vendor requirements or recommendations, industry-recognized benchmarks, and the data that you collect.

## Workload Characterization

It is unlikely that each system in your environment is a separate entity that has its own workload characterization. Most, if not all, network environments have systems that depend on other systems or are even intertwined among different workloads. This makes workload characterization difficult at best.

Workloads are defined by how processes or tasks are grouped, the resources they require, and the type of work being performed. Departmental functions, time of day, the type of processing required (batch or real-time), companywide functions (such as payroll), volume of work, and much more can be characterized as examples of workloads.

So why is workload characterization so important? Identifying system workloads enables you to determine the appropriate resource requirements for each of them. This way, you can properly plan the resources according to the performance levels the workloads expect and demand.

## Benchmarks for Performance Analysis

Benchmarks are a means to measure the performance of a variety of products, including operating systems, virtually all computer components, and even entire systems. Many companies rely on benchmarks to gain competitive advantage because so many professionals rely on them to help determine what's appropriate for their network environment.

As you would suspect, sales and marketing departments often exploit the benchmark results to exaggerate the performance or benefit of a technology solution. For this reason, it's important to investigate the benchmark results and the companies or organizations that produced the results. Check to make sure that the benchmarks are consistent with other benchmarks produced by third-party organizations (such as magazines, benchmark organizations, and in-house testing labs). If none are available, you should try to gain insight from other IT professionals or run benchmarks on the product yourself before implementing it in production.

Although some suspicion might arise from benchmarks because of the sales and marketing techniques, the real purpose of benchmarks is to point out the performance levels that you can expect when using the product. Benchmarks can be extremely beneficial for decision-making, but they shouldn't be your sole source for evaluating and measuring performance. Use the benchmark results only as a guideline or starting point when consulting benchmark results during capacity analysis. You should also pay close attention to their interpretation.

A list of companies or organizations that provide benchmark statistics and benchmark-related information along with some tools for evaluating product performance include

- Transaction Processing Performance Council (`http://www.tpc.org/`)
- eTesting Labs (`http://www.etestinglabs.com/`)
- Computer Measurement Group (`http://www.cmg.org`)

# Leveraging Capacity-Analysis Tools

A growing number of tools originating and evolving from the Windows NT 4.0, Windows 2000, and Unix operating system platforms can be used in data collection and analysis on Windows Server 2003. Some of these tools are even capable of forecasting system capacity, depending on the amount of information they are given.

Microsoft also offers some handy utilities that are either inherent to Windows Server 2003 or are sold as separate products. Some of these utilities are included with the operating system, such as Task Manager, Network Monitor, and Performance Console (also known as Performance Monitor). Data that is collected from these applications can be exported to other applications, such as Microsoft Excel or Access, for inventory and analysis. Other Microsoft utilities that are sold separately are Systems Management Server (SMS) and Microsoft Operations Manager (MOM).

## Built-in Toolset

Windows Server 2003's arsenal of utilities for capacity analysis includes command-line and GUI-based tools. This section discusses the Task Manager, Network Monitor, and Performance Console, which are bundled with the Windows Server 2003 operating system.

### Task Manager
The Windows Server 2003 Task Manager is similar to its Windows 2000 predecessor in that it offers multifaceted functionality. You can view and monitor processor, memory, application, and process information in real-time for a given system. This utility is great for getting a quick view of key system health indicators with the lowest performance overhead.

To begin using Task Manager, use any of the following methods:

- Press Ctrl+Shift+Esc.

- Right-click the taskbar and select Task Manager.

- Press Ctrl+Alt+Delete and then click Task Manager.

When you start the Task Manager, you'll see a screen similar to that in Figure 23.1.

**FIGURE 23.1**    The Task Manager window after initialization.

The Task Manager window contains the following five tabs:

- Applications—This tab lists the user applications that are currently running. You also can start and end applications under this tab.

- Processes—Under this tab, you can find performance metric information of the processes currently running on the system.

- Performance—This tab can be a graphical or tabular representation of key system parameters in real-time.

- Networking—This tab displays the network traffic coming to and from the machine. The displayed network usage metric is a percentage of total available network capacity for a particular adapter.

- Users—This tab displays users who are currently logged on to the system.

In addition to the Task Manager tabs, the Task Manager is, by default, configured with a status bar at the bottom of the window. This status bar, shown in Figure 23.2, displays the number of running processes, CPU utilization percentage, and the amount of memory currently being used.

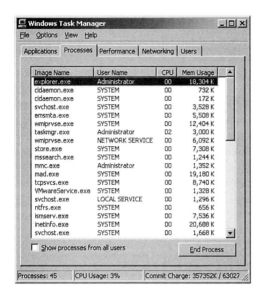

**FIGURE 23.2**  All processes currently running on the system.

As you can see, the Task Manager presents a variety of valuable real-time performance information. This tool is particularly useful for determining what processes or applications are problematic and gives you an overall picture of system health.

There are limitations, however, which prevent it from becoming a useful tool for long-term or historical analysis. For example, the Task Manager can't store collected performance information; it is capable of monitoring only certain aspects of the system's health, and the information that is displayed pertains only to the local machine. For these reasons alone, the Task Manager doesn't make a prime candidate for capacity-planning purposes (you must be logged on locally or connected via Terminal Services to gauge performance with the Task Manager).

### Network Monitor

There are two versions of Network Monitor that you can use to check network performance. The first is bundled within Windows Server 2003, and the other is a part of Systems Management Server (SMS). Although both have the same interface, like the one shown in Figure 23.3, the one bundled with the operating system is slightly scaled down in terms of functionality when compared to the SMS version.

The Network Monitor that is built into Windows Server 2003 is designed to monitor only the local machine's network activity. This utility design stems from security concerns regarding the ability to capture and monitor traffic on remote machines. If the operating system version had this capability, anyone who installed the Network Monitor would possibly be able to use it to gain unauthorized access to the system. Therefore, this version captures only frame types traveling into or away from the local machine.

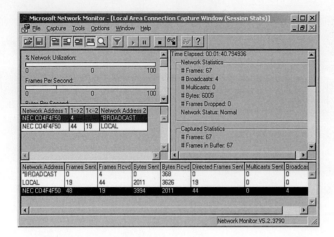

**FIGURE 23.3**
The unified interface of the Network Monitor.

To install the Network Monitor, perform the following steps:

1. Double-click the Add/Remove Programs applet on the Control Panel.

2. In the Add/Remove Programs window, click Add/Remove dialog box.

3. Within the Windows Components Wizard, select Management and Monitoring Tools and then click Details.

4. In the Management and Monitoring Tools window, select Network Monitor Tools and then click OK and then Next.

5. If you are prompted for additional files, insert your Windows Server 2003 CD or type a path to the location of the files on the network. You might be prompted to install the Phone Book Services (PBS) at this point. Choose Yes to continue with the PBS installation.

6. After the installation, locate and execute the Network Monitor by choosing Start, Programs, Administration Tools.

As described previously, the SMS version of the Network Monitor is a full version of the one integrated into Windows Server 2003. The most significant difference between the two versions is that the SMS version can run indiscriminately throughout the network (that is, it can monitor and capture network traffic to and from remote machines). It is also equipped to locate routers on the network, provide name-to-IP address resolution, and generally monitor all the traffic traveling throughout the network.

Because the SMS version of Network Monitor is capable of capturing and monitoring all network traffic, it poses possible security risks. Any unencrypted network traffic can be compromised; therefore, it's imperative that you limit the number of IT personnel who have the necessary access to use this utility.

On the other hand, the SMS version of Network Monitor is more suitable for capacity-analysis purposes because it is flexible enough to monitor network traffic from a centralized location. It also allows you to monitor in real-time and capture for historical analysis. For all practical purposes, however, it wouldn't make much sense to install SMS just for the Network Monitor capabilities, especially considering that you can purchase more robust third-party utilities.

### The Performance Console

Many IT professionals rely on the Performance Console because it is bundled with the operating system, and it allows you to capture and monitor every measurable system object within Windows Server 2003. This tool is a Microsoft Management Console (MMC) snap-in, so using the tool involves little effort to become familiar with it. You can find and start the Performance Console from within the Administrative Tools group on the Start menu.

The Performance Console, shown in Figure 23.4, is by far the best utility provided in the operating system for capacity-analysis purposes. With this utility, you can analyze data from virtually all aspects of the system both in real-time and historically. This data analysis can be viewed through charts, reports, and logs. The log format can be stored for use later so that you can scrutinize data from succinct periods of time.

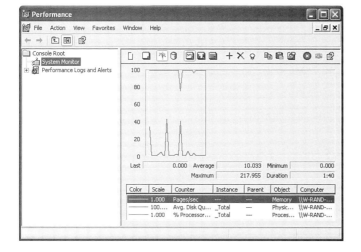

**FIGURE 23.4**
The Performance Console startup screen.

Because the Performance Console is available to everyone running the operating system and it has a lot of built-in functionality, most administrators choose to use this built-in utility.

## Third-Party Toolset

Without a doubt, many third-party utilities are excellent for capacity-analysis purposes. Most of them provide additional functionality not found in the Windows Server 2003 Performance Console, but they cost more too. You might want to evaluate some third-party utilities to get a more thorough understanding of how they might offer more features than the Performance Console. Generally speaking, these utilities enhance the functionality that is inherent to Performance Console, such as scheduling, an enhanced level of reporting functionality, superior storage capabilities, the ability to monitor non-Windows systems, or algorithms for future trend analysis.

Some of these third-party tools are listed in Table 23.1.

**TABLE 23.1**

**Third-Party Capacity-Planning Tools**

| Utility Name | Company | Web Site |
|---|---|---|
| AppManager Suite | NetIQ Corporation | http://www.netiq.com/solutions/ |
| Openview | Hewlett-Packard | http://www.openview.hp.com/ |
| PATROL | BMC Software | http://www.bmc.com/products |
| PerfMan | Information Systems | http://www.infosysman.com/ |
| RoboMon | Heroix | http://www.robomon.com/ |
| Unicenter TNG | Computer Associates | http://www3.ca.com/Solutions/Solution.asp?id=315 |

Although it might be true that most third-party products do add more functionality to your capacity-analysis procedures, there are still pros and cons to using them over the free Performance Console. The most obvious is the expense of purchasing the software licenses for monitoring the enterprise, but some less obvious factors include the following:

- The number of administrators needed to support the product in capacity-analysis procedures is high.

- Some third-party products have high learning curves associated with them. This increases the need for either vendor or in-house training just to support the product.

The key is to decide what you need to adequately and efficiently perform capacity-analysis procedures in your environment. You might find that the Performance Console is more than adequate, or you might find that your network environment requires a third-party product that can encompass all its intricacies.

# Identifying and Analyzing Core Analysis and Monitoring Elements

The capacity analysis and performance optimization process can be intimidating because there can be an enormous amount of data to work with. In fact it can easily become unwieldy if not done properly. The process is not just about monitoring and reading counters; it is also an art.

As you monitor and catalog performance information, keep in mind that more information does not necessarily yield better optimizations. Tailor the number and types of counters that are being monitored based on the server's role and functionality within the network environment. It's also important to monitor the four common contributors to bottlenecks: memory, processor, disk, and network subsystems. When monitoring application servers like Microsoft Exchange systems, it is equally important to understand the various roles each server plays (front-end server, back-end server, bridgehead gateway server, and so on) to keep the number of counters being monitored to a minimum.

## Memory Subsystem Optimizations

As with earlier versions of Windows, Windows Server 2003 tends to use the amount of memory that you throw at it. However, its efficient memory management outperforms its predecessors. Nevertheless, fine-tuning system memory can go a long way toward making sure that each Windows 2003 server has adequate amounts of memory.

Memory management is performed by Windows Server 2003 and is directly related to how well applications on the server perform. Windows Server 2003 also has greatly enhanced memory management and the way it uses virtual memory. This reduces memory fragmentation and enables more users to be supported on a single server or cluster of servers.

**BEST PRACTICE**

### Use the /3GB /USERVA=3000 Parameters

Use the /3GB /USERVA=3000 parameters in boot.ini for application servers like Exchange Server 2003 with more than 1GB of memory installed. This allows Exchange 2003 to manage memory more efficiently and support a greater number of users.

Using the Performance Monitor Console, there are a number of important memory-related counters that can help you establish an accurate representation of the system's memory requirements. The primary memory counters that provide information about hard pages (pages that are causing the information to be swapped between the memory and the hard disk) are

- Memory—Pages/sec. The values of this counter should range from 5 to 20. Values consistently higher than 10 are indicative of potential performance problems whereas values consistently higher than 20 might cause noticeable and significant performance hits.

- Memory—Page Faults/sec. This counter together with Memory—Cache Faults/sec and Memory—Transition Faults/sec counters can provide valuable information about page faults that are not committed to disk because the memory manager has allocated those pages to a standby list also known as transition faults. Most systems today can handle a large number of page faults but it is important to correlate these numbers with the Pages/sec counter as well to determine whether or not each application is configured with enough memory.

Figure 23.5 shows some of the various memory and process counters.

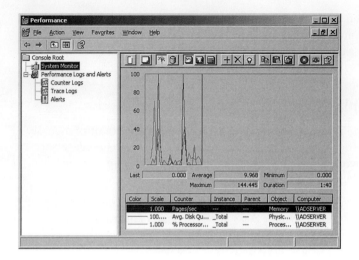

**FIGURE 23.5**
Memory-related counters in
Windows Server 2003.

## Improving Virtual Memory Usage

Calculating the correct amount of virtual memory is one of the more challenging aspects of planning a server's memory requirements. While trying to anticipate growing usage demands, it is critical that the server has an adequate amount of virtual memory for all applications and the operating system.

Virtual memory refers to the amount of disk space that is used by Windows Server 2003 and applications as physical memory gets low or when applications need to swap data out of physical memory. Windows Server 2003 uses 1.5 times the amount of RAM as the default minimum paging file size, which is adequate for many systems. However, it is important to monitor memory counters to determine if this amount is truly sufficient for that particular server's resource requirements. Another important consideration is the maximum size setting for the paging file. As a best practice, this setting should be at least 50 percent more than the minimum value to allow for paging file growth should the system require it. If the minimum and maximum settings are configured with the same value, there is a greater risk that the system could experience severe performance problems or even crash.

The most indicative sign of low virtual memory is the presence of warning events, such as the Event 9582 logged by the Microsoft Exchange Information Store service, that can severely impact and degrade the Exchange Server's message-processing abilities. These warning events are indicative of virtual memory going below 32MB. If unnoticed or left unattended, these warning messages might cause services to stop or the entire system to fail.

## BEST PRACTICE

### Use the Performance Snap-in to Set an Alert for Event ID 9582

Use the Performance snap-in to set an alert for Event ID 9582. This will help to proactively address any virtual memory problems and possibly prevent unnecessary downtime.

To get an accurate portrayal of how a server is using virtual memory, monitor the following counters in the Performance MMC tool:

- *VM Largest Block Size.* This counter should consistently be above 32MB.

- *VM Total 16MB Free Blocks.* This counter should remain greater than three 16-MB blocks.

- *VM Total Free Blocks.* This value is specific to your messaging environment.

- *VM Total Large Free Block Bytes.* This counter should stay above 50MB.

Other important counters to watch closely are as follows:

- *Memory—Available Bytes.* This counter can be used to establish whether the system has adequate amounts of RAM. The recommended absolute minimum value is 4MB.

- *Paging File—% Usage—%.* Usage validates the amount of the paging file used in a predetermined interval. High usage values might indicate that you need more physical memory or need to increase the size of a paging file.

## Monitoring Processor Usage

Analyzing the processor usage can reveal invaluable information about system performance and provide reliable results that can be used for baselining purposes. There are two major processor counters that are used for capacity analysis of a Windows Server 2003 system.

- *% Privileged Time.* Indicates the percentage of non-idle processor time spent in privileged mode. The recommended value is less than 55 percent.

- *% Processor Time.* Specifies the use of each processor or the total processor utilization. If these values are consistently higher than 50%–60%, you should consider upgrading options or segmenting workloads.

## Optimizing the Disk Subsystem Configuration

There are many factors such as the type of file system to use, physical disk configuration, database size, and log file placement that need to be considered when you are trying to optimize the disk subsystem configuration. When optimizing the disk subsystem, there are many choices that need to be made that are specific to the configuration of the existing network environment.

### Choosing the File System

Among the file systems supported by Windows Server 2003 (FAT and NTFS), it is recommended you use only NTFS on all servers, especially those in production environments. Simply put, NTFS provides the best security, scalability, and performance features. For instance, NTFS supports file and directory-level security, large file sizes (files of up to 16TB), large disk sizes (disk volumes of up to 16TB), fault tolerance, disk compression, error detection, and encryption.

### Choosing the Physical Disk Configuration

Windows Server 2003, like its predecessors, supports RAID (Redundant Array of Inexpensive Disks). The levels of RAID supported by the operating system are

- RAID 0 (striping)
- RAID 1 (mirroring)
- RAID 5 (striping with parity)

> **Two Recommended Basic RAID Levels to Use**
>
> There are various levels of RAID but for the context of enterprise servers, there are two recommended basic levels to use: RAID 1 and RAID 5. Other forms of RAID, such as RAID 0+1 or 1+0 are also optimal solutions for enterprise servers. These more advanced levels of RAID are only supported when using a hardware RAID controller. Therefore, only RAID 1 and 5 will be discussed in this chapter.

There are various other levels of RAID that can be supported through the use of hardware-based RAID controllers.

The deployment of the correct RAID level is of utmost importance because each RAID level has a direct effect on the performance of the server. From the viewpoint of pure performance, RAID level 0 by far gives the best performance. However, fault tolerance and the reliability of system access are other factors that contribute to overall performance. The skillful administrator is one who strikes a balance between performance and fault tolerance without sacrificing one for the other.

### Disk Mirroring (RAID 1)

In this type of configuration, data is mirrored from one disk to the other participating disk in the mirror set. Data is simultaneously written to the two required disks, which means read operations are significantly faster than systems with no RAID configuration or with a greater degree of fault tolerance. Because a RAID 1 configuration only has one hard drive controller to handle the writing of information to two or more disks, write performance is slower because data is being written to multiple drives from a single drive controller source.

Besides adequate performance it also provides a good degree of fault tolerance. If one drive fails the RAID controller can automatically detect the failure and run solely on the remaining disk with minimal interruption.

> **Well Suited**
>
> RAID 1 is particularly well suited for the boot drive as well as for volumes containing log files for application and database servers.

The biggest drawback to RAID 1 is the amount of storage capacity that is lost. RAID 1 uses 50% of the total drive capacity for the two drives.

### Disk Striping with Parity (RAID 5)

In a RAID 5 configuration, data and parity information are striped across all participating disks in the array. RAID 5 requires a minimum of three disks. Even if one of the drives fails within the array, the server can still remain operational.

After the drive fails, Windows Server 2003 continues to operate because of the data contained on the other drives. The parity information gives details of the data that is missing due to the failure. Either Windows Server 2003 or the hardware RAID controller also begins the rebuilding process from the parity information to a spare or new drive.

RAID 5 is most commonly used for the data drive because it is a great compromise among performance, storage capacity, and redundancy. The overall space used to store the striped parity information is equal to the capacity of one drive. For example, a RAID 5 volume with three 200GB disks can store up to 400GB of data.

### Hardware Versus Software RAID

Hardware RAID (configured at the disk controller level) is recommended over software RAID (configurable from within the Windows Server 2003) because of its faster performance, greater support of different RAID levels, and capabilities to more easily recover from hardware failures.

## Monitoring the Disk Subsystem

Windows Server 2003 application servers typically rely heavily on the disk subsystem and it is therefore a critical component to properly design and monitor. Although the disk object monitoring counters are by default enabled in Windows Server 2003, it is recommended that you disable these counters until such time that you are ready to monitor them. This is because the resource requirements can influence overall system performance. The syntax to disable and re-enable these counters is as follows:

- `diskperf -n` disables the counter
- `diskperf -y [\\computer_Name]` re-enables the counter

Nevertheless, it is important to gather disk subsystem performance statistics over time.

The primary performance-related counters for the disk subsystem are located within the Physical and Logical Disk objects. Critical counters to monitor include, but are not limited to, the following:

- *Physical Disk—% Disk Time.* Analyzes the percentage of elapsed time that the selected disk spends on servicing read or write requests. Ideally this value should remain below 50 percent.

- *Logical Disk—% Disk Time.* Displays the percentage of elapsed time that the selected disk spends fulfilling read or write requests. It is recommended that this value be 60%–70% or lower.

- *Current Disk Queue Length (both Physical and Logical Disk objects).* This counter has different performance indicators depending on the monitored disk drive. On disk drives storing application databases, this value should be lower than the number of spindled drives divided by two. On disk drives storing filesystem data, this value should be lower than one.

## Monitoring the Network Subsystem

The network subsystem is by far one of the most difficult subsystems to monitor because of the many different variables. The number of protocols used in the network, the network interface cards (NICs), network-based applications, topologies, subnetting, and more, play vital roles in the network, but they also add to its complexity when you're trying to determine bottlenecks. Each network environment has different variables; therefore, the counters that you'll want to monitor will vary.

The information that you'll want to gain from monitoring the network pertains to network activity and throughput. You can find this information with the Performance Console alone, but it will be difficult at best. Instead, it's important to use other tools, such as the Network Monitor, in conjunction with Performance Console to get the best representation of network performance possible. You might also consider using third-party network analysis tools such as sniffers to ease monitoring and analysis efforts. Using these tools simultaneously can broaden the scope of monitoring and more accurately depict what is happening on the wire.

Because the TCP/IP suite is the underlying set of protocols for a Windows Server 2003 network subsystem, this discussion of capacity analysis focuses on this protocol. The TCP/IP counters are added after the protocol is installed (by default).

There are several different network performance objects relating to the TCP/IP protocol, including ICMP, IP, Network Interface, NetBT, TCP, UDP, and more. Other counters such as FTP Server and WINS Server are added after these services are installed. Because entire books are dedicated to optimizing TCP/IP, this section focuses on a few important counters that you should monitor for capacity-analysis purposes.

First, examining error counters, such as Network Interface: Packets Received Errors or Packets Outbound Errors, is extremely useful in determining whether traffic is easily traversing the network. A greater number of errors indicates that packets must be present, causing more network traffic. If a high number of errors is persistent on the network, throughput will suffer. This might be caused by a bad NIC or unreliable links.

If network throughput appears to be slowing because of excessive traffic, you should keep a close watch on the traffic being generated from network-based services such as the ones described in Table 23.2.

**TABLE 23.2**

**Network-based Service Counters to Monitor Network Traffic**

| Counter | Description |
| --- | --- |
| NBT Connection: Bytes Total/sec | Monitors the network traffic generated by NBT connections |
| Redirector: Bytes Total/sec | Processes data bytes received for statistical calculations |
| Server: Bytes Total/sec | Monitors the network traffic generated by the Server service |

# Optimizing Performance by Server Roles

In addition to monitoring the common set of bottlenecks (memory, processor, disk subsystem, and network subsystem), the functional roles of the server influence what other counters you should monitor. The following sections outline some of the most common roles for Windows Server 2003 that also require the use of additional performance counters.

# Terminal Services Server

Windows Server 2003 Terminal Services comes in two flavors: Remote administration mode and Application server mode. The Remote administration mode monitors and services a Terminal Services server remotely. Because it has minimal resource requirements, and therefore is more efficient, this discussion focuses primarily on the Application server mode.

Terminal Services has its own performance object for the Performance Console called the Terminal Services Session object. It provides resource statistics such as errors, cache activity, network traffic from Terminal Services, and other session-specific activity. Many of

> **For More Information on Terminal Services**
> You can find more information on Terminal Services in Chapter 20, "Leveraging Thin Client Terminal Services."

these counters are similar to those found in the Process object. Some examples include % Privileged Time, % Processor Time, % User Time, Working Set, Working Set Peak, and so on.

Three important areas to always monitor for Terminal Services capacity analysis are the memory, processor, and application processes for each session. Application processes are by far the hardest to monitor and control because of the extreme variances in programmatic behavior. For example, all applications might be 32-bit, but some might not be certified to run on Windows Server 2003. You might also have in-house applications running on Terminal Services that might be poorly designed or too resource-intensive for the workloads they are performing.

# Domain Controllers

A Windows Server 2003 domain controller (DC) houses the Active Directory (AD) and might have additional roles such as being responsible for one or more Flexible Single Master Operation (FSMO) roles (schema master, domain naming master, relative ID master, PDC Emulator, or infrastructure master) or a global catalog (GC) server. Also, depending on the size and design of the system, a DC might serve many other functional roles. In this section, AD, replication, and DNS monitoring will be explored.

### Monitoring AD

Active Directory is the heart of Windows Server 2003 systems. It's used for many different facets, including, but not limited to, authentication, authorization, encryption, and Group Policies. Because AD plays a central role in a Windows Server 2003 network environment, it must perform its responsibilities as efficiently as possible. Each facet by itself can be optimized, but this section focuses on the NTDS and Database objects.

The NTDS object provides various AD performance indicators and statistics that are useful for determining AD's workload capacity. Many of these counters can be used to determine current workloads and how these workloads might affect other system resources. There are relatively few counters in this object, so it's recommended that you monitor each one in addition to the common set of bottleneck objects. With this combination of counters, you can determine whether the system is overloaded.

Another performance object that you should use to monitor AD is the Database object. This object is not installed by default, so you must manually add it to be able to start gathering more information on AD.

To load the Database object, perform the following steps:

1. Copy the performance DLL (esentprf.dll) located in %SystemRoot%\System32 to any directory (for example, c:\esent).

2. Launch the Registry Editor (Regedt32.exe).

3. Create the Registry key HKEY_LOCAL_MACHINE\SYSTEM\CurrentControlSet\Services\ESENT.

4. Create the Registry key HKEY_LOCAL_MACHINE\SYSTEM\CurrentControlSet\Services\ESENT\Performance.

5. Select the ESENT\Performance subkey.

6. Create the value Open using data type REG_SZ and string equal to OpenPerformanceData.

7. Create the value Collect using the data type REG_SZ and string equal to CollectPerformanceData.

8. Create the value Close using the data type REG_SZ and string equal to ClosePerformanceData.

9. Create the value Library using the data type REG_SZ and string equal to c:\esent\esentprf.dll.

10. Exit the Registry Editor.

11. Open a command prompt and change directory to %SystemRoot%\System32.

12. Run Lodctr.exe Esentprf.ini at the command prompt.

After you complete the Database object installation, you can execute the Performance Console and use the Database object to monitor AD. Some of the relevant counters contained within the Database object to monitor AD are described in Table 23.3.

**TABLE 23.3**

**AD Performance Counters**

| Database Counter | Description |
| --- | --- |
| Cache % Hit | The percentage of page requests for the database file that were fulfilled by the database cache without causing a file operation. If this percentage is low (85% or lower), you might consider adding more memory. |
| Cache Page Fault Stalls/sec | The number of page faults per second that cannot be serviced because there are no pages available for allocation from the database cache. This number should be low if the system is configured with the proper amount of memory. |
| Cache Page Faults/sec | The number of page requests per second for the database file that require the database cache manager to allocate a new page from the database cache. |

**TABLE 23.3**

**Continued**

| Database Counter | Description |
|---|---|
| Cache Size | The amount of system memory used by the database cache manager to hold commonly used information from the database to prevent file operations. |
| File Operations Pending | The number of reads and writes issued by the database cache manager to the database file or files that the operating system is currently processing. High numbers might indicate memory shortages or an insufficient disk subsystem. |

## Monitoring DNS

The domain name system (DNS) has been the primary name resolution mechanism in Windows 2000 and continues to be with Windows Server 2003. There are numerous counters available for monitoring various aspects of DNS in Windows Server 2003. The two most important categories in terms of capacity analysis are name resolution response times and workloads, as well as replication performance.

The counters listed in Table 23.4 are used to compute name query traffic and the workload that the DNS server is servicing. These counters should be monitored along with the common set of bottlenecks to determine the system's health under various workload conditions. If users are noticing slower responses, you can compare the query workload usage growth with your performance information from memory, processor, disk subsystem, and network subsystem counters.

**TABLE 23.4**

**Counters to Monitor DNS**

| Counter | Description |
|---|---|
| DYNAMIC UPDATE RECEIVED/Sec | Dynamic Update Received/sec is the average number of dynamic update requests received by the DNS server in each second. |
| RECURSIVE QUERIES/Sec | Recursive Queries/sec is the average number of recursive queries received by the DNS server in each second. |
| RECURSIVE QUERY FAILURE/Sec | Recursive Query Failure/sec is the average number of recursive query failures in each second. |
| SECURE UPDATE RECEIVED/Sec | Secure Update Received/sec is the average number of secure update requests received by the DNS server in each second. |
| TCP QUERY RECEIVED/Sec | TCP Query Received/sec is the average number of TCP queries received by the DNS server in each second. |
| TCP RESPONSE SENT/Sec | TCP Response Sent/sec is the average number of TCP responses sent by the DNS server in each second. |
| TOTAL QUERY RECEIVED/Sec | Total Query Received/sec is the average number of queries received by the DNS server in each second. |
| TOTAL RESPONSE SENT/Sec | Total Response Sent/sec is the average number of responses sent by the DNS server in each second. |

**TABLE 23.4**

**Continued**

| Counter | Description |
| --- | --- |
| UDP QUERY RECEIVED/Sec | UDP Query Received/sec is the average number of UDP queries received by the DNS server in each second. |
| UDP RESPONSE SENT/Sec | UDP Response Sent/sec is the average number of UDP responses sent by the DNS server in each second. |

Comparing results with other DNS servers in the environment can also help you to determine whether you should relinquish some of the name query responsibility to other DNS servers that are less busy.

Replication performance is another important aspect of DNS. Windows Server 2003 supports legacy DNS replication, also known as zone transfers, which populate information from the primary DNS to any secondary servers. There are two types of legacy DNS replication: incremental (propagating only changes to save bandwidth) and full (the entire zone file is replicated to secondary servers).

Full zone transfers (AXFR) occur on the initial transfers and then the incremental zone transfers (IXFR) are performed thereafter. The performance counters for both AXFR and IXFR (see Table 23.5) measure both requests and the successful transfers. It is important to note that if your network environment integrates DNS with non-Windows systems, it is recommended to have those systems support IXFR.

**TABLE 23.5**

**DNS Zone Transfer Counters**

| Counter | Description |
| --- | --- |
| AXFR Request Received | Total number of full zone transfer requests received by the DNS Server service when operating as a master server for a zone |
| AXFR Request Sent | Total number of full zone transfer requests sent by the DNS Server service when operating as a secondary server for a zone |
| AXFR Response Received | Total number of full zone transfer requests received by the DNS Server service when operating as a secondary server for a zone |
| AXFR Success Received | Total number of full zone transfers received by the DNS Server service when operating as a secondary server for a zone |
| AXFR Success Sent | Total number of full zone transfers successfully sent by the DNS Server service when operating as a master server for a zone |
| IXFR Request Received | Total number of incremental zone transfer requests received by the master DNS server |
| IXFR Request Sent | Total number of incremental zone transfer requests sent by the secondary DNS server |
| IXFR Response Received | Total number of incremental zone transfer responses received by the secondary DNS server |
| IXFR Success Received | Total number of successful incremental zone transfers received by the second- |

**TABLE 23.5**

**Continued**

| Counter | Description |
|---------|-------------|
|  | ary DNS server |
| IXFR Success Sent | Total number of successful incremental zone transfers sent by the master DNS server |

If your network environment is fully Active Directory–integrated, the counters listed in Table 23.5 will all be zero.

### Monitoring AD Replication

Measuring AD replication performance is a complex process because of the many variables associated with replication. They include, but aren't limited to, the following:

- Intrasite versus intersite replication

- The compression being used (if any)

- Available bandwidth

- Inbound versus outbound replication traffic

Fortunately, there are performance counters for every possible AD replication scenario. These counters are located within the NTDS object and are prefixed by the primary process that is responsible for AD replication—the Directory Replication Agent (DRA).

# Summary

Although most organizations pay little attention to performance tuning and optimization, performing basic steps to monitor a server and to track performance statistics helps organizations better understand the operation of their systems. By setting realistic business operation policies along with monitoring system performance, when a problem arises, the administrators of the organization have a better idea what the normal operation of the system is, and can statistically analyze information to isolate problems more easily.

Additionally, performance optimization helps an organization minimize bottlenecks or inefficiencies that can lead to reliability problems and possibly system failure. Performance management helps an organization improve operational effectiveness, and creates a network that can run more efficiently.

# 24

# Scaling Up and Scaling Out Strategies

**A**s networks grow from a few servers supporting a few hundred users to a large farm of servers supporting several thousand users it's important to understand how to scale services to support greater user loads. This chapter offers solutions on how to take some common services to the next level and allow them to support large numbers of users.

# Size Does Matter

Any time a server is needed the first question is always "How big a server should I order?" If the server is too big for its role, money is wasted. If the server is too small it will have to be upgraded or replaced long before its useful life runs out and that costs money too. The trick for IT administrators is to purchase a server that is just right. In doing so they are able to not only make their users happy but also keep the accounting department happy.

It is important to note that the size of a server should bring to mind not only the amount of processing capacity and storage but also the physical size and requirements of the server. Most companies don't have limitless space in the data center nor do they have infinite power and cooling. Minimizing the footprint of the server can go a long way towards controlling costs and increasing overall system stability. The other item that must be addressed is the scalability of the server. Is it upgradeable? Does it have the capacity to grow as the environment grows? If not, how will that be handled? Although the answers to those questions will vary based on application and environment, this chapter endeavors to answer those questions and give you insight into the options for scaling various technologies.

## Determining Your Needs

There are many factors that will influence the purchase of a new server. The most obvious factor is the role of the server. Although there are many decision points that are applicable to most any server there are also several issues specific to particular roles of servers that must be addressed. Those specifics are covered in the following sections.

# Building Bigger Servers

The simplest path to scaling an application to handle a greater load is improving the hardware. Nowhere is this more apparent than in building a bigger server. *Bigger* in this sense refers to a server with high-speed processors, usually several of them, and a fully populated bank of memory. These are the big iron of the client server world and are designed to be not only fast but also stable and easily managed.

## Beefy Single Boxes

The most common way to scale a server to handle more users or a greater load is to simply upgrade to a bigger box. Upgrading to a higher clock speed processor or a new generation of processor can add significant performance to a server. Adding memory or a faster disk subsystem can also help out performance. Always analyze a system that is going to be upgraded to determine where the bottleneck is on the server. Focus on upgrading that

> **Windows 2003 and Multiple Processors**
> Windows 2003 is much better about dealing with multiple processors than previous versions of Windows. Windows 2003 can support up to 64 processors right out of the box.

subsystem for the largest performance gains. By increasing the performance of the system it will be able to scale further and support more users.

## Multinode Clusters

Sometimes building a bigger server isn't an option. A server might be as big as it can be. If you can't add more processors or faster processors or more memory it might be time to look at getting the server some help. Creating multinode clusters enables you to scale a system beyond what a single server could do. Active/Active clusters can literally double the capacity of a system. The area where this concept adds the most performance is in places where it is not feasible to split users off to another system. This is most commonly seen with databases. Sites that have multiterabyte databases often can't realistically split the data across multiple databases. In these situations the key to scaling out the database is via clustering. Windows 2003 Enterprise offers support for clusters of up to eight nodes. This represents a paradigm shift in how Windows can scale to support high-demand applications. Many Microsoft applications like SQL 2000 and Exchange 2000 were built with clustering in mind.

**Requires Technologies Like SAN or NAS**
Creating clusters of more than two nodes requires technologies like SAN or NAS to provide the shared storage. A shared SCSI enclosure only works for two node clusters. Always work with the hardware vendor to ensure that servers are certified to work with Windows 2003 clustering.

# Building Server Farms

The computer industry is like a pendulum. It swings back and forth between two extremes of computing styles. In the old days it was common to see large groups of computers working together on a common task. This was mostly due to a lack of processing power. As processors became more powerful the industry swung in the opposite direction, moving toward single massively powerful computers. Recently the pendulum has returned toward distributed computing. Not unlike a pendulum, each swing covers less and less distance. In the case of the computer industry the pendulum has swung to a point where groups of computers work together to support a specific need. These groups are commonly referred to as Server Farms. *Server Farms* consist of servers, usually configured identically, a common source of data, and a load-balancing device. The Server Farm is able to scale performance by simply adding more servers to the farm. Some of the larger farms in the industry deal with applications like Computational Chemistry where literally thousands of servers will work together in a farm to perform complex mathematical modeling.

# Avoiding the Pitfalls

Simply buying the biggest, meanest server you can with the most memory isn't always the best plan for a server. Scaling without planning can often result in more problems than it fixes. By avoiding the pitfalls associated with scaling technologies to handle larger loads, you can build an environment that is not only high performance but also low maintenance.

## Buying the Wrong Hardware

All too often administrators purchase a server upgrade for a specific application to run on and it ends up being slower than the old system. As counterintuitive as this might seem, it demonstrates a lack of understanding of some types of applications. Knowing the idiosyncrasies of an application is critical to purchasing hardware for it. An application that is Floating Point Unit–intensive will respond favorably to a system with a large L2 cache. Moving an FPU-intensive application to a newer server with a higher clock speed but lower L2 cache can result in the application actually being slower. Applications that are write-intensive, such as databases, often run faster on independent disks than they do on a RAID 5 subsystem because of the parity check involved on disk writes. Whenever possible you should discuss server selection with the vendor of the application the server is being purchased for and get concrete performance numbers for various hardware configurations. Often the hardware vendors can supply performance numbers for popular applications on their hardware as well. Clever administrators arm themselves with as much information as possible before making hardware purchases.

## Is the Application Multiprocessor-Capable?

Many times servers are purchased with multiple processors. All too often people believe that if one processor is good, two must be better. Often the additional processors can add a significant amount of performance to a system. Unfortunately, not all applications are able to take advantage of multiple processors. Before purchasing a multiprocessor server that is destined to run a specific application you should research the application and determine if it will take advantage of the additional processor. If it won't, you should consider taking the money saved on the secondary processor and upgrading the primary processor.

> ### Windows System Resource Manager
>
> Windows System Resource Manager enables you to limit not only the amount of resources used by an application but also tailor its usage to a specific processor. By limiting less important applications and tailoring the desired application of a specific processor, applications can be made to run faster and further scale their ability to support end users.

If a multiprocessor system is inherited and the application it will run is not able to take advantage of the processor there are still ways to improve performance over a single processor server. Through the use of Processor Affinity you can assign a particular process to run on a specific processor. Any threads spawned by the process will automatically inherit the affinity. This means that a particular application can be assigned to the second processor while the first processor handles all the other Windows-related tasks. In this way the application is not affected by the operating system and runs faster than it could have on the first processor alone.

## Protecting Against System Outages

One of the pitfalls of buying big servers is the tendency to load up the basket with multiple eggs. Although consolidating servers into a single powerful server has been shown to reduce costs in the IT environment it also opens the door to single points of failure. A clever administrator understands that part of scaling an environment is ensuring that individual servers don't get out of hand.

Administrators often fall victim to the affordability of disk space. When a server runs low on space it is very easy to add more disks to the chassis or add an external chassis. This creates two dangerous situations. First of all there is a single server holding a tremendous amount of important data. This makes it very difficult to perform maintenance on the server. If it is a database server the sheer volume of the data might result in database maintenance taking longer than an available maintenance window. If the server fails there will be many users who need to access the data that is now unavailable. It is critical to determine at what point it makes sense to scale up the server by adding a server. Technologies such as DFS, which hide the physical server structure, enable an administrator to add file servers to an environment without altering user configurations or mappings.

The second danger to allowing servers to bloat before splitting off more servers is backup and restore. If a file server has so much data that it would take more than eight hours to restore it, it is probably time to split off data onto a separate server.

Although server consolidation is a good thing, don't fall into the trap of consolidating blindly. Look at the capacity of your backup and restore system and determine the most capacity you can restore in a reasonable period of time. If the data is going to overshoot that number (you've been monitoring disk space, right?) its time to add a server.

## Ensuring that Your Facilities Can Support Your Systems

By and large, administrators are experts in the area of technology. They understand servers, they understand IO, and they understand applications. They spend all their time thinking about the next great server and how to tweak it for maximum performance. Ask an administrator how many amps his server draws on startup and how many BTUs of heat it produces and his eyes will go dull.

Far too often administrators purchase server hardware without regard for how it will affect facilities. Knowing how much power the servers draw and knowing how the electrical circuits in the data center are provisioned is critical to avoiding unnecessary system outages. Knowing things like HVAC capacity of the data center is critical in making informed decisions about hardware. It's depressing to have a 4TB SAN arrive only to find out the data center can't support its electrical or cooling needs. That can be an expensive oversight.

It's also important to avoid falling into the trap of always adding servers. It used to be a very common practice to scale Web sites by simply adding more and more Web servers. It was not uncommon to hear of sites that had more than a thousand front-end Web servers. Even with 1U servers that is 42 servers per rack. That's 24 racks of servers. A typical rack with servers installed

> **Look Beyond the Plug**
>
> When considering 220V hardware it is important to not only determine whether the data center can support 220V but to look beyond the plug. Determine whether you can support 220V at your UPS. If there is a recovery site you must ensure that it can also support the 220V devices.

takes up six square feet of space. That's 144 square feet just for Web servers. Companies with data centers will understand the cost associated with that amount of data center space. Factor in the 1000amp current draw and the amount of heat generated and you will quickly realize that blindly adding servers isn't the best method.

# Making It Perform

> **Never Over Clock the Processor on a Production Server**
>
> Never let the desire for performance overshadow the need for stability. No matter how tempting it might look on paper, never over clock the processor on a production server.

One of the easiest ways to scale a system is to purchase the system with parts that are known to be able to support the current load and two to three years of anticipated growth. Factors such as the number of processors, the amount and type of memory, and the disk subsystem work together to determine the maximum capacity of the server. Careful choices here will allow you to get the most bang for your buck.

## Choosing the Right Processor Type

There are many processors on the market today. Sixty-four bit processors have already hit the market and 32-bit processors are faster than ever. With 64-bit operating systems reaching the market it can be quite tempting to jump on the bandwagon of 64-bit processing. When you are

> **Always Ask for Benchmarks and Let the Numbers Tell the Story**
>
> Not all 64-bit applications will take advantage of a 64-bit processor and operating system. Just because an application is ported to 64 bit doesn't mean that it is optimized for 64 bit. Always ask for benchmarks and let the numbers tell the story.

faced with this decision it is critical to do the research and make sure it's the right decision. Don't be fooled by 64-bit processors and 64-bit operating systems. If the application isn't 64 bit the system will run it in a backwards compatible mode. More often than not this will result in slower performance than a high-end 32-bit processor. As more and more 64-bit applications are released this will become less and less of an issue.

## Eliminating Unnecessary Services

By reducing the number of unnecessary services running on a server the overall performance of the server can be enhanced. Services that need to be present but don't require a lot of resources can be tightly controlled by Windows System Resource Manager. A side benefit of removing unnecessary services is decreased exposure to security vulnerabilities. You should exercise common sense in determining what services should be removed. Although a Web server might not need the printer spooler service, it might still need the server service. More information on this type of tuning can be found in Chapter 23, "Tuning and Optimization Techniques."

## Not All Memory Is Created Equal

Many of today's servers are using a type of memory known as DDR. *DDR* stands for Double Data Rate, which means that data can be transferred on both the upswing and downswing of the electrical cycle. This effectively doubles the speed of the memory. This speed is based on the front side bus speed of the motherboard, which in turn determines the speed of the processor. DDR memory is rated by the speed at which it is capable of running. For example PC3500 memory is capable of running at 433Mhz. The competing memory standard is RDRAM or RamBUS. RamBUS is also rated based on the speed at which it can run. For example RamBUS is offered as RamBUS1066. This runs at 1066Mhz and is designed to run with a system that supports a 533Mhz FSB. Not unlike processors, people tend to automatically associate clock speed with performance. This can be misleading because the real story is told by the memory bandwidth. RDRAM1066 is capable of 4.2GB/sec of transfer whereas PC3500 DDR is capable of 3.5GB/sec. Suddenly the gap has closed.

To further confuse the issue, memory is rated in terms of its latency. Most server memory is rated with a cache latency of 2.5. Memory with a cache latency of 2.0 is noticeably faster and will allow shrewd administrators to squeeze every ounce of performance from their servers.

> **If the Server Vendor Certifies the Memory, You Have Options**
>
> When purchasing memory for a server ask the server vendor if any other brands of memory are certified for use in his server. Oftentimes third-party companies produce memory that is faster and less expensive than the OEM memory from the server manufacturer. Think of the primary server manufacturers and ask yourself which of them are memory companies. If the server vendor certifies the memory, you have options.

## Planning for Disk Subsystems

There are many ways to access disks on a server. Careful planning of the disk subsystem will enable you to take full advantage of space and performance now and enable you to scale storage and performance later as the need for additional capacity arises.

Current SCSI controllers are capable of up to 320MB of combined throughput. It is important to understand that this is the speed of the bus and not the speed of the SCSI drives. Unless the system is running multiple disks, an Ultra 320 controller isn't necessarily going to be faster than an Ultra 160 controller.

Fiber channel controllers have even greater throughput than SCSI controllers. Using Fiber channel to connect to locally attached drive arrays or Storage Area Networks can result in amazing disk IO performance.

Although IDE technologies have long lagged behind SCSI solutions, current generation Serial ATA drives offer very attractive pricing for excellent disk performance. Serial ATA RAID controllers (RAID 0,1,0+1) offer even better performance with the option of redundancy. For systems like Web servers in a Web farm, Serial ATA can be a very viable alternative to more costly SCSI drives.

# Scaling the Active Directory

When a company becomes very large it can be a challenge to make sure the environment can properly scale to support the expanding Active Directory. As more and more objects are added to Active Directory and as more and more fields are used the domain controllers can become more and more taxed. Many companies take an approach of making all the domain controllers identical in terms of hardware and configuration. This greatly reduces the support load of the servers. To do this it is important to properly size the domain controllers to handle the load. Toward this end, Microsoft offers a tool called the Active Directory Sizer Tool.

## Active Directory Sizer Tool

In a perfect world, each domain controller would be capable of handling the entire authentication load of the entire environment. In this way if the entire network went to hell in a handbasket, users would still be able to authenticate to get to resources. In the real world this is actually a very realistic option. The difficulty comes in determining just how beefy a server must be to support the entire user base. Luckily Microsoft offers a specific tool that was developed for exactly this reason. It is called the Active Directory Sizer Tool. By following a simple wizard and having the necessary information about the enterprise you can determine the required specifications for the domain controllers. This tool takes into account factors such as Exchange 200x, typical user activity, and replication schedules. Although it is not an exact science it does provide a good starting point for determining the hardware specification of the domain controllers. Do not forget to factor in room for growth. If a company has a policy for replacing hardware on a regular schedule you must take that period of time of growth into account.

Based on user inputs and internal formulas, this tool can provide estimates for the number of

- Domain controllers per domain per site.
- Global Catalog servers per domain per site.
- CPUs per machine and type of CPU.
- Disks needed for Active Directory data storage.
- Amount of memory required.
- Network bandwidth utilization.
- Domain database size.
- Global Catalog database size.
- Inter-site replication bandwidth required.

Additional information on the Active Directory Sizer Tool can be found on the Microsoft Web site at http://www.microsoft.com/windows2000/techinfo/planning/activedirectory/adsizer.asp.

# File Locations Matter

On any application that uses a database and log files, it behooves you to pay careful attention to where files are placed on the system. In a perfect world the operation system would have its own set of spindles, the swap file would have a separate set, the database would have another set, and finally the log files would have a fourth. The concept is that any spindle can be read or written independently of any other set of spindles. The side benefit of this is that if the spindles supporting the database were to fail, this would not affect the log files. This would greatly aid the recovery process for the database.

Active Directory is an application that uses a database and log files. By placing the database and log files on separate disks, you enable the system to read and write both of these simultaneously. This eliminates bottlenecks where the log files aren't written until the database access is done. Similarly by placing the operating system on its own set of disks, operating system tasks that access the disk will not affect the database or logs. Placing the swap file on its own set of disks is perhaps the most critical of all. The swap file is read from and written to almost constantly. If this activity had to compete with the OS, the database, and the log files, overall performance of the system would suffer.

> **Many Companies Would Rather Mirror Disks than Break Out the Roles**
>
> Because of cost constraints and disk backplane capacity it is often not realistic to break up the OS, swap file, database, and logs to the degree mentioned previously. For system resiliency, many companies would rather mirror disks than break out the roles. When faced with this compromise on a domain controller you can prioritize the functions as follows with regards to which function should get its own spindle first:
>
> Swap file
>
> NTDS.DIT
>
> Active Directory logs

# Configuring Your Disks the Right Way

The optimal configuration for a domain controller is for the operating system to be mirrored on a pair of drives. Each of the drives should be on their own channel of their own controller. This protects against disk failure and controller failure. The swap file should also be on a pair of mirrored drives with each drive on its own channel of the same two controllers running the OS. A third pair of drives should be mirrored in the same manner as the OS drives and these should hold the log files. The drives for the Active Directory database should also be mirrored in the same manner as the prior drives. If the database will be larger than a single drive it is preferred to run mirrored stripe sets (RAID 0+1) for the database. This is preferred over RAID 5 because of the performance hit on writes that is associated with RAID 5.

RAID 0+1 combines the performance of striping with the redundancy of mirroring. Striping multiple disks allows each disk to be read or written simultaneously. This allows the disk performance to scale nearly 1:1 with additional disks. RAID 5 uses a parity check that requires reading all the disks in the RAID and determining the parity value to write. This configuration results in good read speed but reduced write speed. The parity allows the RAID to lose one disk and still operate based on the ability to re-create the value on the missing drive. This also allows the RAID to rebuild the data on the missing disk when it is replaced.

## Understanding Your Replication Topology

Properly scaling Active Directory goes beyond simply sizing the domain controllers and optimizing the location of files. When active directory becomes very large it is critical to address the replication topology. Logical placement of bridgehead servers helps to break up replication traffic. Rather than force all domain controllers to replicate back to a hub site, plan out replication to reduce traffic across slow links. If a network had a main office in San Jose, an office in New York, and an office in New Jersey and the New Jersey office connected only to New York it would not be optimal to have a hub and spoke replication back to the main office in San Jose. By allowing New York to act as a bridgehead with New Jersey using New York as a preferred bridgehead, replication traffic would be reduced. If the domain controller in New York failed, the domain controller in New Jersey could still replicate with the domain controllers in San Jose assuming site link bridging was still enabled. Site link bridging is enabled by default.

> ### KCC in Windows 2003 Is Greatly Improved from the Version in Windows 2000
>
> By default, site link bridging is enabled. The KCC in Windows 2003 is greatly improved from the version in Windows 2000. Replication traffic in Windows 2003 is also reduced as a result of replicating attribute level changes instead of entire user objects. This being the case, it is still important to monitor the KCC to ensure that replication is occurring correctly.

If an Active Directory site is going to have more than one domain controller one of the DCs should be configured as a bridgehead server. This allows the other DCs in that site to get their replication from the local server. Without this type of architecture it would be hard to scale Active Directory across a large environment. The use of site link bridging is useful for creating simple redundancy but as an environment grows the Knowledge Consistency Checker—the function that determines replication across bridged site links—is unable to scale and manually managed site links are required. A good rule of thumb is to check the environment against a complexity formula. To determine if the topology is too complex for the KCC to handle, a complexity formula is used:

$(1 + D) * S^2 <= 100,000$ (where D = Number of Domains and S = Number of Sites in your network)

# Scaling for the File System

> ### Scalability is the key to reducing operation costs
>
> By properly scaling file servers it is possible to consolidate file servers. This reduces hardware costs and maintenance costs, and frees up valuable space in the data center. Scalability is the key to reducing operation costs.

As companies begin to take advantage of new technologies such as Volume Shadow Copy, Redirected Folders, and desktop backups, there is a need for larger and larger file servers. The issue becomes that as more users are accessing the systems the servers are unable to keep up with the demand. Increasing the available disk space on servers only encourages users to store more data and this serves to further affect performance. Because historically the amount of data stored per user has consistently grown, the only option is to increase scalability of the file servers.

## Disk IO Is Critical—SCSI/RAID/IDE

Most modern servers come with a SCSI controller for the disk subsystem with the option of a hardware RAID controller. It is important to distinguish a hardware RAID from a software RAID. The easy way to distinguish them is that a hardware RAID is RAID "all the time." A software RAID is only RAID after the operating system has started. Software RAID requires processor time and is generally less efficient. Hardware RAID traditionally offers more advanced features in the area of distributing memory caches and in dynamic reconfigurations such as adding drives to an existing array.

SCSI comes in many flavors—Wide, Ultra, Ultra Wide, Ultra 160, Ultra 320. Each of these flavors refers to a specific type of drive it supports and an overall bandwidth of the bus. Ultra 320, for example, has a total bandwidth of 320MB/sec. The important thing to note is that the bandwidth of the controller doesn't have anything to do with the bandwidth of a drive. An Ultra 320 hard drive doesn't have a throughput of 320MB/sec. The advantage of the controller having that amount of bandwidth is that it is able to control multiple hard drives before it becomes the bottleneck in the system. This allows a server to scale more efficiently because adding hard drives will increase performance until they saturate the bus. When this occurs you have the option of adding more controllers and reallocating disks such that none of the controllers are oversubscribed.

RAID traditionally refers to a Hardware RAID controller with an attached set of disks. RAID has the ability to take attached disks to another level. By writing to the disks in a specific manner a system can gain the ability to increase read and write performance and offer the ability to continue serving data even after disk failures have occurred. RAID is offered in several levels, each with different characteristics.

Using RAID over single attached disks allows servers to scale well because data is protected and access to data is improved. RAID technologies allow larger numbers of users to be supported on file servers. Striping disks allows the aggregate space to be treated as a single disk. This enables an administrator to surpass the physical limitations of a single disk.

## BEST PRACTICE

### Always Be Aware of the Implications

When making cache settings on a RAID 5 subsystem always be aware of the implications. Allowing write caching on a RAID 5 volume nearly eliminates the write penalty associated with RAID 5 as long as the cache is not full. Failure to commit the write cache to disk will almost always result in file corruption. Ensure that the cache has a functional battery backup if the plan for the RAID 5 calls for write caching. Some controllers allow the cache to be physically moved to another controller without losing the RAID configuration or any of the data stored in the cache. This allows the drives to be moved to another system and the cache flushed to disk.

## BEST PRACTICE

### RAID Types

RAID 0 is referred to as a striped disk array. The data is broken down into blocks and each block is written to a separate disk drive. The first block goes to the first drive, the second block to the second drive, and so on for all the drives and then the writes go to the first disk and follow sequentially. I/O performance is greatly improved by spreading the I/O load across many channels and drives because by having multiple read/write heads the disks can be accessed simultaneously. This scales performance in a nearly 1:1 manner.

RAID 1 is referred to as mirrored disks (or duplexed if there are two controllers). Any data that is written to disk 1 is written to disk 2 as well. There is no performance gain but if disk 1 fails there is an exact mirror of the data on disk 2 that can be utilized by the server.

RAID 5 is Independent Data disks with distributed parity blocks. This essentially means that as blocks are written as 0s or 1s the values are added up for n−1 drives and the resulting 0 or 1 (remember, this is binary and we are checking parity, so two 1s become a 0) is written as a parity bit on the remaining drive. In RAID 5 the parity is distributed across all drives. RAID 3 is a similar concept except that the parity is kept on a dedicated drive. This had a disadvantage of the parity drive seeing more accesses than any other drive and it became a bottleneck, as such it is rarely if ever seen in modern networks. RAID 5 has good read performance because the drives are read simultaneously and the additional heads will scale performance. Writes, on the other hand, suffer a penalty due to the need to check parity and possibly rewrite it. By having the parity bit a RAID 5 system can continue running if a drive is lost. When the drive is replaced the calculated parity is written back to the disk.

RAID 6 is similar to RAID 5 but with the addition of a second parity disk. This allows the system to survive the failure of two disks in the array. It suffers from even worse write performance and is rarely seen in use.

RAID 0+1 is a combination of striping and mirroring. The disks are striped for performance and mirrored for redundancy. It is the least efficient use of disks but it results in the best overall performance for applications that are both read- and write-intensive.

There are other forms of RAID (2, 7, 53, and so on) but they are rarely seen in production either because of a lack of performance advantage or because they are proprietary in design.

## When Does an Environment Justify Using SAN/NAS?

As requirements for data storage and data access become extreme a server with locally attached SCSI or RAID storage can become unable to keep up with the rate of requests for data. Network operating systems such as Windows, Unix, or even Linux are very good at handling and servicing data requests but eventually they become overtaxed and another technology must be employed.

NAS stands for Network Attached Storage. SAN stands for Storage Area Network. These two technologies differ in one key area. NAS utilizes file level access and SAN utilizes block level access. SAN allows another system to believe that a portion of the SAN is local raw disk. NAS uses an additional abstraction layer to make another system believe that a portion of its disk is a virtual local disk. SAN is generally higher performance and is often used on databases because the performance is so high. NAS has only recently entered the area of databases as improvements in its technology and associated abstraction layers have resulted in performance that is sufficient for databases. NAS and SAN have a big advantage over attached storage in that they do not run a full operating system that was designed with hundreds of tasks in mind. They have very dedicated cores that are designed purely for high performance data access. The other key area in which NAS and SAN differ is in their method of attachment. NAS runs over ethernet (TCP/IP) and can take advantage of an existing LAN environment. The use of ethernet somewhat limits the bandwidth available to NAS. SAN, on the other hand, runs over fiber channel. This technology has much greater bandwidth than Ethernet but is also significantly more expensive. Not unlike most things in life, as performance goes up, so does cost.

NAS and SAN offer great flexibility in their ability to centrally manage storage and dynamically allocate space to servers. Some technologies such as large node clustering and large application farms would be nearly impossible without NAS or SAN.

When an environment gets to the point where the file servers are unable to service user requests for data in a timely manner or when attached storage capacity is simply exceeded it is time to strongly consider a NAS or SAN. For applications like Terminal Server farms, where users will attach to the system on any of the nodes, it is highly advisable to store the user's files on a SAN or NAS device. This ensures

> **Fiber Channel**
>
> Fiber channel can be run across tremendous distances. Companies often use fiber channel networks to maintain mirrored data in other states. The bandwidth combined with the long haul features makes fiber channel a very valuable technology to use with data storage.

high performance access to these files from any server in the farm. Without this type of central storage, management of users and their data would be very difficult.

## Remember RAM-disks?

Some situations call for extremely fast access to data but not necessarily large volumes of data. Computational analysis, databases, and system imaging software are just a few examples of applications that could benefit from extremely fast access to read-only data in the under 2GB range. This type of situation can greatly benefit from the use of RAM-disks. By partitioning off a chunk of system memory and treating it as a disk you can get memory speed performance for applications that traditionally accessed disks. Although this information can be written back to disk for storage, it somewhat defeats the purpose of the RAM-disk. By preloading information into the RAM-disk the system can spool out the data as fast as the network interface can handle. For situations like imaging hundreds and hundreds of desktops from a single server image the increase in performance can be stunning. Although Windows 2003 does not natively offer a RAM-disk, there are several third-party RAM-disk programs available such as RamDisk Plus from Superspeed or SuperDisk from EEC Systems.

> **RAM-disks Are Best Suited to Read-only Data**
>
> RAM-disks lose all data when the power is turned off. Ensure that the data will be committed to disk upon shutdown if the data will be read/write. Be aware that a system crash will result in any new data in the RAM-disk being lost. RAM-disks are best suited to read-only data.

## Distributed File System

Another great way to scale file server performance is through Distributed File System. DFS essentially enables you to hide the file servers behind an abstracted layer. Instead of accessing shares in the traditional method of \\fileserver\share the user attaches to \\dfsshare\share. The DFS structure is comprised of links to other file shares. This hides the location of the data from the user. The advantage of this is that shares can be moved to larger servers without the user having to remap her resources. Replicas of the data can be created and Active Directory will allow the user to connect to the closest replica of the data. This allows a DFS structure to scale without consuming all available WAN bandwidth. It also offers a level of redundancy to the environment. If a DFS replica is down, users will connect to the next closest source of the data. This gives you tremendous flexibility in scaling the file servers.

> **Excellent Candidate for DFS**
>
> Read-only data that is accessed heavily is an excellent candidate for DFS. By placing multiple replicas of the data on the same network the DFS structure will load balance the access to the data, resulting in excellent end-user performance.

# Scaling for RAS

Companies today are moving toward the philosophy that data should be available anywhere and anytime. Users should be able to access resources from home, from hotels, and even from Internet cafes. Technologies such as Virtual Private Networks, wireless, and modems work together to allow users to access their data. Setting up basic remote access systems can be fairly straightforward. Scaling these systems is another situation entirely. Companies like AT&T support literally millions of users in their Remote Access systems.

> **Never Compromise Security Policies**
>
> Don't let the scaling of RAS get in the way of network security. Never compromise security policies to increase VPN or RAS performance.

## Hardware Cryptographic Accelerators

VPNs are an amazing way to take advantage of the Internet as a backbone network for remote access. Windows 2003 offers support for both Point-to-Point Tunneling Protocol and Layer 2 Transport Protocol (with IPSec) as VPN technologies. Windows 2003 does a pretty good job of handling these services but as administrators attempt to scale this access to larger and larger numbers of users they quickly discover that the VPN takes up a fair amount of system resources. Rather than just add more and more RAS servers, a clever administrator can increase performance by using a hardware cryptographic accelerator. A cryptographic accelerator offloads encryption tasks from the CPU and performs them on dedicated hardware. This allows a RAS server to greatly increase the number of simultaneous connections it can service. This also allows administrators to

> **A Hardware IPSec Accelerator Is Probably Overkill**
>
> In many environments, the Internet bandwidth becomes the VPN bottleneck long before the VPN server does. If a company only has a T-1 connection to the Internet, a hardware IPSec accelerator is probably overkill.

enforce a higher level of encryption than they would have otherwise used because of perform-ance constraints.

## When to Make the Move from Software to Hardware

Many hardware RAS solutions on the market offer features and levels of performance not found in Windows 2003 Routing and RAS. One of the primary factors in moving to an appliance for remote access is to move away from a multipurpose operating system like Windows 2003 to a more dedicated operating system. Because RAS devices are often run parallel to the firewall the security of the system is of paramount performance. By eliminating the general purpose code these appliances are able to greatly mitigate their exposure to security exploits.

When looking at hardware VPN/RAS devices pay special attention to whether they support native VPN clients. Having the ability to use PPTP or L2TP/IPSec can be a great advantage in not having to purchase or manage a third-party VPN client.

> **PPTP Security**
>
> The industry often gives PPTP a pretty hard time about its security. White papers were published accusing PPTP of being susceptible to a "man in the middle attack." It is impor-tant to point out that the security flaw exposed was not in PPTP but in MS-CHAP, the authentication protocol that was used in PPTP at the time. This flaw has long since been fixed in MS-CHAPv2. This is the authen-tication protocol used for PPTP in Windows 2000 and Windows 2003.

## Multiplexing for Modem Support

Companies that maintain their own dial-up services can take advantage or newer technologies to reduce their costs and maintenance efforts. When looking at adding analog lines for modems, always look into getting an aggregated line and a multiplexer. In many areas it is cheaper and easier to get a T-1 line than it is to get 10 analog lines. The T-1 is cheaper, takes up less space in the Intermediate Data Frame, and has the capacity for a total of 23 analog lines. Always work closely with the telecom group to see what facilities you already have in place and take advan-tage of them whenever possible.

Software modems take this concept to another level. By plugging a single T-1 into a Software Modem device the device creates up to 23 virtual modems that act exactly like physical modems. This is a more cost-effective modem solution and it takes up less space in the data center. Most ISPs use virtual modem technologies to support their dial-up users.

## Taking Advantage of Multihoming Your Internet Connection

As companies become more and more dependent on their VPN environments they often look into making the VPN more resilient. Redundant VPN hardware is usually the first upgrade with things like bandwidth being second. Multihoming the Internet connection is an upgrade that is often overlooked. By attaching to multiple ISPs a company can protect against failures of their upstream providers. Additionally, by multihoming a network can become closer to other specific networks. For example, if a company had its Internet connection through one company and was using dial-up services through another, there is no guarantee as to the performance when going from one network to another. Traffic from ISP A will hit the Internet through a public access point as quickly as possible and eventually reach ISP B. From there it would reach the company's VPN system. By attaching the company's VPN system to ISP B as well (ISP B being the provider of the dial-up services with POPs in every city) there is a much more direct path back to the VPN system. This situation not only improves performance by reducing latency and hop count but it acts as a secondary route for Internet connectivity. Technologies such as BGP4 (Border Gateway Protocol) allow companies to be reachable via multiple ISPs without having to route only through the primary ISP. This allows a company to scale its VPN and RAS solutions through added capacity and added resiliency.

# Scaling Web Services

For many companies, Web services see more traffic than any other single system. As the company grows its identity grows. As its identity grows, more and more people want to find out about the company. This results in more and more traffic for the Web servers. Companies are using the Web for providing not only information but also for supporting their products. Fully indexed searches, dynamic content, and driver and patch downloads all result in increased loads on the Web servers. The Web services must be able to scale if the company is to keep up with the rest of the industry.

## Beefy Boxes Versus Many Boxes

Traditionally, applications scaled by improving the performance of the hardware. Almost all applications ran on a single server and the only way to make it faster or to increase its capacity was to upgrade the server. Web services introduced the industry to an application where much of the data was static. Even today's dynamic sites are mostly static frameworks with bits of data read from another system. This created an environment where a large portion of the data was read-only. This meant that data could be replicated to multiple locations and updated in batches. Changes would not be made by users to one system and need to be replicated to the others. This was a prime environment in which to use multiple servers and load balancers. By adding Web servers and giving them a local copy of the static content and pointing them to a central source for dynamic content performance could be scaled to amazing levels. Soon the Internet was filled with farms of hundreds of front-end Web servers servicing hundreds of millions of hits each day.

## Using Cryptographic Accelerators for SSL

As the increase in Web server usage swept the Internet, new uses for Web servers were appearing. Traditional brick and mortar companies were doing business on the Internet. Security for these business transactions became a strict requirement. Companies turned to encryption to offer a secure method of doing business on the Internet. SSL, or Secure Socket Layer, became something of a de facto standard for encrypting Web traffic. The use of SSL requires the Web server to perform certain cryptographic processes on data. These processes take up CPU cycles and can quickly bog down a Web server. To continue to scale Web services with SSL, administrators continued to add more and more Web servers. The industry quickly realized that this was not an optimal solution and SSL accelerators were created. By offloading cryptographic processes onto a dedicated

> **SSL accelerators**
>
> Many load balancers, also known as layer 4-7 switches, are offering SSL acceleration. Other SSL accelerators come in the form of PCI cards destined for the servers themselves.

hardware device the CPU is freed up to perform other tasks. SSL encryption loads can reduce the performance of a Web server by as much as 75%. An SSL accelerator can return that performance without having to add servers. This reduces maintenance tasks and warranty costs and frees up valuable data center space.

## n-tier Application Model

Many Web-based applications start their lives as a single box that is a Web server, an application, and a data store. This works well for small applications and keeps the data neatly bundled in a single system. As these applications are scaled, a single box is often not sufficient to keep up with the needs of the application. To scale these types of applications it is useful to take the application to an n-tier model. By separating the database from the application an administrator is able to dedicate the performance of a system to being a database. This allows the system to be built and tuned with a specific database in mind. This allows it to scale well. The application layer often has different requirements as well. It might be demanding enough to warrant multiple application servers running in a load-balanced group to offer enough performance to keep up with the application. The Web layer can be scaled like any other Web server. By load-balancing a group of Web servers, they can be scaled to meet the demands of the users. By pointing them to the load-balanced application layer, they can take advantage of the distributed processing of the application. Those applications draw their data from the database and feed it up into the Web presentation layer. This type of model scales very well. As components of the system prove too demanding to share resources with other components, they are simply split off onto dedicated hardware.

## Scaling Web Services via Web Farms

When the Dot Com boom first started to hit companies scrambled to build systems powerful enough to keep up with the demands of their users. Early Dot Com companies put up powerful Unix systems to run their Web sites. It was soon realized that this was a very inefficient method. Because the Dot Com world required resources to be accessible 24 hours a day, seven days a week it became very expensive to maintain redundant Unix systems. The concept of the Web Farm caught on very quickly. By running multiple Web servers the load from the user base was distributed across the systems through the use of a load-balancer. With this architecture, the environment could run with very inexpensive servers. The stability of the systems was not a great concern because if a server failed the other servers would take up the load. If the load became too high the administrator could simply add more Web servers to the farm. This became the de facto standard for high traffic Web sites. By replicating the content or by having the servers draw their content dynamically from another source the systems could be brought online very quickly and easily. Sites using this methodology have scaled to the point of being able to support more than 300 million hits per day.

# Scaling for Terminal Services

Terminal services have changed drastically over the years. Early versions of terminal services had issues with multiple processors, they didn't have the ability to load balance, and they had no ability to leverage local client resources. Third-party add-ons to Terminal Services addressed these types of issues and increased the ability to scale Terminal Services into larger and larger deployments. The current version of Terminal Services in Windows 2003 has natively addressed these concerns and has proven its ability to scale to very large implementations.

## Big Processors Versus Multi-Processors

Current processor technologies allow servers to perform incredible amounts of computing. Single servers can host literally hundreds of simultaneous users. Windows 2003 Terminal Services is able to scale performance nearly 1:1 with the addition of multiple processors up to four processors. Although Terminal Services can be run with more processors, benchmarking has shown that scaling beyond four processors results in greatly diminishing returns.

## Memory, Memory, and More Memory

Terminal Services can be a fairly memory hungry beast. Exact memory requirements will vary dependant on the types of users accessing the system and the applications running on the system itself. A safe rule of thumb is 16MB per user if he is running specific applications and 32MB per user if he is running a desktop session. Memory for the system itself should be added to this value to determine the total memory needed for the terminal server. Without enough memory to support the users the individual user's performance will suffer. Sufficient memory is needed to properly scale Terminal Services.

## Terminal Service Farms

To support very large numbers of Terminal Services users it is necessary to go beyond one or two Terminal Servers and into a full Terminal Service farm. Because of the unique needs of Terminal services there are a few components that are critical to the success of the farm. Some applications require the tracking of a session state. A Web server that is load-balanced might need the user to return to a specific Web server that was tracking the user's actions in order to make an application work properly. Terminal Services takes this concept much further. Terminal Services give the user the capability to disconnect from the session but have the applications continue to run. For this reason it is an absolute necessity for a user to reconnect to his original session. This is accomplished via the Session Directory.

By having Terminal Servers join the Session Directory, the Session Directory Servers will track which users are on which Terminal Servers. This allows users who are intentionally or unintentionally disconnected to return to their original session when they reconnect. Because of the importance of this role, it is recommended that the Session Directory be run on a cluster.

Because users of a Terminal Services farm can conceivably connect to any server in the farm it is important that their personal resources be reachable from any session. It is best to think of a user's terminal server session as a disposable resource. Nothing unique to that user should be stored on a Terminal Server. The easiest way to accomplish this is through the use of Terminal Server profiles and redirected folders. These folders should redirect to a central file store. This file store could potentially be used by hundreds of Terminal Servers and therefore thousands of Terminal Server users. Use of NAS with a clustered head is highly recommended for this role. To make sure that users don't store data locally to the session the session should be locked down via GPOs. Decisions on whether or not to allow users to connect to their local host are left to the individual administrator.

The responsible administrator will take the time to lock down the servers application by application to prevent users from altering resources that they shouldn't have access to.

## Improving Scalability by Load Balancing Applications

Windows 2003 offers load balancing amongst Terminal Servers. For some environments, this isn't enough. Several third-party vendors have added the concept of Application Load Balancing to Terminal Services. This means that if a user wanted to run Word their request would reach an Application Load Balancer and it would check to see which server offering Word had the lowest load. This is the server that the user would be connected to. This allows an administrator to load balance all of her servers to a single name and IP address and not have to install all applications on all servers. This can be especially helpful when running applications that have specific local peripheral requirements.

# Summary

In this chapter you saw that there are two primary ways to scale a technology. The first way is to improve the hardware on which the technology runs. Servers with multiple processors, loads of memory, and high performance disk subsystems are a great way to get a technology to support more users.

You learned that most technologies can be scaled by adding more of the same item and balancing the load across them. By creating these farms, you can scale an application to handle far more users than a single system ever could.

You saw how dedicated hardware devices like accelerators can increase performance beyond the original system's capabilities. Dedicated operating systems can also serve to further scale applications by removing unnecessary services and therefore removing potential security flaws.

Third-party applications can serve not only to extend the functionality of systems like Web servers and Terminal Servers but also they can add scalability by offering load distribution technologies that were not originally present.

By taking advantage of these features and implementing best practices you can scale almost any application to support huge numbers of users and performance loads. By carefully planning the applications, you can scale without falling into the trap of making a system unmanageable.

# 25

# Utilizing Storage Area Networks

**F**ew items in the data center invoke more awe and respect than the shiny black monolith that is the SAN. *SANs*, or *Storage Area Networks*, are extremely high-performance collections of disks that can be sliced and diced dynamically and attached to remote systems as though they were directly attached. SANs differ from traditional DAS, or Direct Attached Storage, in that the disks are no longer attached to the local system through SCSI or IDE connections. The SAN is viewed as a cloud and is literally a separate high-speed network with the sole purpose of connectivity between hosts and high-speed disks. From the server's point of view, the remote disk acts exactly the same as the locally attached disk. By consolidating the disks into a central location, you are able to take advantage of situations that just weren't possible in the past.

This chapter compares and contrasts Storage Area Networks, Direct Attached Storage, and Network Attached Storage (NAS), and shows you when to take advantage of one technology over another. This chapter will explain the requirements of each technology to help you avoid common mistakes when choosing a storage technology. It will also touch on industry best practices for using NAS and SAN technologies with specific applications.

# Defining the Technologies

To understand how and when to use technologies like NAS or SAN it is important to understand what they are and what they offer. The technologies differ in how they are used and what advantages they provide. Many administrators assume that they need SAN when often a NAS will suffice. Because IT budgets are far from limitless, it is to your advantage to know that you aren't overbuying for your solution.

## What Is a SAN?

A Storage Area Network is a high-speed special-purpose network or subnetwork that connects various data storage devices with associated data servers on behalf of a larger network of users. Typically, a SAN is but part of an overall network of computing resources for an enterprise. A SAN is usually located in relative proximity to other computing resources, such as databases and file servers, but might also extend to remote locations for backup and archival storage. These remote locations are traditionally connected via wide area network carrier technologies such as asynchronous transfer mode (ATM) or Synchronous Optical Networks (SONET).

It is very important to understand that the SAN is more than just the chassis that contains the disks. It includes the RAID controllers for the disks, the Fiber Channel switching fabric, and the Host Bus Adapters that reside in the data servers. SANs are traditionally connected to hosts via Fiber Channel. Although it can be fairly easy to support dual arbitrated fiber loops in a corporate environment, keep in mind that one of the primary benefits of SAN is the ability to do block-level mirroring to another SAN. If this SAN is located remotely, up to 1,000km away with current Fiber technology, a company needs to have fiber between the two locations. A fiber connection across those kinds of distances can be quite expensive.

**Zero Latency**

Although most SAN manufacturers refer to the performance of their products as having *zero latency* it is important not to misinterpret this. Zero latency refers to the fact that Fiber Channel has extremely low overhead and doesn't add additional latency. The laws of physics, on the other hand, are still in effect. A 1,000km fiber run will still take 7 milliseconds roundtrip.

SAN technologies excel in the area of disk performance. Fiber channel networks regularly push 2GB/sec of throughput. Although SCSI technologies can move data at up to 320MB/sec, they are limited to less than 25 feet of distance. SAN, not unlike SCSI, is seen by the host system as RAW disk. This is also referred to as a block-level technology. In the past, database applications required block-level access to the disk as well as the "near 0 latency" offered by SAN.

## What Is NAS?

Network attached storage (NAS) is a hard disk storage technology that uses its own network address rather than being attached directly to the host computer that is serving applications or data to a network's users. By removing storage access and its management from the host server, both application programming and files can be served faster because they are not competing for the same processor time. The network-attached storage device is attached to a local area network via Ethernet and given an IP address. File requests are mapped by the host server to the NAS device.

Network-attached storage consists of hard disk storage, including multidisk RAID systems, and software for configuring and mapping file locations to the network-attached device. NAS software can usually handle a number of network protocols, including Microsoft's Internetwork Packet Exchange, Common Internet File System and NetBEUI, Novell Netware Internetwork Packet Exchange, and Sun Microsystems Network File System. Configuration, including the setting of user access priorities, is usually possible using a Web browser though many NAS offerings

> **A Single MAC Address Conversation Cannot Span Multiple Network Interfaces**
> When considering network architecture to support a NAS device, remember that when bonding multiple Ethernet interfaces, a single MAC address conversation cannot span multiple network interfaces. If the NAS is on Gigabit Ethernet and a server has a quad fast Ethernet card, it will only talk to the NAS device at 100MB/sec even though it has 400MB/sec of potential throughput.

require command line configuration. Most NAS manufacturers include specialized software for allowing specific applications such as SQL or Exchange to take advantage of special functions provided by the NAS. These functions include things like mirroring, failover, automated recovery, and snapshotting.

NAS has the advantage of using existing Ethernet technologies that are much less expensive than Fiber technologies. With the availability of 10GB Ethernet, NAS is able to compete with Fiber Channel–based technologies even with the added overhead of Ethernet over Fiber Channel.

## What Is DAS?

Direct Attached Storage (DAS) is the traditional "local disk" that most administrators are accustomed to. Technologies like IDE and SCSI are used to connect drives or RAIDs to the host computer. Direct Attached Storage has many advantages in the area of performance and cost. With SCSI technologies like Ultra 320, which can transfer 320MB/sec of data across the bus and controllers with large amounts of cache memory, DAS is well situated to provide fast and stable disk performance. The disadvantage of DAS is that the management load of each of these DAS subsystems increased linearly with the number of servers. This can eventually become unwieldy as there is a lack of centralized management.

With the advent of Serial ATA and Serial ATA RAID controllers, IDE devices are becoming more and more viable for systems that need fast access to large amounts of data that won't see huge numbers of transactions. Systemlike backup servers that will cache to disk before spooling to

> **IDE Technologies Can Compare Favorably to SCSI Technologies**
>
> Although IDE technologies can compare favorably to SCSI technologies in the area of seek time and bus bandwidth, they can't compete in the area of IO transactions per second. Most applications that require large amounts of disk are IO bound, not bandwidth bound. Be sure to understand the IO requirements of an application before choosing disk technologies.

tape can benefit from the speed and low cost of Serial ATA devices. IDE drives almost always lead SCSI drives in the area of size and are always less expensive. IDE RAID controllers offer excellent performance at much lower costs than their SCSI equivalents. IDE-based RAID controllers don't handle large numbers of requests as well as SCSI-based RAID controllers. IDE-based RAIDs are still limited to four devices. This isn't always an issue as SATA drives of 250GB or more are commonly available. A 1 Terabyte SATA RAID can be built for well under $1,500. With throughput of over 180MB/sec, Serial ATA RAID can be a very tempting DAS technology.

# When Is the Right Time to Implement NAS and SAN Devices?

There are many reasons to implement a NAS or SAN solution in favor of DAS. If the requirements for storage consolidation, reduction in server count, centralized management of disk resources, SLA recoverability times, or near real time mirroring of data justify the cost of a SAN or NAS solution it is time to explore those options. To make an informed decision about when to make the switch it is important for you to pass through several phases:

1. *Analyze*—Gather usage metrics and performance metrics. Determine how storage is being used and how it affects the business processes.

2. *Plan*—Determine the current limitations of your storage solutions. Prioritize the problems and determine if there is a better way. Don't fall into the trap of doing things just because they were always done a particular way.

3. *Develop*—Build the proposed solution for testing. Perform benchmarking to show improvements over the old methods.

4. *Pilot*—Test the solution and improve it based on user feedback. Educate the user population on how to take full advantage of the new functions and determine the improvements in efficiencies.

5. *Deploy*—Deliver the solution to the masses.

Following this methodology will not only streamline the process of implementing new and more efficient storage technologies but also the process will provide valuable data to help upper management buy into the upgrades and support the storage program.

## Analyzing Your Storage Needs

The first phase of any good project is an in-depth analysis of the environment and its needs. In the case of Storage Systems it is critical to identify any systems with special requirements. This would include systems that require multiple layers of redundancy, systems that are under extremely tight Service Level Agreements, and systems that cannot tolerate a loss of data.

Another key area to understand is the capacity requirements of the enterprise. If an investment is going to be made in storage it is a good idea to plan for several years of growth. Look at the number of servers in the environment. If additional servers have been added simply because that is the way things were always done, it is time to look at shifting the philosophy to doing things because they are the right way to do them.

### Disk Drives Get Larger, Faster, and Cheaper Each Year

Disk drives get larger, faster, and cheaper each year. When planning for the future, keep expandability in mind. By buying a partially filled chassis now and adding additional disks later, you can take advantage of falling disk prices and save money over the long run and still get the full capacity they need and the benefits of fewer chassis.

## Planning the Storage Solution

Storage technologies can be very confusing. In most situations, valid arguments can be made for using any of the available technologies. This is a situation in which it makes a lot of sense to get your vendors involved. Contact your potential vendors and let them know what your storage requirements are. Often times they have worked with other companies with similar needs and can provide valuable insight into what worked and what didn't. Given the costs of a large storage system, you can't afford to do it wrong.

After you have an idea of what you'd like to implement, find out if there are reference accounts that you can contact to determine if they were happy with the solution they implemented. Some companies will try to get you to commit to the latest greatest versions of their software and firmware. Large storage environments are a big investment and business processes will depend heavily on it. Ensure that you are implementing a stable and well-tested solution.

### Does This Decision Support the Goals of the Project?

There are a tremendous number of options when it comes to storage solutions. When in doubt about a decision, always refer back to the original goals of the project and ask yourself "Does this decision support the goals of the project?"

## Developing the Storage Solution

After you have determined the needs, explored the options, and come up with a plan, the real fun can begin. Any solution that will become part of the critical path of business must be developed and tested in a controlled lab environment. This is the part of the project where policies and procedures start to take form. Practice runs of mirroring, failing over of resources, and recovery of systems will ensure that the solution will be able to support the needs of the company.

This development phase will identify several requirements that are not usually thought of during the planning phase. Most specifically these requirements are in the area of facilities. Most SAN devices are fairly large. An EMC Symetrix and Connectix, for example, will take up a full rack each. With heat generation more than 3,000BTUs, HVAC resources will need to be considered. Also keep in mind that most SAN and NAS solutions require 220V to run them. Ensure that planned data center locations have appropriate space, cooling, and power. Power should include not only the standard AC feed, but battery backup as well. Be aware of any special requirements of the SAN or NAS. Some SAN devices on the market will void their warranty if they are placed within five feet of any solid objects.

## BEST PRACTICE

### Be Sure to Carefully Document the Entire Installation and Configuration Process

Be sure to carefully document the entire installation and configuration process. Not only will it make troubleshooting easier, but also it will provide the full roadmap for Pilot implementation.

## Piloting the Storage Solution

After the solution has been well tested in the lab, it's time to break it in limited production. Even extensive testing in a lab cannot always fully test all possible scenarios that a storage system will see in production. The best way to try to break the solution is to let users have access to it. Rolling the storage solution into a limited Pilot program will enable you to gather feedback about the performance of the system as well as feedback on the policies and procedures that will support the system. It's also a great time to get support staff trained on a system that they will likely end up supporting in full production.

## BEST PRACTICE

### Pilot the Storage Solution with an Engineering or Development Group

If possible, pilot the storage solution with an engineering or development group. If anyone can break your implementation or find flaws in the process, they can.

## Deploying the Storage Solution

After the system has gone through a final feedback loop from the pilot phase it is time to put the system into production. After following these steps you should have a well thought out solution that meets the current and future needs on the company. The solution will have been well tested and will encompass tweaks and improvements that came from the various testing phases. Performance metrics will be known and monitoring points determined. Now the company can begin to enjoy the benefits of the new storage solution.

# Designing the Right Data Storage Structure

A code vault that stores source code and enables programmers to check code in and out so that they can work on it locally on their systems probably doesn't justify a SAN with 28 platters. An Exchange 2003 Cluster that supports 3,000 users probably could. When designing a storage structure it is critical to understand your own needs.

## Choosing the Right Connectivity

All the high-speed disks in the world won't amount to much if you can't get the data to and from the servers quickly. In a NAS environment, the network itself is the biggest concern for performance. Most NAS devices on the market use very fast *heads* that are literally dedicated computers with high performance processors and loads of memory. With SCSI RAID controllers on board, they can easily saturate multiple 100MB Ethernet connections. Attaching such a device to a low-end switch would result in the NAS running in an extremely restricted manner. Strongly consider using a switch that will enable you to use a gigabit connection.

Consider creating a separate network for the NAS environment. Say, for example, that the NAS is going to support a number of Exchange servers. By multi-homing the Exchange servers, they would have one Ethernet connection that faced the users and provided connectivity to the mail clients, whereas the other interface would be dedicated to NAS traffic. This would allow each interface to run unfettered by the traffic associated with the other network. This also enables you to upgrade only a subset of the network to improve performance and save money. The traffic of the database transaction back to the NAS device by Exchange would be much greater than the traffic associated with users viewing their mail because the traffic that would normally go to the local disk would now be traveling across the Ethernet via the Virtual Disk driver that connects the NAS to the Exchange server.

When selecting network gear for a NAS *out-of-band* network, focus on packets per second. Whenever possible, build this NAS network with multiple switches that are cross-connected. Connect each server to both switches with the NICs in a teamed mode. This will not only add bandwidth but also will create redundancy for the network layer. Odds are if the application warranted the use of a NAS device, it deserves redundancy at the network level as well.

## Slicing and Dicing the Available Disk

Simple physics tells you that you'll get improvements in performance as you add more disks to an array. Because each drive's read/write head can operate simultaneously you get a fairly linear improvement as drives are added. NAS and SAN offer the advantage of dynamically increasing the size of a volume without taking the volume offline. This allows for the addition of even more spindles.

Although it's possible to later resize a volume from a NAS or SAN, you must be careful not to over subscribe the device. Devices that support snapshots of the data reserve twice the volume size that they claim for capacity. So in order to make 100GB available to a server, the NAS would

> ### Never Underestimate the Power of Multiple Spindles
>
> Never underestimate the power of multiple spindles. For applications like Exchange that are very IO-intensive, a quad processor Xeon 1.6 GHz with 4GB of memory and seven local disks can support up to 1,000 heavy users. When the number of attached disks was increased to 112, the system was able to support more than 11,000 heavy users.

reserve 200GB on itself. This ensures that it is able to complete all transactions. This function can be disabled on most devices but it is not recommended. This removes the protection from oversubscription of the disks.

# Adding in Fault Tolerance for External Storage Systems

When implementing centralized storage solutions, you are often placing a large number of very important eggs into a single basket. SAN and NAS manufacturers understand this and have spent a lot of research and development dollars on building in Fault Tolerance into their offerings. There are many options available to the end user; some of the fault tolerance options are as follows:

- RAID Configurations—RAID levels 0+1 and 5 are most common. RAID level 6 offers the ability to lose two drives at a time and not lose data.

- Triple Mirroring—This enables you to snap off a mirror so that data becomes static for purposes of backup. Meanwhile the system still has mirrored drives for fault tolerance. This is most commonly used with databases.

- Log Shipping—Most SAN and NAS devices can copy log files in near real time to another SAN or NAS so that databases can be copied regularly and log files can be kept in synch remotely.

- Geographic Mirroring—SAN and NAS devices offer in-band and out-of-band options for mirroring data across wide distances. Whereas SCSI has a 25-foot limitation, Fiber Channel can locate a device up to 1,000km away.

- Snapshotting—By flagging disk blocks as being part of a particular version of a file and writing changes to that file on new blocks, a NAS or SAN device can take a snapshot of what the data looked like at a point in time. This enables a user to roll back a file to a previous version. It also enables you to roll back an entire system to a point in time almost instantly.

- Clustering—NAS devices that use heads to serve data offer dual heads so that if one fails, the other will continue to serve data from the disks.

- Redundant power systems—Any good SAN or NAS will offer multiple power supplies to protect against failure. Take advantage of the separate power supplies by attaching them to separate electrical circuits.

- Redundant back-planes—Many NAS and SAN devices will offer redundant back-planes to protect against hardware failure.

■ Hot Standby Drives—By having unused drives available in the chassis, the device can replace a failed disk instantly with one that is already present and ready for use. Be sure to monitor the SAN or NAS device to see if a disk has failed and been replaced. It can be easy to miss because there would be no interruption to service.

> **RAID 5 Is Not Recommended**
>
> RAID 5 is not recommended for any application that performs write transactions more than about 15% of the time. This is due to the fact that each write transaction requires reading multiple disks and recalculating and writing of parity bits.

# Combining Hardware Fault Tolerance with Windows Server 2003 Technologies

Windows Server 2003 possesses several technologies that improve system availability and recoverability with Direct Attached Storage. These same technologies work very well with NAS and SAN devices as well.

## Distributed File System with NAS or SAN

Distributed File System has come a long way with Windows Server 2003. The ability to pre-stage data, the ability to mirror the DFS root, and improvements in control of replication topologies have all helped companies to adopt and take advantage of Distributed File System. Although things have gotten better, many administrators still find that there are too many limitations to the functionality of File Replication Services. FRS can't deal properly with roaming profiles and it often replicates data unnecessarily. For example, most antivirus products flag files that they have recently scanned. FRS will misinterpret this as a modification to the file and will queue it up for replication to all of its partners.

Many administrators are finding that the native replication functions of NAS and SAN devices are a much better way to maintain replication for DFS replicas. By having Windows Server 2003 servers mount those replicas and present them as nodes in the DFS tree, they are able to achieve enhanced usability in their DFS structures. This adds an additional layer of redundancy because NAS or SAN mirrored replicas are automatically presented to users if a local copy were to fail.

## Leveraging Logical Disk Manager

Most administrators are very familiar with the Logical Disk Manager that comes built into Windows. This is the interface that is regularly used to mount new disks, create partitions, and format drives. Administrators who are a bit more advanced have no doubt learned the benefits of being able to mount disks to folders rather than drive letters. Very large powerful servers that serve multiple tasks no longer have to worry about running out of drive letters.

Most SAN and NAS devices on the market offer management plug-ins that enable them to be managed through the existing Logical Disk Manager. Through hardware abstraction the remote disk is made to look like a local disk. This enables you to perform much of the management of the remote resources through an interface that they already know. This reduces the requirements to retrain administrative staff on a new technology.

## Remote Storage Management

Remote Storage, the Windows version of Hierarchical Storage Management (HSM), enables you to increase disk space on a server without physically adding more hard disks. Remote Storage automatically moves data back and forth between high-cost, faster disk drives and low-cost, high-capacity storage media. This traditionally meant moving data from Direct Attached Storage to either a lower performance server or a very low cost but high capacity storage media such as a tape library or rewritable DVD or DC media. Remote Storage monitors the amount of space available on local NTFS volumes, and when the amount of free space dips below the low water line, it transfers eligible files from the primary storage to the secondary storage. Users can still see and access archived files but they are actually seeing links to the files stored on the lower cost media. This frees up storage on the file server without requiring the purchase and installation of additional hard disks. The Remote Storage service also works with the Removable Storage service to access any removable media used for remote storage.

In an environment that uses NAS or SAN for storage, this concept can be moved up one tier. In most cases, the NAS or SAN device will replace a number of servers. These are servers that would normally be retired. Rather than scrap all the servers, you can take a subset of the servers and salvage the disks from all the systems and distribute them across the remaining servers. Those servers would be relegated to storing low demand data only. This would enable you to still lower the overall number of servers in the enterprise that require management.

Optionally these "lower tier" servers could be low-end servers with IDE RAID devices attached to them. Given the current prices and sizes of IDE drives, a 1-TB server could be built for well less than $5,000. Because it wouldn't be holding "primary" data, it would be acceptable to take the hit in performance and reliability that comes with IDE drives. This could allow for an environment where high demand and highly important data could live on redundant and high performance SAN/NAS devices. Data that hadn't been accessed in some time could be moved to the IDE RAID systems where the data would still be retrieved quickly. Data that hadn't been accessed in long periods of time would be moved to tape or rewritable media for long-term storage.

## Integrating Backups with NAS and SAN

Many administrators have faced the challenge of dealing with narrow windows of opportunity for performing backups. Given a choice, every department would request that their systems only be backed up between 2 a.m. and 3 a.m. so that they wouldn't suffer a performance hit while users might be accessing them. This is especially difficult in environments where systems are used globally. The challenge with narrow backup windows is that data cannot be spooled to tape fast enough to meet the time commitments. One of the easiest ways to improve this performance is to perform the remote backups to disk.

By using a NAS or SAN device to buffer the backups, you create an environment where the NAS or SAN becomes the backup device. Backups are written directly to the NAS/SAN at impressive speeds. Outside the backup windows, the data is backed up from the NAS/SAN to tape for long term storage. The added benefit of this model is that 90% of restore requests are for data from the previous evening. By having that data on disk on the SAN/NAS, the restore process is also much

> **SAN-attached Tape Devices**
>
> SAN-attached tape devices range from single drive single tape devices all the way up to office-sized backup systems with dozens of drives and literally thousand of available tapes. Robotic arms drive on tracks around the device scanning and moving tapes back and forth between drives, storage slots, and mail slots.

faster than it would have been from tape. SAN devices often support what is known as serverless backups. This means that the SAN itself controls the tape device and writes the data to it without the need for a traditional backup server.

## Leveraging Disk Quotas on NAS or SAN Devices

Disk quotas were introduced as a long overdue feature in Windows. For a long time, you had to worry about users storing inordinate amounts of data in their user directory and filling up the entire volume. Any other users whose home directories were on the same volume would suffer through no fault of their own. In an environment that makes user directory space available on a NAS or SAN will appreciate the safety that comes with being able to enforce quotas through Windows Server 2003. Imaging having to explain to your management that your brand new 4-TB SAN is already full because your users have filled it with "personal" data.

## Using Encrypted File System to Protect Files on the SAN or NAS

One of the greatest concepts ever put into use is the OSI Model. In a nutshell, the concept is that if you have a series of layers that work together than anything that can be abstracted to look like one of those layers will automatically work with the rest of the layers. In the case of SAN or NAS, a driver is used to make the remote storage look just like regular attached storage. After that is done, the rest of the system will treat the abstracted drive like another locally attached drive. This means that technologies like EFS will automatically work with the remote disk. Users can continue to encrypt data on the SAN or NAS and administrators can continue to manage EFS keys and agents the way that they always have.

# Best Practices for SAN and NAS

SAN and NAS manufacturers have provided a number of technologies that make it easier to integrate their products with specific software products. Because these products having been available for a number of years, best practices around these implementations have come about and can help you avoid common pitfalls with SAN and NAS usage.

## Exchange with NAS/SAN

When implementing a NAS or SAN solution in a Microsoft Exchange environment, there are many different interpretations on the best way to implement the solution. Some of the recommended best practices are as follows:

- Run multiple Host Bus Adapters in each Exchange server with each HBA connected to a different Fiber Channel switch. This will allow for failover if one of the Fiber Channel switches should fail.

- Backups should be performed at the storage group level rather than the mailbox level. Mailbox-level backups are very processor-intensive for the Exchange server.

- Separate logs files from databases onto different drive sets. This will improve overall throughput as well as improve recoverability in the case of a NAS/SAN failure.

- Replicate databases hourly to another device for disaster recovery. Logs should be replicated every few minutes. This will limit potential mail loss to one log replication interval.

- Always use integrated tools if they are available, such as Network Appliance's SnapManager for Exchange 2000. They will greatly simplify management and recoverability of the product for which they were designed.

- Always plan for space reservation on a volume. If the database will grow to 80GB and will have snapshots taken for recoverability, reserve 160GB of space on the device.

- Avoid placing multiple Virtual Logical Disks or LUNs on the same volume. This could result in databases and log files being on the same volume. This would complicate system recovers if the volume were to fail.

## SQL with NAS/SAN

A Microsoft SQL environment can leverage NAS and SAN technologies to improve storage management and storage solution implementation. Some of the recommended best practices for implementing a NAS or SAN device in a SQL Server environment are

- Separate database from each other by placing them on separate VLDs or LUNs on different volumes to maximize read/write performance.

- Place databases and log files in separate VLDs or LUNs on different volumes to not only improve read/write performance but to enhance recoverability.

- Run multiple Host Bus Adapters in each SQL Server with each HBA connected to a different Fiber Channel switch. This will allow for failover if one of the Fiber Channel switches should fail.

- Depending on the access pattern, a single hard disk can support roughly 150 I/O operations per second (IOPS). It is important to understand the I/O rate during peak load to estimate the number of disk drives needed to support the I/O load. For example, a RAID group size of eight disks (seven data and one parity) can at most support 7 * 150 IOPS = 1,050 IOPS

- Always take into account database growth to avoid having to constantly expand the volume. When possible, operate with extra free volume space. Maintaining extra free volume space will decrease a possible volume fragmentation rate and will also prevent sudden "out of space" events. When a volume's free space is very limited I/O performance could suffer.

When implementing a NAS solution, some of the technological solutions that can improve operational performance need to be taken into account. As an example, the following fictitious organization with the following requirements for a SQL Server can be modeled for a NAS configuration:

- Initial database size of 80GB

- Database growth rate is estimated to be 15% per month

- Change rate of the current database is estimated to be 15% per month

- Snapshot requirement is four Snapshots per day with a total of 12 Snapshots (three days)

- Default RAID group size is 72GB * 8 devices

- The administrator wants to expand the volume at most every six months

- The growth and change rates are estimates, so extra volume space has been requested, and the customer realizes that a volume always has to operate with some free space to decrease the possible fragmentation rate, or I/O performance could suffer; therefore, an extra 20% free space per disk drive will be allocated as a free-space buffer

- The average I/O rate is about 1.5MB per second and the peak rate is about 3MB per second

Based on the statistical information for this organization, the resulting analysis and projections can be as follows:

- The database size after six months will be about 144GB.

- About 1.6GB of the database will change every month after six months, which is equal to 0.12GB per four hours.

- The minimum space requirement after six months will be (144GB * 2) + (0.12GB * 12) = 290GB.

- A 72GB disk drive has 68GB usable file space, and because 20% is allocated as extra free space, only 55GB is usable per disk drive. Hence, six disk drives are needed for data and one disk drive for parity, for a total of seven disk drives. However, it is important for performance reasons to always configure complete RAID groups; therefore, the volume will be created with eight disk drives. If the rate of growth is consistent over time the volume will have to be expanded with another RAID group after six or seven months.

- The estimated peak load was 3MB per second, which is equal to about 770 IOPS. Because seven data disk drives can support 1,050 IOPS, a RAID group size of eight will be sufficient to support both space requirements and I/O load requirements.

## File Servers with NAS/SAN

File servers are based typically on small individual files as opposed to large blocks of structured information as in a SQL or Exchange environment. Best practices found in creating a NAS or SAN environment for file servers are as follows:

- Allocate only the space needed for a particular server. If users have access to infinite space, they'll find a way to fill it.

- Use third-party file comparison tools to determine when duplicate information is being stored on a separate file server.

- Snapshot the data regularly to enable users to recover their own files across multiple versions of the file.

- Consolidate file servers to a location where they can have very high-speed access to the NAS device. If possible, plug in the servers to the same blade on the network device to avoid sending traffic across the backplane.

- Enforce quotas on user data areas to prevent users from consuming all available space.

- Critical data should be mirrored to another location to ensure rapid recoverability.

- Data should be backed up to long-term storage media such as tape to maintain sufficient data history

- Run multiple Host Bus Adapters in each file server with each HBA connected to a different Fiber Channel switch. This will allow for failover if one of the Fiber Channel switches should fail.

- Users should be trained on any tools that will be available to them for tasks such as recovering deleted data or recovering an older version of an existing folder.

## Backup Systems

When configuring NAS or SAN devices as part of a backup, fault tolerance, disaster recovery, or business continuity structure, the configurations and optimization are much different than for file servers or database servers because the information is primarily stored for redundancy purposes. Some of the best practices for building a backup system NAS or SAN environment are as follows:

- Use configurations that maximize data throughput. Because data will only stay on the NAS or SAN for short periods of time and will be immediately spooled to tape, there is not a large need for redundancy at the SAN or NAS. RAID 0 is a good choice for this.

- The backup system should be connected to the high demand hosts via a dedicated network. This allows the backup to occur without interference from user-facing traffic.

- If using a SAN for the backups, consider using a SAN-attached tape device to spool the data for long term storage.

- For databases that cannot be acquiesced for purposes of backup, use a triple mirror configuration. This allows the third mirror to be broken and brought to a static state. This mirror can then be backed up to tape. After the backup occurs, the third mirror is reattached and synchronized with the system. During the backup process, the system is still protected by the second mirror.

- Run multiple Host Bus Adapters in each file server with each HBA connected to a different Fiber Channel switch. This will allow for failover if one of the Fiber Channel switches should fail.

## Active Directory Integration

Building a NAS or SAN environment in a Windows environment can leverage Active Directory and be integrated into the Directory for authentication, security, and management purposes. Some of the best practices for integrating Active Directory for NAS and SAN devices are as follows:

- NAS devices authenticate against the domain by which they are accessed. To ensure that this still works when a domain is upgraded to Active Directory, be sure to point the NAS at a DNS that holds the appropriate service records (SRV).

- Windows Server 2003 domains default to using only NTLM v2 or Kerberos and require the digital signing of communications. Ensure that any NAS devices present in the enterprise can support these requirements.

- NAS devices ACL resources based on SIDs. If a domain upgrade will involve migrating objects from another domain, be sure to either maintain the SID history or re-ACL the NAS device.

## Terminal Servers

Although a service that runs on Windows 2003, Windows Terminal Services operates similar to multiple workstations as opposed to a limited number of database servers. Some of the best practices in optimizing Windows Terminal Services in a NAS or SAN environment are as follows:

- Store user profiles on a NAS or SAN device to ensure fast access to the profile from any Terminal Server in the farm.

- Store applications on the NAS or SAN device. This allows the new Terminal Servers to be pointed to the existing applications for rapid deployment.

- Store user data on a NAS or SAN device. Due to the high IO requirements of multiple terminal servers potentially needing to reach a given user's data, only a NAS or SAN device spanning a large number of drives will be capable of providing adequate performance.

- Build VLDs or LUNs based not only upon space requirements but on IO requirements as well. Depending on the access pattern, a single hard disk can support roughly 150 I/O operations per second (IOPS). It is important to understand the I/O rate during peak load to estimate the number of disk drives needed to support the I/O load. For example, a RAID group size of eight disks (seven data and one parity) can at most support 7 * 150 IOPS = 1,050 IOPS.

- Store user data and applications on separate VLDs or LUNs. This enables you to easily lock down application files across the entire disk without affecting user-by-user access to their unique data or profiles.

## Booting from NAS/SAN

Some network solutions require certain network functions to load upon server boot-up whereas other applications are independent of server boot functions. When configuring a NAS or SAN device for system boot-up, some of the best practices for configuration are as follows:

- If the Host Bus Adapter supports it, booting a server directly from the SAN without any local hard drives is an easy way to replace failed servers.

- Terminal access type computers can be built by booting via BOOTP and receiving their operating system image from a NAS device. This greatly simplifies management of specialized stations. Using a NAS device for this will greatly improve scalability due to its ability to support higher IO rates.

- Replicate live systems to a test lab SAN by mirroring the data from servers that boot via the SAN. This allows isolated testing with data that is identical to the live system.

# Recovering from a System Failure

Having data stored on a SAN or NAS device can greatly reduce recovery time for failed systems. By having replicas of data on other devices, data can be reattached to a system in case of a system failure. In the situation where a server was booting its operating system off a SAN device, the Host Bus Adapter can simply be placed in similar hardware and the system will come right back up.

In the case of system failure due to data corruption, a SAN or NAS will enable you to roll the system back to a point in time before the corruption occurred based on the number of snapshots available.

If a system fails due to actual disk failure on the VLD or LUN that it was attached to, a system can be brought back up quite quickly if the data on that VLD or LUN was mirrored to another

NAS or SAN device. By simply remapping the VLD or LUN the system can be made functional again in a very rapid manner.

Mirroring and snapshotting are the keys to using NAS or SAN to make a system more easily recoverable than it would have been with DAS. Simple planning like keeping servers standard in their brand and configurations, always using the same brand and model of HBA or NIC, and keeping Fiber Channel switches standard across the enterprise enables you to have an environment where failed components can be replaced from a standard set of spare parts and the system brought up immediately.

Even in cases where entire sites fail due to storm, earthquake, or fire, systems can be brought back up quite rapidly in a failover location if the data was mirrored. Using SAN or NAS to perform this mirroring ensures a much greater level of confidence that the data was replicated correctly, even for databases that remain hot on a 24 by 7 schedule. Recoverability from both a site and a system level make SAN or NAS integrated environments much more resilient and reliable.

# Leveraging NAS and SAN Solutions for Server Consolidation

One of the most popular uses for NAS and SAN devices is to reduce the number of servers in the environment by consolidating servers and server functions. Rather than have dozens and dozens of file servers with locally attached storage, a smaller number of servers with NAS- or SAN-attached storage can serve the same purpose.

## Consolidating the Number of Exchange Servers

Exchange servers were traditionally sized based not only on performance potential but also on the time needed to recover a system. Administrators knew that if they had a four-hour Service Level Agreement for system recovery they could count on using half that time to recover data from tape and half that time to perform the recovery tasks. This meant that they could only have as much local storage as they could recover in two hours. So if a backup/restore system could restore 16GB of data in two hours and each user was allowed 100MB of storage, the maximum number of users on the system would be 160. For a company of 1,600 users, this would mean 10 Exchange servers would be required to support the four-hour SLA.

By placing the mailbox stores onto a NAS or SAN device that can be mirrored and snapshotted, the recoverability time for a 16GB database would drop to mere minutes. Now the bottleneck would become the performance of the server itself and possibly the IO rate of the NAS or SAN. Odds are that the systems that had been purchased for the ability to support 160 users would be dual processor systems with a Gig or two of memory. By reducing the server count to two and fully populating those two systems with memory taken from the retired systems, the two systems with NAS- or SAN-based mailboxes could easily support the 800 users each and still meet the four-hour recovery time required by the SLA.

This would result in the reduction of eight Exchange servers which would free up OS licenses and hardware as well as reduce the effort required to manage the data center.

## BEST PRACTICE

### Consolidating Exchange Servers

When consolidating Exchange servers, consider taking some of the newly freed up Exchange servers to be used to cluster the remaining Exchange servers or place them in the lab to be use for recovery and testing of patches.

## Consolidating the Number of File Servers

Most companies grow their file server environment in an organic manner. This is to say that as different groups in the company come up with needs for data storage, additional file servers are brought up. This can be an expensive process in that each of these file servers requires not only hardware but also an operating system, antivirus software, management software, space in the data center, facilities like cooling and electricity, and many other expenses. Users take storage for granted because drive prices are relatively inexpensive and they believe that disks can just be added and added forever so that they can fill it.

This results in a difficult to manage environment for the IT professional. When system patches become available it can be quite an event to ensure that potentially hundreds of file servers are up to date. Companies that enforce a life cycle for their servers find themselves replacing more and more servers each year.

NAS and SAN devices offer a solution to this problem. By consolidating the storage of data and presenting this data to the user community through a smaller number of high-performance file server clusters, you can ensure that users have reliable access to the files they need. At the same time, you can greatly reduce the management overhead of the vast number of servers and reduce costs across the board.

In environments where file servers are brought up simply to provide better access for local users, you can leverage technologies like DFS and mirroring to make data available to each location. Through DFS and site locality, users can ensure that they are reaching the closest copy of a file without any sort of user interaction. By leveraging a SAN or NAS at each major location administrators can still reduce the number of file servers at each location and maintain the same if not better level of support.

# Summary

This chapter has introduced us to the concepts of Network Attached Storage and Storage Area Networks as options to improve performance and manageability over traditional Direct Attached Storage. We've seen how SAN and NAS can be used to manage data more effectively through the reduction of servers.

Applications like Exchange can be made to support much larger numbers of users through the leveraging of large numbers of disks. Performance scales nearly 1:1 as additional disks are added. Plus adding additional disks allows an application to support more IO operations per second, which is critical to database applications.

You've seen how advanced technologies like snapshotting enable you to back up data regularly on the device itself so that users can recover their own data without having to involve administrators.

NAS implementations work with existing Ethernet infrastructures and impart additional loads on them that must be planned for. You've seen that a strong network is the key to good NAS performance.

This chapter discussed some common Microsoft applications that work well with both NAS and SAN storage. You've learned that SAN provides block-level access to the disk, whereas NAS provides file-level access. Some applications require SAN but most can work with NAS.

SAN and NAS offer you greater performance and enables you to perform geographic mirroring that was previously impossible for the application itself. As Ethernet and Fiber Channel technologies continue to improve and as prices continue to fall you will find NAS and SAN becoming more and more common in the IT world.

# PART VIII

## Business Productivity Solutions

26 User File Management and Information Lookup

# 26

# User File Management and Information Look-up

Throughout the preceding chapters, this book has provided useful tips and explanations of the many features and benefits available in the Windows Server 2003 operating system. In this chapter, the focus will take you a step further by introducing Microsoft technologies that will leverage the Windows Server 2003 platform to provide the next level of data administration.

File management and information retrieval have always been core Information Systems services benefiting from their own best practices and procedures. With an awareness of the key role these IS services play in any business enterprise, Microsoft has developed tools and services that greatly enhance the functionality, usability, and development of file management, team collaboration, and data lookup. Windows SharePoint Services and the new Office suite play a role in these new services that will be deployed in conjunction with Windows Server 2003 to help today's administrators with the daunting task of managing the company's knowledge and enhancing overall productivity.

This chapter shows how each of the new technologies fit into an organization's knowledge management solution and provides tips on how and when to deploy them.

# Enabling Collaboration with Windows SharePoint Services

Windows SharePoint Services (WSS) is a downloadable Windows Server 2003 component used to create Web sites for information sharing and collaboration. SharePoint products and technologies are not new to the product offerings by Microsoft. What was previously released as SharePoint Team Services has now evolved into WSS. Like SharePoint Team Services, WSS is focused on creating sites for teams of information workers to make it easy for users to work together on documents, tasks, contacts, events, and other information. In addition, team and site managers can coordinate site content and user activity easily. The Windows SharePoint Services environment is designed for easy and flexible deployment, administration, and application development.

## New Features in Windows SharePoint Services

WSS is both an update to and a revision of SharePoint Team Services. As such, it offers several new features making it a more compelling alternative to third-party offerings. This section highlights some of these revisions with a concentration on information sharing and collaboration. Some of the new features built in to Windows SharePoint Services include

- *Document Versioning*. Document versioning allows team members to automatically keep backup copies of files whenever updates are saved to a document library hosted on a team site. Additionally, team members can check out a document to lock it while editing, preventing other users from overwriting or editing it inadvertently.

- *Improved Lists and Views*. Picture libraries, issue tracking lists, and calendar views are available components of team sites. Moreover, list owners can approve or reject items that are submitted to a site list and add comments. List owners can also apply permissions to a list, allowing only specific users to make changes. List templates can be saved and used as components on different team sites.

- *Support for Web Parts*. Each list in a site is a Web part that allows easy customization and personalization just by using the browser. Users can customize default Web parts or add new Web parts to a page.

- *Self-Service Site Creation*. After WSS is deployed, users have the ability to create sites on demand without involving the IT department by using Self-Service Site Creation. Site creation and management is still available through SharePoint Central administration.

■ *Improved Storage Options*. All documents, metadata, and site data can be stored in a database. You can choose to leverage SQL or MSDE to store all the data related to a site. This improves reliability by ensuring complete transactional integrity of the data, and enables the scale-out architecture.

■ *Improved Searches through Indexing*. When using SQL as a back-end database, WSS provides full-text indexing to provide site-wide searching of sites on the server.

■ *Improved Security*. WSS works with IIS 6.0 security methods, Windows Authentication, SQL Server authentication, and can be integrated with Active Directory.

## Deployment Options and Scenarios

By allowing all site data to be stored in a SQL Server database, the extensibility of a Windows SharePoint Services solution is greatly enhanced. Now, WSS covers deployment scenarios from a single server, single Web site solution to a full enterprise-level distributed server farm. The following sections cover the options available to you when leveraging WSS to provide team collaboration and information sharing to any size organization.

### Small Organization Deployment

For a small organization, WSS can be deployed on a single server and can take advantage of an existing SQL Server to hold the database information or can use the MSDE option that can be included with the installation of WSS. To support a larger number of Web sites, WSS can be configured to leverage an existing SQL Server to host the site database.

To ease administration and enhance the end-user experience in the small organization scenario, you should include the following features in the WSS deployment:

■ Enable Self-Service Site Creation to allow users to build sites as needed.

■ Enable full-text searching so users can quickly find the information and documents they need.

> **WSS and MSDE**
>
> When WSS is installed using the default settings, the Setup program automatically installs MSDE (Microsoft Data Engine) and uses it to create the database for the Web site(s). No additional configuration steps are required to create the database. This installation scenario offers you the ability to host several Web sites without a lot of overhead.

### Large Organization Deployment

For large organizations with administrators familiar with managing server farm solutions, the WSS deployment can be configured with a distributed solution. These types of solutions will use a SQL Server back-end, which in turn might be hosted on a server cluster. The Web front-end component of WSS can be distributed and sites hosted across several servers as well to provide fault tolerant redundancy and load balancing.

Large WSS deployments can benefit in terms of efficiency and enhanced user experience by taking advantage of the following recommendations:

- *Use existing Web servers.* You can host the Web front-end component of WSS on existing Web servers that are hosting other Web applications. Features in IIS 6.0 allow for greater efficiency in hosting multiple applications on a single Web server.

- *Install language packs.* If the organization is globally distributed, you can take advantage of WSS's language packs. This allows for site creation in different languages around the world while maintaining a central administration.

- *Prompt for site use confirmation, and automatically deleted unused Web sites.* You can configure WSS to delete sites automatically that are no longer being used. Prompts are sent out to the configured owner (and secondary contact) associated with a site after a certain level of inactivity. This will conserve database space and resources on the SQL Server(s).

- *Leverage domain groups.* To ease administration, it is recommended to set permissions on a group level as opposed to individuals when managing Web sites in a large WSS deployment.

### Host WSS Sites on the Internet

Although WSS is ideal for setting up collaborative team sites on a company's intranet, this technology solution can be extended to the Internet as well. Especially if the company is an Internet Service Provider (ISP), the scalability and security of WSS can be leveraged to host public and private Web sites on the Internet. As with the large organization deployment, ISPs can use distributed WSS solutions with a SQL server back-end. Features within IIS 6.0 will keep different Web server processes isolated from one another.

Additionally, ISPs can configure their WSS solution to take advantage of these features:

- *Set Quotas for Sites.* WSS allows you to set quotas for the amount of space a particular Web site will take on a database server. ISPs can set different rates for the size of the Web sites.

- *Use WSS in Active Directory Account Creation Mode.* This allows for the automatic creation of user accounts in configured OUs on the ISP's Active Directory domain. SharePoint site owners will then have the ability to create user accounts or invite users to collaborate on a Web site where existing domain accounts for those users do not already exist.

- *Provide Automatic Site Backups.* This provides the site owners the capability to roll back to previous versions of their site without administrative overhead or technical service calls.

### Using WSS with an Extranet

Finally, if a given organization collaborates with a partner organization, WSS can be used to set up team Web sites across an extranet. In this scenario both intranet and extranet users are able to view and interact with the same documents and information.

This solution is accomplished by using two virtual servers. One virtual server is configured with an internal address and uses Windows authentication. The other virtual server is configured with an external address and uses a different authentication method (using SSL for example). Both virtual servers are then configured to point to the same content, so that changes made from one access point are reflected on the data accessed from the other access point.

Because this solution provides access to a Web server from outside the firewall, it is important to secure the integrity of the server. Of course, this is a topic that takes the reader all the way back to Chapter 1, "Securing Windows Server 2003." At a minimum, you will want to employ an antivirus solution and perhaps block certain file extensions on the server.

## Preparing for the Deployment

Providing a detailed description of installing and configuring WSS is outside the scope of this book, but it might be helpful for administrators considering WSS to be aware of some of the prerequisites and requirements involved with a WSS deployment.

The server that hosts the Web components of WSS depends on the operating system that is used. Enterprise and Datacenter editions of Windows Server 2003 have a greater hardware requirement than the standard server version. Because WSS can only be installed on servers that have the Windows Server 2003 operating system, it is best to follow the requirements for the OS when planning for the Web server.

With this in mind, the Web server hosting WSS installed with the Standard version of Windows Server 2003 should have at least a 550Mhz processor. WSS on an Enterprise Edition OS should have at least a 733Mhz processor. The recommended minimum RAM on either edition should be at least 512MB.

As noted earlier, WSS requires the Windows Server 2003 operating system. This can be either Web, Standard, Enterprise, or Datacenter edition.

WSS requires the NTFS file system. Further, the server must be configured as a Web server, which means it needs to have IIS 6.0 running with ASP.NET in Worker Process Isolation Mode. If the target server has been upgraded to Windows Server 2003 from Windows 2000, the Worker Process Isolation Mode will need to be manually changed.

To set the worker process isolation mode in IIS 6.0, follow these steps:

1. Open Internet Information Services Manager.

2. Right-click on Web Sites, and choose Properties.

3. On the Services tab, uncheck Run WWW service n IIS 5.0 isolation mode, as shown in Figure 26.1.

Internet Explorer 5.5 is the recommended minimum level of browser installed on the Web server although it will function with IE 5.01 and Netscape Navigator 6.2 or later.

WSS requires a database either on the server on which it is running, or in the case of a distributed solution, a separate server. The database requirement for WSS can be either

> **SQL Server and MSDE**
>
> If SQL Server is not installed on the server when WSS is installed, MSDE is installed automatically. If the command-line interface is used to install WSS, a separate server can be specified to use as the database.

Microsoft SQL Server 2000 with Service Pack 3, or Microsoft Data Engine (MSDE) 2000 with Service Pack 3. In order to have multiple back-end databases, WSS requires SQL Server 2000.

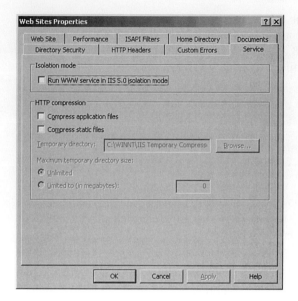

**FIGURE 26.1**
Preparing IIS 6.0 for Windows SharePoint Services.

Because WSS is a Web-based solution, the client side requirements simply involve having a browser. Microsoft Internet Explorer 5.01 is the minimum requirement, although IE 5.5 is recommended. Netscape Navigator 6.2 or later will also work. To save documents to the Web site directly from a Microsoft Office product, Microsoft Office 2003 is required. Microsoft Office 2003, and its relevant features, will be discussed in a later section of this chapter.

## Comparing SharePoint Portal Server with Windows SharePoint Services

Another technology designed to build effective information sharing and collaboration is SharePoint Portal Server 2003. Built on the foundation of SharePoint Portal Server 2001, SPS 2003 provides additional collaborative features, application integration, and personalization to the enterprise knowledge worker. SPS 2003 is an enterprise portal that provides a central place to access, manage, share, and interact with relevant information, documents, applications, and people for quicker and better decisions, effective teaming, and streamlined business process through a familiar integrated user experience and mainstream platform.

From this description, it might appear that SPS 2003 provides the same functionality as WSS. Although in some ways this is true, there are some key differences between the two products. For administrators looking to streamline their knowledge workers' business environment and productivity through SharePoint products and technologies, it is important to understand what sets SPS 2003 apart from WSS.

As has been described in the previous section, WSS is the engine for creating Web sites that enable information sharing and document collaboration. The primary objective of WSS is to take file storage to a new level, moving away from simply saving files to a network share to collaboratively sharing information with team sites. These sites provide communities for team collaboration, empowering users to collaborate on documents, tasks, contacts, events, and other information. WSS can be seen as proliferating *smart places*.

SPS 2003 takes advantage of WSS, connecting and aggregating these *smart places* which in turn facilitate *smart organizations*. SPS 2003 uses the technology of WSS to create sites that are portal pages, the components of which are Web parts and SharePoint document libraries. Through the use of portal pages, users can publish information and documents stored in their WSS sites to the entire organization.

Fundamentally, SPS 2003 can be seen as a tool to aggregate the disparate information contained in multiple Web sites across different business processes into a single solution with familiar management tools.

# Expanding on the File and Data Management Capabilities of Windows 2003

File and Data management has evolved considerably as a standard IT service. The ease and supportability of managed data improve drastically when you progress from sharing files from individual workstations to sharing files on network shares, e-mail public folders, and intranet Web sites. Microsoft has supported and improved the various methods by which data can be shared and managed at each progressive level. The following sections highlight these improvements and guide you in the direction of effective practices to increase the productivity of knowledge workers.

## Simple File Sharing in Windows XP

File sharing between workstations is a concept as old as the first connected personal computers. Making a file or directory available from one machine so that a group or user can access those files from another machine is perhaps the most common file sharing method available. Because this practice is still common in small office environments, Microsoft continues to make this functionality easier for the end user to accomplish. In Windows XP, Microsoft introduces the concept of *Simple File Sharing*.

The Simple File Sharing UI is available in a folder's properties and configures both share and NTFS file system permissions. Access permissions are configured in Simple File Sharing at the folder level and apply to the folder, all the files in that folder, child folders, all the files in child folders, and so on. Files

> **Simple File Sharing**
>
> Note that even if Simple File Sharing is enabled on an XP Professional workstation, the interface will not be available after that machine has been added to a domain.

and folders that are created in or copied to a folder inherit the permissions that are defined on their parent folder.

Windows XP Home Edition–based computers always have Simple File Sharing enabled. Windows XP Professional-based computers that are joined to a workgroup have the Simple File Sharing UI enabled by default. Windows XP Professional-based computers that are joined to a domain use only the classic file sharing and security interface. When the Simple File Sharing UI (located in the folder's properties) is used, both share and file permissions are configured.

To turn Simple File Sharing on or off in Windows XP Professional follow these steps:

1. Double-click My Computer on the desktop.

2. On the Tools menu, click Folder Options.

3. Click the View tab, and then click to select the Use Simple File Sharing (Recommended) check box to enable Simple File Sharing as shown in Figure 26.2. (Click to clear this check box to disable this feature.)

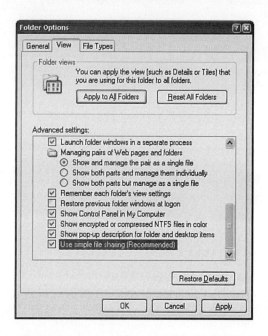

**FIGURE 26.2**    Enabling simple file sharing in Windows XP.

If Simple File Sharing is enabled or disabled, the permissions on files are not changed. The NTFS and share permissions do not change until the permissions are changed in the interface. If permissions are set with Simple File Sharing enabled, only Access Control Entries (ACEs) on files that are used for Simple File Sharing are affected.

## Controlling File Sharing in Active Directory

As workstations begin to share files in a domain environment, it becomes much more difficult to manage data if files are being shared from individual workstations. For this reason, the role of File Server plays a key role in networked knowledge worker environments. With the introduction of Active Directory, Microsoft has provided the system administrator a more effective means by which to enhance file and data management. Network shares that once were mapped via login scripts can now be published in Active Directory making them easily searchable to the knowledge worker.

Moreover, using the Group Policy features available in Active Directory, you can manage how the workstations in the domain environment access shared network files. Primarily the use of Group Policy settings for the management of Offline Files will enhance the knowledge worker's access to shared network files.

> **Simple File Sharing**
>
> Note that even if Simple File Sharing is enabled on an XP Professional workstation, the interface will not be available after that machine has been added to a domain.

By using the Offline Files feature, knowledge workers can continue to work with shared network files even when they are not connected to the network. If the connection to the network is lost, the view of shared network resources that have been made available offline remains the same as when connected. The access permissions to those files and folders are the same as if they were connected to the network. When the status of the connection changes, an Offline Files icon appears in the notification area and a reminder balloon appears over the notification area to notify the user of the change.

When the network connection is restored, any changes made while working offline are updated to the network by default. When more than one person on the network has made changes to the same file, each user will have the option of saving the offline version of the file to the network, keeping the other version, or saving both.

Using either Computer or User based Group Policies, you can control how workstations can leverage the Offline Files feature. Offline Files settings are located in the Group Policy Editor under the following two contexts:

- Computer Configuration/Administrative Templates/Network/Offline Files
- User Configuration/Administrative Templates/Network/Offline Files

These settings can be used to enable/disable the Offline Files feature, set mandatory network paths, set synchronization behavior, and more. How managed the knowledge worker environment is determines the amount of control these policies should incorporate.

## Intranet File Sharing

Intranet file sharing represents the next level of file and data sharing management because it moves the focus of the knowledge worker from the context of the network share to the Web browser and Web site. Microsoft introduced this concept with SharePoint Team Services (STS), which provided a Web site engine that would index shared data for searching by team members granted access to the site.

As with many new technologies, STS was met with challenges. STS proved to be difficult for administrators to manage, and difficult for knowledge workers to leverage. Early efforts at Intranet file sharing provided a great concept, but many users trying to post their files for collaboration on team sites ran into difficulties. As system administrators had to learn how to manage the new Web site functionality, they also needed to add support to their end users trying to post and access documents. For some environments the technology seemed to require additional IT resources to maintain support which lead to a rather lukewarm reception.

## File Sharing Using WSS

Building on the sound concept of Web-based file sharing and collaboration first presented in STS, Microsoft has developed Windows SharePoint Services (WSS) alleviating much of the confusion and administrative overhead found in the earlier product. Improvements found in WSS that are key to data management are summarized in the following list and will be elaborated on in the proceeding sections of this chapter:

- Integration into the Windows Server 2003 File Services. This alleviates the problems associated with posting files to an intranet site.

- Uses the same File/Save functionality in Office applications. Users have the capability to save to and access files from WSS Web sites directly by using the office applications with which they are already familiar.

- Data indexing is improved for better searching capabilities.

- Flexibility in database options. Information can be stored in classic network fileserver data, or can leverage MSDE or Microsoft SQL back-end databases for enhanced scalability and redundancy.

- Documents can be revision controlled. This preserves backup copies of data whenever updates are saved to a document library hosted on a team site.

# Simplifying File Sharing with Office 2003

With WSS, knowledge worker team members can create a team intranet site, and then upload files using a browser. With Microsoft's new Office suite, interaction with WSS can also be conducted directly through the Office programs used to create and modify the shared documents. Microsoft Office Word 2003, Microsoft Office Excel 2003, or Microsoft Office PowerPoint 2003 are each integrated with Microsoft Windows SharePoint Services. Key areas where this integration can simplify file sharing between knowledge workers Document Workspaces, the Shared Workspace task pane, and shared attachments.

## Document Workspaces in Windows SharePoint Services

A Document Workspace site is a Microsoft Windows SharePoint Services site that is specifically targeted for the collaboration of one or more documents. Team members can easily work together on a shared document either by working directly on the Document Workspace copy or by working on their own copy, which they can update periodically with changes that have been saved to the copy on the Document Workspace site.

The documents can be accessed through a browser by typing in the URL for the workspace, or with Office 2003 applications, directly through the application.

## Shared Workspace Task Pane

The Shared Workspace task pane, shown in Figure 26.3, opens automatically when a user opens a document that is stored in a document library.

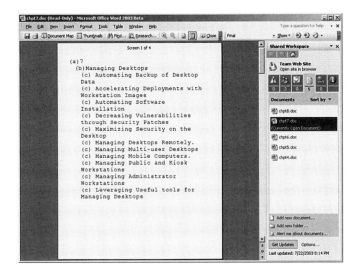

**FIGURE 26.3**
The shared workspace task pane.

To open the Shared Workspace task pane manually so you can add a document to an existing workspace or create a new one, choose Shared Workspace from the Tools pull-down menu within an Office 2003 application.

In addition to displaying Web site data in the Members, Tasks, Documents, and Links tabs, the Shared Workspace task pane provides information about the active document on the Status and Document Information tabs:

- Status—This tab lists important information about the current document, such as whether the document is up to date, whether it is in conflict with another member's copy, and whether it is checked out.

- Document Information—This tab displays properties associated with the document, such as when it was last modified. If the document library where the document is stored defines custom properties for documents, those custom properties are also displayed on the Document Information tab.

## Shared Attachments

When a team member sends a file as a shared attachment in Outlook 2003, a Document Workspace site is created for the attachment in the Microsoft Windows SharePoint Services site specified by the sender. The Document Workspace created will take the same name as the attached file.

The sender of the shared attachment becomes the administrator of the particular Document Workspace, and all the recipients become members of the Document Workspace. The recipients are then added to the contributor site group.

Recipients can open the attachment, or they can follow the link that is added automatically to the message. The link goes to the home page of the Document Workspace, where a copy of the e-mail attachment is stored in the Shared Documents Library.

# Improving Data Lookup with Indexing

By implementing WSS, you provide knowledge workers the capability to search through the entire Web site content on a particular virtual server. The searching capabilities of WSS have been improved from those offered with FrontPage 2002 and STS v1. In STS, searching was implemented through Internet Information Services (IIS) catalogs. This limited searches to documents on the file system. This limitation prevented users from being able to search the contents of lists or discussion board items. With the introduction of WSS, and its ability to leverage SQL Server 2000 for database information, the searching capabilities have been expanded to include all site content. Because all site content is contained in the database, it can be fully indexed for data lookup.

## Understanding Searching in WSS

To make Web site searching available to knowledge workers through WSS, the back-end database implemented must be SQL Server 2000. Using the MSDE back-end does not provide this functionality. WSS uses the SQL Server 2000 full-text searching feature to search for Web site content.

The search engine on a Windows 2003 server can create a search index on a per virtual server basis. This means that search is either turned on or off for all top-level Web sites and subsites on a particular virtual server. Subsites inherit the search settings from parent sites. If search has not been enabled for a virtual server, the search links will not appear in the Web sites that reside on that virtual server.

### Searching Features for Web Site

Another way to get searching features for Web site content is to implement SharePoint Portal Services 2003. In fact, SPS adds several search features not available to SQL Server 2000, including survey lists, attachments to list items, and Office 2003 file properties (such as "Author").

When full-text search is enabled in Windows SharePoint Services, a new empty catalog is created by default. Content is added to this catalog as it is added to the particular Web site. Aside from enabling and disabling full-text search, any search management or monitoring must be done from within SQL Server 2000 with the SQL Server administration tools.

When users search SharePoint sites by using SQL Server full-text searching, the search is performed by using a FREETEXT statement. Using FREETEXT allows searching by intent—all terms are stemmed, so that the query looks for all inflectional forms of each query term. For example, if a user queries for "construct", the query also returns results including "construction", "constructed", "constructing", and so on.

Although WSS with SQL Server 2000 is an appropriate solution to provide search capabilities to small and medium sized organizations, it is important to understand the limitations that this implementation might pose to large server farm type deployments. Search catalogs in SQL Server 2000 can use up to 40 percent of the hard disk space that data uses. Moreover, there is a hard limit of 256 search catalogs per server. There will be performance issues when a search catalog table reaches one million rows.

**BEST PRACTICE**

**Offer Searching Functionality to Only a Limited Number of Sites**

Consider offering searching functionality to only a limited number of sites when hosting Web sites based on Windows SharePoint Services inside a large organization. Choose those sites based on the appropriateness for search for its users and/or content.

Another item to keep in mind with SQL Server 2000 is that although it performs linguistic analysis on full-text search catalogs, it can only support one language per database. As mentioned earlier in the chapter, WSS can support multiple languages. So, if a large-scale WSS deployment is intended to support indexing across multiple languages this will require additional SQL Servers to support.

## Enabling Indexing

Before knowledge workers can begin to search the Web site's contents, the searching function must be enabled. To enable search, you must install the full-text searching feature for SQL Server 2000, and then proceed to enable search in WSS.

Full-text searching is usually installed by default on SQL Server 2000, but if this has not been done initially, it can be added easily through the SQL Server Setup tools. To install full-text indexing on SQL Server 2000, perform the following steps:

1. Run the SQL Server 2000 Setup program.

2. On the setup screen, click SQL Server 2000 Components, and then click Install Database Server.

3. From the Welcome screen, click Next.

4. On the Computer Name screen, select the computer type, and then click Next.

5. When the Installation Selection panel is displayed, select Upgrade, Remove, or Add Components to an Existing Instance of SQL Server, and then click Next.

6. From the Instance Name panel, clear the Default check box, and then in the Instance Name box, select your SQL Server instance for Windows SharePoint Services and click Next.

7. Select Add Components to Your Existing Installation, and then click Next.

8. On the Select Components panel, in the Sub-Components list, select Full-Text Search as shown in Figure 26.4, and then click Next.

9. Click Next again to begin the installation.

10. Click Finish.

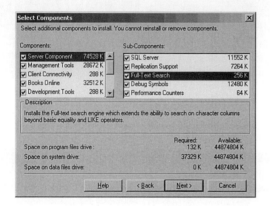

**FIGURE 26.4**   Adding full-text search to SQL Server 2000.

After SQL Server 2000 has been configured to support full-text searching, you can enable search for Windows SharePoint Services. To enable searching for WSS, perform the following steps:

1. On the server computer running Windows SharePoint Services, click Start, point to All Programs, point to Administrative Tools, and then click SharePoint Central Administration.

2. Under Component Configuration, click Configure Full-Text Search.

3. In the Search Settings section, select the Enable Full-Text Search and Indexing check box as shown in Figure 26.5.

4. Click OK.

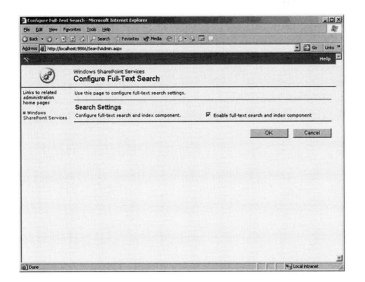

**FIGURE 26.5**
Enabling full-text search for a virtual server in WSS.

# Taking Advantage of Revision Control Management

Using conventional methods for managing documents, particularly in the network file share model, there are no built-in revision controls that protect the integrity of data. In the most primitive cases, there is no revision control and old documents are simply replaced when they are updated. In several other cases, revision control is ad hoc and operational procedures designed to maintain a level of control often fail or are confusing. What you are left with is a file structure that resembles Figure 26.6.

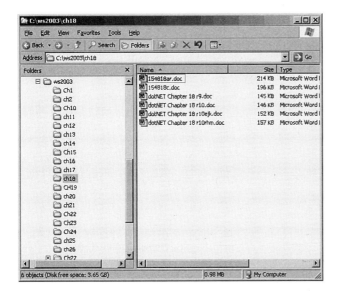

**FIGURE 26.6**
Conventional revision control.

The file structure displayed in Figure 26.6 is an example of how companies try to maintain a level of history over the course of a particular document's development. This example demonstrates the difficulty in standardizing the process because it appears that there are a couple of different naming conventions being used for the same document. It also demonstrates the challenge to clearly present the exact progression or history of the document, or to even specify which file is the latest revision. This method also invites the possibility for more than one user collaborating on the document to make changes that do not end up in the most current working version.

One of the key benefits of WSS is that it gives knowledge workers a clear and consistent method for maintaining versions of documents. It also protects the integrity of the data in documents through a check-in/check-out functionality so that collaborative users do not step on the efforts of other team members.

## Document Versioning

Document versioning allows collaborating team members to keep multiple versions of a document. If a change needs to be reversed, a knowledge worker with the appropriate rights can restore the previous version and continue working. A Version History command is included on the drop-down list users see when they click the arrow next to a document name and on the toolbar in the Edit Properties page for the document.

The Version History command is also available in client applications compatible with WSS, such as the programs found in Office 2003. When the user clicks Version History, a list of the previous versions of the document appears. The user can open an old version, restore a version (replacing the current version), or delete an old version.

**Saving Files**

If the user saves the file again, without closing the file, a new version is not created. If the user closes the application he or she is using to edit the file, and then opens it and saves the file again, another version is created.

**Preserving Data Integrity**

To preserve the integrity of data, only members of the Administrator and Web Designer site groups for a site can determine whether document versioning is enabled for a particular document library.

Versions are automatically created whenever a user updates a document in a document library on a site in which versioning has been enabled. It is important to understand under what circumstances versions are created. Versions are created

- When a user checks out a file, makes changes, and checks the file back in.

- When a user opens a file, makes changes, and then saves the file for the first time.

- When a user restores and old version of a file (and does not check it out).

- When a user uploads a file that already exists, in which case the current file becomes an old version.

Document versioning is enabled through the Settings page for each particular document library. To enable document versioning for a document library, perform the following steps:

1. Navigate to the list, and on the left link bar, click Modify settings and columns.

2. On the Customize Document Library page, click Change General Settings.

3. On the Document Library Settings page, in the Document Versions section, under Create a Version Each Time You Check In a File to This Web Site, click Yes as shown in Figure 26.7.

4. Click OK.

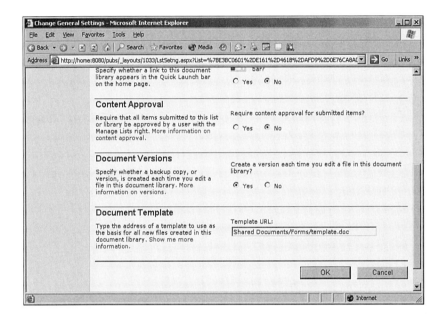

**FIGURE 26.7**
Enabling document versioning for a document library.

## Check-in and Check-out Function for Document Management

Checking documents in and out allows users to obtain exclusive write access to a document, eliminating potential data loss and the need to merge changes from collaborative authors. When a user checks a document out, that user is the only user who can save changes to the document. Other users can read the document, but they cannot make changes. The user who has the document checked out can update the document, and see the latest version of the document, but other users will not see the updates until the document has been checked back in.

In the event that a checked-out document becomes lost or corrupt, members of the Administrator and Web Designer site groups for that site can override a document check-out if necessary, and force the document to be checked in with the previous version.

> **The Cancel Check-out Right**
> Individual users can also be assigned the Cancel Check-out right without having to be made a member of the administrator or Web designer site groups.

Assuming the user has the appropriate rights, a user can cancel a checked-out document and return it to the previous version by performing the following steps:

**1.** Navigate to the document, click the down arrow next to the document's title, and then click Check In.

**2.** On the Check In page, select Discard Changes and Undo Check Out, and then click OK.

**3.** On the confirmation message that appears, click OK to check in the document.

# Hierarchical Storage Management

WSS can be used to manage data in a hierarchical fashion by creating a top-level Web site with subsites to divide site content into distinct separately manageable sites. The top-level sites can contain several subsites; subsites in turn can also contain several subsites. The entire structure of top-level and subsites, called a Web site collection, can be managed centrally.

This structure allows knowledge workers to have a main working site for the entire team, plus individual working sites or shared sites for side projects. Top-level Web sites and subsites allow different levels of control over the features and settings for sites.

The hierarchy in WSS is similar to the hierarchy in Active Directory, which is structured with a top-level domain, with Organizational Units (OUs) comprising the sub divisions. Like AD, administration of subsites in WSS can be delegated to Team administrators. A subsite administrator would only have access to control settings and features of his particular subsite, without requiring control at the top-level site.

Depending on the level of control that is desired for a particular Web site collection, you can individually create and control the entire hierarchy, or can allow users to create their own top level Web sites.

## Creating a Top-Level Web Site

Web site creation can be performed from SharePoint Central Administration or from the command prompt. To create a top-level Web site from SharePoint Central Administration, perform the following steps:

**1.** Under Virtual Server Configuration, click Create a Top-level Web site.

**2.** On the Virtual Server List page, click the virtual server under which you want to create the top-level Web site.

**3.** To create a site under a predefined URL path for the virtual server, on the Create Top-level Web Site page, select Create Site Under This URL; in the Site name box, type the name for the top-level Web site; and then in the URL path box, select the path to use.

> **Creating the Full URL**
>
> The name and URL path are combined with the server name to create the full URL to the site. For example, on `http://servername`, if you create a top-level Web site at the `/sites` URL path, and use Site001 as the name, the full path to the new top-level Web site is `http://servername/sites/site001`.

4. To create a site at a predefined URL path, select Create Site at This URL, and then in the URL path box, select the URL to use for the top-level Web site.

5. In the Site Collection Owner section, type the account name (in the form DOMAIN\username) and e-mail address (in the form someone@example.com) for the user who will be the site owner and administrator.

6. In the Site Language section, select the language to use for the top-level Web site.

7. Click OK.

As a best practice for enterprise environments, at step 5, identify a user as the secondary owner of the new top-level Web site. In the event that the primary owner of the site is unavailable for an extended period of time, the secondary owner receives all the notifications directly related to the site and can respond accordingly.

## Self-Service Site Creation

Depending on the amount of customization and control you want to allow users, you can let them create either top-level Web sites or sub-sites. The Self-Service Site Creation feature gives users the ability to create top-level Web sites on their own. This feature enables the knowledge worker to manage data (they can do it themselves) and reduces administrative overhead.

The user does not need administrator permissions on the server or virtual server, only permissions on the Web site where Self-Service Site Creation is hosted. The user simply enters some basic information and the new top-level Web site is created with the user as the owner and administrator.

Users can also create subsites of any site for which they have the Create Sites and Workspaces right. The Create Sites and Workspaces right is included in the Administrator site group by default, so any member of the Administrator site group for a site can create a subsite of that site.

Self-Service Site Creation is enabled at the Configure Self-Service Site Creation page for the virtual server that will host the sites. When Self-Service Site Creation is enabled, an announcement is added to the home page of the top-level Web site on that virtual server, with a link to the sign-up page. Users can click the link to go to the sign-up page and create their sites.

To enable Self-Service Site Creation for a virtual server, use the Configure Self-Service Site Creation page for that virtual server, and perform the following steps:

1. On the SharePoint Central Administration page, under Virtual Server Configuration, click Configure Virtual Server Settings.

2. From the Virtual Server List page, click the virtual server to enable.

3. With the Virtual Server Settings page displayed, under Automated Web Site Collection Management, click Configure Self-Service Site Creation as shown in Figure 26.8.

4. In the Enable Self-Service Site Creation section, next to Self-Service Site Creation Is, select On.

5. To require two contact names for each site, select the Require Secondary Contact check box.

6. Click OK.

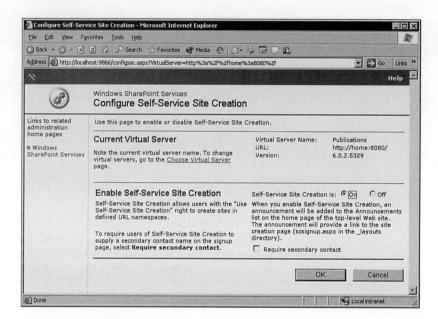

**FIGURE 26.8**
Enabling self-service site creation.

# Implementing Information, Communication, and Collaboration Security

Every IT organization places security as a top priority for the systems and services it provides. Security as it relates to managing the knowledge and data of the company is equally paramount. Just as this book begins with an account of security measures and best practices in Windows Server 2003, it seems fitting to complete the book on the same note.

For traditional data and user management, Windows Server 2003 leverages the NTFS file system, Active Directory, and group Policies as detailed in Chapter 5, "Managing User Rights and Permissions." As Windows SharePoint Services is installed on Windows Server 2003, the best practices detailed in that chapter also apply here. In addition to security practices that leverage the file system and Active Directory, though, WSS has its own security measures built in to ensure that data managed through the SharePoint is equally secure.

## WSS Security

Many of the security measures of WSS have been touched on in various points throughout the chapter. The following is a rundown of features that maximize secure data management through SharePoint technologies:

- *User Authentication.* The process used to validate the user account that is attempting to gain access to a Web site or network resource. The administrator manages security using Windows users and security groups either locally or at the domain level.

- *SharePoint Administrators Group.* A Microsoft Windows user group authorized to perform administrative tasks for WSS. When WSS is installed, this unique administrative group is created.

- *Site Groups.* A means of controlling the rights assigned to particular users or groups in WSS Web sites. Similar to delegation of control in Active Directory, site groups help to distribute the management of data in the WSS framework. There is a predefined list of site groups for each Web site (Administrators, Web Designers, and so on). Granting a user a particular level of access to a Web site is accomplished by assigning that user to a site group.

- *Administrative Port Security.* A means of controlling access to the administrative port for WSS. Help secure the administrative port by using Secure Sockets Layer (SSL) security or by configuring the firewall to not allow external access to the administration port, or both.

- *Microsoft SQL Server Connection Security.* When SQL is an integrated component of the WSS solution, there is an additional layer of security added. Use either Windows Integrated authentication or SQL Server authentication to connect you to your configuration database and content database.

- *Firewall Protection.* A firewall helps protect your data from exposure to other people and organizations on the Internet. WSS can be placed either inside or outside the organization's firewall depending on the function it will play. If WSS will be used to create an extranet or to provide services on the Internet, it is a best practice to use a DMZ network configuration to protect the WSS server.

## Internet Explorer Enhanced Security

By default, Windows Server 2003 provides a set of security settings called Internet Explorer Enhanced Security Configuration. These settings limit the types of content that a user at the server can view using Internet Explorer, except for sites listed in the Local intranet and Trusted sites zones. For example, by default, scripting on Internet pages will not run when the site is accessed from the server.

The goal of these settings is to help ensure that a local user on the server will not download a virus or other harmful files from the Internet and infect the server. This is especially pertinent to Web servers. The security features of Internet Explorer Enhanced Security Configuration do not affect remote users viewing content on the server, only users running Internet Explorer on the server computer itself.

Using Internet Explorer Enhanced Security Configuration on a Web Server running WSS prevents some code necessary for viewing site pages or HTML administration pages from running. Again, remote users with proper access rights can still view the pages correctly, but a user running Internet Explorer on the server computer will be unable to view or administer the site. Note also that the user at the server computer will be unable to view and administer a remote SharePoint site because of the security settings.

| |
|---|
| **Adding All the URLs for Virtual Servers** |
| If you choose to add all the URLs for virtual servers and domain named sites to the Local Intranet zone of IE in a Web farm implementation, this must be done on each front-end server that is participating in the WSS Web farm. Depending on the size of the implementation, this could be a time-consuming process. |

There are ways to get around this security issue so that a local user can run the necessary scripts from the WSS server and still maintain a level of security:

- For simple SharePoint installations, the local administrator can run WSS by using the default localhost name. By default, the SharePoint Central Administration link uses the localhost naming method. This method is not a good option for more complex SharePoint installations that use host-header based site or Web farms.

- The recommended workaround that preserves the highest level of security involves adding the URLs for all of the hosted virtual servers to the Internet Explorer Local intranet zone. In a Web farm, the administrator must also add the URLs of all domain named sites to the list of local intranet sites.

- Internet Explorer Enhanced Security can also be uninstalled. This is perhaps the least secure alternative. If you are not concerned about users working locally at the Web server, this will resolve any problems with scripts running as expected. This alternative requires the least amount of time to configure as the Internet Explorer Enhanced Security can be uninstalled quickly using Add or Remove Windows Components.

# Summary

Windows SharePoint Services elevates knowledge management to a new level. Rather than simply storing files in network shares, knowledge workers can now leverage file versioning, check-in check-out protection, and flexible customizable Web views to share company data. Despite the fact that WSS was engineered to scale to large Web farm style deployments that can accommodate worldwide collaboration, WSS runs just as well and is quickly deployed in small business and departmental environments. Finally, even though the knowledge worker gains the flexibility and customizing features of a Web-based application, WSS preserves a high level of security through a variety of built-in security measures while leveraging the improved security of Windows Server 2003.

# Symbols

# A

## B

## C

*How can we make this index more useful? Email us at indexes@samspublishing.com*

# V

# X-Z

# Your Guide to Computer Technology

www.informit.com